I0887836

East African Community Law

The Editors are grateful to Allen & Overy LLP, the European Union and the Europa Institute of the University of Leiden for making Open Access publication of this book possible.

ALLEN & OVERY

Universiteit Leiden
Europa Institute

This is an open access title distributed under the terms of the Creative Commons Attribution-Noncommercial 4.0 Unported License (CC-BY-NC), which permits any non-commercial use, distribution, and reproduction in any medium, provided the original author(s) and sources are credited.

East African Community Law

Institutional, Substantive and Comparative EU Aspects

Edited by

Emmanuel Ugirashebuja
John Eudes Ruhangisa
Tom Ottervanger
Armin Cuyvers

BRILL
NIJHOFF

LEIDEN | BOSTON

BRILL OPEN Copyright 2017 by Emmanuel Ugirashebuja, John Eudes Ruhangisa, Tom Ottervanger, and Armin Cuvyers

Library of Congress Cataloging-in-Publication Data

Names: Ugirashebuja, Emmanuel, editor.
Title: East African Community law : institutional, substantive and comparative EU aspects / Edited by Emmanuel Ugirashebuja, John Eudes Ruhangisa, Tom Ottervanger, Armin Cuyvers.
Description: Leiden : Brill Nijhoff, 2017. | Includes bibliographical references and index.
Identifiers: LCCN 2017000988 (print) | LCCN 2017001613 (ebook) | ISBN 9789004322066 (hardback : alk. paper) | ISBN 9789004322073 (E-book)
Subjects: LCSH: Law—East African Community. | Law—European Union countries. | International and municipal law—East African Community. | Law—International unification. | Comparative law.
Classification: LCC KQC117 .E27 2017 (print) | LCC KQC117 (ebook) | DDC 349.2676—dc23
LC record available at https://lccn.loc.gov/2017000988

Typeface for the Latin, Greek, and Cyrillic scripts: "Brill". See and download: brill.com/brill-typeface.

ISBN 978-90-04-32206-6 (hardback)
ISBN 978-90-04-32207-3 (e-book)

Koninklijke Brill NV incorporates the imprints Brill, Brill Hes & De Graaf, Brill Nijhoff, Brill Rodopi and Hotei Publishing.
All rights reserved. No part of this publication may be reproduced, translated, stored in a retrieval system, or transmitted in any form or by any means, electronic, mechanical, photocopying, recording or otherwise, without prior written permission from the publisher.
Authorization to photocopy items for internal or personal use is granted by Koninklijke Brill NV provided that the appropriate fees are paid directly to The Copyright Clearance Center, 222 Rosewood Drive, Suite 910, Danvers, MA 01923, USA. Fees are subject to change.

This book is printed on acid-free paper and produced in a sustainable manner.

Contents

Preface IX
Notes on Contributors XI

1 The Road to East African Integration 1
Wanyama Masinde and Christopher Otieno Omolo

1A The Road to European Integration 22
Armin Cuyvers

2 The Institutional Framework of the EAC 43
Wilbert T.K. Kaahwa

2A The Institutional Framework of the EU 79
Armin Cuyvers

3 The Legal Framework of the EAC 103
Elvis Mbembe Binda

3A The Legal Framework of the EU 119
Armin Cuyvers

4 The Scope, Nature and Effect of EAC Law 139
John Eudes Ruhangisa

4A The Scope, Nature and Effect of EU Law 161
Armin Cuyvers

5 External Relations and the EAC 182
Leonard Obura Aloo

5A External Relations and the EU 196
Armin Cuyvers

6 General Principles Governing EAC Integration 202
Khoti Chilomba Kamanga and Ally Possi

6A General Principles of EU Law 217
Armin Cuyvers

7 **Judicial Protection under EAC Law: Direct Actions** 229
John Eudes Ruhangisa

7A **Judicial Protection under EU Law: Direct Actions** 254
Armin Cuyvers

8 **Preliminary References under EAC Law** 265
Emmanuel Ugirashebuja

8A **Preliminary References under EU Law** 275
Armin Cuyvers

9 **The EAC Common Market** 285
Kennedy Gastorn and Wanyama Masinde

9A **The EU Common Market** 293
Armin Cuyvers

10 **Free Movement of Goods in the EAC** 303
Leonard Obura Aloo

10A **Free Movement of Goods in the EU** 326
Armin Cuyvers

11 **Free Movement of Workers in the EAC** 345
Caroline Kago and Wanyama Masinde

11A **Free Movement of Persons in the EU** 354
Armin Cuyvers

12 **Freedom of Establishment and the Freedom to Provide Services in the EAC** 365
Kennedy Gastorn

12A **Freedom of Establishment and the Freedom to Provide Services in the EU** 376
Armin Cuyvers

13 **Free Movement of Capital and East African Monetary Union** 392
Elvis Mbembe Binda

13A **Free Movement of Capital and Economic and Monetary Union in the EU** 410
Armin Cuyvers

14 **EAC Competition Law** 433
Joyce Karanja-Ng'ang'a

14A **EU Competition Law** 454
Pieter Van Cleynenbreugel

15 **Judicial Enforcement and Implementation of EAC Law** 467
James Otieno-Odek

16 **Harmonization in the EAC** 486
Aleem Tharani

Bibliography 501
Index 536

Preface

The East African Community (EAC) is a regional intergovernmental and supranational organization currently comprising the Republics of Burundi, Kenya, Rwanda, South Sudan, the United Republic of Tanzania, and the Republic of Uganda. Established in 2000, the EAC aims at widening and deepening co-operation among its Partner States in, among others, political, economic and social fields.

The organization has established a Customs Union (2005) and a Common Market (2010), and is in the process of establishing a Monetary Union. Its ultimate objective is to establish a complete political (con)federation. It emphasizes strong participation of the private sector and civil society. The accomplishment of these objectives requires an elaborate and functionally-purposed institutional framework.

The EAC aims at far deeper integration than envisioned by its predecessor, whilst simultaneously avoiding the mistakes that led to the failure of previous attempts at East African integration. Important safeguards include a gradual approach to integration and guarantees to ensure an equitable division of the benefits of integration.

There is a general consensus that the European Union (EU) was an important source of inspiration and provided a normative model for the EAC. Indeed the EAC Treaty and the Protocols have adopted and adapted significant parts of the EU's institutional and legal framework. The normative appeal of the EU in this regard can also be readily understood. Despite all the past *and* present failures and challenges facing the EU, no objective observer can deny the benefits of European integration in terms of peace, stability and prosperity. What started 60 years ago as a Community between six Member States in a Europe destroyed by two world wars has now developed into the most peaceful and prosperous block in the world.

Consequently, there are lessons to be learned from the European experience, including the crucial role of the law and of lawyers in the process of integration, be they judges, lawmakers, civil servants, academics or practitioners. The law is one of the most powerful and indispensable instruments to achieve true integration, as effective integration requires some form of supranational legal system. That is what we mean by "Integration through law". Awareness of the possibilities the law offers, therefore, is extremely important for any form of regional integration.

The main challenges facing the EAC today in this regard are how to safeguard the quality of the increasing body of Community law, how to monitor compliance, and how to make EAC law binding and enforceable within national legal systems. All of these are challenges that the EU has faced in the past and is still facing, and where both the success and the failures of the EU may be of comparative use to the EAC, certainly considering the many similarities in the institutional and legal framework of both and the similarities of the challenges faced.

The main purpose of this book, initiated by the Leiden Centre for the Comparative Study of EAC law (LEAC) in close cooperation with Hon. Justice Dr Ugirashebuja, the current President of the East African Court of Justice, is to be a source of information and education for all those involved in shaping, improving and studying integration in the EAC. By comparing each aspect of both institutional and substantive EAC law with its nearest counterpart EU law, we hope to have created a vital tool to better understand and move forward the integration process in East Africa.

Considering these aims, we are proud that, thanks to the generous support of the law firm Allen & Overy LLP, the European Union and the Europa Institute of the University of Leiden, this book will not just be available in printed form but will also be freely available online via a completely Open Access agreement with Brill Publishers.

We have been fortunate to find excellent authors from the different EAC Partner States, all leading experts in their respective fields, enabling us to cover all legal aspects of the EAC. We are very grateful for their wonderful contributions and constructive participation in this ambitious project. In addition, we have greatly benefitted from the excellent research and editorial assistance provided by Ties Boonzajer Flaes, Louise O'Callaghan, Brenden Fourie, Timothy Kawira, Carlota de Paula Coelho, and Merel Valk, as research assistants of the LEAC. We are much indebted to them for, among other things, ensuring consistency between the chapters. As always, however, responsibility for the final product remains with the authors and editors.

Emmanuel Ugirashebuja
John Eudes Ruhangisa
Tom Ottervanger
Armin Cuyvers
November, 2016

Notes on Contributors

Leonard Obura Aloo
Lecturer, School of Law, University of Nairobi; Legal Practitioner, Mwaura & Wachira Advocates, Nairobi, Kenya.

Elvis Mbembe Binda
The author is a trained lawyer and a lecturer at the School of Law of the University of Rwanda where he teaches i.a Economic and Financial Law with an emphasis on the EAC regional economic integration. He obtained a PhD at the University of Utrecht and is President of the Initiative for Peace and Human Rights (IPHR).

Armin Cuyvers
Assistant professor of EU law at the Europa Institute of Leiden University; Co-Director of the Leiden Center for East African Community Law (LEAC); PhD, Leiden; Mjur Oxford; Visiting Fellow "European Political Strategy Centre" of the European Commission (Brussels).

Kennedy Gastorn
Secretary General of the Asian-African Legal Consultative Organization (AALCO). The author was previously a Professor at the University of Dar es Salaam where he headed the Department of Public Law of the School of Law. The views expressed are purely those of the author and may not in any circumstances be regarded as stating an official position of the AALCO.

Wilbert T.K. Kaahwa
Former Counsel to the East African Community (July 2000-January 2015). He now works as the Director and Lead Consultant for M/s Attune Interlink Consultants Limited in which capacity he has been engaged as Senior Legal Consultant at the African Development Bank (Abidjan, Cote d'Ivoire), as Legal Advisor by M/s SAI Consulting Engineers Pvt Limited (Ahmedabad, India) and M/s Carelink Uganda Limited (Kampala, Uganda).

Caroline Kago
Chairperson Department of Private Law, Kenyatta University School of Law, Nairobi, Kenya, Advocate of the High Court of Kenya. The Author is a PHD Candidate at the University of the Witwatersrand, and holds an LL.M from the University of Western Cape, South Africa, and an LL.B University of Nairobi.

Khoti Chilomba Kamanga

Associate Professor, Department of Public Law, University of Dar es Salaam. Ph.D., Patrice Lumumba University (Moscow), *LL.M.* in European Union Law, University of Amsterdam.

Joyce Karanja- Ng'ang'a

Partner and Head of Competition, Bowmans Kenya, Advocate of the High Court of Kenya, member: Law Society of Kenya, International Bar Association. Author: Mergers and Acquisitions Review, Kenya Chapter (2015), The African and Middle Eastern Antitrust Review 2014: Kenya Issues and Challenges in Competition, The COMESA Merger Assessment Guidelines, 2014 explained; The American Bar Association: Essentials of Merger Review (2011,2012), Nature of Law: Broadcasting Regulations (2010), Reform of Kenyan Company Law (2011).

Wanyama Masinde

Director of the Centre for Regional Integration, Founding Director of the Institute for Regional Integration and Development (IRID) at the Catholic University of Eastern Africa, Nairobi, Kenya. The author also served as a Regional Integration Policy and Strategy Advisor to the Government of Kenya, is a Visiting Professor at several academic institutions in Africa, including the UN Africa Institute for Economic Planning & Development.

James Otieno-Odek

Judge of the Court of Appeal and Director of the Judiciary Training Institute of the Republic of Kenya. He is also an Associate Professor of Law at the University of Nairobi. The views expressed are purely those of the author and may not in any circumstances be regarded as stating the position of the Judiciary Kenya or the University of Nairobi.

Christopher Otieno Omolo

Lecturer at the Institute for Regional Integration and Development (IRID) at the Catholic University of Eastern Africa (CUEA), Nairobi, Kenya; Coordinator of the IRID Master of Arts program in Regional Integration. The author holds a Master of Public Policy (specializing in European Public Policy and International Affairs and Development) from the Willy Brandt School of Public Policy at the University of Erfurt, Germany, and a B.A. from the University of Zimbabwe.

Tom Ottervanger

Of Counsel and former Partner at the law firm Allen & Overy LLP (Brussels/Amsterdam); Professor of European and Competition law at the Europa Institute of Leiden University; Chair of the Leiden Center for East African Community Law (LEAC); Visiting Professor LUISS University, Rome; deputy-Justice at the Court of Appeal in The Hague.

Ally Possi

The author (LLB (Mzumbe), LLM Cape Town) is an advocate of the High Court and a lecturer at the Law School of Tanzania. He has a PhD from the University of Pretoria. The major area of his research concerns human rights and aspects of international courts.

John Eudes Ruhangisa

Judge of the High Court of Tanzania; Founding Registrar of the East African Court of Justice 2001-2014; former professor of law at Tumaini-Makumira University, Tanzania, Visiting Professor at i.a Pretoria University (South Africa), Tanzania-German Centre for Postgraduate Studies in Law (TGCL) (Dar es Salaam), Catholic University (CUEA) (Nairobi). He has written extensively on human rights, constitutional law, environmental law, regional integration. PhD in law from the University of London (SOAS). The views expressed are purely those of the author and may not in any circumstances be regarded as stating the position of the Tanzanian judiciary.

Aleem Tharani

Partner in the Corporate and Commercial Department of Anjarwalla & Khanna, specialized in energy, natural resources and infrastructure project development and finance. The author *inter alia* holds a Postgraduate Diploma in Law from the Kenya School of Law (2006), a Diploma in Legal Practice (Dist.) from Nottingham Law School, UK (2006) and an LL.B (Hons.), from the Victoria University of Manchester, UK (2005).

Emmanuel Ugirashebuja

President of the East African Court of Justice, previously *inter alia* Dean of the Law School, University of Rwanda (2009–2014); former Member of the Superior Council of Judiciary (2009–2014); Member of the Supreme Council of prosecution (2009–2014); and Senior Lecturer at the National University of Rwanda. The author holds a PhD and an LLM in Law from the University of Edinburgh, and an LLB. From the University of Rwanda.

Pieter Van Cleynenbreugel
The author (Ph.D., KU Leuven, LL.M, Harvard) is Professor of European Union law at the University of Liège, Belgium, where he also presides the Institut d'Etudes Juridiques Européennes. Previously, assistant professor at the Europa Institute, Leiden University. His research focuses on the public and private enforcement of competition law and on EU administrative law.

CHAPTER 1

The Road to East African Integration

Wanyama Masinde and Christopher Otieno Omolo

1.1 Introduction: African Regionalism in a Global Perspective

In recent times, the world has witnessed on the one hand, a trend towards globalization, which has resulted in a "more interconnected world economy and world society" characterized by fewer and less significant trade borders, and is associated with the decline of the nation-state, and on the other, a trend towards regionalization and cooperation between states or groups of states.[1] Gamble, citing Kenichi Ohmae, observes that economic activity in the contemporary global economy no longer coincides with traditional political and cultural fault lines, so much so that the nation-state is fast being rendered irrelevant, at least as a unit of analysis.[2] The post-Cold War era has particularly featured a resurgence of regionalism across the globe, with both old regional blocs being revived and new ones formed. Many reasons have been advanced to account for the revival of regionalism, including, the end of the Cold War and "the erosion of the Cold War alliance systems", the unreliability of the General Agreement on Tariffs and Trade (GATT), and the many economic and democratic developments in the developing world.[3] The success story of the European regionalization experiment has also been cited as a factor that has inspired the recent wave of regionalism.[4]

1 Eiassen, K.A., & Monsen, B. (2001). Comparison of European and Southeast Asian Integration. In M. Telò, *European Union and New Regionalism: Regional Actors and Global Governance in a Post- Hegemonic Era* (pp. 111–135). Burlington: Ashgate, at 113; Gamble, A. (2001). Regional Blocs, World Order and the New Medievalism. In M. Telò, *European Union and New Regionalism: Regional Actors and Global Governance in a Post-Hegemonic Era* (pp. 21–39). Burlington: Ashgate. at 21.

2 Gamble, *supra* note 1, at 23.

3 Eiassen & Monsen, *supra* note 1, at 113.

4 El-Affendi, A. (2009). The Perils of Regionalism: Regional Integration as a Source of Instability in the Horn of Africa? JOURNAL OF INTERVENTION AND STATEBUILDING, 3 (1), at 1. See further on the example of EU integration EU Chapter 1 detailing the road to European integration.

© WANYAMA MASINDE AND CHRISTOPHER OTIENO OMOLO, 2017 | DOI 10.1163/9789004322073_002
This is an open access chapter distributed under the terms of the CC-BY-NC License.

1.2 The Post-Hegemonic Era and the Search for a New Multilateral Equilibrium

Most analysts have generally cited the "post-hegemonic condition" of the post-Cold War international system as constituting the congenial background for the resurgence of regionalism. The post-hegemonic condition, to cite Padoan, is a "situation in which no single country can provide unilaterally, the public goods required for the operation of the (international) system".[5] The post-hegemonic world is also said to be a world in "a state of institutional disequilibrium", that is, a state in which there is "an excess demand for international public goods" as a result of the combination of, a decrease in supply because of the erosion of the power of the hegemon, and an increase in demand, because of globalization".[6] This condition is ascribed to the decline of the United States as a hegemon in the last few decades. The United States had emerged as a new hegemon after the Second World War, and had led the successful reconstruction of the global political economy in the 1950s and 1960s, guaranteeing "the conditions for a safe liberal world order".[7] However, the economic turbulences of the 1970s and 1980s led to "the erosion of the economic supremacy of the United States" and resulted in the decline of its hegemonic power and ability to supply public goods, thereby rendering the world susceptible to "mercantilists and protectionist policies" by nation-states.[8]

Regionalism, against this view, is perceived, not just as the result of the "convergence of trade and investment activities" by different groups of nation-states, but, as "a policy pursued as a response to the failure of the post-hegemonic world in providing international goods".[9] Regionalism has therefore been pursued as an attempt to provide a sort of new multilateral equilibrium in the absence of a hegemonic power. Proponents argue that regionalism can contribute to global governance by providing solutions to the demand for public goods, and conditions for new multilateralism. Telò, for instance, points out that regionalism is a good precondition for multilateralism since interaction

5 Padoan, P.C. (2001). Political Economy of New Regionalism and World Governance. In MarioTelò, European Union and New Regionalism: *Regional Actors and Global Governance in a Post-hegemonic Era* (pp. 39–59) Burlington: Ashgate, at 40.

6 Padoan, *supra* note 5.

7 Gamble, *supra* note 1, at 26.

8 Gamble, *supra* note 1, at 26.

9 Padoan, *supra* note 5.

between states and international organizations is easier at the regional level.[10] He also notes that regionalism enhances stability in international regimes because it implies "issue linkages" for instance, between economic, security, monetary and trade issues, which in turn leads to exchange of information, and provides security.[11]

1.3 New Regionalism and Globalization

An important subject within the discourse on regionalism has been its relationship with the nation-state and with globalization. There have been debates about the roles played by the nation-state and international economics and world politics in the emergence of new regionalism. Telò has, for instance, argued that both factors are responsible for the development of new regionalism. He contrasts between domestic or internal factors, and the systemic or exogenous economic and political factors, which he argues, constitute the causes of the recent wave of regionalism.[12] By domestic factors he means, the combination of the desire of nation-states to rescue their sovereignty and maintain or recover international bargaining power; the private interest of industries lobbying and networking on a regional basis; the "internal functional spillover" resulting from regional cooperation agreements; and the desire of developing countries to cope with global competition.[13]

The major systemic factor in the development of regionalism, Telò explains, has been globalization, understood as the combination of the international forces, political actors and multinational organizations shaping the "relations and hierarchies between states, economic interests and regions of the world".[14] Telò sees regionalism as the nation-state's response to a two-pronged threat which globalization poses to its existence. On the one hand, he sees regionalism—regional trade liberalization and cooperation arrangements—as a measure that enables nation-states and companies to "cope with the risks and opportunities of the global market and to absorb new multilateral rules".[15] On the other hand, he perceives regionalism as a

10 Telò, M. (2001). *European Union and New Regionalism: Regional Actors and Global Governance in a Post-hegemonic Era*. Burlington: Ashgate, at 13.

11 Telò, *supra* note 10.

12 Telò, *supra* note 10, at 4.

13 Telò, *supra* note 10, at 4.

14 Telò, *supra* note 10, at 4.

15 Telò, *supra* note 10, at 6.

response by nation-states to the threat of financial, technological and market globalization to the traditional "territorial state power".[16] According to this perspective, regionalism rescues national authority by enabling states to pool their authority at a regional level, in the face of the weakening or decline of national sovereignty. Telò observes that traditional state power—sovereignty—has been under threat, not only from technological and market globalization, but also from domestic "social factors, political pressures, and democratic authority".[17] Hence, regionalism does not only rescue the nation-state from global political and economic forces, but, by creating a new supranational framework within which different actors express themselves, limits the "fragmenting and disintegrating impact of subnational regionalism, ethnic fundamentalism and the proliferation of movements (agitating) for self-determination".[18]

Regionalism thus helps countries cope with traditional deficiencies of the nation-state, and to respond accordingly to a globalized economy. The nexus of regionalism with globalization is a subject much discussed in the literature of regionalism, and thus demands more than a cursory treatment here. As already noted, the resurgence of regionalism has been closely associated with the rise of globalization, which has been an important feature of the world economy since the 1980s. There is a consensus that there has been an evolution in the functioning of the world economy and in the operations of multinational corporations, driven by rapid technological advances, increased volumes and increased liberalization of trade, and unimpeded financial flows.[19] Whereas this evolution has brought massive benefits in terms of increased volumes of trade, and increased investment and growth, it has also brought with it challenges for governments. Globalization and liberalization have, for instance, been associated with the weakening of the government's control over their national economies, and in fact exposed domestic economies to external shocks.[20] Telò, rephrasing Gamble, has noted that "globalizers" speak of "hyper-globalization" as constituting the threat to which regionalism seeks to

16 Telò, *supra* note 10, at 7.

17 Telò, *supra* note 10, at 7.

18 Telò, *supra* note 10, at 7.

19 Eiassen & Monsen, *supra* note 1, at 113.

20 Eiassen & Monsen, *supra* note 1, at 113; Jenkins, C., & Thomas, L. (2001). African Regionalism and the SADC. In M. Telò, *European Union and New Regionalism: Regional Actors and Global Governance in a Post-hegemonic Era* (pp. 153–177). Burlington: Ashgate, at 159.

respond. By hyper-globalization he refers to "a new-liberal" vision of the global economy as "cosmopolitan"; characterized by a "fast convergence of national economies" and an increasing autonomy of transnational companies, global financial markets, and private and public networks.[21] "Hyper-globalization" exacerbates the crisis of territorial sovereignty, and in the extreme, renders the state all together, superfluous. Governments react to globalization by setting up regional blocs to enhance their competitiveness in the new global framework. In fact, Telò observes, regionalism is not only the state's alternative to globalization, but also constitutes the state's gateway to the global economy.[22] This point is best illustrated by Vasconcelos in his discussion of MERCOSUR. He states that MERCOSUR is a project generated by globalization, and born from the awareness of Member States like Brazil and Argentina of the difficulties the nation-states, with their sovereignty deprived of potency, face "on their own to benefit from globalization and to meet the economic and security challenges it brings".[23] Jenkins and Thomas reiterate this point in regard to African regionalism, arguing that regionalism should be perceived not just as an alternative to trade liberalization but as a step in "a process of greater integration into international markets".[24] Referring to the South African Development Community (SADC), they state that regional integration, by creating larger markets, could enable SADC to compete in the global economy.[25]

Regionalism and globalization are said to be complementary, even if they bear conflicting tendencies. Gamble notes, quite rightly, that both globalization and regionalism comprise complex processes of social change with unique patterns of social interaction of actors, which occur independently of the state.[26] This is reiterated by Telò who observes that regionalism and globalization are two components of the same "historical process of strengthening interdependence and weakening the state's barriers to free trade …".[27]

---

21 Telò, *supra* note 10, at 9.

22 Telò, *supra* note 10, at 9.

23 Vasconcelos, Á. d. (2001). European Union and Mercosur. In M. Telò, *European Union and New Regionalism: Regional Actors and Global Governance in a Post-hegemonic Era* (pp. 135–153). Burlington: Ashgate, at 137.

24 Jenkins, *supra* note 20, at 137.

25 Jenkins, *supra* note 20, at 137.

26 Gamble, *supra* note 1, at 27.

27 Telò, *supra* note 10, at 1.

1.4 The European Integration as the Primer for New Regionalism

Another feature of new regionalism has been its association with the European Union (EU). There is a general consensus amongst theorists of regional integration that the success story of EU integration has provided both the inspiration and the normative model for the new wave of regionalism throughout the world. It is no surprise therefore that much of the analysis of the phenomenon of new regionalism has featured, almost invariably, a comparative study of the EU and other regional organizations. Telò observes that specialists have approached regionalism from the perspective of the EU, focusing on the comparison of regional arrangements with the EU, and on the evolution of the EU as "both a workshop of institutional innovation and an international entity" in the post-Cold War era.[28] The present work of course contributes to this larger comparative exercise, even if hoping to avoid some of its traps.

The EU has quite explicitly, in its external relations, contributed to the development of regional cooperation in many parts of the world. The setting up of inter-regional cooperation is in fact seen as an important element in the EU's self-consciousness as a new global actor. As Vasconcelos has noted, the global actorship of the EU has consisted in building a new form of multilateralism based on "areas of regional integration and on the experience of supranational regulation of the relations between states", that is, it seeks to turn the international system into "a 'community' on the basis of the success of its own model, which is then extrapolated into the wider world".[29] For this reason, the EU has sought to establish partnerships with regional organizations throughout the world, and now supports the development of regionalism in Asia, Latin America, and Africa. Many regional blocs have been created or re-invented to emulate, or in reaction to, the success story of the EU.

The extrapolation of the EU model has of course not been without challenges. The EU model's incompatibility with some regions of the world has been reported. El-Affendi, for instance, cites the incompatibility of this model of integration with the Third World economies as a major impediment to the growth of regionalism in Africa.[30] He argues that the success of the EU model depends on the emergence of strong and diversified economies, "and presupposes economic complementarity and a strong political commitment" to overcome asymmetrical benefits and costs of integration.[31] However, it suffices

28 Telò, *supra* note 10, at 3.

29 Vasconcelos, *supra* note 23, at 150.

30 El-Affendi, *supra* note 4, at 5.

31 El-Affendi, *supra* note 4, at 5.

to state, as Telò aptly does, that the future of new regionalism is "intrinsically linked to the evolving EU".[32] Although one must remain acutely aware of the risks of too direct or simplistic a comparison, the EU therefore remains the primary comparative model.

1.5 Regionalism in Africa: A Historical Perspective

The fire of new regionalism enkindled in the heart of Europe has also been raging across the continent of Africa. Indeed, regionalism itself is not a new phenomenon in Africa. Some of the world's oldest custom unions are found in Africa, a legacy of colonialism. Whereas we associate the African regional trade integration initiatives since the 1960s with what Telò has called the "economic regionalism" (which emerged alongside US-centered multilateralism of the same period), the actual urge for the unification of the African continent predates the African Independence.[33]

There has always existed in the collective consciousness of Africa, at least in Sub-Saharan Africa, a view that the geographical fault lines that created different African states divided a previously united people. Thus, since the Independence, there have been persistent calls for African Unity. Even if, in the subsequent decades following the Independence, the rather idealistic dream of a politically united Africa, tempered by the complex realities of nation-building, has given way to more modest forms of integration, Africa has remained steadfast in its belief that its welfare is predicated on the unity of the continent.

As Olivier has noted, African regionalism in the post-colonial era has evolved chronologically, in episodes, beginning with the anti-colonial fervor of the immediate post-Independence period which featured a clamor for unification under such slogans as "African Unity", "African Fraternity" and "Pan-Africanism".[34] This episode envisaged a unification process that would lead to the creation of a single African political state—the United States of Africa. Ironically, the institutional embodiment of this dream—the Organization for African Unity (OAU)—would have as one of its main objectives, the defence of the sovereignty of the nation-state inherited from colonialism, a principle that is credited with undermining the integration projects in Africa.

---

32 Telò, *supra* note 10, at 90.

33 Telò, *supra* note 10, at 13.

34 Olivier, G. (n.d.). Regional Integration in Africa: A Political Perspective. *Unpublished Manuscript*, 1–18, at 8.

Olivier has cited this paradox, noting that despite all the rhetoric about African Unity at the formation of the OAU, the "state-centric (confederal) Westphalian model of sovereignty was accepted and institutionalized as the ruling paradigm and political lode star".[35] Hence, whereas one would expect that because of a sense of identity that "manifests so prominently" in Sub-Saharan Africa, it would be easier to achieve African Unity, than in a more heterogeneous region like Europe, this would never be the case.[36] African Unity would remain largely elusive in the decades after Independence. The first attempts at regional integration were hamstrung by several factors, including, "lack of clear leadership and the iron law of impenetrable national sovereignty", and the failure to move beyond minimalist-intergovernmental cooperation.[37] The efforts at integration were further compounded by the subversive post-colonial leadership "driven by the expediency and power-political considerations", and the twin burdens of nation-building and consolidation of national identities.[38]

The second episode featured a shift from the idealism of the Pan-Africanist project to a more modest approach to regional integration, focusing on the "sub-regional economic domain of market-driven intra-state, or extra-territorial cooperation".[39] In the 1960s and 1970s, many African states were tempted into forming regional economic blocs. These attempts basically involved pooling some competencies of domestic regulation and policy at a supranational level. Many regional blocs sprouted across the continent within this framework for example, the SADC, the original East African Community (EAC) and the Economic Community of West African States (ECOWAS). However, this form of regionalism was impeded, again, by the lack of will on the part of the states to cede any power to any supranational body.

A third phase in the evolution of African integration happened at the instigation of a combination of systemic factors. In the 1980s, the United Nations through its Economic Commission for Africa (ECA) supported the Lagos Plan of Action (LPA) and the Full Act of Lagos (FAL), initiated by the OAU, as part of its efforts to revitalize the African economy in the wake of the failure of the post-colonial economic strategies of the preceding decades.[40] The plans proposed a new Pan-African approach to Africa's economic problems

35 Olivier, *supra* note 34, at 6.
36 Olivier, *supra* note 34, at 6.
37 Olivier, *supra* note 34, at 1.
38 Olivier, *supra* note 34, at 6.
39 Olivier, *supra* note 34, at 8.
40 Olivier, *supra* note 34, at 9; El-Affendi, *supra* note 4, at 3.

that included the establishment/revitalization of three Regional Economic Communities (RECs) as a step towards continental integration. They included the revitalization of the already existing, ECOWAS in West Africa, the establishment of the Preferential Trade Area (PTA) in 1981 for Eastern and Southern African states, and the Economic Community for Central African States (ECCAS) in 1983.[41] Olivier remarks that the LPA was indeed an important phase in the evolution of regional integration for re-introducing such pan-Africanist themes like "African solidarity, collective self-reliance and self-sufficiency, economic progress on self-sustaining socio-economic development, reducing its dependence vulnerability vis-à-vis 'external nations'".[42] The LPA underscored the importance of regionalism for African economic progress, expressly urging that "efforts towards African economic integration" be pursued with "renewed determination" so as to create a continental framework for cooperation.[43]

The Abuja Treaty of 1991 marked the beginning of another phase in the evolution of African integration. The Abuja Treaty was an improvement on the LPA. While indicting the African leadership with failure to confront Africa's economic problem, the Abuja Treaty reiterated the importance of regional integration, and in fact set the timeline for full continental economic integration at 2025.[44] The Abuja Treaty recommended the rationalization of RECs to address the problem of multiple membership African states.[45] It envisaged the ultimate continental integration which would culminate in the African Economic Community (AEC) which would be achieved progressively, beginning with the revamping of existing, or the development of new RECs, as building blocks.[46] The immediate post-Abuja Treaty era saw the revitalization of main regional economic blocks. Within its framework, the PTA was replaced by the Common Market for Eastern and Southern Africa (COMESA) in 1993.[47]

Perhaps the most important phase in African integration was set off by the Sirte summit of 2001 which replaced the OAU with the African Union (AU). Olivier has noted that the launching of the AU marked the beginning of the "ultimate episode in African integration".[48] The AU, Olivier observes,

41 El-Affendi, *supra* note 4, at 3.

42 Olivier, *supra* note 34, at 10.

43 Olivier, *supra* note 34, at 10.

44 El-Affendi, *supra* note 4, at 3.

45 African Development Bank. (2016). *Eastern African Regional Integration Strategy Paper* (2011–2015). REGIONAL DEPARTMENTS—EAST (OREA/OREB). African Development Bank, at 1.

46 African Development Bank, *supra* note 45.

47 El-Affendi, *supra* note 4, at 3.

48 Olivier, *supra* note 34, at 12.

essentially perpetuates the OAU paradigm of integration, emphasizing the OAU's foundational principles of "unity, solidarity, cohesion and co-operation".[49] However, whereas it generally upholds the Westphalian nation-state concept that has dominated the past integration projects, it adopts a weaker form of sovereignty, providing for intervention in the member states, "in respect of 'grave circumstances' or if requested by member states to restore peace and security".[50] In the words of Olivier, the AU waters down the old African dictum of "non-interference: to "non-indifference".[51]

The AU also has the quality of being a remote replica of the EU. By its structure and objectives, it exemplifies the type of regionalism that belongs to the species of new regionalism. Olivier has observed that even though the EU and AU are *sui generis* organizations in different ways, they nevertheless share some structural and even foundational philosophical underpinnings.[52] He identifies convergence in the intellectual underpinnings of integration, and the role perceptions of both organizations. He observes, for instance, that both the AU and EU emerged against backgrounds of nation-state failures: just as the "idea of Europe" evolved as a "remedy against nationalistic wars", the "idea of Africa" has similarly been inspired by anti-colonial sentiments, and the past failures of African nation-states.[53] Moreover, he adds, just as the EU has evolved out of the acknowledgement by post-war Europe that unity would be essential for survival in the bi-polar Cold War world dominated by the United States and the Soviet-Union, African integration has also been inspired by the appreciation of the need for unity in the face of the Cold War and Western economic dominance in the post-colonial era.[54]

The AU also shares the structural framework of the EU, having adopted such institutions as the Commission, the Council, and the Parliament, even if each of these are endowed with less power compared to those of the EU. Of course, for obvious reasons, many differences abound between the two organizations. Perhaps most noteworthy is the fact, as Vines has observed, that the AU came into existence fully formed and therefore did not have to confront

49 Olivier, *supra* note 34, at 12.
50 Olivier, *supra* note 34, at 12.
51 Olivier, *supra* note 34, at 12.
52 Olivier, *supra* note 34, at 1.
53 Olivier, *supra* note 34, at 1.
54 Olivier, *supra* note 34, at 1.

some of the challenges that the EU faced in its evolution.[55] This also means that it did not have any accession criteria and there was no threshold of democratic or economic behaviour that a state needed to attain before admission. Whereas the EU integration has evolved in a linear succession, from simple preferential trade area, to free trade area, through customs union, common market, economic union, towards, ultimately, political union, the AU has adopted a more "top-down" approach to integration, that began with the mega unification projects embodied in OAU/AU, and then moving to the RECs.[56] Still, the EU integration, because it has been a success, provides the best model for the kind of regionalism to which Africa aspires.

The AU and the RECs initiated within its framework, have exemplified new regionalism both in origins and objectives. There is a considerable discontinuity between the pre-Sirte summit regionalism and regionalism after the summit. Indeed, after the Abuja Treaty of 1991, regionalism in Africa has been mainly driven by the fear of marginalization of the continent in the new world order characterized by regionalism on the one hand, and globalization on the other. As observed above, the new wave of African regional integration has also been instigated by systemic factors such the international community (the United Nations), and the European Union.

However, as Olivier notes, regional integration in Africa still constitutes at best, a "work in progress" en route to deeper regional integration, and compared to the EU which it holds as a model, it is still in its "rudimentary stages".[57] The political union, which would feature deeper institutional integration, is yet to be achieved, and is conditioned, as rightly reported by Telò, by the "heterogeneity and pre-democratic" nature of the nation-states.[58] Many factors, such as the weight of the colonial past, "the legacy of the Cold War, the cultural, religious, and linguistic diversity, the unique relation between state and society," and together with the perennial problems of under development, the lack of harmonization between national economies, and indeed the ever present political tensions between and within Member States, have conspired to slow down the process.

55 Vines, A. (2013). *A Decade of African Peace and Security Architecture.* International Affairs, 89 (1), 89-1-9, at 95.

56 Olivier, *supra* note 34, at 15.

57 Olivier, *supra* note 34, at 5.

58 Telò, *supra* note 10, at 77.

1.6 African Regionalism: A Factor in the Decline of the Post-Colonial State?

The debate on the relationship between regional integration and the nation-state in Africa is a prominent feature of the discourse on African regionalism, just as it has featured prominently in the discourse on new regionalism in general. As already observed, the place of the state within the framework of regional integration has constituted an essential fault line in the theoretical debates about new regionalism. In Africa, the strong hold of the Westphalian paradigm of state sovereignty—a legacy of colonialism—on politics and economics, has limited the efforts for regional integration to minimalist intergovernmentalism.

The assertion of a strong form of state sovereignty has repeatedly been cited as one of the contributing factors to the failure of regional integration in Africa. There is no doubt that Africa recognizes the importance of regionalism for political and economic progress, but it seems African governments wish this were achievable without having to cede their authority, or shift their loyalties to some continental federal or supra-national institution which they cannot control; or rather that regionalism should complement rather than supplant their national projects. In fact, as Oyugi explains, the governments have preferred to view regionalism as an instrument that supplements or enhances or protects the role of the nation-state.[59] Proponents of this view have also held that regionalism rescues rather than weakens the nation-state in Africa, and provides a gateway for the continent into the global political economy.

Africa's experiment with the Westphalian state system has been notably characterized by dismal failure. Anadi has observed that the independent African states were, in the first place, never "really negotiated states"; they were imposed by colonialism against the consent of the nationalities and thus, always struggled for legitimacy.[60] Lacking legitimacy, the states have relied heavily on force to sustain power, and consequently could not "sufficiently harness the advantages of 'political plurality and ethnic diversity' in nation building".[61] With attention and resources diverted towards strengthening

59 Oyugi, E. (2009). East African Community—the Third Round: A People, Market or State-driven Regionalisation project? *EAC 10th Anniversary Symposium: Role of Non-State Actors in Deepening EAC Integration* (p. 9). Arusha: East African Community, at 2.

60 Anadi, S.K. (2005). *REGIONAL INTEGRATION IN AFRICA: The case of ECOWAS*. Zürich: Zürich University, at 19.

61 Anadi, *supra* note 60.

legitimacy, the states therefore have never been able to pay due attention to the development of sustainable socio-economic and political institutions. The weaknesses have also rendered the African state vulnerable to the forces of globalization. In the post-independent era, the African state has witnessed several conflicts, some of which have in fact threatened its very existence.[62] The case of the African state has typified the inability of the nation-state to singularly provide "public goods". Like every part of the world, regionalism has presented Africa with an opportunity to address the failures of the nation-state and to respond to the threat of globalization. It is within this context that the East African Community, to which we now turn, came into existence.

1.7 Regionalization in the East African Community

An African Development Bank (AfDB) Strategy Paper on Eastern African Regional Integration reports that the Eastern African region has the largest number of RECs and intergovernmental bodies in Africa, with each of the 12[63] countries in the region possessing membership of six of the eight RECs recognized by the AU.[64] Six of the twelve Eastern African countries—Burundi, Kenya, Rwanda, Tanzania, Republic of South Sudan and Uganda, constitute a regional bloc known as the East African Community (EAC). The EAC defines itself as a regional intergovernmental organization that aims at "widening and deepening co-operation among member states in, among others, political, economic and social fields for their mutual benefit".[65] The organization has established a Customs Union (2005) and a Common Market (2010), and is in the process of establishing a Monetary Union. Its ultimate objective is to establish a complete political Union—a "Political Federation of the East African States".[66]

62 Anadi, *supra* note 60.

63 *See* Fig. 1, East Africa' (African Development Bank Website) <http://www.afdb.org/en/countries/east-africa/> accessed 31 July 2016.

64 African Development Bank, *supra* note 45, at v.

65 http://www.eac.int/faqs, EAC. (2013). *Home: About EAC*. Retrieved April 9, 2016, from An East African Community Website: http://www.eac.int/index.php?option=com_content&view=article&id=1:welcome-to- eac&catid=34:body-text-area&Itemid=53.

66 EAC, *supra* note 65.

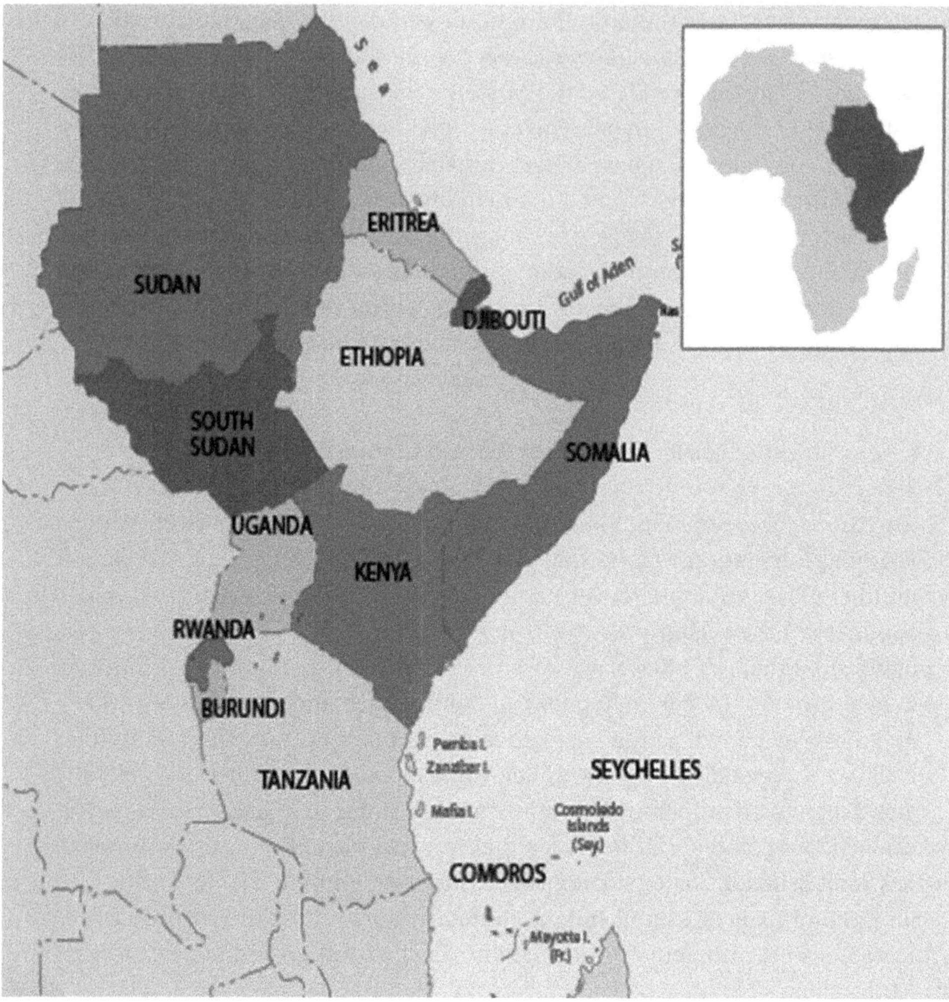

FIGURE 1.1 *Map of Eastern Africa.*[67]
SOURCE: AFRICAN DEVELOPMENT BANK WEBSITE (2016).

1.8 The Defunct EAC

The EAC is, like the AU, a reincarnation of a defunct predecessor. The history of regional integration in East Africa can be traced to the late 19th century, in the very early days of colonialism in the region. As noted in the preamble

67 'East Africa' (African Development Bank Website) <http://www.afdb.org/en/countries/east-africa/> accessed 31 July 2016.

to the Treaty for the Establishment of the East African Community, the formal and social integration in the region can be traced to the construction of the Kenya-Uganda Railways from 1897–1901, the establishment of the Customs Collection Center for Uganda in Mombasa in 1900, and the East African Currency Board and the Postal Union, in 1905.[68] These were later followed by the establishment of the Court of Appeal for East Africa in 1909, the Customs Union for Uganda, Tanganyika and Kenya, then under British administration, in 1919, among other regional initiatives.[69]

Perhaps the most significant milestone in the process of regional integration at this stage was the formation of the East African High Commission in 1948, to strengthen economic links between the three countries.[70] The Commission established a unified income tax for the three countries. It was succeeded by the East African Common Services Organization, which was established in 1961 to coordinate such regional service organizations as the East African Posts and Telecommunications, the East African Railways and Harbors, the East African Airways, the East African Air Aviation Services and the East African Development Bank.[71] In 1967, a treaty—The Treaty for the East African Cooperation—was signed by three East African nations—Kenya, Tanzania and Uganda—establishing the East African Community, and succeeding the East African Common Services Organization.[72] Under the Treaty, the three nations agreed to cooperate in a wide array of economic and social issues. The Community fostered cooperation in many areas within the region, and was considered at the time a model of regional integration and development. The integration achieved under the Community was so deep that it was, as Kiraso has observed, "in all but name, a federal government".[73] However, in 1977, barely a decade after it came into existence, the EAC collapsed. Several reasons have been advanced to explain why the Community collapsed. Shivji explains it rather aptly:

---

68 EAC. (2010). *Home: Treaty Establishing the East African Community*. Retrieved April 08, 2016, from East African Community Website: http://www.eac.int/treaty/index.php?option=com_content&view=article&id=75&Itemid=156, at 3.

69 EAC, *supra* note 68, at 4.

70 Kiraso, B.B. (2009). EAC Integration—Enabling Peace and Security Architecture. *EAC Peace and Security Conference* (p. 18). Kampala: East African Community, at 2; Reith, S., & Boltz, M. (2011). The East African Community Integration: Between Aspiration and Reality. Ambition for and Reality of the East African Community in a Globalized World (pp. 91–107). Dar es Salaam: Konrad Adenauer Stiftung, at 92.

71 Kiraso, *supra* note 70.

72 EAC, *supra* note 68, at 5.

73 Kiraso, *supra* note 70.

> The East African Community formed in 1967, which attempted to address one of the deep-rooted scourges of colonialism, uneven development, also fell victim to the forces of compradorialism and imperialism. It is not necessary to go into details. Suffice it to say that the limited economic unity could not be sustained in absence of a durable political framework. And a durable political framework could not be developed in absence of political unity.[74]

The Treaty that would re-establish the Community more than two decades later points to "lack of strong political will, lack of strong participation of the private sector and civil society in the cooperation activities, the continued disproportionate sharing of benefits of the Community among Partner States due to the differences in their levels of development and lack of adequate policies to address the situation" as the contributing factors to the collapse of the Community.[75]

Many analysts have cited the strong intergovernmental (interstate) structure of the Community, and the ideological differences between the leaders of the Member States as the main reasons for the collapse. For example, in the 1970s, Tanzania was drifting towards Socialism, while Kenya adopted a Capitalist system and this ideological incongruence played out in the Community. Mugomba has pointed out also that beyond ideology, regional conflict, and external systemic penetration, the East African Community integration was also subverted by such factors as "the growing 'radicalization' of regional politics, including the proliferation of Marxist-oriented regimes in Eastern and Southern Africa; Kenya's contribution to the 'development of underdevelopment' within the Community and the Common Market, as well as the increasingly conservative, authoritarian, and defensive position of Kenyatta's regime both at home and in the region".[76] Furthermore, the collapse of the Community is also blamed on governance challenges such as the absence of mechanisms to address corruption, non-respect for rule of law, and impunity.[77]

---

74 Shivji, I.G. (2009). Pan-Africanism and the Challenge of East African Integration. *EAC 10th Anniversary Symposium* (13–14 November, 2009): Pan-Africanism and the Challenge of East African Integration (p. 11). Arusha: East African Community, at 6.

75 EAC, *supra* note 68.

76 Mugomba, A.T. (1978). Regional Organizations and African Underdevelopment: the Collapse of the East African Community. The Journal of Modern African Studies, 16 (2), *The Journal of Modern African Studies*, at 270.

77 Kiraso, *supra* note 70, at 1.

The collapse of the Community led to the dismemberment of its jointly-operated services, with each Member State assuming direct control over regional services within its territorial boundaries. Regional projects—railways, ports, harbors, postal services and airlines—were all now managed separately. However, even with the collapse of the Community, the East African states still acknowledged the advantages of integration for the region and it was always hoped that the Community would be revived at some later date. Therefore, the Mediation Agreement of 1984, which set the criteria for dividing the EAC's assets and liabilities, also included a provision for the future re-establishment of the Community.[78]

1.9 The Re-establishment of the EAC

Steps were taken to reestablish the Community at two summits of the head of states held in 1993 and 1997. In 1993, a Permanent Tripartite Commission for Cooperation was set up to oversee the drafting of a treaty for the establishment of the EAC, and in November 1999, the Treaty for the reestablishment of the East African Community was signed by the heads of state of Kenya, Uganda and Tanzania. The Treaty entered into force on 7th July 2000. Two new members, Rwanda and Burundi, acceded to the Community in 2007 and the Republic of South Sudan in 2016, bringing its membership to six. The new-look EAC therefore constitutes a larger bloc than its defunct predecessor and with a combined population of more than 143.5 million people, land area of 1.82 million square kilometers, and a combined Gross Domestic Product of $110.3 billion, it constitutes a key driver of regional integration in the entire East African region.[79]

The EAC has already achieved some of its objectives; it has managed to establish a Customs Union (2005) and a Common Market (2010), and is in the process of establishing a Monetary Union.[80] However, in light of its ambitious objectives, these achievements are rather modest. The Community aims ultimately to have a "prosperous, competitive, secure and politically united Eastern Africa"—a Political Federation of the East African States.[81]

78 Kiraso, *supra* note 70, at 4.

79 EAC Secretariat. (2012). *East African Community Facts and Figures*—2012. Arusha: East Africa Community.

80 EAC, *supra* note 65. See further chapters 9, 10, and 13 on these developments.

81 EAC, *supra* note 68.

As stated in its founding Treaty, Article 5(1), the objective of the Community is to develop policies and programs aimed at "widening and deepening cooperation among Partner States in political, economic, social and cultural fields, research and technology, defense, security and legal and judicial affairs for mutual benefit".[82]

The EAC thus aims to provide the public goods which the Member States cannot individually provide. As Reith and Boltz rightly observe, few of the many African regional blocs have set their sights so high.[83] Even the more established organizations like COMESA, SADC and ECOWAS do not have a provision for political union in their founding treaties. By its integration process, and objectives, the new EAC typifies the regional blocs that have been spawned by the new wave of regionalism. It takes for its model the EU, and has adopted the EU's institutional framework—it is highly institutionalized. The new EAC also aims at far deeper integration than envisioned by its predecessor. The EAC has also provided in the founding Treaty, for safeguards against the fatal mistakes that led to the collapse of its predecessor, including, a gradual approach to integration; decentralization of powers from the Summit to the Council of Ministers; provision for people-centered and private-sector driven integration; inclusion of civil society as key stakeholders; and, stringent withdrawal procedures.[84]

However, questions still linger over the viability of this renewed attempt at integration in the East African region. Analysts have warned that unless the leading decision-makers in the EAC temper their rhetoric with some measure of action, the current attempt may, like the previous EAC, flounder. Reith and Boltz have noted that the EAC "is strong on paper, but weak in the implementation of its decision", and risks losing the support of civil society and becoming "the scapegoat of national politics".[85] Immediately after the collapse of the first integration project, Mugomba had warned that no attempt at integration would be successful until there was an ideological consensus among partner states, the acceptance of a common economic strategy, and a willingness to tackle the asymmetries of regional distribution of integration benefits and losses.[86] While these factors no longer constitute a real threat to integration, the project nevertheless faces other, even greater challenges.

82 EAC, *supra* note 68.

83 Reith & Boltz, *supra* note 70, at 91.

84 Kiraso, *supra* note 70, at 4.

85 Reith & Boltz, *supra* note 70, at 91.

86 Mugomba, *supra* note 76.

There are many challenges to be overcome to realize the integration to which the EAC aspires. The AfDB Strategy Paper on Regional Integration in the Eastern African Region lists four key challenges to successful regional integration, which are also true with regard to the EAC: weak institutional and human capacity of the RECs and national implementation units; poor performance of regional organizations which impedes their capacity to deliver expected benefits of integration; limited capacity to mobilize the participation of private sector actors in the structures and processes of integration, and insecurity and cross-border conflicts.[87]

The key challenge faced by the EAC is its ambitious nature weighed against its capacity. The EAC has adopted a tight integration plan that is scheduled to progress through the stages of integration "at a gallop"—with the customs union, the common market, monetary union, and the political federation all being achieved within set time frames. However, as the EU integration (which the EAC seeks to emulate) has shown, regional integration is a complex process that requires much time, and serious resources. The EAC's ambitious goals are inconsistent with the reality of its capacity, and the capacity of its Member States to achieve them. According to the AfDB Strategy Paper, the regional organizations in the East African region, including the EAC lack the adequate capacity and resources to plan, coordinate, and monitor the processes required to further the integration.[88] For instance, it has no capacity to design complicated corridor investment projects, or for monitoring and evaluation mechanisms for the integration processes.[89] The process of integration is further compounded by the reluctance of Member States of the organizations to cede requisite competences to regional bodies, which has meant that regional institutions have little power to make decisions that would enhance integration. The AfDB Strategy Paper also cites lack of convergence of attitudes towards regional integration as one of the challenges with which the Community is confronted.[90] Together with the reluctance of the governments to cede sufficient authority to the regional institutions, and to enact legislation and regulations necessary to guide the integration process, the regional concerns and priorities are often also not really reflected in the national policies—the governments simply do not accord the regional integration project due regard.

87 African Development Bank, *supra* note 45, at vii.

88 African Development Bank, *supra* note 45, at vii.

89 African Development Bank, *supra* note 45, at vii.

90 African Development Bank, *supra* note 45, at 13.

Furthermore, due to the reluctance of states to cede power to supranational bodies, the EAC is characterized by an excessive state monopoly over decision-making processes and institutions which in turn poses a serious challenge to successful integration. The EAC defines itself as an intergovernmental organization, and even though it has made provisions for the inclusion of other actors in its decision-making process, the monopoly of the decision-making process still rests with the governments of the states, leaving non-state actors and the civil society locked out of the integration process.

Moreover, effective and deeper integration in the EAC is greatly inhibited by the insecurity and political instability in the region. The AfDB Strategy Paper acknowledges that apart from offering the Member States the opportunity to achieve "better connectivity and enhance prosperity by collectively investing in growth and development to fight poverty, the EAC could also be a tool for resolving the many conflicts that have ravaged the East African region".[91] Each of the five Member States, with the exception of Tanzania, has experienced at least one conflict—ethnic or civil—in the last two decades and each of the states is neighbored by at least one country experiencing one conflict or another. Security is indeed a "Public Good" that the nation-states have not been able to provide individually, and for which they need collectivity to provide. The AfDB Strategy Paper points out that the rampant political conflicts in the region constitute, a "regional public "bad" that frightens investors, inhibits development and stifles economic growth", and consumes resources that are badly needed for productive activities.[92] Thus, it is underlined that the resolution of conflicts and the maintenance of peace and security constitute essential conditions for successful regional integration in the East African region.

1.10 EAC Integration as an Antidote to the Failure of the State in the East African Region

Lamenting Africa's moral crisis at the turn of the twenty first century, the Ghanaian Philosopher, Kwame Gyekye remarked:

> Confronted with a deep and resilient development crisis, with frequent military disruptions of the democratic political process resulting, inevitably, in political instability, uncertainty, and confusion, and with a poor demonstration of political morality resulting in pervasive and rampant

91 African Development Bank, *supra* note 45, at 16.

92 African Development Bank, *supra* note 45, at 16.

> political corruption[,]... African life on the eve of the twenty-first century is not only confused but at a low ebb.[93]

The catalogue of the failures of the post-colonial African state is inexhaustible. Africa's fifty years of experiment with the Westphalian nation-state has been anything but successful. The African state has also, in the last few decades, had to contend with the phenomenon of globalization—the combination of the international forces, political actors and multinational organizations—which, analysts argue, threaten its very existence. It is against the acknowledgement of the limitations and failures of the state, on the one hand, and the threat of globalization, on the other, that the debate on the new wave of regionalism in Africa has been carried out. The question has been whether the maddening rush by Africa for the formation of regional blocs in the recent years—most African states have overlapping membership in many regional organizations—is itself a concession of the limitations of the states in the light of the challenges with which the continent is confronted, and whether indeed regionalism constitutes the continent's best response to the failures of the state and to the threats posed by globalization.

This section has analysed the EAC in the context of the resurgence of regionalism across the globe in the last few decades and has probed the claim that new regionalism is the world's, and indeed Africa's, response to the decline and failure of the nation-state, and the threat of globalization.

---

93 Gyekye, K. (1997). *Tradition and Modernity: Philosophical Reflections on the African Experience.* New York: Oxford University Press.

CHAPTER 1A

The Road to European Integration

Armin Cuyvers

1.1 A Bumpy but Rewarding Road …

The European Union (EU) has achieved a unique level of political and economic integration. More than 500 million European citizens share an area of Freedom Security and Justice and an internal market that forms the largest economic bloc in the world. 19 national currencies have been 'integrated' into a single European currency, further enabling trade and increasing wealth. To achieve and sustain such integration, strong institutions have been built, novel legal and political mechanisms have been developed, and substantial powers have been shared at the Union level, all whilst maintaining the ultimate authority and democratic legitimacy of the Member States.

This high level of integration has wielded enormous benefits in terms of wealth, stability and influence. For despite the vital importance of good law and institutions, part of the real secret behind integration is that it ultimately forms a win-win for all players involved. For states, citizens and businesses alike, integration can provide vital economic and political benefits. What is more, in our globalizing reality, integration is also necessary to retain the economic and political significance of individual states. As markets, companies and the digital world transcend borders, so must states transcend their own borders and cooperate to retain their relevance.

At the same time, European integration has been a long and bumpy road, and the process is far from complete. For despite its long-term benefits, it remains a challenge to properly structure regional integration and to overcome short-term obstacles and conflicts of interest. How, for example, to balance the influence and interests of different Member States, how to divide the benefits and costs of integration, or how to structure democracy at the supranational level? Over the years, therefore, the EU has faced many challenges and set-backs as it pioneered the process of regional integration and tried to adapt how we govern to the reality that needs to be governed. *Brexit* only forms the most recent example of such a set-back and of just how challenging it is to develop regional integration that is effective and legitimate, and that can resist short-term nationalistic reflexes, especially in times of (economic) crises and uncertainty. So far, however, the EU has always overcome such set-backs,

© ARMIN CUYVERS, 2017 | DOI 10.1163/9789004322073_003
This is an open access chapter distributed under the terms of the CC-BY-NC License.

usually deepening integration as a result, in part because of the ultimate desirability and necessity of regional integration as set out above, although the fall-out of *Brexit* of course still has to become clear.

It is the long and bumpy road travelled by the EU that will be discussed in the different EU companion chapters in this book. These companion chapters provide concise overviews of different fields of EU law and discuss the key legal tools that were developed to turn integration from an aspiration into a reality. Considering the comparative objective of this book, the primary focus of these companion chapters is on the foundational rules, mechanism and doctrines of EU law that still provide the basis for European integration today, and that might provide useful inspiration for East African integration now. For more comprehensive or specific discussions on particular issues of EU law each chapter will refer the reader to more specialized literature. In this way, the companion chapters also hope to function as a portal for those wanting to engage in more in depth comparative EAC-EU analysis on particular topics.[1]

Despite their comparative ambitions, the EU companion chapters of course fully recognize the significant differences between the EU and the EAC, and consequently the need for tailor-made EAC solutions that fit the unique potential of East Africa in the 21st century. Comparison can never be a cut-and-paste exercise.[2] Nor do the EU companion chapters assume that the 'European way' is per definition the 'best' and should therefore always be followed. Quite the contrary: the EU offers more than enough failures and mistakes to learn from, and these failures are often at least as instructive as the EU successes. Instead of simplistically transplanting EU norms to the EAC, therefore, the aim of the companion chapters is first to distill the different *legal solutions*

1 For those interested in further exploring EU law also see the Massive Open Online Course (MOOC) 'The Law of the European Union: An Introduction 'developed by the Europa Instituut of Leiden University and available online for free via Coursera.

2 See on the challenges of comparison *inter alia* V.C. Jackson, 'Comparative Constitutional Law: Methodologies', in: M. Rosenfeld and A. Sajó (eds) *The Oxford Handbook of Comparative Constitutional Law* (OUP 2012), 54, V.C. Jackson, 'Methodological Challenges in Comparative Constitutional Law' 28 *Penn State International Law Review* (2010), 319, M. Tushnet, 'Comparative Constitutional Law', in: M. Reimann and R. Zimmermann (eds), *The Oxford Handbook of Comparative Law* (OUP 2006), 1226, G. Frankenberg, 'Comparing constitutions: Ideas, ideals, and ideology—toward a layered narrative', *International Journal of Constitutional Law* (2006), 439, P. Legrand, 'The Impossibility of "Legal Transplants"' 4 *Maastricht Journal of European and Comparative Law* (1997), 111. and classically O. Kahn-Freund, 'On Uses and Misuses of Comparative Law', 37 *Modern Law Review* (1974), 1.

that were developed to meet the different challenges of regional integration. Subsequently, in conjunction with the primary EAC chapters and preferably in a combined effort between EAC and EU experts, it can be further explored how such legal solutions may be translated and adapted to the EAC context. With the benefit of almost 60 years of European hindsight, such a joint effort could hopefully help the EAC to avoid some of the detours taken by European integration, shortening the path towards EAC integration and removing some of the bumps. This is especially so as the EAC has adapted significant parts of the EU institutional and legal framework in its Treaties and Protocols.

This first companion chapter discusses the development of the EU from a Community of six focused on Coal and Steel to a deeply integrated Union of 28. Considering the limited size of this chapter and the rich history of European integration, the discussion focusses on the main developments and most formative crises.[3] Consequently, this chapter first discusses the failed attempts at European integration that preceded the EU, as well as other forms of cooperation in Europe from which the EU should be distinguished. It then charts how the process of European integration got underway, and how it gradually widened and deepened as more and more Member States joined and European integration came to cover more and more policy areas. This discussion will include the different Treaties signed as well as some of the major crises and events faced by the EU, both to present the whole picture of the integration process and to demonstrate how crises may actually form vital and integral parts of integration. The chapter concludes with a brief discussion of Brexit, the most recent fundamental challenge to European integration that may contain useful lessons for the EAC, including on the question of how to deal with the possible withdrawal of Partner States.

3 For more detailed discussions on the history of European integration and it main drivers see *inter alia* P. Craig & G. De Búrca, *EU Law: texts, cases and materials* (OUP, 2015, 6th edition), D. Chalmers, G. Davies and G. Monti, *European Union Law* (CUP, 2010), G. Majone, *Dilemmas of European Integration: The Ambiguities and Pitfalls of Integration by Stealth* (OUP, 2005), A. Moravcsik, *The Choice for Europes: Social Purpose and State Power from Messina to Maastricht* (Cornell University Press, 1998), or G. Delanty, *Inventing Europe: Idea, Identity, Reality* (Macmillan, 1995).

1.2 The Idea of European Integration: From Failed Attempts to a Union on Coal and Steel

The idea of uniting 'Europe' has been around for a long time, even if the meaning of 'Europe' itself has never been static.[4] Several kings, emperors and dictators have obviously tried to 'unite' Europe by force. However, there also is a long history of proposals to unite Europe in a more peaceful and cooperative manner. In 1693, for example, William Penn already developed a confederal proposal for Europe in his 'Essay Towards the Present and Future Peace of Europe'. In 1814, the French philosopher Saint-Simon, even came surprisingly close to the EU institutional framework we find today, even planning the capital for his Union close to Brussels.[5]

These early ideas, however, never gained real traction. They went against the grain of European history, which, in the age of Westphalia, moved towards ever more centralized and powerful nation-states.[6] Instead of cooperation and sharing authority, the trend was to concentrate authority in the state and to make the state increasingly absolute. Two world wars, however, drastically changed the near sacred status of the sovereign state. World War I lasted from 1914 until 1918, leaving over 16 million dead. After this war, the League of Nations was established, a kind of predecessor to the United Nations, to prevent future wars. This relatively weak intergovernmental organization, however, failed, and could not prevent a second World War from erupting between 1939 and 1945. Total deaths due do the Second World War are estimated between 60 to 80 million. This includes the systematic extermination of over 11 million people, mostly Jews, in the Holocaust.

Both world wars had truly brought home the devastating nature and effect of modern industrial warfare, especially once linked to nationalism and absolute nation-states. Once nationalism, centralized nation-states and modern weaponry were combined, the effects were simply unconscionable. Consequently,

---

4 See for example D. De Rougemont, *The Idea of Europe* (New York, MacMillian, 1965), G. Delanty, *Inventing Europe: Idea, Identity, Reality* (Basingstoke, Macmillian, 1995), J. Le Goff, *The Birth of Europe* (Oxford, Blackwell, 2005), or R. McKitterick, *Charlemagne: the Formation of a European Identity* (Cambridge, CUP, 2008).

5 See his 1814 'Plan de la Réorganisation de la société européenne', or 'Plan for the Reorganisation of the European Society'.

6 See for a further discussion of the Peace of Westphalia, traditionally seen as the 'birth' of the modern, sovereign nation-state, and the subsequent evolution of the concept of sovereignty in Europe A. Cuyvers, *The EU as a Confederal Union of Sovereign Member Peoples, Exploring the potential of American (con)federalism and popular sovereignty for a constitutional theory of the EU*, (Leiden, 2013).

preventing future wars became of paramount importance. Never again, *nie wieder, jamais*, became the rallying cry for European integration, as well as for other international attempts to impose some limits and controls on European states. For if states cannot be trusted to always control themselves, the logical conclusion was that another layer of control, *above* the state, was necessary to provide a safe-guard.[7]

At the international level, the UN was established in 1945, with the UN Security Council receiving unique competences on the legal use of force.[8] In Europe, the Council of Europe was established in 1949, with a focus on democracy, the rule of law and human rights. The Council of Europe, which today has 47 Members, is best known for the European Court of Human Rights (ECtHR) in Strasbourg, which applies the European Convention on Human Rights (ECHR). The core idea behind the ECHR is precisely to have a fundamental rights court outside and above the state, so that it can offer protection *against* the state where necessary. Primary protection of fundamental rights, therefore, remains at the national level, but the ECtHR forms a safeguard where the state fails to respect fundamental rights. The Council of Europe, however, should not be confused with the EU. The Council of Europe is an independent, separate international organization, with a different and more limited mandate. It also is a less far reaching form of integration, and does not even come close to the level and scope of supranational integration achieved in the EU.

The first step in the creation of what would become the EU, however, was only taken with the famous Schuman declaration of 9 May 1950.[9] In this declaration, largely drafted by Jean Monnet, Schuman proposed the creation of a European Coal and Steel Community:

> Europe will not be made all at once, or according to a single plan. It will be built through concrete achievements which first create a de facto solidarity. The coming together of the nations of Europe requires the

7 This narrative obviously leaves out the often atrocious acts of European states outside the EU as, sadly enough, these acts never played as central a role in uniting Europe as the destruction European states visited on themselves.

8 See especially Title VII of the UN Charter and the powers of the UN Security Council contained therein.

9 On the failure of two other attempts concerning political and military integration see for example E. Fursdon, *The European Defence Community: A History* (Macmillan, 1980) and R. Cardozo, 'The Project for a Political Community (1952–2), in R. Pryce (ed), *The Dynamics of European Union* (Croom Helm 1987).

> elimination of the age-old opposition of France and Germany. Any action taken must in the first place concern these two countries.
>
> With this aim in view, the French Government proposes that action be taken immediately on one limited but decisive point: It proposes that Franco-German production of coal and steel as a whole be placed under a common High Authority, within the framework of an organisation open to the participation of the other countries of Europe.
>
> The pooling of coal and steel production should immediately provide for the setting up of common foundations for economic development as a first step in the federation of Europe, and will change the destinies of those regions which have long been devoted to the manufacture of munitions of war, of which they have been the most constant victims.
>
> The solidarity in production thus established will make it plain that any war between France and Germany becomes not merely unthinkable, but materially impossible. The setting up of this powerful productive unit, open to all countries willing to take part and bound ultimately to provide all the member countries with the basic elements of industrial production on the same terms, will lay a true foundation for their economic unification.
>
> This production will be offered to the world as a whole without distinction or exception, with the aim of contributing to raising living standards and to promoting peaceful achievements. With increased resources Europe will be able to pursue the achievement of one of its essential tasks, namely, the development of the African continent.
>
> In this way, there will be realised simply and speedily that fusion of interest which is indispensable to the establishment of a common economic system; it may be the leaven from which may grow a wider and deeper community between countries long opposed to one another by sanguinary divisions.
>
> By pooling basic production and by instituting a new High Authority, whose decisions will bind France, Germany and other member countries, this proposal will lead to the realisation of the first concrete foundation of a European federation indispensable to the preservation of peace.

Without condoning in any form the reference to Africa, the central idea behind the Schuman declaration was to create a supranational authority over Coal and Steel, which were at that time the two central commodities for industrialization and war. In addition, the declaration already contained the interconnection of peace and prosperity that was to become central to European integration. On the one hand, economic integration formed a tool to ensure peace: once key industries were integrated war would become an (economic) impossibility. On the other hand, economic development and increased prosperity also formed an end in itself for a Europe ravaged by war. Continued peace, moreover, would also contribute to prosperity as nothing undermines continued prosperity as armed conflict.[10]

The European Coal and Steel Community was established in 1952 by the six 'founding members' France, Germany, Italy, Belgium, Luxemburg and The Netherlands, and contained the vital supranational elements suggested by Schuman and Monnet.[11] Most importantly, a supranational High Authority was established, the later Commission, which could take binding decisions within its own mandate.[12] The supranational nature of the ECSC distinguished it from 'normal' intergovernmental organizations, and allowed it to be far more effective and successful.

1.3 From Coal and Steel to the European Community

In 1957, following the success of the ECSC, two additional organisations, both clearly supranational in character, were created: the European Atomic Agency (EAA), and the European Economic Community (EEC).[13] In contrast to the ECSC and the EAA, however, the EEC was not limited to specific sectors such as coal and steel or atomic energy, but covered the entire economy. The EEA and the EEC were established by the same six countries that also pioneered the establishment of Coal and Steel Community.

Of these three organisations it is the EEC that developed furthest and contributed most to the economic integration in Europe.[14] Its growth over the past decades, both in scope as in membership, has been quite impressive.

10 See on this combination also EU Chapter 9.

11 Treaty establishing the European Coal and Steel Community (Paris, 18 April 1951).

12 See further on this point EU Chapter 2.

13 The Treaty establishing the European Atomic Energy Community (Euratom) and the Treaty establishing the European Economic Community (also known as the Treaty of Rome), (Rome, 25 March 1957).

14 In fact the ECSC itself no longer exists. As the ECSC Treaty was concluded for a limited period of 50 years, it expired in 2002 with all the assets and activities of the ECSC being subsumed into the EU.

1.3.1 *Development of the EEC*

The development of the EEC was, of course, gradual, but certain crucial stages in its development can be singled out. After the initial successes and enthusiasm, the first critical challenge came in the 1960s and 1970s. During this time, and largely due to the political resistance by French president De Gaulle, the EEC had slowly retreated to a more intergovernmental way of functioning. In June 1965 the situation escalated when De Gaulle walked out of negotiations, and for more than half a year the French refused to participate at all, a situation that became known as the 'empty chair crisis'. This crisis was resolved in January of 1966 with the Luxembourg Accords, but at a very high price. Under the Luxembourg Accords, every Member State could declare that a certain proposal being discussed in the Council touched on 'very important national interest', which would then obligate the others not to vote on the proposal at all. *De facto*, the Luxemburg Accords gave every Member State a veto whenever they wanted to claim one, and they did so frequently. The increasingly frequent use of vetoes blocked decision-making, undermined the supranational assumptions underlying the EEC, and led to a long period of political stagnation.[15]

During this period of political stagnation, it was the European Court of Justice (CJEU) that kept the process of integration going, *inter alia* with its seminal judgments on the direct effect and supremacy of EU law, as well as on the free movement rights of companies and individuals.[16] For when political decision-making on EU legislation was blocked, the CJEU was able to interpret and apply EU primary law, as contained in the different Treaties, and develop it into an effective system of rights and obligations. The case law of the CJEU thereby helped to keep European integration alive and relevant, but also provided an impetus for the political revival of European integration and the internal market.

This revival came with Single European Act of 1986 (SEA), which was the first large Treaty amendment since 1957.[17] The SEA placed the 'single market' at the forefront of European integration, and, with that renewed economic focus managed to energise the Communities. For example, it created an ambitious aim to finalize the internal market by 31 December 1992, created new competences to that end, and allowed decision-making by qualified majority, removing the blockage created by the Luxembourg Accords.[18]

---

15 See J-M. Palavret et al. (eds.) *Visions, Votes and Vetoes: Reassessing the Luxembourg Compromise 40 Years On* (Peter Lang, 2006).

16 See for a discussion of this seminal case law EU Chapters 4 and 9–13.

17 The Single European Act (Luxembourg, 17 February 1986), OJ [1987] L169.

18 See further EU Chapter 9 on the SEA and its importance.

The SEA indeed contributed to a new energy for European integration, especially concerning the internal market where a flurry of legislative activity ensued. Already in 1992, however, the EU was faced with a truly existential event: the fall of the Berlin Wall in November 1989 and the subsequent collapse of the Soviet Union.[19] The fall of the Berlin Wall not only led to German reunification, and hence a major power shift in the EU, but also to fundamental questions as to the political nature of the EU and the role of the EU on the international stage.

1.3.2 *From European Community to Full European Union*

The new political reality could also be seen in the 1992 Treaty of Maastricht, an important milestone in European integration.[20] Maastricht formally broadened the scope and ambitions of European integration to Common Foreign and Security Policy (CFSP) and Justice and Home affairs (JHA), taking it clearly beyond economic integration alone. At the same time, Member States were unwilling to grant supranational authority over such sensitive fields as justice and foreign policy.[21] Consequently, Maastricht created the so-called 'temple' structure, a rather uncommon model in constitutional design. Three separate 'pillars' were created. The first pillar was formed by the former EEC, which was renamed the 'European Community (EC)' to reflect its extended ambit. This first pillar remained supranational in character. The Common Foreign and Security Policy (CFSP) and Justice and Home affairs (JHA) formed two separate, essentially intergovernmental, pillars. Jointly, these three pillars supported the 'roof' of the temple, being the European Union. At this stage of integration, therefore, the European Community remained the supranational heart of European integration, whereas the name 'European Union' only referred to the wider construct based on the three pillars.

The Treaty of Maastricht also introduced EU Citizenship and further empowered the European Parliament as part of a broader attempt to improve the democratic legitimacy and functioning of the EU.[22] Moreover, it contained a commitment to the creation of an Economic and Monetary Union (EMU),

---

19 See on the enormous impact of this event for the EU *inter alia* L. van Middelaar, *The Passage to Europe. How a Continent Became a Union* (Yale University Press, 2014), chapter 6.

20 Treaty on European Union (Maastricht Treaty) (7 February 1992, Maastricht), OJ [2992] C 191.

21 See further EU Chapter 5.

22 See further EU chapter 2 on the development of the European Parliament and EU Chapter 11 on the concept of EU Citizenship.

including the introduction of a single currency (the euro), and provided a detailed roadmap for its development.[23]

The Treaty of Maastricht, therefore, contained several far reaching ambitions, but ran into severe difficulties. The ratification of the Treaty was first rejected in a Danish referendum, only received 51% of votes in a French referendum, and was heavily fought over in the UK. Only after a second referendum in Denmark in May 1993 could the Treaty enter into force. The difficult and contested ratification of Maastricht proved a sign of a wider disenchantment with European integration, as popular support for the project decreased from well over 70% in 1990 to around 50% in 1996.

Subsequent Treaties failed to address these concerns and the different problems associated with the Maastricht Treaty. The Treaty of Amsterdam, which came into effect on May 1st 1999 was markedly less ambitious in its goals and achievements. Besides renumbering the existing Treaties, the main alterations lay in the free movement of persons, the wider use of the co-decision procedure, and the introduction of a possibility of 'closer cooperation' between Member States. The main goal of the Amsterdam Treaty, which was to prepare the EU for the approaching enlargement with ten new Member States, was certainly not achieved, but rather postponed to the Nice Summit of 2000. The Treaty of Nice, however, also failed to achieve sufficient results. The compromises reached were complex and not sufficient to deal with the enlargement or the other structural challenges facing the EU.

Consequently, already one year after Nice, the 2001 Laeken declaration of the European Council called for a 'deeper and wider debate about the future of the European Union'. The Laeken declaration led to the creation of a 'European Convention' to discuss the future of the EU, and to draft a 'European Constitution' which would enable the EU to develop further and to deal more satisfactorily with the issues raised by enlargement. In 2004, the Convention indeed led to a new Treaty entitled the 'Treaty establishing a Constitution for Europe'.[24]

The Constitutional Treaty was certainly no traditional, statal constitution and did not intend to create a European federation. At the same time, the new Treaty did purport to further constitutionalise European integration and reflect the deep integration reached in Europe.[25] In line with these constitutional

---

23 The EMU is discussed in more detail in EU Chapter 13.

24 OJ [2004] C 310.

25 See on the contested question of whether the EU Treaties constitute a Constitution inter alia B. De Witte, 'The European Union as an international legal experiment', in: G. de Búrca and J.H.H. Weiler, *The Worlds of European Constitutionalism*' (CUP, 2012),

ambitions, the Constitutional Treaty was put to a vote in national referenda, where it suffered a humiliating defeat. On 29 May 2005, 55 per cent of the French voters said no, and on 1 June 2005 even 62 per cent of the Dutch voters rejected the Constitutional Treaty.

The precise grounds for these rejections can be debated, and over two-thirds of all Member States did ratify, but the rejection of the Constitutional Treaty was a major set-back for the EU. After a two year 'period of reflection', work was started in 2006 on what would become the Lisbon Treaty.[26] In 2007 a relatively short Intergovernmental Conference (IGC) was held that hammered out a new Treaty largely based on the text of the Constitutional Treaty.[27] The new Treaty was signed on 13 December in Lisbon, hence officially becoming 'the Lisbon Treaty'.[28] The Lisbon Treaty survived the national ratification process and different constitutional challenges brought against it, though at a further price in legitimacy, and entered into force on 1 December 2009.[29] Consequently, the Treaty of Lisbon established the legal framework for the EU currently in place.

1.3.3 *The Legal Framework after Lisbon*

Since the Treaty of Lisbon, the EU is based on two Treaties of equal legal value: the Treaty on European Union (TEU) and the Treaty on the Functioning of the

19, D. Grimm, 'Types of Constitutions', in: M. Rosenfeld and A. Sajó (eds) *The Oxford Handbook of Comparative Constitutional Law* (OUP, 2012), 99, A. Von Bogdandy and J. Bast (eds), *Principles of European Constitutional Law* (2nd edn, Hart, 2010), N. Walker, 'Big 'C' or small 'c'' 12 *European Law Journal* (2006), 12, S. Douglas-Scott, *Constitutional Law of the European Union* (Pearson 2002), or G. De Búrca, 'The Institutional Development of the EU: A Constitutional Analysis', in: P. Craig and G. de Búrca (eds), *The Evolution of EU law* (OUP, 1999), 55.

26 See European Commission, *The Period of Reflection and Plan D* (Com(2006)212,2 and the EU Council Declaration of 25 March 2007, par. 3.

27 See for an impressive overview M. Dougan, 'The Treaty of Lisbon 2007: Winning Minds, not Hearts' 45 *CMLRev* (2008), 617.

28 Treaty of Lisbon (13 December 2007, Lisbon), OJ [2007] C 306.

29 See especially in this regard the judgment by the German Constitutional Court on the compatibility of the Lisbon Treaty with the German Constitution in BVerfGE, 2 BvE 123,267, 2 BvE 2/08 (2009) *Lissabon Urteil* as discussed inter alia by D. Grimm, 'Comments on the German Constitutional Court's Decision on the Lisbon Treaty. Defending Sovereign Statehood against Transforming the European Union into a State', 5 *European Constitutional Law Review* (2009), 353, C. Schönberger, 'Lisbon in Karlsruhe: Maastricht's Epigone at Sea', 10 *German Law Journal* (2009), 1201, and F. Schorkopf, 'The European Union as An Association of Sovereign States: Karlsruhe's Ruling on the Treaty of Lisbon; 10 *German Law Journal* (2009), 1220.

European Union (TFEU).[30] In addition, Article 6 TEU declares that the Charter of Fundamental Rights of the European Union shall have the same legal value as the Treaties. Even though it was not politically feasible to include the Charter directly into the text of the Treaties, therefore, the Charter does form part of EU primary law and has the same hierarchical status as the TEU and the TFEU.[31]

Importantly, Lisbon also removed the pillar structure introduced by the Treaty of Maastricht. Formally, therefore, there are no more pillars and the European Community no longer exists but has been replaced by the European Union. This unification of EU law was one important aim of Lisbon. At the same time, however, Member States were still not willing to subsume foreign policy under a supranational approach. Consequently, Title V of the TEU creates a special, largely intergovernmental regime for the Union's external action and the Common Foreign and Security Policy (CFSP). The result of this special regime can be described as a kind of 'hidden' pillar for external relations. Within this hidden pillar Member States remain the key actors in most areas of external policy, excluding areas such as trade.[32]

With the Treaty of Lisbon, two decades of almost constant Treaty change and turmoil came to a close. In these 20 years of Treaty making the EEC developed into a three pillared temple capped by a European Union, only to subsequently morph into a complete European Union with its own citizens and currency. During these decades, however, multiple important factors remained constant as well, including many of the foundational doctrines of EU law and free movement set out in later chapters. In addition, the EU retained its key focus on peace and prosperity, even if new objectives and competences were added.

Considering the significant political and legal difficulties encountered during these Treaty changes, and because finding unanimity with 28 Member States has proven far from easy, the expectation after Lisbon was that no major Treaty revision would be attempted for at least some time, even though the project of integration itself is of course far from finished.[33] The prospect of *Brexit* may alter this prediction, even though it may also be possible to deal

30 The Treaty of Lisbon only served to create these two Treaties, meaning one refers to the provisions in these Treaties directly, and not to the Treaty of Lisbon as such when citing EU law.

31 See also EU Chapter 3 on the hierarchy of norms within EU law and EU Chapter 6 on the application and scope of the Charter.

32 See on the special nature and status of external relations and the CFSP further EU Chapter 5.

33 See for the rules on Treaty change Article 48 TEU. Further see on the use of international law instrument where Treaty change proved unfeasible, for example during the euro crisis, EU Chapter 13.

with a withdrawal of the UK from the EU without opening the 'Pandora's box' of general Treaty revision, in which many Member States may seek to change the fundamental set-up of the EU in their own (short-term) interests. Before we turn to a brief discussion of *Brexit*, and the likelihood of a first ever *reduction* in EU membership, however, the next section first describes the enlargement of the EU from a group of six to a group of 28 Member States, an important process that should be considered in parallel with the political and legal development set out above.

1.4 Here and Back Again: From Enlargement to *Brexit*

1.4.1 *Enlarging the EU*

As indicated above, the EU started out as a Community of six 'Founding Members', being Germany, France, Italy, The Netherlands, Belgium and Luxembourg. From the very start, however, the relevant Treaties always envisaged the accession of new members.[34] An option that has been intensively used, and has had a major impact on the nature and development of the EU.[35]

After accession of the UK had been blocked by De Gaulle in 1961 and 1967, the first enlargement of the EU took place in 1973 when Denmark, Ireland and the UK joined. In 1981 Greece joined the EU as well, with Spain and Portugal joining in 1986 and Austria, Finland and Sweden becoming Member States in 1995. The biggest single enlargement took place in 2004 when ten primarily Eastern European countries joined the EU, being Cyprus, the Czech Republic, Estonia, Hungary, Latvia, Lithuania, Malta, Poland, Slovakia and Slovenia. In 2007, these countries were joined by Bulgaria and Romania, which were not yet deemed ready in 2004. The last enlargement took place in 2013 when Croatia became the 28th Member State of the EU. At the time of writing, moreover, Albania, The former Yugoslav Republic of Macedonia, Montenegro, and Serbia are in the waiting room wanting to join the EU, albeit that for most, accession may take a very long time. Bosnia and Herzegovina and Kosovo have been promised the prospect of joining when they are ready. Turkey forms a very special case as its accession to the EU was already envisioned by the 1963 Ankara Association agreement, yet its accession currently seems further away than ever due to growing political tensions and conflicts.

---

34 Art. 237 of the Treaty of Rome, for example, already provided that 'any European state may apply to become a member of the Community'.

35 See for an overview and analysis, including of the 'enlargement fatigue' the may have arisen by now, C. Hillion, 'EU Enlargement', in: P. Craig and G. De Búrca (eds): *The Evolution of EU Law* (2nd edn., OUP 2011), 187 et seq.

Even if the EU may currently suffer from 'enlargement fatigue', one of the open questions of EU integration therefore remains: 'where does Europe stop'? To accede, however, candidate countries have to follow an increasingly long and arduous path. To begin with, any state that wishes to join must first request permission to become a member from the Council.[36] The Council then decides by unanimity, after consulting the Commission and receiving the assent of the European Parliament. If these requirements are met, an accession agreement will be negotiated with the applicant, usually with the Commission negotiating on behalf of the EU. If an accession agreement is reached this agreement must then be ratified unanimously by all the Member States.[37]

1.4.2 *Downsizing the EU?*

At the time of writing, however, the EU is more concerned with existing Member States leaving the EU than new Member States joining. On 23 June 2016, 51.9%, or 17.410.742 of the British voters chose to leave the EU. With a turnout of 72,2%, a large minority of 48,1%, or 16.141.241 of the voters, opted to remain. The 'Leave' camp therefore won the day with a difference of 3,8% or 1.269.501 votes.[38] The new British Prime Minister, Theresa May, has since indicated that 'Brexit means Brexit'—whatever that may mean by itself—and that she intends to start the formal procedure for withdrawal before the end of March 2017.[39]

The precise outcome of *Brexit* will largely be decided on the field of politics, and not in the legal arena. In addition, with the withdrawal of a Member State, the EU is entering new territory, with very little precedents to guide it.[40] Nevertheless, law will certainly have a role to play, and there are at least several

36 See, reaffirming this notion even in the face of impressive enlargement to the East, the 1992 European Council Conclusions (*EC Bulletin 6–1992*, 1.4.) together with the conditions established for such accession in Copenhagen the next year. See also K.E. Smith, 'The Evolution and Application of EU Membership Conditionality', in: M. Cremona (ed), *The enlargement of the European Union* (OUP 2003), 105 et seq.

37 Art. 49 TEU.

38 The outcome of the referendum therefore invalidates the earlier 'deal' between Cameron and the other 27 Heads of State and Government, see par. 4 of the European Council Conclusions of 19 February 2016, EUCO 1/16.

39 See for example the speech of May on 2 October 2016 to the conservative convention in Brighton.

40 Contrary to what is sometimes claimed, the cases of Algeria and Iceland do not provide relevant guidance, see A. Tatham, '"Don't Mention Divorce at the Wedding, Darling!" EU Accession and Withdrawal after Lisbon' in Andrea Biondi, Piet Eeckhout and Stefanie Ripley (eds), *EU Law after Lisbon* (OUP 2012), 143 and F. Weiss, 'Greenland's Withdrawal from the European Communities' (1985) 10 ELR, 173.

rules and principles that will guide and influence the process of *Brexit*. Several of the most important ones will be briefly set out below, focusing on the nature and background of Article 50 TEU, the process for the withdrawal, and the nature and number of agreements that will to be concluded for *Brexit* to become a reality.[41]

1.4.2.1 The Nature and Background of Article 50 TEU

Long before the Treaty of Lisbon, the general consensus was that Member States could leave the EU.[42] After all, it was hardly conceivable that the EU could keep a Member State in against its will, even though the precise modalities of leaving were far from clear.[43] The right to leave the EU, however, was only explicitly recognized in Article I-60 of the Constitutional Treaty. After the rejection of this Treaty, as discussed above, the right to withdraw from the EU was codified by the Treaty of Lisbon in Article 50 TEU, which reads:

---

41 For further analysis please see P. Craig, '*Brexit*: a drama in six acts' 2016 (4) *European Law Review*, 447, N. Walker, 'The European Fallout' *German Law Journal Brexit Supplement (2016)* 126, G. Davies, 'What Does It All Mean?', *German Law Journal Brexit Supplement (2016)* 7, B. De Witte, 'Near-membership, partial membership end the EU constitution', (2016) (4) *European Law Review*, 471, R.J. Friel, 'Providing a Constitutional framework for withdrawal from the EU: Article 59 of the Draft European Constitution' (2004) 53 ICLQ, p. 407, S. Berglund, 'Prison or Voluntary Cooperation? The Possibility of Withdrawal from the European Union' (2006) 29 *Scandinavian Political Studies*, p. 147, F. Harbo, 'Secession Right—An Anti-Federal Principle? Comparative Study of Federal States and the EU' (2008) 1 *Journal of Politics and Law*, p. 132, J. Herbst, 'Observations on the Right to Withdraw from the European Union: Who are the "Masters of the Treaties"?' (2005) 6 GLJ, 1755, H. Hofmeister, '"Should I Stay or Should I Go?"—A Critical Analysis of the Right to Withdraw From the EU' (2010) 16 ELJ, 589, A. Lazowski, 'Withdrawal from the European Union and Alternatives to Membership' (2012) 37 *ELRev*, 523, P. Nicolaides, 'Withdrawal from the European Union: A Typology of Effects' (2013) 20 MJ, 209, Jean Claude Piris, 'Should the UK withdraw from the EU: legal aspects and effects of possible options', Fondation Robert Schuman / European Issues n°355 / 5th May 2015, A. Tatham, '"Don't Mention Divorce at the Wedding, Darling!" EU Accession and Withdrawal after Lisbon' in A. Biondi, P. Eeckhout and S. Ripley (eds), *EU Law after Lisbon* (2012), 128, and last but far from least, C. Hillion, 'Accession and Withdrawal in the Law of the European Union', in: A. Arnull and D. Chalmers (eds): *The Oxford handbook of European Law* (OUP 2015), 126.

42 See also A. Cuyvers, *The EU as a Confederal Union of Sovereign Member Peoples—Exploring the potential of American (con)federalism and popular sovereignty for a constitutional theory of the EU* (Diss. Leiden, 2013), 88 a.o., as well as K. Widdows, 'The Unilateral Denunciation of Treaties Containing no Denunciation Clause' (1983) 53 *British Ybk Intl L*, 102 and paragraph 55 of the *Maastricth Urteil* (BVerfGE 89, 155) of the German Constitutional Court.

43 Cf. K. Lenaerts and P. van Nuffel, *Constitutional Law of the European Union* (Thomson, 2005), 363.

1. *Any Member State may decide to withdraw from the Union in accordance with its own constitutional requirements.*
2. *A Member State which decides to withdraw shall notify the European Council of its intention. In the light of the guidelines provided by the European Council, the Union shall negotiate and conclude an agreement with that State, setting out the arrangements for its withdrawal, taking account of the framework for its future relationship with the Union. That agreement shall be negotiated in accordance with Article 218(3) of the Treaty on the Functioning of the European Union. It shall be concluded on behalf of the Union by the Council, acting by a qualified majority, after obtaining the consent of the European Parliament.*
3. *The Treaties shall cease to apply to the State in question from the date of entry into force of the withdrawal agreement or, failing that, two years after the notification referred to in paragraph 2, unless the European Council, in agreement with the Member State concerned, unanimously decides to extend this period.*
4. *For the purposes of paragraphs 2 and 3, the member of the European Council or of the Council representing the withdrawing Member State shall not participate in the discussions of the European Council or Council or in decisions concerning it.*
5. *A qualified majority shall be defined in accordance with Article 238(3)(b) of the Treaty on the Functioning of the European Union.*
6. *If a State which has withdrawn from the Union asks to rejoin, its request shall be subject to the procedure referred to in Article 49.*

This affirmation and codification of the right to withdraw served several purposes. Firstly, it was an important symbolical recognition of the ultimate sovereignty of the Member States. They remained the ultimate *Herren der Verträge*, or Masters of the Treaty.[44] This recognition also was intended as a reassurance and legitimization of deeper integration: as Member States could always leave, the implication was that any deeper integration confirmed their implicit consent.[45]

---

44 A. Tatham, '"Don't Mention Divorce at the Wedding, Darling!" EU Accession and Withdrawal after Lisbon' in A. Biondi, P. Eeckhout and S. Ripley (eds), *EU Law after Lisbon* (2012), 148.

45 C. Hillion, 'Accession and Withdrawal in the Law of the European Union', in: A. Arnull and D. Chalmers (eds): *The Oxford handbook of European Law* (OUP 2015), 126, F. Harbo, 'Secession Right—An Anti-Federal Principle? Comparative Study of Federal States and the EU' (2008) 1 *Journal of Politics and Law*, 132.

Secondly, Article 50 TEU was intended to draw the question of withdrawal within the scope of EU law itself. Instead of question of Public International Law, withdrawal from the Union should become a question of EU law itself.[46] Thirdly, Article 50 TEU was also intended, at least partially, to make the process of leaving the EU unattractive. As will be discussed further below, for example, the withdrawing Member State is placed in a difficult negotiation position by the short two-year period in principle provided to complete the withdrawal.[47] These different aims and objectives of Article 50 TEU should be kept in mind when interpreting and applying this brief, rather open, and sometimes vague provision.

1.4.2.2 The Process of Withdrawal under Article 50 TEU

Article 50 TEU provides that a Member State must first decide to withdraw from the Union 'in accordance with its own constitutional requirements.' Subsequently, the Member State must 'notify the European Council of its intention' to leave.[48] The formal process of withdrawal only starts after a notification has been handed in. Until the UK hands in its notification, therefore, nothing changes in its legal position under EU law, and the EU is formally not even allowed to open negotiations with the UK on its exit.[49]

Once a notification has been handed in, the question may arise if a Member State may also *revoke* its notification to withdraw. One could argue that the two-year period in Article 50 TEU would be undermined if a Member State could revoke its notification, and that the option of revoking a notification might allow abuse by Member States.[50] Indeed the parties and the UK High

---

46 See for an alternative view L.F.M. Besselink, 'Beyond Notification: How to Leave the Union without Using Article 50 TEU', U.K. Const. L. Blog (30th Jun 2016) (available via <http://ukconstitutionallaw.org>).

47 Cf. J. Herbst, 'Observations on the Right to Withdraw from the European Union: Who are the "Masters of the Treaties"?' (2005) 6 GLJ, 1757–8. At the same time the two year limit also forms a protection for the Member State that wants to withdraw, as it cannot be kept in the EU against its will.

48 As we have seen so far, this has raised the question of UK constitutional law if the UK government is allowed to submit a notification under the Royal Prerogative, or whether it needs an act of Parliament to do so. At the time of writing, the appeal to the Supreme Court against the High Court decision in R (on the application of Miller and Dos Santos) v Secretary of State for Exiting the European Union [2016] EWHC 2768 is still pending.

49 See also point two of the statement after the informal European Council of 27 to 29 June 2016.

50 See for example S. Lechner en R Ohr, 'The Right of Withdrawal in the Treaty of Lisbon: A Game Theoretic Reflection on Different Decision Processes in the EU,' CEGE

Court in *R (on the application of Miller and Dos Santos) v Secretary of State* simply assume that revoking a notice is not possible, and that a notice, once given, therefore means a one way ticket to leaving the EU.[51]

On closer inspection, however, the more correct interpretation seems to be that a notification under Article 50(2) TFEU can be revoked. To begin with, it is hard to imagine that the European Council would actually refuse a Member State to remain in the EU, certainly if the revocation of the notification to withdraw was given after a new election or a new referendum. In addition, however, it can be argued that a refusal to accept the revocation of a notification of withdrawal would also violate the EU's obligation of sincere cooperation, its obligation to strive towards an 'ever closer union' and its obligation to protect and safeguard the EU citizenship of all British subjects that stand to loose their citizenship after a *Brexit*.[52]

Once a notification has been given by the UK, however, a two year clock starts to tick. If no withdrawal agreement has been agreed *and entered into force* within two years, the UK will automatically and unilaterally leave the EU without any agreement on its withdrawal or its new relation with the EU.[53] This scenario is one road towards the so called 'hard *Brexit*' and can be compared to the scenario where one partner comes home and discovers that the locks have been changed.

Article 50(3) TEU, however, does allow the European Council, by unanimity and with the consent of the UK, to extend this period. Moreover, Article 50(3) TEU does not limit the length or the number of such extensions that may be agreed. The requirement of unanimity, however, means that any Member State may veto an extension, thereby potentially driving the UK towards a hard exit.[54]

During the negotiations on its withdrawal, moreover, the UK remains a full Member of the EU, with all the rights and all the obligations of an EU Member.

Discussion Papers, No. 77, October 2008, Center for European, Governance and Economic Development research, Georg-August-Universität, Göttingen (2008), p. 4. Available via <http://www.uni-goettingen.de/de/60920.html>.

51 R (on the application of Miller and Dos Santos) v Secretary of State for Exiting the European Union [2016] EWHC 2768, par. 4.

52 See by analogy Case C-135/08 *Rottmann* ECLI:EU:C:2010:104 and Case C-34/09 *Zambrano* ECLI:EU:C:2011:124.

53 Article 50(3) TEU.

54 Cf on this point the testimony by Sir David Edward concerning the risks for the UK in assuming an extension will be granted, as cited in par. 44 of the House of Lords European Union Committee Report of 4 May 2016 'The process of withdrawing from the European Union', available via <http://www.publications.parliament.uk/pa/ld201516/ldselect/ldeucom/138/138.pdf>.

This also means that any extension of the two year period automatically lead to a prolonged EU membership of the UK, which might be politically unacceptable to the more impatient *Brexiteers*. The only exception to the rights of the UK after it notifies its intention to leave is that the UK Prime Minister and UK ministers may no longer 'participate in the discussions of the European Council or Council or in decisions concerning it.' The extent of this conclusion will depend on how broad or narrow an interpretation is given to the vague concept of 'concerning it'.[55]

1.4.2.3 The Outcome: Two or Three Agreements?

A last point to be addressed, aside from the content of the new relationship between the EU and the UK which will not be discussed here, is how many and what kind of agreements need to be concluded to realize a *Brexit*, and what the relation between these agreements must be.[56] Article 50 TEU itself clearly requires at least two agreements: one agreement on the withdrawal itself and one, probably far more elaborate, agreement on the new relation between the EU and the UK.[57]

Crucially, both agreements have a different legal basis, and therefore have to be adopted under different procedures. The withdrawal agreement is based on Article 50 TEU itself, and forms an agreement between the EU and the UK alone. As discussed, this withdrawal agreement under Article 50 TEU has to be approved by the European Parliament and concluded by the Council by qualified majority. With the exception of the UK, therefore, the other Member States will not be parties to this withdrawal agreement, which also means

---

55 See on this point C. Hillion, 'Accession and Withdrawal in the Law of the European Union', in: A. Arnull and D. Chalmers (eds): *The Oxford handbook of European Law* (OUP 2015), 126, as well as the *Editorial Comments* of the Common Market Law Review on Brexit, 53 (2016) *Common Market Law Review*, 1.

56 For an overview of the different models for the new relationship between the EU and the UK, none of which seem to offer much hope, see inter alia S. Dhingra en T. Sampson, 'Life after Brexit: What are the UK's options outside the European Union?' Centre for Economic Performance, *London School of Economics Working PaperBrexit 01*, and HM Government, 'Alternatives to membership: possible models for the United Kingdom outside the European Union' March 2016, available via <https://www.gov.uk/government/uploads/system/uploads/attachment_data/file/504604/Alternatives_to_membership_-_possible_models_for_the_UK_outside_the_EU.pdf>.

57 Cf. also the House of Lords European Union Committee Report of 4 May 2016 'The process of withdrawing from the European Union', point 31. See also A. Tatham, '"Don't Mention Divorce at the Wedding, Darling!" EU Accession and Withdrawal after Lisbon', in: A. Biondi, P. Eeckhout en S. Ripley (red.), *EU Law after Lisbon*, (OUP, 2012), 128.

that the withdrawal agreement does not require ratification by the individual Member States.

The agreement on the new relation, however, will almost certainly be a mixed agreement between the EU and the 27 remaining Member States on the one side, and the UK on the other.[58] This agreement will most likely be based on Articles 37 TEU and 217 and 218 TEU concerning respectively the CFSP and association agreements. Consequently, the agreement on the new relationship will first have to be approved by the European Parliament and subsequently adopted by unanimity in the Council.[59] Subsequently, however, because of its mixity, the agreement on the new relationship will also have to ratified by the UK and each of the 27 remaining Member States. In turn, these national ratifications may lead to additional referenda or constitutional challenges.[60]

The *procedure* for the withdrawal agreement, therefore, is already simpler and more straightforward than the procedure for the agreement on the new relationship. In addition, the *substance* of the agreement on the new relation is also far more complex and extensive than the substance of the withdrawal agreement, which could in theory be one paragraph. To illustrate, CETA, the trade agreement between the EU and Canada, which is legally and politically less complex than *Brexit*, already took more than seven years, and a successful completion is far from certain.

Because the agreement on the new relation is procedurally and substantively far more complex than the withdrawal agreement, however, it is likely that the withdrawal agreement can be completed before the agreement on the new relationship. In addition, it is also unlikely that a comprehensive new agreement on the new relationship between the EU and the UK can even be completed within the two year period. This creates a serious problem as in terms of substance and effect the withdrawal agreement and the agreement on the new relationship are difficult to separate.[61] After all, if the withdrawal agreement enters into force *before* the agreement on the new relationship is in place, the UK is *de facto* kicked out of the EU without a new deal, and has to negotiate its new relationship with the EU from outside the EU and its internal market.

58 See further EU Chapter 5 on the concept of mixed agreements.

59 Article 218(8) VWEU.

60 See also *Editorial Comments*, (2016) 53 *Common Market Law Review*, 1.

61 See also B. De Witte, 'Near-membership, partial membership end the EU constitution', (2016) (4) *European Law Review*, 471.

If one wants to avoid such an indirect hard *Brexit*, only two options seem available, and both are problematic. The first option is to link the entry into force of the withdrawal agreement to the entry into force of the agreement on the new relationship. This would mean that the UK would only withdraw from the Union after the entire agreement on the new relationship has been finalised and ratified by the EU and all 27 Member States. The price to be paid for this approach, which could guarantee a seamless transition to the new status of the UK, is a prolonged EU membership of the UK. After all, it is almost certain that a comprehensive agreement on the new relationship cannot be concluded and ratified within two years. It may be difficult for the British government to convince the *Leave* supporters that they should wait so long for their 'liberation' from the EU, and the Brexiteers would want to push a Brexit through before the general elections that must ultimately be held on 7 May 2020.

The second option is to link the withdrawal agreement to a third, *transitional* agreement. This transitional agreement would govern the relationship between the EU and the UK after *Brexit* for as long as it takes to conclude a final agreement on the new relation.[62] The problem of this second option, however, is that concluding a transitional or interim agreement may be almost as complex and time consuming as concluding the final agreement on the new relationship itself. For, to begin with, the transitional agreement will have to cover many of the same points as the final agreement. In addition, the transitional agreement will inevitably form a benchmark for the final agreement and may be in place for a long time, meaning all parties may negotiate just as hard as for the final agreement.

If it proves impossible to find an agreement on a transitional agreement within the period of two years, however, we seem left with a choice between a hard *Brexit*, and a seriously prolonged EU Membership of the UK. Neither of these choices is very appealing, but this is of course primarily due to the fundamentally flawed assumption behind *Brexit* that it is possible to enjoy the benefits of integration without sharing a certain amount of sovereignty at the regional level, as the long and bumpy road towards EU integration has illustrated.

62 C. Hillion, 'Accession and Withdrawal in the Law of the European Union', in: A. Arnull en D. Chalmers (red.), *The Oxford handbook of European Law*, (OUP, 2015), 126.

CHAPTER 2

The Institutional Framework of the EAC

Wilbert T.K. Kaahwa

2.1 Introduction

2.1.1 *Conceptual Background*

In the law of international organizations such as the United Nations (UN), continental organizations such as the European Union (EU) and the African Union (AU) and regional organizations including the Association of South East Asian Nations (ASEAN), the Common Market for Eastern and Southern Africa (COMESA) and the Southern African Development Community (SADC) the term "institutional framework" often refers to the legal framework that guides the pursuit of such organizations' objectives. The term can also refer to the systems of formal laws, regulations, and procedures, and informal conventions, customs, and norms that shape socioeconomic activity and behavior. However for the purposes of this book, this Chapter will only highlight the formal organizational set-up established by the Treaty for the Establishment of the East African Community ("the Treaty"). The second part, the legal framework of the EAC, will be discussed in Chapter 3.

The importance and relevance of the institutional framework in the East African Community (EAC) can be traced to three facts. Firstly, the EAC has revived an inter-state co-operation system, whose historical antecedents and systematic development between 1967 and 1977 had given rise to an elaborate organizational framework of organs and service commissions. The Treaty for East African Co-operation 1967 had established institutions such as the East African Authority,[1] the East African Legislative Assembly,[2] Ministers of the Community,[3] the Common Market Council,[4] the Communications Council,[5] the Economic Consultative and Planning Council,[6] the Finance Council[7]

1 Articles 46–48.
2 Articles 56–60.
3 Articles 49–51.
4 Articles 30–31, 53(a), 54.
5 Articles 53(b), 54, 55.
6 Articles 53(c), 54, 55.
7 Articles 53(d), 54,55.

© WILBERT T.K. KAAHWA, 2017 | DOI 10.1163/9789004322073_004
This is an open access chapter distributed under the terms of the CC-BY-NC License.

and the Research and Social Council;[8] corporations such as the East African Airways Corporation, the East African Harbours Corporation, the East African Railways Corporation, the East African Posts and Telecommunications Corporation;[9] judicial bodies such as the Court of Appeal for East Africa;[10] the East African Industrial Court;[11] specialized bodies such as the East African Development Bank,[12] the East African Community Service Commission[13] and the East African Tax Board;[14] and specialized departments, and services including the East African Medical Research Council and the East African Trypanosomiasis Institute.[15]

Secondly, the renewal and reconceptualization of co-operation among the United Republic of Tanzania, the Republic of Kenya and the Republic of Uganda in 1993 underscored the importance of an institutional framework. This renewal obliged the countries to explore and identify further areas for future co-operation and to work out concrete arrangements for co-operation,[16] and therefore the need for an institutional framework became inevitable. This was reflected in the institution-creating overtones of the Agreement for the Establishment of The Permanent Tripartite Commission for Co-operation Between the Republic of Uganda, the Republic of Kenya and the United Republic of Tanzania[17] and the Protocol on the Establishment of a Secretariat of The Permanent Tripartite Commission for Co-operation Between the Republic

8 Articles 53(e), 54, 55.

9 Articles 71–79.

10 Articles 80–81.

11 Article 85.

12 Articles 21–22.

13 Articles 62–64.

14 Article 88.

15 East African Community, *The East African Community; A Handbook 1972*, Arusha, East African Community Information Division, 1970.The bodies and institutions included the Meteorological Department, the Freshwater Fisheries Organisation, the Industrial Research Organisation, the Institute of Malaria and Vector-Borne Diseases, the Institute for Medical Research, the Leprosy Research Institute, the Marine Fisheries Research Organisation, the Pesticides Research Organisation, the Agriculture and Forestry Research Organisation, the Trypanosomiasis Research Organisation, the Tuberculosis Investigation Centre, the Veterinary Research Organisation and the Virus Research Institute.

16 *See* Article 14.02 of The East African Community Mediation Agreement 1984.

17 Agreement for the Establishment of a Permanent Tripartite Commission for Co-operation Between the Republic of Kenya, The United Republic of Tanzania and the Republic of Uganda; see particularly Articles 1–5.

of Uganda, the Republic of Kenya and the United Republic of Tanzania.[18] Jointly, these instruments established a Permanent Tripartite Commission for Co-operation and a Secretariat.

Thirdly, the Community is a creature of modern dynamics in regionalism. According to Heitne *"the new regionalism differs from the old regionalism (which was based on security interests in the bi-polar cold war context) in that it is a spontaneous process from within a region, is more comprehensive and multi-dimensional and encourages non-state actors and incorporates issues of accountability and legitimacy."*[19] The EAC has grown as a channel for economic integration rather than as a consequence of mainly political solidarity as did, for example, other erstwhile organizations in Africa.[20] New regionalism necessitates organized structures for the purpose of effective and sustained realization of objectives. Indeed McCormick, with specific reference to the EU, argues that, *"integration is effectively driven by institutionalized structures. For example, the European Union has evolved and is driven by an elaborate structure consisting of the European Commission, the Council of Ministers, the European Parliament, the European Court of Justice, the European Council and specialized agencies".*[21]

In its objectives as provided under the Treaty, and unlike the situation that obtained under the defunct East African Community (1967–1977), its predecessor the East African Common Services Organisation (1961–1967), and the colonial arrangement under the East African High Commission (1947–1961), the current integration process aims at achieving more than trade liberalization and harmonization in infrastructure and services. To use Amerasinghe's approach to the classification of international organizations, the EAC is *"an inter-governmental, supra-national and closed organization"*[22] that seeks to

---

18 *Ibid.*, Article 5; See also The Protocol on the Establishment of a Secretariat of The Permanent Tripartite Commission for Co-operation Between The Republic of Uganda, The Republic of Kenya and The United Republic of Tanzania.

19 Bjorn Heitne, *Development Regionalism in New Directions* In *Development Economics (Growth, Environmental Concerns and Government in the 1990s)* Ed by Mats Lundahl and Benno J. Ndulu, London Routledge, 1996 pp. 160–164.

20 Such as The Organisation of African Unity and the Southern African Development Co-ordination Conference.

21 John McCormick, *The European Union, Politics and Policies* 4th Edn, (Philadelphia, Westview Press 2008), pp. 109–226.

22 C.F. Amerasinghe, *Principles of the Institutional Law of International Organizations*, 2nd edn, Cambridge, Cambridge University Press, 1996 pp. 9–13; See also Henry G. Schermers and Niels M. Blokker, *International Institutional Law*, The Hague, Martinus Nijhoff

widen and deepen integration with the systematic establishment of a Customs Union, a Common Market, a Monetary Union and ultimately a Political Federation.[23] It also emphasizes strong participation of the private sector and civil society in its co-operation programmes and activities.[24] The accomplishment of these objectives requires an elaborate and functionally-purposed institutional framework.

2.1.2 *Legal Basis for the Institutional Framework*

Since the Community is an organisation established by states through a treaty, the law applicable to its institutional framework is international law. The legal basis for the institutional framework is found in Article 9 of the Treaty, which stipulates that—

> 1. *There are hereby established as organs of the Community:*
>   (*a*) *the Summit (of Heads of State);*
>   (*b*) *the Council (of Ministers);*
>   (*c*) *the Co-ordination Committee;*
>   (*d*) *Sectoral Committees;*
>   (*e*) *the East African Court of Justice;*
>   (*f*) *the East African Legislative Assembly;*
>   (*g*) *the Secretariat; and*
>   (*h*) *such other organs as may be established by the Summit.*
> 2. *The institutions of the Community shall be such bodies, department and services as may be established by the Summit.*
> 3. *Upon the entry into force of this Treaty, the East African Development Bank established by the Treaty Amending and Re-enacting the Charter of the East African Development Bank, 1980 and the Lake Victoria Fisheries Organisation established by the Convention (Final Act) for the Establishment of the Lake Victoria Fisheries Organisation, 1994 and surviving institutions of the former East African Community and shall be designated and function as such.*

Publishers, 1995 pp. 33–44, and Ray August, et al., *International Business Law: Text, Cases and Readings*, New Jersey, Pearson Education International, Fifth Edition, 2009, pp. 22–23.

23 Articles 2 and 5 of The Treaty for the Establishment of the East African Community.

24 Articles 5(3)(g), 127–129 of The Treaty for the Establishment of the East African Community.

4. *The organs and institutions of the Community shall perform the functions, and act within the limits of the powers conferred upon them by or under this Treaty.*[25]

This Treaty outline does not create a distinct institutional framework, it rather creates four policy-making and administrative organs and sectoral committees. These are i.e. the Summit of Heads of State ("the Summit"), the Council of Ministers ("the Council"), the Co-ordination Committee, the Secretariat and an unspecified number of sectoral committees. This feature could have been intended for the reason that the Treaty is underlain by the preponderance of the Partner States' continuous policy rationalization and harmonization. In such a scenario a more definite category of organs in the policy domain could neither have been provided for with certainty nor foreseen. Apart from the policy organs, the Treaty creates advisory and supervisory organs; the East African Court of Justice ("the Court"), as the judicial arm of the institutional framework; and the East African Legislative Assembly ("the Assembly") as the legislative arm. The Treaty also takes cognizance of institutions.

In a manner corresponding to the Treaty's providing for co-operation in almost all spheres of economic, social, cultural, political and other endeavors for the Partner States' fast, balanced and sustainable development, the basis for the institutional framework leaves room for the creation of such other organs and institutions as the Summit may, in the discharge of its functions deem necessary.

It is important to observe that the Partner States subscribe to an undertaking that *"Community organs, institutions and laws shall take precedence over similar national ones on matters pertaining to the implementation of [the] Treaty".*[26] Therefore contrary to what may occur in practice, this undertaking in institution-building pinpoints the supremacy of the Community's organs and institutions in leading the process of integration.

It must be further observed that in the discharge of their respective functions the organs and institutions are bound by the fundamental and operational principles of the Community. Critical among these principles under the Treaty are those that stress a *"people-centered and market-driven co-operation"*[27] and the application of subsidiarity,[28] both of which are critical tenets in the

---

25 Article 9 read together with Articles 10–12, 13–16, 17–19, 20–22, 23–47, 48–65, and 66–73.

26 Article 8(4).

27 Article 7(1)(a).

28 Article 7(1)(d); the principle of subsidiarity emphasizes multi-level participation and the involvement of a wide range of stakeholders in the process on integration.

establishment of a single market and investment area. In the discharge of their respective functions, including during deliberations and decision-making, the organs and institutions are bound by such procedure as they are empowered by the Treaty to determine.[29] In-built institutional measures such as key ministerial consultations and engagement of the private sector and civil society are supportive of the institutional decision-making process.[30]

2.2 Analytical Overview of the Main Organs

The roles of the different organs and institutions seem to mirror the Partner States' intended metamorphosis, outlined in Article 5(2) of the Treaty, from a co-operation arrangement through integration into a political federation most presumably with a single government. Therefore in a manner reflective of the theory of separation of powers the Court is the judicial organ of the Community,[31]the Council is the main policy organ[32] and the Assembly is the legislative organ of the Community.[33]

It is important not only to highlight the nature of each organ and institution, by reference to its composition and functions and responsibilities, but also to highlight some fundamental challenges and contradictions facing each organ or institution.

2.2.1 *The East African Legislative Assembly*

The Assembly consists of elected members who are elected by the National Assemblies of the Partner States (elected members); ex-officio members consisting of the Ministers responsible for East African Affairs from each Partner State; the Secretary General; and the Counsel to the Community.[34] Regarding the elected members Article 50(1) of the Treaty provides that *"The*

29 Pursuant to Articles 12(5),15(4),19(3),42 and 60 the Summit, the Council, the Co-ordination Committee, the Court and the Assembly have determined their respective rules of procedure.

30 These measures include regular meetings and consultations among key Ministers responsible for East African Community Affairs, Finance, Justice; Central Bank Governors; the business community under the auspices of the East African Business Council; and the Secretary General's annual forums with identified private sector and civil society organizations.

31 Article 23.

32 Article 14.

33 Article 49(1).

34 Article 48(1).

National Assembly of each Partner State shall elect, not from among its members, nine members of the Assembly, who shall represent as much as it is feasible, the various political parties represented in the National Assembly, shades of opinion, gender and other special interest groups in that Partner State, in accordance with such procedure as the National Assembly of each Partner State may determine".[35] The current membership of the Assembly is 52, with nine elected members from each of the five Partner States and seven ex-officio members.

The Assembly is *the Community's legislative organ.*[36] It is also charged with among other functions, liaising with the national assemblies of the Partner States on matters relating to the Community,[37] debating and approving the budget of the Community,[38] considering annual reports of the Community[39] and discussing all matters pertaining to the Community.[40] It is, to this extent, expected to be the people's representative on matters relevant to the efficient functioning of the Community.

In order to comply with the Community policy of popular participation in the achievement of its objectives and to reflect the people-centered approach of the Community, the views expressed in the debates of the National Assemblies are taken into account in the Assembly. By the same token, reports on debates of the Assembly are also passed to the National Assemblies for their consideration.[41]

The Assembly's legislative process is undertaken through enactment of Bills initiated by the Council;[42] or introduced through motions by any Member of the Assembly provided that such a motion relates to the functions of the Community.[43] However, the Treaty envisages a restriction on the initiation of legislation, namely, the requirement that the Assembly shall not proceed on any Bill, including an amendment to a Bill that makes provision for the imposition of any charge upon any fund of the Community; the payment, issue or withdrawal from any fund or the Community of any moneys not charged thereon or the increase in the amount of any such payment, issue or withdrawal; and the remission of any debt due to the Community. Nor can the

35 Article 50(1).
36 Article 49(1).
37 Article 49(2)(a).
38 Article 49(2)(b).
39 Article 49(2)(c).
40 Article 49(2)(d).
41 Article 65.
42 Article 14(3)(b).
43 Article 59(1).

Assembly proceed on any motion that makes provision for such purposes.[44] Article 58 of the Treaty outlines the voting procedure in the Assembly, and stipulates that voting shall be determined *"by a majority of the votes of the members present and voting"*[45] and furthermore that ex-officio members are not entitled to vote.[46]

The Assembly's relatively wide ambit on legislation must be seen against the thrust of the Partner States in the current integration process. Given the fact that the Community has already established a Customs Union, a Common Market and a Monetary Union, the laying of a strong and effective legislative mechanism becomes a *sine qua non* for both current institutional development and the future constitutional basis of the Community. It is against this background that the Assembly has since inauguration been able to enact basic fundamental laws such as the East African Community Emblems Act 2003, the East African Community Interpretation Act 2003 and the Acts of the Community Act 2003; institutional development laws such as the East African Legislative Assembly (Powers and Privileges) Act 2003, the Summit (Delegation of Powers and Functions) Act 2007, the Inter-University Council for East Africa Act 2008, the East African Legislative Assembly Members Election Act 2011 and the East African Community Parliamentary Institute Act, 2012; and annually enacted Appropriation Acts whose purpose is to make appropriation out of Community's budgets as approved by the Assembly.

Most critically to integration the Assembly has also enacted laws that are supportive of the Partner States' policy rationalisation and harmonization such as the East African Community Customs Management Act 2004, the East African Community Competition Act 2006, the Lake Victoria Transport Act 2007, the East African Community Joint Trade Negotiations Act 2008, the East African Community Standardisation, Quality Assurance, Metrology And Testing Act 2008 and the East African Community Budget Act 2009.[47] In this category are also the East African Community Civil Aviation Safety and Security Oversight Agency Act 2009, the East African Community Service

44 Article 59(2).

45 Article 58(1).

46 Article 58(2).

47 The effectiveness of regional legislation is settled by the provisions of the Treaty (*Article 8—and especially paragraphs 4 and 5 thereof*) to the effect that Community laws shall take precedence over similar national ones on matters pertaining to the implementation of the Treaty. Therefore once enacted, published and gazetted Community legislation becomes binding on the Partner States.

Commission Act 2010, the East African Community Conflict Management Act 2012, the East African Community Risk Reduction and Management Act 2012, the East African Community Vehicle Axle Load, Act 2013, the East African Community One Stop Border Posts Act 2013, the East African Elimination of Non-Tariff Barriers Act 2014, the East African Community Co-operative Societies Act 2014, the East African Community Integration (Education) Act 2014, the East African Community Electronic Transactions Act 2015, the East African Community Creative and Cultural Industries Act 2015, the East African Community Electronic Transactions Act 2015, the East African Community Persons with Disability Act 2015 and the East African Community Forests Management and Protection Act 2015 which are yet to be assented to by the Heads of State.[48]

The trend in the Assembly's enactment of regional legislation is in quantitative contrast with past regional practice. During the period 1961–1977, the integration process witnessed the enactment of only 35 Acts of the (now defunct) Community. The Assembly's trend is also more advanced and focused when contrasted with that of the Pan-African Parliament and the legislative forums of other regional economic communities like SADC, the Economic Community of West African States (ECOWAS) and COMESA. The SADC Parliamentary Forum is a policy making and deliberative body that approves the SADC budget, makes recommendations to the SADC Summit, considers and makes recommendations on treaties and promotes SADC objectives and programmes. However, the Parliamentary Forum does not legislate and will only serve as a legislative body when in future it assumes, as is anticipated, a regional parliamentary structure. Likewise, the ECOWAS Parliament is a forum for ensuring dialogue, consultation and consensus on matters pertaining to the promotion of integration but has no legislative function. Moreover, the Protocol Establishing the Pan-African Parliament does not provide for a legislative role among this AU organ's powers and functions.

However, as much as the legislative momentum is bound to remain on course, a few hurdles will have to be addressed, mainly through EAC intra-organ consultative processes. These hurdles include logistical shortcomings, which prevent the Assembly and relevant Committees from discharging work strictly in conformity with legislative programmes; the Council's slow and

48 By the provisions of Articles 62 and 63, once a Bill has been enacted it is submitted to the Heads of State for assent.

protracted initiation of Bills;[49] and Partner States' delays and intransigence in conferring precedence of Community laws over similar national laws.

Moreover, the Assembly has been criticized for exuding a lack of institutional ownership of the Community within the population of East Africa. In this regard, Mukandala has long argued that the Assembly's *"set up leaves a lot to be desired"* on the basis that *"members of the Assembly are elected not directly by the East African electorate, but by the National Assembly of each Partner State. Although those elected are supposed to represent the various political parties and shades of opinion, they still will not be direct representatives of the people. As a result they will not have a constituency in the wider population to whom they will feel obliged to report back."* Furthermore, Mukandala notes that "[s]*ince their election is a caucus process, it will not involve wide ranging campaigns that can educate people on the Community. This is a lost opportunity for the cause of the Community to be known, its problems and prospects to be debated, appreciated and understood*".[50] However, one may plausibly counter argue that besides the European Parliament there is no directly elected international assembly in the world's integration processes.

Mukandala's views are vindicated by the fact that the current process of electing the members of the Assembly has often given rise to national parliamentary challenge and related litigation. In *Prof. Peter Anyang' Nyong'o & 10 others v Attorney General of Kenya & 2 Others* [*Others Intervening*],[51] the Claimants sought an interpretation and application of the Treaty, regarding the validity of the nomination and election of Kenya's nine representatives to the Assembly. The Claimants contended that Kenya's National Assembly did not undertake an election within the meaning of Article 50 of the Treaty and that the Election Rules made by Kenya's National Assembly (*The Treaty for the Establishment of the East African Community* (*Election of Members of the Assembly*) *Rules 2001*) for the purpose of conducting the said elections infringed the provisions of Article 50. In support of their claim, evidence was submitted to show that Kenya's National Assembly only approved

49 Bills which have pended action by the Council for long include The Lake Victoria Basin Commission Bill 2008, The East African Privately-Funded Infrastructure Bill 2009, The East African Community Assets Protection Bill 2012 and The East African Community Disaster Preparedness Bill 2013.

50 Rwekaza Mukandala, *'Political Co-operation'* in *EAC: Perspectives on Regional Integration and Co-operation in East Africa*, EAC Secretariat, Arusha/German Agency for Technical Co-operation (GTZ), 2000, pp. 101–103.

51 EACJ Ref. No. 1 of 2006.

names submitted by two political parties. The Court held that the bottom line for compliance with Article 50 is that the decision to elect is a decision of and by the National Assembly; however the evidence adduced led to only one conclusion, namely that the National Assembly of Kenya neither undertook nor carried out an election within the meaning of Article 50 of the Treaty.

In *Democratic Party and Mukasa Mbidde v Secretary General of the East African Community & Attorney General of Uganda*[52] the Applicants complained of inaction on the part of the Government of the Republic of Uganda and its Parliament to amend the 2006 Rules of Procedure of Parliament for the election of Uganda's representatives to the Assembly as earlier directed by the Constitutional Court of Uganda.[53] They further contended that the intention to conduct elections of the Assembly Members under the un-amended 2006 Rules contravened the Treaty in as far as the rules discriminated and limited the freedom and right of the Democratic Party and its members to associate in vying for election as representatives in the Assembly. The Applicant's sought orders to have the Government of the Republic of Uganda and its Parliament conform to the provisions of Article 50 of the Treaty. The Court held that the 2006 Rules did not conform to the Treaty and restrained the Parliament of the Republic of Uganda from conducting the elections unless and until it amended the impugned 2006 Rules to conform to Article 50 of the Treaty.

In both cases, and later in *Among A. Anita v The Attorney General of Uganda and Secretary General of the East African Community*[54] and *Antony Calist Komu v Attorney General of The United Republic of Tanzania*,[55] the Court upheld the spirit, tenor, language and intent of Article 50(1) of the Treaty. The Court emphasized the requirements of an "election" accommodating all political parties and shades of opinion in actualizing the requirements of that provision, as opposed to a "selection". The moral of these cases is that the institutional framework could do better with strict compliance with the Treaty or, better still, with representation to the Assembly constituted through universal adult suffrage.

52 EACJ Ref. No. 6 of 2011.

53 Uganda Constitutional Court Petition No. 28 of 2006: Jacob Oulanyah v Attorney General of the Republic of Uganda.

54 EACJ Ref No. 6 of 2012.

55 EACJ Ref No. 7 of 2012.

2.2.2 *The Summit of Heads of State*

The Summit, which together with the Council and the Secretariat constitutes the executive arm of the Community, consists of the Heads of State or Government of the Partner States.[56] A *"Head of State"* is defined to mean *"a person designated as such by a Partner State's Constitution"*[57] and a *"Head of Government"* means *"a person designated as such by a Partner State's Constitution".*[58] On the basis of definitions in national Constitutions and interpretation of national laws of the Partner States, both terms refer to Presidents, Vice Presidents and Prime Ministers.

The Summit is principally charged with—

(*a*) *giving general directions and impetus as to the development and achievement of the objectives of the Community;*[59]
(*b*) *considering annual progress reports and such other reports submitted to it by the Council as provided for by the Treaty;*[60] *and*
(*c*) *reviewing the state of peace, security and good governance within the Community and the progress achieved towards the establishment of a Political Federation of the Partner States;*[61]

The Summit is also responsible for—

(*a*) *appointing Judges of the East African Court of Justice (and designate the President, the Vice President, the Principal Judge and the Deputy Principal Judge);*[62]
(*b*) *handling membership issues such as admitting foreign countries into the Community;*[63] *handling sanctions on, and suspension and expulsion of errant Partner States;*[64]

---

56 Article 10.
57 Article 1.
58 *Ibid.*
59 Article 11(1).
60 Article 11(2).
61 Article 11(3).
62 Articles 24(1), 24(4), 24(5).
63 Article 3(5).
64 Articles 143, 146, 147.

(c) *initiating the process towards the establishment of a Political Federation by directing the Council to undertake the process;*[65] *and*
(d) *approving protocols and other annexes to the Treaty.*[66]

The Summit's functions are arguably limited to overall policy direction, whereas implementation, operational policy and similar decisions are made by organs subordinate to the Summit. It is also important to note that some of the functions of the Summit may, through an Act of the Community, be delegated to the Council or the Secretary General.[67] This position represents a *volte-face* from the defunct East African Community whose institutional arrangement reflected a deep seated involvement of the East African Authority which similarly was comprised of Heads of State and whose failure to meet and make decisions has often been cited as one of the reasons for the collapse of that earlier integration arrangement.[68]

The functioning of the Summit also observes the principle of the separation of powers. Firstly, the separation of powers is emphasized by the fact that in giving general directions and impetus as to the development and achievement of the objectives of the Community, the Summit may be said to operate through the Council from whom it receives reports for consideration.[69] Secondly, there is no operational linkage with the Court or with the Assembly. The requirement that each of the members of the Summit assents to Bills enacted by the Assembly does not create such a linkage. Reference to "legislative powers" in the provision of the Treaty for an Act on delegation of the powers of the Summit[70] has sometimes been misconstrued to suggest that the Summit may encroach on the Assembly's domain. However, this reference may have been framed only with regard to assent to Bills. It too, therefore, cannot create such a linkage.

---

65 Article 123(6).

66 Article 151(2).

67 Articles 11(5), 11(6), 11(7). It is the actualization of these provisions that gave rise to the enactment of The Summit (Delegation of Powers and Functions) Act 2007.

68 Sam G. Nahamya, *Regional Economic Disintegration: Tensions, Conflicts and Causes—the Case of the East African Community*, Fort Collins, Colorado State University, 1980. See also Juma Volter Mwapachu, *Challenging The Frontiers of African Integration: The Dynamics of Policies, Politics and Transformation in the East African Community*, Dar es Salaam, E&D Vision Publishing Limited, 2012 p. 55.

69 Article 1.

70 Article 11(6).

The role of the Summit has been subject to judicial scrutiny in *The East Africa Law Society & 5 Others v the Attorney General of the Republic of Kenya & 4 Others.*[71] The Applicants challenged the legality of an amendment to the Treaty which had been adopted by the Summit and which, among other things, created new grounds upon which a Judge of the Court could be removed to include situations where that Judge is removed from that office for misconduct or due to inability to perform the functions of the office for any reason; where the Judge resigns from that office following allegation of misconduct or of inability to perform the functions of the office for any reason; or where a Judge is subject to investigation by a tribunal or other relevant authority of a Partner State with a view to his or her removal from an office referred. The amendments also empowered the Summit to suspend a Judge from the exercise of the functions of his or her office on those grounds. It was contended by some people that the amendment was motivated by the desire to 'punish' judges of the Court for their decision in *Prof. Peter Anyang' Nyong'o & 10 Others v The Attorney General of Kenya & 5 Others* which had gone against, and allegedly "embarrassed" a Partner State. It was further argued that the amendment was in violation of the Treaty provisions in so far as it did not comply with the procedures governing amendments to the Treaty—including consultations. A key issue was whether failure to carry out wide consultations on the proposals for the amendments to the Treaty constitutes an infringement of the Treaty.

The Court, while rightly leaving the amendments intact, held *inter alia* that—

(a) there was a deliberate attempt in the formulation of the Treaty to ensure that East Africans, for whose benefit the Community was established, participate in protecting the integrity of the Treaty;
(b) the principle of people-centered cooperation is also applicable to the Treaty amendment process. Until more elaborate modalities are evolved as the Community continues to grow, the resolve to allow participation of the private sector and civil society recited in the preamble, and the objective to enhance and strengthen partnerships with the private sector and civil society enunciated in Article 5(3)(g), provide adequate guidelines; and

71 EACJ Ref No. 3 of 2007.

(c) the introduction of automatic removal and suspension of judges of the Court on grounds raised or established in any one Partner State, and applicable to only those in judicial or public office, may endanger the integrity of the Court as a regional court.

The decision may generally reflect dictates of good governance. However, the Court also decided that *"the correct construction of Article 150(5) of the Treaty must be that the provision directs the Secretary General to submit proposed amendments and comments received from Partner States to the Summit not later than the expiry of a period of 90 days. There is no express or implied requirement for the Partner States to carry out any consultations, nor is the Secretary General required to hold proposed amendments and comments received from Partner States until expiration of that period"*.[72] Indeed some scholars like Kasaija have asserted that the application was in effect dismissed and the amendments themselves were not bad per se.[73]

2.2.3 *The Council of Ministers*

The Council consists of the Ministers responsible for East African Community Affairs, the Attorney General and such other Ministers as each Partner State may determine.[74] A *"Minister"* in relation to a Partner State means *"a person appointed as a Minister of the Government of that Partner State and any other person, however entitled, who, in accordance with any law of that Partner State, acts as or performs the functions of a Minister in that State"*.[75] The term *"Attorney General"* means *"the Attorney General of a Partner State"*.[76]

The Council is the policy organ in as far as implementation of the Treaty provisions and integration programmes are concerned.[77] The Treaty does not define the term *"policy"*. From an economic and political point of view, *"policy"* should mean a set of principles to broadly guide decisions and achieve rational outcomes in a given process. With regard to the Community, policy

72 *Ibid.*, p. 25.

73 Philip Kasaija, *The State of Constitutionalism in East Africa: The Role of the East African Community (EAC)-2007* In *Constitutionalism in East Africa* Ed by Wanza Kioko, Kampala Foundation Publishers, 2009 pp. 16–17.

74 Article 13.

75 Article 1.

76 *Ibid.*

77 *Op. cit.*, footnote 31.

should relate to the agreed approach towards the realization of the primary or strategic objectives of the Community as provided under the Treaty.

This key function of the Council is vindicated by the fact that the Treaty bestows on the Council—

(a) advisory roles *vis-à-vis* all other organs and institutions e.g. to the Summit with regard to the salaries and other terms and conditions of service of the Judges of the Court and Members of the Assembly; the appointment of Deputy Secretaries General of the Community; and expansion of country membership of the Community;[78]
(b) binding supervisory roles in the sense that *"Subject to the provisions of the Treaty, the regulations, directives and decisions of the Council taken or given in pursuance of the provisions of this Treaty shall be binding on the Partner States, on all organs and institutions of the Community other than the Summit, the Court and the Assembly within their jurisdictions, and on those to whom they may under this Treaty be addressed."*;[79] powers to establish institutions such as those necessary to administer the Common Market and those like specific sectoral councils and sectoral committees;[80] and
(c) power to establish institutions such as those necessary to administer the Common Market and those like specific sectoral councils and sectoral committees;[81] and
(d) power to consider and approve policy rationalization and harmonization undertakings in the various areas of co-operation.[82]

Apart from assisting the Summit in the performance of its functions (including the implementation of the decisions and directives of the Summit), and the said supervisory powers the Council is required to—

---

78 Articles 3(6), 25(5), 51(2) and 68(2).

79 Article 16.

80 The Council may establish sectoral councils (Article 14(3)(i)), creates sectoral committees and may establish institutions for the administration of the Common Market (Article 76(3)).

81 The Council may establish sectoral councils (Article 14(3)(i)), creates sectoral committees and may establish institutions for the administration of the Common Market (Article 76(3)).

82 This power applies to progress in all areas of co-operation provided in Chapters Eleven to Twenty Seven of the Treaty.

(a) *promote, monitor and keep under constant review the efficient functioning and development of the Community* and in this regard, *to consider measures that should be taken by the Partner States in promoting the attainment of the objectives of the Community;*[83]
(b) *initiate and submit Bills to the Legislative Assembly;*[84]
(c) *consider the Budget of the Community (once prepared by the Secretary General);*[85]
(d) *make staff and financial rules and regulations;*[86] *and*
(e) *submit annual progress reports to the Summit.*[87]

For the purpose of ensuring administrative support to the discharge of its functions the Council is required to engage the Counsel to the Community, the Registrar of the Court, the Clerk of the Assembly, heads of institutions and other members of staff of the Community in employment.[88]

The current Council can be contrasted to its predecessor, which existed under the framework of the defunct EAC. Notably, in comparison to the Ministers of the Community, the current Council is significantly less powerful.[89] This contraction of powers is important as the powers bestowed on the Council are crucial for ensuring that decisions are taken on time and that implementation is effectively monitored. For example, directives and regulations are the main conduits through which the objectives of the Customs Union, the Common Market and the Monetary Union are expected to be achieved.[90]

The Council's policy symbiosis with the Assembly is borne out by the latter's consideration and enactment into law of the former's Bills. The Council's

83 Articles 14(2), 14(3)(f).

84 Article 14(3)(b).

85 Article 14(3)(e) read together with Article 132(2).

86 Article 14(3)(g).

87 Article 14(3)(h).

88 Articles 45, 49(2)(f), 69 and 70.

89 Juma Volter Mwapachu, *Challenging The Frontiers of African Integration: The Dynamics of Policies, Politics and Transformation in the East African Community*, Dar es Salaam, E&D Vision Publishing Limited, 2012 p. 56. See also *op. cit.*, footnote 3.

90 *See for example* Article 39(1)(c) of The Protocol on the Establishment of the East African Community Customs Union, Articles 10(4), 12(3), 19(6), 23(3), 36(2), 41(4), 42(3), 42(5), 43(5), 44(3), 47(2) and 51 of The Protocol on the Establishment of the East African Community Common Market and Article 27 of The Protocol on the Establishment of the East African Community Monetary Union.

dependence on the Court is founded on the provision that *"The Council may request advisory opinions from the Court."*[91]

The Council's discharge of functions has resulted in the development of several programmes and projects in different areas of co-operation as outlined by the Treaty and using development strategies as bases. The Council's impact on the development of the institutional framework is borne out by the fact that it is the Council that proposes the establishment of new organs, institutions and offices. It is also the Council that is empowered to grant observer status in the Community to inter-governmental and civil society organisations.[92]

Action by the Council was first subject to judicial scrutiny in *Calist Mwatela and 2 Others v East African Community*[93] where the Court also underlined the separation of powers within the Community's institutional framework. The Applicants challenged the validity of the meeting of the Sectoral Council on Legal and Judicial Affairs held between the 13th and 16th of September 2005. They contended that a decision reached at that meeting to the effect that three Bills originally introduced into the Assembly by way of private member motions but which had been taken over by the Council should be withdrawn from the Assembly ran contrary to the Treaty and should be rendered null and void. The Court decided—

(a) the Treaty has not bestowed any power on the Council to take over Bills without observance of the Assembly Rules and the only lawful way of withdrawing Bills which have become property of the Assembly, as the three Bills had become, is under Rule 34 of the Assembly Rules which provides for a Motion to be introduced in the Assembly for that purpose; and

(b) in light of Articles 14 and 16 of the Treaty, the decisions of the Council have no place in areas of jurisdiction of the Summit, Court and the Assembly.

2.2.4 *The Secretariat*

The Secretariat, headed by the Secretary General of the Community, is responsible for, among other functions—

91 Article 36.

92 Under different protocols; Article 3(5)(b).

93 EACJ Ref No. 1 of 2005.

(*a*) *initiating, receiving and submitting recommendations to the Council, and forwarding of Bills to the Assembly;*
(*b*) *the initiation of studies and research related to, and the implementation of, programmes for the most appropriate, expeditious and efficient ways of achieving the objectives of the Community;*
(*c*) *the strategic planning, management and monitoring of programmes for the development of the Community;*
(*d*) *the undertaking either on its own initiative or otherwise, of such investigations, collection of information, or verification of matters relating to any matter affecting the Community that appears to it to merit examination;*
(*e*) *the co-ordination and harmonization of the policies and strategies relating to the development of the Community;*
(*f*) *the general promotion and dissemination of information on the Community to the stakeholders, the general public and the international community;*
(*g*) *the submission of reports on the activities of the Community to the Council;*
(*h*) *the general administration and financial management of the Community;*
(*i*) *the mobilization of funds from development partners and other sources for the implementation of projects of the Community;*
(*j*) *the submission of the budget of the Community to the Council for consideration;*
(*k*) *preparing draft agenda for the meetings of the organs of the Community other than the Court and the Assembly;*
(*l*) *the implementation of the decisions of the Summit and the Council;*
(*m*) *the organization and the keeping of records of meetings of the institutions of the Community other than those of the Court and the Assembly;*
(*n*) *the custody of the property of the Community; and*
(*o*) *the establishment of practical working relations with the Court and the Assembly.*[94]

The key role played by the Secretariat in the Community's institutional framework received judicial recognition in *Timothy Alvin Kahoho v Secretary General.*[95] An issue as to whether the decision of the 13th Summit of Heads of

94 Article 90(1).

95 EACJ Ref No. 1 of 2012.

State Decision to mandate the Secretariat to propose an action plan on, and a draft model of the structure of the East African Federation was in contravention of the operational principles under the Treaty and the Partner States' undertaking to implement the Treaty. In deciding the issue in the negative, and recognizing that the Secretariat is the only organ created to steer the ship of integration by implementing decisions of all the other Organs, the Court stated *inter alia* that: *"While addressing this issue, it behooves us to address in a few words the critical role that the Secretariat plays in the affairs of the Community, generally."* Prof. Sam Turyamuhika writes as follows:[96]

"The current EAC Secetariat has been typified as powerless, meetings and workshop organizer, minute taker etc." We take a different view of that harsh and unfair judgment. The EAC Secretariat is the fulcrum on which the wheels of integration rotate. The Summit, the Council of Ministers, the Co-ordination Committee and Sectoral Committees are all part-time and meet only as often as their functions require. Yet, the Secretariat slogs, day in, day out, to ensure that the ship of integration remains afloat. The Community, in our view, is like a giant ship owned by shareholders (the people of East Africa);the Summit is like a Board of Directors and the Council, is like the Management. The Captain is the Secretary-General and the crew are the staff in the Community. To call the Captain and crew, useless, and denigrate their role in keeping any ship on the high seas on course, is to say that the shareholders or the Board of Directors can single-handedly and without any input from those that physically man the ship, sail that ship from a distance. The Summit represents the owners of the ship, and its duty is to decide where the ship goes and should always act in the best interests of the shareholders. The Summit thus meets periodically to assess progress and regularly inform the shareholders of the profits (benefits) from the operations of the ship. The Council, Co-ordination and Sectoral Committees are the Summit's agents in overseeing progress aforesaid. Without the Captain and crew, the ship can barely survive the storms and other perils that are prevalent in high seas including attacks by pirates. We digressed to make the point that, our reading and understanding of Articles 11, 14, 18, 21 and 71 of the Treaty, which create the functions of the Organs of the Community, is that the Secretariat is the only Organ created by Article 9 of the Treaty to steer the ship of integration by implementing decisions of all the other Organs and its crucial role thereby ought to be recognized and supported".[97]

96 Sam Turyamuhika, In *The Drive Towards Political Integration in East Africa*, Ed by Isabelle Waffubwa and Joseph Clifford Birungi, p. 173.

97 *Ibid.*, paragraphs 48–49.

The main challenge facing the Secretariat relates to it responsibility concerning *"the implementation of the decisions of the Summit and the Council".* This is regarded as challenging because the Secretariat lacks the administrative mechanism and resources to police the Partner States in their general undertaking as to the implementation of the Treaty, certainly when compared for example to the European Commission.[98] Indeed Mwapachu aptly observes that the lack of executive authority is among the many challenges facing the Secretariat as *"[w]ith no tangible executive authority whereby every act of the Community is subjected to sovereign interests and concerns of the Partner States, the movement towards the realization of a robust EAC integration not to speak of achieving the EAC goal is clearly slow tracked."*[99] However, the responsibility for the co-ordination and harmonization of the policies and strategies relating to the development of the Community[100] should be a strength in the desired role for the Secretariat to steer a supranational organization.

2.2.5 *The East African Court of Justice*

The Court is the *"judicial body"* of the Community.[101] The role of the Court, which has both a First Instance Division and an Appellate Division, is to ensure the adherence to law in the interpretation and application of the Treaty.[102] The Court is composed of a maximum of fifteen Judges: a maximum of ten appointed to the First Instance Division and maximum of five appointed to the Appellate Division.[103] Its Judges are appointed *"by the Summit from among persons recommended by the Partner States who are of proven integrity, impartiality and independence and who fulfil the conditions required in their own countries for the holding of such high judicial office, or who are jurists of recognised competence in their respective Partner States."*[104] This appointment is subject to the restriction that no more than two Judges of the First Instance, or one Judge of the Appellate Division shall be appointed on the recommendation of the same Partner State.[105]

For purposes of adjudicating between legal and natural persons the Court—

---

98 See in this regard also the powers of the European Commission as discussed in EU chapter 2.

99 *Op. cit.*, footnote 90, pp. 41–42.

100 Article 71(1)(e).

101 Article 23.

102 Articles 23 and 27.

103 Article 24(2).

104 Article 24.

105 Article 24(1) (a)–(b).

(*a*) *is competent to accept and adjudicate upon all matters pursuant to the Treaty for purposes of determining the legality of any act, regulation, direction, decision, action or matter; to this extent the Court's jurisdiction also covers references by the Partner States, references by the Secretary General, Community Staff disputes, matters arising out of arbitral proceedings;*[106] *and*

(*b*) *may also be called upon to give advisory opinions regarding questions of law arising from the provisions of the Treaty.*[107]

Initially the Court's jurisdiction was limited to ensuring adherence to law in the interpretation and application of the Treaty.[108] However, for the purpose of ensuring conflict resolution and confidence building in the region it has always been envisaged by the Treaty that the Court shall have such other original, appellate, human rights and other jurisdiction as should be determined by the Council at a suitable date. In 2015, the Court's jurisdiction was extended to cover trade and commercial disputes and disputes arising out of the implementation of the Protocol on the Establishment of the East African Monetary Union.

Notwithstanding its broad jurisdiction, the Court is not designed to deny national courts their respective jurisdictions in accordance with the respective municipal laws.[109] In this regard, the Court can handle cases stated for preliminary rulings on matters of the Treaty.[110]

To date the Court should be credited with having generated not only regional jurisprudence but also public confidence in the integration process. It is important for the public to know that the Partner States and the organs and institutions of the Community cannot avail of impunity for any wrongdoing under the Treaty. The Court's decisions in *Prof. Peter Anyang' Nyong'o & 10 others v Attorney General of Kenya & 2 Others [Others Intervening]*[111] and *Democratic Party and Mukasa Mbidde v Secretary General of the East African Community & Attorney General of Uganda*[112] are of particular significance to institutional development as they are examples of the Court upholding the rule of law within the Community's institutional framework.

---

106 Articles 27, 28, 29, 30, 31 and 32.

107 *Op. cit.*, footnote 89.

108 *Op. cit.*, footnote 99.

109 Article 33.

110 Article 34.

111 *Op. cit.*, footnote 51.

112 *Op. cit.*, footnote 52.

The Court's decisions in *East Africa Law Society v Secretary General East Africa Law Society*[113] and *East African Center for Trade Policy and Law v Secretary General*[114] are also worth highlighting as far as the EAC institutional development is concerned. In both cases Article 24 (1) (e) of the Protocol Establishing the East African Community Customs Union (which establishes an East African Trade Remedies Committee to handle matters pertaining inter alia to rules of origin, anti-dumping, subsidies and countervailing measures and safeguard measures), and Article 54(2) of the Protocol for the Establishment of the East Africa Community Common Market (which empowers competent judicial, administrative or legislative authority or any other competent authority to handle disputes arising out of the implementation of the Protocol) were in issue. The provisions were impugned for allegedly being inconsistent with Articles 27(1) and 38(1) and (2) and by establishing "parallel adjudicatory bodies" or allowing national courts and other institutions to handle Customs and Common Market disputes, infringing on the jurisdiction of the East African Court of Justice. The Court held in both cases that—

(a) the dispute settlement mechanisms created under the Customs Union and Common Market Protocols do not exclude, oust or infringe upon the interpretative jurisdiction of the Court; but are merely alternative dispute resolution mechanisms intended for the speedy and effective resolution of trade disputes by experts in technical and specialized areas; any submission that this Court lacks jurisdiction over disputes arising out of the interpretation and application and implementation of the Protocols cannot be sustained;
(b) the impugned provisions of both Protocols are not in contravention of or in contradiction with the relevant provisions of the Treaty; and
(c) the establishment of the Committee on Trade Remedies or the conferring of jurisdiction upon national judicial, administrative or legislative mechanisms would not prevent Partner States from complying with Article 8 (1) (a) (which imposes on each individual Partner State an obligation to ensure that objectives of the Community are kept in mind during the planning and allocation of resources processes) and Article 8 (1) (c) (which contains a prohibition on

113 EACJ Ref. No. 1 of 2011.
114 EACJ Ref. No. 9 of 2012.

each individual Partner State to take any measure that is likely to jeopardize the achievement of the Treaty).[115]

The jurisprudence of the Court further demonstrates the Court's adherence to the separation of powers. For instance, in *Mbidde Foundation Limited and Rt Hon Margaret Zziwa v Secretary General of the East African Community and The Attorney General of Uganda*[116] the Court, in declining to intervene in the Assembly's process of impeachment of Rt Hon Margaret Zziwa as Speaker of the Assembly as sought by the Applicants, upheld the rule on separation of powers.

The Court remains faced with challenges such as difficulties associated with the enforcement of judgments and rulings as provided for under Articles 38 and 39 of the Treaty; the need for a balance between adjudicating in the primary interests of litigants and the strict application of stringent provisions of the Treaty such as that on limitation of actions as provided under Article 30(2) of the Treaty; and the possibility of the Judges, who pursuant to Article 140(4) of the Treaty (until the Court is declared fully operational), find themselves working under circumstances of "double allegiance" because they remain judicial officers in the Partner States' respective judiciaries and can only serve the Court in circuits sanctioned upon permission by the Chief Justices taking into account the business at their respective national Courts.

The Court can be strengthened through measures including the determination that the Court is fully operational as this would enable the Judges to serve on a permanent rather than *ad hoc* basis; and consideration of possible amendments to the Treaty in relevant areas of concern such as the need to establish a nexus between the trade dispute mechanisms established under the Customs Union and the Common Market Protocols and the Court as the judicial arm of the Community charged with the interpretation of the Treaty. There is also a need for continued discourse on the possibility of future inclusion of crimes against humanity (as an aspect of criminal jurisdiction, and an offshoot of universal human rights jurisdiction) within the Court's jurisdiction. This is informed by the fact that some of the divisions in the Partner States' High Courts handle crimes similar to those established under the Rome

115 See in this regard also the case law of the European Court of Justice on its exclusive jurisdiction as set out in EU chapter 2, for instance in Opinion 2/13 on the accession of the EU to the ECHR.

116 EACJ Applications Nos. 5 & 10 of 2014.

Statute of the International Criminal Court and the fact that only four of the Partner States are party to that Statute.[117]

2.3 Analytical Overview of Other Institutions and Bodies

2.3.1 *The Co-ordination Committee*

The Co-ordination Committee consists of *"Permanent Secretaries responsible for East African Community Affairs and such other Permanent Secretaries as each Partner State may determine"*.[118] Principally, the Co-ordination Committee is charged with submitting reports and recommendations to the Council either on its own initiative or upon request by the Council on the implementation of the Treaty. The Co-ordination Committee is responsible for co-ordinating the activities of the Sectoral Committees and to that extent it is an organ to which Sectoral Committees are answerable.[119]

Furthermore, the Co-ordination Committee is charged with implementing *"the decisions of the Council as the Council may direct"*.[120] It is submitted that this seems to be superfluous as the implementation of the integration agenda is an obligation and undertaking of the Partner States. Moreover, even if this was not the case, the Co-ordination Committee, which only makes recommendations as opposed to decisions, would not be the apt organ to implement the decisions of the Council.

2.3.2 *Sectoral Committees*

The Sectoral Committees are established by the Council on the recommendation of the Co-ordination Committee.[121] They are primarily responsible for the preparation of comprehensive implementation programmes and setting out priorities for different sectors of co-operation. They are also charged with monitoring and keeping under constant review the implementation of the Community's sectoral programmes.[122]

117 The Republic of Rwanda is not party to the Rome Statute.

118 Article 17.

119 Article 18. Compare in this regard also the role of COREPER in the EU, as discussed in EU chapter 2.

120 *Ibid.*

121 Article 20.

122 Article 21.

2.3.3 *Institutions of the Community*

The institutions of the Community so far established by the Summit are: the East African Civil Aviation Safety and Security Oversight Agency, the East African Health Research Council, the East African Kiswahili Commission, the East African Science and Technology Commission, the Inter-University Council for East Africa and the Lake Victoria Basin Commission. The surviving institutions of the former East African Community, which are now deemed to be institutions of the new Community, are the East African Development Bank and the Lake Victoria Fisheries Organization.[123]

The development of the institutions has been necessitated by the Partner States' imperative to articulate the scope and necessary institutional mechanism for achieving objectives in different areas of co-operation. Accordingly, the establishment of the East African Civil Aviation Safety and Security Oversight Agency is a consequence of the Partner States' co-operation in civil aviation and civil air transport; the establishment of the East African Health Research Council, the East African Science and Technology Commission may be attributed to expanded co-operation in health, science and technology; the establishment of the Inter-University Council for East Africa, the Lake Victoria Basin Commission and the East African Kiswahili Commission was necessitated by the Partner States' respective undertakings to revive an erstwhile Inter-University Council, to establish an apex body for the management of Lake Victoria and the development of Kiswahili as a *lingua franca* of the Community.

2.3.3.1 East African Civil Aviation Safety and Security Oversight Agency (CASSOA)

The East African Civil Aviation Safety and Security Oversight Agency (CASSOA), like the preceding East African Directorate of Civil Aviation,[124] is required

123 The definition of "surviving institutions" in the Treaty's Article 1 also includes the East African Civil Aviation Academy, Soroti and the East African School of Librarianship. However the Community has not repossessed these two as was anticipated. According to Article 14.01 of The East African Community Mediation Agreement 1984, Kenya, Tanzania and Uganda agreed *that "the Soroti Civil Flying School, the East African Development Bank, the East African Inter-University Committee, the Eastern and Southern African Management Institute, and the East African Community Library Services shall continue to function as joint East African institutions or common services, as the case may be, and agree to make appropriate arrangements for the financing and operation thereof".*

124 Within the institutional framework of the defunct Community, the Directorate of Civil Aviation was charged with among other roles the provision of technical services for aviation safety, initiation of aviation legislation, pilot training.

"to promote the safe, secure and efficient use and development of civil aviation within and outside the Partner States; assist the Partner States in meeting their safety and security oversight obligations and responsibilities under the Convention on International Civil Aviation 1944; and provide the Partner States with an appropriate forum and structure to discuss, plan and implement common measures for safe and orderly development of international civil aviation".[125]

Prominent among the functions of the CASSOA are to *"strengthen the Partner States' institutional framework for aviation safety and security; co-ordinate the Partner States' civil aviation safety and security oversight activities; foster the Partner States' timely implementation of International Civil Aviation Organisation regional air navigation requirements plans, standards and practices; evaluate the status of aviation safety and security in the Partner States; and facilitate the Partner States' sharing of technical expertise and facilities in civil aviation."*[126]

2.3.3.2 East African Development Bank (EADB)

The East African Development Bank (EADB), which was established in 1967 under the Treaty for East African Cooperation is a development finance institution with the objective of promoting and strengthening socio-economic development and regional integration.[127] Following the breakup of the defunct East African Community in 1977, the EADB was re-established under its own Treaty: the Treaty Amending and Re-enacting the Charter of the East African Development Bank (1980). The member countries are currently Kenya, Tanzania, Rwanda and Uganda. The Republic of Burundi has also applied for membership.

To the extent that the EADB plays a threefold role of lender, adviser and development partner, it may be regarded as a catalyst in the pursuit of the Partner States' undertaking to *"co-operate in financing projects jointly in each other's territory, especially those that facilitate integration within the Community."*[128]

---

125 Protocol on the Establishment of the East African Community Civil Aviation Safety and Security Oversight Agency, Article 4.

126 *Ibid.*, Article 5.

127 Article 1 of The Treaty Amending and Re-enacting the Charter of the East African Development Bank, 1980.

128 *Ibid.*; read together with Articles 8–18.

2.3.3.3 East African Health Research Commission

The East African Health Research Commission (EAHRC) has a vision for *"high quality health research for purposes of improvement of the health and well-being of the peoples of the Community."*[129] The EAHRC aims at *"improving the health of the citizens in the Partner States through capacity building and poverty reduction by promoting, co-ordinating and formulating policies for effective utilization of results from health research".*[130]

Specifically the EAHRC seeks to, among other functions *"strengthen health research collaboration and co-ordination; promote the application of knowledge obtained from health research; promote the development of human resource capacities in health research; promote exchange and dissemination of health research information; and facilitate the creation of health research databases; liaise with national, regional and international health institutions; and develop quality assurance processes and address common intellectual property rights relevant to health in the Partner States".*[131]

2.3.3.4 East African Kiswahili Commission

The East African Kiswahili Commission has a vision *"to be the leading body in the promotion and coordination of the development and usage of Kiswahili for regional unity and sustainable socio-economic development in Partner States".*[132]

The Commission mainly aims at "*strengthening national, regional and international communication through the use of Kiswahili in East Africa and beyond; developing Kiswahili as a regional language expressing and conveying African values with respect to issues of gender equity, human rights and democracy; encouraging collaboration in regional research and assisting the Partner States to develop centers of advanced study and research in Kiswahili; assisting the Partner States to offer quality education for the production of Kiswahili teachers and communicators in all sectors of society; promoting curriculum reform to equip citizens with the Kiswahili literary and linguistic skills and knowledge which meet the needs of the East African society and conform to the development plans of East Africa; developing quality assurance processes, through harmonization of Kiswahili language education programmes, curricula and certification,*

129 Protocol on the Establishment of the East African Health Research Commission, Articles 2, 3.

130 *Ibid.*, Article 3.

131 *Ibid.*, Article 7.

132 Protocol on the Establishment of the East African Kiswahili Commission, Articles 2, 3, 5 and 6.

in order to ensure that teaching and research in Kiswahili achieve and maintain acceptable standards; and assisting governments and other appropriate bodies and authorities with the development of strategies for adequate investment in the promotion of Kiswahili in East Africa and beyond".[133]

For the purposes of achieving these objectives, the Commission plays an advisory, collaborative and co-ordination role.[134]

2.3.3.5 East African Science and Technology Commission (EASTECO)

The East African Science and Technology Commission (EASTECO) is charged with promoting and co-ordinating the development, management and application of science and technology in the Partner States.[135] EASTECO is therefore expected to *"co-ordinate and facilitate the activities of the Partner States and national science and technology institutions in promoting the development and application of science, technology and innovation in all aspects including policy development, administrative issues, resource mobilization and utilization, research and development, product and project development".*[136]

2.3.3.6 Inter-University Council for East Africa (IUCEA)

The mission of The Inter-University Council for East Africa (IUECA) is *"to encourage and develop mutually beneficial collaboration between Member Universities, and between them and Governments and other organizations".*[137]

IUECA is therefore charged mainly with "*strengthening regional communication among the universities; initiating, assisting and encouraging the development of East African higher institutions of learning; encouraging collaboration in regional research; mobilizing universities to offer quality education; promoting curriculum reform in order to equip graduates with the skills and knowledge that meet the needs of employers and conform to the development plans of East Africa; and developing quality assurance processes in order to ensure that teaching and research achieve and maintain international standards".*[138]

---

133 *Ibid.*, Article 7.

134 *Ibid.*, Article 8.

135 Protocol on the Establishment of the East African Science and Technology Commission, Article 5.

136 *Ibid.*, Article 6.

137 The Inter-University Council for East Africa Act 2008, Sections 3 and 4.

138 *Ibid.*, Section 6.

2.3.3.7 Lake Victoria Basin Commission (LVBC)

The Lake Victoria Basin Commission (LVBC) was established for the management of the Lake Victoria Basin. The LVBC is responsible for coordinating the sustainable development agenda of the Lake Victoria Basin.[139]

The broad functions of the institution are *"to promote, facilitate and coordinate activities of different actors towards sustainable development and poverty eradication of the Lake Victoria Basin" through the harmonization of policies, laws, regulations and standards; the promotion of stakeholders' participation in the sustainable development of natural resources; promotion of capacity building and institutional development; promotion of security and safety on Lake Victoria; promotion of research and development; monitoring, evaluation and compliance with policies and agreed upon actions; preparation and harmonization of the Partner States' negotiating positions against any other state on matters concerning the Lake Victoria Basin; consideration of reports from the Partner States' institutions on their activities relating to the management of the Basin under The Lake Victoria Basin Commission Protocol; and initiation and promotion of programmes that target poverty eradication".*[140]

2.3.3.8 Lake Victoria Fisheries Organisation (LVFO)

The primary functions of the Lake Victoria Fisheries Organisation (LVFO), established by the Convention (Final Act) for the Establishment of the Lake Victoria Fisheries Organisation, 1994, are to build cooperation among the Member States, to harmonize domestic laws and regulations for the sustainable use of the living resources of Lake Victoria, and to develop and adopt conservation and management measures.[141]

LVFO is charged with *"promoting the proper management and the optimum utilization of the fisheries and other resources of Lake Victoria; enhancing the capacity building of existing institutions and developing additional relevant institutions, in cooperation with existing institutions and other international, regional and non-governmental organizations; creating a forum for discussion regarding environmental and water quality initiatives affecting the Basin and maintaining a liaison with existing bodies and programs; conducting research regarding water quality in Lake Victoria; encouraging, recommending, coordinating and, as appropriate, undertaking relevant training and extension activities concerning the fisheries; considering and advising on the effects of the introduction of*

139 Protocol For the Sustainable Development of Lake Victoria Basin, Articles 33–42; read together with Articles 3–32.

140 *Ibid.*

141 The Convention (Final Act) for the Establishment of the Lake Victoria Fisheries Organisation, 1994, Article II.

non-indigenous aquatic animals or plants into Lake Victoria or its tributaries and adopting measures related to the introduction, monitoring, control or elimination of such animals or plants; serving as a clearing house and databank for information on Lake Victoria's fisheries and promoting the dissemination of information; adopting budgets, seeking funding, formulating financial management plans and allocating funds for the Organisation's activities in furthering the purposes of the Convention (Final Act) for the Establishment of the Lake Victoria Fisheries Organisation, 1994."[142]

The institutions that are already in place have several achievements to their name, for instance, CASSOA's harmonization of regional aviation safety and security regulations and technical guidance materials; EADB's growing range of financial services in real and property development, infrastructure development, trade finance, capital markets development, business advisory services etc.; IUCEA's strengthening of higher education quality assurance processes and enhancement of regional research management; and LVBC's Lake Victoria Water and Sanitation Project, Mt Elgon Regional Ecosystem Conservation Programme and the Mara Basin Project.

Establishment and projection aside, the nature and structure of the new institutions raises a few queries. Whereas the LVBC, the EAHRC, EASTECO and the East African Kiswahili Commission are supposed to be legal personalities, their establishment has not, contrary to policy, been based on an Act of the Community but on protocols i.e. international agreements. In some cases the process of establishing an institution on a strong legal and statutory basis has been protracted. For instance, the East African Civil Aviation Safety and Security Oversight Agency Bill has never been fully assented to, even though it was enacted in 2009. Furthermore, although these institutions are required to report to the Council, the procedure for this is not harmonized because some of the institutions are also required as legal entities to report to their own corporate boards, as is the case with the EADB. They may also be required to report to Ministerial councils, which are arguably external in composition to the Community's institutional framework, as is the case with the LVFO. Furthermore, because there is no common basis for the establishment of the institutions the Secretary General's negotiations with the Partner States for the grant of privileges and immunities to them and their staff is not as accordant as it should be. There is therefore need to establish a policy framework indicating the exact relationship of the organs and institutions *inter se*. The moot point is whether the institutions are meant to be specialized agencies with a distinct legal personality of their own or subsidiary organs only exercising delegated powers.

---

142 *Ibid.*

2.3.4 *Other Bodies, Departments and Services*

Other bodies, departments and services within the framework should include—

(a) The East African Community Trade Remedies Committee established to handle disputes and investigate on matters relating to rules of origin, subsidies and countervailing measures etc.;[143] and such bodies, departments and services as may be established pursuant to the Customs law of the Community for purposes of administering the Customs Union;[144]
(b) Such institutions as may be established or authorized by the Council for purposes of administering the Common Market;[145] and
(c) The East African Central Bank;[146] institutions responsible for financial services (surveillance, compliance, enforcement) and statistics; and The East African Monetary Institute[147] within the context of administering The East African Monetary Union.

2.4 Challenges to the Institutional Framework

Institutional and governance challenges associated with managing international organizations, such as Partner States' overemphasis on national sovereignties, inadequate resources, underdeveloped infrastructure and slow implementation of decisions face the Community's institutional framework. Critical among these are the excesses of the requirement of consensus in decision-making, interface challenges and challenges to the safeguarding of the Community's international status.

2.4.1 *Decision-Making by Consensus*

Decision making by the Summit and the Council and the making of recommendations by the Co-ordination Committee are guided by the principle of consensus. In the case of the Council, this applies to the making of policy

---

143 Protocol on the Establishment of the East African Community Customs Union, Article 24.

144 *Ibid.*, Article 34.

145 Protocol on the Establishment of the East African Community Common Market, Article 46 read together with Article 76(3) of the Treaty.

146 Protocol on the Establishment of the East African Community Monetary Union, Article 20.

147 *Ibid.*, Articles 21 and 23 respectively.

decisions, directives and regulations pertaining to the development and progression of the integration process as provided under the Treaty. In this regard, the Treaty provides that—

(a) *"for purposes of the discharge of functions, the decisions of the Summit shall be by consensus"*;[148] and
(b) *"subject to a Protocol on decision-making the decisions of the Council shall be by consensus"*.[149]

The Protocol on Decision Making by the Council provides that—

1. *The decisions of the Council on the following matters shall be by consensus:*
   (a) *Granting of observers status to an inter-governmental organization or civil society organization;*
   (b) *Making of the financial rules and regulations of the Community;*
   (c) *Submission of the annual budget of the Community to the Legislative Assembly;*
   (d) *Approval of the expenditures of the Community;*
   (e) *Establishment of any sectoral council or committee under the Treaty;*
   (f) *Submission of Bills to the East African Legislative Assembly;*
   (g) *Policy decisions made pursuant to Article 14(3) (a) of the Treaty;*
   (h) *Decisions on what should be recommended to the Summit on:*
      (i) *Amendment of the Treaty;*
      (ii) *Approval or amendment of any protocol;*
      (iii) *Admission of new members*
      (iv) *Imposition of sanctions;*
      (v) *Suspension of a member;*
      (vi) *Transformation into a political federation; and*
      (vii) *Expansion of areas of co-operation.*
2. *All other decisions of the Council shall be by simple majority.*[150]

The requirement on consensus has been replicated in the Rules of Procedure for the Summit, the Council and the Coordination Committee.[151] Accordingly,

148 *Ibid.*, Article 12(3).
149 *Ibid.*, Article 15(4).
150 Article 2.
151 See Rule 13 of the Rules of Procedure of the Summit, Rule 13 of the Rules of Procedure of the Council and Rule 13 of the Rules of Procedure of the Co-ordination Committee (which apply mutatis mutandis to all lower committees and bodies).

this requirement directs the making of all institutional or organizational policy decisions (which create direct obligations on the organs and institutions) and all operational decisions (which are necessitated by the Community's direct and substantive operations).

The Treaty does not define the term "consensus" in terms of, for example unanimity, or absolute, simple, qualified or other majority. However, the Court has given guidance as to the definition of consensus within the Community framework: *"a general agreement among the members of a given group or community, each of which exercises some discretion in decision making agreements. Achieving consensus requires serious treatment of every group member's considered opinion. Once a decision is made it is important to trust in members' discretion in follow-up action. In the ideal case, those who wish to take up some action want to hear those who oppose it, because they count on the fact that the ensuing debate will improve the consensus. In theory, action without resolution of considered opposition will be rare and done with attention to minimize damage to relationships".*[152]

Consensus as applied in the Treaty and protocols is not only a decision-making mechanism at the policy level for the Summit and the Council and in the other executive organs of the Community; it is also a mechanism that emphasises "all Partner States' representation" for a quorum at all meetings.[153]

The context of the Protocol on Decision Making suggests that all key policy matters such as the transformation of the integration process into a political federation or achieving key milestones like the Customs Union, the Common Market, the Monetary Union and institution building have to be arrived upon on the basis of consensus. Any EAC framework in such areas necessitates prior agreement/consensus by all the Partner States. Mwapachu has observed that *"this protocol could have set out, as in the European Union, a matrix of issues that would require different forms or modalities of decision-making—unanimity, consensus, qualified majority etc. Unfortunately and given the backdrop of the demised EAC and the remaining excess baggage in the Partner States regarding issues of differential stages of economic development, the protocol retained a strict requirement for all decisions made by the Council".*[154]

The only significant exception to the preponderance of consensus in decision-making is in respect of suspension or expulsion of a Partner State in case

152 EACJ Application No. 1 of 2008, p. 29.

153 Rules of Procedure.

154 *Op. cit.*, footnote 90, p. 57. See on different forms of decision making in the EU also EU chapter 2, and for the crucial importance of decision making by Qualified Majority Voting for the internal market, EU chapter 9.

of failure to observe and fulfill the fundamental principles and objectives of the Treaty or gross and persistent violation of such principles and objectives.[155]

As elaborated by Schermers and Blokker, decision-making by consensus ensures "general acclamation" or "common feeling" or "concurrence of feelings", acknowledges differences in power and interests and obviates "majoritarianism"; it has therefore been adopted by many international organizations.[156] However, as has often been the case in the Community, it is a time-consuming method in which decisions may often have their intention watered down. It is also over-tied to "all Partner States' representation" for a quorum at meetings.

2.4.2 *Interface Challenges*

The achievement of the objectives of the Community depends on how cohesive and co-ordinated the organs and institutions are in the discharge of their respective functions. Although the Treaty and relevant protocols spell out the different functions of the organs and institutions, a primary or literal interpretation of the Treaty suggests that the intention of the Partner States, as contracting parties, is that the organs and institutions should play their roles with one ultimate objective—development of the Community for the benefit of the people of East Africa. Therefore, the introduction and maintenance of a mechanism for cordial and collaborative inter-facing and inter-relationships between the organs and institutions is unassailable.

Besides providing for the applicability of the principle of asymmetry and requiring the Secretariat to establish *"practical working relations with the Court and the Assembly"*[157] the Treaty does not establish a mechanism for intra-organ/institution collaboration. With the Assembly, the Council and the Court each vying for optimum discharge of obligations, misunderstandings and institutional clashes do occur. Therefore, collaboration is more of an outcome of necessity in given cases than a substratum for regular operations. Regrettably, collaboration is not seen in the practice of the EAC and clashes between the different organs and institutions are evident, for example, the Assembly allowing a motion on a Bill like the Lake Victoria Basin Commission Bill which is not supported by the Council;[158] or the Assembly enacting Bills such as the East African Community Trans-Boundary Ecosystem Management Bill 2011, the East African Community Polythene Materials Control Bill 2011, the East African Community Human and Peoples' Rights Bill 2011, the East African

155 Article 148.

156 Henry G. Schermers and Niels M. Blokker (1995), International Institutional Law, Martinus Nijhoff Publishers, The Hague, pp. 505–885.

157 Article 71(1)(o).

158 *Op. cit.*, footnote 90, p. 145.

Community HIV and AIDS Prevention and Management Bill 2012 and the East African Service Commission Bill 2010, all of which have not been assented to by the Summit.

Moreover, lack of a clear collaborative basis has the potential to generate unnecessary duplication of efforts among the organs and institutions. Since this challenge arises out of the fact that each organ pursues the accomplishment of its mandate to the best of its ability, the panacea lies in overall institutional review and amendment of the Treaty.

2.4.3 *Challenges to the Safeguarding of the Community's International Status*

It is part of *jus cogens* that for purposes of effectively discharging their functions *"international organisations should be entitled to the grant of privileges and immunities for their assets, properties and representatives"*.[159] The Treaty recognizes the international legal personality of the Community and invariably the Community's institutional framework.[160] In this regard, the Treaty cognizant of the Community's legal capacity as a body corporate with perpetual succession, provides that—

(a) the Community shall enjoy international legal personality;[161] and that

(b) persons employed in the service of the Community including staff, experts and consultants shall enjoy immunities and privileges while performing services to the Community.[162]

In practice the realization of the international status is afflicted by both the Partner States' insistence on national sovereignty and, *a fortiori*, their reluctance to agree on a common platform premise on the nature and extent of immunities and privileges. As a result the conclusion of headquarters agreements as bases for the grant of immunities and privileges for Community organs, institutions, staff and other persons in the employ of the Community remains largely streaked from one Partner State to another country to country. This is notwithstanding the Secretariat's long outstanding proposal for the conclusion of a protocol that would be a common yardstick for the conclusion of such agreements.

---

159 Malcolm N. Shaw (1997), International Law, Cambridge University Press, Cambridge, pp. 923–929.

160 Articles 138 read together with Articles 4 and 8.

161 *Ibid.*

162 Article 73 read together with Article 72.

CHAPTER 2A

The Institutional Framework of the EU

Armin Cuyvers

2.1 An Evolutionary Supranational Framework

This chapter discusses the original institutional set-up of the European Union as well as the key evolutionary steps that led to its current institutional reality.[1] The initial institutional framework forms an important comparator for the EAC today, which is still in its relatively early days. The evolutionary developments are both important to indicate which institutional challenges may arise in the future and to illustrate what possible solutions and their consequences are. In addition, they serve as an illustration of those areas where the institutional system of the EU was also not yet sufficiently developed in the beginning, and those areas where the system got it right from the beginning.

To simplify comparison, this chapter first discusses each institution in turn, following the sequence of discussion in the EAC chapter. In addition, each section will refer to some of the standard works on the different institutions for those who would like to engage in a further comparison.

2.2 From Assembly to Parliament

What became the 'European Parliament' started life as a relatively powerless 'European Assembly' of the European Coal and Steel Community (ECSC).[2] This Assembly was not directly elected but consisted of representatives of national

1 On this issue also see G. De Búrca, 'The Institutional Development of the EU: A Constitutional Analysis', in: P. Craig and G. de Búrca (eds), *The Evolution of EU law* (OUP 1999), 55.

2 See chapter II of the 1951 Treaty of Paris (ECSC Treaty). For a more elaborate discussion of the European Parliament see amongst others P. Dann, 'The Political Institutions', in: A. Von Bogdandy and J. Bast (eds), *Principles of European Constitutional Law* (2nd ed., Hart Publishing 2010), 247, D. Earnshaw and D. Judge, *the European Parliament* (2nd edn, Palgrave 2008), R. Corbett, F. Jacobs and M. Shackleton (eds), *The European Parliament* (7th edn, John Harper Publishing 2007), M. Westlake, '"The Style and the Machinery": The Role of the European Parliament in the EU's Legislative Process', in: P. Craig and C. Harlow (eds), *Lawmaking in the European Union* (Kluwer, 1998), ch. 5, or P. Pierson, 'The Path to European Integration: A Historical Institutionalist Analysis' 29 *Comparative Political Studies* (1996), 123.

© ARMIN CUYVERS, 2017 | DOI 10.1163/9789004322073_005
This is an open access chapter distributed under the terms of the CC-BY-NC License.

assemblies or parliaments (the so called double-mandate). The Assembly, moreover was largely an advisory body without formal powers. Most importantly, it could not adopt or block legislation. The Assembly only had the right to be consulted, and its opinions or comments were not binding on the other institutions. It is fair to say, therefore, that in the early days of European integration the Assembly played only a minor role, and real democratic representation of national interest was done via the Council.

One of the main evolutionary trends in the institutional history of the EU, however, is the gradual empowerment of what is now the European Parliament. As the EU sought to increase its democratic legitimacy, each consecutive Treaty-amendment gave more and more power to the European Parliament. With the Single European Act of 1968, for example, the Assembly was formally renamed the 'European Parliament', an important symbolical step.[3] As of 1979, the European Parliament became directly elected through national elections. With the Treaties of Maastricht, Amsterdam, Nice and especially Lisbon, the European Parliament also got increasing powers over the budget and legislation. Today, the European Parliament controls the budget and is co-legislator in the large majority of fields covered by EU competences.[4] As such, the European Parliament has actually accrued more formal rights and powers than several Member State parliaments. With this background in mind, let us turn to the current composition, powers and operation of the European Parliament.

2.2.1 *Composition of the European Parliament*

The European Parliament consists of 751 members including its President, who are elected for a period of five years.[5] One of the major issues in the European Parliament is the division of seats. On the one hand, there are significant differences in the population of each Member State. Germany, for example, has over 80 million inhabitants, where Malta only has around 450.000. If Malta were given an equal number of MEP's to Germany, this would seriously undermine the vote of German citizens. Vice versa, if seats in the European Parliament would be divided proportionally, the influence of Maltese citizens would be negligible.

3 Article 3 SEA.

4 See Article 14(1) TEU. For the ordinary legislative procedure, in which the European Parliament acts as a co-legislator with a veto right and the power to table amendments, see Article 294 TFEU.

5 Article 14(2) TEU.

The solution chosen in the EU is to use a *degressively proportional system*. No Member State shall have less than six, or more than 96 MEP's. The result is that the citizens of smaller states are (heavily) overrepresented, whilst those of large states are underrepresented, but that nevertheless the populations of bigger states retain far greater influence on the whole.[6]

According to the TEU, the function of MEP's is to represent 'the Union's citizens'. Consequently, they should represent the people and not the Member States as such. At the same time, MEP's are elected in national elections and seats are divided per Member State. A Danish citizen, therefore, can only cast his vote for a Danish candidate in the Danish elections for the European Parliament. No European parties exist either. This also means that national parties usually retain control of national lists for the European Parliament, and therefore of who is ultimately elected.[7] These factors mean that MEP's retain linked to the Member States and represent the different *member peoples* as such rather than all EU citizens as a whole.[8]

2.2.2 *Functions and Powers of the European Parliament*

The three primary functions of the European Parliament concern legislation, the budget, and political control. In terms of legislation, the starting point is that the European Parliament does not have the right of initiative. Only the European Commission, and in a few cases the Council, can initiate legislation.[9] The legislative powers of the Parliament, therefore, revolve around amending and adopting Commission proposals.

---

6 For the serious, if not always convincing, concerns of the German Constitutional Court concerning this system of representation and the principle of 'one man, one vote', see BVerfGE, 2 BvE 123,267, 2 BvE 2/08 (2009) *Lissabon Urteil.*

7 See for an alternative suggestion the plan developed by former MEP Andrew Duff, calling for transnational lists for the election of 25 MEP's, creating a truly European election. The serious national political opposition to this proposal reflects the remaining national focus and foundation of the European Parliament. See European Parliament, Committee on Constitutional Affairs, Second Report on a proposal for a modification of the Act concerning the election of the Members of the European Parliament by direct universal suffrage of 20 September 1976, A7–0027/2012, 1 February 2012.

8 A. Cuyvers, *The EU as a Confederal Union of Sovereign Member Peoples, Exploring the potential of American (con)federalism and popular sovereignty for a constitutional theory of the EU*, (Diss. Leiden, Wöhrmann 2013), 313.

9 The Parliament may, however, request the European Commission to investigate a certain topic or to develop a legislative proposal on a certain field (Article 225 TFEU). The Commission may ignore or reject such requests, but of course does so at its own peril, and is legally obligated to state reasons.

The precise powers of the Parliament, moreover, depend on the legal basis underlying the proposed legislation.[10] Under most legal bases, including the vital Article 114 TFEU on the internal market, the so called 'ordinary legislative procedure' applies.[11] Under this procedure the European Parliament is a full co-legislator that can veto legislation and can propose amendments. The adoption of legislation, however, always requires the approval of the Council of Ministers as well.

In addition to the ordinary legislative procedure, two main special legislative procedures exist as well, each with increasingly reduced powers for the European Parliament. Firstly, under the consent procedure, the Council formally adopts an act, but the European Parliament must give its consent. Here the Parliament can block an act, but not (formally) amend it. Secondly, under the consultation procedure, the Parliament only has to be consulted. It is the Council that adopts the act and that may also reject or ignore any observations made by the Parliament. Clearly under this last procedure the power of the European Parliament is limited. At the same time, the European Parliament can of course always threaten to use its blocking powers in *other* ongoing legislative procedures to incentivize the Commission and Council to take its views into serious consideration.

The European Parliament must also consent to the multi-annual five year framework for EU expenditure, and may veto the annual budgets based on this framework.[12] On the expenditure side, therefore, the Parliament has significant powers. On the revenue side, however, the power of the Parliament is limited. Most crucially, Parliament, and the EU as a whole, lack the power to directly levy taxes, and thereby to increase its own revenues when desired. It is the Member States that retain ultimate control over taxing and the revenue available to the EU. To put the relative financial power of the EU and its Member States into perspective, the EU controls just over 1% of European GDP, whereas most Member States control around 50% of their national GDP.

The main power of the Parliament in terms of political control concerns the appointment and dismissal of the Commission. To begin with, the European Parliament must approve the candidate-president of the European Commission, who is nominated by the European Council, taking into account the outcome of the elections for the European Parliament. In 2014, however, the European Parliament for the first time used this power of approval to increase its control over the selection of the Commission President as

---

10 On legal bases and EU competences see chapter 3.

11 Article 294 TFEU. Before Lisbon this procedure was known as the co-decision procedure.

12 Articles 312(1) and 314 TFEU.

such. Most political groupings in the European Parliament selected their own candidate for the Commission presidency, the so called *Spitzenkandidaten*. The Parliaments position was that the European Council should then select the candidate of the political grouping that won the elections for the European Parliament, as this would increase the democratic legitimacy of the Commission. As it turned out, the political grouping of Juncker, the European People's Party (EPP), became the largest. Juncker, however, faced strong political opposition, especially from the UK. Despite this opposition, Juncker was eventually selected by the European Council and approved by the Parliament. It now remains an open question of EU law whether this has created a legally or politically binding precedent, or whether the next time round the European Council will select its own candidate, daring the Parliament to actually reject the candidate it puts forward.

Once the Commission President has been approved, the Parliament also has to approve the entire College of Commissioners as assembled by the President and the Member States. Equally, the European Parliament has the power, at any time, to dismiss the entire Commission.[13] Both the power to approve and to dismiss the Commission, however, only applies to the Commission as a body. The Parliament does not have the formal right to reject or dismiss individual Commissioners, even though it can place effective political pressure on a Commissioner to withdraw or resign 'voluntarily', or on the President of the Commission to withdraw or dismiss an individual Commissioner.[14]

In addition to its powers of approval and dismissal, Parliament also has the right to challenge the validity of any EU legal act before the Court of Justice of the European Union (CJEU), to request answers or reports from most other institutions, and to receive a report from the President of the European Council after each summit.[15] In addition, the European Parliament of course organizes hearings and debates, and tries to exert its influence via resolutions.

---

13 Article 17(7) TEU. Under Article 234 TFEU such a motion of censure requires a two-thirds majority.

14 See Article 17(6) TEU on the power of the Commission President to dismiss individual Commissioners. See on this point also the Order of the CJEU in Case C-394/15 P *Dalli v. Commission* ECLI:EU:C:2016:262 as well as the interinstitutional agreement between the Parliament and the Commission on this point: <http://ec.europa.eu/dgs/secretariat_general/relations/relations_other/docs/framework_agreement_ep-ec_en.pdf>.

15 Articles 263, 249, 284(3), 228 TFEU and Article 15(6)(d) TEU. On the direct action under Article 263 TFEU, see further chapter 7. On the effective use of litigation by the Parliament, which is also of interest to the EALA, see for example M. McCowan, 'The European

2.2.3 *Operation of the European Parliament*

As there are no pan-European parties, but MEP's also do not represent their Member State as such, the European Parliament is organized in Political Groupings. These groupings bring together MEP's from the different national parties that are ideologically more or less aligned, such as social-democrats, liberals, or Christian-democrats.[16] These Political Groupings, and their leadership, wield most political power in the European Parliament.

The European Parliament, moreover, is organized as a 'working' Parliament. Most of the work of the Parliament is carried out in Committees, where MEP's from the different Political Groupings work on specific subjects.[17] Most issues are settled in Committee before they reach the plenary for a confirmation vote by the plenum. Consequently, when one is interested in a specific field or act, it is crucial to focus on the debates in the relevant Committee. In most cases, including in the adoption of legislation or tabling amendments, the Parliament decides by an ordinary majority.[18]

2.3 The European Council

Today, the European Council today is one of the most powerful and interesting institutions of the EU.[19] This makes it all the more interesting that the institution did not even exist at the conception of the EU. It was only with the Treaty of Lisbon in 2009 that the European Council, the EU counterpart of the EAC Summit, formally became an institution of the EU.[20] Long before that time, however, the European Council already was a *de-facto* institution of the EU.

Parliament before the Bench: ECJ Precedent and EP Litigation Strategies' (2003) 10 *JEPP* 974.

16 For an overview of the eight current Political Groupings see <http://www.europarl.europa.eu/aboutparliament/en/20150201PVL00010/Organisation-and-rules>.

17 For an overview of the Committees see <http://www.europarl.europa.eu/committees/en/parliamentary-committees.html>.

18 Article 231 TFEU.

19 See for example Editorial Comments 'An ever Mighty European Council' 46 *CMLRev* (2009), 1383, and for an elegant and insightful discussion of this body, L. Van Middelaar, The Passage to Europe, How a Continent became a Union' (2014, Yale University Press). For a more general overview see amongst others U. Puetter, *The European Council and the Council: New Intergovernmentalism and Institutional Change* (OUP, 2014), or J. Werts, *the European Council* (Harper, 2008).

20 Article 15 TEU.

The European Council started life as an informal meeting of Heads of State. It was created during the Paris summit of December 1974, on the initiative of then French President Valéry Giscard d'Estaing as an informal forum for discussion.[21] The first actual European Council took place in Dublin on 11 March 1975. Even though the European Council did not have any formal powers, or even formal existence, under the EU Treaties, a body comprising all Heads of State or Government obviously wields significant power and influence. Over time, and as European integration deepened, European Council meetings gradually became more frequent, and the role of the European Council became more prominent. The role and existence of the European Council was subsequently formally recognized for the first time in the Treaty of Maastricht in 1992. It was only with the Treaty of Lisbon, however, that the European Council became of the seven official institutions of the EU.

2.3.1 *Composition of the European Council*

First and foremost, the European Council consists of all the EU Heads of State or Government.[22] Where a Member State has both a Head of State and a Head of Government, such as Germany and France, it is up to the Member State to indicate which one of the two represents the highest political authority and hence will attend the European Council. For Germany, the prime-minister (or *Bundeskanzler*) attends, instead of the President of the German Republic, who has more of a ceremonial function. In France, the situation is reversed, as the French President wields the highest political authority, not the French prime-minister.

Since Lisbon, the European Council has a permanent president. This President is elected by the European Council itself for a period of two and a half years, renewable once. So far, the president has always been a former head of state or government himself.[23] The President primarily coordinates and builds consensus as he chairs sessions and manages the agenda.

The President of the European Commission is also *ex officio* a member of the European Council, although she does not represent a Member State and

21 See on the evolution of the European Council and its significance for European integration also L. van Middelaar, *The Passage to Europe. How a Continent Became a Union* (Yale University Press, 2014).

22 Article 15 TEU.

23 The first President of the European Council was Herman van Rompuy, the former Belgian Prime minister. As of 2014, the second President is Donald Tusk, former Prime-Minister of Poland.

therefore has a different position. The High Representative for Foreign Affairs, on the other hand, is not a full member but may 'take part' in the work of the European Council.

2.3.2 *Functions and Powers of the European Council*

In line with its political weight, the main function of the European Council is to lay out the general direction the EU should take and provide the political leadership to get there. As the Treaties officially term it, the European Council shall 'provide the Union with the necessary impetus for its development' and 'define the general political directions and priorities thereof.'[24] Increasingly, however, the European Council is also the institution that steps in in times of crisis. Both during the euro crisis and the refugee crisis, for example, it was the European Council that took center stage and decided on many crucial issues. In *Brexit* as well, the European Council will likely play a leading role. As they say in Brussels, these issues are '*Chefsache*', requiring the political authority of the European Council to take actual decisions.

The function of crisis management, however, sits somewhat uneasily with the limited formal powers of the European Council, which were primarily formulated with the agenda-setting function in mind.[25] The European Council can adopt conclusions and take decisions, but has no explicit legislative or executive powers. Consequently, it cannot initiate legislation, adopt EU laws, spend EU money or take executive action. Formally, moreover, it has no direct authority over other institutions such as the Commission or the Council of Ministers. In practice, however, the European Council can often act through the other institutions, or through the Member States they collectively control. After all, the Council of Ministers, that does have legislative powers, is composed of national ministers that usually answer to their own Heads of State and Government sitting in the European Council. The European Commission usually also has clear incentives to cooperate with the European Council, especially in crisis situations where action is needed, as well as additional Member State funds. Overall, therefore, the functions of the European Council are steadily increasing, as are its (informal) powers to fulfill these additional functions. The shifts this increasingly executive role of the European Council lead

24 Article 15 TEU.

25 L. van Middelaar, 'Taking decisions or setting norms. EU Presidences between executive and legislative power in a crisis-driven Union', in: Steunenberg et al. (eds), *Fit for the Future. Reflections from Leiden on the functioning of the EU* (Eleven International Publishing, Den Haag, 2016), 11 and L. van Middelaar, 'The return of politics: The European Union after the crises in the euro zone and Ukraine', *Journal of Common Market Studies* 54 (2016) n° 3, 495.

to in the nature and functioning of the EU form one of the major institutional and constitutional questions of the moment.

2.3.3 *Operation of the European Council*

The European Council meets at least twice every six months, but can meet much more often where developments require. In the context of *Brexit*, moreover, the European Council holds 'informal' meetings of the 27 remaining Member States. Almost always, the European Council decides by consensus. One of the key functions of the President of the European Council, therefore, is to prepare meetings well, explore the political lay of the land, and find the zone of possible agreement before the meeting. This is not to say that the European Council cannot be the scene of vehement debate and disagreement, but, as all participants know, the result has to be a consensus.

One telling detail about the functioning of the European Council is that it normally meets with just its members, no advisors being present. This means that the Heads of State and Government normally meet without any civil servants or ministers, adding to the intimacy and intensity of the meetings and the collegial nature of the body.

2.4 The Council of Ministers of the EU

Not to be confused with the European Council, the Council of Ministers is the representative body of the Member States in the EU.[26] The Council has been one of the main institutions since the ECSC and fulfills many different functions. Consequently, the Council is hard to pin down into one of the traditional categories of the *Trias Politica*. It is a body that consists of the national executives, forms part of the EU legislature but also plays an important role in the execution of EU law and policies. The Council itself, moreover, only forms the top of the iceberg, as the institution rests on a large amount of committees of national civil servants preparing its work.

---

26 For a more elaborate analysis of the Council see *inter alia* U. Puetter, *The European Council and the Council: New Intergovernmentalism and Institutional Change* (OUP, 2014), F. Hayes-Renshaw and H. Wallace, *The Council of Ministers* (2nd edn, Macmillan, 2006), M. Westlake and D. Galloway, *The Council of the European Union* (3rd edn, Harper Publishing, 2004).

2.4.1 *Composition of the Council*

As its name appropriately suggests, the Council of Ministers is composed of ministers of the different Member States.[27] The actual ministers attending a meeting of the Council, however, depends on the topic of discussion. On questions of finance, for example, it will be the ministers of finance that meet, on questions of transport the ministers of transport, etc.[28] All in all, the Council meets in ten different configurations. There is no formal hierarchy, but the General Affairs Council, composed of the Ministers of Foreign Affairs, has a general coordinating role.[29] Despite this coordination, one of the major challenges facing the Council is safeguarding consistency between the different configurations.

The Eurogroup is an *informal* body comprised of the finance ministers of the Eurozone countries. The Commissioner for Economic and Financial Affairs, Taxation and Customs as well as the President of the European Central Bank may also take part in Eurogroup meetings. As such, the Eurogroup is not formally a part of the Council.[30] At the same time, during the 'informal' meetings, which normally take place right before the Economic and Financial Affairs (ECFIN) configuration of the Council, Eurogroup members can coordinate their position and hence influence the ultimate decisions taken in the Council. Consequently, the Eurogroup in practice has an important impact on the functioning of the Council.

2.4.2 *Functions and Powers of the Council*

The main functions of the Council concern legislation and the budget, policy making, coordination of execution and the foreign policy of the EU.[31] In addition, the Council prepares the work for the European Council and follows up on European Council conclusions.

With the European Parliament and the European Commission, the Council is part of the EU legislature. Unlike the Parliament, there are no legislative procedures that exclude the Council. Consequently, no legislation

---

27 Article 16 TEU.

28 Where the issues being discussed touch on multiple portfolio's, more than one minister may attend, voting power not being affected.

29 For an overview, see <http://www.consilium.europa.eu/en/council-eu/configurations/>.

30 The Eurogroup started in 1998, but its existence was first recognized in the Lisbon treaty via Article 137 TFEU and Protocol 14 on the Eurogroup. This recognition, however, does not alter the informal status of the Eurogroup.

31 Article 16 TEU.

can be adopted without the Council, even though in most cases the Council needs the European Parliament to pass a law.[32] Equally, the Council determines the budget, together with the European Parliament. Through the Council, therefore, the Member States retain their influence over EU legislation and the budget, even though, as we will see below, the Council can often decide by a qualified majority, meaning no single Member State can block legislation.

The Council also plays a particularly important role in foreign relations. Considering the political sensitivity of foreign relations, this area has remained largely intergovernmental. Member States simply were unwilling to surrender this field to full supranationalism. Consequently, the Foreign Affairs Council, and the Member States, retain a primary role in foreign policy. In many fields of foreign affairs, for example, the Commission does not have the right of initiative, and the Council can decide without the European Parliament. Nevertheless, over time, the role of both the Commission and the Parliament in external relations has clearly increased. To better coordinate EU foreign policy, the Treaty of Lisbon also introduced the High Representative of the Union for Foreign Affairs and Security Policy.[33] This almost impossible job comes with three hats. The High Representative simultaneously is a Vice-President of the European Commission for foreign affairs, chairs the Foreign Affairs Council, and as High Representative heads the European External Action Service (EEAS), the diplomatic body of the EU. As we shall see in chapter 5, however, the stage has become increasingly crowded when it comes to EU foreign relations, with the High Representative, the President of the European Commission, the President of the European Council, the rotating President of the Council of Ministers and the different Heads of State and Government competing for position. Even on this crowded stage, however, and despite the role of the European Council in major international crises, the Council remains the central institution for EU external relations competences.

2.4.3 *Operation of the Council*

Most Council configurations meet around once or twice a month, usually in Brussels. The Council has a rotating presidency. Every six months, a new Member State takes over the presidency, which currently means that a Member

32 The Council can delegate certain authority to adopt acts to the European Commission, or grant the Commission the power to adopt implementing acts, but these acts remain under the ultimate control of the Council itself and do not form legislative acts under EU law. See Articles 289–291 TFEU.

33 Article 18 TEU.

State holds the presidency once every 14 years.[34] The presidency *inter alia* sets the agenda, chairs meetings, represents the Council internally and externally, and tries to find consensus, and in doing so can exercise a certain albeit limited influence over decision making.[35] To ensure consistency with such frequent rotations, three Member States together form a so called *troika*, that should coordinate their consecutive presidencies. Since Lisbon, moreover, both the Foreign Affairs Council and the Eurogroup have permanent presidencies. The Foreign Affairs Council is chaired by the High Representative, whereas the Eurogroup elects its own president for renewable periods of two and a half years.[36] These permanent presidencies aim to increase consistency, coherence and the capacity to act in times of crises for these vital groups.

In terms of *decision making* the Council uses different mechanisms, ranging from simple majority voting, via qualified majority voting to unanimity. Of these mechanisms, qualified majority voting, or QMV in EU lingo, is the most important and common one. A qualified majority requires at least 55% of the Member States (usually fifteen) that together represent at least 65% of the EU population. By requiring at least fifteen states this formula protects smaller Members States, ensuring that they remain relevant for decision making. The population requirement, on the other hand, respects the larger populations represented by the more populous states.[37] In the resulting balance, smaller states are overrepresented but in absolute terms the biggest states wield most influence.

QMV has been vital for the success of the EU. Initially, the Council primarily operated via unanimity. Especially with more and more Member States joining, however, decision making by unanimity can lead to paralysis because each Member State can block an entire proposal. Over time, therefore, the Member

34 Articles 16(9) TEU and 236(b) TFEU. The order is determined in Decision 2007/5/EC, EURATOM [2007] OJ L1/11. In light of *Brexit*, the UK has indicated it will not assume its presidency in 2017.

35 Cf. for the pre-Lisbon situation A. Warntjen, 'Steering the Union: The Impact of the EU Presidency on Legislative Activity' (2007) 45 *JCMS*, 1135.

36 Article 18(3) TEU and Protocol 14 Article 2.

37 See Articles 16(4) and 238(2) TFEU. Conversely, a blocking minority requires at least four Member States, meaning that even three Member States that represent more than 35% of the EU population cannot block legislation. After heated negotiations, moreover, the Lisbon treaty also introduced a transitional scheme which can be invoked by Member States until 31 March 2017, and which makes it easier for certain states like Poland to block legislation. See Article 16(5) and the Protocol on transitional provisions.

States agreed to switch to QMV in ever more areas.[38] This switch of course reduces the ultimate control a Member State has over legislation. At the same, this loss should also not be exaggerated. To begin with, even in QMV areas, the Council always strives for consensus and tries to avoid a vote. In approximately 80% of cases that fall under QMV the Council decides by consensus.[39] In practice, therefore, states are not often outvoted, although the *possibility* of a vote alone of course already affects the negotiations, and may promote the willingness to compromise. Since Lisbon the Council meets in public when it deliberates or votes on a draft legislative act, so as to increase transparency.[40]

2.4.3.1 COREPER and Committees

As stated, the Council only forms the tip of a legislative iceberg. Directly below the Council sits COREPER (*Comité des représentants permanents*), a body of permanent representatives of the Member States in Brussels.[41] COREPER is split into COREPER I, which consists of the deputy representatives, and COREPER II, which consists of the permanent representatives or ambassadors of the Member States to the EU. COREPER prepares all the meetings of the Council. It designates files as either A or B matters. A matters are already agreed in COREPER and only require rubberstamping by the Council. B matters are the more complex dossiers on which the Council itself must decide.[42] In turn, the work of COREPER is prepared by over 250 different working groups of *national* civil servants. It is in these working groups that the national experts of the civil service meet, negotiate and draft, and that vital preparatory work is done. Here as well it is vital to understand how the EU institutional system builds on and is integrated with the national systems, as opposed to some separate federate bureaucracies.

---

38 The Single European Act of 1986 formed a watershed moment in this regard, as decision making by QMV was accepted for the vital field of the internal market (now Article 114 TFEU).

39 Most of the cases that do come to a vote, moreover, concern agriculture and fisheries, and therefore directly opposed and quantifiable interests. See F. Hayes-Renshaw, W. van Aken and H. Wallace, 'When and Why the Council of Ministers of the EU Votes Explicitly' (2006) 44 *JCMS*, 161, 165 or M. Matilla, 'Contested Decisions: Empirical Analysis of Voting in the Council of Ministers' (2004) 43 *EJPR*, 29.

40 Article 16(8) TEU. These public sessions can even be followed via live streams. Of course this does not prevent Ministers from negotiating in more private settings.

41 Article 16(7) TEU and 240(1) TFEU.

42 On the significant influence of COREPER also see M. Westlake and D. Galloway, *The Council of the European Union* (3rd edn, Harper Publishing, 2004), 201.

2.5 The European Commission

The European Commission is the supranational body that represents the general European interest.[43] It participates in legislation, forms part of the EU executive, and has several semi-judicial and enforcement powers. The European Commission also represents one of the important institutional innovations that sets the EU apart from 'normal' international organizations.[44] Right from the start, with the High Authority of the ECSC, the need was felt for a supranational body that could safeguard the effectiveness of rules and defend the common interest instead of more direct national interests. History had shown that purely intergovernmental institutions would not suffice to turn the EU's ambitions into reality. The Commission, therefore, is one of the most characteristic EU institutions and a key ingredient to the EU's success. The EU Commission, moreover, is a far more developed institution than the EAC Secretariat, both in terms of competences and staff. At the same time, the power of the Commission should also not be overstated. The Commission functions within an institutional balance with the European Council, the Council and the European Parliament. Each of these institutions represent their respective interests, and needs the others to realize its aims. The Commission, therefore, is not the 'government' of the EU.[45] It does, however, provide a vital authority that can help draft and adopt rules that take the general European interest into account and subsequently enforce those rules to turn them into a living reality.

2.5.1 *Composition of the Commission*

The College of Commissioners consists of one Commissioner per Member State.[46] The Commission has a president and a number of vice-presidents, one

---

43 See more generally on this important and interesting institution D. Spence (*ed*), *The European Commission* (3rd edn, Harper, 2006), Temple Lang, 'How Much do the Smaller Member States Need the European Commission: The Role of the Commission in a Changing Europe' 39 *CMLRev* (2002), 315, or L Hooghe, *The European Commission and the Integration of Europe* (CUP, 2002).

44 Cf. D. Curtin and M. Egeberg, 'Tradition and Innovation: Europe's Accumulated Executive Order' (2008) 31 *West European Politics*, 639.

45 Cf. also D. Curtin, *Executive Power in the European Union: Law, Practises and the Living Constitution* (OUP, 2009).

46 Although Article 17(4) TEU states that as of 1 November 2014 the Commission will be reduced to two-thirds of the Member States, this reduction was blocked by a decision from the European Council as enabled by the last sentence of this paragraph. This decision was linked to the first Irish no to Lisbon, after which Ireland received a promise that

of which is the High Representative discussed above.[47] All commissioners are appointed for a five year, renewable term.[48] Commissioners should represent the general interest of the Union. They must hence be 'completely independent' from their own Member States and may not accept any instructions.[49]

The appointment of the Commission starts with the selection of its President. Taking into account the results of the election to the European Parliament, the European Council proposes a candidate, which must then be elected by the European Parliament.[50] The President-elect then works with the Council to assemble the rest of the commissioners, based on the lists of names suggested by the Member States, and to divide the different portfolio's between them. Subsequently, the College of Commissioners has to be approved, as a body, by the European Parliament.[51] Once in office, the Commission can also be fired, again only as a body, by the European Parliament.[52] In addition, the President has the authority to ask individual Commissioners to resign.[53]

Each Commissioner has a personal *Cabinet* of around eight persons to support her work. The real manpower of the Commission is located in the different Directorates-General, where about 25.000 civil servants work on

---

it could keep its Commissioner, and other Member States then wanted the same. See Conclusions of the European Council of 11 and 12 December 2008, par. 2 (17271/1/08).

47 In 2014, Jean-Claude Juncker, as President of the Commission, introduced a system with one *first Vice-President* (Frans Timmermans) and multiple ordinary Vice-Presidents. This system is based on the discretionary power of the Commission President.

48 Article 17(3) TFEU.

49 Article 17(1) and (3) TFEU.

50 In 2014 the European Parliament for the first time applied the so called '*Spitzenkandidaten*-procedure' whereby each political faction in the Parliament nominated its own candidate for Commission President. The Parliament claimed that the European Council would then be obligated to select the candidate of the faction that won the elections for the European Parliament. After a long political battle, the European Council indeed selected Jean-Claude Juncker, the wining candidate. It is as yet unclear, however, if this now forms a binding convention of EU law, or if the European Council can or will ignore the EP candidate next time.

51 Formally, therefore, the European Parliament cannot reject individual Commissioners, but only accept or reject the entire Commission, a nuclear option. In practice, the Parliament does organize individual hearings for the Commissioners, and can pressure the President-elect to withdraw one or more of his candidates.

52 Article 234 TFEU.

53 Article 17(6) TFEU. See also Case C-394/15 P *Dalli v Commission* ECLI:EU:C:2016:262. In addition, the Court of Justice of the EU, on the application of the Council or the Commission, may compulsorily retire a Commissioner as well under Article 245 TFEU. See on this point Case C-432/04 *Commission v. Cresson* [2006] ECR I-6387.

particular areas such as Agriculture, Competition, Migration or Trade. These Directorates-General do not report to individual Commissioners, but work for the Commission as such. This increases the relative autonomy of these Directorates-General, which has both benefits and some draw-backs.

2.5.2 *Functions and Powers of the Commission*

The Commission has a broad array of functions and powers, ranging from the administrative, via the legislative to the quasi-judicial. Like the Council, therefore, it is hard to fit the Commission in the traditional model of the *Trias Politica.*

Firstly, the Commission participates in legislation. In most areas except the Common Foreign and Security Policy the Commission has the *exclusive* right of initiative. Consequently, a proposal from the Commission is usually necessary for any legislation to be adopted.[54] During the legislative process, moreover, the Commission retains the right to withdraw its proposal, which gives it continued influence over the legislation. In addition, legislative acts of the Council and Parliament often *delegate* significant rule-making or implementing powers to the Commission.[55] The Commission is then requested, for example, to fill-in a framework directive with more specific rules or to adopt implementing acts.[56] Combined, these powers give the Commission serious legislative and quasi-legislative powers. This power also ensures a strong voice for the general European interest in EU legislation.

Secondly, the Commission is best known for being the EU 'executive', although the EU *administration* may be a more precise term.[57] The Commission administers the EU's revenue and budget and is also in charge of many EU programs. In

54 Article 17(2) TFEU. The Commission also has the initiative for the budget, see Article 314(2) TFEU. Note though that in practice most proposals are initiated by the Commission on the basis of request by other institutions (Article 225 and 241 TFEU), the need to update legislation, or international obligations. Around 5% of proposals are fully based on the Commissions own initiative for new legislation. See the House of Lords European Union Committee, *Initiation of EU Legislation* (22nd Report, 2007–08 Session).

55 See Article 290 and 291 TFEU.

56 Often, where power is delegated to the Commission, the use of this power is overseen by Committees of Member State representatives. These Committees sometimes can refer a matter back to the Council. This entire process of supervision is known as 'Comitology'. See Regulation 182/2011/EU laying down the rules and general principles concerning mechanisms for control by Member States of the Commission's exercise of implementing powers, *OJ* [2011] L 55/13, and the Framework Agreement on relations between the European Parliament and the European Commission, *OJ* [2010] L 304/47.

57 Cf. H. Hoffmann and A. Türk (eds), *EU Administrative Governance* (Edward Elgar, 2006).

addition, the Commission plays a central role in negotiating agreements with third countries, including accession treaties, and in maintaining international relations on behalf of the EU, except in the field of the Common Foreign and Security Policy.[58] During the *Brexit* negotiations, for example, the Commission is also likely to play a central role in negotiating the actual legal technicalities of withdrawal, even if the main political decision making will take place in the European Council and the Council.

Although the Commission therefore fulfills vital administrative functions, again its role should not be overstated. To begin with, its administrative capacity is limited, certainly when one compares the Commission staff of around 25.000 with the tens of millions of civil servants employed by the Member States. A key role for the Commission, therefore, is to coordinate with the much larger national bureaucracies, which are the primary implementers of EU law and policies. The EU administration should therefore be seen as a compound structure, where the EU administration must cooperate with national administrations to be effective.[59] Even at the EU level itself, moreover, the Commission does not have the capacity to provide all the executive and administrative capacity needed, especially in highly technical areas that require a lot of expertise. For that reason, over 40 regulatory agencies have been developed. These agencies have widely varying powers and tasks, ranging from mere advisory powers to enforcement and rule setting powers. They cover specific fields such as Food Safety, Chemicals or Medicines, and form an important part of the EU administration. Most of these bodies cooperate with the Commission, but they are nevertheless separate and distinct legal entities, that wield significant power.[60]

Thirdly, the Commission has important enforcement and quasi-judicial functions and powers. To begin with, the Commission is the so called 'watch dog' of EU law. It checks whether Member States fully comply with EU law. If they do not, the Commission may start an infringement procedure. A Member State is then first given notice and given a chance to explain or where necessary to improve its compliance with EU law. If the Member State does not comply, the Commission may bring the Member State before the Court of Justice.[61] The

---

58 EEA and High Representative.

59 D. Curtin, *Executive Power in the European Union: Law, Practises and the Living Constitution* (OUP, 2009), A. Cuyvers, *The EU as a Confederal Union of Sovereign Member Peoples, Exploring the potential of American (con)federalism and popular sovereignty for a constitutional theory of the EU*, (Diss. Leiden, Wöhrmann 2013), 141.

60 See also M. Busuioc, *European Agencies: Law and Practises of Accountablity* (OUP, 2013).

61 Article 258 TFEU.

CJEU, when it finds a violation, may then order the Member State to comply, or in a second round of infringement impose a (serious) fine.[62] In a large majority of cases, however, Member States already comply with the suggestions of the Commission before the case proceeds to court.[63] This general role of the Commission as guardian of the Treaties has proven especially important as experience has shown that Member States will rarely police each others compliance with EU law, largely due to the political costs of doing so. An effective power of enforcement and infringement therefore seems an important building block for successful regional integration.

The Commission also has special and far reaching powers in the enforcement of EU competition law. The Commission itself can impose fines on companies that partake in prohibited cartels or abuse a dominant position on the EU market.[64] The Commission may also order Member States to recover illegal or unlawful state aid granted to undertakings.[65] As the recovery order of over 13 billion euro in the case of Ireland and Apple demonstrates, these can be far reaching powers, even if all Commission decisions can be challenged before the Court of Justice.

2.5.3 *The Functioning of the Commission*

The Commission formally functions under the principle of collegiality. This principle means that all decisions should be take collectively by the College of Commissioners, and that the College is also collectively responsible for all decisions taken. Only minor decisions, or 'acts of management' may be delegated to individual Commissioners.[66] In practice, most decisions are prepared by one or more Commissioners and then approved by the College in its weekly Wednesday meeting. Only a limited number is discussed, and an even lower number is put to a vote, as consensus is the preferred outcome. When the College votes, however, it only requires an ordinary majority.

Over time, moreover, the functioning of the Commission has become increasingly 'presidential', as the President of the Commission acquired more and more power and influence. The President is of course elected first and therefore already involved in the initial selection of Commissioners and the division of portfolios. In addition, the President may also reallocate or change portfolios during the term of office, take over certain policy fields, or even

62 Article 260(2) TFEU. See for more details chapter 7.

63 Cf Case C-286/12 *Commission v Hungary*, ECLI:EU:C:2012:687.

64 Articles 101, 102 and 105 TFEU, as well as Regulation 1/2003 [2003] OJ L1/1.

65 Articles 107 and 108 TFEU.

66 Case C-137/92 P *Commission v. BASF* [1994] ECR I-2555.

request individual Commissioners to resign.[67] More generally, the President sets the political agenda and direction of the Commission as a whole, and also represents the Commission in the European Council, the European Parliament, and the world at large. In 2014, President Juncker moreover used his powers to introduce the new post of 'first Vice-President' and to give all Vice-Presidents of the Commission the power to block proposals from Commissioners in 'their' project teams. It is to be seen if these innovations will be taken over in later Commissions.

2.6 The European Court of Justice

The European Court of Justice is the judicial body of the EU, and has been part of the institutional set-up from the start.[68] It ensures 'that in the interpretation and application of the Treaties the law is observed.' The Court of Justice has played a crucial role in the success of European integration, especially in the creation of an effective internal market and the development of EU law. Indeed the Court has been a vital engine for integration during several deep crises, and has helped shape the process known as 'integration through law', which helped the EU to become an effective supranational organization without becoming a federal state. For where substantive power largely remains with the Member States, law becomes a crucial tool for effective integration.[69]

---

67 Article 17(7) TFEU. Of course the President normally will check this with the relevant national governments as well.

68 See on this important institution and its role in European integration generally K. Alter, *The European Court's Political Power: Selected Essays* (OUP, 2009), or G. de Burca and J.H.H. Weiler, *The European Court of Justice* (OUP, 2001). For a nice overview and discussion of several seminal cases of the CJEU and the role they played in European integration see M.P. Maduro and L. Azoulai (eds), *The Past and Future of EU Law: The Classics of EU law Revisited on the 50th Anniversary of the Rome Treaty* (Hart Publishing, 2010).

69 See famously M. Cappelletti, M. Seccombe, and J.H.H. Weiler, *Integration Through Law—European and the American Federal Experience, Vol. I* (De Gruyter 1986), and J.H.H. Weiler, 'The Transformation of Europe' 100 *Yale Law Journal* (1991), 2403. For a further discussion on the importance of rule *by* law for (con)federal organization see A. Cuyvers, *The EU as a Confederal Union of Sovereign Member Peoples, Exploring the potential of American (con)federalism and popular sovereignty for a constitutional theory of the EU*, (Diss. Leiden, Wöhrmann 2013), 180.

Like the Commission, the Court is a truly supranational body. It has compulsory jurisdiction over all EU law.[70] The Court can therefore ensure that EU law is interpreted properly and coherently in all different Member States, and that all parties respect their obligations.[71] The Court thereby forms another of the crucial institutional innovations that set the EU apart from 'ordinary' international organizations and that contributes to the actual effectiveness of the EU. Without the Court it can safely be said the EU would never have come close to the level of integration reached today. Again, however, the power of the Court and EU law should also not be overstated. Ultimately integration succeeds because it serves the needs of the Member States and the Member Peoples, not just because of the law. Rather, the law is simply one necessary tool in allowing integration to bring concrete benefits to all parties involved. In addition, the Court of Justice heavily relies on a close cooperation with national courts, as it obviously cannot oversee the application of EU law to over 500 million people. Much of the credit for making EU law work, therefore, is also owed to the national courts.

2.6.1 *Composition of the Court of Justice*

The *institution* entitled the 'Court of Justice of the European Union' actually consists of two courts. The highest of these is somewhat confusingly also called 'the Court of Justice of the European Union'. The second, lower court is now called the 'General Court', but was previously entitled 'the Court of First Instance' (CFI). In addition, the Treaty allows for specialized courts to be set up, for example in the field of intellectual property.[72] So far, however, only the Civil Service Tribunal was set up in this manner to adjudicate staff cases, only to be scrapped in 2016 after the enlargement of the General Court.[73]

The Court of Justice consists of one judge per Member State and 11 Advocates-General that provide legal opinions to assist the Court in its work. The General Court also used to consist of one judge per Member State, but in 2016 was enlarged to two judges per Member State to increase its capacity. Judges and Advocates-General are appointed by common accord of the governments of the Member States, after each Member State nominates its own

70 The only main exception concerns the Common Foreign and Security Policy, see Article 24(1) TEU and Article 275 TFEU. For other, smaller, limitations see Article 269 and 276 TFEU.

71 On the vital importance of the Courts complete jurisdiction over all aspects.

72 Article 19(1) TEU.

73 Council Decision 2004/752/EC, Euratom of 2 November 2004, establishing the European Union Civil Service Tribunal [2004] OJ L333/7.

candidate.[74] Before being appointed, however, the suitability of candidates must be assessed by a panel of seven members, comprised of former members of the Court of Justice and the General Court, members of national supreme courts or lawyers of recognized competence.[75] Judges and Advocates-General are appointed for renewable periods of six years.[76] Both courts choose their own presidents for renewable periods of three years.

2.6.2 *Powers and Functions of the Court of Justice and the General Court*

The general function of both EU Courts is to ensure that EU law is observed throughout the EU. The main power they have to fulfill this function is the final say on the interpretation and application of EU law. Ultimately, it is always up to the CJEU to determine both the scope and the correct interpretation of EU law, and *all* national and EU bodies are bound by this interpretation. The CJEU jealously safeguards this ultimate say on the interpretation and application of EU law. For example, the CJEU has so far blocked the setting up of any alternative courts or bodies that would have the power to interpret parts of EU law but would not be subject to the jurisdiction of the CJEU itself.[77] This strict position is largely to safeguard the unity and coherence of Union law, which could suffer if its interpretation differed per Member State or if multiple separate bodies could interpret it independently from each other. The jurisdiction of the EU Courts, moreover, is obligatory, and cannot be rejected by the Member States in individual cases. On this point, therefore, we see a clear difference between the exclusive and ultimate jurisdiction of the CJEU, and the more fragmented jurisdiction of the East African Court of Justice.

Concerning the relationship between the Court of Justice and the General Court, it can generally be said that the General Court acts as a court of first instance for individuals and companies, whereas most other issues go straight to the CJEU.[78] For example, the CJEU deals with cases between the institutions

---

74 Articles 253 and 354 TFEU.

75 This is the so called 'Article 255 panel'. The conclusions of the panel are not made public, but it is known that several judges have been rejected based on the opinion of this panel.

76 This system has been criticized as it creates the risk that judges avoid 'upsetting' their own Member State so as to not endanger their reappointment. In practice, however, this risk is largely avoided by the fact that judgments are given by the Court as such, and no dissenting opinions are given, which usually hides the opinion of individual judges.

77 See especially CJEU Opinion 2/13 on the draft agreement providing for the accession of the European Union to the Convention for the Protection of Human Rights and Fundamental Freedoms ECLI:EU:C:2014:2454.

78 For a more detailed overview of these legal remedies see the companion chapters 7 and 8.

and conflicts between the EU and Member States,[79] including infringements.[80] In addition, the CJEU answers preliminary references from national courts, has appellate jurisdiction over the General Court on points of law, and may provide opinions on international agreements.[81] The General Court, on the other hand, hears all actions by individuals and companies challenging an EU act, also in the field of competition law, holding the EU liable for non-contractual damages.[82] Although the General Court is not formally bound by the judgments of the Court of Justice, it considers itself *de facto* bound to follow the jurisprudence of the CJEU.[83]

In the future, the General Court may also receive the power to answer certain preliminary references.[84] It is important to note, however, that neither the CJEU nor the General Court have a general appellate jurisdiction over national courts. It is never possible, therefore, to appeal a judgment from a national court to the General Court or the CJEU directly.

2.6.3 *The Functioning of the Court of Justice and the General Court*

The Court of Justice normally sits in chambers of five or three judges. In complex or important cases, or where a Member State or an institution so requests, the CJEU will sit as a 'Grand Chamber' of 15 judges. Such judgment also tends to carry greater weight. In truly exceptional cases the CJEU can sit as a 'full court' with all 28 judges. Clearly such judgments carry special significance.[85] The CJEU normally receives a written Opinion from an Advocate-General on a case, even though under certain expedited procedures it decides to only hear the Advocate-General orally or to do without an opinion altogether.

The General Court hears most cases in chambers of three judges, but may also sit in chambers of five or in some cases with a single judge.[86] Where the case requires, however, the General Court may also sit as a Grand Chamber of 15 or a full court.[87] The General Court does not yet have Advocates-General, but may

79 Except for conflicts between Member States and the Commission, the ECB or the European Council, see Articles 263 and 265 TFEU.

80 See Articles 258, 259, 260, 263, and 265 TFEU.

81 Articles 118(11), 265 and 267 TFEU.

82 Articles 263, 265 and 340 TFEU.

83 Kadi II GC.

84 Article 256(3) TFEU.

85 See Article 251 TFEU together with the Statute of the Court (n. 205), art. 16, as well as Case C-370/12 *Pringle* ECLI:EU:C:2012:756.

86 See Council Decision 1999/291 [1999] OJ L114/52, and the Statute (n 205) Art. 50.

87 Idem.

acquire them in the future. In addition, the General Court can exceptionally ask one of tis judges to act as an Advocate-General in a particular case.[88]

The General Court and the Court of Justice do not issue dissenting opinions. As one of the core functions of the EU courts is to guard the unity and consistency of EU law, it is important that they speak with one voice. One consequence of this choice is of course that decisions may form compromises between different views within the EU courts, which may undermine their clarity and internal consistency. At the same time, such compromise judgments also fit with the collective nature of European integration, which should take different views into account. They also prevent the dangerous fragmentation that can take place where strong dissenting views may threaten the uniform application of EU law, especially in Member States whose national interests are best served by the minority view.

One major challenge for the functioning of the CJEU, as for all EU institutions, is posed by the 24 official and working languages of the EU. Although the Courts predominantly use French as a working language, judgments need to be translated into all official languages, and parties are allowed to submit written and oral pleadings in their own language. The CJEU therefore requires a very large, and highly specialized, team of lawyer-linguists, and translation actually forms a major source of delay.

2.7 Other Institutions and EU Bodies

In addition to the institutions discussed above, Article 13 TEU also establishes the European Central Bank (ECB) and the Court of Auditors (CoA) as formal EU institutions, bringing the total to seven. The ECB is an independent central bank with the exclusive competence over monetary policy of Eurozone (including interest rates), and the primary task of ensuring price stability. Its governing body is composed of representatives of Member State central banks together with the board of the ECB itself.[89] Especially after the euro crisis the ECB has acquired an increasingly central position, which will be discussed in more detail in chapter 13.

The Court of Auditors checks the books of the EU. It examines the accounts of all revenue and expenditure of the Union, and checks if these

88 Statute (n 205) Article 49.

89 Article 282(1) TFEU and Protocol no 4 on the statute of the European System of Central Banks and of the European Central Bank.

are in accordance with the rules. A negative opinion, however, will not block expenditure.[90] The CoA consists of one member per Member State.

As will also be clear from the above, moreover, the institutions only form the top layer of all EU bodies that allow the EU to function and fulfill its many tasks. Especially important are the over 40 agencies and the many committees in which national civil servants meet, as these provide the EU with the vital expertise, capacity, and bridge to the national administrations where most of the work has to be done. As long as the overwhelming majority of administrative and executive capacity remain with the Member States, after all, the institutional structure and functioning of the EU must reflect and support the multilevel nature of the EU. Conversely, as national systems become such a vital part of supranational regional integration, each national system must also gradually adapt and evolve to include its new functions with the EU system, an evolution that has not yet been completed in the EU and that is causing part of the problems the EU is experiencing today.

90 Article 285 TFEU.

CHAPTER 3

The Legal Framework of the EAC

Elvis Mbembe Binda

3.1 Attribution, Scope and Nature of Competence

The competence of the East African Community (EAC) as an intergovernmental organization is not stated *expressis verbis* in the Treaty for the Establishment of the East African Community (the Treaty). Unlike the EU where the powers of the supranational organization were clearly defined from the onset as to be distinguished from the competence of the Member States, in the EAC the situation is quite blurred.[1] In fact, the competence of the EAC can rather be implied from the objectives of the Community as broadly set in Article 5 of the Treaty.

According to Article 5(1), the objective of the Community is to "develop policies and programmes aimed at widening and deepening co-operation among the Partner States in political, economic, social and cultural fields, research and technology, defense, security and legal and judicial affairs, for their mutual benefit". Obviously, this is a very broad objective that embraces all the imaginable aspects of Community life. However, the Community's competence is limited to enhancing cooperation in specific areas that the Partner States agreed to undertake in common.[2] As far as these fields are concerned, it can be considered that a portion of competence has been conferred by the Partner States to the EAC, which is henceforth entitled to act within the limits of the powers conferred upon to it.[3] This includes making policies, enacting legislations, making regulations, issuing directives, taking decisions, making recommendations, or giving opinions to further the objectives of the community.

Pursuant to Article 8(1)(b) the Partner States have an obligation to work in close collaboration with the EAC institutions in the coordination of

---

* The author gratefully recognizes that paragraph 3.3, of this chapter was written by Professor K. Gastorn.

1 See the clear listing under Art. 3 of the Treaty of Rome (1957) and its modification in subsequent EU Treaties, including the current Articles 4–6 TFEU. For a further overview see EU Chapter 3.

2 See their list in the next section.

3 Art. 9(4) of the EAC Treaty.

© ELVIS MBEMBE BINDA, 2017 | DOI 10.1163/9789004322073_006
This is an open access chapter distributed under the terms of the CC-BY-NC License.

their economic and other policies in order to achieve the objectives of the Community.[4] This provision can be construed as enabling a kind of concurrent competence between the Partner States and EAC. Therefore, this means the conferred competence to the Community on some matters does not imply that the Partner States have automatically lost their authority to act on the same matters. Actually, the Partner States are entitled to continue making and applying their own policies and laws—even on matters under the competence of the EAC—as long as the latter has not yet made a common rule applicable to all of the Partner States. In other words, the competence of the Partner States ends where that of the Community start being exercised.[5]

Looking at the EU competence typology,[6] it can be inferred from various provisions that the EAC Treaty has consecrated a general regime of shared competence between the Community and the Partner States.

3.2 Main Competences of the EAC

The Treaty does not contain a single article that exhaustively lists the areas or powers that the Partner States intend to confer to the Community. The wording of the Treaty is rather very subtle and requires attention to find out whether a specific area of competence has been transferred to the EAC. In fact, Treaty provisions generally impose obligations directly on the Partner States in terms such as "the Partner States shall..." and "the Partner states agree...", which confirms that the EAC is a Partner States-led organization in accordance with its intergovernmentalist integration approach. However, some paragraphs are inserted under those articles to legitimize the intervention of EAC institutions either by reserving to them a fair amount of latitude to determine the course of a certain action or by entrusting them with the power to act with immediate effect, with effect on a certain specified time or as soon as certain requirements are met.[7] It has been suggested that whenever a provision contains such a paragraph, it should be construed as conferring competence to the Community.[8]

4 Art. 4(1)(b) of the EAC Treaty.

5 A.G. Toth, 'The Principle of Subsidiarity in the Maastricht Treaty', (1992) 29 *Common Market Law Review* 1079, p. 1080. Compare in this regard also the discussion in EU Chapter 3 on the nature of shared competences in the EU.

6 See Art. 2 of the Treaty on the Functioning of the European Union (TFEU).

7 See for instance arts. 75(2), (3) and (4); 76(2) and (3); 80(2); 84(1); 85; 86; etc.

8 A.G. Toth, *op. cit.*, p. 1081.

In line with this, a careful reading of various Treaty provisions suggests that the Partner States intended to confer powers to the Community in the following areas:

(i) Trade liberalization and development, including the establishment of a Customs Union and a common market (Articles. 75–78);
(ii) Investment and industrial development (Articles. 79–80);
(iii) Standardization, quality assurance, metrology and testing (Article. 81);
(iv) Monetary and financial matters, including the free movement of capital (Articles. 82–88);
(v) Infrastructure and services (Articles. 89–101);
(vi) Development of human resources, science and technology (Articles. 102–103);
(vii) Free movement of persons, labor, services, right of establishment and residence (Article. 104)
(viii) Agriculture and food security (Articles. 105–110)
(ix) Environment and natural resources management (Articles. 111–114);
(x) Tourism and wildlife management (Articles. 115–116);
(xi) Health, social and cultural activities (Articles. 117–120)
(xii) Enhancing the role of women in socio-economic development (Article. 121)
(xiii) Political matters (Articles. 123–125);
(xiv) Legal and judicial affairs (Article. 126)

This list is not exhaustive as, pursuant to Article 131, the Partner States may decide to extend their scope of co-operation to other fields. Besides, in addition to the competence in areas mentioned in these general provisions, it should be understood that the EAC also has implied competences in any other domain not listed above as long as such competence is necessary to perform the activities under these areas in order to achieve the Treaty objectives.

3.3 The Principle of Variable Geometry and Enhanced Co-operation

As an operational principle of the Community, the principle of variable geometry is the principle of flexibility that allows for progression in co-operation among a sub-group of Partner States in a larger integration scheme in a variety of areas and at different speeds.[9] The principle of variable geometry rests on the rationale that in any given community some members are able to integrate more than others in a variety of areas and at different speeds. It is not a rule of exclusion, it simply allows Partner States to jointly agree on issues but implement them at different speeds.

The concept of variable geometry is also known as the principle of flexibility, differentiated integration, enhanced co-operation, Europe *à la carte*, concentric circles, and multi-speed Europe.[10] That means, the concept of enhanced cooperation as practiced in the EU where a limited number of EU members may cooperate in an area without other members is associated with the concept of variable geometry in the context of the EAC.

In the context of the EAC, the principle of variable geometry is not developed. However, the East African Court of Justice has opined that the principle of variable geometry is in harmony with the requirement for consensus in Council decision-making. Adding that, the principle is a strategy of implementation of Community decisions and not a decision making tool itself and it therefore guides the integration process.[11]

As much as the principle of variable geometry is viewed as a necessary means of enabling those ready to proceed, and hoping the remaining States follow later, it has the danger of creating a small community within a community that might ultimately endanger the cohesion of the larger community. The EACJ accordingly advised that the principle of variable geometry should be resorted to as an exception, not as a rule since institutionalized flexibility might lead to a breakup of the Community or its transformation into a mere free trade area.[12] It is advised that in a young community like the EAC, the principle of legal unity should be stressed instead of variable geometry.[13]

---

9 Arts. 1(1) and 7(1)(e) of the EAC Treaty.

10 See http://www.euro-know.org/europages/dictionary/v.html (30 Sept 2013); Bomberg, E., et al., *The European Union: How does it work?* (OUP 2012), p. 163.

11 In the Matter of a Request by the Council of Ministers of the East African Community for an Advisory Opinion, Application No. 1 of 2008, In the East African Court of Justice at Arusha First Instance Division [Coram: Johnston Busingye, PJ; Mary Stella Arach-Amoko, DPJ; John Mkwawa, J; Jean-Bosco Butasi, J; Benjamin Patrick Kubo, J].

12 See http://www.euro-know.org/europages/dictionary/v.html) (30 Sept 2013); In the Matter of a Request by the Council of Ministers of the East African Community for an Advisory Opinion, Application No. 1 of 2008, In the East African Court of Justice at Arusha First Instance Division [Coram: Johnston Busingye, PJ; Mary Stella Arach-Amoko, DPJ; John Mkwawa, J; Jean-Bosco Butasi, J; Benjamin Patrick Kubo, J]; M.J. Maalim, *The United Republic of Tanzania in the East African Community: Legal Challenges in Integrating Zanzibar*, (PhD Thesis, University of Dar es Salaam, 2013), p. 56.

13 R. McAllister, *European Union: An Historical and Political Survey* (Routledge 2010), p. 91.

According to Henry Kibet Mutai, the principle of variable geometry was incorporated in the EAC Treaty primarily to allay the concerns of Tanzania and Uganda, which feared that, given their relatively low levels of development, their economies ran the risk of being swamped by Kenyan goods if they were obliged to liberalize at the same rate.[14]

The design of variable geometry as a negotiation strategy and as a strategy of implementation of agreed activities is complex and difficult. The concept of variable geometry suits a larger group of countries among which a subset is initially willing to enter an agreement.[15] It first appeared in EU Treaties and has later arisen in other negotiations particularly in the World Trade Organization as a possible way of breaking the impasse in failed negotiations, such as the GATTs opt-in agreements on Technical Barriers and Government Procurement.[16]

In the EU, variable geometry started with the 1990 Schengen Convention relating to the free movement of person among the Schengen States where Ireland and the UK were not willing to remove controls on the intra-EU movement of non-EU nationals.[17] Then again in 1991 where 11 Member States of the EU signed the Social Policy Agreement relating to employment and working conditions, but the UK opted out. In 1992, the European Economic and Monetary Union (EMU) adopted the common currency, the euro, and common monetary policy under the European Central Bank. The UK, Ireland and Denmark immediately refused to sign and thereby retained their own currencies, with Ireland joining at a later date.[18]

In the EU, the principle of variable geometry was first formalized in the 1997 Treaty of Amsterdam, then christened as 'closer co-operation', largely in response to the UK's and Denmark's opt-outs on European Monetary Union, the UK's and Ireland's exemptions from the Schengen Agreement and Denmark's

14 As quoted in J.V. Mwapachu, *Challenging the Frontiers of African Integration: The Dynamics of Policies, Politics and Transformation in the East African Community*, (E&D Vision Publishing, Dar es Salaam 2012), p. 365.

15 P. Lloyd, '*The Variable Geometry Approach to International Economic Integration*', University of Melbourne, p. 51. See http://journals.usb.ac.ir/Business/en-us/Articles/Article_172/ (accessed 15 November 2013).

16 P. Lloyd, *op. cit.*, p. 56.

17 C. Barnard, *The Substantive Law of the EU: The Four Freedoms*, (OUP 2010), pp. 524–527; Lloyd, Peter, '*The Variable Geometry Approach to International Economic Integration*', *supra*, pp. 53–54.

18 P. Lloyd, *op. cit.*, p. 54. See also EU Chapter 13 on the development of EMU in the EU, and the problems this has created.

opt-out on anything to do with a common EU defence policy.[19] These opt-outs had already created de facto variable geometry.

Today, variable geometry agreements and the '*acquis communautaire*' are the two main tracks of greater integration within the EU. The '*acquis communautaire*' refers to EU's total body of legislation or what has so far been achieved by the EU.[20] However, the acts adopted in the framework of the variable geometry bind only participating Member States and they do not in formal terms constitute part of the *acquis* that has to be accepted by candidate states for accession to the EU. According to Peter Lloyd, variable geometry has the following features.[21] First, it is an opt-in agreement devised by a proper subset of a larger group of countries. It is therefore an opt-in strategy as opposed to *à la carte* practices of opting out.[22] Second, its benefits are restricted to the subset of countries. Third, it is a union of temporary steps towards the eventual inclusion of all members into the negotiated arrangements.

In the EAC, this principle found practical application when Kenya, Rwanda and Uganda decided in 2013 to fast-track some integration projects such as the establishment of a single customs territory, a single tourist visa and the use of national identity card as travel documents for their citizens to cross their mutual borders.[23] Tanzania and Burundi were not ready to be involved. Therefore, based on the principle of variable geometry, Kenya, Rwanda and Uganda launched the projects and left it open to the discretion of Burundi and Tanzania to join whenever they deem appropriate.

---

19 (http://www.euro-know.org/europages/dictionary/v.html) (30 Sept 2013).

20 S. Hargreaves, *EU Law*, (OUP 2009), p. 18. Also see Y. Usui, "Constructing an East Asian Acquis", in Nkamura, Tamio (ed), *East Asian Regionalism from a Legal Perspective: Current features and a vision for the future*, (Routledge 2009), pp. 231–243.

21 P. Lloyd, *op. cit.*, pp. 58 and 63.

22 J. Janning, '*European Democracy and Variable Geometry. How a multi-speed Europe complicates the Union's democratic legitimacy*', (2013), p. 2. See https://ip-journal.dgap.org/en/ip-journal/topics/european-democracy-and-variable-geometry (accessed 25 December 2013).

23 See G. Ajumbo, 'Is Variable Geometry Leading to the Freagmentation of Regional Integration in East Africa?', available on http://www.afdb.org/en/blogs/integrating-africa/post/is-variable-geometry-leading-to-the-fragmentation-of-regional-integration-in-east-africa-12524/ last access on 15 November 2016.

3.4 Legal Instruments

3.4.1 *Treaty and Protocols*

The EAC legal landscape consists of the Treaty and protocols concluded by the Partner States to enhance their cooperation in agreed areas. In principle, each protocol spells out its objectives, scope and any institutional framework needed for cooperation and integration. According to Article 151 of the Treaty, each protocol becomes an integral part of the Treaty after signature and ratification following the approval by the Summit on the recommendation of the Council.

So far, more than a dozen protocols have been ratified and are in force.[24] Among them, three deserve to be mentioned given their paramount significance for the regional integration process in the EAC. The first protocol is the Protocol on the Establishment of the East African Customs Union which entered into force in 2005 with the main aim of eliminating internal tariffs and other charges of equivalent effect as well as non-tariff barriers in order to smoothen the free movement of goods between the Partner States. The second is the Protocol on the Establishment of the East African Common Market in force since 2010.[25] This Protocol focuses on the free movement of labor, services and capital while fostering the freedom of establishment and that of residence for EAC Partner States' nationals. The third protocol worth mentioning is the Protocol on the Establishment of the East African Community Monetary Union. This Protocol entered into force in 2015 after its ratification by all the Partner States with the objective to "promote and maintain monetary and financial stability aimed at facilitating economic integration to attain sustainable growth and development of the Community".[26]

---

24 *Inter alia* can be mentioned Protocol on the Decision-Making by the Council of the East African Community [2001]; Protocol on the Establishment of the East African Kiswahili Commission [2007]; the Protocol on Combatting drug trafficking in the East African Community [2001]; Protocol on Standardization, Quality Assurance, Metrology and Testing [2001]; Protocol on the Establishment of the East African Civil Aviation Safety and Security Oversight Agency [1999]; Protocol on the Establishment of the East African Science and Technology Commission [2008]; Protocol on Peace and Security [2013]; Protocol on the Establishment of the East African Health Research Commission [2008]; Protocol for the Sustainable Development of Lake Victoria Bassin [2003]; Protocol on Environment and Natural Resources Management [2006]; etc.

25 See also Chapter 9, 10, 11 and 12 for a more detailed discussion of these Protocols.

26 Art. 3 of EAC Monetary Union Protocol as well as Chapter 13.

Each of these protocols embodies, respectively and successively, the attainment of the first three key stages of the EAC regional integration process, i.e. customs union, common market and monetary union as affirmed in paragraph fifteen of the preamble to the Treaty. The Protocol on the Establishment of a Political Federation, the ultimate stage of EAC regional integration, is still in an embryonic draft stage.

Acts and regulations are enacted for the implementation of Treaty protocols. In relation to the protocols mentioned above, one could name the East African Custom Management Act (2004) and the East African Community Customs Union (Rules of Origin) Rules as amended to date, and the six annexes[27] to the Common Market Protocol as some of the acts and regulations in force in the EAC.

3.4.2 *General Principles*

The Treaty makes a distinction between fundamental principles of the Community and its operational principles.[28] On the one hand, according to Article 6, the achievement of the objectives of EAC regional integration is governed by fundamental principles of (a) mutual trust, political will and sovereign equality; (b) peaceful co-existence and good neighborliness; (c) peaceful settlement of disputes; good governance including adherence to the principles of democracy, the rule of law, accountability, transparency, social justice, equal opportunities, gender equality, as well as the recognition, promotion and protection of human and peoples rights in accordance with the provisions of the African Charter on Human and Peoples' Rights; (e) equitable distribution of benefits; and (f) cooperation for mutual benefit.

On the other hand, Article 7 provides for operational principles that must be observed for the practical achievement of the objectives of the Community. These are principles of (a) people-centered and market-driven cooperation, (b) the provision by the Partner States of an adequate and appropriate enabling environment, such as conducive policies and basic infrastructure;

---

27 Annex 1: The East African Community Common Market (Free Movement of Persons) Regulations; Annex 2: The East African Community Common Market (Free Movement of Workers) Regulations; Annex III: The East African Community Common Market (Right of Establishment) Regulations; Annex IV: The East African Community Common Market (Right of Residence) Regulations; Annex V: The East African Community Common Market Schedule of Commitments on the Progressive Liberalization of Services; and Annex VI: The East African Community Common Market Schedule on the Removal of Restrictions on the Free Movement of Capital.

28 See for a detailed discussion in this point also Chapter 6.

(c) the establishment of an export oriented economy for the Partner States in which there shall be free movement of goods, persons, labor, services, capital, information and technology; (d) the principle of subsidiarity which emphasizes on multi-level participation and the involvement of a wide range of stake-holders in the process of integration; the principle of variable geometry allowing for progression in cooperation among groups within the community for wider integration schemes in various fields and at different speeds; (f) the equitable distribution of benefits accruing or to be derived from the operations of the Community and measures to address economic imbalances that may arise from such operations; the principle of complementarity; and (h) the principle of asymmetry. In addition to these principles, good governance also appears as one of the operational principles of the EAC.

The treaty-makers found it judicious to erect two principles that at the same time form fundamental and operational principles of the Community. These are the principle of equitable distribution of the benefits of the Community and the principle of good governance.[29] This is not by chance. To understand the reason for this choice, one may want to refer to paragraph 4 of the preamble to the Treaty where the "continued disproportionate sharing of benefits of the Community among the Partner States" and the "lack of adequate policies to address this situation" are deplored as some of the main reasons that caused the collapse of the former EAC in 1977.

In fact, right after independence, Uganda and Tanzania already started complaining that the British system had favored Kenya which became more industrialized than her two other Partner States. This allegedly caused serious trade imbalances whose manifestation was that Uganda and Tanzania imported from Kenya more than they could export. They contended that this situation was actually fostered by the customs union which became fully-fledged among them in 1940. As a result of the customs union's common external tariff, it was difficult for products from third countries to penetrate the Community market. Hence, Uganda and Tanzania had to import quasi-exclusively from Kenya. This situation contributed a lot to the economic development of Kenya, but to the detriment of the other two EAC countries. According to Uganda and Kenya, this was one of the materializations of the inequitable sharing of the benefits of the Community.[30] The Kampala agreement and the treaty establishing the former EAC attempted to address this issue of inequitable distribution of the benefits of the community in 1964 and in 1967, respectively. However,

---

29 See Arts. 6(e) and 7(f) for the principle of equitable distribution of the benefits; and arts. 6(d) and 7(2) for the principle of good governance.

30 See on this point also further Chapters 9 and 13.

this was in vain. It is probably to highlight the fatality of this issue in order to urge the Partner States to find an effective solution that Treaty-makers resolved to make the "equitable distribution of the benefits of the Community" one of its dualist general principles under Articles 6 and 7.

On the other hand, good governance as a general principle is one of the pillars that supports the entire EAC architecture. In this sense, the EACJ held that the principle of good governance has to be observed as it is "foundational, core and indispensable to the success of the integration agenda".[31] Good governance acts as the steering principle to ensure that both the Partner States, and EAC organs and institutions are effectively and efficiently converging towards the achievement of the integration objectives.

Apart from the principle of variable geometry and that of good governance which have been addressed by the EACJ, the scope and the practical meaning of other general principles enshrined in the Treaty are not yet ascertained. While the concrete meaning of the principle of variable geometry was asked to the Court by the Council in order to break a deadlock in which its decision-making seemed to be trapped,[32] the scope and the practical meaning of the principle of good governance was rather an outcome of EAC citizens' activism.

In fact, for some reasons, the Treaty-makers subjected the human rights jurisdiction of the EACJ to the adoption of an ad hoc protocol.[33] As this protocol is still awaited, pursuant to Article 30 of the Treaty that gives quality to "any person who is resident in a Partner State" to refer a case on the unlawfulness of any Partner State's act, regulation, directive, decision or action to the EACJ, EAC nationals resorted to Article 6(d) that provides for good governance as a fundamental principle of the Community to bypass the human rights jurisdictional confinement imposed on the EACJ. According to Article 6(d) good governance is defined as encompassing "adherence to the principles of ... rule of law ... as well as the recognition, promotion and protection of human and peoples rights ..." Therefore, it was quite straightforward for applicants to claim that human rights violations by a Partner State form an infringement of Articles 6(d) and 7(2) of the Treaty. The EACJ did not hesitate to uphold that while it could not assume jurisdiction to "adjudicate human rights disputes, [the Court] will not abdicate from exercising its jurisdiction of the interpretation under Article 27(1) *merely because the Reference includes*

31 Reference No. 5 of 2011, *Samuel Mukira Mohochi v. The Attorney General of the Republic of Uganda*, Judgment, 17 May 2013, para 36.

32 See Application No. 1 of 2008, *Advisory Opinion*, 13 September 2008. For more details on the principle of variable geometry in the EAC Treaty, see *supra* (section 3.3.).

33 Art. 27(2) of the Treaty.

allegations of human rights violations".[34] Hence the Court concluded that the principle of good governance in Articles 6(d) and 7(2) of the Treaty contains a clear intention of the Treat-makers to safeguard individuals against arbitrary governance and ill treatment by totalitarian leader, or mob rule.

This ruling paved the way for several other human rights cases based on the violation of the principle of good governance.[35] Accordingly, good governance has become the most used general principle of the Treaty. This contributed a lot to the clarification of the definition of good governance and to the framing of its substantial scope.

3.4.3 *Regulations, Directives, Decisions, Recommendations and Opinions*

Article 8(2)(b) provides for the obligation of the Partner States to confer upon Community legislation, regulations and directives the force of law within their territories. However, the Treaty does not define what the Community's regulations, directives or decisions are; nor does it provide a clear hierarchy or procedural differences between them. Therefore, arguing on the difference of their respective binding force could be difficult. Indeed, Article 16 of the Treaty that touches this issue of the binding force of the Community's regulations, directives, decisions, recommendations, and opinions rather focuses on those taken by the Council, by stipulating that they are binding on the Partner States, on all organs and institutions of the Community other than the Summit, the Court and the Assembly within their jurisdictions. This is understandable as the Council is the policy organ of the Community.[36] In addition, pursuant to Article 11(5) of the Treaty the Summit can delegate some of the powers (including legislative powers) conferred to it to the Council. However, this does not

---

34 Reference No. 1 of 2007, *James Katabazi v. Secretary General of the East African Community and the Attorney General of the Republic of Uganda*, Judgment of 1 November 2007, para. 41 [emphasis supplied].

35 See for instance: Reference No. 1 of 2010, *Honorable Sitenda Sibalu v. the Secretary of the EAC, Attorney General of Uganda, Honorable Sam Njuba, and the Electoral Commission of Uganda*, Judgment of 30 June 2011; Reference No. 7 of 2010, *Mary Ariviza and Okotch Mondoh v. Attorney of Kenya and Secretary General of the East African Community*, Judgment of 30 November 2011; Reference No. 30 of 2010, *Independent Medico Legal Unit v. Attorney General of Kenya*, Judgment of 1 March 2013; Reference 4 of 2011, *Omar Awadh and Six Others v. Attorney General of Kenya and Attorney General of Uganda*, Judgment of 15 April 2013; and Reference No. 8 of 2010, *Plaxeda Rugumba v. Secretary General of the EAC and Attorney General of Rwanda*, Judgment of 1st December 2011; Reference No. 9 of 2012, *East African Center for Trade Policy and Law v. Secretary General of the EAC*, Judgment of 9th May 2013.

36 Art. 14(1) of the Treaty.

answer the question of the difference in both the nature and the binding force of EAC acts. Even a look at the EAC Protocol on the Council's decision-making does not provide the expected distinction.

Therefore, it can be noticed that the concern of the Treaty-makers was more to establish a hierarchy between the acts of the Community and those of the Partner States than to make a clear internal distinction between Community acts. This is clearly highlighted in Article 8(4) that provides for the precedence of Community laws over the similar ones of the Partner States. It means that in case of conflict EAC legislation, regulations, and directives, recommendations and opinions should take precedence over any Partner States' national acts of a similar effect.[37]

3.5 Legislation and Decision-making

This section addresses the legislative process of bills by the East African Legislative Assembly, the law-making institution of the EAC, and sheds light on the Council's decision-making.

3.5.1 *Legislative Procedures*

The Treaty confers power to initiate legislation to both the Council of Ministers and the East African Legislative Assembly (the Assembly). This implies a dichotomist approach to the EAC legislative process. On the one hand, there is the Council Bill initiated by the Council[38] and directly introduced to the Assembly for the first reading. On the other hand, there is the Private Member's Bill that can be initiated by any member of the Assembly.[39]

A Private Member's Bill is introduced by way of motion to which is attached the proposed draft of the bill. The Counsel to the Community has the obligation to provide reasonable professional assistance in drafting the bill to any Assembly member who intends to move a Private Member's Bill before it can be compiled by the clerk in order to be attached to the motion.[40] In case the motion is carried, the clerk of the Assembly has the responsibility to print and publish the concerned bill in the Gazette,[41] as it is a rule that every bill has to be printed and published in the Gazette before its introduction to

37 See further on this issue Chapter 4.

38 See Art. 14(3)(b).

39 See Art. 59(1) of the Treaty and Rule. 64(1) of EALA Procedure.

40 Rule 64(2),(3) and (4) of the EALA Procedure.

41 Rule 64(6) EALA Procedure.

the Assembly.[42] It is worth mentioning that although Assembly members are entitled to introduce a Private Member's Bill, such a bill cannot be proceeded if its purpose would amount to the imposition of any financial charge upon any Community's fund, either directly or indirectly.[43] Moreover, a bill, motion or amendment that is likely to result in the derogation from the enjoyment of human rights cannot be introduced before the Assembly.[44]

After introduction, every bill (either Council Bill or Private Member's Bill) has to be read three times before being passed. The first reading is a kind of introduction of the bill to the Assembly. It consists of an aloud reading of the short title of the bill by the clerk. Afterwards, the bill is referred to the Committee which should analyze it and present its report to the Assembly within 90 days. This deadline can be extended for an extra period of 30 days with the permission of the Assembly if the Committee fails to complete its report within the given period.[45] The work of the Committee is not ceremonial but rather is very critical as it is at this stage that the relevance of the bill is assessed. In order for a bill to progress, the Committee needs to be convinced that there is a positive balance between the advantages and the disadvantages of the bill. In case the Committee needs an external expertise to make its mind, it may be allowed to appoint experts for advice.[46] The Committee's assignment also involves conducting widespread consultations with members of the Council of Ministers, representatives of Partner States' institutions related to the matter of the bill, national parliaments, and the citizens who are basically the final beneficiaries of EAC acts.[47]

If after this scrutiny process the Committee finds that relevant amendments should be done to the bill, it may recommend so. Furthermore, the Committee,

---

42 Rule 61 EALA Procedure. Exception to the publication rule is when a given bill is declared to be of an urgent nature by the Assembly on a motion by any EALA member. In this case the bill may be introduced without publication and such a bill may be taken through all the legislative stages in one day (Art. 62 EALA Procedure).

43 Art. 59(2) of the Treaty.

44 Rule 63 of the EALA Procedure. This is a strong token for the protection of human rights by the EALA, and the EAC at large.

45 Rule 66(6) of the EALA Procedure.

46 EAC, 'Report of the Capacity Building Workshop for the Committee on General Purpose: "The Legislative process of Bills: From Initiation, enactment to oversight on enacted law"', Nairobi, 6–9 August 2014, p. 3 online at http://www.eala.org/new/index.php/key-documents/reports/500-capacity-building-workshop-for-the-eala-committee-on-general-purpose?path=, accessed on 15 November 2016.

47 *Ibid.* Public consultation occurs through public hearing workshops that the committee has to undertake in all Partner States.

through its chairperson, has competence to review and accept proposals for correction of blatant misprints and punctuation errors in the bill without any formal request from a member of the Assembly.[48]

When the Committee is satisfied of the bill's relevance, it is submitted to the second reading upon the request of the Council chairperson or the Assembly member who initiated the bill, depending on whether it is a Council Bill or a Private Member's Bill. The report of the Committee is presented to the whole Assembly by the chairperson of the Committee. This opens the bill to debate on its merits and principles, which will have the consequence of sending the bill to its next level, the Committee of the Whole House.[49] This Committee is constituted of all the members of Assembly and is chaired by the Speaker who acts for this specific purpose as the chairperson of the Committee of the Whole House. At this stage, the Assembly proceeds with an article-by-article review and adoption of the bill. When amendments are suggested, they are debated and eventually adopted.

At the end of the second reading, the bill is submitted with the permission of the Speaker to the Assembly for the third reading, either immediately or on a day decided by the Speaker.

However, even after a bill is set for the third reading, any member can request that a given provision be deleted, amended or added.[50] However, this must be done before the third reading is introduced. In case a bill is suggested for a partial or whole amendment, it should go back through the procedure of the Committee of the Whole House as described above until the bill is adopted.[51] The third reading constitutes the adoption of the bill by the Assembly,[52] and indicates that the bill is ready to be sent to each of the EAC Heads of States for their assent.

A bill becomes an act of the Community when it receives the assent of all the Heads of State of the Community. In case one or more Heads of States

---

48 Rule 67(3) of EALA Procedure.

49 Rule 69 of EALA Procedure.

50 Rule 72(1) of EALA Procedure.

51 Rule 72(3) of EALA Procedure.

52 It is noteworthy that the EALA decides on all questions by a majority of votes of the elected members present and voting on the basis of one person one vote. The speaker or the chairperson of committee does have neither an original nor a casting vote (Rule 54 of EALA Procedure). Thus, if on an issue votes of the members are equally divided, the motion should be lost (art. 58(4) of the Treaty). Ex-officio members by virtue of article 48(1)(b) of the treaty (minister, assistant minister in charge of EAC, the secretary general and the counsel to the community) do not hold a voting right in the deliberations of the EALA. See Art. 58(2) of the Treaty.

withhold their assent to a bill, a notification is sent to the Speaker who informs the Assembly about this occurrence. The returned bill and the reason why assent was withheld are laid on the table of the Assembly by the member who initiated that bill for further referral to the relevant Committee in order to undergo scrutiny of the clauses objected by the Heads of State.[53]

3.5.2 *Decision-making and Delegation of Powers*

The Council is the policy organ of the EAC.[54] For this reason, this section is mainly dedicated to the decision-making by this organ. According to Article 15(4) of the Treaty, "the decisions of the Council shall be by consensus", subject to a Protocol on the Decision-making.[55] However, the provisions of this Protocol suggest that consensus is just one of the two modes on which Council decisions can be made. In fact, Article 2 of this Protocol exhaustively lists matters that require consensus. It includes granting observer status to an intergovernmental organization or civil society organization; making the financial rules and regulations of the Community; submission of the annual budget to the Assembly; approval of the expenditures of the community; establishment of any sectoral council or committee under the Treaty; submission of Bills to the Assembly; decision policy-making for the efficient and harmonious functioning and development of the community; and decisions on what should be recommended to the Summit on matters such as the amendment of the Treaty; the approval or amendment of any protocol; the admission of new members, the granting of observer status to foreign countries; the imposition of sanctions; the suspension of a member; the transformation into a political federation; and the expansion of areas of cooperation.

All other decisions are taken by simple majority.[56] This provision may raise the question of knowing whether simple majority should also be used when the Council is acting pursuant to powers delegated to it by the Summit. As a reminder, Article 11(5) and (6) of the Treaty stipulates the possibility of power delegation from the Summit to the Council or to the Secretary General. The Summit may delegate any of its Treaty-conferred powers except the giving

53 Rule 73(5) of EALA Procedure. In this case, the procedure to be followed is the same as the one prescribed by art. 72 applicable in case a member of the EALA suggests the amendment of a bill after the second reading but before the third reading.

54 Art. 14(1) of the Treaty.

55 See on the vital importance of the shift towards Qualified Majority voting in EU decision-making further EU Chapters 2 and 3.

56 Art. 2(2) of the Protocol on the Decision Making by the Council of the East African Community [2001].

of general directions and impetus; the appointment of judges to the EACJ, the admission of new members and granting of observer status to foreign countries; and assent of bills.[57] Given that the decisions of the Summit are made by consensus,[58] and yet the Protocol on the decision-making of the Council does not mention the exercise of summit powers by the Council among the matters to be decided upon by consensus, one may wonder whether such decisions are also made by simple majority pursuant to Article 2(2) of this protocol on the decision-making of the Council. Obviously, this does not seem to be the intention of the Treaty-makers especially that this would eventually have a consequence of turning this delegation into an alteration of the Summit competence. Therefore, it makes sense to suggest that when the Council is deciding by virtue of the powers delegated to it by the Summit, such decision should be made by consensus as at that time the Council is not acting as the Council but rather as the Summit (in the name and on behalf of the Summit).

57 Art. 11(9) of the Treaty.

58 Art. 12(3) of the Treaty.

CHAPTER 3A

The Legal Framework of the EU

Armin Cuyvers

3.1 Introduction

This chapter provides a brief overview of the main competences of the EU, as well as the tools and processes the EU has to translate these competences into legal action. In other words, what may the EU actually do, and how does it act?[1] In addition, this chapter touches on a question that is increasingly important for the EU, certainly after Brexit, and that may become of increasing importance to the EAC as well: variable geometry. To what extent can integration differ per Member State or per group of Member States, or must all states integrate at the same pace? We begin, however, with the question which competences the EU actually has, and how competence can be determined in a concrete case.

3.2 Conferral, Scope, Nature and Use of EU Competences

Fundamentally, the EU remains an organization established by its Member States. Consequently, the EU does not have a general competence to act in whatever field it wants to. In EU-speak, this is often summarized by saying the EU has no *Kompetenz-Kompetenz*.[2] Instead, the EU only has those powers *conferred* on it by the Member States via the different Treaties.[3] All powers that have not been transferred to the EU remain with the Member States.[4]

1 See generally on these issues *inter alia* L. Azoulai (ed), *The Question of Competence in the European Union* (OUP, 2014), A. Von Bogdandy and J. Bast (eds), *Principles of European Constitutional Law* (2nd ed., Hart Publishing 2010), A. Estella, *The EU Principle of Subsidiarity and its Critique* (OUP, 2002), P. Craig, 'Subsidiarity: A Legal and Political Analysis' (2012) 50 *JCMS* 72, or S. Weatherill, 'Competence Creep and Competence Control' (2004) 23 *YEL*, 1.

2 Cf. the German Constitutional Court in BVerfGE, 2 BvE 123,267, 2 BvE 2/08 (2009) *Lissabon Urteil* or BverGE 2 BvR 1390/12, 2 BvR 1421/12, 2 BvR 1438/12, 2 BvR 1439/12, 2 BvR 1440/12, 2 be 6/12 (2012) *ESM Treaty*.

3 D. Chalmers, *European Union Law* (CUP 2007), 140.

4 Of course, deciding where the boundaries of existing powers lie becomes a crucial element here.

© ARMIN CUYVERS, 2017 | DOI 10.1163/9789004322073_007
This is an open access chapter distributed under the terms of the CC-BY-NC License.

The basic principle of conferred powers is laid down in Articles 4, 5(1) and (2) TEU, which provide that:

> 1. *The limits of Union competences are governed by the principle of conferral. (...)*
> 2. *Under the principle of conferral, the Union shall act only within the limits of the competences conferred upon it by the Member States in the Treaties to attain the objectives set out therein. Competences not conferred upon the Union in the Treaties remain with the Member States.*

If the EU wants to act in a certain field, therefore, it must first have received the competence from the Member States to do so. Concretely, this delegation of competences in the Treaties is done via *legal basis provisions*. These are provisions in the TEU or TFEU that explicitly give the EU the competence to act in a certain field, and that also indicate the legislative process the EU should follow to adopt such acts.[5] These legal bases can be very limited and specific, such as Article 157(3) TFEU, which only allows the EU to regulate in the field of sex equality in employment and occupation:

> The European Parliament and the Council, acting in accordance with the ordinary legislative procedure, and after consulting the Economic and Social Committee, shall adopt measures to ensure the application of the principle of equal opportunities and equal treatment of men and women in matters of employment and occupation, including the principle of equal pay for equal work or work of equal value.

Other legal bases, however, are very open and wide-ranging. Article 114 TFEU on the creation of the internal market, the most important legal basis in EU law, provides a good example of such a broad legal basis. Article 26 TFEU states that EU should create one internal market.[6] This provision itself, however, only provides the *objective* of creating a market. It does not provide a legal basis to turn this objective into reality by adopting legal acts. This legal basis can be found in the first paragraph of Article 114 TFEU:

---

5 See case 45/86, *Commission v. Council*, [1987] ECR 493. Such legal bases must be distinguished from the broader articles that determine the values and objectives of the EU, such as Articles 2 and 3 TEU. Such Articles only indicate what the EU should aspire to, but do not give the competence to adopt any acts.

6 See for a further discussion of EU internal market law EU chapters 9–13.

> Save where otherwise provided in the Treaties, the following provisions shall apply for the achievement of the objectives set out in Article 26. The European Parliament and the Council shall, acting in accordance with the ordinary legislative procedure and after consulting the Economic and Social Committee, adopt the measures for the approximation of the provisions laid down by law, regulation or administrative action in Member States which have as their object the establishment and functioning of the internal market.

Article 114 TFEU, therefore, empowers the EU to adopt legislation to harmonize all national laws that may hinder the free movement of goods, services, capital or people and therefore obstruct the internal market. Such a far-reaching power of course also raises the question where the *limits* of EU competences lie, and who gets to decide on these limits. After all, as we know from the Commerce Clause in the US Constitution, almost anything can be said to affect the internal market, as almost all rules will have some (indirect) effect on cross-border-trade.[7] Once we have established that the EU has been attributed a certain power, like regulating the internal market, we must then answer the additional question where the limits of this power lie.

3.2.1 *The Scope of EU Competences*

Crucially, when it comes to delineating EU competences, the line judge is the CJEU, and not the Member States or the EU legislative institutions.[8] Even though the EU does not have *Kompetenz-Kompetenz*, it is an EU institution that determines the scope of the competences that have been conferred by the Member States.[9] This exclusive power of the CJEU to determine

7 J.H. Choper, R.H. Fallon, Y. Kamisar, and S.H. Shiffrin, *Constitutional Law* (10th edn. Thomson 2006), 87 and 91. Further see T.W. Merril, 'Towards a Principled Interpretation of the Commerce Clause', 22 *Harvard Journal of Law and Public Policy* (1998), 31, and D. McGimsey, 'The Commerce Clause and Federalism after Lopez and Morrison: The Case for Closing the Jurisdictional-Element loophole', 90, *California Law Review* (2002), 1675. Different from the US, however, the EU has less effective political counterbalances.

8 Case C-376/98 *Tobacco Advertising I* [2000] ECR I-8419, C-380/03 *Tobacco Advertising II* [2006] ECR I-11573, Case C-358/14, *Poland v Parliament and Council* (Tobacco Advertising III) ECLI:EU:C:2016:323, Joined Cases C-293 and 594/12 *Data Retention Directive*, ECLI:EU:C:2014:238.

9 As will be discussed further below, not all national supreme courts accept this absolute claim of the CJEU in its full extent, although in practice it is the CJEU that determines the limits of EU competences. Of course the Member States do retain the option of changing the EU Treaties if they disagree, even though this requires unanimity of 28 states, and therefore is not often a realistic option.

competence is important for the stability and effectiveness of the EU. Just imagine if each individual Member State or national court would be able to decide, for every single peace of EU legislation, whether the act was *ultra vires* or not. Similarly, the review by the EU Courts, and not the EU political institutions, also means that the EU political institutions must respect the nature and limits of EU competences as well.

In determining the scope of EU competences, the CJEU follows a teleological, or purposeful approach. It looks at the objectives and ambitions of the EU, and interprets EU competences in such a way that these objectives may be realized.[10] The main argument is that the Member States intended to give the EU the necessary powers to realize its objectives, as it were the same Member States that formulated these objectives in the first place. The result of this teleological approach is that the CJEU often chooses a rather expansive interpretation that increases EU competences. The best example of this purposeful approach, and its expansive effects, is the (in)famous *Tobacca Advertising* case law.[11]

The tobacco cases concerned a directive prohibiting all advertising and sponsorship of tobacco products.[12] The main legal basis for this act was the internal market clause of Article 114 paragraph 1 TFEU.[13] The Council, the European Parliament and the Commission claimed that the many differences in national laws on tobacco advertising were a threat to the internal market. If Italy allowed tobacco advertising but Sweden did not, for example, Italian newspapers or journals with tobacco advertisements could not be sold in Sweden, hindering their free movement. Germany, however, claimed that the real objective of the directive was to reduce smoking and protect public health. This was problematic according to Germany because the EU only has very limited competences in the field of public health. In fact, Article 168(5) TFEU explicitly prohibits harmonization in the field of public health, even though it also does obligate the EU to ensure 'a high level of human health protection' in all Union policies and activities.[14]

---

10 S. Douglas-Scott, *Constitutional Law of the European Union* (Pearson 2002), 261.

11 Case C-376/98 *Tobacco Advertising I* [2000] ECR I-8419 and C-380/03 *Tobacco Advertising II* [2006] ECR I-11573. For a recent addition in this debate also see Case C-358/14, *Poland v Parliament and Council* (Tobacco Advertising III) ECLI:EU:C:2016:323.

12 Directive 98/43.

13 Under the old, pre-Lisbon and Amsterdam numbering this was still Article 100A and 95 EC respectively.

14 With certain limited exceptions in Article 168(4) TFEU that were not applicable in this case.

In two landmark judgments the CJEU first held that the directive did exceed the competence under Article 114 TFEU as it was overly broad. For example, it also included advertisements on objects that would never cross the border.[15] An amended directive, however, which excluded these objects, was later upheld by the CJEU. These judgments contain two key findings concerning the delineation of EU competences. The first is the low threshold the CJEU requires before allowing the use of Article 114 TFEU. The second is that, once this low threshold has been met, EU measures based on the market competence of Article 114 TFEU may *also*, or even *predominantly* pursue other objectives, including public health. The reasoning of the CJEU here is exemplary and an important window into the logic of effectiveness that shapes EU law and contributes to its actual success. The CJEU first reiterates the fundamental principle of attribution:

> Those provisions, read together, make it clear that the measures referred to in Article [114(1)] of the Treaty are intended to improve the conditions for the establishment and functioning of the internal market. To construe that article as meaning that it vests in the Community legislature a general power to regulate the internal market would not only be contrary to the express wording of the provisions cited above but would also be incompatible with the principle embodied in Article [5 TEU] that the powers of the Community are limited to those specifically conferred on it.
>
> Moreover, a measure adopted on the basis of Article [114] of the Treaty must genuinely have as its object the improvement of the conditions for the establishment and functioning of the internal market. If a mere finding of disparities between national rules and of the abstract risk of obstacles to the exercise of fundamental freedoms or of distortions of competition liable to result therefrom were sufficient to justify the choice of Article [114] as a legal basis, judicial review of compliance with the proper legal basis might be rendered nugatory. (...)[16]

The CJEU therefore insists that a measure can only be based on a legal basis if it 'genuinely' pursues the objective behind that legal basis, which it is for the Court to assess. Both in *Tobacco Advertising I* and in *Tobacco Advertising II*,

---

15 The directive also allowed Member States to impose stricter norms, but did not provide for a free movement clause (*Tobacco I*, paras. 101 a.o.). See on this issue the further discussion on the free movement of goods in chapter 10.

16 *Tobacco Advertising I*, paras. 83–84.

however, the CJEU subsequently held that there was a sufficient risk to free movement, now *or in the future*, to justify the use of Article 114 as a legal basis:

> It is clear that, as a result of disparities between national laws on the advertising of tobacco products, obstacles to the free movement of goods or the freedom to provide services exist or may well arise.
>
> In the case, for example, of periodicals, magazines and newspapers which contain advertising for tobacco products, it is true, as the applicant has demonstrated, that no obstacle exists at present to their importation into Member States which prohibit such advertising. However, in view of the trend in national legislation towards ever greater restrictions on advertising of tobacco products, reflecting the belief that such advertising gives rise to an appreciable increase in tobacco consumption, it is probable that obstacles to the free movement of press products will arise in the future.[17]

The EU therefore has a competence to regulate under Article 114(1) TFEU where there is an actual or potential obstacle, now or in the future to any of the fundamental freedoms.[18] Even the risk of *potential future obstacles*, therefore, is sufficient to create a competence under Article 114 TFEU.

Once this already low threshold for the use of Article 114 TFEU has been met, moreover, the CJEU held that the EU was also allowed to pursue *other objectives* than the internal market, including public health:[19]

> Furthermore, provided that the conditions for recourse to Articles [114], 57(2) and 66 as a legal basis are fulfilled, the Community legislature cannot be prevented from relying on that legal basis on the ground that public health protection is a decisive factor in the choices to be made. On the contrary, the third paragraph of Article129(1) provides that health requirements are to form a constituent part of the Community's other

---

17 *Tobacco Advertising I*, paras. 96–97.

18 Cf. amongst many other confirmations of this line Case C-491/01 *British American Tobacco* [2002] ECR I-11453, par. 60, case C-434/02 *Arnold André* [2004] ECR I-11825, par. 30, case C-210/03 *Swedish Match* [2004] ECR I-11893, par. 29, or joined cases C-154/04 and C-155/04 *Alliance for Natural Health* [2005] ECR I-6451, par. 28. Measures are not allowed, however, on a 'mere finding of disparity between national rules'.

19 Note also in this regard that, even though the EU has no competence in public health, Article 168 TFEU does obligate the EU to take public health into account in all its legislation.

> policies and Article [114](3) expressly requires that, in the process of harmonisation, a high level of human health protection is to be ensured.[20]

When safeguarding the internal market, therefore, the EU may also pursue other objectives, further increasing the scope of EU competences. Here the CJEU clearly applied a very expansive doctrine of attribution to make sure the EU has sufficient competences to reach its objectives.[21] Many further examples can be given. In the *Ship Source Pollution* cases, for example, the EU could use its environmental competence to require Member States to impose criminal sanctions for the dumping of ship waste, as this was absolutely necessary to make the environmental competence effective.[22] In *ESMA*, the CJEU upheld that the competence under Article 114 TFEU includes the power to create agencies with far reaching powers.[23] In *Digital Rights Ireland* the CJEU found that Article 114 TFEU could also be used to require the retention of meta-data from telephones, as the diverging rules on data retention formed a risk for free movement.[24] Perhaps the most far-reaching example can be found in the *Kadi-I* saga.[25] Here the CJEU invented the notion of an 'implicit underlying objective', which could be transformed into a competence via Article 352 TFEU.[26]

---

20 *Tobacco Advertising I*, par 88.

21 For further examples see, amongst others, the *Ship Source Pollution* cases, where the EU could use its environmental competence to require Member States to impose criminal sanctions for the dumping of ship waste, as this was absolutely necessary to make the environmental competence effective. In *ESMA*, the CJEU upheld that the competence under Article 114 TFEU includes the power to create agencies with far reaching powers. In *Digital Rights Ireland* the CJEU found that Article 114 TFEU could also be used to require the retention of meta-data from telephones, as the diverging rules on data retention formed a risk for free movement.

22 Case C-176/03 *Commission v Council* (*Ship Source Pollution I*) [2005] ECR I-7879. The EU is not competent, however, to determine the 'type and level' of criminal sanction. See case C-440/05 *Ship Source Pollution II* [2007] ECR I-9097 par. 70. After Lisbon the EU has, however, received further, and more explicit, competences in the field of criminal law. See especially art. 82–86 TFEU.

23 Case C-270/12, *UK v Parliament and Council* (*ESMA*), ECLI:EU:C:2014:18.

24 Case C-301/06 *Ireland v Parliament and Council* (Data Retention), ECLI:EU:C:2009:68.

25 For a further analysis of these cases see A. Cuyvers, '"Give me one good reason": The unified standard of review for sanctions after Kadi II', 51(6) *Common Market Law Review* (2014), 1759, and A. Cuyvers, 'The Kadi II judgment of the General Court: the ECJ's predicament and the consequences for Member States'. *European Constitutional Law Review*, 7, 481.

26 Joined cases C-402/05 P and C-415/05 P *Kadi I*, par. 226.

The expansive interpretation of competences followed by the CJEU has of course been criticized in many Member States, and one could say that the CJEU comes close to granting a general competence under Article 114 TFEU.[27] At the same time, the purposeful approach of the CJEU has been vital for enabling the EU and allowing it to be effective. As it only has a limited number of competences, these competences need to provide sufficient space for the EU to actually achieve its aims.[28] Moreover, it must also not be forgotten that it is the political institutions, including the Member States as represented in the Council of Ministers, that first adopt legal acts, and hence are of the opinion that these acts fit within a certain competence. The CJEU only reviews these acts once adopted. It is not the CJEU, therefore, that expands EU law all by itself, but rather the CJEU that empowers the political institutions to achieve EU objectives by following a purposive and permissive doctrine of competences.

3.2.2 *The Nature of EU Competences*

In addition to establishing the existence and the scope of EU competences, it is also important to understand the *different types* of EU competence. For the EU has three different types of competences, being exclusive competences, shared competences and supporting competences.[29]

3.2.2.1 Exclusive Competences

An exclusive competence means that Member States transfer all their authority in a certain area to the EU, and hence have no powers left to regulate that field themselves. Even if the EU has not yet acted on a certain issue, say developing a trade agreement with a new state like South Sudan, Member States are not allowed to act nationally. The only way to act in an area of exclusive competence is via the EU.

Exclusive competences, therefore, are the most far reaching competences the EU has. This also explains why there only are a few exclusive competences,

27 Cf. P. Van Cleynenbreugel, 'Meroni Circumvented? Article 114 TFEU and the EU Regulatory Agencies', 21 *Maastricht Journal* 1 (2014), 64–88.

28 Note though that Article 352 TFEU also provides a residual competence for the EU. Where the Treaty provides an objective, but no explicit competence, Article 352 TFEU may be used as a fallback competence. The use of Article 352 TFEU, however, requires unanimity in the Council, and also separate approval of some national parliaments.

29 R. Schütze, 'The European Community's Federal Order of Competences A Retrospective Analysis', in: M. Dougan and S. Currie (eds), *50 Years of the European Treaties: Looking Back and Thinking Forward* (Hart Publishing 2009), 63.

as in most fields Member States are not willing to transfer all their authority to the EU. Article 3 TFEU provides an overview of the areas of exclusive competences:

> 1. *The Union shall have exclusive competence in the following areas:*
>   (*a*) *customs union;*
>   (*b*) *the establishing of the competition rules necessary for the functioning of the internal market;*
>   (*c*) *monetary policy for the Member States whose currency is the euro;*
>   (*d*) *the conservation of marine biological resources under the common fisheries policy;*
>   (*e*) *common commercial policy.'*

In these areas, such as the customs union or the common commercial policy, it was deemed necessary to have one coherent EU policy. For example, the EU customs union can only work effectively if all Member States use the exact same rules and rates. Similarly, the common commercial policy (CCCP) requires the EU to act as a single block externally. The effectiveness of this policy would be undermined if Member States could also negotiate trade deals bilaterally. Hence the decision was taken to create exclusive competences in these fields.

3.2.2.2 Shared Competences

The second, and largest group of competences are shared. As their name already indicates, these competences are shared between the EU and the Member States. This means that both the EU and the Member States are allowed to act in areas of shared competence. Article 4 TFEU provides an overview of the many and broad shared competences of the EU:

> 1. *The Union shall share competence with the Member States where the Treaties confer on it a competence which does not relate to the areas referred to in Articles 3 and 6.*
> 2. *Shared competence between the Union and the Member States applies in the following principal areas:*
>   (*a*) *internal market;*
>   (*b*) *social policy, for the aspects defined in this Treaty;*
>   (*c*) *economic, social and territorial cohesion;*
>   (*d*) *agriculture and fisheries, excluding the conservation of marine biological resources;*

> (*e*) *environment;*
> (*f*) *consumer protection;*
> (*g*) *transport;*
> (*h*) *trans-European networks;*
> (*i*) *energy;*
> (*j*) *area of freedom, security and justice;*
> (*k*) *common safety concerns in public health matters, for the aspects defined in this Treaty.'*

Such shared competences create the risk of conflict: What if a Member State and the EU both legislate to protect consumers on-line, for example, but the different regulations conflict? Three main principles regulate such conflict. Firstly, EU law always trumps national law, be it of an earlier of a later date. If there is a conflict, the EU law therefore trumps the national law.[30] Secondly, once the EU regulates a certain topic within a shared competence it 'occupies the field', which means that the Member States lose the authority to regulate this topic as well. As soon as the EU acts in an area of shared competences, therefore, the Member States lose their competence on the issue covered by the EU act. For example, if the EU regulates the nicotine content of cigarettes under the shared internal market competence, Member States lose their competence to regulate nicotine content themselves. They remain competent, however, to regulate other topics such as tar content or the size of cigarettes. How much authority Member States have left in the areas of shared competences, therefore, depends on how much EU legislation has already been adopted. Thirdly, even on those issues where Member States remain competent to act, the principle of sincere cooperation obligates them not to undermine the effectiveness or objectives of existing EU obligations.[31]

3.2.2.3 Supporting, Coordinating and Supplementing Competences

Supporting, coordinating and supplementing competences are the third, and most limited, type of EU competences. These are areas where the Member States retain their authority to regulate, but where the EU can help out, for example by coordinating national policies or providing subsidies. In contrast to shared competences, EU action under a supporting competence does not occupy the field. Even if the EU acts, therefore, national competences are not reduced. Article 6 TEU provides an overview of these more secondary competences:

30 Also see the general discussion on the supremacy of EU law in EU chapter 4.

31 Article 4 TEU.

> The Union shall have competence to carry out actions to support, coordinate or supplement the actions of the Member States. The areas of such action shall, at European level, be:
> (*a*) *protection and improvement of human health;*
> (*b*) *industry;*
> (*c*) *culture;*
> (*d*) *tourism;*
> (*e*) *education, vocational training, youth and sport;*
> (*f*) *civil protection;*
> (*g*) *administrative cooperation.'*

One of the most successful examples of a supporting competence is the Erasmus programme allowing students to study abroad. The area of education is so sensitive and connected to national identity that the EU has received no competences to harmonize. The EU, therefore, cannot regulate curricula or school systems. The EU has, however, received the competence to support and supplement national education policy, for example by providing subsidies to certain programmes, or sharing best practises between Member States. The Erasmus programme is one example of such supporting action.

3.2.2.4 The Residual Competence of Article 352 TFEU

Article 352 TFEU forms an intriguing and important addition to the entire system of EU competences. It provides a residual competence where the Treaties do provide an objective but, even under the expansive interpretation of the CJEU, no competence can be found in any of the legal basis provisions:

> If action by the Union should prove necessary, within the framework of the policies defined in the Treaties, to attain one of the objectives set out in the Treaties, and the Treaties have not provided the necessary powers, the Council, acting unanimously on a proposal from the Commission and after obtaining the consent of the European Parliament, shall adopt the appropriate measures. Where the measures in question are adopted by the Council in accordance with a special legislative procedure, it shall also act unanimously on a proposal from the Commission and after obtaining the consent of the European Parliament.[32]

Besides an interesting legal conundrum, Article 352 TFEU creates a form of residual competence to ensure that objectives can be realized, and hence

32 Article 352 TFEU.

further ensures EU effectiveness.[33] Here the EU system for attribution again has similarities to the federate US approach under the necessary and proper clause.[34] Article 352 TEU in fact even goes one step further, as the text of the necessary and proper clause only refers to the *powers* of the federal government, not the objectives.

The use of Article 352 TFEU, however, does require unanimity in the Council, which of course limits its use. In addition, because of its openness, some, including the *Bundesverfassungsgericht*, see it as a limited form of amendment, and hence require approval by the German parliament for any use of Article 352, further complicating the use of this residual competence.[35]

3.3 The Use of EU Competences: The Principles of Subsidiarity and Proportionality

Having a competence does not automatically mean that you should also use it, or use it to its fullest extent. Once it is established that the EU has a certain competence, therefore, two new questions arise: 1) when should the EU use a certain competence, and 2) how far should the EU go when using that competence? These questions are governed by the principles of subsidiarity and proportionality.

Under the principle of subsidiarity the EU 'shall act only if and in so far as the objectives of the proposed action cannot be sufficiently achieved by the Member States.'[36] Even if there is a competence, EU action is only called for where the Member States cannot achieve a similar result themselves. Although subsidiarity is a legal principle, it is highly political in nature, and difficult to adjudicate. The primary subsidiarity check takes place in the political

---

33 A. Dashwood, 'Article 308 as the Outer Limit of Expressly Conferred Community Competence', in: C. Barnard and O. Odudu (eds) *The Outer Limits of European Union Law* (Hart Publishing 2009), 35 et seq.

34 See however also the attempt to at least somewhat limit the potential this opens up in Declaration No. 41 on art. 352 TFEU. For example, art. 352 TFEU is not to be used in relation to such lofty aims as 'promoting peace'.

35 See especially its *Lissabon Urteil* of 30 June 2009, BVerfGE, 2 BvE 2/08. On the other hand also see Opinion 2/94 *Accession to the European Convention on Human Rights* [2006] ECR I-929, and the limits imposed by the CJEU therein. Further see J.H.H. Weiler, *The Constitution of Europe: Do the New Clothes have an Emperor?* (CUP 1999), 54–55.: 'No sphere of the material competence could be excluded from the Community acting under art. 352 TFEU'.

36 Article 5(3) TEU.

institutions and the national parliaments.[37] The CJEU primarily checks the formal subsidiarity requirements, for example if a legislative act actually contains a paragraph assessing subsidiarity. Logically, subsidiarity only applies to shared competences and not to exclusive competences, where the Member States are no longer allowed to act anyway.

If the EU should act, the principle of proportionality demands that 'the content and form of Union action shall not exceed what is necessary to achieve the objectives of the Treaties.'[38] For example, where a limited directive harmonizing product labels for chocolate would suffice, the EU should not adopt a regulation completely regulating the manufacturing of chocolate. Like subsidiarity, the principle of proportionality is also rather political, and hence left primarily to the political institutions.[39]

3.4 Variable Geometry and Enhanced Cooperation

If the EU has a competence, and if it is allowed to use it, a further question that arises is if this competence may only be used where all Member States participate or if it may also be used by a smaller sub-set of Member States. This question brings us to the problem of variable geometry and flexibility.

The default position is that all Member States participate in any EU action. Especially as the EU expanded, however, the need was felt for more flexibility. As with the euro, for example, some Member States wanted to integrate faster and deeper than others. How much flexibility should be allowed, and in what form, however, has always been a highly contentious point. On the one hand, it is argued that flexibility is simply necessary in so large a union. In addition, flexibility may ultimately deepen integration as it allows a 'coalition of the willing' to intensify integration in certain fields, with other Member States probably joining later. On the other hand, it is feared that a 'Europe of

---

37 See Protocol (No. 1) and (No. 2) on subsidiarity and the role of national parliaments that may give 'yellow' or 'orange' cards to legislative proposals where they think they infringe the principle of subsidiarity. On the complex nature of these concepts also see P.J.G. Kapteyn and P. VerLoren van Themaat, '*Introduction to the Law of the European Communities*' (3rd edition, Kluwer 1998), 233 et seq.

38 Article 5(4) TEU and the Protocol on the application of the principles of subsidiarity and proportionality.

39 At least in the field of competence determination. As we shall see in chapters 9–13, the CJEU does closely scrutinize proportionality where restrictions on free movement are concerned.

multiple speeds' is only the first step towards the unravelling of the EU, as it would undermine the necessary coherency and unity within the Union.

In practice, a great deal of flexibility already exists in today's EU.[40] Often this has been achieved by opt-outs in the Treaties, including accession treaties. For example, only 19 of the current 28 Member States participate in the Euro.[41] Similarly, some Member States, notably the UK, have an opt-out for Schengen, which lifts the borders between participating states, even though some non-EU states do participate. In the larger picture, there is also the European Economic Area (EEA) and the European Free Trade Agreement (EFTA) that provide a kind of alternative membership to the EU internal market.[42]

In addition to these existing forms of flexibility, Lisbon also further developed the Treaty mechanism for enhanced cooperation.[43] This mechanism allows a group of at least nine Member States to establish closer cooperation with each other *within* the framework of EU, and whilst using EU institutions and competences. They may only do so, however, as a last resort. This means that they must first try to achieve the desired objective with all Member States, and may only resort to enhanced cooperation where this objectively proves impossible.[44] The enhanced cooperation, furthermore, must always be open to other Member States that want to join. So far, however, this mechanism has only been used twice to adopt rules on divorce and Union patents, as the procedure is quite burdensome.

A third mechanism to allow for flexibility is to conclude international agreements between all or a group of Member States. Such agreements are often intimately connected with EU law, but formally qualify as international agreements between the Member States. The Fiscal Compact or the ESM Treaty provide clear examples of this practice, that is welcomed by some and seen as a threat to the 'Community method' by others.[45]

---

40 Cf already B de Witte, D. Hanf and E. Vos, *The many faces of Differentiation in EU law* (2001, Intersentia).

41 Of these, the UK, Denmark and Sweden even have a formal or informal exemption from the obligation to join the euro zone at some stage. See further EU chapter 13 on EMU.

42 See on these existing forms of flexibility and alternative membership also G. Davies, 'What Does It All Mean?', *German Law Journal Brexit Supplement* (2016), en B. De Witte, 'Near-membership, partial membership and the EU constitution', (2016) (4) *European Law Review*, p. 471.

43 Article 20 TEU and Articles 326 to 334 TFEU.

44 Article 20(2) TEU and Joined Cases C-274/11 and C-295/11 *Spain and Italy v Council* (Enhanced Cooperation), ECLI:EU:2013:240.

45 P. Craig, 'The Stability, Coordination and Governance Treaty: principle, politics and pragmatism', 37(7) 2102 *European Law Review* p. 231. See also the evidence given by

None of these mechanisms, however, seem to provide both the flexibility that seems necessary and the safeguards that are required to guarantee the unity and stability of European integration. Especially with *Brexit* looming, therefore, the search is on for alternative mechanisms and models that offer both, and that may satisfy those Member States that want deeper integration and those that want to remain more on the sidelines but remain part of the EU.[46] Current suggestions include, for example, the creation of several circles of integration, which range from a deeply integrated core with even a common military to less integrated 'outer circles' that primarily participate in economic integration, although it is as yet wholly unclear if it is actually feasible to separate these areas. In any event the question of flexibility and variable geometry is an important one for the EU, and will likely only increase in importance for the EAC as well. Consequently, it would seem an important area for further research and comparison.

3.5 EU Legal Instruments

Where the EU has a competence, it can only act through one of the legal instruments provided for in Article 288 TFEU, being regulations, directives, decisions, recommendations and opinions.

A regulation can best be described as an EU law. From the moment of its publication a regulation applies fully and directly in all Member States. Regulations require no national implementation, rather it is even prohibited to transpose a regulation into national law. Consequently, once a regulation has been adopted and published, it is the applicable law throughout the entire EU.

A directive, on the other hand, is an indirect instrument addressed to the Member States. The directive tells Member States to achieve a certain result, for example giving a right of residence of three months to all EU citizens.[47] The Member States must then implement this directive in their national law,

---

M. Dougan and P. Craig for the European Scrutiny Committee of the House of Commons. House of Commons—European Scrutiny Committee, Treaty on Stability, Coordination and Governance: impact on the rule of law (62nd report, 27 March 2012).

46 See in this context also the 'Cameron-deal' that was supposed to prevent Brexit, and the right of the UK not to participate in deeper integration, as well as the obligation of the UK not to interfere where other Member States would like to integrate more deeply. See the European Council Conclusions of 18–19 February 2016, Annex I, EUCO 1/16. For analysis see "Editorial comments: Presiding the Union in times of crisis: The unenviable task of the Netherlands' (2016) 53(2) *Common Market Law Review*, 327–328.

47 Directive 2004/38.

where they are free to choose the best national means and methods of doing so. Usually, Member States are given a period of two years for this implementation. Individuals and companies subsequently rely on the national laws transposing the directive, not on the directive itself.[48] The directive, therefore, is a less intrusive measure, as it allows Member States to make certain choices and to integrate a certain rule into their own national law and legal system. At the same time, directives also carry a higher risk of divergence between Member States, as the implementation may differ between Member States and as some Member States may fail to implement a directive or may implement it incorrectly.[49]

Decisions are legally binding acts addressed to specific addressees, and hence are not of general application. Examples are Commission decisions that grant specific farmers a subsidy or impose a fine on certain companies for violating of EU competition law. Recommendations and opinions, on the other hand, have no binding legal force. They can still have legal effect, for instance as soft law or via the principle of legitimate expectations, but are not binding as such.

3.6 EU Legislation and Decision-making

Where the EU wants to use a competence, for instance to adopt a regulation or a directive, it must act via one of the decision-making procedures provided for in the Treaty or secondary legislation.[50] These procedures, therefore, regulate *how* the EU can act. The most important decision making procedures that will be discussed here are the ordinary legislative procedure set out in Article 294 TFEU and the two main special legislative procedures.[51]

48 For the complex doctrine on the potential direct effect of directives see EU chapter 4.

49 As we shall see in EU chapter 7, it is then up to the Commission to check whether a directive has been implemented correctly and to start infringement proceedings where necessary.

50 For a discussion of non-legislative decision-making within the different institutions, see chapter 2, as these procedures often entail the Institutions taking decisions on their own and under their own internal rules, such as under Articles 31 TEU or 31, 106(3), 236, 290 or 291 TFEU. The discussion here will focus on the legislative decision-making procedures. For secondary legal bases see Case C-133/06 *Parliament v Council* (Secondary Legal Basis) [2008] ECR I-3189.

51 Pre-Lisbon this procedure was known as the co-decision procedure, in light of the important role for the European Parliament as co-legislator with full rights. See also EU chapter 2.

3.6.1 *The Ordinary Legislative Procedure*

The ordinary legislative procedure involves the Commission, the European Parliament and the Council in up to four 'rounds'owhen trying to adopt legislation. The procedure starts with the Commission submitting a proposal to the European Parliament and the Council for the first reading. The Parliament then adopts a position whereby it rejects the Commission proposal, accepts the proposal or, more commonly, proposes several amendments. The position of the Parliament is then communicated to the Council. If the Council approves with the position of the European Parliament, the act is adopted, and the procedure is finished. If the Council does not agree, it shall adopt its own position, for instance suggesting different amendments, and communicate this position to the European Parliament and the Commission. The Commission will then give its own views on the position of the Council to the Parliament.

The position of the Council and the views of the Commission then form the starting point for the second reading. If the Parliament agrees with the position of the Council at the end of the first reading, the act will be adopted as formulated by the Council. If the Parliament simply rejects the position of the Council, the proposed act is not adopted, and the procedure stops. Alternatively, however, the European Parliament may again suggest amendments. The Commission then gives an opinion on the amendments proposed by the Parliament, after which the ball is back again in the court of the Council. By a qualified majority the Council can then either approve all amendments by the Parliament and adopt the act, or, if it does not agree, convene a so called Conciliation Committee.[52]

The Conciliation Committee is composed of an equal number of representatives of the Council and the European Parliament. These representatives negotiate with each other and have six weeks to arrive at a text that is acceptable for both institutions.[53] The Commission also takes part in this Committee to advise and suggest possible compromises. If no compromise is reached, the act is not adopted. If a joint text can be agreed upon, however, the procedure continues to the third reading.

---

52 For a discussion of the qualified majority voting procedure see EU chapter 2. If the Commission has given a negative opinion on certain amendments of the European Parliament, however, the Council may only adopt these by unanimity. This requirement further safeguards the position of the Commission at this stage of the legislative procedure.

53 The representatives of the Council thereby have to approve the outcome with a qualified majority, the representatives of the Parliament by a normal majority, following the voting rules of their respective institutions.

In the third reading, the European Parliament, by normal majority, and the Council, by qualified majority, each have six weeks to either accept or reject the compromise text drafted by the Conciliation Committee, no further amendments being allowed. If one or both of the institutions reject the text, the procedure ends and no act is adopted.

The ordinary legislative procedure therefore truly casts the Council and the European Parliament as co-legislators, and also provides significant influence to the Commission. As can already be guessed from the many different rounds, however, the ordinary legislative procedure can also take quite some time. Largely for this reason, the *trialogue* has been invented. Essentially, the trialogue moves the Conciliation Committee up to the first round. Instead of exchanging amendments for two rounds, a Committee with representatives from the Council and the Parliament is immediately set op to negotiate a joint text. This joint text is subsequently submitted to the Council and Parliament for an up or down vote, without any further amendments being allowed. The main advantage of the trialogue is its speed, certainly when compared against a normal ordinary legislative procedure. The downsides of trialogues, however, include the reduced space for open and transparent debate, as most of the negotiation takes place behind closed doors, and no further amendments are allowed. Benefits and advantages, therefore, have to be carefully weighed in practice.

3.6.2 *Special Legislative Procedures*

In addition to the ordinary legislative procedure, there are also some *special* legislative procedures. The key difference between special legislative procedures and the ordinary legislative procedure is the role played by the European Parliament. In special legislative procedures the Parliament always plays a more limited role.[54] The two main special legislative procedures are the Consent procedure and the Consultation procedure.

Under the Consent procedure, the European Parliament must consent to an act but does not have the power to table amendments. Formally, therefore, it can only say yes or no to the proposal on the table.[55] Under the Consultation procedure, Parliament only has to be consulted, i.e. given a chance to express its view on a proposal. Parliament, however, cannot block legislation under

---

54 Also see Article 289(2) TFEU. Particular legal bases can add certain additional elements to special legislative procedures.

55 See for examples of the consent procedure Articles 49 and 50 TEU, or 19(1), 218 and 352 TFEU.

this procedure. Usually, moreover, consent procedures require unanimity in the Council, preserving a veto for all Member States.[56]

3.6.3 *Determination of Legislative Procedure and the Qualification of Legislative Acts*

Which legislative procedure should be used for a specific act is determined by the legal basis. Each legal basis simply indicates the required procedure. Article 114(1) TFEU, for example, requires the ordinary legislative procedure, whereas Article 115 TFEU requires the special consultation procedure.[57]

The procedure used for the adoption of an act also determines its qualification as a legislative or a non-legislative act. Here again the rule is very simple. All measures adopted via the ordinary legislative procedure or a special legislative procedure qualify as *legislative acts*.[58] This qualification is linked to the involvement of the parliament. Vice versa, all acts adopted via non-legislative procedures are non-legislative acts. This qualification is purely formal. It only depends on the procedure used, and does not look at the content of the act at all. The qualification of an act as legislative is relevant for the hierarchy of acts in the EU. Because they partake in the democratic legitimacy of the European Parliament, legislative acts are hierarchically placed above non-legislative acts. The qualification as legislative or not-legislative, moreover, is also relevant for the remedies available against an act, as will be further discussed in chapter 7.

3.6.4 *Delegation and Implementation*

Often, EU legislative acts only provide a framework that needs to be further developed or implemented. The Council and the Parliament can decide to leave this task to the Commission, for example because it requires a certain administrative expertise or because they want to focus on more high level activities. In this context the EU Treaties distinguish between delegation and implementation.

56 See for examples Articles 103(1), 109 and 115 TFEU.

57 A complication can arise where an act must be based on multiple legal bases and the different legal bases cannot be combined. The selection or combination of legal bases in such cases is governed by Cases C-300/89 *Commission v Council* (Titanium Dioxide), ECLI:EU:C:1991:244, Case C-338/01 *Commission v. Council* (AGGF) [2004] ECR I-4829, Case C-411/06 *Commission v. Parliament and Council* (shipment of waste) ECLI:EU:C:2009:518, and Case C-166/07 *Parliament v. Council* (Irish Fund) [2009] ECR I-7135.

58 Article 289(3). See also on this point Case C-583/11 P *Inuit Tapiriit Kanatami and others v Parliament and Council*, ECLI:EU:C:2013:625.

Under the process of *delegation* a 'legislative act may delegate to the Commission the power to adopt non-legislative acts of general application to supplement or amend certain non-essential elements of the legislative act.'[59] The delegated powers, however, may not concern the 'essential elements of an area', which must be dealt with in the legislative act itself.[60] The use of delegated powers, moreover, can be subject to control by the Parliament and the Council.[61]

Sometimes legislation also requires further implementation at the EU level, for instance where the Commission has to grant subsidies based on a legislative act establishing a subsidy scheme.[62] To this end, a legislative act may grant implementing powers to the Commission, or less commonly to the Council. These implementing powers can be significant and far-reaching in practice. For that reason, they are usually controlled by committees of national experts, reporting back to the Council and/or the European parliament, and with different powers of checking the Commission. This entire system of committees checking the implementation of EU law by the Commission is usually referred to as Comitology.[63]

The precise border between delegation and implementation can be difficult to draw in practice, as both can be very similar. For adopted acts, however, this should not create any headaches as each act is required to indicate, in its title, if it is delegated or implementing.[64]

---

59 Article 290(1) TFEU.

60 See also ECJ, Case C-427/12 *Commission v Parliament and Council* (Biocidal Products), ECLI:EU:C2014:170.

61 Article 290(2) TFEU.

62 In addition, Member States of course always have the general obligation to implement EU law as well. See both the general obligation of sincere cooperation in Article 4(3) TEU and the specific obligation in Article 292(1) TFEU.

63 See Regulation 182/2011/EU laying down the rules and general principles concerning mechanisms for control by Member States of the Commission's exercise of implementing powers, OJ 2011 L 55/13.

64 Articles 290(3) and 291(4) TFEU.

CHAPTER 4

The Scope, Nature and Effect of EAC Law

John Eudes Ruhangisa

4.1 Introduction

4.1.1 *The Aim*

This chapter examines the scope and origins of EAC law as well as its strength and validity with regards to the Partner States. It does so with a view to analyzing the relevance of EAC law within the integration process. The importance of law within a regional bloc cannot be overstated, as there cannot be meaningful integration without a solid regulatory framework to provide guidance to the process. Undoubtedly, EAC law is a regulatory framework envisaged by the Partner States to direct and control the integration process. However, having the law scribed on paper is one thing, whereas giving effect to the law is another. This chapter, in the spirit of studying this dichotomy, assesses the status and effect of EAC law bearing in mind the fact that EAC has all the characteristics of a supranational organization.[1]

4.1.2 *The Structure*

In this chapter we open the discussion by examining the various sources of EAC law as provided by the Treaty which is the principal partnership accord as well as the parent instrument of the Community. With this background the study in this chapter goes on to analyze the range within which EAC law exerts its operation. The influence and consequence of EAC law in the national legal order is then evaluated before we proceed to look into the hierarchical relation

* Hon. Justice Prof. John Eudes Ruhangisa, judge of the High Court of the United Republic of Tanzania and former registrar of the East African Court of Justice.

1 For more and detailed discussion on the supranational character of EAC see John Eudes Ruhangisa, "From Rules to Reality: Creating a Legal Community for the EAC", *A Key Note Address to the Second LEAC Conference on East African Integration Through law, organized by Leiden University in Collaboration with the East African Court of Justice, Held at EAC Headquarters*, Arusha, Tanzania 5th May, 2016. See also Mbembe Binda, "Good Governance and Foreign Direct Investment: A Legal Contribution to a Balanced Economic Development in the East African Community", *PhD Thesis*, Utrecht University, The Netherland, 25th August 2015, at page 89.

© JOHN EUDES RUHANGISA, 2017 | DOI 10.1163/9789004322073_008
This is an open access chapter distributed under the terms of the CC-BY-NC License.

of this law vis-à-vis national law. The chapter will conclude with a discussion on how EAC law relates to other regional and international law.

4.2 Sources of EAC Law

In order to explain the scope of EAC law it is important to first consider its sources. Each country or region has its own sources of law, which largely influence its legal system. The most common sources of law are Constitutions, Parliamentary legislation (statutes), judicial decisions, treaties, protocols and circulars issued by various policy organs. In the EAC regime, the sources of law are: the Treaty for the Establishment of the East African Community (the Treaty) which came into force on 7th July 2000, following its ratification by the Partner States; Acts of the East African Legislative Assembly; decisions of the East African Court of Justice; Protocols; and formal directives and decisions of the policy organs of the Community.[2]

Within the EAC framework, the Treaty is the main source of Community law and it outlines the areas of cooperation on which the Partner States of the Community have agreed to cooperate. Under the Treaty it is agreed that, with a view to strengthening their cooperation, the Partner States are resolved to adhere to the fundamental and operational principles that shall govern the achievement of the objectives set out in the Treaty and to the principles of international law governing relationships between sovereign states. In this regard, the relevant provisions of the Treaty are: Article 5 on the Objectives of the Community; Article 6 on the Fundamental Principles of the Community; Article 7 on the Operational Principles of the Community; and Article 8 on the general undertaking as to implementation. For their mutual benefit, Partner States have agreed to cooperate in the following fields: political, economic, social, cultural, research, technology, defense, security, and legal and judicial affairs.

In modern democracies, the legislative function of the State is a preserve of the legislature (Parliament). This power is normally enshrined in the Constitution, which is the mother of all laws in a particular state.[3] In the EAC, the Treaty regulates the powers and functions of the organs and institutions

2 According to the East African Community structure the policy organs of the Community are mainly two: the Summit of Heads of State and the Council of Ministers.

3 For example Article 64 (1) of the Constitution of the United Republic of Tanzania, 1977 which provides that "legislative powers in relation to all Union matters and also in relation to all other matters concerning mainland Tanzania is hereby vested in Parliament". Also Article

of the Community in the same way that Constitutions regulate the affairs of states. Article 49 (1) of the Treaty vests the lawmaking function in the East African Legislative Assembly (the Assembly) as it provides that *"The Assembly shall be the legislative organ of the Community."*[4] The Assembly plays its legislative role in the Community by passing Bills and having them assented to by the Head of States in the Summit. The Bills that have been duly passed and assented to are styled as Acts of the Community and are published in the East African Community Gazette.

However, under common law tradition, in the course of performing their duties, other state organs such as the judiciary can make law as well. Judges are not supposed to make laws as their duty is to interpret it, but through statutory interpretation a judge can make law. This is where the saying "[j]udges make law" derives its origin.[5] The legal systems in the United Kingdom are based largely on judge-made law. Judge-made law is law developed through decisions by judges in the course of deciding cases brought before them. This is what is famously called "common law" or case-law. Although after the 17th Century new laws and law reforms in England have increasingly been brought about through Acts of Parliament, usually inspired by policies of the Government of the day, the development of case law still remains an important source of law. A statement of law made by a judge in a case can become binding on later judges and can in this way become the law for everyone to follow.[6]

The legal systems of the three founding countries of the EAC,[7] which incidentally were under British colonial control, are Common law. It is this background that not only influenced their respective Constitutions, but also the Treaty and the respect they give to the binding decisions of the East African Court of Justice (EACJ).

The EACJ is the judicial body of the Community whose role, under Article 23 of the Treaty, is to ensure adherence to law in the interpretation and application of and compliance with the Treaty. The EACJ has exercised its mandate of interpretation under Article 27 of the Treaty by hearing and determining

---

94 (1) of the Kenya Constitution provides that "[t]he legislative authority of the Republic is derived from the people and, at the national level, is vested in and exercised by Parliament."

4 Article 49 (1) of the Treaty, *Ibid.*

5 Frederick Schauer, Do Cases Make Bad Law?, 73 U. Chi. L. Rev. 883 (2006). "It is thus no longer especially controversial to insist that common law judges make law."

6 Jan Komárek, Judicial Lawmaking and Precedent in Supreme Courts, (LSE Law, Society and Economy Working Papers 4/2011), http://ssrn.com/abstract=1793219.

7 The Republic of Kenya, the Republic of Uganda and the United Republic of Tanzania. The Republic of Burundi and the Republic of Rwanda acceded to the Treaty on 18th June 2007 and became full members on 1st July 2007.

cases relating to infringement and contravention of the Treaty. Under Article 36 of the Treaty, the EACJ gives advisory opinions regarding questions of law arising from the Treaty which affect the Community. The EACJ also has jurisdiction under Article 32 of the Treaty to hear and determine any matter arising from an arbitration clause contained in a contract or agreement which confers such jurisdiction to which the Community or any of its institutions is a party or; arising from a dispute between the Partner States regarding the Treaty if the dispute is submitted to it under a special agreement between the Partner States concerned; or arising from an arbitration clause contained in a commercial contract or agreement in which the parties have conferred jurisdiction to it. The Court can also hear and give preliminary rulings on matters referred to it by the national courts or tribunals of a Partner State concerning interpretation or application of the provisions of the Treaty or the validity of the regulations, directives, decisions or actions of the Community. Invariably the judges of the EACJ through judicial pronouncements have also made laws in the course of interpreting the Articles of the Treaty and developing regional jurisprudence.

One example is the landmark case of *Callist Andrew Mwatella & 2 Others vs. EAC*.[8] In this historic[9] case the applicants challenged the legality of the actions of the Council of Ministers and the Secretariat in assuming control over Assembly-led Bills. The Council had purported to withdraw four Private Members' Bills from the Assembly. The application before the Court questioned the right of the Council to delay the presentation of the Bills to the House. It also challenged the validity of the meeting of the Sectoral Council on Legal and Judicial Affairs (the Sectoral Council) held on 13th to 16th September 2005 and the decisions taken by it to write to the Speaker attempting to withdraw the Bills pending before the Assembly, including the recommendation to legalize decisions through Protocols not through Community Acts. The application sought an order by the Court that the report of the Sectoral Council meeting held on 13th to 16th September 2005 was null and void *ab initio* and requested the Court to find that all decisions, directives and actions contained in or based on it were null and void.

The Court found that the Sectoral Council on Legal and Judicial Affairs was not constituted per Treaty, in particular Article 14 which provided that the Council of Ministers shall "*establish from among its members*" only Sectoral Councils and that Sectoral Council members were restricted to "Ministers" as defined by the EAC Treaty. The Court found that Kenya and Tanzania were

---

8 *Reference No. 1 of 2005.*

9 It is a historic case in the sense that it was the first ever case to be filed in the Registry of the Court since 2001 when the Court was inaugurated.

represented by non-ministers (including Attorney Generals) at the disputed meeting of 13th to 16th September 2005 and therefore the meeting was not properly constituted and did not amount to a lawful Sectoral Council meeting. In this regard, its decision regarding the two Bills was *ipso facto* invalid. However, the Court employed a prospective annulment principle as opposed to retrospective annulment in order not to take the Community back to square one on matters that the improperly constituted meeting had already decided. It was this particular decision of the Court that led to an amendment of the Treaty thereby validating participation of Attorney Generals in the Sectoral Council for Legal and Judicial Affairs.[10]

On another issue the Court found that under Article 59 (1) any Member of the Assembly may introduce a Bill. The Council does not have exclusive legislative initiative to introduce Bills in the Assembly. It held that the Assembly owns all Bills once tabled in the Assembly, whether they came initially by way of Private Members' Bills or Community Bills. As such, permission of the Assembly would be required for withdrawal of any Bill. Such approval must be sought and obtained through a motion passed by the Assembly and could only be withdrawn by the member from whom it originated. In this case the Council of Ministers was not the originator of the Bill. Thus, the Bill could not be withdrawn by the Council of Ministers as purportedly done. All the Council could do was to delay the debate.

As regards to the relationship between the Council and the Assembly, the Court found that each has its own enumerated areas of competency.[11] It held that the Assembly is a creature of the Treaty as are the other Organs of the Community and its competencies lie only with matters conferred upon it by the Treaty, as is the case with all other Community Organs. In this regard, the Assembly could only legislate on matters on which the Partner States had surrendered sovereignty to the EAC.

By interpreting these Articles of the Treaty, the Court dutifully discharged its major function under the Treaty and provided guidance for future operations of the affairs of the Community Organs. The Court boldly told the Ministers and the Attorney Generals that they had overstepped their boundaries and that this was not acceptable in the realm of integration, where institutions are created and given specific mandates to facilitate the integration agenda.

10 Article 13 of the Treaty for the Establishment of the East African Community was subsequently amended to recognize the Attorneys General as Members of the Council by adding sub article (c).

11 Article 14 (3) (c) and Article 16.

Moreover, the Court, in order not to cripple the activities of the Community, invoked the doctrine of prospective annulment.[12]

The EACJ has also played its interpretative role in the case of *Attorney General of the Republic of Kenya vs. Independent Medical Legal Unit*[13] where the disputed issue among the parties regarded the interpretation of Article 30(2) of the Treaty. The raised issue was whether Article 30(2) of the Treaty, which provides a time limitation of two months, can be extended where there is a *"continuous violation of human rights."* The Appellate Division held that the Treaty does not grant the EACJ any express or implied jurisdiction to extend the time limit of two months.

Other cases where the Court has performed its interpretative role and developed the Community jurisprudence include *Christopher Mtikila vs. The Attorney General of the United Republic of Tanzania and the Secretary General of the East African Community;*[14] *Prof Peter Anyang' Nyong'o & others vs. AG of Kenya & 5 Others;*[15] and *East African Law Society and 4 Others vs. Attorney General of Kenya and Others.*[16]

The Council of Ministers is the policy organ of the Community. The role of the Council is to make regulations, issue directives, take decisions, make recommendations and give opinions which are binding on the Partner States; on all organs and institutions of the Community other than the Summit; the Court and the Assembly within their jurisdictions; and on those to whom they may under the Treaty be addressed.[17] Thus, the Council also plays a law-making function within the Community.

If we were to rank the sources of EAC law hierarchically, there is no doubt that the Treaty leads in this arrangement as it specially presents itself in the integration process the way national constitutions lead in creating the rest of the laws in the respective countries. Likewise, in any regional organization it is the treaty that stands on top of the legal order as a groundnorm from which all laws derive their strength and origin. Protocols, being creatures of the Treaty, come next in the lineage of sources of law in the EAC. However, for ease of enforceability, and to give them effect, the contents and spirit of the protocols have to be translated into law by the Assembly through the legislative process. Likewise, the decisions or directives of the Council of Ministers or of

12 *Reference No. 1 of 2005.*

13 Appeal No. 1 of 2011.

14 Reference No. 2 of 2007.

15 Reference No. 1 of 2006.

16 Reference No. 3 of 2007.

17 Article 14 (3)(d) and Article 16 of the Treaty.

other policy organs of the Community have to be translated into law in order to give them a binding effect and make them enforceable in the court of law.

In any case, a Council decision cannot legally contravene the legislation of the Assembly. If it does, wittingly or unwittingly, such decision of the Council shall be *ultra vires* the law and therefore void to the extent it contravenes that legislation. Could this be one of the reasons for the Council of Ministers' reluctance or very slow pace in presenting Bills that translate the protocols into Acts of the Assembly? For quite some time the Council of Ministers has been uncomfortable with demands and even attempts to translate the protocols into law. This prompted three members of the Assembly to seek the Court's intervention in the case of *Callist Andrew Mwatella & 2 others vs.* EAC (*Supra*), where the Council decided to hold the Private Members' Bills[18] that were sent to the Council for input. The Council was of the strong view that there was no need for specific legislation in those areas since the relevant protocols, the Treaty and Council decisions were adequate.

It is important to note that in 2013 the Council of Ministers proposed an amendment to the Treaty which would somewhat ensure its full control of the Assembly. This was at the instance of one Partner State which was not happy with a Private Members' Bill that sailed through to become an Act of the Assembly. It failed however, when the remaining three Partner States declined to support the proposal to amend the Treaty. The proposed amendment intended to remove the part of Article 59 that states as follows: "*subject to the rules of procedure of the Assembly, any member may propose any motion or introduce any Bill in the Assembly.*"[19] If the said proposed amendment sailed through, it would have substantially reduced the amount of legislation for passing through the Assembly, as most Bills are proposed by private members.

It is legitimate to state that there has been a running tension between the Council of Ministers and the Assembly, with the former heavily relying on protocols and Summit directives to move forward key aspects of the integration agenda, something viewed as a slight by the Assembly. This is particularly seen in the relationships between Protocols and Acts, whose contents can overlap.[20]

---

18 The East African Community Trade Negotiation Bill, The East African Community Budget Bill, The East African Community Immunities and Privileges Bill, and The Inter-University Council for East Africa Bill.

19 At the 25th Meeting of the Council of Ministers held in Bujumbura in August, Tanzania proposed that article 59 of the Treaty be amended to remove the part that states that "subject to the rules of procedure of the Assembly, any member may propose any motion or introduce any Bill in the Assembly."

20 EAC Regulatory Capacity Review.

The Assembly is not in favour of protocols, because they limit its flexibility, while the Council prefers protocols, which are its own creation and within its control.

4.3 Scope of EAC Law

The scope of EAC law mostly covers matters related to the adherence to, application of, and compliance with the Treaty. This means that EAC law restricts itself only to the areas of cooperation as identified and agreed upon by the Partner States and it is within these areas where EAC law takes precedence over similar laws of Partner States. The agreed areas of cooperation are: political, economic, social and cultural fields, research and technology, defence, security and legal and judicial affairs.[21]

Although the EAC Partner States have expressed, through the Treaty, their common desire of ceding some elements of their sovereignty to the EAC (a supranational organization), they still maintain a considerable degree of sovereignty. In this regard it is only in the identified areas of cooperation that they have relinquished some sovereignty as it is only in these areas that Partner States are under an obligation to harmonize their policies and laws. Likewise, it is only in these areas that the Assembly can legislate. This scenario introduces the pertinent question of when and where EAC law can be relied upon. This question has two limbs, "when" and "where". The answer to "when" is partly found in the discussion above but may also be personal. Legal persons (natural persons and fictitious persons such as corporations) may invoke EAC law at any time, if their rights under the Treaty have been infringed or violated by a Partner State or an institution of the Community. The Treaty clarifies this view by providing that "any person who is resident in a Partner State may refer for determination by the Court, the legality of any Act, regulation, directive, decision or action of a Partner State or an institution of the Community on the grounds that such Act, regulation, directive, decision or action is unlawful or is an infringement of the provisions of this Treaty."[22]

The answer to the second limb of the question, "where", is also answered by the Treaty in Articles 33 and 34. While the EACJ exercises jurisdiction over disputes that arise out of the Treaty, this jurisdiction is not exclusive to the EACJ; national courts also share part of this jurisdiction. The Treaty provides that except where jurisdiction is conferred on the Court by the Treaty, disputes

21 Article 5 (1) of the Treaty, *op. cit.*

22 Article 30 of the Treaty.

to which the Community is a party shall not on that ground alone, be excluded from the jurisdiction of the national courts of the Partner States.[23] This appears strange and contradictory when the same Treaty goes on to say that decisions of the EACJ on the interpretation and application of the Treaty shall have precedence over decisions of national courts on a similar matter.[24]

It is the role of the Court to ensure that rules are adhered to in the course of integrational pursuits, and that the rights of the citizens are respected across the region. For there to be consistency in the way integration issues are being handled, EACJ decisions on integration matters should prevail over national courts and other tribunals, per Article 33 (2), despite Article 33 (1) calling for national courts to share jurisdiction with EACJ on Community matters.

Furthermore, the EACJ's jurisdiction is circumscribed by other judicial mechanisms that have been introduced by subsequent Protocols to the Treaty. This can be seen in both the Customs Union Protocol and the Common Market Protocol. Article 41(2) of the Customs Union Protocol, which deals with dispute settlement, establishes committees to handle disputes arising out of the Protocol and gives these committees finality in determining such disputes. The Court is excluded and denied a role in the entire process except if a party challenges the decision of the Committee on grounds of *fraud, lack of jurisdiction* or *other illegality*.[25]

Again, under Article 54(2) of the Common Market Protocol, jurisdiction to entertain Common Market related disputes has mainly been given to national courts the EACJ is given a very limited role. The national courts are responsible for dealing with complaints by businesses and citizens to protect their rights under EAC regulations. However, as stated earlier, while the national courts are given first priority on matters concerning the enforcement of rights and freedoms arising out of the Common Market Protocol, Article 33(2) of the Treaty recognizes EACJ decisions on the interpretation of the Treaty and Community law as being superior to national court decisions on the same matter. This tendency of ousting the jurisdiction of the EACJ is not conducive to the integration agenda and has the effect of undermining the Court itself and hindering the development of uniform regional jurisprudence.

---

23 Article 33 (1)of the Treaty.

24 Article 33 (2) of the Treaty.

25 Harold R. Nsekela, Overview of the East African Court of Justice, A Paper Presented During the Sensitisation Workshop on the Role of the EACJ in the EAC Integration, Imperial Royale Hotel, Kampala, Uganda, 1st–2nd November, 2011. See on the different situaiotn under EU law, where the CJEU has always claimed exclusive ultimate jurisdiction, EU Chapter 4.

Upon the opportunity to make a judicial pronouncement on the systematic erosion of its jurisdiction, the EACJ, while answering the issue whether it lacks jurisdiction over disputes arising out of the implementation of the Customs Union and the Common Market Protocols and after examining the impugned Articles of the Protocols, tried to find a way of guarding its jurisdiction by making the following finding:

> …we do not find, within the Customs Union and the Common Market Protocols, a provision that confers jurisdiction to resolve disputes arising from the interpretation of provisions of both Protocols either to an organ of a Partner State or of the Community, save this Court.[26]

The Court concluded that it has jurisdiction over disputes arising out of the interpretation and application of the Treaty which, for re-emphasis, includes the Annexes and Protocols thereto. However, the Court did not take time to either expound on the relevance of the impugned Articles of the Protocols or explain the intention of the Partner States in including the provisions which appear to suggest that the Court does not have jurisdiction over these matters. This issue is exemplified when the said impugned Articles of the Protocols are read together with a proviso to Article 27(1) of the Treaty which states:

> Provided that the Court's jurisdiction to interpret under this paragraph shall not include the application of any such interpretation to jurisdiction conferred by the Treaty on organs of Partner States.

Throughout the hearing of the case the Counsel to the Community who represented the Respondent kept the Court under constant reminder of the intention of those who framed the impugned Articles of the Protocols, the exercise he coordinated, as being to oust the jurisdiction of the Court in these matters.

The submission by the Counsel to the Community about the Court not having jurisdiction over such matters had been the position consistently taken by the Partner States. This view can be found in the submission by Mr. Amos Wako, the then Attorney General of the Republic of Kenya, during the hearing of an Application for temporary injunction in the famous *Anyang' Nyong'o* case[27] where he said:

---

26 Case of East African Law Society v. The Secretary General of the East African Community, Reference No. 1 of 2011, at pg 23 of the Judgment.

27 *Peter Anyang' Nyong'o and 10 Others v. The Attorney General of the Republic of Kenya and 5 Others*, Reference No. 1 of 2002.

> ... Since you have an Article in the treaty which is specific to that issue, Article 52 then you have no jurisdiction. This is because the matter for deciding on the validity of election is a matter for the national courts and not this court [EACJ]. In other words, at the stage in which we are today, with your limited jurisdiction, you should not wittingly or unwittingly, assume jurisdiction on matters on which the Treaty itself has said should be determined by the national courts.[28]

When the Court in its ruling rejected the Attorney General's argument on this, the Treaty was immediately amended to mark the Partner States' seriousness and a proviso to Article 27 (1) was added. The added amendment basically reflected the above Attorney General's views. Considering this background, it is likely that the purpose for including the impugned controversial dispute settlement provisions in the two Protocols was to oust the jurisdiction of the Court, an outcome which would arguably be detrimental to integration.[29]

4.4 The Effect of EAC Law in the National Legal Order

The EAC Treaty came into force upon ratification by all three founding Partner States and upon the Partner States successfully depositing the instruments of ratification with the Secretary General.[30] Once this was completed, the Treaty became part of the law of the land but it had no special position within the individual Partner States' legal framework until it was formally accepted by their respective Parliaments. The EAC Partner States have dualist as opposed to monist systems regarding the relationship between their respective national law and international law or other regional law. In monist States, international or regional law does not require to be translated into national law, but it is simply incorporated and has an automatic effect in national or domestic systems. On the contrary, dualist States, the category to which the EAC Partner States belong, accentuate the difference between national and international law, and

28 Pg 65 of the typed court proceedings of 24/11/2006 in the case *of Peter Anyang' Nyong'o and 10 Others v. The Attorney General of the Republic of Kenya and 5 Others*, Reference No. 1 of 2002. [Emphasis added].

29 Compare in this regards also Opinion 2/13 on the draft agreement providing for the accession of the European Union to the Convention for the Protection of Human Rights and Fundamental Freedoms ECLI:EU:C:2014:2454, and the rules of the jurisdiction of the CJEU discussed in EU Chapter 4.

30 Article 152 of the Treaty.

require the translation of international law such as Treaties and Protocols into national law by way of ratification or domestication. Therefore, in order to give effect to the Treaty, the Partner States had to incorporate it into their national legal systems by way of ratification/domestication.[31] This incorporation was achieved by the passing of domestic legislation that gave effect to the Treaty within each national legal system.[32] This is as provided by Article 8(2) of the Treaty which stipulates that:

> Each Partner State shall, within twelve months from the date of signing this Treaty, secure enactment and the effective implementation of such legislation as is necessary to give effect to the Treaty, and in particular—
> (*a*) *to confer upon the Community the legal capacity and personality required for the performance of its functions; and*
> (*b*) *to confer upon the legislation, regulations and directives of the Community and its institutions as provided for in this Treaty the force of law within its territory.*[33]

In accordance with this Treaty provision, each Partner State enacted a specific law to give effect to the Treaty within the domestic legal order. In the case of Uganda for example, this law is the East African Community Act of 2002 (EAC Act). The EAC Act gives the force of law in Uganda to the Treaty[34] since the Treaty provisions are also part of the law of the land[35] and can be enforced and allowed in Uganda.[36] In the case of the United Republic of Tanzania, through its Legislature the law was enacted to domesticate the Treaty.[37] It is this particular Act, No. 4 of 2001 that provides for giving effect to the provisions of

31 Articles 152 *Ibid.*

32 For Tanzania see The Treaty for the Establishment of the East African Community Act, 2001 (Act No. 4 of 2001 / Cap 411). For Uganda see East African Community Act, 2002, for Kenya see The Treaty Establishing the East African Community Act (No. 2 of 2000), for Rwanda see Law No. 29/2007 of 27/06/2007, and for Burundi the information that was obtained during research was that Burundi has no specific law in place domesticating the treaty as the country ascribes to the principle of Monism. Accordingly when EAC Treaty was ratified it became part and parcel of the laws of Burundi. As such there was no need for enacting another law domesticating EAC Treaty.

33 Article 8 (2) of the Treaty, *op. cit.*

34 Section 3 (1) of East African Community Act, 2002 (Uganda).

35 Dora Byamukama, "The EAC Treaty has the force of law in Uganda", *op. cit.*

36 Section 3 (2) of the East African Community Act, *op. cit.*

37 The Treaty for the Establishment of the East African Community Act, 2001 (Act No. 4 of 2001 / Cap 411).

the Treaty for the Establishment of the East African Community and for connected purposes. This law applies to Tanzania Mainland as well as to Tanzania Zanzibar.[38]

In my view, the directive of Article 8(2) of the Treaty in relation to EAC law goes against direct effect. This is a major difference with EU law, and perhaps the breeding ground for problems in the future as integration gains momentum.[39]

Arguably this legal requirement for domestication of the Treaty and the Protocols[40] represents an escape clause for direct effect of international agreements as commonly understood under Public International Law. However, there is no such requirement for ratification of EAC laws enacted by the Assembly in exercise of its legislative powers. EAC laws, therefore, take immediate and automatic effect in the Partner States after being signed by the Head of States of the Partner States. In other words, EAC laws have direct effect and take precedence over similar laws in the Partner States.[41]

The effect of EAC Protocols is unclear. Arguably the domestication of the Treaty by the Partner States was by extension and by necessary implication the domestication of the Protocols thereto as the Protocols form an integral part of the Treaty.[42] The ambivalence here is whether subsequent Protocols signed by the EAC would by effect of the domesticated Treaty be automatically binding on the Partner States without being ratified first. The Treaty makes the situation even more confusing when it categorically provides that each Protocol shall be subject to signature and ratification by the parties thereto.[43]

Within the EAC structure, the Assembly is the only Organ mandated to enact the laws for the Community.[44] By the term "laws", we refer to Acts of the Assembly as opposed to other legal instruments[45] originating outside the Assembly framework. Invariably the Assembly passes legislation the way National Parliaments legislate for the respective Partner States. However,

38 Section 1 (2) *Ibid.*

39 Compare in this regard also EU Chapter 4 on the conditions for direct effect of EU law. under EU law, moreover, this direct effect depends on EU law itself, not on the national laws transposing EU law.

40 According to Article 151 (4) of the Treaty, Protocols are integral parts of the Treaty.

41 They can be compared in that sense to EU Regulations.

42 Article 151 (4) of the Treaty, *Ibid.*

43 Article 151 (3), *Ibid.*

44 Article 49 (1) of the Treaty, *Ibid.*

45 Other legal instruments include for example Protocols, Memorandum of Understanding, Regulations and Rules. Regulations and Rules are subsidiary legislation made by various authorities which derive the authority to do so from the Treaty, Protocol or any Principal Act made by EALA.

according to the Treaty as earlier highlighted, the legislation to domesticate the Treaty, effectively conferred upon the Community legislation, regulations and directives, the force of law within its territory such that once passed as an Act of the Community then that law so enacted by the Assembly should also become a law domesticated, as provided under Article 8(2) (b) highlighted above.

Accordingly, under Article 8 (2) (b) any Community law enacted by the Assembly, as well as the regulations and directives of the organs of the Community have a direct effect such that there is no further ratification or re-domestication of any EAC law required subsequent to the domestication of the Treaty by the Partner States. One such example is the Customs Management Act, 2004 which was enacted by the Assembly to replace the respective customs laws of the Partner States.[46] This Community law did not undergo any ratification procedure in the Partner States.

The EACJ decisions on EAC matters do not only bind the Community and its organs but also the Partner States and their respective institutions including national courts. The EACJ has to remain steadfast in the discharge of its functions as although under the Treaty the Partner States have undertaken to maintain the rule of law this does not necessarily translate into practice. The Partner States have demonstrated the lack of it especially when the Court ruled in the case of *Anyang' Nyongo'* in 2006 temporarily halting the business of the Assembly. The Partner States immediately embarked on a process of amending the Treaty which was also another subject of a Reference by the East African Law Society.[47] The Court stood its ground and even in the subsequent judgments in the case of *Anyang' Nyong'o* and that of *the East African Law Society* it declared the process of amending the Treaty and some provisions introduced in the Treaty as infringing the same Treaty.

The Partner States have under Article 38 of the Treaty undertaken to accept and implement the judgments of the EACJ. Under Article 33 of the Treaty, decisions of the Court on interpretation and application of the Treaty have precedence over decisions of national courts on similar matters. This specific Article has implications for the national Courts as the decisions of the EACJ can therefore be used as precedents in the national courts.

---

46 Other such laws include: The East African Community standardization, Quality Assurance, Metrology and testing Act, 2006; The East African Community Competition Act, 2006; The Lake Victoria Transport Act, 2007.

47 East African Law Society and 4 Others v. Attorney General of Kenya and Others, Reference No. 3 of 2007.

Although the EACJ does not have execution mechanisms whereby it can compel the Partner State to comply with its decisions, there has not been any instance where the Partner States have declined to comply with the Court's decisions. This can be evidenced from the cases of *James Katabazi & 21 Others vs the Attorney General of the Republic of Uganda and the Secretary General of the East African Community*;[48] *Plaxeda Rugumba vs the Attorney General of the Republic of Rwanda*;[49] *Prof Anyang' Nyongo & 10 Others vs the Attorney General of the Republic of Kenya and 5 Others*.[50] In these cases the Court made declarations that the acts of the Partner States were in contravention of the Articles of the Treaty with which the Partner States complied by taking steps to correct or rectify the Act, regulations, directives, decisions or actions that had infringed the Articles of the Treaty. A good example is the case of *Anyang' Nyongo'* where the Republic of Kenya had to review its rules of elections of Kenyan representatives to the Assembly in order to comply with Article 50 of the Treaty. Moreover, in the case of *Katabazi* suspects of terrorism were released by the state security agent which had initiated court martial criminal proceedings against them notwithstanding the fact that they were civilians and during which the suspects were denied bail and legal representation.

The effect of the EACJ not having execution mechanisms of its own is that under Article 44 of the Treaty it will depend on the process of execution in the Partner States regarding matters of pecuniary nature. However, where execution regards matters where the Court has made declaratory decisions then it will rely on the goodwill of the Partner States to implement or comply with the decisions of the Court.

4.5 The Hierarchy between EAC Law and National Law

Essentially, a discussion on the hierarchy between EAC law and national law is a discussion on which of the two sets of law is superior to the other if they were to be placed on a ladder to determine the order of precedence. This goes with the examination on the usefulness of EAC law to the people living in the Partner States.

In order to complement Article 8 (2) (b), the Treaty goes on to state categorically that Community organs, institutions and laws shall take precedence

48 *Reference No. 1 of 2007*.

49 *Reference No. 8 of 2010*.

50 *Reference No. 1 of 2006*, This case is reported in EALS Law Digest, 2005–2011, pp. 173–195, published by EALS with leave of EACJ.

over similar national ones on matters pertaining to the implementation of the Treaty. Further the Partner States are under a general obligation to make the necessary legal instruments to confer precedence of Community organs, institutions and laws over similar national ones. It is this particular character of precedence of Community institutions and Community laws that makes the EAC a supranational organization as opposed to an intergovernmental one.[51] This, in essence, means that if there is a Community law on Customs Management, for example, like the East African Community Customs Management Act, 2004 this law automatically takes precedence over similar national laws on matters pertaining to the Treaty.[52] This view is supported by the essence of Section 3 of the East African Community Customs Management Act, 2004 which provides that *"The Directorate of Customs as established by the Council under the Treaty shall be responsible for the initiation of policies customs and related trade matters in the Community and coordination of such policies in the Partner States".*

The hierarchy of EAC Law over national law can also be found in Article 33 of the Treaty read together with Article 27 on Jurisdiction of the Court and Article 34 according to which national courts may refer matters on issues of interpretation of the Treaty for a preliminary ruling by the EACJ. This is one of the rare opportunities where national courts, at all levels, are given a chance to interact with an international court through litigation. When faced with a case requiring the application or the interpretation of the Treaty or any other EAC law, the national courts are required to refer the matter to the EACJ for preliminary ruling.[53] Unlike other regional and international courts there is no requirement under the EAC Treaty that a party must exhaust local remedies before coming to the EACJ. A party may file a case with the EACJ in respect of a violation or infringement of an Article without having to exhaust local remedies as long as he/she is resident in a Partner State.[54]

Under Article 33(2) of the Treaty, decisions of the EACJ on matters of interpretation and application of the Treaty have precedence over decisions of the national courts on similar matters. Article 34 of the Treaty also provides

---

51 It is interesting to note that whereas the Treaty recognizes East African Community as a supranational organization, the EAC Secretariat and the Partner States degrade it to the status of being an intergovernmental organization, and this is the meaning of EAC as posted on the EAC web site. Compare in this regard also the central importance of the supremacy of EU law for the nature and effectiveness of the EU, as described in EU Chapter 4.

52 See Dora Byamukama, "The EAC Treaty has the force of law in Uganda", *New Vision News Paper*, Kampala, Uganda, 25th November, 2015.

53 Article 34 of the Treaty, *op. cit.*

54 Section 30 (1) of the Treaty, *op. cit.*

that where a question is raised before any court or tribunal of a Partner State concerning the interpretation or application of the provisions of the Treaty or validity of the regulations, directives, decisions or actions of the Community, that Court or tribunal shall, if it considers that a ruling on the question is necessary to enable it to give judgment, request the Court to give a preliminary ruling on the question. The implementation of this provision requires the national judge before referring the issue to the EACJ to first satisfy himself that the following two conditions are fulfilled:[55]

1) A question concerning the interpretation or application of the Treaty or a question concerning the validity of the regulations, directives, decisions or actions of the Community must be raised in a case before him;
2) A ruling on the question must be necessary to enable the national judge to give judgment in the particular case.

With regards to the first condition, namely that *"a question of Treaty interpretation must be raised"*, the national court is solely entitled to appreciate whether or not a particular case raises a question of interpretation or application of the Treaty or a question concerning the validity of the regulations, directives, decisions or actions of the Community. The answer by the EACJ to the question raised by national courts in the reference for preliminary ruling is binding on the court that made the reference and on other national courts when subsequently faced with a similar issue. The Treaty is silent as to who should raise this question. Arguably, the question could be raised by any party to the case before the national judge or by the judge himself/herself.

However, it follows from the second condition that any such question does not necessarily need to be referred to the EACJ for a preliminary ruling. The question must be necessary in order for the national court to give its judgment. This of course leaves the national court very wide discretion to ascertain whether a decision on a question of Community law is necessary to enable it to give its judgment. In the exercise of this discretion, the national courts must be guided by a number of principles which are not provided for in the Treaty.[56]

---

55 See for further details on this procedure under EAC and EU law Chapter 8 and EU Chapter 8.

56 Harold R. Nsekela, "Cooperation between the East African Court of Justice and the national courts of Partner States", *A Paper presented during the United Republic of Tanzania Judges Conference*, Arusha, Tanzania, 31 August, 2009.

To fill this void the EACJ formulated and published guidelines for national judges wishing to refer questions to the EACJ for preliminary ruling.[57]

The issue of hierarchy between EAC law and national law was discussed in a reference for preliminary ruling to the EACJ made by the High Court of Uganda under Article 34 of the Treaty in the proceedings involving *The Attorney General of the Republic of Uganda and Tom Kyahurwenda*.[58] The High Court of Uganda had referred for a preliminary ruling on two questions:

(a) Whether the provisions of Articles 6, 7, 8 and 123 read together with Articles 27 and 33 of the Treaty are justiciable in the national courts of Partner States; and
(b) Whether the provisions of Articles 6, 7, 8 and 123 read together with Articles 27 and 33 of the Treaty are self-executing and confer sufficient legal authority on the national courts of the Partner States to entertain matters relating to Treaty violations and to award compensation and/or damages as against a Partner State.

At paragraphs 50 and 51 of its ruling the Court stated as follows:

50. The Court holds that by resorting to the use of the word ***"shall"*** *in Article 34 and having regard to the raison d'etre of the preliminary ruling procedure expounded above, it was the intent and purpose of the framers of the Treaty to grant this Court the exclusive jurisdiction to entertain matters concerning interpretation of the Treaty and annulment of Community Acts.*

51. The Court deems it important to distinguish the application of the Treaty from interpretation of the same as found in Article 34. Whereas, as we held above, interpretation is the preserve of this Court, the same is not necessarily the case for the application of the Treaty by the national courts to cases before them. It would defeat the purpose of preliminary reference mechanism if the Court's interpretation of Article 34 of the Treaty extended to "application of treaty provisions". The purpose for the mechanism is for the national courts to seek

---

57 *The EACJ-Court Users Guide*, page 35 (Guidelines on a Reference for Preliminary Ruling).

58 Case Stated No. 1 of 2014. This Preliminary Reference arose out of a Miscellaneous Application before the High Court of the Republic of Uganda ("the High Court") arising from Civil Suit No. 298 of 2012 between Tom Kyahurwenda and The Attorney General of Uganda. The High Court stayed the proceedings pending the preliminary ruling of the East African Court of Justice ("the Court").

interpretation of the Treaty provisions in order that they may then apply them to a case at hand. Hence, to interpret Article 34 as requiring "application of the Treaty provision" to be excluded from the purview of national courts would ***"lead to a result which is manifestly absurd or unreasonable".*** *In this regard, Article 32 (b) of the Vienna Convention on the Law of Treaties cited above acknowledges an absurdity exception to the literal interpretation of any Treaty.*

52. *The national courts seek interpretation from this Court in order to be empowered to apply the Treaty provisions to the facts of the case(s) before them.*

In conclusion the Court held that:

(*a*) *Article 34 of the Treaty for the Establishment of the East African Community grants this Court exclusive jurisdiction to interpret the Treaty and to invalidate Community Acts.*
(*b*) *National courts and tribunals are entitled to entertain matters involving the violation of the Treaty and the application of the provisions of the Treaty within the context of Articles 33 and 34.*
(*c*) *Decisions of this Court in the interpretation of the Treaty take precedence over decisions of the national courts and tribunals on similar matters.*
(*d*) *Articles 6, 7 and 8 of the Treaty are justiciable before the national courts and tribunals of the Partner States.*
(*e*) *While they remain inoperative, Paragraphs 2, 3 and 4 of Article 123 of the Treaty are not justiciable both before this Court and before the national courts and tribunals.*

In *East African Law Society vs the Secretary General of the East African Community, Reference No. 1 of 2011* the Court held that:

> As Partner States, by virtue of their being the main users of the Common Market Protocol on a daily basis, it would be absurd and impractical if their national courts had no jurisdiction over disputes arising out of implementation if it did not provide for right of individuals to invoke it before national courts.

From the above explanation and cases, it appears that national courts can entertain matters related to Community law in respect of application of the Treaty but when it comes to interpretation of the Treaty it is the sole jurisdiction of the EACJ. With regard to Article 33(2) which provides that the decisions of the Court on the interpretation and application of the Treaty shall have precedence over decisions of national courts on a similar matter, the court opined at paragraph 60 that reading the Article together with Articles 27 and 34 it would be that the framers of the Treaty envisaged a situation where it is possible to contract out of the general norm of the EACJ having sole jurisdiction as to interpretation; and to give instead, concurrent jurisdiction of interpretation on a given subject matter to both the Court and the national courts. In such case the interpretation of the EACJ takes precedence.

It also appears that the Court has concurrent jurisdiction with the national courts. This matter was discussed in two cases where the Court was of the view that the Treaty needs to be amended to rectify this. In the case of *East African Law Society and 4 Others vs the Attorney General of Kenya and 3 Others*[59] the Court observed the need to amend the new proviso that was introduced in Article 27(1) on Jurisdiction of the Court that states "*Provided that the Court's jurisdiction to interpret under this paragraph shall not include the application of any such interpretation to jurisdiction conferred by the Treaty on organs of Partner State*". This proviso should also be read together with Article 30(3) that provides "*The Court shall have no jurisdiction under this Article where an Act, regulation, directive, decision or action has been reserved under this Treaty to an institution of a Partner State*". It should also be read together with 33(1) "*Except where jurisdiction is conferred on the Court by this Treaty, disputes to which the Community is a party shall not on that ground alone, be excluded from the jurisdiction of the national court of the Partner States*". The Court has reiterated in several decisions as those mentioned hereinabove expressed the need to amend the Treaty in order to clear the confusion.

4.6 The Relationship between EAC Law and Other Regional and International Law

As indicated earlier in this work, the EAC Partner States have dualist as opposed to monist systems regarding the relationship between their respective national law and international or regional law. This means that international law has to be national law as well otherwise it will not be considered as law in dualist systems and judges cannot apply it nor can citizens rely on it.

59 *Reference No. 3 of 2007.*

As the EAC is not, as of yet, considered to be a state, any international or other regional laws are of no effect to the EAC as a Community but only bind the individual Partner States that subscribe to that particular international law. In that case the usual dualist state procedure has to be followed for such international or regional law to be applied in a particular Partner State where EAC law has direct effect.

Arguably, the only international law that the Treaty recognizes and adopts within the EAC legal framework is the African Charter on Human and Peoples Rights which is explicitly mentioned in Article 6 of the Treaty:

> *The fundamental principles that shall govern the achievement of the objectives of the Community by the Partner States shall include:*
> *a)* . . .;
> *(b)* . . .;
> *(c)* . . .;
> *(d)* *good governance including adherence to the principles of democracy, the rule of law, accountability, transparency, social justice, equal opportunities, gender equality, as well as the recognition, promotion and protection of human and peoples rights in accordance with the provisions of the African Charter on Human and Peoples' Rights.*[60]

While, the EACJ is not bound by decisions of other regional and national courts, such decisions are considered to be of persuasive authority. The EACJ has drawn a lot of inspiration from the revolutionary case law of the Court of Justice of the European Union (CJEU) which can be evidenced in many of its judgments where it has cited some of the cases of the CJEU. This shows that the EACJ recognizes the potential advantages of the European notions of autonomy and primacy of Community law.[61] Other regional Courts such as the SADC Tribunal and the COMESA Court of Justice have also gained inspiration from the decisions of the EACJ when handling cases before them and vice versa.

Furthermore, in playing its role of interpretation of the EAC Treaty the Court has largely drawn inspiration from the Vienna Convention on of the Law of Treaties and from other sources of persuasive value.

60 Article 6 of the Treaty, *op. cit.*

61 See further on these concepts EU Chapter 4.

4.7 Conclusion

The discussion in this chapter has examined the sources of EAC law, its scope and its supranational character. It has been pointed out that the supranational character of EAC law as envisaged under the Treaty to a large extent puts the Partner States in a very difficult situation for they are not wholly ready to cede a substantive part of their sovereignty. This creates a dichotomy in that Partner States still wish to maintain their full sovereignty whereas their commitments under the Treaty demand them to cede part of their sovereignty to a the Community. This is a paradoxical situation which Partner States find themselves in whenever they are called upon to propose Bills for legislation by the Assembly. As a result, Partner States prefer Protocols to Acts of the Assembly, the position that is vehemently opposed by the members of the Assembly who resort to tabling Private Members' Bills.

CHAPTER 4A

The Scope, Nature and Effect of EU Law

Armin Cuyvers

4.1 Introduction: 'the very foundations of EU law'[1]

This chapter deals with some of the most foundational doctrines of EU law, including supremacy and direct effect.[2] These doctrines have been vital for the success of the EU, also in the early days of European integration. It can safely be said that without these doctrines the EU would never have been as successful and effective as it has been. Considering their vital role in EU integration, it may even be said that direct effect and supremacy form essential elements for any regional system that truly wants to be effective and deliver concrete benefits to its citizens.[3] Both doctrines, therefore, are of vital interest to the EAC as well.

---

1 This chapter gratefully builds on the LEAC research report by T. Ottervanger and A. Cuyvers, 'The functioning of the East African Community: Common market, Court of Justice and fundamental rights, a comparative perspective with the European Union' (Europa Instituut Leiden, 2013), pp. 1–206, and the excellent master Thesis of Merel Valk, written in 2015 under supervision of the LEAC, entitled 'The Rule of the European Court of Justice and the East African Court of Justice: Comparing Potential Judicial Strategies for Early Stage Integration'. (on file with the author).

2 For further reading on these issues see inter alia See for one among several classics B. de Witte, 'Direct Effect, Supremacy, and the Nature of the Legal Order', in: P. Craig and G. De Búrca (eds), *The Evolution of EU Law* (OUP 1999), 209 et seq, or the updated version in P. Craig and G. De Búrca (eds), *The Evolution of EU Law* (2nd ed. OUP 2011), 324, as well as the different contributions in M.P. Maduro and L. Azoulai (eds) *The Past and Future of* EU *Law: The Classics of EU law Revisited on the 50th Anniversary of the Rome Treaty* (Hart Publishing 2010), especially see P. Pescatore, 'Van Gend en Loos, 3 February 1963—A View from Within', 1, B. de Witte, 'The Continuous Significance of *Van Gend en Loos*', 9, F.C. Mayer, '*Van Gend en Loos*: The Foundation of a Community of Law', 16, and of course D. Halberstam, 'Pluralism in *Marbury* and *Van Gend*', 26, as well as N. Fennely, 'The European Court of Justice and the Doctrine of Supremacy: *Van Gend en Loos; Costa v. ENEL; Simmenthal*', 39, and I. Pernice, '*Costa v. ENEL and Simmenthal*: Primacy of European Law', 47.

3 C.F. Nyman-Metcalf, Papageorgiou, *Regional Integration and Courts of Justice*. 1st ed. (Insertia, 2005), p. 6. Mattli, *The Logic of Regional Integration: Europe and Beyond*. 1st ed. (Cambridge University Press, 1999, p. 74. Also: De Burca, Scott. *Constitutional Change in the EU. From Uniformity to Flexibility?*. 1st ed. (Hart Publishing, 2000), p. 63.

© ARMIN CUYVERS, 2017 | DOI 10.1163/9789004322073_009
This is an open access chapter distributed under the terms of the CC-BY-NC License.

Before we look closer at the legal *effect* of EU law, however, it is necessary to first look at the *scope* of EU law, that is the question when and where EU law actually applies. For even EU law can only have direct effect and supremacy in those cases where it applies in the first place. The question of scope, moreover, is equally relevant for the EAC as the precise scope of EAC law seemingly has not yet been settled yet, but will equally be of crucial importance for the success of regional integration in East Africa.

4.2 The Scope of EU Law

When one talks about 'the scope' of EU law, one basically asks which cases are governed by EU law. When two Portuguese companies conclude a contract for IT services in Portugal, for example, does EU law apply? And what if an American undertaking imports products into Ireland, or participates in an American cartel that affects the EU market? Or is EU law applicable when a Spanish region directly awards a multi-million contract to a Spanish company?

Just as EU law determines the limits of EU competences, the CJEU also held that EU law determines its own scope.[4] Whether a certain issue falls under EU law, therefore, is a question of EU law, not of national law. Moreover, the mere fact that a certain issues *also* falls under national law, does not mean it does not fall under EU law, as both can apply at the same time. The exclusive jurisdiction of the CJEU over the scope of EU law is also necessary to ensure the unity of EU law and to enable the CJEU to remain the ultimate arbiter of EU law. After all, if other courts could determine the scope of EU law, they could prevent the Court of Justice from safeguarding the correct interpretation and application of EU norms in certain cases, simply by declaring them outside the scope of EU law. Reducing the scope of EU law would then become an escape route for Member States or national courts to escape or reduce the direct effect and supremacy of EU law. Control over the scope of EU law, consequently, should also be seen as an important precondition for supremacy and direct effect, just like the ultimate jurisdiction over the correct interpretation and application of EU law.[5]

4 Case C-617/10 *Akerberg Fransson*, ECLI:EU:C:2013:105.

5 See already on this point Case C-459/03 *Commission v Ireland* [2006] ECR I-4635, as well as the much discussed CJEU Opinion 2/13 on the draft agreement providing for the accession of the European Union to the Convention for the Protection of Human Rights and Fundamental Freedoms ECLI:EU:C:2014:2454.

4.2.1 *EU Actions and the Scope of EU Law*

Logically, all actions by EU institutions and bodies fall under the scope of EU law. All EU legislation and all decisions from EU institutions and bodies, therefore, have to comply with EU law, including all fundamental rights guaranteed within the scope of EU law.[6] More complicated is the question when actions by Member States fall under the scope of EU law.[7]

4.2.2 *Member State Actions and the Scope of EU Law*

Essentially, there are three ways in which Member State actions fall under the scope EU law. Firstly, any Member State action falls under the scope of EU law when the Member State is *implements or applies* EU measures.[8] Any national legislation implementing a directive, for example, falls under the scope of EU law.[9] Consequently, if an individual challenges a national act that implements or applies an EU rule, that decision falls under the scope of EU law. So for example, where two companies start legal proceedings against each other, and one company relies on a national law that implements an EU directive, this dispute between two private parties will fall under the scope of EU law.[10]

Secondly, any Member State action that *derogates* from EU rules or rights also falls under the scope of EU law.[11] This category *inter alia* includes all cases where a Member State action restricts free movement. In *Schmidberger*, for example, Austria allowed a demonstration that blocked the Brenner Pas, one

6 See for a highly principled position of the CJEU on this point the Kadi-saga: Joined cases C-402/05 P & C-415/05 P *Kadi I* [2008] ECR I-6351, and Case C-584/10 P *Commission v. Kadi* (Kadi II). or further analysis of these cases see M. Avbelj, F. Fontanelli and G. Martinico (eds), *Kadi on Trial* (Routledge, 2014), as well as A. Cuyvers, '"Give me one good reason": The unified standard of review for sanctions after Kadi II', 51(6) *Common Market Law Review* (2014), 1759, and A. Cuyvers, 'The Kadi II judgment of the General Court: the ECJ's predicament and the consequences for Member States'. *European Constitutional Law Review*, 7, 481.

7 See for a discussion in the context of the Charter K. Lenaerts, 'Exploring the Limits of the EU Charter of Fundamental Rights' (2012) 8 EUConst, 375.

8 See for example already case 5/88 *Wachauf* [1989] ECR 2609, paras 17–19, or Case 249/86 *Commission v. Germany* [1989], ECR 1263, or Case C-578/08 *Chakroun* [2010] ECR I-1839.

9 For recent examples see amongst many others Case C-399/11 *Melloni* ECLI:EU:C:2013:107, Case C-131/12 *Google v. Spain* ECLI:EU:C:2014:317 or Case C-300/11 *ZZ* ECLI:EUC:2013:363.

10 For a further delineation of what exactly qualified as 'implementing EU law', see inter alia Case C-206/13 *Cruciano Siragusa* ECLI:EU:C:2014:126, par. 25, Case C-40/11 *lida* ECLI:EU:C:2012:691, case C-87/12 *Ymeraga* ECLI:EU:C:2013:291, par. 41, and Case C-198/13 *Julian Hernandez* ECLI:EU:C:2014:2055, par. 34.

11 See for example Case C-260/89 *ERT* [1991] ECR I-2925. Similarly see for example Case C-470/03 *AGM-COS.MET* [2007] ECR I-2749 or Case C-390/12 *Pfleger* EU:C:2014:281.

of the main transport routes to southern Europe. The Court held that allowing this demonstration restricted the free movement of goods enjoyed by a transport company. Even though the Court found the restriction justified in the end, the mere fact that Austria had restricted free movement was enough to bring the dispute under the scope of EU law.[12] As many national laws will in some way affect the free movement of goods, services, establishment, persons or capital, this second ground significantly expands the scope of EU law.

In addition to the two grounds set out above, there also is a third, rather vague ground for bringing a case under the scope of EU law. The CJEU sometimes finds that a case does not involve an implementation or a derogation of EU law, but nevertheless falls 'within the scope of EU law' in a *generic sense* because there is a sufficient link between the national act and EU law. The case of *Fransson*, for example, concerned Swedish tax penalties and a criminal prosecution that were not directly based on EU law, nor did they derogate from EU law. Nevertheless the CJEU found these penalties came under the scope of EU law because they were *also* designed to protect the collection of VAT, and therefore the financial interest of the EU.[13] This indirect and partial link was sufficient to bring the case under the scope of EU law in the generic sense. In *Kücükdeveci*, the CJEU brought a case under the scope of EU law primarily because the *subject matter* of the case was covered by a directive, even though the directive did not apply itself.[14]

Some further guidance on this third category of scope was given more recently in *Hernandez*, where the CJEU held that scope 'presupposes a degree of connection between the measure of EU law and the national measure at issue which goes beyond the matters covered being closely related or one of those matters having an indirect impact on the other.'[15] Despite this clarification, however, this ground for scope remains relatively opaque and unpredictable. These same qualities, of course, may also be part of the appeal to the CJEU, as it sometimes may be in need of a ground to extend the scope of EU law beyond implementation or derogation.[16]

---

12 Case C-112/00 *Schmidberger* [2003] ECR I-5659.

13 Case C-617/10 *Fransson* ECLI:EU:C:2012:340, paras. 24–28.

14 Case C-555/07 *Seda Kücükdeveci v Swedex GmbH & Co. KG*, [2010] ECR I-365.

15 Case C-198/13 *Julian Hernandez* ECLI:EU:C:2014:2055, par. 34.The CJEU thereby referred to its earlier case law in Case 149/77 *Defrenne* EU:C:1978:130, paras. 29 to 32, Case C-299/95 *Kremzow* EU:C:1997:254, paras. 16 and 17, Case C-144/04 *Mangold* EU:C:2005:709, par. 75, and *Siragusa* EU:C:2014:126, paragraph 24.

16 For the more specific rules on the scope of EU law in the field of competition law, also see companion chapter 14. Essentially the scope of EU competition law is linked to the effect of the anti-competitive behavior on the EU market, as held in Joined cases C-89/85,

4.3 Direct Effect of EU Law

Direct effect is one of the hallmarks of the EU legal order. *Van Gend en Loos*, the case which established direct effect and the autonomy of the EU legal order has a near mythical status as the alpha and omega of the EU legal order.[17] The essence of direct effect is as simple as it is fundamental. Direct effect means that individuals and companies can rely on EU law before all national courts and public bodies, just as they can on national law. EU law, therefore, is not some foreign or international law that must first be imported into the national legal order to have legal effect.[18] Rather, direct effect means that EU *law is part of national law*.

This section first outlines the establishment of the direct effect of Treaty provisions in *Van Gend en Loos*, the criteria that a Treaty provision has to meet to have direct effect, and the main arguments given by the CJEU to justify direct effect of EU law. Subsequently, this section discusses the direct effect of secondary EU law. This discussion will also touch on the main complexities surrounding direct effect, including the direct effect of general principles and directives as well as the difference between vertical and horizontal direct effect.

4.3.1 Van Gend en Loos: *Establishing Direct Effect of Treaty Provisions*

Van Gend en Loos illustrates how small cases can make good law. The judgment concerned the company of Van Gend en Loos that wanted to import the rather unspectacular chemical ureaformaldehyde into the Netherlands from Germany. The Netherlands wanted to impose an import duty of 8%, which was higher than the import tariff that applied when the Netherlands joined

---

C-104/85, C-114/85, C-116/85, C-117/85, C-125/85, C-126/85, C-127/85, C-128/85 and C-129/85 *Woodpulp I* ECLI:EU:C:1993:120.

17 Case C-26/62 *Van Gend en Loos v Netherlands Inland Revenue Administration*, EU:C:1963:1. Direct effect and supremacy have inter alia been referred to as the 'grounding principles' in: K. Lenaerts and Gutierrez-Fons, The Constitutional Allocation of Powers and General Principles of EU law' (2010) *Common Market Law Review*, 1631, or the 'twin pillars' in: S. Prechal, 'Does Direct Effect Still Matter?' (2000) *Common Market Law Review*, 1047. The Court referred to them 'essential characteristics' in Opinion 1/19 *Draft Agreement relating to the creation of the European Economic Area* [1991] ECR I-6979, para. 21.

18 At least as would be required in dualist systems. In pure monist systems even public international law can have direct effect, albeit based on the monist constitution. For a very far reaching position on this point see Cour de Cassation (Belgium), 27 May 1971, S.A. *Fromagerie franco-suisse 'Le Ski'* (1971) RTD eur 495.

the EEC. Van Gend en Loos argued that this increase violated what was then Article 12 of the EEC Treaty, which read:

> Member States shall refrain from introducing between themselves any new customs duties on imports or exports or any charges having equivalent effect, and from increasing those which they already apply in their trade with each other.[19]

In its defense, the Dutch government argued that Article 12 EEC was an international obligation only directed at the state, and that a private company like Van Gend en Loos could not rely on it. The CJEU disagreed, and held that Treaty provisions could have direct effect if they met three cumulative conditions:

i. The measure must be sufficiently clear and precise;
ii. It must be unconditional, and;
iii. It must leave no legislative discretion to the Member State.

Jointly, these criteria essentially require that, to be directly effective, a rule of EU law actually gives a right to an individual, and that this right can be sufficiently determined on the basis of the Treaty provision alone, without requiring further legislative action by the Member State. For example, imagine an EU rule saying that all Member States must strive to provide reasonable studying grants to all students. This norm is vague and requires implementation by Member States to determine the actual right. How much would the grant be per month, for example, and who precisely would be entitled to it? In contrast, an EU rule holding that all people registered at a university have a right to a four year state sponsored grant of €250 per month, would be sufficiently clear and precise, as one can determine the core elements of an unconditional right from the provision itself. In practice, the CJEU is rather flexible in finding direct effect. It is enough if the core elements or the minimal content of a right can be determined.[20]

---

19 At this stage of European integration, not yet all import tariffs had been abolished. Rather, during the transitional stage, only increases were prohibited as gradually all tariffs were reduced to zero.

20 Case 43/75 *Defrenne* [1976] ECR 455. See for an example of which key elements must be sufficiently clear for a right to exist also Case C-479/93 *Francovich* [1995] ECR I-3843. By now, moreover, the CJEU has been able to rule on the direct effect of all Treaty provisions. When one is in doubt, therefore, if a certain Treaty provision fulfills the requirements for direct effect, this can simply be checked via the case law of the Court of Justice.

Applying these criteria in In *Van Gend en Loos*, the CJEU held that the prohibition to increase customs duties in Article 12 EEC was sufficiently clear, precise and unconditional. As a clear prohibition, furthermore, it required no further implementation.[21] Consequently, Article 12 EEC had direct effect, and the company of Van Gend en Loos could directly rely on it to challenge the Dutch increase in import tariffs.

4.3.2 *Justifying Direct Effect of EU Law*

By holding that EU Treaty provisions could apply directly, the CJEU took a monumental step towards differentiating the EU legal order from 'normal' public international law and ensuring that EU law would become a living reality rather than just another legal norm that applied only between states. Most importantly, the CJEU determined that individuals and companies derived certain rights directly from EU law and that they could directly enforce these rights at the national level.

With this single judgment, the CJEU transformed millions of individuals and companies into EU law policemen that could make sure Member States respected their rights under EU law. This greatly increased the enforcement of EU law. After all, it is extremely unlikely that the Commission would have ever started an infringement proceeding against the Netherlands over something as minor as increasing the tariffs for ureaformaldehyde to 8%. For a transport company like Van Gend en Loos, however, such an increase was important enough to undertake legal action. The principle of direct effect, therefore, linked the enforcement of EU law to the self-interest of individuals and companies, self-interest being one of the more reliable incentives that legal systems can rely on. For no matter how technical or 'minor' an EU rule may seem, there is likely a company or individual deeply affected by it.

To support its monumental ruling, the CJEU essentially relied on four, interconnected arguments derived from the 'spirit, general scheme and the wording' of the Treaty.[22]

Firstly, the CJEU pointed out that the EEC Treaty 'is *more* than an agreement creating mutual obligations between the Member States' alone, as it must have been intended to include individuals as well. Here the CJEU *inter alia* refers to the aim of establishing a common market. The functioning of such a market necessarily concerns individuals as 'stakeholders'. One simply cannot have

21 *Van Gend en Loos*, therefore, also forms a good authority for the conclusion that prohibitions will usually be sufficiently clear, precise and unconditional to have direct effect.

22 Note that the wording only comes last, further underscoring the fundamental as well as the creative exercise in *Van Gend en Loos*.

a market without involving the market actors, so the logic goes.[23] This logic is then further supported by the Preamble of the EEC which 'refers not only to government but also peoples'. Both the text and the objective of the EEC Treaty, therefore, imply that it was intended to be more than just another international treaty only creating rights and obligations between states. Rather, the EEC Treaty was intended to be something more, a legal instrument that unlike traditional international law also included individuals as its objects and subjects.

This finding that the EEC Treaty must be more than an ordinary Treaty connected to the CJEU's second and even more fundamental argument on the nature and autonomy of the EEC legal order:

> ...the Community constitutes a new legal order of international law for the benefit of which states have limited their sovereign rights, albeit within limited fields, and the subject of which comprise not only Member States but also their nationals.[24]

The EEC Treaty, therefore, created a whole new legal order, and this legal order is *autonomous* from the Member States that created it.[25] Both the Member States and individuals are members of this new autonomous legal order, and both can therefore rely on it directly. The autonomy of the EU legal order, and the fact that Member States have actually limited their sovereign rights to create it, also explains why it is EU law itself that can determine its own direct effect.

Thirdly, the CJEU supports these two teleological arguments with a more textual and straightforward argument: the existence of the preliminary reference procedure.[26] The CJEU points out that the preliminary reference procedure allows national courts to ask questions to the CJEU on the correct interpretation and application of EEC law. This possibility implies, according to the CJEU, that these national courts were presumed to apply EEC law directly. Why, after

---

23 F. Mayer "*Van Gend en Loos:* The Foundation of a Community of Law" in Maduro, Azoulai, *The Past and Future of EU law.* 2nd ed. (Hart Publishing, 2010), p. 20.

24 *Van Gend en Loos*, EU:C:1963:1.

25 Cf. also K. Lenaerts, "The Court of Justice as the Guarantor of the Rule of Law Within the European Union" in: G. De Baere and J. Wouters, *The Contribution of International and Supranational Courts to the Rule of Law"*, 1st ed. (Edward Elgar Publishing Limited, 2015), 243.

26 Article 177 EEC, now Article 267 TFEU. See for a more detailed discussion of this remedy EU Chapter 8.

all, would national courts ask preliminary questions on EEC law to the CJEU if these courts were not even allowed to apply EEC law in the first place? The indirect remedy of the preliminary reference, therefore, implies the direct effect of EU law.

Fourth, and most fundamentally, however, the CJEU seems to base direct effect on *effectiveness*. If the Member States seriously wanted the EEC to achieve its objectives, they must have accepted the direct effect of EEC law, for without direct effect the EEC could not work.[27] Not only is the participation of individuals necessary to achieve objectives such as the internal market, it is also necessary to ensure the effective enforcement and application of EU law. In the words of the CJEU:

> The vigilance of individuals concerned to protect their rights amounts to an effective supervision in addition to the supervision entrusted by Articles 169 and 170 to the diligence of the Commission and of the Member States.[28]

This logic of effectiveness seems to be the most fundamental reason underlying direct effect, as well as many other key principles of EU law.[29] If the ambitions of the EU are to be taken seriously, the EU legal order must be conceived as something that goes far beyond an ordinary international treaty. Innovations such as direct effect, therefore, are a necessary price to pay for effective regional integration, and as Member States surely must have wanted to create an effective regional organization, the CJEU also assumes they intended to pay this price. Consequently, even though it may not have been made explicit in the EEC Treaties, the CJEU found that the potential direct effect of Treaty provisions was inherent in EEC law.[30]

---

27 For an explicit reference to the *effet utile* of EU law also see Case C-9/70 *Franz Grad v Finanzamt Traunstein* ECLI:EU:C:1970:78.

28 *Van Gend en Loos,* EU:C:1963:1.
Referenced to as a "prophetic" statement, since the preliminary reference procedure seems to have "... effectively become the infringement procedure for the European citizen". See: "*Van Gend en Loos,* 3 February 1963—A View from Within" in: Maduro, Azoulai, *The Past and Future of EU law.* 2nd ed. (Hart Publishing, 2010), p. 7.

29 Also see EU chapter 6 on the general principles of EU law.

30 Note that even unwritten General Principles of EU law, which are also pat of EU primary law, can also have direct effect if they are sufficiently clear, precise and unconditional. Precisely because of their generality, many principles of EU law may struggle to meet this criterion, but for example the general principle prohibiting discrimination on the basis of age has been found to be directly effective. See Case C-144/04 *Mangold* [2005]

Treaty provisions, moreover, usually have both vertical and horizontal direct effect. Vertical direct effect refers to situations where parties rely on EU law against the state, or any entity wielding public authority.[31] Horizontal direct effect concerns situations where none of the parties wield any public authority, for example in a dispute between two private companies. Even in such purely horizontal situations, where no party wields any public authority, the CJEU has found that most Treaty provisions apply directly and can therefore be relied upon against each other. For example, the Belgian stewardess Defrenne could rely directly on then Article 119 EEC, at least to the extent that it required equal pay for equal work for men and women.[32] Equally, Mr. Angonese could rely on the freedom of workers against a private bank in Italy, which would only hire staff with a language certificate awarded in Bolzano.[33] For some Treaty provisions, including those on the free movement of goods and services, however, the CJEU seemingly has not yet fully made up its mind.[34]

4.3.3 *Direct Effect of other EU Norms*

Van Gend en Loos only established the direct effect of Treaty provisions. The question therefore remained if secondary EU law could also have direct effect, and if so under what conditions.[35] By now the CJEU has also ruled on the direct effect of all forms of secondary legislation enumerated in Article 288 TFEU, being regulations, directives, decisions, recommendations and opinions. In

---

ECR I-9981 and Case C-555/07 *Kücükdeveci* ECLI:EU:C:2010:21. The possible direct effect of the Charter of Fundamental rights of the EU remains a more contested issue, as the CJEU has so far avoided ruling on it. At the same time, any rights embodied in the Charter may also form General Principles of EU law as such, and in that capacity enjoy direct effect if they meet all the criteria. On the direct effect of the Charter see Case C-282/10 *Dominguez*, ECLI:EU:C:2012:33, and especially the Opinion of AG Trstenjak in this case, as well as Case C-176/12 *AMS* ECLI:EU:C:2014:2. For a further discussion on the nature of EU General Principles as such see EU chapter 6.

31 See for examples Case 152/84 *Marshall I* [1986] ECR 723, Case 71/76 *Thieffry* [1977] ECR 765, Case C-309/99 *Wouters* [2002] ECR I-1577, par. 120, Case 13/76 *Dona* [1976] ECR 1333, or Case 36/74 *Walrave and Koch* [1974] ECR 1405.

32 Case 43/75 *Defrenne* ECLI:EU:C:1976:56.

33 Case C-281/98 *Angonese* [2000] ECR I-4139.

34 See Case C-171/11 *Fra.bo* ECLI:EU:C:2012:453, as well as Case C-341/05, *Laval un Partneri* ECLI:EU:C:2007:809.

35 For a more elaborate overview of the different regimes and requirements for direct effect, in a comparative perspective to the US, see K. Lenaerts 'Constitutionalism and the Many Faces of Federalism' 4 *American Journal of Comparative Law* (1990), 208, 212. et seq.

addition, the CJEU has clarified that international agreements concluded by the EU law can also have direct effect.

4.3.3.1 Direct Effect of Regulations

The potential direct effect of directives is inherent in their very nature. As Article 288 TFEU provides, a regulation 'shall be binding in its entirety and *directly applicable* in all Member States.'[36] Regulations, therefore, do not require any support of or conversion into national law to directly apply in the national legal orders of the Member States. At the same time, this does not mean that all parts of all regulations apply directly. To be directly effective, a provision in a directive must also be unconditional, sufficiently clear and precise, and require no further implementation.[37] For if a provision in a regulation does not contain a sufficiently specific right, there simply is nothing that can be applied directly.

4.3.3.2 Direct Effect of Directives

The possible direct effect of directives is one of the more complex and potentially confusing parts of EU law.[38] The starting point, however, is very clear. Directives normally do not have direct effect. As Article 288 TFEU states, directives are addressed to Member States, not to individuals. If all goes well, Member States implement directives in their own legal order within the prescribed period. Individuals can then rely on the national law implementing the directive, and do not need to rely on the directive itself. If directives are implemented timely and correctly, therefore, they never acquire direct effect.

Problems arise, however, where Member States fail to implement a directive or implement a directive incorrectly. In such cases, individuals are unable to rely on a national implementing law to enforce any rights that the directive may have given them. To fill this gap, and make sure Member States do not get away with not implementing directives, the CJEU has found that directives can have vertical direct effect where they have not been correctly implemented and the implementation period is over. Compared to Treaty provisions and

---

36 The existence of regulations, therefore, also provides a possible counterargument to the reliance of the CJEU on the preliminary reference procedure as proof of the fact that the EEC Treaty should have direct effect. The existence of directly effective regulations could have been sufficient explanation for the inclusion of the preliminary reference procedure in the EEC Treaty.

37 See for example C-403/98 *Azienda Agricola Monte Arcosu v Regione Autonoma della Sardegna* ECLI:EU:C:2001:6, paras 28–29.

38 For a more general analysis see S. Prechal, *Directives in EC law* (2nd edn., OUP 2005).

regulations, therefore, directives must meet some additional requirements in order to have direct effect. The cumulative requirements for a provision in a directive to have direct effect are as follows:

i. The provision must be sufficiently clear and precise;
ii. It must be unconditional, and;
iii. It must leave no legislative discretion to the Member State.
iv. In addition, the implementation period must have passed, and;
v. The directive has not been implemented or has not been implemented correctly.[39]

Directives, therefore, cannot have direct effect before the implementation period has expired.[40] Moreover, the CJEU has consistently ruled that directives can only have so-called *vertical* direct effect. This means that the direct effect of directives can only be relied upon against the state or emanations of the state. Directives can never have *horizontal* direct effect, which means they cannot be relied upon against other individuals.[41] In a conflict between two individuals, for example two private companies litigating over a commercial contract, neither party can therefore directly rely on any EU directives, even if these directives grant them a clear, precise and unconditional right.

The lack of horizontal direct effect of directives creates a certain gap in the legal protection of individuals and the effectiveness of EU law. Where Member States for example fail to implement a directive on consumer protection, consumers cannot invoke their rights under the directive against private companies violating these rights.[42] The CJEU has, therefore, developed several other doctrines to at least reduce the impact this gap has and to ensure the

39 See for example Case C-41–74 *Van Duyn* ECLI:EU:C:1974:133, paras. 4–7, Case C-148/78 *Criminal proceedings against Tullio Ratti* ECLI:EU:C:1979:110, para. 46. Also note that there is a general obligation on National Courts to interpret national law in conformity with EU law. Even if a directive has not (yet) been implemented by a Member State, therefore, the national court is obliged to interpret national law in line with the directive. Only where this would require an interpretation *contra legem* is a national court allowed to choose an interpretation of EU law that conflicts with a directive. This obligation, moreover, applies to all EU norms, even those that are not directly effective. See Case C-397–403/01 *Pfeiffer* [2004] ECR I-8835.

40 Even before the implementation deadline has expired, however, Member States are obligated to refrain from acting in ways that might nullify the effect of the directive, see Case C-129/96 *Inter-Environment Wallonie* ECLI:EU:C:1997:628, par. 50.

41 Case C-152/84 *Marshall* EU:C:1986:84, par. 48, Case C-91/92 *Faccini Dori* [1994] ECR I-3325.

42 See for example Cases 189 & 190/94 *Dillenkofer v Germany*, ECLI:EU:C:1996:375.

effectiveness of EU law as much as possible. To begin with, the CJEU employs a very wide conception of the State, and therefore of vertical situations. Bodies that wield some form of public authority will rather quickly qualify as a part of the State, and hence have to accept that directives may be relied upon against them directly.[43] In addition, the CJEU allows for so called *triangular* direct effect and, exceptionally, for *indirect* horizontal direct effect.[44] Even where no direct effect can be created, moreover, the duty of conform interpretation requires that national courts try and interpret national law in conformity with EU law, including directives, even where these do not have direct effect.[45] Although national courts are never obligated to interpret national law *contra legem*, they must try to find a way to read any rights granted by a directive into national law. Lastly, the doctrine of Member State liability allows individuals to sue the Member State for any damages they have suffered due to the failure to (correctly) implement the directive.[46] Ultimately, however, the fact remains that directives in principle do not have direct effect, and never have real horizontal direct effect.

4.3.3.3 Direct Effect of Decisions, Opinions and Recommendations

Decisions can have direct effect.[47] According to the CJEU, the mere fact that the Treaty does not explicitly mention the direct effect of decisions, as it does for regulations, does not mean that decisions lack the capacity for direct effect.[48] The addressee of a decision can, therefore, directly rely on the decision if it is sufficiently clear and precise, unconditional, and leaves no discretion to Member States with regards to its implementation.[49]

Opinions and recommendations, on the other hand, lack binding legal force altogether and hence cannot have direct effect.[50]

---

43 See for example Case C-188/89 *Forster* [1990] ECR I-3313 or Case C-282/10 *Dominguez*, ECLI:EU:C:2012:33.

44 See Case C-201/02 *Wells* [2004] ECR I-723, and Case C-194/94 *CIA Security* [1996] ECR I-220.

45 This duty is part of the duty of sincere cooperation. Case 14/83 *Von Colson & Kamann* ECLI:EU:C:1984:153 and Case C-106/89 *Marleasing*. The duty of conform interpretation, moreover, does apply horizontally.

46 See Cases C-6/90 and 9/90 *Francovich* [1991] ECR I-5357, and Cases C-46 and 48/93 *Brasserie du Pêcheur* [1996] ECR I-1029. For these principles also further see EU chapter 6.

47 Case C-9/70 *Franz Grad v Finanzamt Traunstein* ECLI:EU:C:1970:78, par. 9.

48 Idem, paras. 4–5.

49 Idem, par. 9.

50 In this respect, see also Berry, Homewood and Bogusz, *EU Law—Text, Cases and Materials*. 2nd ed. (Oxford University Press, 2015). 90.

4.3.3.4 Direct Effect of EU International Agreements

International agreements concluded by the EU form an integral part of EU law and can also have direct effect.[51] Formally, the criteria for their direct effect are the same as the criteria for the direct effect of Treaty provisions, meaning a provision in an international agreement has to be legally binding as well as sufficiently clear, precise and unconditional.[52] In practice, however, the CJEU has sometimes been more hesitant to accept the direct effect of international agreements. This hesitation is largely due to the different political and practical consequences of giving full direct to international agreements. The main example in this regard is WTO law, where the CJEU has generally been unwilling to accept the direct application of WTO obligations or decisions from the WTO Dispute Resolution Body.[53]

4.4 The Supremacy of EU law

The principle of supremacy concerns the hierarchical relationship between EU law and national law, and forms the necessary counterpart to the principle of direct effect. What, after all, should happen where an EU rule enters into the national legal order but comes into conflict with a rule of national law? As we shall see, the answer from the CJEU is pretty clear: EU law always has absolute supremacy over all national law. At the same time, the view of most national constitutional courts tends to differ, even though they agree that in almost all cases EU law should indeed trump national law as well.

This section first outlines the principle of supremacy as developed in the case law of the CJEU, as well as the main arguments developed by the Court to support the absolute primacy of EU law. Subsequently, we briefly turn to some of the national responses to this absolute claim, and the functioning of primacy in daily reality.

---

51 On the status of such agreements see Article 216(2) TFEU as well as Case 181/73 *Haegeman* [1974] ECR 449, par. 5 and Opinion 1/91 (*EEA Agreement*) [1991] ECR 6079, par. 37.

52 Case C-12/86 *Demirel* ECLI:EU:C:1987:400.

53 See Cases 21–24/72 *International Fruit Company* [1972] ECR 1219, Case C-149/96 *Portugal v. Council* [1999] ECR I-8395 and Cases C-120 and 121/06 *FIAMM* [2008] ECR I-6513.This despite some complex and not always convincing legal meandering, for example in case C-69/89 *Nakajima* [1991] ECR I-2069 and Case C-280/93 *Germany v. Commission* [1994] ECR I-4873, as seemingly restricted again in Case C-351/04 *Ikea Wholesale* [2007] ECR I-7723.

4.4.1 *From* Costa E.N.E.L. *to Opinion 1/09: Establishing Absolute Primacy of EU Law*

Although the supremacy of EU law was already implicit in *Van Gend en Loos*, the principle was only explicitly established in *Costa E.N.E.L.*, another judgment in the EU law hall of fame:[54]

> The integration into the laws of each member state of provisions which derive from the Community, and more generally the terms and the spirit of the treaty, make it impossible for the states, as a corollary, to accord precedence to a unilateral and subsequent measure over a legal system accepted by them on a basis of reciprocity. Such a measure cannot therefore be inconsistent with that legal system. The executive force of Community law cannot vary from one state to another in deference to subsequent domestic laws, without jeopardizing the attainment of the objectives of the treaty set out in article 5 (2) and giving rise to the discrimination prohibited by article 7.
>
> (...)
>
> It follows from all these observations that the law stemming from the treaty, an independent source of law, could not, because of its special and original nature, be overridden by domestic legal provisions, however framed, without being deprived of its character as Community law and without the legal basis of the community itself being called into question.

In later cases such as *Simmenthal* and *Internationale Handelsgesellschaft* the CJEU confirmed and clarified that the supremacy of EU law also covered national legislation of a later date and national constitutional law.[55] A more recent confirmation of this absolute supremacy doctrine was given in Opinion 1/09:

> It is apparent from the Court's settled case-law that the founding treaties of the European Union, unlike ordinary international treaties, established a new legal order, possessing its own institutions, for the benefit of which the States have limited their sovereign rights, in ever wider fields, and the subjects of which comprise not only Member States but also their nationals. The essential characteristics of the European Union legal

54 Case 6/64 *Costa v E.N.E.L.*, ECLI:EU:C:1964:66.

55 Case 106/77 *Simmenthal*, ECLI:EU:C:1978:139 and Case 11/70, *Internationale Handelsgesellschaft*, [1970] ECR 1125.

> order thus constituted are in particular its primacy over the laws of the Member States and the direct effect of a whole series of provisions which are applicable to their nationals and to the Member States themselves.[56]

From the EU perspective, therefore, the principle of supremacy is very straightforward. EU law has absolute supremacy over all national law, including national constitutional law.[57] Article 4(2) TEU, which protects national identities, does not change this supremacy but only creates an obligation for the EU to respect these identities. Where a conflict arises, therefore, all national courts are obligated, by EU law itself, to disapply the conflicting national law and apply the relevant EU law instead.[58] Note though that the national law is not annulled, but only has to be disapplied to the extent that it conflicts with EU law.[59]

4.4.2 *Justifying Supremacy*

The EU Treaties do not provide an explicit basis for the supremacy of EU law.[60] Supremacy, therefore, is a judge made doctrine developed by the CJEU.

---

56 Opinion 1/09 [2011] ECR I-1137, par. 65.

57 See also Case C-399/11 *Melloni,* ECLI:EU:C:2013:107, paras 58–59, and Ottervanger, Cuyvers, Ammeloot, Croft, Etienne, Gallerizzo, Harrer, Wernitzki, *'The functioning of the East African Community: Common Market, Court of Justice and fundamental rights, a comparative perspective with the European Union'.* Leiden Centre for the Legal and Comparative Study of the East African Community (LEAC), November 2012, p. 31. For the pivotal importance of this doctrine also see J.H.H. Weiler, 'The Tranformation of Europe', 1991 *The Yale Law Journal,* 2414, who also claims that here the relation between national law and Community law is 'indistinguishable from analogous relationships in constitutions of federal states.'

58 This also means that even a court of first instance, which might normally not have the authority to disapply parts of the constitution, derives both the right and the obligation to do so where the constitution conflicts with EU law. Primacy, therefore, also affects the hierarchical ordering of national judicial systems.

59 Cf. for example Case C-10/97 to C-22/97 *Ministero delle Finanze v IN.CO.GE.'90 Srl and 12 others* ECLI:EU:C:1998:498, par, 29.

60 An explicit recognition of supremacy was included in Article I-6 of the Constitutional Treaty, which however never entered into force. In the Lisbon Treaty, this explicit recognition was replaced by Declaration no. 17 Concerning Primacy. Not only is this Declaration very indirect in its recognition of supremacy, as a declaration it also has no legally binding effect. Cf. on the silence of the Treaties on primacy also A. Von Bodandy and S. Schill, Overcoming Absolute Primacy: Respect for National Identity Under the Lisbon Treaty" (2011) *Common Market Law Review,* 1417. And Gingsberg, *Demystifying the European Union: the Enduring Logic of Regional Integration* (2nd edn, Rowman & Littlefield Publishers, 2010), 112.

Consequently, it is important to analyse which arguments were used by the CJEU to justify primacy, also as some of these arguments might also prove relevant in the EAC context.

Logically, the four main arguments of the CJEU to justify primacy bear great resemblance to the arguments underlying direct effect.[61] Firstly, the CJEU returns to its ruling in *Van Gend en Loos* on the autonomous nature of the EU legal order. This autonomy means that EU law determines its own validity, and that its validity cannot be undermined by national law. If EU law could be trumped by national law, after all, its validity would ultimately depend on national law, which would undermine its autonomy.

Secondly, the CJEU bases primacy on the principle of *pacta sunt servanda*, and does so much more explicitly than it did in *Van Gend en Loos*. It holds that the Member States accepted EU law 'on the basis of reciprocity', which means that each Member State promised the others it would respect all its obligations under EU law. If one Member State could unilaterally reject some obligations of EU law by changing its laws or its constitution, this would undermine the reciprocity of EU law.

Thirdly, the CJEU also provides some more textual arguments for the supremacy of EU law. To begin with, it indicates that 'wherever the Treaty grants the States the right to act unilaterally, it does this by clear and precise provisions.'[62] Applying an *a contrario* reasoning, this means that Member States are not allowed to deviate from EU law unilaterally, for example by adopting laws that violate EU law, where the Treaty does not explicitly allow this. In addition, the CJEU points to the definition of regulations in Article 288 TFEU, providing that regulations are 'binding' and 'directly applicable in all Member States.' This binding and direct effect would be effectively 'nullified' if Member States could adopt later national legislation that went against a regulation. Essentially the CJEU here also conflates bindingness and absolute supremacy.

The fourth, and *de facto* the most central argument, however, again concerns the effectiveness of EU law and of European integration as a whole. The CJEU essentially argues that the *effet utile* of EU law would be undermined if Member States could unilaterally overrule parts of EU law. This risk is exacerbated if one takes into account the possible *cumulative effects*. If all Member States would start to deviate from different parts of EU law, even on a limited scale, the collective effect could undermine the unity and coherence of EU law itself. EU law would then differ from Member State to Member State based on national legislation, which is the opposite of the effective and unified regional

61 See also I. Pernice *Costa v ENEL* and *Simmenthal*: Primacy of European Law', in: M. Maduro and L. Azoulai, *The Past and Future of EU law.* (2nd edn, Hart 2010), 47.

62 *Costa v. E.N.E.L.* ECLI:EU:C:1964:66.

system the EU wants to establish. As the CJEU states, this would call into question 'the legal basis of the Community itself'.

From the perspective of the CJEU, therefore, defending the supremacy of EU law is of existential importance for the EU legal order and for European integration as such.[63] Undermining supremacy risks opening the floodgates, as 28 Member States may than (ab)use national law or constitutional principles to limit or distort the uniform application of EU law.[64]

4.4.3 *The National Reception of EU Supremacy*

From the perspective of national courts, and especially of national constitutional courts, however, one may understand a certain hesitation to accept absolute supremacy of EU law, certainly over key principles of national constitutional law. After all, one of the key functions of constitutional courts is to protect their own constitution, as well as the fundamental rights the constitution grants to individuals.

In practice, therefore, almost all national supreme or constitutional courts reject the absolute supremacy as postulated by the CJEU.[65] Only a few national courts come close to accepting absolute supremacy, and this acceptance is linked to the monist nature of their constitution, and not EU law as such.[66] The overwhelming majority of national constitutional courts only accept

---

63 See for a recent example of just how important the CJEU considers this task Opinion 2/13 *Accession of the EU to the ECHR* ECLI:EU:C:2014:2454.

64 Cf. also Case C-399/11 *Melloni*, ECLI:EU:C:2013:107, paras. 58–59, where the CJEU finds that supremacy is an 'essential feature', and it 'cannot be allowed to undermine the effectiveness' of EU law.

65 D. Chalmers, G. Davies, and G. Monti, *European Union Law* (CUP 2010), 190.

66 For Estonia see the conclusion of the Constitutional Chamber of the Supreme Court of Estonia in the Euro Decision, Opinion No. 3-4-1-3-06 of 11 May 2006, par. 16, available in English translation at: http://www.nc.ee. For Belgium see the ruling by the Belgian *Court de Cassation* of 27 May 1971, *S.A. Fromagerie franco-suisse 'Le Ski'* (1971) RTD eur 495, which grants inherent and absolute supremacy to international law, including EU law. This line, which is not based on EU law as such, has been maintained, see for example *Court de Cassation*, 9 Nov. 2004, Pas., 2004, 1745 and *Court de Cassation*, 16 Nov. 2004, Pas., 2004, 1802. A second Belgian highest court, the *Conseild'Etat*, has so far generally followed the line of the *Court de Cassation*, yet following a different reasoning (*Conseil d'Etat* Case 62.922 of 5 November 1996 (Orfinger). J.T., 1997, 254). To complicate matters in Belgium, however, a third highest court was created in 2007, namely the Belgian *Cour Constitutionnelle*, and subsequently chose a different position than the other two courts. The *Cour Constitutionnelle* holds that the authority of EU law derives from the Belgian constitution, and hence must be limited by it as well. (*Cour Constitutionnelle* 16 October. 1991, No. 26/91 and *Cour Constitutionnelle*, 3 February 1994, No. 12/94). For the Netherlands

a more relative form of EU supremacy that is based on and limited by the national constitution.[67] The general line of reasoning is that Member States did accept a certain form of primacy when they joined the EU, as primacy is a necessary element of EU law. However, this primacy is ultimately *based on* the national constitution, and therefore also subject to any limitations that the national constitution imposes, such as fundamental rights or core constitutional values.[68] In addition, because the EU is based on conferred powers, any *ultra vires* actions would not bind the Member States either.[69] This means that it is ultimately up to the national constitutional courts to decide in specific cases if EU law manifestly violates certain key principles or provisions of the national constitution, or is *ultra vires*, and if it is, to disapply the relevant parts of EU law within 'their' national legal order.[70]

---

see *Hoge Raad*, 2 November 2011, LJN AR1797, R.O. 3.6, *Hoge Raad* 1 October 2004, LJN AO8913 and *Raad van State* 7 July 1995, AB 1997, 117.

67 For an overview of the classic national case law see A. Oppenheimer (ed) *The Relationship Between European Community Law and National Law: The Cases Vol I and II* (CUP 1994 and 2003).

68 For several typical examples of this reasoning see the Czech Constitutional Court, Pl. ÚS 19/08, 26 November 2008 *Lisbon I*, and Pl. ÚS 29/09, 3 November 2009 *Lisbon II*, the Hungarian Constitutional Court, Decision 143/2010 (VII. 14.) AB, of 12 July 2010 *Lisbon Treaty*, the German *Bundesvefassungsgericht* in BVerfGE, 2 BvE 123,267, 2 BvE 2/08 (2009) *Lissabon Urteil*, the Italian Corte Costituzionale, Decision No. 348 and No. 349, 24 of October 2007 confirming the *controlimiti* doctrine, the Conseil constitutionnel, Decision 2004–2005 DC of 19 November 2004, *Traité établissant une Constitution pour l'Europe*, Conseil constitutionnel, Decision 2600–540 DC of 27 July 2006, *Loi transposant la directive sur le droit d'auteur*, or the Spanish Constitutional Court Declaration 1/2004 of December 13 2004 on the Constitutional Treaty, (BOE number 3 of 4 January 2005), the UK Supreme Court in *R (on the application of HS2 Action Alliance Limited) (Appellant) v The Secretary of State for Transport and another (Respondents)* (https://www.supremecourt.uk/decided-cases/docs/uksc_2013_0172_judgment.pdf), or the Polish Constitutional Court in its decision on Poland's Membership in the European Union (Accession Treaty), 11 May 2005 (Polish Constitutional Tribunal), http://www.trybunal.gov.pl/eng/summaries/documents/K_18_04_GB.pdfn.

69 See for example the judgment of the German Constitutional Court in BVerfGE 89, 155 (1993) *Maastricht Urteil*, or the reasoning of the Czech Constitutional Court in its judgment of 31 January 2012, *Landtova* Pl. ÚS 5/12.

70 See for instance the ruling of the Polish Constitutional Court of 11 May 2005, K18/04 on Polish accession to the EU, or the Constitutional Court of Lithuania in joined cases No. 17/02, 24/02, 06/03 and 22/04, judgment of 14 March 2006. Cf. also B. De Witte, 'Direct Effect, Supremacy, and the Nature of the Legal Order', in: P. Craig and G. De Búrca (eds), *The Evolution of EU Law* (2nd ed. OUP 2011), 356: 'Everywhere the national constitution remains at the apex of the hierarchy of norms, and EU law is to trump national law only

It should be stressed that so far the differing views on the basis, scope and limits of EU supremacy have largely remained in the realm of theory and principle. In the day-to-day practice, the primacy of EU law, certainly over non-constitutional national law, is generally accepted.[71] Moreover, even in cases where important principles are at stake, national courts generally try to avoid an open conflict, or at least conflicting judgments.[72] The CJEU, in return, has often incorporated concerns of the national high courts into its case law, for example improving the protection of fundamental rights or granting a certain leeway to a Member State on a politically or culturally sensitive issue.[73] The only open conflict so far, where a national constitutional court has openly declared a judgment of the CJEU *ultra vires*, is the *Landtova* judgment of the Czech Constitutional Court, which concerned the sensitive issue of pensions after the dissolution of Czechoslovakia into the Czech Republic and Slovakia.[74]

From one perspective, precisely this lack of a formal and linear hierarchy, or 'pluralism', within the EU legal order can be seen as valuable in itself. It can be said to reflect the cooperative nature of the EU that depends on shared values and dialogue, rather than on force or formal authority.[75] In any event the

---

under the conditions, and within the limits, set by the national constitution.' Also see the discussion in this context of the European Union Act of 2011, including its 'sovereignty clause' in art. 18 in P. Craig, 'The European Union Act 2011: Locks, limits and legality' 48 *CMLRev* (2011), 1881.

71 G. de Búrca, 'Sovereignty and the Supremacy Doctrine of the European Court of Justice', in: N. Walker (ed), *Sovereignty in Transition* (Hart Publishing 2006), 454. See also House of Lords *R v Secretary of State for Transport ex. p. Factortame* (No. 2) [1991] A.C. 603 or the French *Conseil constitutionnel*, in Decision 2004–2005 DC of 19 November 2004, *Traité établissant une Constitution pour l'Europe*.

72 For a recent, very high stake, example of a dialogue where ultimately the German Constitutional Court accepted the position of the CJEU see the OMT saga resulting in the OMT decision [2016] - 2 BvR 2728/13, 2 BvR 2729/13, 2 BvR 2730/13, 2 BvR 2731/13, 2 BvE 13/13, summary available via http://www.bundesverfassungsgericht.de/SharedDocs/Entscheidungen/DE/2016/06/rs20160621_2bvr272813.html.

73 See *inter alia* Case 11/70 *Internationale Handelsgesellschaft* [1970] ECR 1125, or Case C-391/09 *Runevič-Vardyn and Wardyn* [2011] ECLI:EU:C:2011:291.

74 Judgment of 31 January 2012, *Landtova* Pl. ÚS 5/12, and the analysis by J. Komarek, 'Czech Constitutional Court Playing with Matches: the Czech Constitutional Court Declares a Judgment of the Court of Justice of the EU Ultra Vires' 8 *European Constitutional Law Review* (2012), 323.

75 See on the concept of pluralism especially N. MacCormick, *Questioning Sovereignty: Law, State and Nation in the European Commonwealth*' (OUP 1999), N. Walker, 'The Idea of Constitutional Pluralism', 65 *The Modern Law Review* (2002), 317, or M.P. Maduro,

EU demonstrates that 'the system can work' even where there is disagreement on such a fundamental point. From another perspective, however, this open disagreement also reflects the still unfinished nature of the EU, and that even now the EU still seems to be in a transitional phase. In addition, as long as this disagreement remains open, there is the risk that a more serious conflict arises that does threaten the stability of the EU, for example in the context or aftermath of Brexit. From this perspective, the search remains on for a more mature and nuanced doctrine of supremacy that can accommodate sufficient respect for national constitutional principles whilst still preserving a sufficient level of unity and coherence of EU law.[76] A quest that the EAC can join, benefiting from the experiences in the EU, when searching for a doctrine of supremacy that fits within its own legal and political context.

'Contrapunctual Law: Europe's Constitutional Pluralism in Action' in: N. Walker (ed), *Sovereignty in Transition*, (Hart 2006), 501.

76 For a first attempt to create such a 'softer' variant of supremacy along *confederal* lines A. Cuyvers, *The EU as a Confederal Union of Sovereign Member Peoples, Exploring the potential of American (con)federalism and popular sovereignty for a constitutional theory of the EU*, (2013, Diss. Leiden), available via, https://openaccess.leidenuniv.nl/handle/1887/22913.

CHAPTER 5

External Relations and the EAC

Leonard Obura Aloo

5.1 Introduction

An important element of co-operation between states is co-operation in external relations. In this Chapter some aspects of the external relationships of the East African Community (EAC) will be addressed. The relationships between the East African Community, other international organisations and states will be considered. Some comments will be made about the relationship between the Community and its Partner States. To begin with the Chapter considers the Community's capacity to enter into external relations or its external competence. The EAC coordination of Partner States' positions in foreign relations, defence and trade matters will then be considered. Given its significance, the Chapter will briefly address trade negotiation between the EAC and the European Union (EU). A comment will be made about the EAC's relations with the African Union and other regional economic communities. The Chapter concludes by evaluating the extent of the EAC's external competence.

5.2 External Competencies of the East African Community

5.2.1 *The East African Community Acting Directly in External Relations*

The objectives of the EAC are to develop policies and programmes aimed at widening and deepening co-operation among the Partner States in political, economic, social, and cultural fields, research and technology, defence, security and legal and judicial affairs.[1] The ultimate goal of the EAC is a political federation.[2] For these goals to be achieved, there is an inevitable demand that the Partner States transfer or surrender some level of sovereignty to the EAC and its institutions.[3] Coordination presupposes some level of joint action. In

---

1. EAC Treaty Article 5(1).
2 EAC Treaty Article 5(2).
3 Oppong, R.F. "Re-imagining International Law: An Examination of Recent Trends in the Reception of International Law Into National Legal Systems in Africa" 30 *Fordham Int'l L.J.* 296 (2006) 299.

© LEONARD OBURA ALOO, 2017 | DOI 10.1163/9789004322073_010
This is an open access chapter distributed under the terms of the CC-BY-NC License.

relations with external parties it presupposes that the organisation will have some level of capacity to interact with the third parties, in other words that the organisation will have external legal capacity. There is considerable debate about the exact nature of the international legal personality of inter-governmental organisations.

Coordination in the external relations of EAC states is not a new development. Under the defunct EAC, for example, Tanzania, Uganda and Kenya, in 1969, entered into an agreement—the Arusha Agreement—with the then European Economic Community.[4] This Agreement granted certain concessions regarding access of goods from Tanzania, Uganda and Kenya to the European Economic Community.[5] The tradition of entering into external agreements has continued into the current treaty arrangements. The question that remains is, to what extent can the Community enter into external arrangements and are those arrangements binding on the Partner States and what governs the Community's capacity to enter into these arrangements? To address these questions, the legal personality of the Community and its functions and powers need to be examined.

A reading of the current Treaty for the Establishment of the East African Community (the EAC Treaty) does not reveal a clear provision conferring upon the EAC a general competence with regard to foreign agreements. Article 138(1) of the EAC Treaty accords the EAC international legal personality.[6] This provision is similar to Article 47 of the Treaty on European Union, which explicitly recognises the legal personality of the EU.[7] However, Article 138(1) of the EAC Treaty appears to be pointed internally at the Partner States of the EAC. This internal outlook is suggested by both its full title 'Status, Privileges and Immunities' and its content in dealing with headquarter agreements and immunity of staff.[8] Article 138(1) of the EAC Treaty, therefore, covers the privileges and immunities of the EAC within the territory of the Partner States rather than the EAC's capacity to enter into external

4 *Agreement establishing an association between the United Republic of Tanzania, the Republic of Uganda and the Republic of Kenya and Annxed Documents*, Brussels, 1969. See also Mukwaya, A.K.K. "A Survey of Relationships between the European Union and the East African States", 1961–1980. *East Afr. Geogr. Rev* Vol 19, No. 2 pp. 73092, 1997.

5 Cosgrove-Twitchett, C. *Europe and Africa: from association to partnership*. Surrey: Saxon House 1978 p. 146; see also Zartman, W. *The Politics of Trade negotiations between Africa and the European Economic Community*. Princeton, Princeton University Press, 1971.

6 EAC Treaty Article 138(1).

7 Article 47 Treaty on European Union. See also EU Chapter 5 on the external standing and competences of the EU.

8 EAC Treaty Article 138(2) and (3).

relationships. This 'internal' orientation is also seen in Article 4(1) of the EAC Treaty which indicates that the Community shall have capacity, within each of the Partner States, of a body corporate with perpetual succession, and shall have power to acquire, hold, manage and dispose of land and other property, and to sue and be sued in its own name.[9]

Although Article 4(1) of the EAC Treaty indicates that the EAC can sue and be sued in its own name, the Partner States undertake under the Treaty to grant the Community and its officers the privileges and immunities accorded to similar international organisations within the Partner States' territory.[10] There is thus an apparent paradox with the EAC Treaty indicating, on the one hand, that the EAC can sue and be sued in its own name while, on the other hand, requiring the Partner States to grant the EAC similar immunities as accorded to international organisations.

Article 4(2) of the EAC Treaty provides that:

> ... the Community shall have powers to perform all the functions conferred upon it by this treaty and to do all things, including borrowing, that are necessary or desirable for the performance of those functions.[11]

Article 9(4) indicates that the organs and institutions of the Community shall perform the functions, and acts within the limits and powers conferred upon them by or under the Treaty.[12]This restrictive framing has, however, not prevented the EAC from activities in external relations. The argument may be made that an inter-governmental organisation can derive its competence from a wider reading of its respective treaty. It has been argued by Fin Seyersted that the legal capacity of an inter-governmental organisation to perform sovereign and international acts is like those of states—not confined to what can be positively deduced from their constitutions but comprises all acts which are not precluded by their constitutions and which do not impose new obligations upon parties who are not subject to their jurisdiction.[13] However, it is recognised that it is only to the extent that other subjects of international law

9 EAC Treaty Article 4(1).

10 EAC Treaty Article 138(3); article 72(3) requires each partner state to respect the international character of the responsibilities of the institutions and staff of the Community.

11 EAC Treaty Article 4(2).

12 EAC Treaty Article 9(4).

13 Seyersted, F. "Objective International Personality of Intergovernmental Organizations: Do their Capacities Depend Upon The Conventions Establishing Them?" *Nordisk Tidsskrift for International Ret* 34 p. 3.

recognise a regional body as a member of the international community that it can take initiatives and play an active role in the international arena.[14]

However, apart from the general aspiration in the statements, the EAC Treaty itself is silent on the actual authority and power of the Community as far as external relations are concerned.[15]

The theoretical arguments notwithstanding, the reality is that the EAC has acted directly, for example the Community has signed development aid agreements with third countries[16] and has received diplomats.[17] The Summit, the highest organ of the EAC, can also direct action on behalf of the EAC, for example, designating the Chairperson of the Summit to sign an accession treaty with a new Partner State.[18] A key example is the decision by the Summit to have the Partner States of the EAC negotiate as a bloc in matter of the African Caribbean and Pacific Countries, European Union (EU) and the World Trade Organisation (WTO) that was arrived at in 2002.[19]

5.2.2 *Co-ordination of Activities of Partner States*

The EAC Treaty requires the Partner States to develop policies and programmes aimed at widening and deepening co-operation among the Partner States in political, economic, social and cultural fields, research and technology, defence, security and legal and judicial affairs for the mutual benefit of the Partner States.[20] Having provided for the areas of co-operation, the EAC Treaty proceeds to indicate the manner in which this co-operation will be achieved.

---

14 Mathinjsen, P.S.R.F *A Guide to European Union Law*. Thomson Sweet & Maxwell London 2007 p. 491; article 38–39 Vienna Convention on the Law of Treaties.

15 Compare in this regard also the discussion in EU Chapter 5, as in the EU many of the external competences of the EAC also were derived by the CJEU from the internal competences, as no explicit competences had been granted in the Treaty.

16 For example EAC Grant Agreement with the Federal Republic of Germany signed on the 23rd January 2016 see http://www.eac.int/news-and-media/press-releases/20160123/eac-germany-sign-37-million-euros-agreement-support-regional-integration.

17 EAC receives Finnish Ambassador see http://www.eac.int/news-and-media/press-releases/20160122/eac-secretary-general-receives-credentials-finnish-ambassador.

18 East African Community *Joint Communiqué 17th Ordinary Summit of the East African Community Heads of State* item 11 see http://www.eac.int/news-and-media/statements/20160302/joint-communique-17th-ordinary-summit-east-african-community-heads-state—Directing the Chairperson to sign the accession treaty with South Sudan.

19 See *Communiqué of the 6th Extraordinary Summit of East African Community Heads of State* held in Arusha on 20th August 2007 referring to the Summit of April 2002. (Communiqués and other sources refer to the Summit of 14th April 2002, the Communiqué of the Summit is dated 11th April 2002).

20 EAC Treaty Article 5(1).

Article 5(2) of the EAC Treaty indicates the steps that will be taken in the journey to ultimate Political Federation: the Customs Union, a Common Market and the Monetary Union.[21] The EAC Treaty then lists the approaches to co-operation: the Fundamental Principles of the Community; the Operational Principles of the Community; and a General Undertaking as to Implementation.[22] The terms co-operation and co-ordination are recurrent themes throughout these provisions. For example, one of the fundamental principles of the Community is co-operation for mutual benefit,[23] and one of the operational principles is people centred and market driven co-operation.[24]

The Partner States have given a general undertaking, to amongst other things, pass legislation conferring the Community with legal capacity and personality required for the performance of its functions and to confer the legislation, regulations, and directives of the Community and institutions with the force of law within each Partner States territory.[25] The Partner States are also required to give Community law precedence over similar national laws in matters covered by the Treaty.[26]

The EAC Partner States have agreed to co-operate in various areas and ultimately to form a political federation. It can be concluded that, at least by their intention, some element of sovereignty has been ceded to the EAC. The classical definition of sovereignty is "independence from authority of any other state and equality with it in international law".[27] To the extent that the Partner States have pooled their decision making there is some ceding of sovereignty. The main responsibility for the achievement of the aims of the EAC is, however, retained by the Partner States who are ultimately in control of the process.

The EAC is a permanent entity that is established for an unlimited period.[28] The fact that the ultimate aim is a political federation implies that the Treaty will have achieved its aims once a political federation is achieved. It can therefore be argued that the EAC, in the present form, is intended to exist until political federation is achieved. A Partner State can withdraw from the EAC Treaty provided the Partner States National Assembly resolves by not

21 EAC Treaty Article 5(2).

22 EAC Treaty Articles 5(3), 6, 7 and 8.

23 EAC Treaty Article 6(f).

24 EAC Treaty Article 7(1)(a).

25 EAC Treaty Article 8(2).

26 EAC Treaty Articles 8(4) and (5).

27 Moregenathu, Hans. *Politics Among Nations*. Alfred Knoff. New York. 1950.p. 249.

28 EAC Treaty Article 144.

less than two thirds majority of all members entitled to vote and the Secretary General of the Community is given twelve months notice of the intention to withdraw.[29] A Partner State may also be suspended or expelled from the EAC.[30]

The fact that the Partner States are in control can be evidenced by the provision that decision making under the EAC Treaty is largely by consensus.[31] The main organs of the EAC are:[32]

(a) The Summit comprising head of government of the Partner States that gives general direction towards the realisation of the goals of the Community.[33]
(b) The Council of Ministers which is the main decision making body comprising ministers of the partner states responsible for regional co-operation and such other Ministers as the Partner States may determine.[34]
(c) The Co-ordinating Committee made up of permanent secretaries responsible for regional co-operation. It co-ordinates the activities of the sectoral committees and reports to the Council.[35]
(d) The Sectoral Committees which are established by the Council on recommendation of the respective Co-ordinating Committees. They develop and monitor the implementation of the programmes of the EAC.[36]
(e) The East African Court of Justice
(f) The East African Legislative Assembly
(g) The Secretariat

The Summit decision making process is by consensus.[37] The consensus approach protects national interests as, effectively a Partner State can veto the decision of the Summit.

Moreover, under the earlier East African Community, the East African Court of Appeal in *Okunda v Republic* had held that the national constitutions were

29 EAC Treaty Article 145.
30 EAC Treaty Articles 146 and 147.
31 EAC Treaty Article 12(3).
32 See summary in Lumumba, P.L.O. "The East African Community Two: Destined to Succeed or Doomed to Fail?" LSKJ 5(1)(2009) pp. 105–132 at p. 121.
33 EAC Treaty Chapter 4.
34 EAC Treaty Chapter 5.
35 EAC Treaty Chapter 6.
36 EAC Treaty Chapter 7.
37 EAC Treaty Article 12(3).

superior to the provisions of the Treaty.[38] In this case a prosecution was instituted by the Attorney-General of the Republic of Kenya against two persons under the provisions of the Official Secrets Act of the East African Community without the consent of the Counsel to the Community as required by the Act. Under the Constitution of Kenya, at the time, the Attorney-General controlled prosecutions. There was therefore an apparent conflict between the Constitution of Kenya and the Official Secrets Act of the East African Community. The High Court of Kenya held that the Act of the Community was void to the extent of the inconsistency with the Constitution of Kenya. On appeal, the East African Court of Appeal, which at the time severed all the Partner States of Community held that the Constitution of Kenya was paramount and any law, whether it be of Kenya or the Community, or of any other country which had been applied in Kenya, which was in conflict with the Constitution was void to the extent of the conflict.

The legacy of the East African Court of Appeal decision in *Okunda v Republic* continues to inform the position of EAC laws *vis-a-vis* the national constitutions. Decisions and actions at the EAC level are controlled by the national constitutional set up. Any authority surrendered to the EAC has to be done, it appears, within the constitutional context of the individual country.

5.3 Specific Co-operation in Foreign Policy

The EAC Treaty requires that Partner States establish common foreign and security policies.[39] The objective of the common foreign and security policies include:

(a) safeguarding the common values, fundamental interests and independence of the Community
(b) strengthening the security of the Community and its Partner States in all ways
(c) developing and consolidating democracy and the rule of law and respect for human rights and fundamental freedoms
(d) preserving peace and international security among the partner states
(e) promote co-operation at international fora, and

38 *Okunda v Republic* [1970] E.A. 453.

39 EAC Treaty Article 123(1).

(f) enhance the eventual establishment of a Political Federation of the Partner States[40]

The Partner States have bound themselves under the EAC Treaty to co-ordinate actions in international organisations and international conferences.[41]

The co-ordination in this area has been characterised by a cautious approach by the Partner States in yielding sovereignty to the EAC. This is shown by the fact that the implementation of the provisions of the Treaty on co-operation on political matters were to become operative when so determined by the Council. The Treaty also requires the Council to prescribe in detail how this co-operation is to be implemented.[42] The provisions are not yet operational. The East African Court of Justice (EACJ) has been called upon to consider the justiciability of the provisions of the EAC Treaty on political cooperation. In the case of *Attorney General of Uganda v Tom Kyahurwenda* the EACJ considered the question and ruled that the provisions of paragraphs 2, 3 and 4 of Article 123 of the Treaty on political co-operation are not justiciable before the EACJ or local courts until the provisions are operationalised.[43]

The EAC currently cites the joint support for citizens of the Community for international level positions as a tangible result of the co-ordination of efforts in the Partner States international relations.[44] This promotion of a relatively minor achievement of co-ordination indicates the reluctance of the Partner States to yield greater authority to the EAC. A draft protocol on foreign policy co-ordination has been published.[45] The provisions of the draft protocol further indicate a cautious approach as it calls mainly for collaboration rather than the yielding of any authority to the Community. For example, the draft protocol calls for "collaboration" in diplomatic and consular activities, multilateral diplomacy, and in economic and social activities.[46] The approach of the draft is cautious and calls for collaboration rather than action by the EAC. Furthermore, caution is emphasised by the fact that the protocol remains a draft and a final version is yet to be concluded.

---

40 EAC Treaty Article 123(3) (a)–(f).

41 EAC Treaty Article 123(4), see also Articles 5, 6, 7, 123, 124 and 125 of the EAC Treaty.

42 EAC Treaty Article 123(5).

43 *Attorney General of Uganda v Tom Kyahurwenda* Case Stated No. 1 of 2014.

44 www.eac.int/legal/index.

45 *Draft East African Community Protocol on Foreign Policy Co-ordination* Arusha March 2010.

46 *Draft East African Community Protocol on Foreign Policy Co-ordination* Arusha March 2010 article 5, 6 and 7.

The EAC has concluded a Protocol on Peace and Security[47] and a Protocol on Corporation in Defence Affairs.[48] Notably, these two protocols call for collaboration and do not themselves cede any decision making or action to the Community itself.

In the area of trade negotiations, the co-ordination effort has been institutionalised through the EAC Trade Negotiations Act of 2008.[49] The Act was initiated as a private member's bill in the East African Legislative Assembly.[50] The objectives of the Act include the establishment of joint negotiation of the Partner States in bilateral, regional and multilateral trade.[51] The Act creates a Commission known as the East African Joint Trade Negotiation Commission which is the mechanism the Partner States use to negotiate as a bloc in matters relating to regional and multilateral trade.[52] The Joint Trade Negotiation Commission is tasked with conducting trade negotiations on behalf of the Partner States of the EAC.[53] The Joint Trade Negotiation Commission comprises two members nominated by each Partner State, the Secretary General of the EAC as a *ex-offico* member, one *ex-offico* member designated by the designated Ministry of each Partner State. The Director General of the Joint Trade Negotiating Commission is also an *ex officio* member.[54]

The negotiating mandate of the Joint Trade Negotiating Commission is given in writing by the Summit acting through the Council.[55] Notwithstanding the existence of the Joint Trade Negotiating Commission, the co-ordination has not been seamless and implementation of the Act has not been a smooth process.[56] The Partner States still send individual delegations to international trade negotiation forums and enter into multilateral trade agreements as

47 *East African Community Protocol on Peace and Security* Arusha February 2013.

48 *East African Community Protocol on Co-operation on Defence Affairs* Arusha April 2012.

49 The East African Trade Negotiations Act of 2008.

50 EALA Achievements 2001–2009 bill initially introduced in 2003 http://www.eala.org/new/index.php/the-assembly/achievements.

51 The EAC Trade Negotiations Act of 2008. Section 2.

52 The East African Trade Negotiations Act of 2008. Section 3 and 5.

53 The East African Trade Negotiations Act of 2008. Section 5(1)(c).

54 The East African Trade Negotiations Act of 2008. Section 6.

55 The East African Trade Negotiations Act of 2008. Section 12.

56 Ayeko, F. "East African States Still Negotiate Trade Pacts as One Despite 2008 Law" *The East African* Monday, October 4 2010 http://www.theeastafrican.co.ke/news/EAC%20states%20still%20to%20negotiate%20trade%20pacts/-/2558/1024814/-/9f3mip/-/index.htm.

individual countries.[57] There has been apparent reluctance to implement the Trade Negotiations Act.[58] This could be because, as indicated above, the Act was initiated as a private member's bill and not by the Secretariat or by the Partner States. As will be seen below negotiating with the EU, for example, has seen apparent conflicts between Partner States.

5.4 EAC and EU Relationships

As noted above the EAC-EU relationship has a long history dating back at least to the 1969 Arusha Agreement between Tanzania, Uganda and Kenya and the European Economic Community.[59] In the early 1970s, the three East African countries joined other African, Caribbean and Pacific states in a bloc, the ACP, to negotiate with the European Economic Commission. The negotiations resulted in the first Lomé Convention in 1975 (Lomé I).[60] The Lomé Convention was renegotiated and renewed three times: the second Lomé II was signed in 1980; Lomé III in 1985;[61] and Lomé IV in 1990.[62] The Lomé Convention's provisions were viewed by other states as being incompatible with the General Agreement on Tariffs and Trade (the GATT) and subsequently the WTO. This resulted in complaints filed before the GATT, WTO and also the European Court of Justice.[63] The Lomé Convention's trade provisions included

57 Ayeko, F. "East African States Still Negotiate Trade Pacts as One Despite 2008 Law" *The East African* Monday, October 4 2010 http://www.theeastafrican.co.ke/news/EAC%20states%20still%20to%20negotiate%20trade%20pacts/-/2558/1024814/-/9f3mip/-/index.htm.

58 Seatini. *Uganda's Trade Negotiation Framework*. September 2013 p. 16.

59 *Agreement establishing an association between the United Republic of Tanzania, the Republic of Uganda and the Republic of Kenya and Annxed Documents*, Brussels, 1969.

60 The First Lomé Convention Lomé I (Negotiations began in 1973 and lasted for eighteen months. The convention was signed on 28th February 1975 and cam into force on 1st April 1976. See Babarinde, O.A. *The Lomé Convention and Development: An Empirical Assessment*. Brookfield: Avebury Press 1994 p. 20; Oumar Sy, S. "The Birth of the ACP Group" *The Courier* No. 93 September- October 1985 pp. 51–56. Full text see *The Courier* No. 31 Special Issue march 1975.

61 For full text see *The Courier* No. 89 January-February 1985.

62 For full text see *The Courier* No. 120 March-April 1990; Lomé VI bis The courier No. 155 January-February 1996.

63 DS 27 European Communities—Regime for the Importation, Sale and Distribution of Bananas (Complainants: Ecuador; Guatemala; Honduras; Mexico; United States) see https://www.wto.org/english/tratop_e/dispu_e/dispu_status_e.htm; Federal Republic of Germany v Council of the European Union.

trade preference arrangements including tariff rates that differed from the Most Favoured Nation (MFN) rate and discriminated against other developing countries as it granted more generous treatment than offered by the EU's generalised system of preferences. The regime also had four protectionist protocols on beef and veal, rum, bananas and sugar.[64]

The Lomé Conventions were replaced in the year 2000 with a new agreement, the Contonu Agreement, between the ACP countries and the EU.[65] Under Article 36(1) of the Cotonou Agreement, the EU and the ACP countries agreed to negotiate Economic Partnership Agreement (EPAs) which would be compatible with the WTO.[66]

Negotiations between the EAC and EU began immediately, and progressed for over a decade. The EU set 1st October 2014 as a deadline upon which the EAC states would forfeit their preferential treatment and revert to the less generous generalised system of preferences.[67] The result would be that exports from Kenya to the EU would face higher tariffs while those from the other EAC Partner States would continue to enjoy duty free access to the EU under a component of the EU generalised system of preferences—the Everything But Arms arrangement.[68]

The negotiation of the EU-EAC EPA was concluded in October 2015 and was expected to be ratified by October 2016.[69] However, internal timelines have been missed, for instance an expected signing in July 2016 was missed resulting in speculation that the ratification is facing difficulty.[70] Furthermore, following

64 Grynberg, R. *The WTO incompatibility of the Lomé Convention trade provisions* Asia Pacific School of Economics and Management Working Paper 1998.

65 Agreement between the ACP and the EC the Contonu Agreement 2000. The agreement was revised in 2005.

66 Article 36(1) Cotonou Agreement; Gathii, James T. The Cotonou Agreement & Economic Partnership Agreements.

67 Ongónge, L. "The EAC-EU Economic partnership Agreement: Context, Content and Consequences". *Trade Notes*. Institute of Economic Affairs. Nairobi 2015.

68 Kenya Human Rights Commission. The ABC of the EAC-EU Economic Partnership Agreement (EPA). Kenya Human Rights Commission. Nairobi; Ongónge, L. "The EAC-EU Economic partnership Agreement: Context, Content and Consequences". *Trade Notes*. Institute of Economic Affairs. Nairobi 2015.

69 The European Commission. *Economic Partnership Agreement between the EU and the Eastern Africa Community* (*EAC*) October 2015 http://trade.ec.europa.eu/doclib/html/142194.htm.

70 Ssemuwemba, Anne M. ЁPA Negotiations: Is EAC at the crossroad?" *The Daily Monitor* Tuesday, August 2 2016 http://www.monitor.co.ug/Business/Prosper/EPA-negotiations--Is-EAC-at-the-crossroads-/688616-3325520-kg10mdz/index.html.

the vote by Britain to exit the EU in June 2016, the EAC Partner States' position on the future of the EU-EAC EPA appear to be divergent.[71]

The negotiations with the EU indicate a coordinated approach by the EAC Partner States. However, the Partner States do enter into the agreements individually and where national interest dictate, they can proceed even if contrary to the agreed coordinated position.

5.5 EAC and Other Regional Communities

Although the EAC Partner States aim at forming a political federation, this has not prevented the Partner States from joining different regional integration communities (RECs). The Partner States of the EAC are members of various other RECs including COMESA,[72] SADC[73] and IGAD.[74] Indeed Eastern Africa has the largest number of RECs and intergovernmental regional bodies on the continent.

Membership on EAC Partner States in other RECs

	COMESA	IGAD	SADC
Burundi	*	*	
Kenya	*	*	
Rwanda	*		
South Sudan		*	
Tanzania			*
Uganda	*	*	

71 Kidanka, Christopher. "Tanzania dodges EPA to Protect Industrialisation, budget" The East African July 16, 2006; Bangaba, Julius. "Leaders Urge Review of EU-EAC Trade Deal" *The East African* July 23, 2016 http://www.theeastafrican.co.ke/news/Leaders-urge-review-of-EAC-EU-trade-deal/2558-3307650-ua000vz/index.html.

72 COMESA- Common Market for Eastern & Southern Africa see http://www.comesa.int/.

73 SADC- Southern Africa Development Community see http://www.sadc.int/.

74 IGAD—Intergovernmental Authority on Development see http://igad.int/.

The multiple memberships of the various RECs can result in the duplication of roles and conflicting goals and policies.[75] Membership of the different RECs can also allow a country to play on the differentials of timings, commitments and tariffs in the various RECs and can be a source of divided loyalty.[76]

It is with this realisation that COMESA-EAC-SADC held a tripartite summit in October 2008 during which it was agreed to establish a tripartite free trade area.[77] The co-operation is not however between the various RECs but through the member states themselves making commitments.

5.6 EAC and African Union

As early as 1980 under the then Organisation for African Unity (OAU), the Lagos Plan of Action for the Economic Development of Africa called for the eventual convergence of various regional trade liberalisation regimes to form the African Common Market.[78] The commitments in this plan were made concrete in 1991 when African countries signed the Treaty Establishing the African Economic Community (AEC) also known as the Abuja Treaty.[79] The Abuja Treaty came into operation in 1994 and provides a framework for continental integration. The Abuja Treaty is expected to take shape in six phases over a period of thirty-four years.[80] The phases require the co-ordination and harmonisation of both tariff and non-tariff systems in the various RECs on the continent with a view to establishing a continental customs union. The various RECs are to be consolidated and then merged into a single block.

The EAC Treaty requires the Partner States to accord special co-operation with the African Union, the United Nations and other international organisations and bilateral and multi-lateral development partners interested in the objectives of the Community.[81] As part of this effort the EAC enjoys observer status within the African Union. The EAC Secretary General is invited to the

75 African Development Bank. *East African Regional Integration Strategy Paper 2011–2015* September 2011.

76 AFRODAD. *Regional Integration and Debt in East Africa.* High Gloss Prints Harare 2003 p. 23.

77 United Nations Economic Commission for *Africa Assessing Regional Integration in Africa V Towards an African Continental Free Trade Area* Addis Ababa 2012 p. 21.

78 The Organisation of African Unity. *Lagos Plan of Action for Economic Development of Africa 1980–2000.* Lagos 1980 paragraph 250 (iv).

79 Treaty Establishing the African Economic Community 1991.

80 Treaty Establishing the African Economic Community 1991.

81 EAC Treaty Article 130(4).

African Union Summit and is in charge of all relations with the African Union. In 2012, the EAC posted a liaison person to the African Union. The African Union also has a liaison person at the EAC Secretariat.

However, the EAC's activities with the African Union are limited and do not involve actions that would directly bind any of the EAC Partner States. Partner States act independently albeit perhaps in a coordinated manner.

5.7 Conclusion

The EAC does have a limited amount of external competence. The areas where it has been applied is receiving envoys and entering into agreements with development partners. The EAC Partner States have not yielded significant sovereignty to the EAC and instead have adopted a co-ordinated approach to negotiations with third parties. The formal structure for co-ordination, the EAC Joint Trade Negotiation Act is yet to be fully implemented.

This co-ordination approach leaves each individual Partner State entering into multilateral and bilateral agreements as an individual state andwhere domestic interests dictate it, the Partner States will pull away from the co-ordinated position. However, with political federation as the ultimate goal, the Partner States will have to consider moving beyond mere co-ordination in external relations and grant the EAC greater external competence.

CHAPTER 5A

External Relations and the EU

Armin Cuyvers

5.1 Introduction

The area of EU external relations is a complex one. Over time, the EU has gradually developed more competences to act externally, but the competences of the EU vary significantly over the different areas of external policy.[1] Institutionally, the area is complex as well. Multiple EU actors and the Member States all want to exert their influence, crowding the international stage. This 'multiple-actor-syndrome', however, merely reflects one of the fundamental dilemmas of EU external relations: in principle it would be good if the EU could speak with one voice, but in most fields of external relations Member States are simply unwilling to transfer the powers to the EU that this requires.

In line with the comparative aim of this book, the present Chapter focusses on the development of EU external relations in the early days, especially on the creation of implied external competences where the Treaties did not provide for explicit ones. In addition, it discusses the legal principles developed by the CJEU to ensure that Member States do not undermine the external policies of the EU with their own foreign policy. First, however, this Chapter briefly discusses the institutional landscape in EU foreign affairs, which is still haunted by the ghost of Kissinger.[2]

5.2 'Who do I call': The Crowded European Stage

According to EU mythology, Henry Kissinger once complained in exasperation: 'if I want to talk to Europe, who do I call?' Even though he may actually never

1 See also for the major changes in this field after Lisbon P. Van Elsuwege, 'EU External Action after the Collapse of the Pillar Structure: In Search of a New Balance Between Delimitation and Consistency' (2010) 47 *CMLRev*, 987.

2 For more general overviews of EU external relations see for example G. De Baere, *Constitutional Principles of EU External Relations* (OUP, 2008), P. Eeckhout, *EU External Relations Law*, (OUP, 2011), or B. Van Vooren and R.A. Wessel, *EU External Relations Law: Text, Cases and Materials* (CUP, 2014).

© ARMIN CUYVERS, 2017 | DOI 10.1163/9789004322073_011
This is an open access chapter distributed under the terms of the CC-BY-NC License.

have said this, the story survives as it so aptly captures one of the problems of EU external representation. There is no single institution or person that has the general authority to represent the entire EU, such as the US President or Secretary of State. Instead, multiple actors are usually involved.[3]

To begin with, in many external fields, certainly in the Common Foreign and Security Policy (CFSP), the European Council and especially the Council of Ministers are the central actors, also demonstrating the often intergovernmental character of this field.[4] Certainly in non-CFSP external relations, however, the Commission also plays an important role in representing the EU externally, for example also in negotiating international agreements on behalf of the EU.[5] In addition, in areas where the EU and the Member States share a competence, all 28 Member States may also be active themselves.[6]

The Treaty of Lisbon tried to streamline the external representation of the EU by creating the office of the High Representative of the Union for Foreign Affairs and Security Policy, who is supposed to 'conduct the Union's common foreign and security policy'.[7] As the High Representative is simultaneously the Vice-President of the Commission for CFSP, the chair of the Foreign Affairs Council and may take part in the work of the European Council, the hope was that this function could unite the external representation of the EU and silence Kissinger once and for all. At the same time, however, the Treaty of Lisbon also created a permanent President of the European Council, who shall 'at his level and in that capacity, ensure the external representation of the Union on issues concerning its common foreign and security policy.'[8] Similarly, the responsibility of the President of the European Commission to represent the EU externally was not removed, nor was the external role of the rotating presidency of the Council.

An example of the complications that may arise with so many actors was provided when President Obama refused to come to a Summit in Spain in May 2010. Again as EU mythology has it, the President of the European Council, the High Representative, the President of the Commission, the President of the European Parliament, the Member State holding the rotating presidency

3 See also C. Tomuschat, 'Calling Europe by Phone' Guest Editorial 2010 (47) *CMLRev*, 3.

4 See generally title V of the TEU. For a general introduction of the different EU Institutions see EU Chapter 2.

5 See Article 17(1) TEU and Article 118 TFEU.

6 See on this situation also C. Hillion, and P. Koutrakos (eds) *Mixed Agreements Revisited* (Hart, 2010).

7 Article 18 TEU.

8 Article 15(6) TFEU.

of the Council and several of the heads of State or Government of individual Member States could not agree on protocol, including on the question who would shake Obama's hand first.[9] Clearly this is only an anecdotal illustration of the underlying problem identified above: the EU has no single institution with the authority and legitimacy to pick up the phone on behalf of the entire EU. As long as that is the case, the EU will need to coordinate and cooperate, and hence cannot be as unified externally as some would like.

5.3 EU External Competences

As discussed in EU Chapter 3, the EU is based on the principle of conferral. Consequently, it only has those competences conferred on it by the Member States, also in the field of external relations.[10] In this regard Article 21 TFEU first spells out the *objectives* of the EU. Subsequently, Title V of the TEU (CFSP),[11] and Part V of the TFEU (non-CFSP external policies) provide the EU with most of its explicit external competences to actually realize these objectives.[12]

When the EEC was created in 1957, however, the Community lacked almost all of the explicit external competences it has today. The Treaty of Rome only provided for two explicit external competences: the Common Commercial Policy and the conclusion of Association agreements.[13] This lack of external competences created a problem, as the (then) Community often had to act externally, already to be able to achieve its *internal* objectives. In line with its general teleological approach to competences, the CJEU developed the doctrine of *implied powers* to deal with this lacuna. Three types or categories of implied powers were developed by the CJEU.

The first category of implied powers was created in the seminal case of *AETR*. This judgment concerned the question if the (then) Community had the competence to sign an external agreement concerning the work of crews of vehicles engaged in international road transport (the AETR agreement). It is relevant to note that the EU already had adopted legislation on this topic *internally*, but the Treaty provided no express competence to adopt an agreement on this point *externally*. The CJEU held that:

9 See also A. Rosas and L. Armati, *EU Constitutional Law*, (Hart, 2010).

10 Article 4 and 5 TEU and Opinion 2/94 *Accession to the ECHR* [1996] ECR I-1759, par. 24.

11 See particularly Articles 24 and Article 37 TEU.

12 See especially Articles 207, 208, 209, 212, 214, 216, 218.

13 Articles 113 and 238 EEC.

> Although it is true that Articles 74 and 75 do not expressly confer on the Community authority to enter into international agreements, nevertheless the bringing into force, on 25 March 1969, of Regulation No. 543/69 of the Council on the harmonization of certain social legislation relating to road transport (OJ L 77, p. 49) necessarily vested in the Community power to enter into any agreements with third countries relating to the subject-matter governed by that regulation.
>
> This grant of power is moreover expressly recognized by Article 3 of the said regulation which prescribes that: 'The Community shall enter into any negotiations with third countries which may prove necessary for the purpose of implementing this regulation'.
>
> Since the subject-matter of the AETR falls within the scope of Regulation No. 543/69, the Community has been empowered to negotiate and conclude the agreement in question since the entry into force of the said regulation.
>
> These Community powers exclude the possibility of concurrent powers on the part of Member States, since any steps taken outside the framework of the Community institutions would be incompatible with the unity of the Common Market and the uniform application of Community law.[14]

The use of the internal competence, in other words, had created an (implied) external competence. The CJEU thereby connected the existence and use of an internal competence to the existence of an external competence, greatly expanding the capacity of the (then) Community to act externally.

The second category of implied powers concerns those cases where the internal power to act for the attainment of a specific objective itself necessitates external action.[15] Some internal market rules, for example, may have an inherently international aspect.[16]

A third 'implied' external competence can be found in Article 352 TFEU. The residual competence granted by this provision may also be used for external action where an EU action is necessary to attain a Treaty objective but no explicit of implied power can be found in the Treaties.[17]

---

14 Case 22/70 *AETR* [1971] ECR 263, paras. 28–31. Also see Cases 3, 4, and 6/76 *Kramer* [1976] ECR, 1279 paras. 19–20 and Opinion 1/03 ECLI:EU:C:2006:81, par. 115.

15 See Opinion 1/76 *Laying-up fund* [1977] ECR 741, par. 3 as well as Opinion 1/03 ECLI:EU:C:2006:81, par. 115.

16 In Opinion 1/76 regulating transport on the river Rhine, for instance, could only be achieved by international action as it needed to include non-EU Member States.

17 See Case 22/70 *AETR* [1971] ECR 263, par. 95.

Through these three types of implied powers, the CJEU created a significant capacity for the EU to act externally based on internal competences and legislation already adopted inside the EU. With the Treaty of Lisbon, the extensive and often complex, case law of the CJEU on implied external powers has been codified in Article 216 TFEU.[18] For the EAC, however, especially the initial case law, linking internal competences to external competences via a logic of unity, coherence and effectiveness, may be most relevant.

5.4 Sincere Cooperation and the Negative Obligations of Member States

A last issue that may be relevant to the EAC, considering the fact that the Partner States participate in multiple international and regional bodies, is the obligation of EU Member States not to undermine or frustrate EU external action. The precise obligation of Member States in this regard depends on the nature of the EU external competence at stake.

In areas where the EU has an exclusive external competence, such as in the Common Commercial Policy (CCP) or the Customs Union, Member States are in principle not allowed to act externally at all, unless they have permission from the EU to do so.[19] Consequently, where Member States participate in an International Organization, like the G20, and issues are discussed that touch on an exclusive competence of the EU, they are under a legal obligation to act in the interest of the EU rather than to defend their own interests.[20]

In areas where the EU and the Member States share the competence, the principle of pre-emption usually applies.[21] This means that Member States are no longer allowed to act externally themselves if the EU has exercised its shared competence. If the EU already has concluded an international agreement on the free movement of workers, for instance on the mutual recognition

18 P. Eeckhout, *EU External Relations Law*, (OUP, 2011), 112.

19 See also the similar effect of exclusive competences for the Member States internally, as discussed in EU Chapter 3.

20 F. Amtenbrink, N. Blokker, S. Van den Bogaert, A. Cuyvers, K. Heine, C. Hillion, J. Kantorowicz, H. Lenk and R. Repasi, *The European Union's Role in the G20*, (2015) Working paper for the scientific bureau of the European Parliament, 41 and J. Wouters, J. Odermatt and T. Ramopoulos, "The EU in the World of International Organizations: Diplomatic Aspirations, Legal Hurdles and Political Realities", in: Leuven Centre for Global Governance Studies, *Working Paper* no. 121.

21 See on this point R. Wessel and B. Van Vooren, *EU External Relations Law: Text, Cases and Materials* (CUP, 2014), 103.

of diplomas, Member States can no longer act externally on this point. The pre-emptive effect in external relations, however, goes much further. The CJEU has given a very far reaching interpretation to the principle of sincere cooperation, holding that Member States are precluded from all unilateral action that is may adversely affect the realization of a Treaty objective. The *PFOS* case provides an illustration of just how far this obligation may extend.[22] In *PFOS* Sweden wanted to have a certain chemical added to Annex A to the Stockholm Convention on Persistent Organic Pollutants, which fell under a shared competence with the EU. Despite several requests, the Commission and Council had not acted on this point, neither approving nor rejecting Sweden's request. Briefly put, the Council had only started the process of coming to a joint position. The mere fact that the Council had discussed the issue in Council and was adopting a common position, however, already pre-empted Sweden from acting unilaterally. Even the initial stages of undertaking an EU external action, therefore, may pre-empt the right of Member States to act externally on their own.

The duty of sincere cooperation also leads to a general obligation of cooperation on Member States, and an obligation not to frustrate or undermine the effectiveness of EU external actions in any way. Even if Member States are acting in a field where the EU has no competence or has not used its shared competence, therefore, they are under an obligation not to use their own competence in a way that might undermine the effective attainment of EU objectives in another field.[23] This obligation does not amount to a general obligation for Member States to coordinate all national external actions.[24] In some cases, however, the duty of sincere cooperation may lead to a positive obligation on Member States to ensure coherence.[25] Clearly, the extent to which these legal obligations can be enforced in a highly political area is another question, but the main point here is that EU law has developed a set of legal principles and obligations to control the external behaviour of its Member States, even in areas where the EU has only shared or even no external competences.

22 Case C-246/07 *Commission v Sweden (PFOS)* ECLI:EU:C:2010:203.

23 See for example Case C-266/03, *Commission v Luxemburg* [2005] ECR I-4805 or Case C-433/03, Commission v Germany [2005] ECR I-6985.

24 See however Article 21(3) TEU on ensuring 'consistency between different areas of its external action and between these and other policies.'

25 See especially C. Hillion, 'Tous pour un, un pour tous! Coherence in the External Relations of the European Union' in: M. Cremona, *Developments in EU External Relations Law* (OUP, 2008), 10.

CHAPTER 6

General Principles Governing EAC Integration

Khoti Chilomba Kamanga and Ally Possi

6.1 Introduction

This chapter expounds on the general principles which govern the functioning and activities of the East African Community (EAC), while also reflecting on the European Union (EU) integration experience.[1] From the outset, it is important to point out that the 'general principles' are a source of law as well as guidelines to which states in an integration arrangement should adhere. Thus, this chapter is preoccupied with the dual tasks of mapping the principles of the EAC, as set out in the Treaty for the Establishment of the East African Community (the Treaty), as well as examining the broader legal import of these principles. The justification for such an examination is the role these principles play in promoting universally acceptable tenets of good governance, and more importantly, as a source of law, a dispute resolution tool. Central to this chapter is the thesis that beyond and above individual, specific and binding legal rules found in treaties, on statute books, regulations, by-laws, and case law, there are normative prepositions of a more abstract nature, and of 'general applicability', namely general principles.

6.2 General Principles

It has been observed that general principles perform a threefold function, as they "operate as aids to interpretation, as grounds for review, and as rules of law, breach of which may give rise to tortuous liability."[2] As a 'source of law', a general principle serves a 'gap-filling' function to the extent that a *lacuna* arises from the fact that a situation may arise which is not governed by a rule of law, be it statutory or judicial.[3] However, the term "general principles", as

1 See also EU Chapter 6, particularly on the development of fundamental rights as General Principles of EU law in this regard.

2 T. Tridimas (2006), The General Principles of EU Law (2nd ed), Oxford: Oxford University Press, p. 29.

3 *Ibid.* p. 17.

© KHOTI CHILOMBA KAMANGA AND ALLY POSSI, 2017 | DOI 10.1163/9789004322073_012
This is an open access chapter distributed under the terms of the CC-BY-NC License.

used in this chapter, draws inspiration from the Statute of the International Court of Justice (ICJ). The ICJ Statute, an appendage to the United Nations (UN) Charter, is particularly notable for the direction it gives to the "principal judicial organ" of the UN, in respect of applicable law whenever the ICJ is carrying out its adjudication function. The pertinent part of the ICJ Statute enjoins the Court to have recourse, among others, to "general principles of law recognized by civilized nations."[4]

Unfortunately, the ICJ Statute fails to define or characterize such 'general principles'. Therefore, this task inevitably falls on international judicial bodies and experts. The adoption of the UN Declaration on Principles of International Law was one response to the resulting *lacuna*.[5] Experts from the United States of America also joined the fray, to argue that the term 'general principles' as used by the ICJ Statute could mean any of the following five categories:

a) Principles of municipal law recognized by civilized nations;
b) General principles of law derived from the specific nature of the international community;
c) Principles intrinsic to the idea of law and basic to all legal systems;
d) Principles valid through all kinds of societies in relationship of hierarchy and coordination; and
e) Principles of justice founded on the very nature of man as a rational and social being.[6]

However, in the case of the EAC, as well as the EU, the relevant general principles are the source of less controversy, having been either captured by statute, or the subject of numerous judicial pronouncements. The situation in the EU is striking in that many of the principles under discussion have been developed by the case law of the European Court of Justice (ECJ) rather than finding an "explicit" formal basis in the Treaties. Conversely, in the EAC many of these principles are formally prescribed by the Treaty, even though there is

4 Article 38, ICJ Statute, 1945.

5 More precisely, 'Declaration on Principles of International Law Concerning Friendly Relations and Cooperation Among States in Accordance with the Charter of the United Nations' reproduced, among others, in I. Brownlie (ed) (1995), *Basic Documents in International Law* (4th ed), pp. 36–45.

6 L.F. Damrosch et als. (2001), *International Law: Cases and Materials* (4th ed), St Paul, Minnesota: American Casebook Series, p. 118.

of course also scope for unwritten principles to be discovered and developed by the EACJ.[7]

6.3 General Principles Under the EAC Treaty

Upon examination of the Treaty, it is easy for one to conclude that there is a generous intention for EAC integration to be governed by the enshrined Treaty principles. These principles may form a source of law as well as impact upon policy guidelines, with which Partner States should comply. However, it is fair to comment that as there are numerous provisions dealing with general principles,[8] there is a superfluous restatement and repetition of principles to the point of generating incoherence.[9] The structure of the principles within the Treaty is inconsistent, as for instance, some of the principles are stated neatly and explicitly, while others are implicit and, while some form part of the main body of the Treaty, others only find articulation in the preambles.

As indicated above, there are instances of repetition. In the preambles of the Treaty, one encounters the solemn commitment to "adhere ... to the fundamental and operational principles that shall govern the achievement of the objectives [of the Treaty], and to the principles of international law governing relationships between sovereign States." Moreover, provisions which directly and explicitly dedicate themselves to articulating principles of EAC law, are to be found in Articles 6 and 7 of the EAC Treaty. The former carries the title 'Fundamental Principles', whereas the latter, enumerates what are termed 'Operational Principles'. Interestingly, neither of the two Articles proclaims itself to be an exhaustive statement of principles of EAC law.[10]

It is equally important to note the rationale for classifying the principles into the two respective categories. Whereas the 'Fundamental Principles' are of general applicability, the 'Operational Principles' are meant to 'govern the

7 M.E. Mendez-Pinedo (2009), *EC and EEA Law: A Comparative Study of the Effectiveness of European Law*, Amsterdam: Europa Law Publishing, p. 15.

8 According to our count there are no less than 9 provisions, most notably, Articles 5, 6 and 7 dedicated to the issue of general principles.

9 Article 7 (2) substantially repeats the contents of Article 6 (d) with questionable added value.

10 Both provisions contain the important refrain that the respective list "shall include ..." the following principles.

practical achievement of the objectives' of the EAC,[11] a situation suggesting that the former, enjoy a comparatively superior normative status to the latter. If this truly is the case, and we believe that to be so, the overlap between the contents of Article 6 (d) and, Article 7 (2) is rather unfortunate. On the one hand Article 6 (d) reads as follows:

> The fundamental principles that shall govern the achievement of the objectives of the Community by the Partner States shall include [...] Good governance including adherence to the principles of democracy, rule of law, accountability, transparency, social justice, equal opportunities, gender equality as well as the recognition, promotion and protection of human and peoples' rights in accordance with the provisions of the African Charter on Human and Peoples' Rights.[12]

On the other hand Article 7 (2) reads, *verbatim*:

> ... Partner States undertake to abide by the principles of good governance, including adherence to the principles of democracy, the rule of law, social justice and the maintenance of universally accepted standards of human rights.[13]

Visibly, each of the two provisions makes reference to 'good governance', 'democracy', 'rule of law', 'social justice', and 'human rights,' with no apparent justification for the repetition. Only the issues of "equal opportunities" and "gender equality" are unique to Article 6 (d). Our understanding of the basic and primary justification for isolating the general principles outlined in Article 6, and the 'Operational Principles' as set out in Article 7, is to underscore the wider, general applicability of principles in the former category. It therefore is clearly superfluous, to have the same principles articulated in Article 7, since principles of general applicability would apply to any isolated, specific matter anyway. Finally, and perhaps more critically, this repetition leaves us questioning the genuine rationale for the dichotomy of the classification and the attendant legal ambiguity.

---

11 See the opening paragraph of Articles 6, in contrast to Article 7 (1).

12 Art 6 (d) of the EAC Treaty.

13 Art 7 (2) of the EAC Treaty.

6.4 The Principle of Subsidiarity

In recent times, the concept of subsidiarity has gained significant weight and attention within the sphere of international institutional law. The concept implies the presence of authority between different levels of governance, in which the decision making process should start from the lowest level capable of achieving the objectives set. In the process of regional integration, it is a common place to find Partner States within an integration bloc clinging-on to their sovereignty. In order to provide protection to such sovereignty against unnecessary action by the center, principles such as subsidiarity are adopted in the constitutive integration treaties.[14]

The principle of subsidiarity, therefore, forms a compromise on the sensitive themes of state sovereignty and a supranational form of a regional integration block.[15] In the law-making process, subsidiarity provides guidance on the legislative powers of an integration bloc in areas in which both the bloc and the Partner States have common legislative competences. In the EAC, the primary goal of the subsidiarity principle is to ensure decisions, regarding an integration activity, originate from the people; in line with the 'people-centered' integration spirit. In essence, the principle of subsidiarity reaffirms democratic principles, within the context of regional integration.[16]

While relevant, subsidiarity as envisaged by the EAC Partner States' federal regime should be approached with caution. Of course the principle is an important component in the Treaty, overseeing the achievement of the objectives of the EAC as well as being a normative source of law. Undisputedly, subsidiarity sets the tune of interaction between the EAC and its Partner States. The Treaty defines subsidiarity as a 'principle which emphasises multilevel participation of a wide range of participants in the process of economic integration'.[17] For achieving the objectives of the Community, Partner States are required to adhere to the principle of subsidiarity in all activities involving EAC integration.[18] However, the Treaty definition of subsidiarity is not clear. The scope of

14 Historic, nationalist and economic factors cause states and their nationals to advance sovereign ideology overriding integration initiatives. See Ronald Tiersky, 'Europe: International Crisis and the Future of Integration' in Robert Tiersky (ed), Europe Today (2nd edn, Rowman & Littlefield Publishers Inc. 2004) 3.

15 Deborah Cass, 'The Word that Saves Maastricht? The Principle of Subsidiarity and the Division of Powers within the European Community' (1992) 29 C.M.L. Rev. 1107, 1116.

16 Olivia Barton 'An analysis of the principle of subsidiarity in European Union law' (2014) 2 *North East Law Review* 83, 84.

17 Art 1 of the EAC Treaty.

18 Art 7(1)(d) of the EAC Treaty.

its application, as well as judicial and political mechanisms for enforcing the principle are not defined by the Treaty.

In determining whether the principle has been duly adhered to by the EAC, it is important to note that major decisions impacting EAC integration have not been widely debated by Community citizens. Notably, EAC Partner States have shown early signs of violating the subsidiarity principle, by hastily amending the Treaty in 2007, without eliciting the opinion of Community citizens.[19] This trend is contrary to the principle outlined in the EAC Treaty. It is clearly stated that for an 'action to accomplish a legitimate government objective [it] should in principle be taken at the lowest level of government capable of effectively addressing the problem.'[20] When looking at the functioning of the EACJ, there is a genuine question to be asked as to whether non-inclusion of domestic remedy requirement in the EACJ is within the spirit of the subsidiarity principle as provided in the EAC Treaty.

The principle has positives and negatives. It is easy to note that the subsidiarity principle legitimizes the Community for its citizens.[21] It also smoothens the relationship between the Community and its Partner States. However, when the principle is subverted by Partner States for political reasons, it serves as a delaying tactic by Partner States unwilling to implement the Community agenda.

6.5 Variable Geometry

The principle of variable geometry allows Partner States in an integration bloc to implement integration projects at different paces. States within an integration arrangement are allowed to move-forward with integration activities, while leaving others to join at a later date.

As is the case with the principle of subsidiarity, the Treaty fails to clearly define the scope and applicability of variable geometry principle. The Treaty recognises the principle as a policy tool of '…flexibility which allows for

19 Henry Onoria 'botched-up elections, treaty amendments and judicial independence in the East African Community' (2010) 54 *Journal of African Law 74, 88.* See also the case of *East African Law Society and 4 Others v. The Attorney General of Kenya and 3 Others, Reference No. 3 of 2007.*

20 George A. Bermann 'Subsidiarity and the European Community' (1994) 17 *Hastings Int'l & Comp. L. Rev.* 97, 97.

21 Reimer von Borries & Malte Hauschild 'Implementing the subsidiarity principle' (1999) 5 Columbia Journal of Europe Law, 369, 369.

progression in co-operation among a sub-group of members in a larger integration scheme in a variety of areas and at different speeds.'[22] On a quick reading of the Treaty, the principle clashes with the requirement of consensus in the decision making process within the Summit[23] and the Council of Ministers.[24] This was evident when the Council of Ministers approached the EACJ to seek clarity on the scope of application of the variable geometry principle within the EAC.[25]

It was clear that even the top-most officials of the Community could not contemplate the nature and scope on the implementation of one of the founding principles of the Community; a principle derived from their own wisdom. In the quest for an advisory opinion, the EACJ was called upon to clarify the application of the principle of variable geometry *vis-à-vis* the requirement of consensus in the decision making process of the EAC. The Court was of the view that, if diligently applied, the principle of variable geometry is in harmony with consensus, when deliberating on integration decisions.[26] In clarifying, the EACJ stated:

> The Court finds that the principle of variable geometry, as its definition suggests, is a strategy of implementation of Community decisions and not a decision making tool in itself. [...] The Court is of the opinion, therefore, that the principle of variable geometry can comfortably apply, and was intended, to guide the integration process and we find no reason or possibility for it to conflict with the requirement for consensus in decision-making.[27]

22 Art 1 of the EAC Treaty. Variable geometry principle is also described under art 7(1)(e) of the EAC Treaty as '... the Principle of variable geometry which allows for progression in co-operation among groups within the Community for wider integration schemes in various fields and at different speeds.'

23 See art 12(3) of the EAC Treaty.

24 Art 15(4) of the EAC Treaty, subject to the Protocol on Decision-Making by the Council of 2001 under art 2(2), which provides that the decision of the Council is by simple majority, without disclosing the kinds of decisions to be reached by a simple majority.

25 In the matter of a request by the Council of Ministers of the East African Community for an Advisory Opinion, Application No. 1 2008, EACJ, First Instance Division.

26 In the matter of a request by the Council of Ministers of the East African Community for an Advisory Opinion, Application No. 1 2008, EACJ, First Instance Division, p. 29.

27 In the matter of a request by the Council of Ministers of the East African Community for an Advisory Opinion, Application No. 1 2008, EACJ, First Instance Division, p. 33.

The EACJ is simply of the position that the principle of variable geometry is a strategy in realising a decision, which Partner States may agree by consensus. Partner States may agree by consensus to implement certain integration projects, depending on the readiness of some members. It may happen that a particular state may choose to opt out in implementing an integration project, and join the rest at a suitable future time, or may decide to opt out altogether. The EACJ observed further that consensus in the realm of decision making process of the EAC does not imply unanimity, thus there is no need for veto power among Partner States.[28]

The main aim of the principle of variable geometry is to ensure that the integration agenda proceeds, even if unwilling states are reluctant to implement integration activities. Moreover, it is a way of avoiding any internal conflicts by forcing unenthusiastic Partner States to implement a certain program or policy.[29] Learning lessons from the failure of the defunct EAC, the principle attempts to address the issue of inequality among Partner States.[30] However, when applied under political influence, this may lead to the fragmentation of the integration bloc. In 2013, invoking the principle of variable geometry, Kenya, Rwanda and Uganda, under the tag of 'coalition of the willing', held a series of meetings while excluding Burundi and Tanzania.[31] The meetings considered issues relating to the Customs Union, Common Market implementation, regional investment, infrastructure development, and the removal of non-tariff barriers. The move by the three countries was not well-received by the citizens and leaders of Burundi and Tanzania. Furthermore, the principle is at risk of being used as an escape route by an unwilling state to implement integration projects under the shield of the principle of variable geometry.

---

28 Joshua M. Kivuva 'East Africa's dangerous dance with the past: Important lessons the new East African Community has not learned from the defunct' (2014) 10 *European Scientific Journal* 359.

29 In the matter of a request by the Council of Ministers of the East African Community for an Advisory Opinion, Application No. 1 2008, EACJ, First Instance Division, p. 35.

30 *James Thuo Gathi* 'African regional trade agreements as flexible legal regimes' (2010) 35 *N.C.J. Int'l L. & Com. Reg* 571, 623.

31 African Development Bank Group 'Is Variable Geometry Leading to the Fragmentation of Regional Integration in East Africa?' http://www.afdb.org/en/blogs/integrating-africa/post/is-variable-geometry-leading-to-the-fragmentation-of-regional-integration-in-east-africa-12524/ (Accessed on 26 May 2016).

6.6 The Principle of Complementarity

The principle of complementarity has gained prominence in international criminal law following implementation of the Rome Statute.[32] There are different methods through which the principle of complementarity is applied under international law. The principle delineates the relationship between international institutions and those at the domestic level.[33] The principle of complementarity in the EAC Treaty has taken on an economic approach, namely trade complementarity. According to the Treaty, the principle 'defines the extent to which economic variables support each other in economic activity'.[34] The principle of complementarity in the EAC Treaty does not only cover the relationship between the Community itself and its Partner States, but also attempts to create a bridge between the work of the EAC and other African institutions performing activities and functions similar to those of the EAC. Therefore, EAC complementarity operates with regard to both national and other regional and international institutions. Similarly to the principle of complementarity as envisaged in the Rome Statute, EAC complementarity calls upon relevant institutions at the Community and local level to act, when and where their counterparts are unable or less equipped to do so.

6.7 Fundamental Rights as a General Principle of the EAC Law

Respect for human rights and fundamental freedoms is essential in forming strong regional integration.[35] Under contemporary international institutional law, respect for human rights has developed to be an important integration principle. For instance, it is common to find an integration bloc imposing respect for human rights as one of the prerequisites for accession to the bloc.[36]

The EAC Treaty expressly designates the "promotion and protection of human and peoples' rights" as a 'Fundamental Principle' of the EAC. We also find, among the 'Operational Principles' of the EAC, the undertaking by Partner

32 See the Preamble and art 1 of the Rome Statute of the International Criminal Court, UN Doc. A/CONF. 183/9*(1998).

33 Xavier Philippe 'The principles of universal jurisdiction and complementarity: how do the two= principles intermesh?' (2006) 88 *International Review of the Red-cross* 375, 380.

34 Art 1 of the EAC Treaty.

35 See on this point also the gradual development of fundamental rights protection in the EU, that kept pace with the level of integration, as described in EU Chapter 6.

36 See for example Article 3 (3) (b) of the EAC Treaty.

States, to adhere to the "maintenance of universally accepted standards of human rights". The legal principles are the source of EAC law, of which human rights, as they are protected by the Partner States and with the international treaties are incorporated in the EAC Treaty.[37] However, when the EACJ started to receive cases concerning human rights allegations, the Partner States were not shy of vigorously opposing the binding nature of the principles within the EAC Treaty.[38]

The EAC does not have its own human rights catalogue, and therefore, places its reliance on other international sources of rights. The African Charter on Human and Peoples' Rights (ACHPR) is mentioned as one of the normative frameworks to be taken into account when conducting EAC activities,[39] along with 'universally accepted standards of human rights.'[40] If the supremacy of the EAC law is firmly accorded by EAC Partner States, human rights norms in the Treaty have the potential of creating a Community with better human rights standards. In line with this objective, the EACJ itself is of the firm view that the mention of the ACHPR in the EAC Treaty 'was not merely decorative of the Treaty'.[41]

Sadly, however, the EAC Treaty has shied away from taking one important legal step towards giving life to the principle of fundamental rights. The EACJ's jurisdiction in respect of 'interpretation and application' of the EAC Treaty is set out in a manner that is forthright and unequivocal, but not in regard to the question of human rights. The pertinent provision limiting the Court's jurisdiction to determine human rights disputes reads:

> The [EACJ] shall have such other original, appellate, human rights and other jurisdiction as will be determined by the Council at a suitable

37 For a general discussion on principles and human rights in the EU, see Tanja Karakamisheva-Jovanovska 'Legal principles versus fundamental rights post Lisbon' (2013) 15 *Rev. Eur. L.* 41.

38 See for example the submissions of the Attorneys General in the cases of *Mary Ariviza and Okotch Mondoh v. Attorney General of kenya and Secretary General of the East African Community, Reference No. 7 of 2010 (First Instance Division); James Katabazi and Others v. Secretary general of the East African Community, Reference No. 1 of 2007 (First Instance Division); Plaxeda Rugumba v. The Secretary General of the East African Community, Reference No. 8 of 2010 (First Instance Division); and The Attorney General of Rwanda v. Plaxeda Rugumba, Appeal No. 1 of 2012 (Appellate Division).*

39 Art 6(d) of the EAC Treaty.

40 Art 7(2) of the EAC Treaty.

41 Plaxeda Rugumba v. The SG of the EAC & the AG of Rwanda, Ref No. 8 of 2010, First Instance Division.

> subsequent date. To this end, Partner States shall conclude a Protocol to operationalize the extended jurisdiction.[42]

This formulation exposes the reluctance of the drafters of the EAC Treaty towards paving the way for human rights litigation at the EACJ. This reluctance was demonstrated by not only handing the Council an open ended time frame for clarifying EAC human rights laws, but also through the additional requirement that this extended jurisdiction be effectuated through a fresh treaty, essentially requiring a human rights 'Protocol'. Despite these hurdles, intrepid litigants have petitioned the EACJ on matters of a human rights nature. The presence of human rights norms in the EAC Treaty has placed the EACJ at a cross-roads, as it is now receiving more cases with human rights components than other Community norms enshrined in the EAC Treaty.[43]

It should be recalled that human rights did not feature in the now defunct EAC, just as they did not in the early days of the EU integration.[44] The current EAC Treaty recognises human rights, as one of the founding principles of the EAC, however, upon examination of the constitutions of the EAC Partner States, one of the findings that could easily be gathered is the difference in the level of human rights protection. To its credit, despite the Court's explicit lack of jurisdiction to adjudicate human rights matters, it continues to play a leading role in advancing fundamental rights within the EAC. To this end, the Court has been applying law-making strategy in upholding fundamental rights and promoting freedom within the EAC.

In a string of cases, applications have been made, *inter alia*, on grounds of infringements with respect to both 'fundamental' and 'operational principles' of the EAC. They notably include the responsibility to respect human rights in accordance with the ACHPR, and maintenance of 'universally accepted standards of human rights'. A notable example of one of these cases is the case of *James Katabazi*,[45] the first ever case in which the EACJ took head on the issue of its jurisdiction with respect to human rights. The *Katabazi* case opened a Pandora's box of human rights cases, as the Court now receives repeated

42 Article 27 (3).

43 See A Possi 'Striking a balance between community norms and human rights: The continuing struggle of the East African Court of Justice' (2015) 15 *African Human Rights Law Journal* 192–213 http://dx.doi.org/10.17159/1996-2096/2015/v15n1a9.

44 Henrik Karl Nielsen 'The protection of fundamental rights in the law of the European Union' (1994) 63 *Nordic J. Int'l L*, 213 at 213 and in more detail, EU Chapter 6.

45 *James Katabazi & 21 Others* v *Secretary General of the EAC & Attorney General of the Republic of Uganda*, Reference No. 1 of 2007.

reference to human rights infringements.[46] Notably, in *Katabazi*, the Court gives an insightful if not groundbreaking position regarding the respondents' contention that the EAC Treaty does not confer on the EACJ powers to entertain matters pertaining to human rights violations, notwithstanding the contents of Articles 6 and 7.

The Court began by acknowledging how an 'ordinary meaning' of Article 27 (2) of the EAC Treaty justifies the conclusion that the EACJ lacks jurisdiction in matters of human rights.[47] The Court then abandons the 'textual' approach in favor of a 'contextual' one.[48] The Court's dictum observes how important it is to take into account those provisions of the EAC Treaty governing objectives, principles, and obligations of Partner States. Having done so, the Court arrives at its groundbreaking conclusion, which reads:

> While the Court will not assume jurisdiction to adjudicate on human rights disputes, it will not abdicate from exercising its jurisdiction of interpretation under Article 27 (1) merely because the reference [before the Court] includes allegation[s] of human rights violation.[49]

For a long period of time, the position of the EACJ Appellate Division was that the Court will only adjudicate on a matter containing a human rights allegation only if the application contained a cause of action distinct from human rights,[50] for example the rule of law, democracy and good governance. In the recent decision of *Democratic Party v. SG of the EAC and Others*, the EACJ stated as follows:

> The wording "... in accordance with the provisions of the [ACHPR]", creates an obligation on the EAC Partner States to act in good faith and in accordance with the provisions of the Charter. Failure to do so constitutes an infringement of the Treaty. Such violation can be legally challenged before the [EACJ] by virtue of its jurisdiction [...] Articles 6 (d) and 7(2)

---

46 These are found at p. 3 of the judgment and in direct connection to Articles 6 and 7 of the EAC Treaty.

47 See pp. 14–15 of the judgment.

48 For details regarding the issue of interpreting treaties, see, among others, Ian Brownlie, Principles of Public International Law (7th ed), Oxford University Press, 2008, pp. 630–636.

49 See pp. 15–16 of the judgment.

50 *Independent Medical Legal Unit v Attorney-General of Kenya*, Appeal No. 1 of 2011, EACJ Appellate Division.

> of the Treaty empower the [EACJ] to apply the provisions of the Charter, the Vienna Convention, as well as any other relevant international instrument to ensure the Partner States' observance of the provisions of the Treaty, as well as those of other international instruments to which the Treaty makes reference. The role of the Court in the instant Reference, was to ascertain the Partner States' adherence to, observance of, and/or compliance with the Treaty provisions—including the provisions of any other international instruments which are incorporated in the Treaty, whether explicitly [as in Article 6(d)], or implicitly [as in Article 7 (2)].[51]

The *Democratic Party case* is the latest case through which the EACJ has attempted to expand its authority to adjudicate human rights cases. The decision emanated from the Appellate Division of the Court, which was originally reluctant to give straightforward interpretations on human rights norms provided for in the EAC Treaty. The fresh approach by the Court towards human rights cases could be due to the presence of newly appointed judges. If that is indeed the case, their new approach may be tempered by the political attitude of Partner States towards EACJ jurisdiction. This is evidenced by the events leading up to the suspension of the Southern African Development Community Tribunal, an unwanted experience to most human rights litigants in Africa. It also provides a referencing point for Partner States seeking to 'destroy' a 'misbehaving' judicial body. The suspension of the SADC Tribunal demonstrates the negative effects that could emanate should the EACJ seek to overextend their human rights adjudicatory jurisdiction.

6.8 Other Principles

Seemingly, a caveat was entered to the effect that Articles 6 and 7 do not exhaust the range of provisions dedicated to espousing principles of EAC Law. It will be discovered that, besides the preambular section to the Treaty and Articles 6 and 7, there are no less than another half a dozen provisions articulating general principles, sometimes explicitly, and on other occasions implicitly.

The first, within this category, is the provision addressing the fundamental issue as to the 'aims and objectives' of the entire EAC enterprise, and how it is envisaged to unfold. The Treaty explicitly directs that 'Partner States undertake to establish among themselves and in accordance with the provisions of [the Treaty], a Customs Union, a Common Market, subsequently a

51 Appeal No. 64 of 2014, EACJ Appellate Division.

Monetary Union, and ultimately a Political Federation.'[52] At least two further provisions shed light as to the principles governing the manner in which integration is expected to occur. These are the specific provisions in the Treaty relating to the creation of the Customs Union and Common Market. In both instances, the Treaty calls for the negotiation and adoption of a fresh treaty, a "Protocol", to be specific.[53] Read together, these provisions have led some observers to press for the argument that 'gradualism and pragmatism', are among key principles of EAC Law and integration, even if not explicitly acknowledged as such, by the Treaty.

Apart from the above narrated principles, the Treaty is enriched with other principles deserving mention. In order to meet the objectives of the EAC, Partner States are required to conduct their activities and make decisions based on mutual trust, political will and sovereign equality;[54] peaceful coexistence and good neighborliness;[55] peaceful settlement of disputes;[56] equitable distribution of benefits;[57] and cooperation for mutual benefit.[58] Also, Partner States have identified people-centred and market driven cooperation;[59] obligation to provide an adequate and appropriate enabling environment, such as conducive policies and basic infrastructure;[60] establishment of an export oriented economy accompanied with free movement of goods, persons, labour, services, capital, information and technology;[61] and symmetry;[62] as principles which govern the practical achievement of the EAC objectives.[63]

6.9 Conclusion

This chapter has identified what can be termed general principles of EAC Law, and has investigated their wider implications. The justification for general

52 Article 5 (2) of the EAC Treaty.
53 See Articles 75, and 76 of the EAC Treaty.
54 Art 6(a) of the EAC Treaty.
55 Art 6(b) of the EAC Treaty.
56 Art 6(c) of the EAC Treaty.
57 Art 6(e) of the EAC Treaty.
58 Art 6(f) of the EAC Treaty.
59 Article 7(1)(a) of the EAC Treaty.
60 Art 7(1)(b) of the EAC Treaty.
61 Art 7(1)(c) of the EAC Treaty.
62 Art 7(1)(h) of the EAC Treaty. It is also defined under article 1 of the Treaty as 'the principle which addresses variances in the implementation of measures in an economic integration process for purposes of achieving a common objective.'
63 Article 7.

principles is their unique role in promoting the universally accepted tenants of good governance, in addition to their capacity as a 'source of law'. They are consistent with the ideals enumerated in the Statute of the ICJ and also function as guiding tools for achieving integration objectives. In other words, and for this reason, it is the central assumption of this chapter that understanding EAC law requires giving due attention to the issue of EAC general principles. It is observed in this chapter that the development of 'general principles' within the EU evolved in a manner quite distinct from what unfolded in the EAC. In the former, 'principles' of EU law were left to evolve gradually through the jurisprudence of the ECJ, the constitutive instruments of the then European Communities shying away from making any explicit statement on the question. In contrast, the EAC Treaty has given the issue of general principles, generous if not exaggerated attention while case law has been less robust in this regard. Articles 6 and 7 of the EAC Treaty are devoted to principles of the EAC. We also find additional principles littering the EAC Treaty elsewhere, beginning with the preambular section. There is also a troubling repetition in stating the principles, especially between Articles 6 and 7. Nevertheless, conclusively, 'general principles' enshrined in the EAC Treaty constitute a normative source of law and guidelines for achieving the targeted objectives of the EAC integration. It is, therefore, the duty of the Partner States to adhere and uphold the established principles, so as to make EAC integration a reality.

CHAPTER 6A

General Principles of EU Law

Armin Cuyvers

6.1 Legal Dark Matter

In certain ways, general principles can be understood as the dark matter of EU law. They unify the law, fill gaps, and lend weight and legitimacy to the EU legal order as a whole. Like dark matter, moreover, legal principles can be hard to pin down and describe, as often it is their flexibility and fluidity that allows them to successfully fulfil the different role they play. Principles are also intimately connected to values, often giving a legal voice to considerations of morality and social convictions that cannot enter the legal plane directly.[1] Because of their flexibility, general principles may also enable a legal order to evolve and adapt, as the general principles themselves may develop along new realities and responsibilities, but they may also be used to re-interpret rules that block progress.

This Chapter briefly discusses the general principles of EU law. Because the EU legal order knows a great many general principles, and because these principles play many roles, it is impossible to provide anything close to a complete overview here.[2] Instead, taking into account the comparative aim of this book and the limited space available, this Chapter focusses on one issue that may be of particular importance for the EAC: the protection of fundamental rights as general principles of EU law. Several other important principles of EU law including direct effect, supremacy, subsidiarity and proportionality, are discussed in other EU Chapters.[3]

1 See for example R. Dworkin, '*Taking Rights Seriously*' (Duckworth, 1977), Chapters 1 and 2 and (for a different approach) J. Raz, 'Legal Principles and the Limits of Law', 81 *Yale Law Journal* 823.

2 For two impressive volumes dedicated to General Principles in EU law, which can provide a fuller if still not even complete overview, see T. Tridimas, *The General Principles of EU Law* (2nd edn, OUP, 2006) and X. Groussot, *General Principles of Community Law* (Europa Law Publishing, 2006).

3 See EU Chapters 2, 3, and 4 for the principles of supremacy, direct effect, conferral and subsidiarity. See the EU Chapters on the internal market and free movement for the application of the principle of proportionality and consistency.

© ARMIN CUYVERS, 2017 | DOI 10.1163/9789004322073_013
This is an open access chapter distributed under the terms of the CC-BY-NC License.

Before we engage with the issue of fundamental rights, the next section first provides an overview of the nature, legal basis and functions of general principles in the EU legal order.

6.2 General Principles in the EU Legal Order

Unlike the EAC, many general principles of EU law are unwritten and judge-made, even though over time many have been codified in the Treaty.[4] Many of the more institutional-type of principles can now be found in the beginning of the TEU, such as the principle of sincere cooperation, conferral, Member State equality and the respect for national constitutional identity, subsidiarity, and proportionality.[5] Article 6 TEU, which was only introduced with the 1992 Treaty of Maastricht, now forms the central Treaty provision for the more substantive general principles relating to fundamental rights:

> 1. The Union recognises the rights, freedoms and principles set out in the Charter of Fundamental Rights of the European Union of 7 December 2000, as adapted at Strasbourg, on 12 December 2007, which shall have the same legal value as the Treaties.
> (...)
> 2. The Union shall accede to the European Convention for the Protection of Human Rights and Fundamental Freedoms. Such accession shall not affect the Union's competences as defined in the Treaties.
> 3. Fundamental rights, as guaranteed by the European Convention for the Protection of Human Rights and Fundamental Freedoms and as they result from the constitutional traditions common to the Member States, shall constitute general principles of the Union's law.

Some other provisions, moreover, contain important principles of non-discrimination, including Articles 18, 45 and 157 TFEU. Several important principles of EU law, however, still have no Treaty basis and remain based on the case

4 See on the different categories and types of general principles also A. von Bogdandy, 'Founding Principles' in: A. von Bogdandy and J. Bast (eds), *Principles of European Constitutional Law* (2nd edn., Hart, 2010), 11.

5 See Articles 4 and 5 TEU.

law of the CJEU. These unwritten principles include direct effect, supremacy and effectiveness, three of the most distinctive principles of EU law.[6]

In terms of hierarchical status, the general principles are usually considered part of primary law (certainly when they are codified in the Treaty), or otherwise as a special category of norms that are just below primary law but above all other EU law, including secondary legislation and international agreements signed by the EU. The hierarchical status of general principles is important for the question if principles can even trump the Treaties themselves, and thereby the will of the Member States as 'Masters of the Treaty'. The orthodox position still is that this is not possible, although some recent case law may suggest that there are some core principles that may in some cases acquire a supra-Treaty status.[7]

One of the reasons that EU law has so many general principles, and that these principles play such an important role, is that on many points the Treaties only lay down a very limited and open framework. As we shall see moreover, this limited framework was primarily focussed on economic integration, and less on other legal issues such as fundamental rights. Consequently, it was often up to the CJEU to fill in the general framework, provide protection where necessary, and generally breathe life into the bare bones of the Treaties.

This background of general principles can also be seen in the different functions general principles fulfil in the EU legal order. Although alternative categorizations are possible, one can say principles play at least four key roles. Firstly, general principles can form an aid to interpretation of primary or secondary law.[8] Secondly, because of their hierarchical status, general principles can be used to review the legality of secondary EU law and international agreements

---

6 The CJEU has also accepted multiple other, less far reaching principles in its case law, such as the principle of legal certainty, legitimate expectations or national procedural autonomy. See for example CJEU Case 112/77 *Töpfer*, Case C-453/00 *Kühne & Heitz* [2004] ECR I-8370r Case C-234/04 *Kapferer* [2006] ECR I-2585. For an example of a principle that was rejected, however, see Case C-189/01 *Jippes* ECLI:EU:C:2001:420 on animal welfare. See on direct effect and supremacy also EU Chapter 4.

7 See especially Case C-402/05 P *Kadi* [2008] ECRI-6351, to which we will return below. See for the claim that these principle can trump primary law for example A. Rosas and L. Armati, *EU Constitutional Law* (Hart, 2010), pp. 38–39. For further discussion see. Idriz-Tescan, *Legal constraints on EU Member States as primary law makers: a case study of the proposed permanent safeguard clause on free movement of persons in the EU negotiating framework for Turkey's accession* (Diss. Leiden 2015, Meijersreeks; MI-247) and A. Cuyvers, 'The Kadi II judgment of the General Court: the ECJ's predicament and the consequences for Member States'. 7 (2011) *European Constitutional Law Review*,. 481.

8 See for a far reaching and contested example Case C-402/07 *Sturgeon* ECLI:EU:C:2009:716.

signed by the EU.[9] Third, general principles form an independent basis for Member State liability.[10] Fourth, general principles can be used as 'gap fillers'. Where there is no relevant EU law, or the relevant rules simply do not provide an answer, general principles may be used to fill the gap in EU law in a way that is consistent with the overall body of EU law and the general principles.[11]

As indicated, the remainder of this Chapter focusses on two further topics that may be of particular interest to the EAC, starting with the pervasive, if not always visible, principle of effectiveness.

6.3 Fundamental Rights and General Principles in the EU

Like the EACJ, the CJEU does not have a separate fundamental rights jurisdiction. In other words, individuals cannot go to the CJEU, or even rely on EU law, just because one of their fundamental rights may have been violated. Individuals and companies can only rely on any rights granted by EU law when they are under the scope of EU law, for example because they have moved to another Member State, or because they fall under a piece of EU legislation.

Even though EU law today contains multiple fundamental rights, including a complete EU Charter of Fundamental Rights, these rights themselves, therefore, do not bring an individual within the scope of EU law or create jurisdiction for the CJEU, as will be explained in more detail below. Nevertheless, the EU has developed an effective protection of fundamental rights *within* the scope or EU law, largely through the creation and application of general principles. This is quite an achievement if one considers that, in the beginning of European integration, the Treaties did not refer to fundamental rights at all, and the CJEU even explicitly refused to apply fundamental rights.

This section therefore outlines how the CJEU used general principles to go from a situation in which EU law offered no protection of fundamental rights to a situation where the EU legal order identifies itself as a bastion of fundamental rights protection.

---

9 Joined Cases C-293 and 594/12 *Data Retention Directive* ECLI:EU:C:2014:238.

10 Case C-6/90 and 9/90 *Francovich* [1991] *ECR* I-5357 and Case C-46 and 48/93 *Brasserie du Pêcheur* [1996] *ECR* I-1029.

11 See for example Case C-555/07 *Kücükdeveci* [2010] ECR I-365 or Case 294/83 *Les Verts* ECR 1986 p. 1339.

6.3.1 *Genesis of Fundamental Rights in the EU*

The evolution of fundamental rights in the EU starts with their firm denial by the CJEU in *Stork*.[12] A German company wanted to rely on several fundamental rights contained in the German constitution against a secondary act of EU law. In its reply, the CJEU emphasized the economic nature of the Community:

> under Article 8 of the Treaty the High Authority is only required to apply Community law. It is not competent to apply the national law of the Member States. Similarly, under Article 31 the Court is only required to ensure that in the interpretation and application of the Treaty ... the law is observed. It is not normally required to rule on provisions of national law. Consequently, the High Authority is not empowered to examine a ground of complaint which maintains that, when it adopted its decision, it infringed principles of German constitutional law (in particular Articles 2 and 12 of the Basic Law).

The denial to protect fundamental rights, however, led to increasing concern at the national level. Especially some national constitutional courts were alarmed by a Community that claimed increasing authority, including supremacy over national law, but did not offer fundamental rights protection. This concern was one of the reasons behind the landmark judgment in *Solange I* by the German Constitutional Court (GCC). The GCC held that as long as fundamental rights were not adequately protected in the Community legal order, it reserved the right to disapply Community law in Germany.[13]

Faced with the understandable claim that an increasingly powerful EU should protect fundamental rights, the CJEU changed course. In *Internationale Handelsgesellschaft* and *Nold* the CJEU suddenly 'discovered' that EU law actually did contain fundamental rights in the form of general principles.[14] in *Internationale Handelsgesellschaft*, for example, the CJEU held that:

> However, an examination should be made as to whether or not any analogous guarantee inherent in Community law has been disregarded. In fact, respect for fundamental rights forms *an integral part of the general principles of law* protected by the court of justice.

---

12 Case 1/58 *Stork* ECR 1959 p. 17.

13 BVerfGE 37, 271 (1974) *Solange I*. See also EU Chapter 4 on the importance of this case law for the debate on supremacy of EU law as such.

14 Case 11/70 *Internationale Handelsgesellschaft* [1970] ECR 1125 and Case C-4/73 *Nold* ECLI:EU:C:1974:51.

> (…)
> The protection of such rights, whilst *inspired* by the constitutional traditions common to the Member States, must be ensured within the framework of the structure and objectives of the Community. It must therefore be ascertained, in the light of the doubts expressed by the *Verwaltungsgericht*, whether the system of deposits has infringed rights of a fundamental nature, respect for which must be ensured in the Community.[15]

Similarly, in *Nold* the CJEU found:

> As the court has already stated, fundamental rights form an integral part of the general principles of law, the observance of which it ensures. In safeguarding these rights, the court is bound to draw inspiration from constitutional traditions common to the Member States, and it cannot therefore uphold measures which are incompatible with fundamental rights recognized and protected by the constitutions of those states. Similarly, international treaties for the protection of human rights on which the member states have collaborated or of which they are signatories, can supply guidelines which should be followed within the framework of Community law.[16]

The CJEU, therefore, still refused to directly apply national fundamental or constitutional rights, also because doing so might threaten the autonomy and supremacy of EU law. At the same time, it used the open category of unwritten principles of EU law to create an 'analogous' protection at the EU level. The message to the national courts therefore was, do not worry, you do not need to apply your national constitutional rights, as EU law provides similar protection. In *Nold*, moreover, the CJEU further clarified that it would also take international treaties for the protection of human rights into account when determining the fundamental rights protection offered by the general principles of EU law.

6.3.2 *Consolidation of Fundamental Rights in the EU Legal Order*

Once the principled decision had been taken that the EU legal order protected fundamental rights, the CJEU could further develop and consolidate this protection. This consolidation was also supported by national supreme courts

15 Case 11/70 *Internationale Handelsgesellschaft* [1970] ECR 1125, par. 4 a.o.

16 Case C-4/73 *Nold* ECLI:EU:C:1974:51, par. 13.

responding positively to the *Internationale Handelsgesellschaft* and *Nold* line of case law. The German Constitutional Court, for example, showed its good will by retreating from its *Solange I* position to a more deferential approach in *Solange II*.[17] As long as fundamental rights would be adequately protected by the CJEU, the GCC would not exercise its right to disapply Community law in Germany, although it retained the authority to do so where manifest breaches of fundamental rights would occur.

An important step in the consolidation of fundamental rights as general principles came in *Baustahlgewebe*.[18] In this judgment the CJEU loyally applied the ECHR and the case law of the European Court of Fundamental Rights in Strasbourg (ECtHR), even though the EU was not, and is not, a party to the ECHR. This confirmed the trend of the CJEU *de facto* respecting the ECHR as applied by the Strasbourg court. In addition, *Baustahlgewebe* was the first case where the CJEU actually found a violation of a fundamental right by an EU institution. The following paragraphs of the judgment show the transformation of Article 6 ECHR into a general principle of EU law, which could then be applied by the CJEU:

> It should be noted that Article 6(1) of the EHRC provides that in the determination of his civil rights and obligations or of any criminal charge against him, everyone is entitled to a fair and public hearing within a reasonable time by an independent and impartial tribunal established by law.
>
> The general principle of Community law that everyone is entitled to fair legal process, which is inspired by those fundamental rights(…), and in particular the right to legal process within a reasonable period, is applicable in the context of proceedings brought against a Commission decision (…).[19]

Even though the ECHR or national constitutional rights did not apply directly into the EU legal order, therefore, general principles could be used to 'import' them and transform them into principles that could be applied in the EU legal order.

The recognition of fundamental rights in the EU legal order, and the special significance of the ECHR in this regard, was further consolidated by the 1992 Treaty of Maastricht, which introduced the provision that has now become

17 BVerfGE 73, 339 (1986) *Solange II*.

18 Case C-185/95 P *Baustahlgewebe* ECLI:EU:C:1998:608.

19 Case C-185/95 P *Baustahlgewebe* ECLI:EU:C:1998:608, paras. 20–21.

Article 6(3) TEU. As a result of this provision, fundamental rights as general principles, as well as the relevance of the ECHR, received a direct foundation in the Treaty, further cementing their standing and authority.[20]

6.3.3 *The Ascension of Fundamental Rights: The Charter and Kadi*

Despite the *de facto* application of the ECHR through general principles and their recognition in the Treaty, worries remained that the protection of fundamental rights within the EU might not go far enough, also because the ECHR only provides a minimum level of protection. For this reason, an EU Charter of fundamental rights was drafted, containing both the traditional fundamental rights and some more modern and social rights and 'principles'.

The Charter was first only 'solemnly proclaimed' on 7 December 2007 at the Nice European Council. Consequently, it did not have formal legal binding effect. Rather, it could be used as a tool for the EU to create or interpret the EU general principles that were legally binding. Subsequently, however, the Charter eventually became legally binding after the entry into force of the Lisbon Treaty on 1 December 2009. Somewhat embarrassingly, it was not considered politically opportune to include the Charter into the Treaties directly, this after the debacle of the Constitutional Treaty.[21] Instead, Article 6(1) TEU only refers to the Charter, and declares that it has the same legal value as the Treaty. Consequently, the Charter is now part of EU Primary law, and one of the central sources governing fundamental rights in the EU. This also means that since Lisbon, fundamental rights are both protected under the Charter *and* under the General principles of EU law, which continue to apply.[22]

---

20 At the same time, however, it was the same CJEU that blocked the accession of the EU to the ECHR. It was argued that the importation of ECHR rights by the CJEU carried the risk that the CJEU might, knowingly or unknowingly, get it wrong at some point, and that therefore the EU itself should also accede to the ECHR. The CJEU, however, argued that there was no sufficient legal basis for accession in Opinion 2/94 *Accession by the Community to the European Convention for the Protection of Human Rights and Fundamental Freedoms* ECLI:EU:C:1996:140. After this legal basis was created with the Treaty of Lisbon, however, the CJEU again blocked accession, inter alia because it might undermine the autonomy of EU law. See Opinion 2/13 *on the draft agreement providing for the accession of the European Union to the Convention for the Protection of Human Rights and Fundamental Freedoms* ECLI:EU:C:2014:2454.

21 See EU Chapter 1.

22 See however, section 3.4. below on the scope of the Charter, which is identical to those of the general principles and does not create a general human rights jurisdiction for the CJEU.

In addition to the introduction of the Charter, however, recent years saw another increase in the importance and standing of fundamental rights and general principles in the EU legal order. The key example of this development is the *Kadi* saga. The *Kadi* cases concerned the imposition of sanctions on individuals suspected of supporting terrorism. On 17 October 2001 Kadi, a Saudi national, was placed on a UN sanctions list because he was suspected of supporting Al Qaeda. This UN sanction was based on resolutions of the Security Council under Title VII of the UN charter, and hence claimed absolute primacy over all other international law.[23] The EU automatically took over all UN sanctions, so on 19 October 2001 Kadi was added to the EU sanctions list. As of that moment, all his European assets were frozen. Kadi challenged his EU sanction before the CJEU, arguing inter alia that his fundamental rights to a fair trial and an effective remedy had been violated. Consequently, the Kadi case lead to a direct conflict between EU fundamental rights and a resolution of the UN Security Council under Chapter VII.

The General Court essentially found that, under Article 103 UN Charter, the UN resolution trumped EU law, unless norms of *jus cogens* had been violated.[24] The CJEU, however, took the opposite approach. It stressed the foundational importance of fundamental rights for the EU legal order, holding *inter alia*:

> Art. 307 EC may in no circumstances permit any challenges to the *principles* that form part of the *very foundations* of the Community legal order (…).[25]

Kadi does not yet form a sufficient basis for the conclusion that some general principles may now trump EU primary law. At the same time, it is a striking example of just how far fundamental rights and general principles have come in the EU legal order since the initial denial of the CJEU in *Stork* to apply fundamental rights at all. At the same time, the impressive rise of fundamental rights

---

23 See amongst others Resolution 1904 (2009) and the earlier resolutions mentioned therein, as well as Article 103 of the UN Charter.

24 T-315/01 *Kadi I* [2005] ECR II-3649.

25 ECJ, Case C-402/05 P *Kadi* [2008] ECRI-6351, par. 304. See for multiple other confirmations of the fundamental importance and hierarchical standing of fundamental rights in the EU legal order also paras. 282–326 ECJ. This position was confirmed in Joined Cases C-584/10 P, C-593/10 P and C-595/10 P *Kadi II*, ECLI:EU:C:2013:518. See also A. Cuyvers, '"Give me one good reason": The unified standard of review for sanctions after Kadi II', 51(6) *Common Market Law Review* (2014), 1759.

should not be confused with the creation of a general fundamental rights jurisdiction, as EU fundamental rights only apply within the scope of EU law.

6.4 Protection within the Scope of EU Law Alone

By its very nature, EU law only applies in situations that fall under the *scope* of EU law.[26] Most importantly, this means that purely internal situation, i.e. situations that wholly take place in one Member State without any connection to EU law, do not fall under EU law.[27] In such purely internal situations, EU law does not apply, and hence individuals cannot derive any protection from it. For example, if an Austrian police man were to torture an Austrian citizen in Austria, the case would likely not have any connection to EU law. Consequently, the Austrian citizen could *not* rely on Article 4 of the EU Charter or on the General Principle of EU law that, inspired by Article 3 ECHR, prohibits torture. Naturally, the Austrian citizen will have the protection of the Austrian constitution, as well as the ECHR directly as Austria, as all EU Member States, is a party to the ECHR.

When drafting the Charter, the Member States wanted to make it very clear that the Charter does not extend the scope of EU law, and most certainly does not create a general jurisdiction for fundamental rights violations. As Article 51 of the Charter is at pain to stress:

> 1. The provisions of this Charter are addressed to the institutions, bodies, offices and agencies of the Union with due regard for the principle of subsidiarity and to the Member States *only when they are implementing Union law*. They shall therefore respect the rights, observe the principles and promote the application thereof in accordance with their respective powers and respecting the limits of the powers of the Union as conferred on it in the Treaties.
> 2. The Charter does not extend the field of application of Union law beyond the powers of the Union or establish any new power or task for the Union, or modify powers and tasks as defined in the Treaties.'

---

26 See also EU Chapter 4 par. 2 on the concept of scope.

27 Naturally, all acts by EU institutions or bodies fall under the scope of EU law, and hence under the scope of the Charter as well. Cf also Article 51(1) of the EU Charter.

Despite the fact that Article 51(1) of the Charter only refers to Member States when 'implementing' Union law, the CJEU has held in *Åkerberg Fransson* that the scope of the Charter is the same as the scope of EU law as such:

> Since the fundamental rights guaranteed by the Charter must therefore be complied with where national legislation falls within the scope of European Union law, situations cannot exist which are covered in that way by European Union law without those fundamental rights being applicable. The applicability of European Union law entails applicability of the fundamental rights guaranteed by the Charter.
>
> Where, on the other hand, a legal situation does not come within the scope of European Union law, the Court does not have jurisdiction to rule on it and any provisions of the Charter relied upon cannot, of themselves, form the basis for such jurisdiction.[28]

Over time, the CJEU has clarified that there are three ways of bringing an action by a Member State situation under the scope of EU law, and hence the Charter. Firstly, Member State actions fall under the scope of EU law where the Member State is *implementing EU law*, for example by implementing a directive. Where an individual, for example, is affected by a national law that directly or indirectly implements a directive, she is under the scope of EU law, and hence can also rely on EU fundamental rights.[29] Secondly, Member States fall under the scope of EU law where they are *derogating* from any rule of EU law. For example, any national law that restricts a free movement right, even if it is justified, falls under the scope of EU law.[30] Lastly, and most complexly, the actions of a Member State may also 'generically' fall under EU law. For example, this can be the case where the *subject matter* at stake is covered by an EU directive, even if the directive itself does not directly apply.[31]

28 Case C-617/10 *Åkerberg Fransson* ECLI:EU:C:2013:105, paras. 20–21.

29 See for the broad concept applied by the CJEU, which does not just cover national acts that directly implement a directive, also Case C-617/10 *Åkerberg Fransson* ECLI:EU:C:2013:105, paras. 27–28.

30 See in this context also Case C-112/00 *Schmidberger* [2003] ECR I-5659.

31 See for example Case C-555/07 *Kücükdeveci* ECR I-365, where the dispute was brought under the scope of EU law based on the directive which did not apply horizontally. Once the dispute had been brought under the scope of EU law in this creative manner, the CJEU could apply a general principle of EU law to it. For another creative extension to the scope of EU law see Case C-34/09 *Zambrano* [2011] ECR I-1177.

EU fundamental rights, therefore, have no general application, and the CJEU has no general fundamental rights jurisdiction. Despite these limitations, however, the protection offered by EU fundamental rights was seriously developed and improved by first developing substantive EU rights, both as general principles and via the Treaties, and secondly, by expanding the scope of EU law as such.

CHAPTER 7

Judicial Protection under EAC Law: Direct Actions

John Eudes Ruhangisa

7.1 Introduction

Judicial protection entails the guarantees offered by a legal order to the people as they individually or collectively enforce their rights or seek redress through litigation in the courts of law. In any country, rights on paper conferred by various legislation have little meaning if they cannot be claimed by individuals and be enforced via available legal remedies.

The concept of judicial protection at national level as well as at international level encompasses various elements such as access to justice, the right to an effective remedy and principles of fair trial and due process of law.[1]

The common place where redress or legal remedies can be sought in a national legal order is the court of law. Democratic States therefore are under obligation to provide to the citizens adequate procedural tools for the realization of this mechanism. The East African Community (EAC) as a democratic regional organization which aspires to become a political federation is no exception and therefore, the EAC has developed mechanisms to enable individuals to realize their rights afforded to them under the Treaty for the Establishment of the East African Community (Treaty).

7.2 An Overview

In any active partnership, differences, disagreements or disputes are bound to happen in the course of realizing the agreed terms by the partners. Inevitably, partners in the integration agenda just like partners in a business venture may find themselves disagreeing on some matters and such disagreement necessitates the intervention of a neutral person as an arbiter. The dispute requiring settlement may be between the member countries *inter se*, or the institutions of the organization against a member country or an individual citizen. In many

1 For a discussion on judicial protection see: Linda Mario Ravo "*The Role of the Principle of Effective Judicial Protection in the EU and its Impact on National Jurisdictions*", Ph.D Thesis, University of Trieste, pp. 102–104.

© JOHN EUDES RUHANGISA, 2017 | DOI 10.1163/9789004322073_014
This is an open access chapter distributed under the terms of the CC-BY-NC License.

cases the disputes involve the citizens of the member countries and their governments or citizens among themselves in the course of interacting and enjoying the benefits of integration as provided by the Treaty.

Since disagreements among active partners cannot be avoided, it is important that the contracting partners put in place a mechanism to deal with this eventuality when circumstance deems it necessary.

Being mindful of the above stated possibility and in anticipation of there being disagreements, the founding fathers of the EAC made a provision for the arbiter in the Treaty.[2] The East African Court of Justice (EACJ) was specifically created as one of the ten organs of the Community,[3] and was charged with settlement of disputes arising out of the Treaty.[4] Its major responsibility is to ensure the adherence to law in the interpretation and application of and compliance with the Treaty. The EACJ therefore, as the judicial organ of the Community, provides judicial protection to the citizens of East Africa through judicial pronouncements on matters that are brought before it by anyone seeking judicial protection on a point of EAC law and within the EAC framework.

Indeed the crucial role that both the laws and the courts play in the daily lives of citizens, and the crucial role that legal norms play in managing relationships that exist between sovereign states that intend to deepen or widen their relationship in the form of regional integration, cannot be overemphasized.[5] Undoubtedly, the Court plays a crucial role in the process towards integration of the EAC. This role can be effectively realized through the Court's effective and efficient execution of its mandate as an arbiter in dispute resolution, thereby contributing to confidence building in the region. Invariably the Court by playing its role effectively is expected to enhance the observance and upholding of human rights through good governance and democratic institutions in the region. All these aspirations and objectives must be reflected in the ways the Court conducts its activities including the quality of its judgments and the arbitration awards.

The concept of judicial protection is reflected in the Treaty where it creates legal actions in order that the Partner States, Secretary General, Council of

2 Chapter Eight of the Treaty for the Establishment of the East African Community (The Treaty) is dedicated to the East African Court of Justice.

3 Articles 9 (1) (e) of the Treaty *op. cit.*

4 Article 23 (1) and 27 (1) of the Treaty *op. cit.*

5 RUHANGISA, John, *"Establishing Independent and Effective Regional Courts: Lessons for the SADC Region from the EAC and ECOWAS"*, A Paper presented during the SADC Regional Colloquium on the SADC Tribunal, Johannesburg, South Africa, 12th–13th March 2013.

Ministers, legal and natural persons and employees of the Community are able to approach the Court for a remedy. These include

(*a*) *A situation where a Partner State or an organ or institution of the Community fails to fulfil an obligation under the Treaty or infringes a provision of the Treaty;*[6]
(*b*) *An action to question the legality of any Act, regulation, directive, decision or action of a Partner State for being ultra vires or unlawful or an infringement of the provisions of the Treaty or any rule of law relating to its application or that it amounts to a misuse or abuse of power;*[7]
(*c*) *Where a Partner State has failed to fulfil an obligation under the Treaty or infringes a provision of the Treaty* (not by natural persons);[8]
(*d*) *An action to question the legality of any Act, regulation, directive, decision or action of a Partner State or an institution of the Community whenever such Act, regulation, directive, decision or action is unlawful or infringes the provisions of Treaty;*[9]
(e) *Whenever a dispute arises between the Community and its employees concerning the terms and conditions of employment of the employees of the Community or the application and interpretation of the staff rules and regulations and terms and conditions of service of the Community.*[10]

The only remedy available in the above actions is court declaratory orders,[11] except for actions concerning terms and conditions of service of employees of the Community until when other original, appellate, human rights and other jurisdiction will be determined by the Council at a suitable subsequent date and a protocol concluded to that effect.[12]

Subject to the provisions of Article 27 of the Treaty, any person who is resident in a Partner State may refer for determination by the Court, the legality of any Act, regulation, directive, decision or action of a Partner State or an institution of the Community on the grounds that such Act, regulation, directive,

6 Article 28 (1) of the Treaty *op. cit.*
7 Article 28 (2) *Ibid.*
8 Article 29 *Ibid.*
9 Article 30 of the Treaty *op. cit.*
10 Article 31 *Ibid.*
11 Articles 23(1), 27(1), 33, 34, and 38 of the Treaty.
12 Article 23(2) of the Treaty.

decision or action is unlawful or is an infringement of the provisions of this Treaty.[13]

The actions that can be brought before the EACJ for judicial remedies include: actions for interpretation of the Treaty and Community laws, action for annulment, actions for liability, EAC employees' conflict, reference by national courts on points of EAC law, infringement proceedings, arbitration and advisory opinions. In all these actions, there is no requirement for exhaustion of local remedies as is the case with many regional and international courts.[14]

7.3 The Action for Annulment

An action for annulment is a legal procedure brought before the EACJ questioning the legality of an act/decision by a Partner State or by the organs/institutions of the Community and seeking the review of such acts or decisions. The Court shall annul the act concerned if the impugned act or decision is found to be contrary to the Treaty or any of the Community laws. Such action must be based on the violation or breach of the provisions of the Treaty by either the Partner State, or the organ or institution of the Community. This kind of intervention can be equated to judicial review under Common Law whereby the Court has power to issue the prerogative orders of *mandamus* and *certiorari* against the government, institutions of government or against the agents of government and people in service of the public institutions.

While the legislative and executive organs work towards the creation of an environment which furthers political integration by enacting Community laws and adopting policies for the implementation of these laws, the judicial organ plays the crucial role of interpreting the Treaty and other Community laws and in ensuring respect for the founding principles of the Community. The EACJ has on several occasions been called upon to invoke its powers to interpret the Treaty and other Community laws with a view to measuring the acts of the Partner States or the organs/institutions of the Community against the dictates of the Treaty or Community law. The first case to test the waters in this area originated from the East African Legislative Assembly (the Assembly), in which three members of the Assembly approached the Court in the famous

---

13 Article 30 (1) of the Treaty *op. cit.*

14 *Ibid.*

case *Callist Andrew Mwatela and Others v. The East African Community.*[15] This was also the first case to be filed with the EACJ.

What gave rise to the dispute in *Callist Andrew Mwatela* were four Private Members' Bills[16] which were pending before the Assembly. The Council of Ministers decided that they could take over the Bills seeing as they were policy oriented Bills and had implications on the Partner States sovereign interest. The Sectoral Council for Legal and Judicial Affairs to which the Council forwarded the Bills for their expert input, decided that, rather than having legislative acts enacted by the Assembly, protocols would be sufficient and that the two Bills should be withdrawn from the Assembly. The Secretary General communicated this to the Speaker. Aggrieved by this Council decision, three members of the Assembly brought the case before the EACJ seeking the annulment of the report of the Sectoral Council on Legal and Judicial Affairs including all its decisions, directives and actions contained in or based on it. With reasoned analysis of the issues the Court made the following specific findings, considerations, conclusions and holdings:

1. *That the Council is empowered under Article 14 of the Treaty to establish Sectoral Councils from among its members only. Membership of the Council under that Article is restricted to Ministers.*
2. (*a*) *That for the Council of Ministers to be properly constituted, it must comprise the stipulated quorum of the "representatives of all Partner States", in conformity with Rule 11 of the Rules of Procedure of the Council*
   (*b*) *That the Rule applies to Sectoral Council as well, since the decisions of Sectoral Council are deemed to be decisions of the Council of Ministers under Article 14(3) (i) of the Treaty. Accordingly the establishment of the Sectoral Council of September 2005, was inconsistent with the provisions of Article 14(3)(i) of the Treaty.*
3. *That the meeting of 13th–16th September, 2005 was not lawful meeting of a Sectoral Council; and decisions it handed down in respect of the two Bills were not valid decisions of the Sectoral Council. Therefore the Court ordered annulment of the decisions of the purported "Sectoral Council" However, since that Sectoral Council had been in place from 2001 and had*

15 *Reference No. 1 of 2005.*

16 The East African Community Trade Negotiation Bill, The East African Community Budget Bill, The East African Community Immunities and Privileges Bill, and The Inter-University Council for East Africa Bill.

undoubtedly made a number of decisions which it would be unwise to disturb, the Court was of the considered opinion that this was a proper case to apply the doctrine of prospective annulment—which the Court held to be "good law and practice". Accordingly, the Court ordered that its annulment of this particular Sectoral Council report would not have retrospective effect.

4. (*a*) *The Treaty does not provide for the members of the Council or the Sectoral Council to be represented at meetings by non members*
   (*b*) *This was deliberate, to avoid distortion of the elaborate structural hierarchy of representation of Partner States at the different levels in the organizational framework of the Community, in order to uphold the objective of the separation of the functions of the different organs of the Community.*
5. (*a*) *Ministers of Partner Stats cannot appoint persons who are not Ministers to attend meetings of Sectoral Councils or those of the Council purportedly on their behalf.*
   (*b*) *To do so would be to make inroads into the very clear words of Article 13 of the Treaty.*
6. (*a*) *Although the composition of the Council is established under Article 13 of the Treaty, the total membership is not readily ascertainable, since it is only the membership of Ministers responsible for Regional Cooperation which is static and ascertainable.*
   (*b*) *Apparently membership of additional Ministers is determined by the agenda of a particular meeting of the Council. A more transparent way of knowing the composition of the Council Members should be evolved, to avoid uncertainty and disputes.*

Following the Court's findings, the Treaty was amended to legalize the status of Attorney Generals in the Sectoral Council for Legal and Judicial Affairs by formally recognizing them as members of the Council. After the amendment, the Treaty read:

> The Council shall consist of:
> (*a*) *The Minister responsible for East African Community affairs of each Partner State;*
> (*b*) *Such other Minister of the Partner States as each Partner State may determine; and*
> (*c*) *The Attorney General of Each Partner State*[17]

17 Article 13 of the Treaty [Emphasis added].

Invariably, none of the subsequent requests for annulments was successful to obtain an order with retrospective effect. For example, in the case of *East African Law Society v. The Attorney General of Kenya & 3 Others*,[18] the Court was asked whether the amendments to the Treaty as carried out by the Summit could be stopped. The Court declined to invalidate the amendments and instead declared that the decision on the requirement of involvement of people in the Treaty amendment process shall have prospective application.

In essence the Court hesitated to nullify the impugned amendments but warned the Partner States not to repeat the same mistake in future, and if they did, such amendments would *ipso facto* be null and void. This is technically known as prospective annulment[19] or prospective overruling[20] or the doctrine of temporary validity. Under normal circumstances nullification by the court is prospective, meaning that after the nullification of the action or the law, such act or law so nullified by the court becomes void and of no consequence from the date the court declares the impugned act or law null. This means the impugned affairs remain undisturbed even after the date when the court makes the declaration. It has the effect of outlawing new similar future acts. The doctrine was devised by the Supreme Court of the United States in the case of *Linkletter v. Walker, 381 US (1965) 618* to alleviate the inconveniences which would have resulted from its new decision which was a departure from its previous ruling that impugned the law was constitutional. Likewise the EACJ was mindful of the fact that the Sectoral Council for Legal and Judicial Affairs had illegally taken many decisions of a policy nature concerning the development of the Customs Union. These decisions would be affected and

18 The Applicants filed this Reference challenging the legality of the process for the December 2006 Amendments of the EAC Treaty. The Applicants challenge was not directed to the substance of these amendments. Rather, they challenged the extra-ordinary hasty manner and the impropriety of the amendment process as being an infringement of Articles 1, 5, 6, 7, 8, 9, 11, 26, 38 and 150 of the Treaty: namely, failure to have the mandatory 90 days period for Partner States' comments under Article 150(4) and (5): amending the Treaty while the EACJ was still seized of a live case on the matter (i.e. Reference No. 1 of 2006); and exclusion from the Amendment process of other EAC Organs, State governments, and the people and registered of East Africa.

19 The same approach was adopted by the Court in the case of *Callist Andrew Mwatela and Others vs The East African Community, Reference No. 1 of 2005* when it was called upon to nullify the report of the Sectoral Council on Legal and Judicial Affairs including all its decisions, directives and actions contained in or based on it.

20 For a discussion on prospective overruling see the decision of the Supreme Court of Uganda in the case of *The attorney General vs Paul K. Ssemogerere and Hon. Zachary Olum, Constitutional Appeal No. 3 of 2004 at pages 138–139.*

serious inconvenience would be caused to the advanced stage that had been reached in negotiating the Customs Union Protocol if the EACJ would have nullified all such decisions.[21]

7.4 The Action for Interpretation of the Treaty

In interpreting laws, courts play an important role complementing that of legislators in as far as they give clear and detailed explanations of the content and spirit of the laws. In a context of a regional organization aimed at full integration of Partner States as is the case with the EAC, the judicial pronouncements and interpretation of the Community laws assist the policy makers to have a common understanding of these laws in order to take informed decisions consistent with their spirit during the implementation stage. The EACJ has actively played this role as it transpires from its jurisprudence so far developed.

In the case of *Callist Andrew Mwatella & 2 others v. EAC*,[22] discussed above in relation to annulment, the applicants also requested the Court to interpret various provisions of the Treaty against the actions and decisions of the Council of Ministers and the Sectoral Council for Legal and Judicial Affairs. As outlined, the Council of Ministers and the Secretariat had illegally assumed control over Assembly-led Bills. However, the Council had also purported to withdraw four Private Members' Bills from the Assembly and therefore the application to the EACJ questioned the right of the Council to delay the presentation of the Bills to the House.

The Court found that the Sectoral Council on Legal and Judicial Affairs was not constituted per Treaty, in particular Article 14 which provided that the Council of Ministers shall 'establish from among its members' Sectoral Councils and that Sectoral Council members are restricted to 'ministers' as defined by the Treaty. The Court found that Kenya and Tanzania were represented by non-ministers at the disputed meeting of the 13th to 16th September 2005 and, therefore the meeting was not properly constituted and did not amount to a lawful Sectoral Council meeting. In this regard, its decision regarding the two Bills was *ipso facto* invalid.

---

21 See for the options to limit the retrospective effect of an annulment under EU law EU Chapter 8.

22 *Application No. 1 of 2005*. See also the case of *Christopher Mtikila v. The Attorney General of the United Republic of Tanzania and the Secretary General of the East African Community, Reference No. 08 of 2007*.

On another issue the Court interpreted Article 59 (1) to the effect that any Member of the Assembly may introduce a Bill in the House as the Council does not have exclusive legislative initiative to introduce Bills in the Assembly. The Court held that the Assembly owns all Bills once in the Assembly, whether they came initially by way of Private Members' Bills or Community Bills. As such, permission of the Assembly would be required for withdrawal of any Bill and such approval must be sought and obtained through a motion passed by the Assembly. The Court found that the Bills were already in the Assembly, so could not be withdrawn by the Council of Ministers as purportedly done and that all the Council could do was to delay the debate but could not withdraw the Private Members' Bills.

On the issue concerning the relationship of the Council and the Assembly on legislation, the Court held that the decisions of the Council even on policy issues have no place in areas of jurisdiction of the Summit, Court and the Assembly.[23] It held that the Assembly is a creature of the Treaty like the other organs of the Community and its competence is only on matters conferred upon it by the Treaty as with all Community organs. In this regard, the Assembly could only legislate on matters on which the Partner States had surrendered sovereignty or part thereof to the EAC.

By interpreting these Articles of the Treaty, the Court provided guidance for future operations of the affairs of the Community by its organs and institutions. The Court boldly told the Ministers and Attorney Generals that they had overstepped their boundaries which was not acceptable in any democratic institution.

Another significant case that was brought to the EACJ seeking interpretation of the Articles of the Treaty *vis-à-vis* the actions of a Partner State was *Anyang' Nyong'o & others v. The Attorney General of Kenya & Others*.[24] The main contention in this reference was whether Kenya's process of electing the nine persons deemed to be its members in the Assembly and the rules of the Kenya National Assembly for Assembly elections infringed Article 50 of the EAC Treaty.

The EACJ considered the possible meanings of the expression "the National Assembly shall elect" as stated in Article 50 of the Treaty. The Court found that it can only mean "shall choose by vote" taking the ordinary meaning of the phrase and that reference to "democratic election of persons to political office" is understood to mean election by voting. Furthermore, the Court found that this interpretation of the meaning of "elect" is borne out by the practice in each Partner State of electing the Speaker and Deputy Speaker in the National

---

23 Article 14 (3) (c) and Article 16 of the Treaty, *op. cit.*

24 *Reference No. 1 of 2006.*

Assembly through voting. In all Partner States, the National Assembly executes the function of electing Speaker and Deputy Speaker by voting in one form or another and the extent of discretion of the National Assemblies is to determine what procedure should be applied for the voting. The Court held that the bottom line for compliance with Article 50 is that the decision to elect is a decision of and by the National Assembly not another caucus.

Finally, on whether the Kenyan rules complied with Article 50, the Court held that the election rules partially comply with Article 50 of the Treaty in so far as they provide for proportional representation of political parties. However, there was a significant degree of non-compliance in the failure to make a provision for gender and other special interest representation. The major deviation found in the Kenyan rules was the non-provision for election. The Court held that the election rules and actual process was the antithesis of an election, as the rules "deemed" the nine elected in order to circumvent the express Treaty provision.

7.5 EAC-Employee Conflicts

The jurisdiction of the EACJ includes hearing and determining disputes between the Community and its employees which arise out of the terms and conditions of their employment; the application and interpretation of the staff rules and regulations; or the terms and conditions of service of the Community.[25] This is another area where the Court has not performed well in terms of statistics of cases that have been filed and determined. As of November 2015, only two cases, *Alloys Mutabingwa v. the Secretary General of the East African Community*[26] and *Angela Amudo v. the East African Community*,[27] had been filed.

The former case concerned the claim by Mr Alloys Mutabingwa following the refusal by the Secretariat to compensate him full remuneration for the remainder of contract, which had been cut short by the EAC. Such remuneration was a mandatory requirement under Rule 96(3) of the EAC Staff Rules and Regulations. However, the case could not go for trial as the claimant withdrew his claim.

25 Article 31 of the Treaty, *op. cit.*

26 *Claim No. 1 of 2011.*

27 *Claim No. 2 of 2012.*

In the latter case, Ms Angela Amudo sought a declaration concerning the tenure of appointment given to her which was initially for a period of 20 months with subsequent periodical extensions of the appointment up to 30th April 2012. Amudo submitted that such tenure was *ultra vires*, considering the powers of the Secretary General and his deputies, and also inconsistent with the Staff Rules and Regulations of the Respondent, and as such she was entitled to a contract of employment for a period of 5 years from the date of assumption of duty renewable for another 5 years. The claim was heard by the Court and judgment was partly entered in her favour. Ms Amudo appealed in relation to the part of her claim that she lost, however, the Appellate Division dismissed the appeal and allowed the cross-appeal on the basis that the Appellant's position was not an established position in the Community and therefore Ms Amudo could not have been regarded as a member of staff under the Staff Rules and Regulations.

7.6 Direct Appeals from Other Courts on Points of EAC Law

The jurisdiction of the Court as presently constituted does not include direct appeals from national courts.[28] Instead, the Treaty prescribes the jurisdiction of the Court to include references, by national courts, for preliminary ruling when a question is raised before any court or tribunal of a Partner State concerning the interpretation or application of the provisions of the Treaty or the validity of the regulations, directives, decisions or actions of the Community.[29] The procedure operates so that national courts or tribunals shall, if they consider that a ruling on the question is necessary to enable it to give judgment, request the EACJ to give a preliminary ruling on the question.

Furthermore, under the proviso to Article 27(1), the Court's jurisdiction to interpret the Treaty shall not include the application of any such interpretation to the jurisdiction conferred by the Treaty on organs of the Partner States. This Article should be read together with Article 33 which reads—

---

28 Such direct appeals should be distinguished from the preliminary questions procedure, discussed in Chapter 8, which allows national courts to ask questions to the EACJ during national proceedings, but does not allow parties to appeal to the EACJ.

29 Article 34 of the Treaty, *op. cit.*

(1) *Except where jurisdiction is conferred on the Court by thisTreaty, disputes to which the Community is a party shall not on that ground alone, be excluded from the jurisdiction of the national court of the Partner States.*
(2) *Decisions of the Court on the interpretation and application of this Treaty shall have precedence over decisions of national courts on a similar matter.*

The Court seems to have concurrent jurisdiction with national courts on the interpretation of the Treaty, but decisions of the Court take precedence over decisions of the national courts. This position, as it currently stands, may be a breeding ground for confusion. The EACJ in *The East African Law Society and 4 Others v. The Attorney General of Kenya and 3 Others,*[30] made the following pertinent observation on this issue—

> By the provisions under Articles 23,33(2) and 34, the Treaty established the principle of overall supremacy of the Court over the interpretation and application of the Treaty, to ensure harmony and certainty. The new (*a*) *proviso to Article 27; and* (*b*) *paragraph* (*3*) *of Article 30*, have the effect of compromising that principle and/or of contradicting the main provision. It should be appreciated that the question of what "the Treaty reserves for an institution of a Partner State" is a provision of the Treaty and a matter that ought to be determined harmoniously and with certainty. If left as amended the provisions are likely to lead to conflicting interpretations of the Treaty by national courts of the Partner States.

Also in *Prof. Peter Anyang' Nyongo and 10 Others v. The Attorney General of Kenya and 2 Others and Abdirahim Haitha Abdi and 11 Others*[31], the Court had this to say—

> The purpose of these provisions is obviously to ensure uniform interpretation and avoid possible conflicting decisions and uncertainty in the interpretation of the same provisions of the Treaty. Article 33(2) appears to envisage that in the course of determining a case before it a national court may interpret and apply a Treaty provision. Such envisaged interpretation however, can only be incidental. The article neither provides for nor envisages a litigant directly referring a question as to the

30 *Reference No. 3 of 2007.*
31 *Reference No. 1 of 2006.*

> interpretation of a Treaty provision to a national Court. Nor is there any other provision directly conferring on the national Court jurisdiction to interpret the Treaty.

It is important that this uncertainty in the Treaty provisions should be made clearer by amending the Treaty as appropriate. Therefore the Treaty, protocols and any Community law are the core generators of the work of the Court, and the Court can entertain any dispute arising out of these instruments. However, a continuing number of protocols contradicting the position of the Treaty have been enacted. Other parallel dispute resolution mechanisms (national courts and quasi-judicial bodies) have been established. For instance, Article 41(2) of the EAC Customs Union Protocol which deals with dispute settlement, establishes committees to handle disputes arising out of the Protocol and gives these committees finality in determining the disputes. The Court is left out and therefore denied a role in this process except if a party challenges the decision of the committee on grounds of fraud, lack of jurisdiction or other illegality. Again, under Article 54(2) of the Common Market Protocol, jurisdiction to entertain Common Market related disputes has mainly been given to national courts. At the same time Article 33(2) of the Treaty recognizes the EACJ's decisions on the interpretation of the Treaty and Community law as being superior to a national courts decision on the same matter. Since the EACJ does not form part of the hierarchy of the national judicatures, the Common market related dispute to be handled by national institutions will also follow the relevant national court system in case a party seeks to appeal against the decision of such national institution. This tendency of the Partner States to oust the jurisdiction of their own joint Court, is not conducive to the integration agenda. It has the effect of undermining the Court itself and causing confusion in the development of the uniform regional jurisprudence.[32]

7.7 Appeals as a Remedy

The Treaty provides that appeals from judgments and orders of the First Instance Division shall lie to the Appellate Division.[33] However, there are two areas in the Treaty where such a mechanism may not be appropriate: firstly, on matters of referral of certain disputed questions from the national courts to

32 Compare in this regard also the rulings of the CJEU defending its ultimate authority as final arbiter of EU law, also to protect the unity of EU law, as discussed in EU Chapter 4.

33 Article 35A of the Treaty, *op. cit.*

the EACJ;[34] and secondly, on matters of request for advisory opinions on questions of law arising from the Treaty.[35]

As alluded to earlier a national court or tribunal before which a question arises as to the interpretation or application of the Treaty, is required to request the EACJ to give a preliminary ruling on the matter, in order to enable the national court or tribunal before which the question has arisen to give its judgment on the parent matter. Where should such a referral go to, First Instance Division or Appellate Division? The Court has taken the initiative and invoked its rule-making powers under Article 42 of the Treaty by amending the EACJ Rules of Procedure and introduced Rule 76 to address this issue. Rule 76 (1) provides as follows—

> A request by a national Court or tribunal of a Partner State concerning the interpretation or application of the provisions of the Treaty or validity of any regulations directives, decisions or actions of the Community pursuant to Article 34 of the Treaty shall be lodged in the Appellate Division by way of a case stated.

This may be a stop-gap measure, however, it is imperative that proper jurisdictional boundaries are provided for in the Treaty itself.

To date the national referral jurisdiction has remained essentially dormant in the EACJ with only two referrals from the High Court of Kenya and High Court of Uganda having been filed so far in the registry of the EACJ.[36]

The potential for referral is overwhelming, however, unfortunately, that potential has not been utilised. This failure cannot be attributed to a scarcity of disputed questions in the Partner States' national courts. The paucity of referrals is most likely due to various factors including lack of knowledge and non-awareness concerning the availability of this mechanism. The EACJ, national courts as well as the Bar Associations across the region have to sensitize the litigating public and all other concerned stakeholders about this jurisdiction.

---

34 Article 34 of the Treaty, *Ibid.* See also Rule 76 (1) of the East African Court of Justice Rules of Procedure.

35 Article 36 of the Treaty, *op. cit.* See also Rule 75 (1) of the East African Court of Justice Rules of Procedure.

36 See on this point also chapter 8, as well as the very different situation in the EU as set out in EU Chapter 8.

In the European Union, referrals for preliminary rulings from national courts do make up a significant part of the CJEU's workload.[37] Thus, the jurisprudence of the European Court has seeped down and saturated the roots of the national courts of all European Member States.

7.8 Infringement Proceedings

All proceedings in the EACJ require the Court to interpret either the Treaty or other Community laws in order to determine the issues before it. Infringement proceedings like other actions involve the interpretation of the law *vis-à-vis* the impugned action. A significant number of actions for infringement in the EACJ have largely involved the examination of the facts relating to adherence to the principles of democracy, the rule of law, promotion and protection of human and peoples' rights.

The regional cooperation put in place under the Treaty is people-centered and market driven.[38] If democracy means the rule of the people by the people, and is one of the fundamental principles of the EAC, then the EAC working strategy must focus on participation of all social groups from the bottom to the top.

When it was asked to consider if by reason of failure to carry out wide consultations within Partner States on proposals for amendments, the process constituted an infringement of the Treaty in any way, the Court found that:

> It is common knowledge that the private sector and civil society participated in the negotiations that led to the conclusion of the Treaty among the Partner States and, as we have just observed, that they continue to participate in the making of Protocols thereto. Furthermore, as we noted earlier in this judgment, Article 30 entrenches the people's right to participate in protecting the integrity of the Treaty. We think that construing the Treaty as if it permits sporadic amendments at the whims of officials without any form of consultation with stakeholders would be a recipe for regression to the situation lamented in the preamble of "lack of strong participation of the private sector and civil society" that led to the collapse of the previous Community.[39]

---

37 See the discussion in EU Chapter 8.

38 Treaty, Article 7 (1) (a).

39 *East Africa Law Society and 4 others v. Attorney General of Kenya and 3 others*, type written judgment p. 30.

The Court went on to conclude that:

> [F]ailure to carry out consultation outside the Summit, Council and the Secretariat was inconsistent with a principle of the Treaty and therefore constituted an infringement of the Treaty (...).[40]

As regards, the principle of promotion and protection of human and peoples' rights, it must be noted that for any regional court to be seen as an integrating institution, it has *inter alia* to facilitate the integration process through the recognition of the rights of individuals.

Although explicit human rights jurisdiction is yet to be operationalized, the Court has been courageous enough to ensure that basic rights of individuals are respected. On more than one occasion, the Court has had to consider preliminary objections from defendants alleging lack of *locus standi* by individuals and legal persons. The Court has consistently upheld that individuals and legal persons have access to the Court under Article 30 of the Treaty,[41] which is a basic right to the regional justice mechanism enabling the peoples to "participate in protecting the integrity of the Treaty."[42] An infringement of the rights of the citizens of East Africa by the Partner State or by the organs or institutions of the Community is therefore actionable in the EACJ. However, the Court has strictly entertained such proceedings if and only if the impugned action or decision is by either the Partner State or the organ or institution of the Community. In the case of *Modern Holdings (EA) Limited v. Kenya Port Authority, Reference No. 1 of 2008* the Court held that the Kenya Ports Authority lacked the authority to be sued because it was not an institution of the Community created under Article 9 (2) of the Treaty or a surviving institution of the defunct EAC, instead it was created under section 3 of the Kenya Ports Authority Act as a statutory body with perpetual succession, a common seal and power to sue and be sued in its corporate name.

This ruling has been criticized as it is perceived that the Court "shot itself in the foot". Critics would have wished in the seemingly borderline cases like this that the Court would have made a finding that it had jurisdiction

40 As above p. 31.

41 Cases *Prof. Peter Anyang' Nyong'o and Others v. Attorney General of Kenya and Others; Christopher Mtikila v. The Attorney General of the United Republic of Tanzania and the Secretary General of the East African Community* and *East Africa Law Society and 4 others v. Attorney General of Kenya and 3 others.*

42 *East Africa Law Society and 4 others v. Attorney General of Kenya and 3 Others.*

just like it did in *James Katabazi & 21 others v. The Secretary General of the East African Community & Another*,[43] where even after finding that it had no direct jurisdiction, it still found a way of dealing with the matter. In *Katabazi*, the Court read the Treaty *in toto* and invoked the spirit of the Treaty instead of concentrating on the wording of the Treaty. The Court in that case said *inter alia*:

> Does this court have jurisdiction to deal with human rights issues? The quick answer is: No it does not have.... It is very clear that jurisdiction with respect to human rights requires a determination of the Council and a conclusion of a protocol to that effect. Both of those steps have not been taken. It follows, therefore, that this Court may not adjudicate on disputes concerning violation of human rights per se.... While the Court will not assume jurisdiction to adjudicate on human rights disputes, it will not abdicate from exercising its jurisdiction of interpretation under Article 27 (1) merely because the reference includes allegation of human rights violation.[44]

At the time of inception, the Court of Justice of the European Union had very limited jurisdiction as well, as Karen J Alter said:

> The ECJ was created to fill three limited roles for the member states: ensuring that the Commission and the Council of Ministers did not exceed their authority, filling vague aspects of EC laws through dispute resolution, and deciding on charges of non compliance raised by the Commission or member states.[45]

However, even with that limited jurisdiction, over time the CJEU asserted itself and provided guidance to the policy organs by interpreting the Treaty for prosperity.[46] In the words of Alec Stone Sweet and James A. Caporaso:

> The community treaties started as a set of legal arrangements binding on the member states but with a lot of help from the creative ECJ have evolved into a vertically integrated legal regime conferring legally

43 *Reference No. 1 of 2007*.

44 *Ibid.*, typewritten judgment pp. 15–17.

45 Karen J Alter," Who are the Master of the Treaty"?: European Governments and the European Court of Justice, *International Organization* 52 (1998) 121–147 p. 124.

46 See also EU Companion Chapters 4 and 9.

> enforceable rights and obligations on all persons and entities public and private within the EC territory.[47]

This was not achieved easily since the European Court was first and foremost established with limited roles, just like the EACJ.

The Court has also declined to entertain matters where its jurisdiction is in doubt.[48] In *Prof. Anyang' Nyongo and Others v. the Attorney General of the Republic of Kenya and Others, Ref. No.1 of 2006,* the Court struck out the reference against two individuals for lack of capacity as they were wrongly sued. To clarify on whether a person can bring action under Article 30 against a natural person who commits misfeasance that infringe on provisions of the Treaty the Court held:

> ... A reference under Article 30 of the Treaty should not be construed as an action in tort brought by a person injured by or through the misfeasance of another. It is action to challenge the legality under the Treaty of an activity of a Partner State or of an institution of the Community. The alleged collusion and connivance, if any, is not actionable under Article 30 of the Treaty.[49]

7.8.1 *Infringement Proceedings Initiated by a Partner State*

Ordinarily, infringement proceedings which are initiated by a Partner State, like those instituted by individuals, are ordinary suits that come to the Court by way of reference.[50] As highlighted earlier in this chapter, a Partner State which considers that another Partner State or an organ or institution of the Community has infringed a provision of the Treaty, may refer the matter to the Court for adjudication.[51] Furthermore, the Treaty gives power to a Partner

---

47 Alec Stone Sweet and James A.Caporaso, From Free Trade to Supranational Policy: The European Court and Integration in Waynes Sandholtz and Alec Stone Sweet (eds), *European Integration and Supranational Governance*, Oxford University, 1998, pp. 92–133 at p. 102.

48 *Christopher Mtikila and Others v. The Attorney General of the United Republic of Tanzania, Ref No.2 of 2007.*

49 *Prof. Anyang' Nyongo and Others v. the Attorney General of the Republic of Kenya and Others, Ref. No.1 of 2006*, page 7.

50 This term has no special meaning but it originates from the verb "refer" to represent and distinguish the cases in the East African Court of Justice with those in the national courts where such cases would be known as suits or claims.

51 Article 28 (1) of the Treaty, *op. cit.*

State to refer for determination by the Court, the legality of any Act, regulation, directive, decision or action on the ground that it is *ultra vires* or unlawful or an infringement of the provisions of the Treaty or any rule of law relating to its application or amounts to a misuse or abuse of power.[52]

Despite the availability of this machinery, no single Partner State has ever dared bring action against another Partner State on ground of infringement of the Treaty. This inaction does not mean that there have not been Treaty infringements.[53] Some infringements were, in fact, glaringly obvious. For example, the 2015 unfair and non-peaceful elections in the Republic of Burundi and the subsequent killings or disappearance of people who expressed dissatisfaction with the manner in which the entire election was conducted. Moreover, the post-2007 election violence in Kenya which led to the prosecution of the President and Vice President[54] at the International Criminal Court, as well as the scramble for Mingigo Island between the Republics of Kenya and Uganda are further examples of unabated Treaty infringements.

7.8.2 *Infringement Proceedings Initiated by the Secretary General*

The Secretary General has powers to bring an action against a Partner State for infringement of the Treaty where he considers that a Partner State has failed to fulfil an obligation under the Treaty or has infringed a provision of the Treaty.[55] However, the procedure for actualization of these powers by the Secretary General as laid down by the Treaty is cumbersome and makes it virtually impossible for him to exercise these powers. The Secretary General is required, before approaching the Court, to first submit his or her findings to the Partner State concerned so that Partner State can submit its observations on the findings by the Secretary General.[56]

If the Partner State concerned does not submit its observations to the Secretary General within four months, or if the observations submitted are unsatisfactory, the Secretary General shall refer the matter to the Council which shall decide whether the matter should be referred by the Secretary

52 Article 28 (2) *Ibid.*

53 At one point the Republic of Kenya was about to go to war with the Republic of Uganda, a fellow Partner State quarreling for Migingu a rocky island in Lake Victoria. Even the Kenya 2007/08 post- election violence were never taken to the East African Court of Justice for their potential infringements of the Treaty until they found space in the ICC (The Hague) at the instance of the international community.

54 The charges against these Statesmen and top leaders of the Government of Kenya were subsequently dropped following lack of evidence.

55 Article 29 of the Treaty, *op. cit.*

56 Article 29 (1) of the Treaty *Ibid.*

General to the Court immediately or be resolved by the Council.[57] It is apparent that the Secretary General's powers to bring in Court an action for infringement of the Treaty against a Partner State is subject to two conditions: firstly; the Council should have failed to resolve the matter; and secondly, the Council, having failed to resolve the matter, should have directed the Secretary General to refer the matter to the Court. Short of that, the Secretary General cannot on his own imitative take action against a Partner State which infringes the Treaty. These conditions explain the non-existence of any reference by the Secretary General to date.

7.9 Arbitration before the EACJ

The EACJ can constitute itself as an arbitration tribunal.[58] The Treaty confers arbitration mandate to the Court to the effect that:

> The Court shall have jurisdiction to hear and determine any matter:
> (*a*) *arising from an arbitration clause contained in a contract or agreement which confers such jurisdiction to which the Community or any of its institutions is a party; or*
> (*b*) *arising from a dispute between the Partner States regarding this Treaty if the dispute is submitted to it under a special agreement between the Partner States concerned; or*
> (*c*) *arising from an arbitration clause contained in a commercial contract or agreement in which the parties have conferred jurisdiction on the Court.*[59]

The Court formulated the rules to govern arbitration proceedings after consulting its major stakeholders. These rules wait to be tested as soon as matters are referred to the Court for arbitration. It is a clear fact that, no arbitrator can arbitrate any matter unless the parties appoint him or include a clause in their agreement to the effect that in case of dispute they would all submit themselves to a certain arbitrator for arbitration.

---

57 Article 29 (2) of the Treaty, *Ibid.*

58 See also a discussion by John Eudes Ruhangisa, "Procedures and Functions of the East African Court of Justice", in Kennedy Gastorn, Harad Sippel and Ulrike Wanizek (eds), *Processes of Legal Integration in the East African Community,-TGCL Series 2, Dar es Salaam University Press, Dar es Salaam, 2011, pp. 145–172.*

59 Article 32 of the Treaty, *op. cit.*

Although appointing the EACJ as arbitrator has many advantages *vis-à-vis* other arbitration fora,[60] it is doubtful whether any parties have actually appointed it, as there has not been any litigation to compel the parties to choose the Court. Even the governments of the Partner States have not utilised the seemingly free services of the Court as far as arbitration is concerned but find it easier to go abroad and exclude an institution of their own creation. Lawyers in East Africa have a big role to play in advising their clients of the arbitral jurisdiction of the EACJ especially at the time of drafting commercial agreements.

There could be many reasons for this unusual reaction by the people of East Africa especially the business community. The wait and see tendency could be one of the possible reasons explaining the slow momentum in utilising the Court's arbitral jurisdiction. As the EACJ's arbitral jurisdiction is new, people may hesitate to risk filing their matters in the institute whose workings are unknown. Moreover, the double role being played by the Court, where on the one hand it functions as the Court of Justice and on the other hand as the arbitration tribunal, places it in difficult situation of making its stakeholders understand its definite status. Stakeholders would like to be assured that Judges sitting as arbitrators will behave differently from the way they behave while presiding over matters in court rooms, bearing in mind the fact that arbitration is a specialised discipline of dispute settlement. Arguably, the arbitral jurisdiction puts the eminence of the EACJ as a court of law at risk. Furthermore, the multiple jurisdictions of the Court as the Court of Justice,[61] as a court of human rights,[62] as a labour court[63] and as an arbitration court[64] may negatively impact on its efficiency should all these jurisdictions be fully operationalised.

Despite the Court's efforts in 2006 and thereafter to prepare itself for handling arbitration disputes by providing its Judges with arbitration skills through training, all such Judges have since retired without arbitrating any matter. As a result, the Court has to retrain Judges every time they complete their contractual tenure. The Court has spent a substantial amount of its financial resources to train the Judges who subsequently depart without leaving behind

60 Such advantages include the fact that parties to arbitration are not required to pay arbitrators' fee as the arbitrators are paid by East African Community in their capacities as Judges.

61 Article 27 of the Treaty, *op. cit.*

62 Article 27 (2) *Ibid.*

63 Article 31, *Ibid.*

64 Article 32, *Ibid.*

the fruits of such investment. In effect, the Court has been turned into a training ground for arbitrators who do not benefit it. Since 2001, when the Court was inaugurated, only one case, *Nayebare Alice v. East Africa Law Society,*[65] has been arbitrated. The Claimant's claim was for a total sum of USD 48,387.00, which constituted payment for various employment benefits covering salary emoluments, leave and repatriation allowances, sundry and other termination benefits. In addition, the Claimant prayed for an order that: "the Respondent clears and/or signs the requisite NSSF forms to enable the Claimant access her NSSF savings." The arbitral claim was heard and an award given on 9th May 2014 to the effect that the Claimant was entitled to a monetary award of USD 8,534 plus interest on the amount at the Tanzanian rate from 9th May, 2014 until payment in full and that the Respondent should within 7 days of the award remit USD 724.50 to NSSF as its contribution for the claimant, covering a period between September–December 2004.

7.10 Advisory Opinions of the EACJ

The Treaty confers jurisdiction on the Court to give advisory opinions regarding a question of law arising from the Treaty which affects the Community.[66] This is a rare, if not inexistent, in municipal jurisdiction in common law countries. It was however, sourced from the Court of Justice of the European Union (itself largely of the continental legal systems).[67] Among the organs and institutions of the Community, it is only the Council of Ministers that may request advisory opinions from the Court.[68] It makes sense to make the request for advisory opinions one of the functions of the Council of Ministers which is the policy organ of the Community. However, what is objectionable is to make the Council of Ministers the only and sole organ which can request advisory opinions from the Court. The Council is not an active and operational executive arm of the Community and therefore unable to encounter issues which may require the Court's interpretation or advisory opinion. Ordinarily, it is only issues of policy nature about which the Council may require the Court's opinion. The implementation of the Treaty and the decisions of the executive organs of the Community is the responsibility of the Secretary General.

---

65 *Arbitration Cause No. 1 of 2012.*

66 Article 36, *Ibid.*

67 See EU Chapter 7.

68 Article 14 (4) of the Treaty, *op. cit.*

However, paradoxically, the Secretary General who in the course of executing his duties is likely to encounter challenges that may necessitate judicial pronouncement by way of advisory opinion, has no powers to approach the Court for advisory opinion on any matter. It can be argued that such powers for seeking advisory opinion could be given to the Assembly provided due regard is taken to preserve separation of powers among these two organs. As a result, the Council of Ministers has been hesitant to approach the Court for an advisory opinion although there have been disagreements especially at Council level which the Court would have given its advisory opinion if approached.

Bearing in mind the seriousness of such issues, should advisory opinions be rendered by Court of First Instance, subject to appeal to the Appellate Division or by the Appellate Division, whose decisions are final? There is no guidance in the Treaty on this issue so the Court took a decision to put a request for an advisory opinion, within the jurisdiction of the Appellate Division due to the fact that it is not appealable. Rule 75 (1) of the EACJ Rules of Procedure was introduced to the effect that:

> A request for an advisory opinion under Article 36 of the Treaty shall be lodged in the Appellate Division and shall contain an exact statement of the question upon which an opinion is required and shall be accompanied by all relevant documents likely to be of assistance to the Division.

This was yet another stop-gap measure taken by the Court to fill a void.

Only two cases, *Advisory Opinion No. 1 of 2008 In the matter of a Request by the Council of Ministers of the East African Community for an Advisory Opinion* and *Advisory Opinion No. 2 of 2015 In the matter of a Request by the Council of Ministers of the East African Community for an Advisory Opinion* have since been referred to the EACJ by the Council of Ministers.

In the first request the issues were whether the principle of variable geometry[69] was in harmony with the requirement for consensus in decision-making and whether the principle of variable geometry could apply to guide the integration process, notwithstanding the requirement on consensus in decision-making by the Community's top organs (Summit of EAC Heads of State, and Council of Ministers). The First Instance Division of the Court delivered its opinion on 24th April 2009 that the principle of variable geometry is

69 Under the principle of "Variable Geometry", groups within the East African Community are allowed progression in cooperation for wider integration schemes in different fields and at different speeds. See Article 7 (1) of the Treaty.

in harmony with the requirement for consensus in the decision-making process of the EAC organs. Consensus is a purely decision-making mechanism; while variable geometry is a strategy for implementation of the decisions so made (bearing in mind the capacity of each Partner State to implement the particular decisions). Consensus does not mean unanimity when used in the EAC Treaty.

As for the second and most current request which is pending a ruling on 19th November 2015, the issue was whether forfeiture of a position of a Deputy Secretary General by a Partner State under Article 67(2) of the Treaty for the purpose of making way for an incoming Secretary General from the same Partner State was in effect a withdrawal of such Deputy Secretary General.

The procedure for advisory opinions represents another dormant potential, waiting to be tapped, not only to resolve substantive questions of law that arise, but also to engage the Court which is waiting to contribute to the lively jurisprudence of the region.

7.11 Conclusion

Regional integration has become the world's major inclination due to the effect of globalization. Africa as a continent and East Africa as a sub region has not been left out in this crusade due to the forces that dictate the prevailing world dimension. If any regional integration is to succeed those who are involved in the process should appreciate the need for building strong institutions instead of banking on the rarely available strong individuals to spearhead the process. Whereas effective and strong institutions can endure indefinitely, effective individual leaders come and go.

The EAC model of integration is unique in that it is structured as a State and aims ultimately to become a political federation. All its organs and institutions are working towards the achievement of this challenging goal. The EACJ for its part is participating in the process by providing judicial interpretation of the Treaty and other Community laws and in ensuring respect for the founding principles of the Community. Its jurisprudence so far has proven that the Court has modeled itself to the standards of a respectable and independent organ that encourages public interest litigation.

The peoples of East Africa should know that the integration process on which the EAC has embarked is for them. The rights that flow from the Treaty are for them. They should enjoy them and claim them where necessary through the regional justice mechanism put in place by the Treaty as the Court attempts to create an environment conducive to public interest litigation.

The discussion in this topic has highlighted the judicial protection mechanisms under the Treaty within EAC framework. A section of the population has attempted to seek remedy and realize the rights afforded to them by the Treaty. However, reflecting on the discussion above, it may be questioned as to whether the existing judicial protection mechanisms are as effective as they could or should be.

CHAPTER 7A

Judicial Protection under EU Law: Direct Actions

Armin Cuyvers

7.1 Introduction

This chapter discusses the different direct actions under EU law.[1] The term direct action indicates that these legal actions provide parties with a remedy directly before the Court of Justice or the General Court. Only five direct actions exist under EU law, being the action for annulment, the action for inaction, an action for damages against the EU, the infringement proceeding and the request for an advisory opinion from the CJEU. Most of these actions have a rather limited scope, or like the action for annulment are only open to a very limited category of applicants. The limited availability of direct actions further emphasizes the point already made in chapter 2, namely the crucial role played by national courts in the interpretation and application of EU law.[2] It also helps to explain the central importance of the preliminary reference procedure discussed in EU chapter 8.

7.2 The Action for Annulment

Article 263 TFEU allows certain applicants to bring an action for annulment against all legal acts from EU institutions or other EU bodies, offices or agencies. An action for annulment, however, cannot be brought against EU primary law.[3]

---

1 For a more elaborate analysis on direct actions see amongst many others P. Craig and G. De Búrca, *EU Law* (6th edn, OUP 2015), chapters 12–16.

2 Also see on this point EU Chapter 8 par. 1.

3 For a discussion of the fascinating question if primary law or proposed Treaty amendments can ever violate (even) higher principles of EU law, and for that reason be annulled or disapplied see Unierecht N. Idriz-Tescan, *Legal constraints on EU Member States as primary law makers: a case study of the proposed permanent safeguard clause on free movement of persons in the EU negotiating framework for Turkey's accession* (Diss. Leiden 2015, Meijersreeks;MI-247), or A. Cuyvers, 'The Kadi II judgment of the General Court: the ECJ's predicament and the consequences for Member States'. *European Constitutional Law Review*, 7, pp. 481–510.

© ARMIN CUYVERS, 2017 | DOI 10.1163/9789004322073_015
This is an open access chapter distributed under the terms of the CC-BY-NC License.

These acts may be challenged 'on grounds of lack of competence, infringement of an essential procedural requirement, infringement of the Treaties or of any rule of law relating to their application, or misuse of powers.'[4] Especially considering the inclusion of the catch-all ground of 'infringement of the Treaties' this essentially means that an act can be challenged for any violation of EU law. This includes, for example, the use of an incorrect legal basis as discussed in EU chapter 3, or a conflict with a fundamental right. An EU act can only be annulled, however, where it violates a *higher* norm of EU law. A legislative act adopted under the ordinary legislative procedure, for example, can only be annulled for a conflict with higher norms such as a General Principle of EU law, the Charter, or provisions in the TEU or TFEU, but not for a conflict with lower rules such as delegated or implementing acts.

The most complex and contested issue under Article 263 TFEU concerns the three different categories of applicants that are allowed to bring an action for annulment, and especially the very limited standing of individuals to do so.[5] As EAC law does not impose similar restrictions on individuals that want to bring an action for annulment, a detailed overview on this point would be of limited comparative value. Consequently, this section only gives a general overview of the legal complexities surrounding the standing of individuals under Article 263 TFEU.[6]

The first category, the so-called privileged applicants, consists of the Member States, the European Parliament, the Council and the Commission. These applicants have a general right to start an action for annulment against any EU legal act, without having to prove any legal interest whatsoever.

The second category consists of the Court of Auditors, the European Central Bank and the Committee of the Regions. These semi-privileged applicants may bring an action for annulment against any EU act that affects their own prerogatives. They therefore do have to establish a certain legal interest in the act being challenged, and must prove that this act in some way affects their own powers or responsibilities.

---

4 Article 263(2) TFEU.

5 Cf. T. Tridimas and S. Poli, '*Locus Standi* of Individuals under Article 230(4): The Return of Eurydice?' in: A. Arnull, P. Eeckhout, and T. Tridimas (eds), *Continuity and Change in EU law: Essays in Honour of Sir Francis Jacobs* (OUP, 2008), ch. 5, or S. Balthasar, '*Locus Standi* Rules for Challenges to Regulatory Acts by Private Applicants: The New Article 263(4) TFEU' (2010) 35 *ELRev*, 542.

6 For the very broad standing under the EAC equivalent action see Chapter 7. For a more detailed analysis on standing under Article 263 TFEU see A. Ward, *Judicial Review and the Rights of Private Parties in EU law* (OUP, 2nd edn, 2007).

The third category consists of all natural or legal persons that are not privileged or semi-privileged, usually referred to as 'individuals'. These individuals only have standing to bring an action for annulment against an EU act in one of three scenarios. To begin with, individuals can institute annulment proceedings against an act specifically *addressed* to them. This includes for example companies that receive a decision from the Commission lowering a grant or imposing a fine for a violation of competition law. In such cases, standing will be easy to establish, as the parties will be identified by name in the act they want to challenge.

Additionally, individuals can also bring an action for annulment against an act that is not addressed to them if this act 'is of direct and individual concern to them'. The criterion of direct concern requires that the EU act 'directly affects the legal situation of the individual' and leaves no discretion to those implementing it, such as a Member State.[7] It is the criterion of 'individual' concern, however, that forms the real bottleneck. In the (in)famous *Plaumann* ruling, the CJEU gave an extremely restrictive interpretation of individual concern:

> Persons other than those to whom a decision is addressed may only claim to be individually concerned if that decision affects them by reason of certain attributes which are peculiar to them or by reason of circumstances in which they are differentiated from all other persons and by virtue of these factors distinguishes them individually just as in the case of the person addressed. In the present case the applicant is affected by the disputed Decision as an importer of clementines, that is to say, by reason of a commercial activity which may at any time be practised by any person and is not therefore such as to distinguish the applicant in relation to the contested Decision as in the case of the addressee.[8]

Essentially, the CJEU thereby restricts individual concern to those situations where an act is so specifically affecting a certain party that it is *de facto* addressed to it. The main test the CJEU uses for this purpose is the idea of an 'open group'. Whenever an act affects an 'open group', that is a group to which new members can accede, the member of this group are not individually concerned, even if they can be identified very precisely. In *Plaumann*, for example, the contested act affected importers of clementines. The CJEU held that this

7 Case C-386/96 P *Dreyfus v Commission* [1998] ECR I-2309, par. 43, or Joined Cases C-445/07 P and C-455/07 P *Ente per le Ville vesuviane* [2009] ECR I-7993, par. 45.

8 Case 25/62 *Plaumann* ECLI:EU:C:1963:17, my italics.

is an open group, as any person may decide to become a clementine importer and join this group. As a result, clementine importers were not individually concerned, and had no standing under Article 263 TFEU. Any act, therefore, that affects an open group, such as a certain profession or industry, will not be of individual concern to the members of this group, and consequently they will not be able to bring an action for annulment under Article 263 TFEU.

The interpretation given by the CJEU in *Plaumann* is extremely restrictive, and indeed individuals almost never succeed in proving that they are individually concerned.[9] Despite serious criticism that the *Plaumann* doctrine excessively limits the legal protection of individuals, however, the CJEU has so far refused to soften is approach.[10] The CJEU instead argued that expanding standing for individuals under Article 263 TFEU required a Treaty amendment.

With the Treaty of Lisbon in 2009, the standing for individuals was indeed somewhat extended, albeit in a rather complex way. Individuals can now also bring an action for annulment against 'a regulatory act which is of direct concern to them and does not entail implementing measures.' Under this ground, the restrictive requirement of individual concern no longer has to be met. In its place have come two new requirements, namely that the act is regulatory in nature, and does not require any implementing measures. The term 'regulatory act' however, was new and was not defined anywhere in the Treaty. The CJEU therefore, had to provide its own definition of regulatory action in *Inuit*:

> The General Court concluded, in paragraph 56 of the order under appeal, that 'the meaning of "regulatory act" for the purposes of the fourth paragraph of Article 263 TFEU must be understood as covering all acts of general application apart from legislative acts'. Consequently, a legislative act may form the subject matter of an action for annulment brought by a natural or legal person only if it is of direct and individual concern to them.[11]

9 For a rare example, and a nice illustration of just how specific an act needs to target a particular individual for individual concern to exist, see Case C-309/89 *Codorniu* ECLI:EU:C:1994:197.

10 For an authoritative criticism on this restrictive interpretation, as well as the refusal of the CJEU to change its case law, see the Opinion of Advocate General Jacobs in C-50/00 P *Union de Pequeños Agricultores v Council*, ECLI:EU:C:2002:462, as well as the judgment of the General Court being reviewed and the General Court's openly critical judgment in Case T-177/01 *Jégo-Quéré* [2002] ECLI:EU:T:2002:112.

11 Case C-583/11 P *Inuit* ECLI:EU:C:2013:625, par. 12.

The third possible ground of standing for individuals, therefore, only allows them to challenge non-legislative acts, i.e. acts that were not adopted under a legislative procedure, which do not require any implementation, such as for example some implementing regulations.[12]

All categories of applicants, moreover, must bring their action for annulment within two months, starting from the publication of the measure. If the measure was not published, the time limit starts to run from either the notification to the plaintiff, or, if there was no notification or the plaintiff hears about the measure before notification, from the day on which the measure came to the knowledge of the plaintiff.

7.3 The Action for Inaction

The action for failure to act in Article 265 TFEU can be used where an EU institution, body, office has a legal obligation to act but fails to do so. Again there is a group of privileged applicants, consisting of the Member States, the European Parliament, the European Council, the Council, the Commission and the ECB with unlimited standing. Individuals, on the other hand, only have limited standing, and can only bring an action where the body concerned should have addressed an act specifically to them. Before a plaintiff can start an action for inaction, he or she first must call on the relevant body to act.

The main difficulty for the action of inaction is to prove a sufficiently clear and well-defined obligation to act that can also be enforced by a Court.[13] Partially in light of this difficulty, the action for inaction is not used very frequently.[14]

12 See Article 289(3) TFEU for the concept of legislative act. For an example of a regulatory act that does not require implementation, see Case T-262/10 *Microban* ECLI:EU:T:2011:623.

13 See on this difficulty especially Case 13/83*Parliament v Council* (Transport Policy), ECLI:EU:C:1985:220.

14 For further examples see Case 4/69 *Lütticke* ECLI:EU:C:1971:40 or Case T-395/04 *Air One* ECLI:EU:T:2006:123.

7.4 The Action for Damages

The action for EU liability under Article 30 TFEU should be distinguished from the possibility to hold Member States liable for violations of EU law.[15] Article 340 TFEU can only be used to hold EU institutions and bodies liable for any damages caused by them or their servants. A distinction should further be made between the contractual liability of the EU and the non-contractual liability. Contractual liability of the EU is determined by the law applicable to the relevant contract, and by the national civil court that has jurisdiction under the rules of Private International Law. Only the non-contractual liability of the EU for violations of EU law is determined by EU law itself.

Any party that claims to have suffered damages caused by an unlawful act of an EU institution or body can start an action for damages before the CJEU. The defendant is not the EU as such, but the institutions whose alleged unlawful act has caused the damage. Three criteria have to be met for EU liability to exist: 1) an *illegal act* by an EU institution or body, 2) actual *damage*, and 3) a *causal* relation between the illegal act and the damage.[16] The most complex and restrictive criterion is the existence of an illegal act, which requires a sufficiently serious breach of a rule of EU law intended to confer rights on individuals. In turn, a breach is sufficiently serious where the institution concerned 'manifestly and gravely disregarded the limits on its discretion.'[17] Consequently, the more discretion an institution had, the more difficult it will be to hold it liable for any damages caused by its actions.[18] This means that it is extremely difficult to establish liability of for instance the European Parliament for legislative choices made, but easier to establish liability where the Commission wrongly implements a very straightforward rule that leaves almost no discretion.[19]

Under Article 46 of the Statute of the Court, a time-limit of five years applies.[20]

---

15 On this principle see EU chapter 6 as well as Case C-6/90 and 9/90 *Francovich* [1991] *ECR* I-5357 and Case C-46 and 48/93 *Brasserie du Pêcheur* [1996] *ECR* I-1029. At the same time, the substantive criteria for the non-contractual liability of a Member State for violations of EU law are identical to the ones for EU liability. See Case C-352/98P *Bergadem* [2000] *ECR* I-5291.

16 Case C-352/98P *Bergadem* [2000] *ECR* I-5291.

17 Case C-46 and 48/93 *Brasserie du Pêcheur* [1996] *ECR* I-1029.

18 See for example Case C-472/00 P *Fresh Marine* ECLI:EU:C:2003:399, or for liability of the EU Courts themselves, case C-385/07 P *Der Grüne Punkt* ECLI:EU:C:2009:456.

19 See for example Case T-260/97 *Camar* ECLI:EU:T:2005:283.

20 For the details see Case C-51/05 P *Cantina Sociale* ECLI:EU:C:2008:409.

7.5 The Plea of Illegality

The plea of illegality under Article 277 TFEU is not an independent remedy. Instead, it is an *argument* that parties which are already in front of the CJEU may rely on to question the legality and validity of an EU act.[21] For example, a farmer may bring an action for annulment against a Commission decision refusing to grant the farmer a milk-subsidy. The farmer, as addressee of this decision, is then allowed to start an action for annulment against this Commission decision under Article 263 TFEU. In the context of this annulment procedure, the farmer may then rely on the plea of illegality to challenge *another* relevant EU act, such as the directive on which the Commission decision was based. After all, if the farmer can prove that the directive underlying the Commission decision itself is invalid, this will also affect the validity of the Commission decision itself. The plea of illegality itself, however, does not provide a self-standing remedy.[22]

7.6 Infringement Proceedings

The infringement procedure is another atypical remedy that allows Member States or the European Commission to bring a Member State before the CJEU for violating its obligations under EU law.[23] As it is highly exceptional for Member States to start infringement procedures against each other, also in light of the political costs, it is almost exclusively the Commission that starts infringement proceedings under Article 258 TFEU.[24] Partially because of the reluctance of Member States to infringe each other, the independent and autonomous power of the Commission to start infringement proceedings against Member States has proven of great importance to ensure the respect for EU law.[25]

When considering the infringement procedure, it is important to realize that the main purpose of infringement is not to impose a penalty on the Member

21 Joined cases 31/62 and 33/62 *Wöhrmann* ECLI:EU:C:1962:49.

22 See for an example Case C-11/00 *Commission v European Central Bank*, ECLI:EU:C:2003:395.

23 Articles 258–260 TFEU.

24 So far, only four infringement proceedings were started by Member States against each other, all in situations that were already at an advanced stage of political escalation. See for the most recent example Case C-364/10 *Hungary v. Slovak Republic* ECLI:EU:C:2012:3798.

25 See in this context also the institutional responsibility of the Commission as 'guardian' of the *acquis* as described in EU Chapter 2.

State. Rather, the main purpose is to ensure that EU law is applied correctly, preferably without having to proceed to the CJEU and asking for sanctions.[26] This main purpose is reflected in the set-up of the infringement procedure, which is divided into several stages.

An infringement starts with a first administrative, or pre-litigation, phase, in which the Commission becomes aware of a possible violation of EU law by a Member State.[27] This can either be based on the own investigations of the Commission or on complaints that the Commission received.[28] The Commission then engages in an informal dialogue with the Member State to further explore if EU obligations are indeed not respected, and if that is the case, to request the Member State to make the necessary improvements. If the matter is not solved during the informal dialogue, the Commission can decide to send a letter of formal notice. The letter contains a brief overview of the problems found and allows the Member State to react or make improvements. If the Commission is still not satisfied with the explanation or improvements it can decide to issue a reasoned opinion. This is an important step in the entire proceedings. The reasoned opinion formally has to set out all the complaints that the Commission has concerning the way in which the Member State fulfils its obligations, and must give the Member State a reasonable period to comply.[29] If the Member State does not comply, the reasoned opinion becomes the basis for the next phase, which is the first judicial phase. It has to be stressed though that at this stage over 90% of all infringements have been resolved, as either the Commission has been convinced that there is no violation of EU law or the Member State has already made the necessary improvements to ensure future compliance.

In the first judicial phase the Commission brings the Member State before the CJEU. The case before the CJEU is delineated by the reasoned opinion, and may for example not include any alleged violations that were not already

26 See on this point for example Case 293/85 *Commission v Belgium* (*University Fees*), ECLI:EU:C:1988:40.

27 It does not matter which organ or body of the state actually violated EU law. Under EU law the central government is responsible for the behaviour of all public bodies, including the courts. The infringement, therefore, will always be addressed to the central government.

28 Where the Commission receives complaints from third parties on possible violations of EU law it has absolute discretion to initiate infringement proceedings or not. This allows the Commission to effectively use its limited resources. See Case 247/87 *Star Fruit* ECLI:EU:C:1989:58.

29 Case 293/85 *Commission v Belgium* (*University Fees*), ECLI:EU:C:1988:40, and Case C-304/02 *Commission v France*, ECLI:EU:C:2005:444.

included in the reasoned opinion.[30] If the CJEU agrees with the Commission that the Member State has indeed failed to fulfil its obligations under EU law, it will render a declaratory judgment detailing the failure of the Member State and ordering it to bring an end to the violation.[31] In this first judicial phase, therefore, no sanction is yet imposed on the Member State, as the main aim is still to ensure compliance.[32]

In the exceptional cases where Commission thinks the Member State is not complying with its obligations under EU law and the judgment of the CJEU, it can start the second administrative, or pre-litigation, phase of the infringement procedure.[33] The Commission again starts with an informal dialogue, potentially followed by a letter of formal notice. In the second pre-litigation phase, however, no reasoned opinion is given or necessary, as the dispute is already clearly delineated by the judgment of the CJEU.

If the Commission is still not convinced that the Member State has fully complied at the end of the second pre-litigation phase, it can initiate the second judicial phase. In this phase, the Commission may request the Court to impose a lump sum fine and/or a penalty payment for every day the Member State fails to comply. Ultimately, it is then up to the CJEU to determine if a sanction should be imposed and if so how severe this sanction should be. If sanctions are imposed, however, they can be very serious indeed, running into the tens of millions of euros.[34] So far, Member States have always complied with such penalties when imposed, but if they were not such penalties could probably simply be deducted from any EU subsidies the Member State receives from the EU.

---

30 Cf. Case C-350/02 *Commission v Netherlands*, ECLI:EU:C:2004:389. Also note that the CJEU will judge the situation in the Member State at the end of the reasoned opinion. Any improvements made after the time period allowed in the reasoned opinion has expired will therefore not be taken into consideration by the CJEU, and will not prevent a violation from being found. See already Case 167/73 *Commission v France* (Merchant Navy), ECLI:EU:C:1974:35.

31 Article 260(1) TFEU.

32 Cf. Case 128/78 *Commission v United Kingdom* (Tachographs), ECLI:EU:C:1979:32. See however the exceptional possibility under Article 260(3) TFEU to already impose a sanction in the first judicial phase if the violation at stake was a failure to *notify* the Commission on the measures taken to transpose a directive. If the infringement concerns the incorrect implementation of a directive itself, the normal procedure with two judicial rounds applies.

33 Article 260(2) TFEU.

34 See for example Case C-387/97 *Commission v Greece*, ECLI:EU:C:2000:356 or Case C-304/02 *Commission v France*, ECLI:EU:C:2005:444.

As stated, the infringement procedure is an important instrument in the EU law toolbox to make sure Member States comply with their obligations under EU law. Even if the Commission only has a limited capacity, and hence has to strategically choose which infringements to choose, it still contributes significantly to the effectiveness of EU law and the trust in the overall system. Moreover, most infringement actions are already successful in the first pre-litigation phase, meaning that they do not necessarily have to take very long or become litigious.[35]

7.7 Arbitration Before the CJEU

Under Article 272 TFEU the CJEU has jurisdiction to give a judgment based on any arbitration clause contained in a contract concluded by or on behalf of the EU. This may be in a contract governed by public or private law. In addition, Article 273 TFEU allows for CJEU jurisdiction where any dispute between Member States which relates to the subject matter of the Treaties is submitted to it under a special agreement between the parties.

So far the CJEU has not yet been active under these provisions. In recent years, however, the use of public international law instruments to support or supplement EU action, where collective action under EU law proved impossible, has increased significantly. Increasingly, these fascinating hybrids of EU and Public International law also involve EU institutions outside the boundaries of EU law proper. This includes the grants of jurisdiction to the CJEU. The coming years, therefore, might see some actual uses of these special heads of jurisdiction, which may also be of interest to the comparable heads of jurisdiction enjoyed by the EACJ.[36]

---

35 Of course where disputes become extremely political, such as in the contested changes to the Hungarian constitution, even the infringement procedure might be limited in what it can achieve. See Case C-286/12 *Commission v Hungary*, ECLI:EU:C:2012:687.

36 For such additional jurisdiction of the CJEU see especially Article 8 of the Treaty on Stability, Coordination and Governance in the EMU (Fiscal Compact), signed on 2 March 2012 by all EU Member States except UK and the Czech Republic, as well as the Treaty establishing the European Stability Mechanism, Brussels, February 2 2012 T/ESM 2012/en 1.

7.8 Advisory Opinions of the CJEU

Article 118(11) TFEU allows the Member States, the European Parliament, the Council or the Commission to request an opinion of the CJEU on the compatibility of an envisaged international agreement with the Treaties. If the CJEU finds that the envisioned agreement is not compatible with the Treaties, the agreement may not enter into force, unless the parts that conflict with the Treaties are sufficiently amended. Asking an opinion is not mandatory. Not asking an opinion, however, runs the risk of the CJEU annulling the entire agreement at a later stage if conflicts with the Treaties are found. Such an annulment would of course create even more legal and political headaches, including possible liability towards the other signatories to the agreement.[37]

Over time, the capacity to give legal opinions has led to some of the most important rulings given by the CJEU, often dealing with foundational questions on the nature of the EU legal order itself, and its relation to other legal regimes. This also in part because legal opinions provide the CJEU with the opportunity to settle such questions in a relatively general manner.[38]

---

37 See in this context the recent Opinion 2/15 of the CJEU on the trade agreement between the EU and Singapore, considered to be the model for CETA and TTIP.

38 See for example Opinion 2/94 *Accession to the European Convention on Human Rights* [2006] ECR I-929, Opinion 1/09 *Patent Court* [2011] ECR I-1137, or the highly contentious recent Opinion 2/13 on the draft agreement providing for the accession of the European Union to the Convention for the Protection of Human Rights and Fundamental Freedoms ECLI:EU:C:2014:2454.

CHAPTER 8

Preliminary References under EAC Law

Emmanuel Ugirashebuja

It was envisaged by the drafters of the Treaty establishing the East African Community (EAC Treaty) that the responsibility of applying its provisions belonged concurrently to the national courts and the East African Court of Justice (EACJ). With this responsibility, a potential challenge of ensuring uniform application of the Treaty was envisioned. In order to avoid the likely possibility of inconsistency in the application of Community law, the EAC Treaty embedded a procedure of preliminary rulings. It should be noted that such a procedure had been earlier adopted in the European Union, and there has considerably enhanced the uniform application of EU law in the European setting.[1] Article 34 of the EAC Treaty establishes a procedure which enables domestic courts of EAC Partner States to refer to the EACJ questions on Community law which would help them to arrive at a judgment in a substantive case before them. It provides as follows:

> Where a question is raised before any court or tribunal of a Partner State concerning the interpretation or application of the provisions of this Treaty or validity of the regulations, directives, decisions or actions of the Community, that court or tribunal shall, if it considers that a ruling on the question is necessary to enable it to give judgment, request the Court to give a preliminary ruling on the question.

The following sections will discuss Article 34 of the EAC Treaty in the light of its practical applicability. The first section reviews the standing of national courts and tribunals in the context of the preliminary reference procedure. The second section analyzes the obligation of national courts to refer questions for preliminary rulings. The third section reviews whether there is an obligation on the part of the EACJ to provide an answer in the form of a preliminary ruling to all references made by national courts. The fourth section discusses the nature and effect of the preliminary ruling made by the EACJ. Finally, the fifth

1 See EU Chapter 8 for an analysis of this procedure under EU law and the crucial role it played in European integration.

© EMMANUEL UGIRASHEBUJA, 2017 | DOI 10.1163/9789004322073_016
This is an open access chapter distributed under the terms of the CC-BY-NC License.

section will review the relationship between the national courts and the EACJ in light of the established procedure of preliminary reference.

8.1 Standing of National Courts and Tribunals

National courts and tribunals do not explicitly feature in the judicial architecture of the Community. The only reference to national courts in the Treaty appears in Article 34 of the EAC Treaty establishing the preliminary reference procedure. However, the national courts and tribunals are vital parts of the Community to the extent that they directly apply Community law to the cases before them where relevant. In *East African Law Society v. the Secretary General of the East African Community* (2013), the First Instance Division of the EACJ held that:

> As Partner States, by virtue of their being the main users of the Common Market Protocol on a daily basis, it would be absurd and impractical if their national courts had no jurisdiction over disputes arising out of implementation of the Protocol. Indeed, Community law would be helpless if it did not provide for the right of individuals to invoke it before national courts.[2]

This view of the First Instance Division was adopted by the Appellate Division in *Tom Kyahurwenda* (2015) when it stated:

> This Court agrees with the postulation of the law by the First Instance Division of this Court that it would be absurd if national courts and tribunals were to be excluded from the application of Treaty provisions should the occasion arise before them.[3]

2 Case No. 1 of 2011 *East African Law Society vs. the Secretary General of the East African Community* [2013] (EACJ, 2013) 28. The First Instance Division's view was by *Van Gend Loos* where the ECJ held that: "[t]he fact that Article 169 and 170 of the EEC Treaty enable the Commission and the Member States to bring before the Court a State which has not fulfilled its obligations does not deprive individuals of the right to plead the same obligations, should the occasion arise, before a national court", see Case 26/62 *Van Gend Loos* [1963] ECR 1.

3 Case Stated No. 1 of 2014 *Attorney General of Uganda vs. Tom Kyahurwenda* [2015] (EACJ, 2015) [54].

The starting point for any preliminary reference procedure lies with the question which national courts or tribunals are entitled to ask a question to the EACJ.

Article 34 of the Treaty provides that "where a question is raised before any court or tribunal of a Partner State concerning the interpretation or application of the provisions of this Treaty or the validity of the regulations, directives, decisions or actions of the Community, that court or tribunal shall…". The crucial point is that a question has to be posed by "any court or tribunal" and not any other entity. In the quest to determine what a "court or tribunal" is, the EACJ, in the preliminary ruling on questions posed by the High Court of the Republic of Uganda, drew inspiration from the jurisprudence established by the Court of Justice of the European Union (CJEU) in the *Pretore di Salò v. Persons unknown*.[4] In this case, the CJEU held the following:

> The Court has jurisdiction to reply to a request for a preliminary ruling if that request emanates from a court or tribunal which has acted in the general framework of its task of judging, independently and in accordance with the law, cases coming within the jurisdiction conferred on it by law, even though certain functions of that court or tribunal in the proceedings which gave rise to the reference for a preliminary ruling are not, strictly speaking, of a judicial nature.[5]

Inspired by this landmark case, the EACJ held that:

> …for a national entity to be considered a "court or tribunal" for purposes of preliminary reference, the entity should possess the following attributes: established by law; have permanent existence; endowed with compulsory jurisdiction; have ability to entertain procedures inter partes; apply rules of law; and, be endowed with functional independence.[6]

Any entity which does not fulfil these attributes is not a court or tribunal in the perspective of Article 34 of the EAC Treaty. This would imply that certain tribunals such as arbitral tribunals; commissions of inquiry or tribunals fully controlled by the executive or the legislative arms of government; ad-hoc

4 Case 14/86, *Pretore di Salò v Persons unknown* [1987] ECR 2545. See further on the EU system EU Chapter 8.

5 Case 14/86 *Pretore di Salò v Persons unknown* [1987] ECR 2545 [7].

6 *Tom Kyahurwenda* [40].

tribunals; prosecution authorities; and national competition authorities do not have standing for purposes of referring questions to the EACJ.

8.2 Obligation of a National Court to Refer to the EACJ

This section inquires whether national courts are under an obligation to refer questions to the EACJ and the extent of such an obligation. In *Tom Kyahurwenda*, the Partner States made different contentions regarding the interpretation of Article 34 of the Treaty in as far as the obligation of national courts to refer cases is concerned.

The Republic of Uganda contended that the interpretation of the Treaty was a prerogative of the EACJ and that consequently, national courts, at all levels, were barred from interpreting the Treaty. Uganda argued that the sole purpose of Article 34 was to allow national courts to entertain matters of enforcement of the Treaty, but not its interpretation, which squarely fell under the sole purview of the EACJ. The United Republic of Tanzania, held a similar view. The Republic of Kenya, on her part, argued that, in general terms, without looking at each and every specific Article, the Treaty is justiciable before the national courts. The argument of Kenya essentially meant that the EACJ and the national courts have concurrent jurisdiction on the interpretation of the Treaty, and that the discretion to refer a question to the EACJ lies with a national court when faced with a case involving Community law. The Secretary General of the EAC held a similar view to that of Kenya on the basis that the wording of Article 34 ("... if it considers that a ruling on the question of interpretation or application of the Treaty is necessary to enable it to give judgment"), should be construed to mean that Partner States were endowed with the discretion whether or not to refer a question to the EACJ.

In order to determine the extent of the obligation of national courts to make preliminary reference, the EACJ reviewed the wording of Article 34 of the Treaty, in *Tom Kyahurwenda*.[7] The EACJ held that:

> Article 34 of the Treaty further provides that where a court or tribunal is faced with "... the interpretation or application of the provisions of this Treaty or the validity of the regulations, directives, decisions or actions of the Community, that court or tribunal shall if it considers that a ruling

7 It is important to note here that the EACJ in this case resorted to the canons of interpretation established by the Vienna Convention on the Law of Treaties, in particular, Articles 31 and 32. See, *Tom Kyahurwenda* [33].

> on the question is necessary to enable it to give judgment, request the Court to give a preliminary ruling on the matter". The provision uses the emphatic word "shall". In the general scheme of legal drafting, the use of the word "shall" would presuppose that when the national courts or tribunals are faced with a question of interpretation, application or validity, they have no option, but to refer the matter to this Court.[8]

The EACJ's ruling made it clear that it possesses the monopoly of interpretation of the EAC Treaty. In other words, when any national court is faced with the question of interpreting the Treaty, it has no choice but to refer the question to the EACJ.

In answering to the apparent discretion of national courts in Article 34, the EACJ noted that:

> ... the discretion afforded to national courts by Article 34 is the discretion to refer or not to refer a question of interpretation to this Court. However, the condition precedent to the exercise of this discretion is this: "*if* the national court or tribunal considers that a ruling on the question is necessary to enable it to make a judgment ..." Once a national court or tribunal considers an interpretation to be necessary, then it has no option but to refer the question to this Court. Hence, the discretion is narrow. It is confined to determining whether or not a ruling on the question is necessary to enable the court to make its judgment.[9]

In determining the parameters of the discretion of national courts to determine the necessity to refer a question, the Court noted that the discretion was, "in the great majority of cases," limited to: cases where the Community law is not relevant to the matter before national courts ("an irrelevant question"); cases where the EACJ has already clarified the point of law in its previous cases ("*acte eclairé*"); and, instances where the interpretation of the Community law is obvious ("*acte clair*").[10] Simply put, under Article 34 of the EAC Treaty, a reference must be made unless the national court has recognized any of the above reasons for not doing so.[11]

In *Tom Kyahurwenda*, the EACJ distinguished the discretion endowed to the national courts by the Treaty to refer or not to refer a question for interpretation

---

8 *Tom Kyahurwenda* [41].
9 *Ibid.* [56].
10 *Ibid.* [57].
11 Cf. in this regard the CILFIT doctrine under EU law, discussed in EU Chapter 8.4.

from the obligation to refer where the subject matter involves invalidation of the regulations, directives, decisions or actions of the Community. The EACJ stated that it would be "disastrous were national courts and tribunals permitted to declare Community Acts, regulations, directives and actions invalid in the absence of a ruling to that effect by the East African Court of Justice".[12] It is very clear from this that the EACJ has exclusive powers to invalidate any acts, regulations, directives and actions of the Community and therefore, if such a question arises, a national court is under an obligation to refer to the EACJ.

8.3 Obligation of the EACJ to Provide an Answer

From the outset, it is paramount to note that the role of the EACJ in a preliminary ruling is to interpret Community law and determine the validity of Acts of the Community. The Court cannot apply Community law to the facts of the case at hand. Consequently, the function of the EACJ in a preliminary ruling is to provide an abstract interpretation of Community law. It is also important to mention that the EACJ cannot interpret or apply national law. Hence, the Court can decline to answer a question from a national court where it is called upon to apply Community law to a case before that national court or to interpret or apply national laws.

As a vital condition precedent for the EACJ to provide an answer, there has to be a live case before a national court requesting a preliminary ruling. The rationale for this is that the ultimate purpose of a preliminary reference is to enable a national court to resolve a matter before it. The EACJ will therefore reject a reference where the questions referred are hypothetical in nature. In *Alcon International Limited*, even though it did not come through the channel of preliminary reference, the EACJ adopted the well-known principle of mootness or academic adventure. The Court observed that "the *raison d'être* of Courts of Justice is to give binding decisions to live disputes…" and that in the absence of a live dispute, they may not engage in a "futile and vain exposition of the law".[13] The same outcome would be adopted in the event that a preliminary reference is moot or academic.[14]

It is also important that the question referred should be relevant to the case pending before the national court. Otherwise, the question would suffer the

12 *Ibid.* [48].

13 Appeal No. 3 of 2013 *Alcon International Limited vs. Standard Chartered Bank of Uganda and 2 Others* [2015] (EACJ, 2015) [99].

14 See the similar approach under EU law as set out in EU Chapter 8.5.

same fate as a moot or academic question. In order for the EACJ to be able to deliver a relevant and useful preliminary ruling or to determine whether the question is moot or academic, the reference should contain detailed relevant information about the factual background to the case and/or the relevant provisions of the national law in question.

Once the conditions of a live case and relevance of the question to the case at hand are fulfilled, then the Court is under the obligation of giving an answer in the form of a preliminary ruling. Article 35(1) of the Treaty is very clear in as far as the obligation is concerned. It provides: "The Court [the EACJ] shall consider and determine every reference made to it pursuant to this Treaty in accordance with the rules of the Court and shall deliver in public, a reasoned judgment". The emphatic use of the word "shall" in delivering a judgment would suggest that once a given reference including a preliminary reference satisfies the conditions established by the Rules of Procedure of the EACJ, then the Court is under the obligation to deliver a reasoned judgment.

8.4 The Nature and Effect of the Preliminary Ruling

As discussed above, a preliminary ruling is by its very nature a ruling of the Court and it has all the attributes and effects of any other ruling by the EACJ. The rulings and judgments of the EACJ, as one of the organs of the Community, are binding and take precedence over any national organ of the Partner States. To this end, Article 8(4) of the EAC Treaty provides: "Community organs [including the EACJ], institutions and laws shall take precedence over similar national ones on matters pertaining to the implementation of this Treaty". In an even more specific provision to the rulings of the Court, Article 38(3) of the Treaty provides: "A Partner State or Council shall take, without delay, the measures required to implement a judgment of the Court". Implementation of a judgment of the Court would include the application of a preliminary ruling of the EACJ by both the court which asked the question and also all other courts in EAC Partner States in similar cases. In other words, once the EACJ delivers a preliminary ruling, it is binding on all courts in the Community. To emphasize the binding nature of a preliminary ruling, the EACJ in *Tom Kyahurwenda* held that:

> This Court deems it apposite to draw attention to two points of fundamental importance. The first fundamental point is that this Court's preliminary ruling is binding on the national court or tribunal which has sought a preliminary ruling. The second fundamental point is that a

> preliminary ruling is binding erga omnes (towards all). It is erga omnes in the sense that it is binding on all national courts and tribunals in all Partner States of the Community.[15]

To put it otherwise, the court that made the reference and all other courts in the EAC Partner States that encounter the same subject matter are bound by the operative part of the preliminary ruling. The *Tom Kyaruhwenda* preliminary ruling implies that the ruling is capable of applying retrospectively since it is binding on all national courts. Furthermore, the ruling establishes a precedent which the EACJ will itself follow in similar matters.

It is also important to note that in *Tom Kyaruhwenda* the EACJ decided that since the ruling was a step towards the resolution of the dispute before the Ugandan Court, "the decision as to costs is the matter for that Court [High Court of Uganda] to pronounce in the context of the proceedings before it".[16] As to the costs incurred by the Secretary General and the Partner States in submitting their observations in matters of preliminary references, the EACJ opined that they are not recoverable.[17]

8.5 The Relationship between the National Courts and the EACJ

As previously discussed, the EAC Treaty envisages no particular relationship between national courts and the EACJ, except for Article 34 which creates the procedure of preliminary references, detailed throughout this chapter. The EACJ has so far entertained one preliminary reference in its fifteen years of existence. However, the importance of the preliminary reference procedure should not be gauged from the number of cases referred but the potential it has to significantly impact on the process of the EAC integration through developing Community law.

The success of the preliminary reference procedure lies in the cooperation, or what is widely referred to as a "judicial dialogue" between the EACJ and the national courts. The preliminary ruling procedure promotes preservation of legal unity through uniform interpretation and application of Community law. In stressing the importance of the "judicial dialogue" through the preliminary reference, the EACJ in *Tom Kyahurwenda* stated:

---

15 *Tom Kyaruhwenda* [58].

16 *Tom Kyaruhwenda* [76].

17 *Tom Kyaruhwenda* [76].

> It is of utmost importance to understand the significance of the preliminary ruling procedure. The procedure is the keystone of the arch that ensures that the Treaty retains its Community character and is interpreted and applied uniformly with the objective of its provisions having the same effect in similar matters in all the Partner States of the East African Community. In the absence of this procedure, it is possible that legions of interpretation of the same Treaty would emerge drifting hither and thither, aiming at nothing. This would at best create a state of confusion and uncertainty in the interpretation and application of the Treaty; and at worst, ignite an uncontrolled crisis which would destabilise the integration process. The situation could even be more disastrous were national courts and tribunals permitted to declare Community Acts, regulations, directives and actions invalid in the absence of a ruling to that effect by the East African Court of Justice.[18]

National judges apply Community law as well as the interpretation of the law through preliminary rulings manufactured by the EACJ as part of the Partner States' national laws. The procedure ensures that individual rights under Community law which have been infringed are legally redressed. Preliminary references have created a forum of cooperation between national judges and EACJ judges in resolution of domestic cases with aspects of Community law and further development of Community law.

Even though, as discussed earlier, the importance of the instrument of preliminary reference lies in the appropriate division of labor in the development and application of Community law, it is nonetheless imperative to analyze why the instrument has not generated a voluminous amount of workload for the EACJ as it has in the CJEU.[19] The number of all the references filed in the EACJ is way below those filed annually at the CJEU. It should be noted that, with the exception of the one preliminary reference and the two advisory opinions, the rest of the cases filed in the EACJ have been by persons (both natural and legal).

---

18 *Ibid.* [48].

19 In the ECJ, preliminary reference accounts for over 50% of the Court's workload. In 2014 alone, the total number of references were 622. See further EU Chapter 8. Whereas in the lifespan of the EACJ today, it has received two references and delivered one preliminary ruling.

The EAC Treaty affords individuals the right to directly file cases with the EACJ,[20] whereas such a right of direct action by persons is permitted only exceptionally before the CJEU.[21] It would be a viable assumption that individuals might have opted to use the route of direct action under the EACJ setting and this would explain why preliminary references are very rare as opposed to the CJEU where direct action is restricted.

Another possible explanation of why the preliminary reference procedure has not been used is the absence of knowledge of its existence by both the residents of the Community and judges of national courts. The EACJ has sought to rectify this problem and has embarked on a sensitization program of judges through actively organizing and being part of conferences in the Partner States.

The importance of the preliminary reference instrument as a source of dialogue between national judges and the EACJ cannot be stressed further. With the Court having delivered its first preliminary ruling, it is hoped that it will open the way for many more preliminary references in the future with a view of developing and promoting cohesion of Community law and deeper integration.

---

20 Article 30(1) of the EAC Treaty provides: "Subject to the provisions of Article 27 of this Treaty, any person who is a resident in a Partner State may refer for determination by the Court, the legality of any Act, regulation, directive, decision or action of a Partner State, or institution of the Community on the ground that such Act, regulation, directive, decision or action is unlawful or is an infringement of the provisions of this Treaty."

21 According to Arnull, "If the Court took a liberal approach on the question of the category of acts susceptible to review and the status of the European Parliament in annulment proceedings, its attitude to the standing of private parties has on the whole been more restrictive" *in* Anthony Arnull, *The European Union and its Court of Justice* (2nd edn, OUP, 2006) 69 See for the precise rules on standing before the CJEU also EU Chapter 7.

CHAPTER 8A

Preliminary References under EU Law

Armin Cuyvers

8.1 Introduction

The preliminary reference procedure allows national courts to ask questions on EU law to the Court of Justice of the European Union (CJEU). The importance of preliminary references becomes readily apparent when one realizes the EU has over 500 million citizens and companies, but there are only 84 judges in the EU Court in Luxembourg. Consequently, it is the tens of thousands of national judges that have to uphold and apply EU law in practice. It is these national judges that have to turn EU law into a living, enforceable reality within each Member State.[1]

Because of their central role, it is essential that all these national courts apply EU law correctly and consistently. The application of EU law, after all, should not depend on which national judge you happen to end up with. At the same time, a uniform application of EU law is far from automatic. Each lawyer is shaped by his or her own national legal system and culture, and will unavoidably approach EU law from this national perspective, even if it is often unwittingly so. Without guidance, therefore, it is likely that a British lawyer with a common law background and a French lawyer with a civil law background would arrive at different interpretations of the same EU law concepts, even though these concepts have their autonomous EU meaning and should not be affected by national law. To protect the unity and effectiveness of EU law, therefore, it is essential that the Court of Justice provides guidance on the correct interpretation of EU law, and is enabled to assist national courts that are faced with certain doubts about the right interpretation of EU law.[2]

The preliminary reference mechanism is one of the key instruments enabling the CJEU to provide this guidance, and cooperate with national

1 For more elaborate discussion of the preliminary reference procedure see *inter alia* M. Broberg and N. Fenger, *Preliminary References to the European Court of Justice* (OUP, 2nd edn, 2014), and on the process in new Member States, which maybe of special interest to the EAC, M. Bobek, 'Learning to talk: Preliminary Rulings, the Courts of the New Member States and the Court of Justice' (2008) 45 *CMLRev* 1611.

2 Cf. Opinion 1/09 *Patent Court* [2011] ECR I-1137.

© ARMIN CUYVERS, 2017 | DOI 10.1163/9789004322073_017
This is an open access chapter distributed under the terms of the CC-BY-NC License.

courts. Indeed, many of the most foundational rulings on EU law, including *Van Gend & Loos* and *Costa v. E.N.E.L.* were given in preliminary reference proceedings, further illustrating the importance of this mechanism.[3] This chapter systematically discusses the different legal issues and complications preliminary references may give rise to, and the legal solutions developed in the EU to ensure the proper functioning of this mechanism. To structure this discussion, it follows the different steps of a preliminary ruling procedure, starting with the question of which bodies are allowed to ask references, and if national law is allowed to limit the right of courts to ask a reference. Subsequently, this chapter discusses when national courts may actually have an obligation to ask a preliminary reference, instead of just a right, or conversely, when the CJEU may declare a preliminary reference inadmissible. Lastly, it must be discussed what the CJEU may rule on in a preliminary judgment, and what a national court should do with the preliminary judgment it receives from the CJEU.

8.2 Courts and Tribunals Allowed to Refer a Preliminary Question

Article 267 TFEU states that a preliminary question may be asked by 'any court or tribunal of a Member State'. The CJEU by now has clarified that to qualify as a court or tribunal, a body must meet all, or at least most, of the following criteria to a high degree:

i. It has to be established by law;
ii. It has to be permanent;
iii. It must have compulsory jurisdiction;
iv. It must deal with procedures *inter partes*;
v. It must apply rules of law
vi. And lastly it must be independent.[4]

Whether a specific body qualifies has to be assessed on a case-by-case basis, whereby the CJEU tends to be supportive of the body wanting to refer where possible.[5] The CJEU has, however, adhered to its position that normally arbitral tribunals do not qualify as a court or tribunal under Article 267 TFEU, unless

3 See also F. Mancini and D. Keeling, 'From *CILFIT* to *ERT*: The Constitutional Challenge Facing the European Court' (1991) 11 *YBEL*, 1.

4 See Case C-14/86 *Pretore di Salò* ECLI:EU:C:1987:275, or more recently Case C-210/06 *Cartesio* ECLI:EU:C:2008:723.

5 See for example Case C-408/98 *Abrahamsson* ECLI:EU:C:2000:367.

there is a very close link between the arbitration and the ordinary judicial system of a Member State.[6] This might be understandable as many arbitral proceedings fail to meet many of the criteria given and many arbiters might not even want to ask a reference, taking into account the year and a half it takes on average to get an answer. Yet the inability of arbiters to refer questions to the CJEU is also increasingly problematic. To begin with, arbitration is becoming increasingly common. In addition, the CJEU has also held that arbiters are obligated to respect EU law of public order, such as EU competition law, in their awards. A failure to respect EU law therefore leads to an obligation on national judges to annul an arbitral award and to refuse execution.[7] Arbiters, therefore, are bound by EU law, but are unable to ask guidance on it.

In the EAC context, the EACJ has already directly referred to *Pretore di Salò* in determining which Courts and Tribunals are allowed to refer a question to it.[8] Building on this solid start, one may also consider if these criteria could perhaps be further developed to take the specific context of East Africa into account, for example by including systems of customary law or dispute settlement into the circle of courts and tribunals that are allowed to refer. In addition, the EAC may have an opportunity to reconsider the standing of arbitral awards, and perhaps find a more balanced solution than the one chose in the EU.

8.3 The Sacred Right to Refer

The CJEU has made it very clear that the right of a court or tribunal to refer a question to the CJEU may never be limited.[9] Neither national law nor higher courts are allowed to limit the freedom of a court to refer. For example, national higher courts may not prohibit lower courts to ask a preliminary question in a specific case or on a point they have already ruled upon in an injunction. Similarly, the CJEU held that a French draft-law that would obligate lower courts to first refer a question to the French Constitutional Court before

6 See for example Case C-102/81 *Nordsee* ECLI:EU:C:1982:107 or Case C-377/13 *Ascendi Beiras* ECLI:EU:C:2014:1754.

7 Case C-126/97 *Eco Swiss v. Benneton* ECLI:EU:C:1999:269.

8 See Chapter 8 par.1 and Case Stated No. 1 of 2014 *Attorney General of Uganda vs.and Tom Kyahurwenda* [2015]. (EACJ, 2015) [54].

9 See already Case 166/73 *Rheinmühlen-Düsseldorf* ECLI:EU:C:1974:3.

they could refer a preliminary question to the CJEU violated the right of lower courts under Article 267 TFEU.[10]

No limit may be imposed, therefore, on the right of any court to ask a preliminary reference to the CJEU. By defending this absolute right of national courts, the CJEU also ensures that the channel of communication with lower courts remains open. Any risk that national law or higher courts may try to prevent any questions from reaching the CJEU is thereby addressed. In addition, this allows lower courts to enlist the support of the CJEU when they for example think a ruling of their own supreme court or an act of parliament conflicts with EU law. Lower courts may, justly so, have some reservations before overruling their own supreme courts through the supremacy of EU law, and may hence prefer some confirmation and borrowed authority from the CJEU.[11] At the same time, lower courts must also carefully consider if, in a concrete case, it might perhaps not be better to leave it to the Court of Appeal to refer a question, as at that stage of the proceedings the facts of the case and the relevant legal issues may have been clarified and come into sharper focus.

8.4 A Right or an Obligation to Refer?

Article 267 TFEU makes a distinction between lower courts, which *may* refer a preliminary question and 'a court or tribunal of a Member State against whose decisions there is no judicial remedy', which *shall* refer a question to the CJEU when a question of EU law arises. In some cases, therefore, national courts actually have a legal obligation under EU law to ask a preliminary question.[12]

When deciding if an obligation to refer exists, it is useful to first distinguish between questions on the validity of EU law and questions on the interpretation of EU law. Subsequently, it is necessary to establish which courts fall under the obligation to refer, and which exceptions the CJEU has developed through its case law on the obligation to refer.

10 Case C-188/10 *Melki en Abdeli* ECLI:EU:C:2010:363.

11 See EU chapter 4 on the doctrine of supremacy. One of the effects of this supremacy is that lower courts can escape the normal judicial hierarchy, as their power to overturn or ignore a ruling from their own supreme court, or even a provision of their own constitution, derives from EU law itself, not just from their own judicial authority.

12 The failure to do so may even lead to Member State liability for the breach of this obligation to refer, even if this action will only be successful in extreme cases. See Case C-224/01 *Köbler* [2003] ECR I-10239.

8.4.1 *Questions on Validity versus Questions on the Interpretation of EU Law*

National courts can refer two different kinds of question to the CJEU. The first type of question concerns the validity of EU law. Such a question essentially asks if a certain rule of EU law might be invalid because it conflicts with a higher norm of EU law. In *Digital Rights Ireland*, for example, the High Court of Ireland and the Austrian *Verfassungsgerichtshof* both asked a preliminary question on the validity of the data retention directive, as they thought this directive *inter alia* violated fundamental rights protected under the EU Charter.[13] The second type of questions concerns the interpretation of EU law, and basically asks how a certain rule of EU law should be interpreted.

Since the CJEU is the only court with the authority to declare EU law invalid, national courts are *always* under an obligation to refer a validity question to the CJEU if they want to question the validity of an EU act. National courts are, therefore, allowed to hold that an EU act is valid, but not that an EU act is invalid.[14] Consequently, the entire question of whether a court may or must refer a preliminary question only concerns the second type of questions, being questions on the interpretation of EU law.

8.4.2 *Courts with an Obligation to Refer*

Only courts against whose decision there is no remedy can be under the obligation to refer. This is a factual test that requires a case-by-case assessment. For example, national law may not allow an appeal from a court of first instance to a court of appeal if the monetary interest at stake is too low, or if the case concerns a labor dispute. In such cases, no remedy exists against the court of first instance, and even a court of first instance might be obligated to ask a preliminary reference. It is incorrect, therefore, to summarize Article 267 TFEU as holding that only supreme courts or constitutional courts are under an obligation to refer. The fact that a remedy depends on a supreme court accepting a case, or that an appeal to the supreme court is only allowed on points of law, however, does not make the decision of a court of appeal into a decision

---

13 Joined Cases C-293 and 594/12 *Data Retention Directive*, ECLI:EU:C:2014:238.

14 The only, very limited, exception is that national courts may, in exceptional circumstances where irreparable harm may be caused by enforcing a rule of EU law, provide an interim measure disapplying that rule of EU law in the particular case whilst they await the preliminary ruling of the CJEU on validity. See Case 314/85 *Foto-Frost* [1987] *ECR* 4199.

against which there is no remedy, even if the supreme court in the end refuses to hear the case.[15]

8.4.3 *Exceptions to the Obligation to Refer: The CILFIT Doctrine*

Even where no legal remedy exists, however, national courts may not be obligated to refer a question. In the famous *CILFIT* judgment the CJEU formulated three exceptions to the obligations to refer. Firstly, no obligation exists where the question of EU law 'is not relevant, that is to say, if the answer to that question, regardless of what it may be, can in no way affect the outcome of the case.'[16] Secondly, a reference is not required 'where previous decisions of the Court have already dealt with the point of law in question, irrespective of the nature of the proceedings which led to those decisions, even though the questions at issue are not strictly identical.'[17] This second exception is known as the *acte eclairé* doctrine, and means that courts do not have to ask questions of law that, in their opinion, have already been clarified in previous judgments of the CJEU. Of course whether the question at stake has really been settled by previous CJEU case law is an assessment the national courts has to make.

The third exception is known as the *acte clair* doctrine, and removes the obligation to refer where the correct interpretation of EU law is so obvious for the national court that no reference is deemed necessary. In the words of the CJEU: 'Finally, the correct application of Community law may be so obvious as to leave no scope for any reasonable doubt as to the manner in which the question raised is to be resolved.'[18] This third exception is potentially the most far reaching, as it creates the risk of national courts imposing their own, incorrect interpretation on EU law, either intentionally or unwittingly. For this reason the CJEU adds several warnings to national courts, and implores them to not assume that the correct interpretation is clear too easily:

> Before it comes to the conclusion that such is the case, the national court or tribunal must be convinced that the matter is equally obvious to the courts of the other Member States and to the Court of Justice. Only if those conditions are satisfied, may the national court or tribunal refrain from submitting the question to the Court of Justice and take upon itself the responsibility for resolving it.

15 Case C-99/00 *Kenny Roland Lykkeskog*, ECLI:EU:C:2002:329 and Case C-210/06 *Cartesio* [2008] ECR I-9641.

16 Case 283/81 *CILFIT* ECLI:EU:C:1982:335, par. 10.

17 Idem, par. 14.

18 Idem, par. 16.

> However, the existence of such a possibility must be assessed on the basis of the characteristic features of Community law and the particular difficulties to which its interpretation gives rise.
>
> To begin with, it must be borne in mind that Community legislation is drafted in several languages and that the different language versions are all equally authentic. An interpretation of a provision of Community law thus involves a comparison of the different language versions.
>
> It must also be borne in mind, even where the different language versions are entirely in accord with one another, that Community law uses terminology which is peculiar to it. Furthermore, it must be emphasized that legal concepts do not necessarily have the same meaning in Community law and in the law of the various Member States.
>
> Finally, every provision of Community law must be placed in its context and interpreted in the light of the provisions of Community law as a whole, regard being had to the objectives thereof and to its state of evolution at the date on which the provision in question is to be applied.[19]

At the same time, this does not mean that national high courts must refer every time some doubt remains. After all, it is part of the responsibility of high courts to settle doubts, even if there may be disagreements on the law with or between lower courts. As the CJEU recently clarified in *Ferreira da Silva*:

> In itself, the fact that other national courts or tribunals have given contradictory decisions is not a conclusive factor capable of triggering the obligation set out in the third paragraph of Article 267 TFEU.
>
> A court or tribunal adjudicating at last instance may take the view that, although the lower courts have interpreted a provision of EU law in a particular way, the interpretation that it proposes to give of that provision, which is different from the interpretation espoused by the lower courts, is so obvious that there is no reasonable doubt.
>
> However, so far as the area under consideration in the present case is concerned and as is clear from paragraphs 24 to 27 of this judgment, the question as to how the concept of a 'transfer of a business' should be interpreted has given rise to a great deal of uncertainty on the part of many national courts and tribunals which, as a consequence, have found it necessary to make a reference to the Court of Justice. That uncertainty

19 Idem, paras 17–20. See for further discussion also D. Edward, '*CILFIT* and *Foto-Frost* in their Historical and Procedural Context', in: *The Past and Future of EU Law: The Classics of EU law Revisited on the 50th Anniversary of the Rome Treaty* (Hart Publishing 2010), 173.

> shows not only that there are difficulties of interpretation, but also that there is a risk of divergences in judicial decisions within the European Union.
>
> It follows that, in circumstances such as those of the case before the referring court, which are characterised both by conflicting lines of case-law at national level regarding the concept of a 'transfer of a business' within the meaning of Directive 2001/23 and by the fact that that concept frequently gives rise to difficulties of interpretation in the various Member States, a national court or tribunal against whose decisions there is no judicial remedy under national law must comply with its obligation to make a reference to the Court, in order to avert the risk of an incorrect interpretation of EU law.[20]

Although the CJEU therefore allows the *acte clair* doctrine to be applied where national lower courts disagree, it does not allow it where there is disagreement or confusion between the courts of multiple Member States. Such disagreement between Member States would threaten the uniformity of EU law and indicate the necessity of a preliminary ruling to provide an authoritative EU interpretation.

These exceptions to the obligation to refer, and the leeway granted to national courts by the CJEU, reflect the cooperative nature of the preliminary reference procedure. The CJEU heavily relies on the national courts to refer the important cases to it, and to correctly implement the preliminary rulings it gives. Even though EU law itself is supreme, and national courts are under a legal obligation to implement any preliminary ruling given, the entire preliminary question mechanism depends on mutual respect and a good working relation between the CJEU and national courts. This mutual respect includes trusting national courts, certainly national supreme courts, to assess when a preliminary reference is required and when it is not. Vice versa, national courts must take seriously their duty to refer questions on interpretation, also as referring the right questions allows the CJEU to ensure the correct and uniform interpretation of EU law.

---

20 Case C-160/14 *Ferreira da Silva* ECLI:EU:C:2015:565, paras 41–44.

8.5 Admissibility of Preliminary References

When a national court refers a question, the CJEU is in principle obligated to provide a preliminary answer.[21] Ultimately, however, the CJEU retains the final say over its own jurisdiction, which means that it can also declare preliminary references inadmissible. Generally, the CJEU does not want to reject references, both out of respect for the national courts asking them and because it needs preliminary questions to fulfill its function. The CJEU will even try to 'rescue' poorly drafted questions where possible, so as to provide a helpful response to the national court. Over time, however, the CJEU has developed three general grounds on which a reference may be declared inadmissible.

Firstly, a reference is inadmissible where the question asked is obviously irrelevant to solve the dispute before the national court.[22] Secondly, a reference may be declared inadmissible where the dispute between the parties is hypothetical. This concerns disputes that have been construed by the parties with the sole purpose of acquiring a judicial ruling on a certain question, but where there is no real dispute between the parties.[23] Test-cases, however, are allowed, as long as there is a real dispute concerned. Lastly, the CJEU may also declare a reference inadmissible where the case file sent by the national court does not provide sufficient factual and legal information to usefully answer the questions posed.[24] Of course a national court is then allowed to improve the file and resend it.[25]

The fact that a question asked by a national court has already been clarified in earlier case law, or the correct interpretation is obvious, is not a ground for inadmissibility. These *CILFIT* exceptions only remove the obligation of national courts to refer, they do not remove the right to refer where national courts want to do so.

---

21 See for example case C-220/05 *Auroux* ECLI:EU:C:2007:31.

22 Cf. Case C-293/03 *My* ECLI:EU:C:2004:821 or Case C-152/03 *Ritter-Coulais* ECLI:EU:C:2006:123.

23 Case 244/80 *Foglia* ECLI:EU:C:1981:302 or Case C-225/02 *Garcia Blanco* ECLI:EU:C:2005:34.

24 See for example Case C-567/07 *Sint-Servatius* ECLI:EU:C:2009:593.

25 The CJEU has also provided national courts with a communication providing recommendations on how to submit preliminary references, published in OJ [2012] C 338/1.

8.6 Status and Effect of the Preliminary Ruling

In a preliminary ruling, the CJEU may only rule on the validity of EU law or provide the correct interpretation of a rule of EU law. The CJEU is not allowed to interpret national law, or to settle the underlying dispute between parties. It remains up to the national court to apply the interpretation given by the CJEU to the case at hand. What the CJEU can do, however, is to provide an interpretation of EU law that is so specific, and is so closely linked to the facts of the case, that it *de facto* determines the decision the national court should take.[26] In other cases, the CJEU may only provide a more general interpretation of EU law, and thereby leave a broad discretion to the national court, for example to determine the proportionality of a measure.[27]

A preliminary answer is legally binding on the national court that referred the question to the CJEU.[28] In addition, a preliminary ruling is also binding on all other national courts, as it provides the authoritative interpretation of EU law.[29] Preliminary rulings, therefore, have an *erga omnes* binding effect, and function as legal precedents. Normally, the interpretation provided by the CJEU also has retroactive effect, meaning it determines how the provision should always have been interpreted, also in the past (*ex tunc*).[30] In exceptional cases, however, the CJEU may limit the effect of a preliminary reference in time, for example because legal certainty requires so or the practical implications of *ex tunc* application would be to severe. In *Defrenne*, for example, the CJEU limited the effects of its ruling on equal pay between men and women based on (now) Article 157(1) TFEU, as full retroactive effect would require governments and companies to compensate lower wages going back for more than a decade.[31]

26 See for example Case C-180/04 *Vasallo* ECLI:EU:C:2006:518.

27 See for an overview and analysis of different approaches T. Tridimas, 'Constitutional Review of Member State Action: The Virtues and Vices of an Incomplete Jurisdiction', (2011) 9 *I-CON* 737.

28 Case 52/76 *Benedetti* ECLI:EU:C:1977:16.

29 This obligation also derives from Article 4(3) TEU. See also Joined Cases 28–30/62 *Da Costa* ECLI:EU:C:1963:6.

30 J. Komarek, 'Federal Elements in the Community Judicial System: Building Coherence in the Community Legal System', (2005) 42 *CMLRev*, 9.

31 43/75 *Defrenne v SABENA* (Defrenne II), ECLI:EU:C:1976:56. Also see Case C-262/88 *Barber* ECLI:EU:C:1990:209.

CHAPTER 9

The EAC Common Market

Kennedy Gastorn and Wanyama Masinde

9.1 Introduction

On the 1st July 2010 the East African Community Common Market became operational. The actual negotiations on the establishment of the Common Market started in April 2008 and ended in November 2009 when the East African Community (EAC) Heads of States signed the Protocol on the Establishment of the EAC Common Market.[1] The ratification process was completed by each respective Partner State and, in July 2010, the Common Market came into force.

A common market is essentially an arrangement whereby member or partner countries of a regional economic community operate as a single market for goods, services, capital and labor, having common revenue and trade laws. Two main economic grounds in favor of a common market or absence of internal barriers are: firstly, that freedom of trade and movement tends to bring about that each kind of production undertaken in the area will be endeavored in the sectors that suit it best; and secondly, it tends to ensure that, where there is an advantage in large-scale production of a commodity, it will be produced on large scale in one or a few places, for the whole area, instead of being produced on an uneconomically small scale in a large number of places.[2]

Article 5(2) of the Treaty for the Establishment of the East African Community (the EAC Treaty) enjoins Partner States to establish among themselves a Customs Union, a Common Market, a Monetary Union and ultimately a Political Federation. The Common Market is therefore the second stage of integration after the Customs Union which was achieved through the EAC Protocol on the Customs Union in 2004.[3]

---

1 Gastorn, K. 'The Legal Analysis of the Common Market of the East African Community as Market Freedoms in the Open Market Economy', Law in Africa, 2011:1:143–154.

2 Newman, P., 'The Economics of Integration in East Africa', in Colin T. Leys and Peter Robson (eds), *Federation in East Africa: Opportunities and Problems*, Oxford University Press, London/New York (1965), 58.

3 Pursuant to Article 75 of the Treaty for the Establishment of the East African Community, 1999. The Protocol on the Establishmentof the East African Community Customs Union was signed on 2nd March 2004, and launched in 2005 with the aim of removing tariff and

© KENNEDY GASTORN AND WANYAMA MASINDE, 2017 | DOI 10.1163/9789004322073_018
This is an open access chapter distributed under the terms of the CC-BY-NC License.

9.2 History of Common Market in the Region

The region has rich history of uncoordinated experiences of common markets.[4] Cooperation among the Partner States of the EAC has a history dating back over a century. From 1884 to 1919, Burundi, Rwanda and Tanganyika were one territory (German East Africa) under German colonial rule. Uganda and Kenya existed as separate territories under British colonial rule. The defeat of the German power during the First World War changed the geographical frontiers of German East Africa. Two provinces were split from the territory and became autonomous territories and were renamed Burundi and Rwanda under Belgian colonial rule. The remaining part became Tanganyika (later Tanzania) under British rule, first as a mandate under the League of Nations and later as a trust territory under the rule of the United Nations. In short, the victorious powers divided the previous German territory among themselves under the Versailles Treaty of 1919 in which Germany was forced to surrender all its foreign occupations. By examining the historical development of the region, four stages of common market integration can be noted.

Generally, the pre-colonial African communities were not organized along countries, tribes or ethnic groups. Their identities and vernacular languages simply shaded into one another, and for them cooperation was more important than competition. All this changed when the Europeans came to Africa as colonialists. They invented colonies, drew frontiers across the map at will to exclusively suit their imperial interests and convenience at the whim of few cartographers in London, Berlin or Paris. They also classified peoples of Africa, sorting them out into what they called tribes, producing a whole new ethnic map to show the frontiers of each one. They simply wanted recognizable units they could easily control.

In 1895 the first phase of integration of the region began through the construction of the Uganda railway starting from Mombasa and linking the two countries of Kenya and Uganda. This provided a basis for the first creation of a common market in 1900 between Kenya and Uganda after the latter had made formal customs arrangements with Kenya for Mombasa to become the Customs Collection Centre. In 1905, the common currency (East African Shilling) was introduced in the two countries.[5] Therefore, Kenya and Uganda

---

non-tariff barriers on intra-regional trade, establishment of the common external tariff for goods imported from outside the region, and implementation of the common customs law.

4 See also Gastorn, K., cited *supra* note 1.

5 Apuuli, D.P., 'Fast Tracking East African Federation: Asking the Difficult Questions', Paper Prepared and Presented at a Development Network of Indigenous Voluntary Associations

had by that year passed through the three main stages of integration, namely (a) customs union, (b) common market, and (c) monetary union. The cooperation between Uganda and Kenya was largely facilitated by the fact that both countries were under one colonial master, the British. However, at the time, Tanganyika (then German East Africa) was under German rule and therefore could not easily be brought into this cooperation.

The second phase of the common market took place after the defeat of Germany in the First World War which culminated in the takeover of the territory by the British. The interests of the British could then be better served with Tanganyika joining its empire. Tanganyika was therefore brought within the already established arrangements of cooperation. In 1922, Tanganyika joined the customs union package. In 1933 it had already acceded to the free exchange of locally produced goods and the Postal Union, and finally the Common Market between Tanganyika, Kenya and Uganda was established.

The third phase of the common market was provided for in the Treaty for East African Cooperation[6] adopted by Kenya, Tanzania and Uganda in 1967. The principal common market machineries included the Common Market Council and the Common Market Tribunal.[7] The operation of this common market was very much influenced by historical accidents which ultimately made Kenya take a lead by gaining substantial benefits that accrued from the common market. Uganda also benefited, although not as much as Kenya, while Tanganyika gained the least. Such unequal benefits were among the reasons that led to the collapse of the common market in 1977 which was viewed as slowing down the economic development of some individual states.[8]

After the independence of Tanganyika (1961), Uganda (1962) and Kenya (1963), there was a big interest, especially on the part of Tanganyika, to move towards a political federation, an idea imbued in Pan-Africanism. Tanganyika wanted to build on the already achieved stages of integration, namely customs union, common market and monetary union, and to have a political federation. Tanganyika was also prepared to delay its independence for a year to wait for

(DENIVA), Public Dialogue on Fast Tracking East African Federation Dialogue, Hotel Equatoria Kampala, 24th November, 2006, 5; Ruhangisa, J.E., 'The Institutions of the East African Community (EAC) with Emphasis on the East African Court of Justice', A Course Material for TGCL Students, University of Dar es Salaam (2010), 2 (unpublished).

6 Part II of the Treaty for the Establishment of the East African Community.

7 Part III of the Treaty for the Establishment of the East African Community.

8 Ndegwa, P., 'The Common Market and Development in East Africa', Eastern Africa Publishing House, Kampala (1965), 136.

Kenya and Uganda, so that an East African Federation would be established.[9] Thus in 1963, a Declaration for the establishment of a political federation was signed. From the point of view of Nyerere, then President of Tanganyika:

> A federation of at least Kenya, Uganda and Tanganyika should be comparatively easy to achieve. We already have a common market and run many services through the Common Services Organization which has its own Central Legislative Assembly and an Executive composed of the Prime Ministers of the three states. This is the nucleus from which a federation is the natural growth.[10]

However, disagreements about the idea of a political federation prevented the establishment of the federation and instead the East African Cooperation was instituted. The main issues of disagreement include division of state and federal powers, citizenship, borrowing powers and conceptual structures. In any event, the Prime Minister of Uganda, Hon. Apollo Milton Obote, was instrumental in the failure of the idea of federation as he thought that Uganda might become extinct overnight.[11] Moreover, it was still too soon to aim for a federation, both considering the complexities of federating and given the fact that all the preceding stages of integration were not people-centered and were not systematically and incrementally achieved.[12]

The current Common Market set-up is the fourth phase, built on the ruins of the extinct East African Cooperation that collapsed in 1977. It should be noted that the 1967–1977 East African Common Market, and the Central American Common Market (CACM)[13] were by then frequently cited as the two most economically integrated areas among the least developed countries. In particular, the East African Common Market was viewed as a more perfect customs union with somewhat more coordination of economic policies, while the CACM was more a free trade area.[14]

---

9 Apuuli, D.P., cited *supra* note 6, 5.

10 Apuuli, D.P., cited *supra* note 6, 4.

11 *Ibid.*, 6–7.

12 Gastorn, K., cited *supra* note 1, 147.

13 The CACM was established in 1960 and is headquartered in Guatemala city, and includes Guatemala, Honduras, El Salvador, and Nicaragua, and Costa Rica.

14 Fred H. Lawson (ed), 'Comparative Regionalism', Ashgate (2009), 9.

9.3 Aims and Objectives

The foundation of the current Common Market is derived from Articles 76 and 104 of the EAC Treaty. Article 76 of the Treaty provides that:

1. *There shall be established a Common Market among the Partner States. Within the Common Market, and subject to the Protocol provided for in paragraph 4 of this Article, there shall be free movement of labor, goods, services, capital and the right of establishment.*
2. *The establishment of the Common Market shall be progressive and in accordance with schedules approved by the Council.*
3. *For purposes of this Article, the Council may establish and confer powers and authority upon such institutions as it may deem necessary to administer the Common Market.*
4. *For the purpose of this Article, the Partner States shall conclude a Protocol on a Common Market.*

Furthermore, Article 46 of the Common Market Protocol requires the Council of Ministers to establish an authority or institution to manage the Common Market. This authority is not yet established.

The stated overall objective of the Common Market is to widen and deepen cooperation among the Partner States in economic and social fields for their benefit.[15] The Common Market is the second out of the four envisaged stages for current EAC integration,[16] namely the Customs Union, the Common Market, the Monetary Union, and the Political Federation. The achievement of the above stages is to be governed by the fundamental principles of cooperation for mutual benefit, mutual trust, political will and sovereign equality, good governance, equitable distribution of benefits, and peaceful co-existence and good neighborliness.[17]

The EAC Common Market focuses mainly on four freedoms, namely free movement of goods, free movement of labor, free movement of services, and free movement of capital. It therefore involves the integration or amalgamation of the four markets; (a) the goods market, (b) the labor market, (c) the

---

15 Article 4 of the EAC Common Market Protocol.

16 Article 5(2) of the EAC Common Market Protocol.

17 Article 6 of the EAC Common Market Protocol.

services market, and (d) the capital market.[18] On the account of Article 2(4) of the Common Market Protocol, the right of establishment, the right of residence, and the right of free movement of persons (other than labor) are an integral part of the Common Market. To this end, rights of establishment and residence may be added to as the fifth freedom under the Common Market.

Free movement of goods entails the removal of tariff and non-tariff barriers (barriers to trade), thus easing the movement of goods.[19] Non-tariff barriers do not involve direct payments of money. They are quantitative restrictions and specific limitations that act as obstacles to trade, and which appear in the form of rules, regulations and laws that have a negative impact on trade.[20]

Free movement of labor relates to the unhindered movement of workers within the territories. It entails the principle of non-discrimination in labor laws and policies on grounds of nationality.[21] Article 10 of the Common Market Protocol provides for the free movement of workers and their accompanying spouse or children (family members).

Free movement of services is provided for under Part F of the Common Market Protocol and refers to the movement of services supplied by nationals of the Partner States within the Community. The current schedule of commitments on free movement of services identifies seven sectors to be liberalized, namely (a) business services, (b) communication services, (c) distribution services, (d) education services, (e) financial services, (f) tourism and other related services, and (g) transport services.

Free movement of capital is provided for under Part G of the Common Market Protocol and entails the removal of restrictions on the movement of capital supplied by nationals of Partner States, and the removal of discrimination based on nationality.

The right of establishment is provided for in Article 13 of the Common Market Protocol and entitles a national of a Partner State to undertake and pursue economic activities as a self-employed person, and set up and manage economic undertakings in the territory of another Partner State. It also entitles a self-employed person who is in the territory of another Partner State to join the social security scheme of that Partner State in accordance with its national

18 Tax, S.L., (2010), 'East African Community Integration: Marching towards a Common Market', Paper Presented at the University of Dar es Salaam, East African Community Students' Union, 26th June 2010, 6 (unpublished).

19 Part C of the EAC Common Market Protocol.

20 See on this point also the distinction in EU law between financial and non-financial restrictions to the free movement of goods discussed in EU Chapter 10.

21 Part D of the EAC Common Market Protocol.

laws.[22] The implementation of the right of establishment is done according to the specific regulations.[23]

The right of residence[24] relates to persons from other Partner States who have been admitted to the country as workers[25] or self-employed persons under the right of establishment as provided above.[26] Under this right, citizens of the Partner States would be entitled to a residence permit in the host State provided that they have been employed or self-employed in accordance with the respective national policies and laws of that country. The implementation of the right of residence is also done in accordance with specific regulations.[27]

The abovementioned freedoms are the subject of the following chapters in which they will be discussed in more detail. Suffice it to say at this stage that the Common Market has created opportunities within the region as it seeks to remove all obstacles to intra-community trade and to merge the national markets into one unified market, and thereby make a place where the individual freedom of economic activity would be exercised regardless of borders between Partner States. The unified EAC Common Market encompasses more than 143.5 million people and a combined Gross Domestic Product of $110.3 billion (2014).[28] Opportunities include (a) a deeper understanding and integration of the East Africans which in return would strengthen peace and stability in the region, (b) an expanded market for goods, services, capital, and labor likely to boost and expedite economic and social development in the region, (c) the creation of a strong basis on which common fiscal policies including currency may be established.

9.4 Levels of Economic Integration

In terms of levels of economic integration, a common market is normally the third level, after a free trade area (an area within which customs duties and other trade restrictions between member states are prohibited) and a customs union (a free trade area, together with a system whereby a common duty is charged on goods entering the free trade area from a non-member state).[29]

---

22 Article 13(3) of the EAC Common Market Protocol.
23 Article 13(12) of the EAC Common Market Protocol.
24 Article 14 of the EAC Common Market Protocol.
25 Article 10 of the EAC Common Market Protocol.
26 Article 13 of the EAC Common Market Protocol.
27 Article 14(8) of the EAC Common Market Protocol.
28 EAC Facts & Figures Report 2014.
29 Cf, also EU Chapter 9 on the internal market in the EU.

It is a stage in which there is free flow of factors of production, a common external tariff and no tariffs or quotas. However, the EAC common market today is a label more widely applied than practiced. Also the concept of levels tends to employ stages, the sequence of which is often confusing in practice. For instance, the European Common Market achieved partial free flow of factors of production before it became a full free trade area and customs union in July 1968.[30]

9.5 The Relationship between the EAC Treaty and the Protocols

The EAC Treaty is the basic rule constituting the integration process. In the scheme of constitutional principles within a state, the EAC Treaty is similar to a national constitution or *grundnorm* of the legal orders.[31] The EAC Treaty defines "Treaty" as including its annexes and protocols. Article 1 of the EAC Treaty defines a "protocol" as an agreement that supplements, amends or qualifies the Treaty. Protocols therefore derive their legitimacy and legality from the Treaty and thereby become an integral part of the EAC Treaty.[32]

In principle, protocols are negotiated and concluded "for purposes of spelling out the objectives and scope of, and institutional mechanisms for, cooperation and integration".[33] The protocol is therefore a tool that is used to open up a sector of cooperation between the Partner States.

In the EAC, a protocol may be concluded on any matter specifically provided for in the Treaty. For example, Article 27(2) specifically requires Partner States to conclude a protocol to operationalize the extended jurisdiction of the East African Court of Justice on matters like appellate and human rights jurisdiction. Furthermore, a protocol may be concluded on any matter necessary to achieve the agreed objectives in each area of cooperation. However, each protocol must be approved by the Summit of the Heads of State on a recommendation from the Council of Ministers, and is also subject to signature and ratification by the Partner States.[34]

---

30 Fred H. Lawson, cited *supra* note 15, 8.

31 Mchome, S.E. 'The Treaty of the East African Community: Is it the Equivalent of a National Constitution?', in in Kennedy Gastorn et al. (eds.), 'Processes of Legal Integration in the East African Community', Dar Es Salaam University Press, Dar es Salaam, 83–102.

32 Article 151(4) of the Treaty for the Establishment of the East African Community.

33 Mwapachu, J.V. 'Ten Years of the EAC—Achievements, Challenges and Prospects', in Kennedy Gastorn et al. (eds.), 'Processes of Legal Integration in the East African Community', Dar Es Salaam University Press, Dar es Salaam, 62.

34 Article 151 of the Treaty for the Establishment of the East African Community.

CHAPTER 9A

The EU Common Market

Armin Cuyvers

9.1 Introduction

The internal market is both an end in itself and a means to a higher end.[1] Article 2 of the 1957 Treaty of Rome already declared that the (then) European Economic Community (EEC) aimed to establish a Common Market between the Member States.[2] The EEC, therefore, already had a clear economic objective of increasing economic integration and the living conditions in a Europe impoverished after two world wars.[3] At the same time, the market was also a means to an end. It was thought that by integrating markets and economies, peace and stability would follow. Not only would Member States become accustomed to cooperation and dialogue, economic integration would also lead to a *de facto* solidarity and would make waging war *economically* impossible. The economic costs of conflict would simply become too high, preventing conflicts as long as some form of rational decision making would be in place. It was this dual purpose of the internal market that formed part of the genius of European integration.

This chapter will briefly introduce some of the main features of the EU internal market, focusing on the early stages of integration the combined use of negative and positive integration and the increasing convergence between the freedoms. Subsequently, EU chapters 10 to 13 will separately discuss the four individual freedoms underlying the internal market, being the free movement

1 For a more detailed analyses of the internal market and its development see inter alia N.N. Shuibne, *The Coherence of EU Free Movement Law. Constitutional Responsibility and the Court of Justice* (OUP, 2013), S.C. Barnard, *The Substantive Law of the EU. The Four Freedoms* (4th edn, OUP 2015), or P.J.G. Kapteyn, A.M. McDonnell, K.J.M. Mortelmans, and C.W.A. Timmermans (eds), *The Law of the European Union and the European Communities* (4th revised edition, Kluwer Law International 2008).

2 The objective can currently be found in Article 3(3) TEU. Note that in the early days of European integration the term Common Market was used, as currently in the EAC, before the terminology of an internal market was adopted to stress the complete removal of barriers.

3 See for some economic analysis of the internal market *inter alia* W. Molle, *The Economics of European Integration* (Aldershot, 2006) or J. Pelkmans, *European Integration: Methods and Economic Analysis* (Longman, 1997).

© ARMIN CUYVERS, 2017 | DOI 10.1163/9789004322073_019
This is an open access chapter distributed under the terms of the CC-BY-NC License.

of goods, services and establishment, persons, and capital. We begin, however, with the concept of an internal market as such.

9.2 The Concept of an Internal Market

Article 26 TFEU defines the internal market as 'an area without internal frontiers in which the free movement of goods, persons, services and capital is ensured in accordance with the provisions of this Treaty'. This very broad concept was further developed, albeit still in a very general manner, by the CJEU in its *Schul* judgement:

> The concept of a common market as defined by the court in a consistent line of decisions involves the elimination of all obstacles to intra-community trade in order to merge the national markets into a single market bringing about conditions as close as possible to those of a genuine internal market.[4]

The essential aim of an internal market, therefore, is to make trade between Member States as easy as trade within a single state. Geographic realities such as distance and mountains aside, a Danish company should be able to sell its goods or services just as easily in Italy as in Denmark itself. The main idea is that such an internal market allows all the factors of production, labour, capital and enterprise, to move freely, generating maximum allocative efficiency and hence increasing overall wealth.

An internal market, therefore, is a far reaching form of economic integration. It goes beyond a free trade area and a customs union, as it aims to remove *all* obstacles to free movement and create a market that functions as if all Member States are one country. The ambitious nature of this aim comes into focus when one realizes that almost any national rule may be able to affect free movement, as we shall see in more detail in the coming chapters on the specific free movement rights. Creating an internal market, therefore, is not just an economic but also a major political project. An internal market, however, is not yet the most intense form of economic integration beyond statehood. For in the final step, a full economic union, an internal market is combined with the complete integration of monetary and fiscal policy as well. The EU has moved a long way towards economic union as well, as will be discussed in

4 Case 15/81, *Schul*, [1982] ECR 1982, 1409.

more detail in EU chapter 13, even though that process has run into significant challenges, which other regional systems should try to avoid.[5]

9.3 The Time Line of the EU Internal Market

Something as complex as an internal market cannot be established overnight, already because Member State economies and legal systems need time to adjust. Establishing an internal market, therefore, requires several phases and transition periods. The first step in the development of the EU internal market was the creation of a customs union, on which the internal market, according to Article 28 TFEU, remains based:

> The Union shall comprise a customs union which shall cover all trade in goods and which shall involve the prohibition between Member States of customs duties on imports and exports and of all charges having equivalent effect, and the adoption of a common customs tariff in their relations with third countries.[6]

The crux of a customs union, which forms one step up from a free trade area, is that not only the tariffs and quotas internally, so between members, are removed, but that the members also agree to apply a common tariff externally, so on goods entering the union from outside. Once goods have entered this customs union, they can be moved around freely in the entire union, inter alia removing the need for burdensome rules of origin.[7] The uniformity of the customs regulation then becomes vital, as the conditions for access to the territory of the customs union must be the same in all Member States, which also explains why the customs union is an exclusive competence of the EU.[8]

The customs union was established in phases, allowing Member States to gradually reduce tariffs and adjust, whilst prohibiting new tariffs. The customs union was completed on 1 July 1968, when all 'internal' tariffs between

5 In addition, as also pointed out in Chapter 10, para. 2, these distinctions and steps are theoretical constructs, and 'In practice, regional cooperation does not fit exactly into these theoretical pigeon holes'. In practice integration can blend certain steps or only complete certain steps incompletely.

6 Compare also the former Article 23 EC, holding that 'The Community shall be based upon a customs union (...).'

7 See on the EAC challenges on this point also Chapter 10.3.4.

8 Article 3(a) TFEU.

the (then six) Member States had been removed, and common customs tariff for the entire Community had been established. At this date, however, a real internal market, originally planned to be in place by 1 January 1970, was, still a long way off. In fact, European integration was facing several political crises, and political faith in the entire project had been reduced significantly.[9] During the political stagnation, however, it was the CJEU that picked up the integration gauntlet, as will be discussed in more detail below and the next chapters. It really was the CJEU's case law on free movement that provided the most important contribution to the development of the internal market in the 1960's and 70's. This case law probably saved the project from a complete demise, and progressively turned the internal market into a legal reality.

In the eighties, different political elites in Europe got their second European wind, as economic growth increased and political support for the internal market project picked up. The re-launch of the European internal market that followed is usually linked to an important White Paper on 'Completing the Internal Market' by the Commission that appeared on 14 June 1985.[10] The White Paper laid out an ambitious agenda to create a truly internal market. It included a list of 279 legislative measures that should all be in place by 31 December 1992, the date on which the market should be 'complete'.[11]

Partially based on the economic benefits that such integration would bring,[12] the White Paper was followed by decisive political action in the form of the Single European Union Act (SEA) 1986.[13] Crucially, the SEA both formulated the Treaty objective to create an internal market as now formulated in Article 26 TEU, and provided the political mechanisms to actually create it. One of the most important changes was the introduction of the current Article 114 TFEU, which allowed internal market legislation to be adopted by

9 See also EU chapter 1 for a further description of some of these crises in European integration, which show that the EU has often developed in a pattern of crisis followed by deeper integration.

10 Commission White Paper 'Completing the Internal Market' COM(85)310.

11 This White Paper, therefore, creates an interesting blue print for comparison, for example with the East African Community Elimination of Non-Tariff Barriers Act 2015.

12 See for contemporary analyses for example M. Emerson, M. Aujean, M. Catinat, P. Goybet, and A. Jacquemin, *The Economics of 1992: The EC Commission's Assessment of the Economic Effects of Completing the Internal Market* (OUP, 1988), or P. Cecchini, *The European Challenge 1992: The Benefits of a Single Market* (Gower, 1988). For later analysis see *inter alia* W. Molle, *The Economics of European Integration* (Aldershot, 2006).

13 For further analysis on why the SEA could be adopted politically, aside from economic benefits, see for example P. Craig, 'Integration, Democracy and Legitimacy' in P. Craig and G. de Búrca (eds), *The Evolution of EU Law* (2nd edn, OUP 2010), ch. 1.

qualified majority. This removed the veto-power of each individual Member State, which had often blocked political decision making before.

With new political vigour and qualified majority voting, the internal market project took off, and was for the major part 'finished' in 1992.[14] Work was then started on economic integration with the Maastricht commitment to introduce a single European currency.[15] In addition, work continued to further develop the internal market, which was of course not yet fully finished even though the main aims of the 1992 project had been achieved. Currently, the main areas where the EU internal market needs to be improved concern services and the digital market.[16] After all, the EU internal market was largely developed in a time where the trade in goods made up over 70% of the economy and the internet did not yet exist. In our current digital age and services-driven economic reality, however, some adjustment may be in order. The need for adjustment and modernisation also creates opportunities for more recent forms of regional integration. They can leap-frog ahead and develop their internal market law with these new challenges and opportunities in mind. In addition, newly formed internal markets may also learn from the EU struggles to include a social dimension in the internal market, as a failure to do so may undermine the legitimacy of the market in the longer run.[17]

9.4 Combining Negative and Positive Integration

The EU internal market depends on a combination of negative and positive integration. A full understanding of the internal market therefore requires a proper understanding of both mechanisms, as well as their interaction.

The term negative integration denotes the use of legally enforceable prohibitions that forbid Member States to restrict free movement. For example, Article 34 TFEU prohibits any Member State rule that restricts the free

---

14 See the Commission Recommendation of 12 July 2004 on the transposition into national law of directives affecting the internal market, O.J. [2005], L 98/47.

15 See further EU chapters 1 and 13 on this process.

16 See for more discussion EU chapter 12, as well as the newly launched Commission initiative on the Digital Internal Market, available via <https://ec.europa.eu/priorities/digital-single-market_en>.

17 See on this increasingly problematic issue B, de Witte, 'Non-Market Values in Internal Market Legislation', in N. Nic Shuibhne (ed), *Regulating the Internal Market* (Edward Elgar, 2006), 75 or the 210 Monti report 'A New Strategy for the Single Market, At the Service of Europe's Economy and Society'.

movement of goods unless it can be justified.[18] As this prohibition is directly applicable and supreme, it allows individuals and companies to challenge any national rules that limit their free movement before a national court.[19] Aided by the CJEU and national courts, negative integration therefore allows individuals and companies to act as a kind of legal bulldozers that remove all obstacles to free movement.[20] The functioning of negative integration, moreover, depends on courts and individuals, not on political action. It can therefore survive, or even thrive, in periods of political stagnation.

Negative integration in the EU is based on a collection of Treaty provisions that prohibit restrictions on all four freedoms and provide some exceptions for rules that serve public interests.[21] The structure of the Treaty provisions concerning the different freedoms is very similar. First, the Treaty contains a general prohibition on any obstacles to the specific freedom, then it provides for a limited set of exceptions to the prohibition, based on such issues as public health and national security.[22] As indicated above, the Court of Justice has played a key role in making negative integration effective in the EU. For example, it was the CJEU that found all these prohibitions had direct effect, allowing them to be effectively enforced. In addition, the CJEU developed a very wide definition of restriction, meaning that the free movement clauses could be used to challenge an extremely broad array of national rules that *de facto* limited free movement, even if they were not even indirectly discriminatory.[23] Exceptions, on the other hand, were interpreted narrowly, meaning that it becomes harder for Member State to justify restrictions on public interest grounds.

Negative integration, however, has its limits. To begin with, it can only remove national obstacles, it cannot create new, better laws to replace the ones that have been disapplied. Negative integration also depends on individual actors, which may lead to incoherence as some restrictions are challenged and others are not. In addition, negative integration cannot harmonize

18 See for a further discussion of this prohibition EU chapter 10.

19 See EU chapter 4 on the concept of direct effect and its pivotal importance for EU law.

20 On the importance of national courts in this process also see K. Lenaerts, 'The Court's Outer and Inner Selves: Exploring the External and Internal Legitimacy of the European Court of Justice', in M. Adams, H. De Waele, J. Meeusen and G. Straetmans (eds), *Judging Europe's Judges, The Legitimacy of the Case Law of the European Court of Justice* (Hart, 2013), 40, as well as EU chapter 9.

21 Articles 30, 34, 35, 45, 49, 56, 63 and 110 TFEU.

22 See generally C. Barnard, 'Derogations, justifications and the Four Freedoms', in C. Barnard and O. Odudu (eds.) *The Outer Limits of European Union Law*, (OUP, 2009).

23 See for example Case 8/74, *Dassonville*, [1974], ECR 837, and EU chapters 10–13.

the restrictive laws that are justified and remain in place. After all, many rules that restrict free movement, such as consumer protection or food safety rules, are highly desirable, and can also be justified under EU law. Free movement is not the same as total deregulation. Where all Member States adopt different but justifiable laws on, for example, food safety, however, free movement of food stuffs would still be seriously undermined. A Dutch dairy producer, for instance, would still have to deal with different food laws in each Member State, which *de facto* undermines the free movement of his product.

For all these reasons, negative integration needs to be complemented by so-called positive integration.[24] The concept of positive integration essentially denotes the use of EU legislation to harmonize or replace national laws.[25] Such EU rules can then serve the required public interests, such as food safety, without creating unnecessary obstacles to free movement. For example, the EU could adopt a directive on the minimum standards for dairy products. This directive could provide effective and uniform protection to all consumers in the EU, but would also allow producers that meet these minimum standards to sell their product throughout the entire EU. By harmonizing the level of protection at the EU level, therefore, legislation that protects public interests does not have to create differences between national laws that hinder free movement. Under the *Tedeschi* principle, moreover, free movement prohibitions no longer apply once secondary EU legislation is in place. The free movement clauses cannot be used, therefore, to challenge national restrictions to free movement that are based on EU legislation.[26]

The introduction of harmonization by qualified majority voting under the Single European Act, therefore, was so important because it enabled the

24 Negative integration also creates its own push towards positive integration, for as national rules are set aside, the need arises for EU law to replace them. The East African Community Standardisation, Quality Assurance, Metrology and Testing Protocol and the 2006 East African Community Standardisation, Quality Assurance, Metrology and Testing Act can also be seen as an example, or at least anticipation, of this process.

25 This is often done via directives, usually under Article 114 TFEU, which require all Member States to adopt certain national laws. As a result, all national laws adopt similar provisions, and hence are 'harmonized'. See for the instrument of a directive EU chapter 3.

26 See Case C-5/77 *Tedeschi* ECLI:EU:C:1977:144 and Case C-573/12, *Alands* ECLI:EU:C:2014:2037. Naturally the validity of the EU legislation itself can be challenged, for instance for a violation of free movement principles, under Article 263 TFEU. See EU chapter 7 and K.J.M. Mortelmans, 'The Relationship between the Treaty Rules and Community Measures for the Establishment and Functioning of the Internal Market: Towards a Concordance Rule' (2002), *CMLRev*, 1303.

necessary positive integration to complement the negative integration already spearheaded by the CJEU. In addition to qualified majority voting, however, successful future positive integration also depended on more effective *methods* of harmonization. Initially, the main method used was that of total harmonization. Member States would for instance try to exhaustively regulate all product requirements for a certain product. Such total harmonisation, however, could take a very long time to reach agreement, as all details needed to be agreed upon.[27] After the SEA, therefore, the EU also moved towards a new approach towards harmonization that depended more on the setting of minimum standards and mutual recognition.[28] This new approach significantly sped up harmonization and improved the quality and effectiveness of the legislation adopted.

In line with the interaction between negative and positive interaction described above, each of the different freedoms discussed in the next chapters will show a similar pattern. First, negative integration is used, with the support of the CJEU, to challenge a host of national regulations. Subsequently, EU legislation is gradually developed to harmonize or replace national legislation, whereby increasingly more modern forms of harmonization are employed. Again, more recent forms of economic integration may learn from some of the detours and dead ends in this process of European integration, as they may try to jump directly towards more effective forms of negative and positive integration.

9.5 Convergence in Negative Integration

Before the next chapters discuss each individual freedom separately, however, it is useful to highlight one further overarching development in internal market law, being the gradual convergence of the different freedoms.[29]

27 See already J. Pelkmans, 'The New Approach to Technical Harmonization and Standardization' (1987) 25 *CCMS*, 249 as well as the White Paper of the Commission on this point COM(85)310.

28 See <www.newapproach.org>. See also more generally C. Janssens, *The Principle of Mutual Recognition in EU Law* (OUP, 2013), F. Kostoris Padoa Schioppa (ed), *The Principle of Mutual Recognition in the European Integration Process* (Palgrave MacMillan, 2005) or (on the difficulties of this approach) J. Pelkmans, 'Mutual Recognition in Goods: On Promises and Disillusions' (2007) 14 *JEPP*, 699, and M. Dougan, 'Minimum Harmonization and the Internal Market' (2000) 37 *CMLRev*, 853.

29 See also Niamh Nic Shuibne, *The Coherence of EU Free Movement Law. Constitutional Responsibility and the Court of Justice* (OUP, 2013).

Each freedom depends on different Treaty prohibitions and exceptions. In addition, there are obvious differences between the different freedoms, since goods, services, capital and especially people have some rather significant differences. Nevertheless, the different freedoms also have a lot in common, and share the purpose of creating an internal market. In line with these commonalities, the case law of the CJEU is showing an increasing convergence and unity in the application of free movement prohibitions and exceptions.[30]

This convergence can first of all be seen at the general level. In all freedoms, for example, the CJEU has interpreted the prohibitions very broadly, whereas the exceptions that can justify restrictions are interpreted very narrowly. Equally, for all freedoms the CJEU has accepted a category of non-Treaty based exceptions, the so called Rule of Reason exceptions. The CJEU also applies the principle of mutual recognition to all freedoms, even though it was established in the context of the free movement of goods.[31] Lastly, in most free movement cases, the actual assessment eventually comes down to the proportionality test, which is normally very similar in all freedoms.[32]

By now, however, the convergence extends even further than just the general structure of free movement provisions. Case law from different freedoms is now often used interchangeably. *Futura*, for example, concerned the freedom to provide services, yet the CJEU also refers to case law on establishment, workers, and goods, which apparently are also relevant for services.[33] Such convergence can help to increase legal certainty and promote the unity of internal market law. In light of the differences between the freedoms already referred to above, convergence can of course not be total, and differences do and will probably remain. These for example concern direct horizontal effect, the extra-territorial scope of the freedoms or the detailed legislation regulating free movement of persons. Equally, the Keck-exception has so far not been

30 See inter alia S.C. Barnard, *The Substantive Law of the EU. The Four Freedoms* (4th edn, OUP 2015), 24, or already J. Snell, *Goods and Services in EU Law. A Study of the Relationship between the Freedoms* (OUP, 2002) and H.D. Jarass, 'A Unified Approach to the Fundamental Freedoms', in M. Andenas and W.-H. Roth (eds), *Services and Free Movement in EU Law* (OUP, 2002).

31 Case C-120/78, *Cassis de Dijon* ECLI:EU:C:1979:42.

32 For an overview of this ordinary structure as well as an example of a deviatoin in the context of games of chance see S.C.G. Van den Bogaert and A. Cuyvers: 'Money For Nothing: The Case Law of the EU Court of Justice on the Regulation of Gambling' *Common Market Law Review* 48 (4), 1175.

33 Case C-250/95 *Futura* ECLI:EU:C:1997:239. For further examples of convergence also see Case C-379/87, *Groener* ECLI:EU:C:1989:599, Case C-340/89, *Vlassopoulou* ECLI:EU:C:1991:193, or Case C-19/92, *Dieter Kraus* ECLI:EU:C:1993:125.

applied outside the freedom of goods, and in certain areas the CJEU seems less and less committed to its position that Rule of Reason exceptions can only justify non-discriminatory restrictions.[34]

The following chapters will further explore these similarities and differences, as they systematically discuss the four different freedoms and their development over time. Considering the comparative objective of this book, moreover, these chapters will focus on the initial and foundational case law in the earlier stages of European integration and the basic structure this case law provided to get the European internal market going.

---

34 Joined Cases C-267 & 268/91, *Keck and Mithouard* ECLI:EU:C:1993:905, Case C-2/90, *Commission v. Kingdom of Belgium* ECLI:EU:C:1992:310, and Case C-379/98 *PreussenElektra* ECLI:EU:C:2001:160.

CHAPTER 10

Free Movement of Goods in the EAC

Leonard Obura Aloo

10.1 Introduction

This Chapter addresses the free movement of goods within the East African Community (EAC). A central feature of regional integration and any common market are the "four freedoms"—the free movement of goods, labour, services and capital.[1] Free movement of goods paves the way for the other freedoms and is usually one of the initial steps in the integration process. Free movement of goods is sometimes referred to as the pioneer economic freedom and it is a key component of the East African integration process.[2]

Free movement of goods means that goods can be moved freely within the defined common territory.[3] The idea is that the Community will constitute a single economic area similar to the domestic market of any of the Partner States. It is generally agreed that free trade contributes to wealth creation.[4] Free movement of goods enables a producer in the EAC to have access to a potential market of 143.5 million people.[5]

This Chapter will cover the free movement of goods in the EAC under the Customs Union as well as subsequent developments under the Common Market. Firstly, it will examine the extent to which free movement of goods is envisaged under the Community instruments.[6] Some historical review will

1 East African Community Treaty (adopted 30 November 1999, went into force 7 July 2000) (EAC Treaty) art 76(1): "There shall be established a Common Market among the Partner States. Within the Common Market, and subject to the Protocol provided for in paragraph 4 of this Article, there shall be free movement of labour, goods, services, capital, and the right of establishment."

2 For the similar role movement of goods played in European integration see EU chapter 9 and 10.

3 P.S.R.F., Mathijsen, *A Guide to the European Union Law* (8th edn, Sweet & Maxwell 2004) 173.

4 For the theory of comparative advantage put forward by David Ricardo in 1817 see William J. Baumol & Alan S. Blinder, *Economics: Principles & Policy* (11th edn, South-Western Cengage Learning 2008) 50.

5 EAC Facts & Figures Report (2014).

6 For the reality on the ground, which sometimes does not accord with what reality intended on paper, see East African common market scorecard 2014: tracking EAC compliance in the

© LEONARD OBURA ALOO, 2017 | DOI 10.1163/9789004322073_020
This is an open access chapter distributed under the terms of the CC-BY-NC License.

explain the progression of law under these instruments. Next, there will be a brief examination of the free movement of goods under the Customs Union, including the rules of origin and the rules on elimination of non-tariff barriers. This discussion includes a brief look at developments under the Common Market Protocol. Finally, the chapter examines the question of whether the theory on the free movement of goods accords with the reality experienced by traders.

The Chapter is descriptive and introductory and is intended to enable the reader to navigate through the various EAC instruments dealing with the free movement of goods.

10.2 Historical Development of the Free Movement of Goods in the East African Community

Some understanding of the historical development of free movement of goods in the East African region is necessary in order to contextualise the way in which the EAC has developed and continues to develop its rules on the free movement of goods.[7]

The EAC in its current format comprises six states. The founding Partner States which signed the Treaty for the Establishment of the East African Community (the EAC Treaty) in 1999 were Kenya Tanzania and Uganda. They were subsequently joined by Rwanda and Burundi in the year 2007. South Sudan became the sixth Partner State in 2016.

Free movement of goods has already been a central feature of East African cooperation since early in the last century. As early as 1917, Kenya and Uganda established a Customs Union with the amalgamation of their customs authorities.[8] In 1922, Kenya, Uganda and Tanganyika agreed on a common

---

movement of capital, services and goods (Vol. 2): Main report (English), < http://documents.worldbank.org/curated/en/2014/01/23862386/east-african-common-market-scorecard-2014-tracking-eac-compliance-movement-capital-services-goods-vol-2-main-report> accessed June 28 2016.

7 For a detailed discussion on the early history of co-operation amongst East African countries see Thomas M. Franck, *East African Unity Through Law* (Yale University Press 1964); Y.P. Ghai and J.P.W.B. McAuslan. *Public Law and Political Change in Kenya: A Study of the Legal Framework of Government from Colonial Times to the Present* (Oxford University Press 1970) Chapter 12 and Chapter X above.

8 *Ibid.* 460; Henry Kibet Mutai, *Compliance With International Trade Obligations: The Common Market For Eastern and Southern Africa* (Kluwer Law International 2007) 116–118; *See generally* Thomas M. Franck, *East African Unity Through Law* (Yale University Press 1964); *See*

external tariff. In 1923, free interchange of domestic products was achieved. Four years later the three territories agreed on free movement of imported goods.[9] However, these early arrangements were often not legally secured and depended on the goodwill of the parties.[10] The early Customs Union "was maintained only as a result of inter-territorial negotiations and Kenya-Uganda and Tanganyika retained their separate customs administrations until 1949."[11]

In 1947, the East African High Commission was established through the East African (High Commission) Order in Council.[12] The High Commission's mandate did not cover the Common Market sufficiently, with emphasis being placed instead on the common services.[13] The effectiveness of the Common Market was left to the authority of the Colonial Secretary. Though effective, the benefits of the early Common Market were not evenly distributed amongst the three territories. Just before independence of the three territories in the early 1960s, the problem was significant enough that a Commission to review the workings of the common services and common market was established.[14] Between 1961 and 1967 the East African Common Services Organisation was established, briefly providing an anchor for the Common Market. However, due to an uneven distribution of benefits, Uganda and Tanzania imposed restrictions on the access of Kenyan goods into their territories. Efforts to resolve disputes over these restrictions culminated in the establishment of the Treaty of East African Co-operation in 1967.[15]

This Treaty arrangement lasted between 1967 and 1977 and contained elaborate provisions to cover the free movement of goods within the territories in addition to common external tariffs. Despite these provisions, the 1967–1977 Treaty was plagued by many of the same complaints as its predecessor, namely free movement of goods benefiting Kenya at the expense of the other

---

generally Robert W. Strayer, *The Failure of Closer Union in East Africa 1919–1931* (dissertation, University of Wisconsin-Madison 1966).

9 Y.P Ghai and J.P.W.B. McAuslan. *Public Law and Political Change in Kenya: A Study of the Legal Framework of Government from Colonial Times to the Present* (Oxford University Press 1970) 460.

10 *Ibid.*

11 *Ibid.*

12 East African (High Commission) Order in Council, S.I. No. 2863 of 1947.

13 Y.P. Ghai and J.P.W.B. McAuslan. *Public Law and Political Change in Kenya: A study of the legal framework of government from colonial times to the present.* Nairobi. Oxford University Press. 1970. p. 470.

14 *Ibid.* 472.

15 *Ibid.* 478.

territories.[16] These complaints, coupled with other political factors, led to the eventual collapse of the old EAC. However, the EAC of the 1970s made significant progress towards the free movement of goods within the Community.[17] Lessons drawn from the collapse of the old Community and the pre-independence arrangements continue to inform the approach towards the free movement of goods in the current Community.[18] Specifically, safeguards were built into the framework for integration to ensure that the economies that were relatively less developed were not swamped by goods from the relatively better developed economies. The principles of variable geometry and asymmetry are integral to the EAC Treaty.[19]

Under Article 5(2) of the EAC Treaty, the Partner States undertake to establish among themselves and in accordance with the provisions of the treaty, "a Customs Union, a Common Market, subsequently a Monetary Union and ultimately a Political Federation."[20] In implementing these, the Operational Principles of the Community include the principle of variable geometry, equitable distribution of benefits and principle of asymmetry.[21]

Free movement of goods is an essential feature of a fully-fledged customs union and a given in a functioning common market.[22] Regional economic integration regimes theoretically proceed from the preferential trade area (PTA) where partners offer each other preferential trade terms relative to the rest of the world, to a free trade area (FTA), where trade amongst the partners is conducted free from tariff and non-tariff barriers. Meanwhile, each partner in the

16 Ngila Mwase, 'Regional Economic Integration and the Unequal Sharing of Benefits: Background to the Disintegration and Collapse of the East African Community' (1979) 4 Africa Development 2/3; Y.P. Ghai and J.P.W.B. McAuslan. *Public Law and Political Change in Kenya: A Study of the Legal Framework of Government from Colonial Times to the Present* (Oxford University Press 1970) 478.

17 Ngila Mwase, 'Regional Economic Integration and the Unequal Sharing of Benefits: Background to the Disintegration and Collapse of the East African Community' (1979) 4 Africa Development 2/3.

18 Henry Kibet Mutai, 'Regional trade integration strategies under SADC and the EAC: A comparative analysis' (2011) 1 SADC Law Journal 81, 90.

19 *Ibid.* 85.

20 EAC Treaty Article 5(2).

21 EAC Treaty Articles 7(1)(e), 7(1)(f) and 7(1)(h).

22 Report of the Heads of Delegation to the Foreign Ministers at the Messina Conference, 21 April 1956. This report, which emphasized the benefits of the free movement of goods, was presented at the conference and paved the way for future negotiations which culminated in a European customs union and common market (known colloquially as the Spaak Report).

FTA has an independent trade policy to the rest of the world. Next comes the customs union, where the free trade amongst member states is supplemented by the free movement of goods, and is extended to include free movement of capital, services, labour, and persons and a right of establishment. Finally, the monetary union, has all the aspects of the common market, in addition to cooperation on economic and monetary issues including a common currency.[23]

In practice, regional cooperation does not fit exactly into these theoretical pigeon holes,[24] and the EAC developments are no exception. The developments in the EAC have been pragmatic, from trade liberalisation to a Customs Union and proceeding to the Common Market. However, not all aspects of the Customs Union are fully implemented as of yet.[25]

With this background in mind, we may now discuss the provisions of the EAC legal regime on the free movement of goods.

10.3 Free Movement of Goods

As indicated above, the EAC Treaty was signed on the 30th November 1999. The Protocol on the Establishment of the East African Community Customs Union was concluded five years later in 2004 and implementation began in January 2005. Implementation of the Customs Union was to be progressive for a period of five years. The Partner States have formally eliminated tariffs on goods for intraregional trade. However, measures of equivalent effect, rules of origin, sanitary and phytosanitary measures, additional taxes and charges in addition to technical barriers all remain.[26] Below we examine the framework for the free movement of goods and the way in which the barriers to trade are dealt with in the EAC.

The legal framework of the Customs Union consists of the EAC Treaty; the Protocols; the laws enacted by the East African Legislative Assembly; the

---

23 EAC, *Study on the Establishment of an East African Community Common Market: Final Report* (M.A. Consulting Group, August 2007) 10. See on this point also EU Chapter 9.

24 *Ibid.*

25 *Ibid.* 11; Bela Balassa, *The Theory of Economic Integration* (first published in 1961, Routledge 2011) 2.

26 East African common market scorecard 2014: tracking EAC compliance in the movement of capital, services and goods (Vol. 2): Main report (English), The World Bank/ EAC Secretariat, 4 <http://documents.worldbank.org/curated/en/2014/01/23862386/east-african-common-market-scorecard-2014-tracking-eac-compliance-movement-capital-services-goods-vol-2-main-report> accessed June 28 2016.

regulations and directives of the Council; relevant principles of internal law; and applicable decisions made by the East African Court of Justice.[27] The current institutional framework for the implementation of the Customs Union is made up of regional policy organs and national institutions. In respect of customs, the Council is responsible for policy decisions. The Directorate of Customs coordinates the policy development and the customs authorities in each respective Partner State are responsible for the day-to-day customs operations including revenue collection, accountability and enforcement of the East African Community Customs Management Act (EACCMA).[28] At the national level customs is administered under the revenue authority through national legislation implementing the EACCMA.

10.3.1 *The Protocol on the Establishment of the East African Community Customs Union*

The EAC trade regime is informed by Chapter Eleven of the EAC Treaty which is entitled "Co-operation in Trade Liberalisation and Development". Article 74 of the EAC Treaty provides that in order to achieve the EAC's objectives the Partner States shall adopt an East African Trade Regime and co-operate in trade liberalisation and development in accordance with the regime.

Under Article 75 of the EAC Treaty, the Partner States agreed to establish a Customs Union, details of which were to be contained in a Protocol. Under Article 75(7) of the EAC Treaty, the Partner States agreed to conclude a Protocol on the Establishment of a Customs Union within four years. The EAC Partner States took the unusual route of implementing the free trade area and the customs union simultaneously.[29] The Protocol on the Establishment of the East African Community Customs Union (the Customs Union Protocol) was signed in March 2004.[30]

The EAC Treaty required the Customs Union Protocol to contain certain details including:

---

27 EAC, *Framework for the Attainment of the East African Community Single Customs Territory* (November 2013) 2.1.2(e).

28 East African Community Customs Management Act 2004 (Revised Edition 2009); see also EAC, *Framework for the Attainment of the East African Community Single Customs Territory* (November 2013) 2.1.2(e).

29 Henry Kibet Mutai, 'Regional trade integration strategies under SADC and the EAC: A comparative analysis' (2011) 1 SADC Law Journal 81, 83. Economic literature suggests the conventional approach would be to move from a free trade area to a customs union and then to a common market. In the EAC the first two stages were implemented together.

30 Protocol on the Establishment of the East African Community Customs Union (2004).

(*a*) *Application of the principle of asymmetry;*
(*b*) *The elimination of internal tariffs and other charges of equivalent effect;*
(*c*) *The elimination of non-tariff barriers;*
(*d*) *Establishment of a common external tariff;*
(*e*) *Rule of Origin;*
(*f*) *Dumping;*
(*g*) *Subsidies and countervailing duties;*
(*h*) *Security and other restrictions to trade;*
(*i*) *Competition;*
(*j*) *Duty drawback, refund and remission of duties and taxes;*
(*k*) *Customs co-operation;*
(*l*) *Re-exportation of goods; and*
(*m*) *Simplification and harmonisation of trade documentation and procedures.*[31]

The Customs Union Protocol dealt with these issues in 44 comprehensive articles. The articles are divided into nine parts. These parts cover interpretation; establishment of the East African Community Customs Union; Customs Administration; Trade Liberalisation; Trade Related Aspects; Export Promotion Schemes; Special Economic Zones; Exemption Regimes; and General Provisions.[32]

The Customs Union Protocol provides that the implementation of the Protocol would be progressive over a five year period ending in 2010.[33]

The most significant aspects of the EAC Customs Union Protocol were: the removal of internal taxes on intra-EAC trade; the removal of non-tariff barriers on intra-EAC trade; the introduction of common external trade policy through the Common External Tariff; the introduction of a list of sensitive products that were to be provided with additional protection; and the legal and institutional mechanisms which have been developed to govern free movement of goods within the EAC.[34] Having provided an outline of the Customs Union Protocol, we can now examine how it dealt with each of these major areas.

---

31 EAC Treaty Article 75(1).

32 EAC Customs Union Protocol.

33 EAC Customs Union Protocol Article 11.

34 EAC, *Study on the Establishment of an East African Community Common Market: Final Report* (M.A. Consulting Group, August 2007).

10.3.2 *Removal of Internal Tariffs of Intra-EAC Trade under EACCU Protocol*

As indicated above, elimination of internal tariffs on goods under the Customs Union Protocol was envisioned to be progressive and asymmetrical. The Customs Union Protocol defines goods as:

> [A]ll wares, articles, merchandise, animals, matter, baggage, stores, materials, currency and includes postal items other than personal correspondence, and where any such goods are sold under the auspices of this Protocol, the proceeds of the sale.[35]

Under Article 11 of the Customs Union Protocol, there was an immediate elimination of duty for goods to and from the Republic of Uganda and the United Republic of Tanzania.[36] Goods from Tanzania and Uganda destined for Kenya also enjoyed immediate duty free access on coming into force of the Customs Union Protocol.[37]

However, goods from Kenya destined for Uganda and Tanzania were divided into two categories: firstly, those eligible for immediate duty free access to the markets in Uganda and Tanzania were placed in category A;[38] and secondly, other goods were placed in category B and were eligible for a gradual tariff reduction.[39] Category B goods from Kenya destined for Uganda had a phased reduction of tariffs of 10, 8, 6, 4 and 2 per cent in each of the first to fifth years respectively and thereafter tariff free access would be applied.[40] Category B goods from Kenya destined for Tanzania had a phased reduction of tariffs that was specified in Annex II to the Customs Union Protocol.[41]

Internal tariffs specified in the Customs Union Protocol were not to exceed the Common External Tariff with regard to any of the specified products.[42]

35 EAC Customs Union Protocol Protocol Article 1(1).

36 EAC Customs Union Protocol Article 11(2)(a); The language of the is not unequivocal but the intention is clear.

37 EAC Customs Union Protocol Article 11(2)(b).

38 EAC Customs Union Protocol Article 11(3)(a).

39 EAC Customs Union Protocol Article 11(3)(b).

40 EAC Customs Union Protocol Article 11(4); Annex II to the Protocol in respect to Uganda contains 443 categories of goods each with different schedules for reduction of tariffs, see www.eac.int/customs/index.................... (last accessed 2nd December 2015).

41 EAC Customs Union Protocol Article 11(5); Annex II to the Protocol in respect to Tanzania contains 859 categories of goods each with different schedules for reduction of tariffs, see www.eac.int/customs/index.................... (last accessed 2nd December 2015).

42 EAC Customs Union Protocol Article 11(6).

The current state of implementation of the Customs Union Protocol is that it has now been fully implemented. Since the coming into force of the Customs Union Protocol the Partner States have eliminated internal tariffs and apply a common external tariff. "Goods procured in the region are not subject to import duty when transferred to another Partner State if they meet the rules of origin requirements. The goods are however, subject to domestic taxes (VAT, excise and other levies) levied on international trade upon arrival at the international borders."[43]

10.3.3 *Intra-EAC Trade—Common External Tariff*

In a fully flagged customs union states apply a common external tariff on imports. A common external tariff is a commercial policy towards third countries.[44] In the EAC, due to the progressive approach to integration, there are exemptions to the common external tariff.

Under Article 12 of the Customs Union Protocol the Partner States established a three band common external tariff with a minimum rate of zero per cent, a middle rate of ten per cent and a maximum rate of twenty five per cent in respect of all products imported into the Community.[45] Exceptional measures may be taken to remedy any adverse effects which any Partner State may experience by implementation of the Common External Tariff.[46] Rates higher than 25 per cent are applied to some selected items (termed the sensitive list).[47] These include such items as maize, cement, rice, cotton fabrics, milk and dairy products.[48] The rates are published in the EAC Common External Tariff Handbook,[49] and EAC Gazette Notices.[50]

The EAC Customs Management Act provides the legal framework for the implementation of duties and the Common External Tariff. Section 110 of the EAC Customs Management Act indicates that the rate of duty payable shall be the rate specified under the Customs Union Protocol. Goods originating from the Partner States are to be accorded Community tariff treatment in accordance with the Rules of Origin and the Customs Union Protocol.[51]

43 EAC Customs Union Protocol Article 25(2)(b).

44 P.S.R.F., Mathijsen, *A Guide to the European Union Law* (8th edn, Sweet & Maxwell 2004) 175.

45 EAC Customs Union Protocol Article 12(1).

46 EAC Customs Union Protocol Article 12(3).

47 EAC Trade Report 2014 Section 5.2.; Sensitive Goods.

48 *Ibid.*

49 The EAC Common External Tariff (CET) Handbook.

50 EAC Gazette.

51 The East African Community Customs Management Act Section 111.

The classification of goods is in accordance with a Harmonised Customs Commodity Description and Coding System.[52]

The EAC Partner States are also members of other regional trading arrangements which complicates application of the Common External Tariff. Burundi, for example, is a member of the EAC, the Economic Community of Central African States (ECCAS), the Common Market for Eastern and Southern Africa (COMESA) and COMESA Free Trade Area. Kenya is a member of the EAC, COMESA, and the Intergovernmental Authority on Development (IGAD). Rwanda is a member of the EAC, the ECCAS, COMESA and COMESA Free Trade Area. Tanzania is a member of the EAC and the Southern African Development Community (SADC). Uganda's membership is in the EAC, COMESA, COMESA Free Trade Area and IGAD.[53] The Customs Union Protocol in Article 37 requires Partner States to honour commitments in respect of all other multilateral and international organisations to which they belong. In particular the Partner States are required to identify the issues arising from membership of other integration blocks in order to establish convergence. Article 37 specifically allows Partner States to enter into other regional arrangements although a procedure for notifying other Partner States is provided.[54]

Under Section 112 of the EAC Customs Management Act, notwithstanding the Common External Tariff, preferential treatment is applied to goods imported under the COMESA and SADC arrangements in the Partner States as prescribed by the Partner States legislation and also for other tariff arrangements approved by the Council.[55] The preferential treatment for COMESA and SADC was supposed to cease in 2008, however, the preferential treatment for goods approved by the Council continues.[56] The multiple and overlapping membership of regional trading arrangements complicates the application of the Common External Tariff and makes the EAC Partner States reluctant to eliminate internal boundaries and also increases the significance of the rules of origin regime.[57]

---

52 EAC Customs Union Protocol Art. 8 and 12(4).

53 Adam Ihucha, 'Comesa, Sadc imports get tariff relief again' (*The East African* 5 2013) <http://www.theeastafrican.co.ke/news/Comesa-Sadc-imports-get-tariff-relief-again-/-/2558/1658344/-/ugt2mi/-/index.html> accessed July 6, 2016.

54 EAC Customs Union Protocol Article 37.

55 S. 112 The East African Community Customs Management Act.

56 S. 112 (2) The East African Community Customs Management Act.

57 Ron Sandry, *Intra-REC trade and overlapping membership: review of COMESA, EAC, SADC* (Trade Law Centre, August 2015).

10.3.4 *Removal of Internal Tariffs of Intra-EAC Trade-Rules of Origin*

In order to implement free movement of goods, it is necessary to establish the origin of the goods so as to determine which goods benefit from the rules on free movement and which goods do not. In a fully-fledged customs union, rules of origin are of less significance because states apply a common external tariff.[58] However, in the EAC due to the progressive approach to integration and the exemptions to the Common External Tariff, an absence of rules of origin would result in trade deflection where goods would enter the region via the country with the lowest external tariff which would deny customs revenue to the other Partner States.[59]

Article 14 of the Customs Union Protocol provides for the rules of origin. The rules specify that goods are accepted as being eligible for the Community tariff treatment if they originate from the Partner States.[60] Goods are considered to originate from the Partner States if they meet the criteria set out in the EAC Customs Union (Rules of Origin) Rules specified in Annex III to the Customs Union Protocol.[61]

The EAC Customs Union (Rules of Origin) Rules 2015 are the current edition of these rules.[62] The Rules of Origin provide that the purpose of the rules is to "ensure there is uniformity among Partner States in the application of the Rules of Origin and that to the extent possible the process is transparent, accountable, fair, predictable and consistent with the provisions of the Protocol."[63]

Rule 4 of the Rules of Origin provides two criteria for goods to be considered as originating in the Partner States.

Firstly, goods are accepted as originating in a Partner State where the goods have been wholly produced in the Partner State from which they are

58 What is the Common Customs Tariff, (European Commission) <http://ec.europa.eu/taxation_customs/customs/customs_duties/tariff_aspects/index_en.htm> accessed July 6, 2016.

59 Henry Mutai, 'Regional trade integration strategies under SADC and the EAC: A comparative analysis' (2011) 1 SADC *Law Journal* 81–97 at 86.

60 EAC Customs Union Protocol Article 14(1).

61 EAC Customs Union Protocol Article 14(2) and Article 14(3); East African Community Customs Union (Rules of Origin) Rules, 2015 available at http://www.customs.eac.int/index.php?option=com_content&view=article&id=106&Itemid=135.

62 East African Community Customs Union (Rules of Origin) Rules, 2015 available at http://www.customs.eac.int/index.php?option=com_content&view=article&id=106&Itemid=135.

63 East African Community Customs Union (Rules of Origin) Rules 2015; Rule 2 available at http://www.customs.eac.int/index.php?option=com_content&view=article&id=106&Itemid=135.

consigned.[64] Rule 5 of the Rules of Origin sets out the criteria for determining products as wholly produced in the Partner States. The rule states:

> 1. *For the purposes of rule 4 (a), the following products shall be regarded as wholly produced in a Partner State:*
>   (*a*) *mineral products extracted from the ground or sea-bed of the Partner State;*
>   (*b*) *vegetable products including plant and plant products harvested, gathered or picked within the Partner State;*
>   (*c*) *live animals born and raised within the Partner State;*
>   (*d*) *products obtained from live animals within the Partner State;*
>   (*e*) *products from slaughtered animals born and raised within the Partner State;*
>   (*f*) *products obtained by hunting or fishing conducted within the Partner State;*
>   (*g*) *products of aquaculture, including mariculture, obtained within the Partner State where the fish is raised;*
>   (*h*) *products of sea fishing and other products taken from the exclusive economic zone of the Partner State;*
>   (*i*) *products of sea fishing and other products taken from the waters in the high seas by a vessel of a Partner State;*
>   (*j*) *products manufactured in a factory ship of a Partner State exclusively from the products referred to in sub-paragraph (i);*
>   (*k*) *products extracted from marine soil or subsoil outside the territorial waters of a Partner State provided that the Partner State has the sole right to work on that soil or subsoil;*
>   (*l*) *used articles fit only for the recovery of materials, provided that such articles have been collected from users within the Partner State;*
>   (*m*) *scrap and waste resulting from manufacturing operations within the Partner State; and*
>   (*n*) *goods produced within the Partner State exclusively or mainly from the following—*
>   *i. products referred to in this paragraph; and*
>   *ii. materials which do not contain elements imported from outside the Partner State or which are of undetermined origin.*[65]

64 East African Community Customs Union (Rules of Origin) Rules 2015; Rule 4(1)(a).

65 East African Community Customs Union (Rules of Origin) Rules 2015; Rule 5(1).

Secondly, goods will be considered as originating from the Partner States where the goods are produced in a Partner State incorporating materials which have not been wholly obtained in the Partner State provided that such materials have undergone sufficient working or processing in the Partner State.[66]

Products are considered to meet the criteria of being sufficiently worked or produced on a case-by-case basis when they meet the criteria provided for under the First Schedule of the Rules of Origin.[67]

The current Rules of Origin appear more complex than the previous rules which were based on the percentage of local material or value addition in the product.[68]

Some processes are specifically indicated as not providing origin. These include packaging, bottling, placing in bags, simple mixing of ingredients, simple assembly of components, and simple painting or polishing.[69]

In determining the origin of the goods, energy and fuel; plant and equipment; machines and tools; and goods which do not enter and are not intended to enter into the final composition of the product are considered neutral elements and are not considered part of the goods.[70]

In order to obtain a Certificate of Origin, the Rule of Origins require that an application is made to the competent authority in the consignees Partner State and that application is to be accompanied by documents verifying that the goods meet the required criteria.[71] The Certificate that is issued is valid for a period of six months.[72]

10.4 Elimination of Non-Tariff Barriers to Trade

Free movement of goods will not be achieved, even where the tariffs have been fully eliminated, unless non-tariff barriers are also eliminated. Non-tariff barriers (NTBs) are defined as any device or government practice that directly impedes the entry of imports into a country. They are restrictions other than tariffs that act as obstacles to trade and may be imbedded in government

66 East African Community Customs Union (Rules of Origin) Rules 2015; Rule 4(1)(b).

67 East African Community Customs Union (Rules of Origin) Rules 2015; Rule 6.

68 For discussion of previous rules see Henry Mutai, 'Regional trade integration strategies under SADC and the EAC: A comparative analysis' (2011) 1 SADC *Law Journal* 81–97 at 86.

69 East African Community Customs Union (Rules of Origin) Rules 2015; Rule 7.

70 East African Community Customs Union (Rules of Origin) Rules 2015; Rule 14.

71 East African Community Customs Union (Rules of Origin) Rules 2015; Rule 17.

72 East African Community Customs Union (Rules of Origin) Rules 2015; Rule 21.

laws, regulations, practices and requirements at both the national and local levels.[73] Article 1 of the EAC Treaty defines NTBs as "administrative and technical requirements imposed by a Partner State in the movement of goods."[74] The Customs Union Protocol goes into more detail and defines non-tariff barriers as "laws, regulations, administrative and technical requirements other than tariffs imposed by a Partner State whose effect is to impede trade."[75]

The EAC Secretariat has attempted an operational definition and defines NTBs in the EAC as quantitative restrictions and specific limitations, other than tariffs, that act as obstacles to trade. Such obstacles, it observes, may be embedded in government laws, regulations, practices and requirements at the national and local level. A wide range of measures have the potential of falling within the scope of NTBs. A report prepared for the EAC in 2008 identified numerous NTBs, including non-recognition of EAC Certificates of Origin; import bans of various products including milk, dairy products, multiple road blocks and weighbridges; levies charged on various imports; and road consignment notes required of transports.[76]

Article 75 of the EAC Treaty provides that the Customs Union Protocol will cover amongst other things the elimination of non-tariff barriers.[77] Article 13 of the Customs Union Protocol provides that:

1. *Except as may be provided for or permitted by this protocol, each Partner State agrees to remove, with immediate effect, all the existing non-tariff barriers to the importation into their respective territories of the goods originating in the other Partner States and, thereafter, not to impose any new non-tariff barriers.*
2. *The Partner States shall formulate a mechanism for identifying and monitoring the removal of non-tariff barriers.*[78]

Given the wide variety of measures that can potentially be classified as NTBs the EAC Treaty and implementation organs have developed various approaches

73 Imen Trabelsi, 'Agricultural trade face to Non-Tariff barriers: A gravity model for the Euro-Med area' (2013), 3 *Journal of Studies in Social Sciences* 1, 20–32.

74 EAC Treaty Article 1.

75 EAC Customs Union Protocol Article 1.

76 EAC, *Implementation and Impact of the East African Community Customs Union* (2009).

77 EAC Treaty Article 75(1)(c).

78 EAC Customs Union Protocol Article 13.

to dealing with them.[79] A number of institutions with the responsibility for monitoring the imposition of NTBs have been created. The monitoring is mainly done through reports and investigations. The institutions include the EAC Sectoral Committee on Trade, Industry, Finance and Investment; the EAC Trade Remedies Committee; the EAC Secretariat; and National Monitoring Committees.

The EAC Sectoral Committees are mandated under the EAC Treaty to monitor progress of implementation of the Treaty in their sectors and submit reports.[80] The main Sectoral Committee for the elimination of NTBs is the Sectoral Committee on Trade, Industry, Finance and Investment.

The Trade Remedies Committee was established under Article 24 (1) of the Customs Union Protocol.[81] The main duty of the Committee is to handle matters relating to rules of origin; anti-dumping measures; subsidies and countervailing measures; safeguard measures; and implementation of the Dispute Settlement Mechanism.[82]

National Monitoring Committees work through regional forums that enable the Partner States to exchange experiences. The National Monitoring Committees' reports are sent to the EAC Secretariat through the national ministries.[83]

In 2008, the EAC Council directed the Secretariat to develop a time bound mechanism for the elimination of current and future NTBs.[84] The Secretariat developed the mechanism which guides the process of elimination of NTBs.

10.4.1 *The East African Community Non-Tariff Barriers Act, 2015*

The mechanisms discussed above have been criticised for their failure to significantly reduce NTBs in the EAC.[85] The weakness led the East African Legislative

79 EAC, *Status of Elimination of Non-Tariff Barriers in the East African Community* (2014, Volume 8); Phyllis Osoro, 'The East African Community and Non-Tariff Barriers A Hindrance to the Trade Liberalisation Policy and Legal Proposals for Eliminating Non-Tariff Barriers', University of Nairobi LL.M. Thesis (2015).

80 EAC Treaty Articles 20, 21 and 22.

81 EAC Customs Union Protocol Article 24(1).

82 EAC Customs Union Protocol Article 24(4).

83 National Monitoring Committees …

84 EAC, *East African Community Time Bound Programme for the Elimination of Non-Tariff Barriers*, EAC Arusha 2008.

85 EAC (EABC), *Monitoring Mechanism for Elimination of Non-Tariff Barriers in the EAC* <http://www.eac.int/news/index.php?option=com_docman&task=doc_view&gid=291&Itemid=158>.

Assembly to put in place the process of binding legislation to deal with NTBS.[86] This process culminated in the enactment of the East African Community Elimination of Non-Tariff Barriers Act, 2015 on the 30th March 2015.[87] The Act awaits Presidential assent by the Heads of States of the Member States. Once it receives the necessary assent, it will be the basis for handling NTBS within the EAC.

The short statute has 18 sections divided into five parts. The objective of the Act is to facilitate trade, and create an environment conducive to the movement of goods within the region.[88] The NTBS are categorised according to the World Trade Organisation (WTO) categories set out in the Schedule to the Act.[89] The Schedule has categorised NTBS into seven categories.[90] The categories are government participation in trade and restrictive practices tolerated by government; customs and administrative entry procedures; technical barriers to trade including standards, testing and packaging; sanitary and phytosanitary measures; specific limitations including quantitative restriction, exchange control, export taxes and quotas; charges on imports; and other procedural problems including arbitrariness, discrimination, costly procedures and documentation.

Bureaucratic activities of public officers and institutions of the Partner States which waste time and increase the cost of movement of goods are also specifically designated as NTBS to trade under the Act.[91]

National Monitoring Committees comprising representatives of both public and private sector representatives are to be established for each Partner State.[92] The National Monitoring Committees, as the name suggests, are required to outline the process of elimination of NTBS in the respective Partner States and monitor the process.[93] The National Monitoring Committees are to advise the Partner States on policies and laws that contain or lead to NTBS. Each Partner State is to identify a National Focal Point which is to be a particular Ministry to champion the elimination of NTBS.[94]

86 East African Legislative Assembly, *Official Report of the Proceedings of the East African Legislative Assembly* (Fifth Meeting—Fifth Session—Second Assembly, 2012).

87 The East African Community Elimination of Non-Tariff Barriers Act, 2015.

88 The East African Community Elimination of Non-Tariff Barriers Act, 2015 Article 3.

89 The East African Community Elimination of Non-Tariff Barriers Act, 2015 Article 4.

90 The East African Community Elimination of Non-Tariff Barriers Act, 2015 Schedule.

91 The East African Community Elimination of Non-Tariff Barriers Act, 2015 Article 6.

92 The East African Community Elimination of Non-Tariff Barriers Act, 2015 Article 7 & 7(2).

93 The East African Community Elimination of Non-Tariff Barriers Act, 2015 Article 7(1).

94 The East African Community Elimination of Non-Tariff Barriers Act, 2015 Article 8.

The Act sets out a procedure for the elimination of NTBs. The elimination is to be by mutual consent of Partner states; by implementation of the East African Community Time Bound Programme for Elimination of Identified Non-Tariff Barriers; and through directives of the EAC Council.[95]

The Act provides that where a Partner State fails to eliminate the NTBs the Secretary General shall refer any matter that is not resolved by the Council to the EAC Committee on Trade Remedies.[96] The Council may recommend to the Summit that sanctions are imposed on a Partner State that fails to comply with any directive, decision or recommendation of the Council.[97]

The Act has been criticised for being silent on what action is to be taken against a Partner State which fails to eliminate NTBs.[98] The scheme of the Act may be faulted for relying on the potential beneficiaries of the NTBs for their elimination. The National Monitoring Committees comprising private and public sector officials of a Partner State may not be motivated to eliminate the NTBs that affect goods from third Partner States.

10.5 Harmonisation and Development of EAC Standards

As indicated above, the EAC has recognised that the application of standards can be classified as a NTB and hinder the free movement of goods. In 2001, in order to reduce the chances of the application of different standards acting as a barrier to the free movement of goods, the EAC Partner States concluded the East African Community Standardisation, Quality Assurance, Metrology and Testing Protocol.[99] Furthermore, in 2006 the East African Legislative Assembly passed the East African Community Standardisation, Quality Assurance, Metrology and Testing Act, 2006,[100] which is aimed at the further harmonisation of standards.

---

95 The East African Community Elimination of Non-Tariff Barriers Act, 2015 Article 9.

96 The East African Community Elimination of Non-Tariff Barriers Act, 2015 Article 12 & 15.

97 The East African Community Elimination of Non-Tariff Barriers Act, 2015 Article 16.

98 Phyllis Osoro, 'The East African Community and Non-Tariff Barriers A Hindrance to the Trade Liberalisation Policy and Legal Proposals for Eliminating Non-Tariff Barriers' (2015) University of Nairobi LL.M.

99 The East African Community Standardisation, Quality Assurance, Metrology and Testing Protocol, 15th January 2001.

100 The East African Community Standardisation, Quality Assurance, Metrology and Testing Act, 2006.

10.5.1 *The East African Community Standardisation, Quality Assurance, Metrology and Testing Protocol*

The EAC Standardisation, Quality Assurance, Metrology and Testing Protocol requires that Partner States evolve and apply a common policy on standardisation, quality assurance, metrology and testing of products which are produced and tested within the Community.[101] A common policy on the relationship between the standard bodies in each Partner State, termed Bureauxs, must also be developed.[102] The Protocol requires that Partner States develop capacity in standard enforcement.[103] The Partner States are also required, by the Protocol, to recognise standards developed and adopted by the African Regional Organisation for Standardisation.[104] The Protocol requires that Partner States apply uniform standards and procedures for formulation of national standards and must also adopt and implement East African Standards alongside these national standards.

10.5.2 *The East African Community Standardisation, Quality Assurance, Metrology and Testing Act, 2006*

The EAC Standardisation, Quality Assurance, Metrology and Testing Act, 2006[105] has provided further legal force to the efforts for harmonisation of standards within the EAC. The Act establishes the East African Standards Committee,[106] the Liaison Office,[107] and the East African Accreditation Board.[108] Each of these bodies assists in the efforts towards harmonisation of standards.

101 Article 3.1 of The East African Community Standardisation, Quality Assurance, Metrology and Testing Protocol, 15th January 2001.

102 Article 3.1(b) of The East African Community Standardisation, Quality Assurance, Metrology and Testing Protocol, 15th January 2001.

103 Article 3.1(b) of The East African Community Standardisation, Quality Assurance, Metrology and Testing Protocol, 15th January 2001.

104 Article 4.1 of The East African Community Standardisation, Quality Assurance, Metrology and Testing Protocol, 15th January 2001.

105 The East African Community Standardisation, Quality Assurance, Metrology and Testing Act, 2006 Legal Notice No. 01/2007 of the East African Community.

106 The East African Community Standardisation, Quality Assurance, Metrology and Testing Act, 2006 Legal Notice No. 01/2007 of the East African Community Section 4.

107 The East African Community Standardisation, Quality Assurance, Metrology and Testing Act, 2006 Legal Notice No. 01/2007 of the East African Community Section 5.

108 The East African Community Standardisation, Quality Assurance, Metrology and Testing Act, 2006 Legal Notice No. 01/2007 of the East African Community Section 11.

A detailed examination of the workings of these bodies would be beyond the scope of this work,[109] however, a brief overview is given below.

Among other things, the Standards Committee is required to undertake and coordinate activities related to standardisation, including establishment of procedures for the development, approval, gazetting and withdrawal of East African Standards.[110] The Liaison Office provides administrative support to the Standards Committee. The Liaison Office is the custodian of the catalogue and authoritative texts of the East African Standards that have been adopted. The East African Accreditation Board is made up of the chief executives of the national accreditation bodies. They seek to avoid duplication of functions at the national and regional levels.

Under Section 19 of the EAC Standardisation, Quality Assurance, Metrology and Testing Act, 2006, the Council may declare an East African Standard, or provision of the Standard, to be compulsory. Before such declaration, the Standard has to published in the East African Community Gazette and at least one newspaper of national circulation in each of the Partner States. The Standards Act provides sanctions for the manufacture or distribution of products not in conformity with the standards. The Act provides:

> No person shall manufacture, trade, distribute, sell, supply or bring a product that is within the scope of a compulsory standard into the Community unless the product confirms with the requirements of the compulsory standard.[111]

Partner States are required to apply their national legislation in enforcement of the standards.[112] Partner States are also required to ensure that their regulatory authorities suspend the manufacture, trading and distribution or sale of non-conforming products. Products that do not comply may be removed from the market, returned to the country of origin or confiscated and destroyed.[113]

---

109 For a summary see East African Community *Understanding of the East African Community Legislation on Standardisation, Quality Assurance, Metrology and Testing Act* (*SQMT*) Arusha.

110 The East African Community Standardisation, Quality Assurance, Metrology and Testing Act, 2006 Legal Notice No. 01/2007 of the East African Community Section 4.

111 The East African Community Standardisation, Quality Assurance, Metrology and Testing Act, 2006 s. 22(1).

112 The East African Community Standardisation, Quality Assurance, Metrology and Testing Act, 2006 s. 22(4).

113 The East African Community Standardisation, Quality Assurance, Metrology and Testing Act, 2006 Section 22(3) & (4).

A person aggrieved by a decision under this section may appeal to the East African Standards Committee within 14 days of the decision.[114] The exact authority of the Committee within the domestic and regional judicial framework is not clear and there appears to be an area of potential conflict between the Committee and domestic courts.

Each Partner State is required to notify the Council of the product certification marks within the jurisdiction of the State. The Partner States are required to recognise as equal to their own, product certification marks awarded by national quality systems institutions of the other Partner States.[115]

Pursuant to the powers under Section 29 of the EAC Standardisation, Quality Assurance, Metrology and Testing Act, 2006, the Council of Ministers has made a number of regulations to govern standards making and implementation.[116]

10.6 Free Movement of Goods and The Protocol on the Establishment of the East African Community Common Market

The Protocol on the Establishment of the East African Community Common Market (Common Market Protocol) was signed on the 9th of November 2009, ten years after the signing of the EAC Treaty.[117]

---

114 The East African Community Standardisation, Quality Assurance, Metrology and Testing Act, 2006 Section 22(5).

115 The East African Community Standardisation, Quality Assurance, Metrology and Testing Act, 2006 Section 24(2) & (3).

116 Subsidiary Legislation passed includes:
1) East African Community Standardisation, Quality Assurance, Metrology and Testing (Product Certification in the Partner States) Regulations, 2013. EAC Statutory Instruments Supplement No. 1 of 6th December 2013 EAC Gazette No. 15 6th December 2013. Uganda Printing and Publishing Corporation, Entebbe.;
2) East African Community Standardisation, Quality Assurance, Metrology and Testing (Enforcement of Technical Regulations in Partner States) Regulations, 2013. EAC Statutory Instruments Supplement No. 2 of 6th December 2013 EAC Gazette No. 15 6th December 2013. Uganda Printing and Publishing Corporation, Entebbe;
3) East African Community Standardisation, Quality Assurance, Metrology and Testing (Designation of Testing Laboratories) Regulations, 2013. EAC Statutory Instruments Supplement No. 1 of 6th December 2013 EAC Gazette No. 15 6th December 2013. Uganda Printing and Publishing Corporation, Entebbe.

117 EAC Common Market Protocol.

Under the Common Market Protocol, the Partner States undertake to accord to each other's nationals treatment which is not less favourable than that accorded to nationals of third party states (Most Favoured Nation), and to observe non-discrimination of nationals of other Partner States on grounds of nationality (national treatment).[118] In addition, under Article 5 (2)(c) of the Common Market Protocol, the Partner States agree to eliminate tariff, non-tariff and technical barriers to trade; harmonise and mutually recognise standards; and implement a common trade policy for the Community.[119]

Part C of the Common Market Protocol covers the free movement of goods. Article 6 of the Common Market Protocol indicates that the free movement of goods between the Partner States of the Community is to be governed by the Customs law of the Community specified in Article 39 of the Customs Union Protocol.[120] In addition to the Customs law of the Community, the free movement of goods is to be governed by:

(*a*) *The East African Community Protocol on Standardisation, Quality Assurance, Metrology and Testing;*
(*b*) *The East African Community Standardisation, Quality Assurance, Metrology and Testing Act, 2006;*
(*c*) *The provisions of the Customs Market Protocol;*
(*d*) *Other protocols that may be concluded in the areas of cooperation on sanitary and phyto-sanitary and technical barriers to trade; and any other instrument relevant to the free movement of goods.*[121]

10.7 Free Movement of Goods in the East African Community Theory and Reality

In this part of the Chapter we look at the theory of the EAC free movement of goods regime as spelt out in the regional legal regime reviewed above, against the reality of its implementation. In the last few years, with the assistance of the World Bank, "Score Cards" on the implementation of the EAC Treaty which track the implementation of the provisions of the EAC Treaty and the

118 EAC Common Market Protocol Article 3.
119 EAC Common Market Protocol Article 5(2)(a).
120 EAC Common Market Protocol Article 6(1).
121 EAC Common Market Protocol Article 6(2).

protocols have been prepared.[122] The 2014 Score Card notes that the laws and regulation of the Partner States continue to be a barrier to increased cross-border trade. The progress to eliminating restrictions is slow and new measures are introduced despite the provisions of the protocols. There is, according to the 2014 Score Card, a lenient attitude towards exemptions which is consequently slowing down the development of the EAC Common Market.

The 2014 Score Card notes that, although formally all Partner States have eliminated tariffs on intra-regional trade, measures of equivalent effect to tariffs still remain. It is noted, for example, that certificates of origin are often not recognised by the Partner States. It is also noted that although the Common External Tariff is formally in place, it is not implemented fully due to the fact that the EAC Partner States belong to a multiplicity of different free trade areas.

The 2014 Score Card evaluates the extent to which the Partner States have implemented their obligations under Article 5(2(c)of the Customs Union Protocol. The areas evaluated are, the elimination of tariffs and measures of equivalent effect; the elimination of NTBs; the implementation of a common external tariff and the harmonisation of mutual recognition of sanitary and phytosanitary standards; and standards preventing technical barriers to trade.[123] The general consensus is that more could be done by the Partner States for the Community in order to fully realise free movement of goods within the EAC.

10.8 Conclusion

This Chapter briefly described the EAC regime for the free movement of goods. It has been noted that the current structure of the free movement of goods is

122 East African common market scorecard 2014: tracking EAC compliance in the movement of capital, services and goods (Vol. 2): Main report (English), The World Bank/ EAC Secretariat, 4 <http://documents.worldbank.org/curated/en/2014/01/23862386/east-african-common-market-scorecard-2014-tracking-eac-compliance-movement-capital-services-goods-vol-2-main-report> accessed June 28 2016; see also Maximillan Haller, 'The East African Community (EAC) The Difference between theory and practice based on the example of free movement of goods and services' (University of Sussex, 2014) Master of Arts.

123 East African Common Market Score Card, 2014: tracking EAC compliance in the movement of capital, services and goods (Vol. 2): Main report (English), The World Bank/ EAC Secretariat, 4 <http://documents.worldbank.org/curated/en/2014/01/23862386/east-african-common-market-scorecard-2014-tracking-eac-compliance-movement-capital-services-goods-vol-2-main-report> accessed June 28 2016.

informed by the historical relationships between the Partner States and their experiences, in part experiments, with cooperation. It has been noted that the Customs Union Protocol is very clear on the free movement of goods. In theory free movement of goods is operative within the Community. However, it has been noted that the existence of exceptions and the overlapping membership of regional trade regimes affects the effective implementation of the free movement of goods. There is also discord between the commitments that the Partner States have to free movement of goods and the reality as indicated by their domestic legislation.

CHAPTER 10A

Free Movement of Goods in the EU

Armin Cuyvers

10.1 Goods: The Foundation of the EU Internal Market

When the EU internal market was established, goods accounted for more than 70% of the European economy. Consequently, goods formed the primary focus when the Treaty rules on free movement were drafted, and most of the early internal market cases concerned goods as well. Many of the most fundamental and groundbreaking judgments on the internal market, therefore, were made in the context of goods. As a result, the free movement of goods forms a useful starting point for any analysis of EU free movement law.

This Chapter provides an overview of EU rules on the free movement of goods. In light of the comparative aim of this book, the focus will lie on the main rules and doctrines of negative integration, which were gradually developed in the early days of EU integration and still form the foundation of EU free movement law today. In this discussion, pride of place will go to the case law of the CJEU, which was instrumental in developing the rather vague and general provisions in the Treaties, and turning them into effective rights.[1]

The Treaty framework for the free movement of goods, laid down in Articles 28–37 and Article 110 TFEU, distinguishes between financial and non-financial restrictions. Financial restrictions can either be customs duties or internal taxes that protect national products. Non-financial restrictions, on the other hand, are all national rules that impose quantitative limits on foreign goods or in any other way limit their access to the national market. The reason for removing both financial and non-financial restrictions is to allow goods to be traded freely throughout the entire territory of the EU, ensuring that, for example, the French cannot use their tax laws to block German beer, or the Germans their product standards to bar French wine.

This Chapter discusses the EU rules on financial obstacles before moving on to the rules on non-financial restrictions. Before doing so, however, it is

1 For more detailed discssions see *inter alia* P. Oliver (ed.), *Oliver on Free Movement of Goods in the European Union* (5th edn, Hart, 2010) or C. Barnard, *The Substantive Law of the EU. The Four Freedoms* (4th edn., OUP 2013).

© ARMIN CUYVERS, 2017 | DOI 10.1163/9789004322073_021
This is an open access chapter distributed under the terms of the CC-BY-NC License.

necessary to discuss some preliminary issues, including the concept of a good and the scope of the free movement of goods.

10.2 Goods Falling under EU Free Movement Law

The Treaties do not define 'goods', but the CJEU has defined them as: 'products which can be valued in money and which are capable, as such, of forming the subject of commercial transactions.'[2] This is a very broad definition that can even include electricity or waste that no longer has any commercial value.[3] Fishing rights, on the other hand, formed intangible rights that did not qualify as goods.[4]

The right to free movement applies to all goods that originate from a Member State or that that have been legally brought into free circulation somewhere in the EU.[5] Once a good has been imported into one EU Member State, therefore, it can move just as freely as any good produced in the EU, without requiring any certificate of origin.[6] Free movement rights only apply, however, in cross-border situations. A Czech car, built in the Czech Republic and sold in the Czech Republic, for example, has never crossed a border, and therefore does not fall under EU free movement law.[7] However, a cross-border effect may already be present where a national rule 'facilitates the marketing of goods of domestic origin to the detriment of imported goods', even if the rule only applies to national products.[8] In other words, even if a national rule does

2 Case 7/68 *Commission v. Italy* [1968] ECR 617 and Case C-65/05 *Commission v. Greece* [2006] ECR I-10341.

3 Case C-379/98 *Preussen Elektra* [2001] ECR I-2099 and Case C-2/90 *Wallonian Waste* [1992] ECR I-4431.

4 Case C-97/98 *Jägerskiöld* [1999] ECR I-7319.

5 See Article 29(2) TFEU and Case 2/69 *Sociaal fonds voor de Diamantarbeiders* [1969] ECR 211, paras. 24–26.

6 Case 41/76 *Donckerwolcke* [1976] ECR 1921, para. 17. To enter legally they have to comply with all rules in the EU Common Customs Code and pay the required duties. See Regulation 450/2008 on the Modernised EU Common Customs Code, OJ [2008] L145/1.

7 Note though that the CJEU has sometimes also applied free movement prohibitions against measures that differntiated between regions within a Member State. This apporach might be of particulr interest in the EAC, where some barriers may lie within Member States, for example in Tanzania. See for example Case C-363/93, *Lancry* [1994] ECR I-3957, par. 26 or Case C-72/03 *Carbonati Apuani* ECLI:EU:C:2004:506, par. 22.

8 Case C-321/94, *Pistre*, [1997] ECR I-2343.

not even apply to foreign products but grants a benefit to national products, a cross-border effect is present and EU law applies.

When they apply, the rules on the free movement of goods have direct effect. This means that they can be directly relied on before national courts or other public bodies to challenge any national rule or practise that restricts free movement.[9] Consequently, individuals and businesses do not have to wait for public enforcement against restrictions, but can directly attack them themselves on the basis of EU law.[10] So far, the Treaty provisions on goods, do not yet seem to have horizontal direct effect, even though they can be relied upon against private bodies that wield certain public authority.[11]

10.3 Financial Restrictions

The first category of prohibited restrictions concern financial restrictions, which can either be customs duties and charges having an equivalent effect (Article 30 TFEU), or internal taxation measures restricting free movement (Article 110 TFEU).

10.3.1 *Customs Duties and Charges Having an Equivalent Effect*

Customs duties include any form of payment that has to be made because a good crosses a border, also of a fiscal nature. All customs duties are prohibited under Article 30 TFEU, without exception. In practice, customs duties no longer occur in the EU, which attests to the effectiveness of this prohibition.

Article 30 TFEU, however, also prohibits 'charges having an equivalent effect to customs duties'. This means that Member States are not allowed to adopt other measures that are technically speaking not a customs duty, but in practice have the same effect. Consider, for example, Portugal imposing an obligatory veterinary check at the border and charging a mandatory fee of 10 euros per animal. Such a measure would not be a customs duty, but would have the same effect of increasing the price of imported live stock.

9 The CJEU has even held that a statement by a public official can be a prohibited restriction under Article 34 TFEU. See Case C-470/03, *A.G.M.-COS.MET* [2007] ECR I-2749, par. 58.

10 See EU chapter 4 on the concept of direct effect and supremacy of EU law. For the direct effect of the free movement of goods provisions see inter alia Case 26/62 *Van Gend en Loos* [1963] ECR 1, and Case 74/76, *Iannelli* [1977] ECR 577.

11 See for example Case 311/85 *Vereniging voor Vlaamse reisbureaus* [1987] ECR 3801, paras. 11 and 30, and recently Case C-171/11, *Fra.bo* ECLI:EU:C:2012:453.

To make sure Member States do not develop creative alternative measures to circumvent the prohibition of Article 30 TFEU, the CJEU has given a very broad and effect-based interpretation to the concept of 'charges having an equivalent effect', which covers:

> any pecuniary charge, however small and whatever its designation and mode of application, which is imposed unilaterally on domestic or foreign goods by reason of the fact that they cross a frontier, and which is not a customs duty in the strict sense.[12]

All charges having an equivalent effect are in principle prohibited, as the Treaty provides no possible justifications for them.[13] The CJEU, however, has allowed two very narrow exceptions. Firstly, a charge may be allowed where it covers the actual costs of an inspection required by EU law itself. Where the EU, for example as during the BSE crisis, imposes mandatory health inspections on beef at the border, Member States may recover the costs of these inspections from importers. The charges imposed, however, may never exceed the actual costs of the inspections.[14]

Secondly, charges are allowed where they only form compensation for services rendered to the importer on a voluntary basis. For example, an importer may voluntarily request to use a warehouse with cooling facilities owned by the state whilst awaiting further shipping of the goods. If so, the state may charge a reasonable fee for this service.[15] As soon as there is any form of obligation, directly or indirectly, to make use of a specific service, however, or if there is no real benefit to the individual importer, no charges may be imposed.[16]

10.3.2 *Internal Taxation as a Restriction on Free Movement of Goods*

Member States are also not allowed to effectively recreate customs duties via their internal taxes. Just imagine France imposing an additional VAT of 20% on German cars, which would undo the prohibition of Article 30 TFEU completely.

---

12 Case 24/68 *Commission v Italy* [1969] ECR 193, par. 9. This remains the case 'even if the charge is not imposed for the benefit of the State, is not discriminatory or protective in effect and if the product on which the charge is imposed is not in competition with any domestic product.' See Joined Cases 2/62 and 3/62, *Commission v Belgium and Luxemburg* ECLI:EU:C:1962:45.

13 Case 24/68 *Commission v Italy*, par 10.

14 Case 18/87 *Commission v Germany*, ECLI:EU:C:1988:453.

15 Case 132/82 *Commission v Belgium*, ECLI:EU:C:1983:135, par. 8.

16 See for the strict scrutiny of the CJEU on this point for example *Ford España v Spain* ECLI:EU:C:1989:306, or Case 87/75 Bresciani [1976] ECR 129.

Therefore, even though Member States retain the competence to organize their own tax system, they may not use their taxes to restrict free movement of goods.[17] For 'whenever a fiscal levy is likely to discourage imports of goods originating in other Member States to the benefit of domestic production', it is caught by the prohibition of Article 110 TFEU.[18]

To protect free movement, Article 110 TFEU prohibits both *discriminatory taxation* and more subtle measures that do not discriminate but still have the effect of *protecting national products*. Discriminatory taxes are prohibited in Article 110(1) TFEU, which determines that 'No Member State shall impose, directly or indirectly, on the products of other Member States any internal taxation of any kind in excess of that imposed directly or indirectly on similar domestic products.'

For Article 110(1) TFEU to apply, one must first assess if a tax is imposed on 'similar' products. Here the CJEU primarily looks at the comparability of products from the perspective of the consumer. As the CJEU held in *Commission v France*, similarity must be assessed on the basis 'not of the criterion of the strictly identical nature of the products but on that of their similar and comparable use.'[19] This may lead the CJEU into rather factual assessments involving substances as fruit wine, whiskey or that evergreen of EU law, bananas.[20]

If products are sufficiently similar, one must next assess if the tax at issue discriminates between them, either directly or indirectly. Direct discrimination means that imported products are taxed differently precisely *because* they originate from another Member State. Indirect discrimination, which is more common, means that taxation differs based on a criterion that seems neutral as to nationality, but in reality affects imported goods more than national goods. The case of *Humblot* provides a good example of indirect discrimination, and how Member States may use it to protect their own industries.[21] In *Humblot*, the French tax on cars with more than a 16 cylinder engine volume rose sharply from 1.100 French francs to 5000 francs. It just so happened that no car produced in France had a cylinder engine volume over 16, but many German cars did. The French tax measure, therefore, did not directly discriminate based on nationality, but the criterion of engine volume indirectly discriminated against

17 See inter alia Case 168/78 *Commission v France* [1980] ECR 347.

18 Case 252/86 *Bergandi* ECLI:EU:C:1988:112, par. 25.

19 Case 168/78 *Commission v France* [1980] ECR 347. See also already Case 45/75 *Rewe-Zentral* [1976] ECR 181.

20 Cf. Case 243/84 *Johnnie Walker* [1986] ECR 875 and Case 184/85 *Commission v Italy* [1987] ECR 2013.

21 Case C-112/84 *Humblot*, ECLI:EU:C:1985:185.

imported cars. The CJEU saw through this attempt to indirectly protect French car producers and found the measure to violate Article 110(1) TFEU.[22]

Article 110(2) TFEU may come in play where the products concerned are not similar, but the taxes nevertheless provide indirect protection to domestic products against *competing* importing products.[23] For a tax to be caught by Article 110(2) two conditions must be met. First, the relevant products must be in a competitive relationship. This logically is a lower threshold than the similarity that is required for Article 110(1) TFEU to apply.[24] A competitive relationship essentially concerns substitutability, i.e. the question if consumers might choose product A instead of product B, for example if A becomes 5% cheaper. The classic example of products that are not comparable but do compete is beer and (cheap) wine. In *Commission v. UK*, the tax imposed on wine was more than four times higher than the tax on beer, especially in the case of the lower segments of wine.[25] As in *Humblot*, it just so happens that the UK produces almost no wine, but does produce a lot of beer. Ultimately, the CJEU held that wine and beer were not similar enough to fall under Article 110(1) TFEU, but they were substitutable enough for consumers to be in competition with each other in the meaning of Article 110(2) TFEU, as consumers can switch from beer to wine.

Second, if products compete with each other, the tax may not protect the domestic product. Here the CJEU primarily looks at the effect of the tax on consumers. In *Commission v. UK*, for example, the CJEU found that the much higher taxes on wine did protect the domestic beer, and hence was prohibited under Article 110(2) TFEU, because the tax difference was so high that it affected consumer choices and the tax difference could not be objectively justified on any ground. Member States, therefore, do of course retain the freedom to differentiate their taxes on different products based on objective criteria. For Article 110(2) TFEU to apply, therefore, a real protective effect must be shown, the mere existence of a difference in tax rate is not enough.[26]

---

22 For another example, see Case C-402/09, *Tatu* ECLI:EU:C:2011:219. Directly discriminatory taes can never be justified. Whether indirectly discriminory taxes can ever be justified, even though the Traety provides no exceptions, remains a contested question. See for a case that perhaps provides an opening Case 140/79 *Chemial Farmaceutici v DAF* [1981] ECR 1.

23 On the difficculties that may arise in distinguishing between 110(1) and 110(2) TFEU see for example Case 169/78 *Commission v Italy* [1980] ECR 385 or Case 171/78 *Commission v Denmark* [1980] ECR 447.

24 Case 27/67 *Fink-Frucht* [1968] ECR 223.

25 Case 170/78 *Commission v UK* [1983] ECR 2265.

26 Cf. on the leeway of Member States also Case 243/84*Johnnie Walker* [1986] ECR 875.

Article 30 and 110 TFEU jointly aim to prevent financial obstacles to free movement, The two provisions are mutually exclusive. A case, therefore, can never fall under both provisions. A financial charge is either based on the product crossing the border, and hence a customs duty under Article 30 TFEU, or not, in which case it falls under Article 110 TFEU. For example, if an *identical* charge is levied from both imported and domestic products, this forms an internal tax, even if the tax for imported products just happens to be collected at the border.[27] For in such situations, the charge itself does not depend on the crossing of the border, only the time and place of collection does.

10.4 Non-Financial or Non-Tariff Barriers (NTBs)

As the EAC experience has also shown, real free movement of goods cannot be achieved by just removing financial or tariff barriers.[28] For in practice, trade in goods is obstructed at least as much by so called non-tariff barriers (NTBs) as it is by tariff barriers. For example, consider a producer of child-safety seats in a situation where each Member State has different safety standards for child-safety seats. Even if there are no tariffs and equivalent charges, he will still find it difficult to sell his child-safety seats in other Member States. Not only will he have to meet different standards in all Member States, the national producers he competes with only have to meet their own national safety standards, giving them a competitive advantage. Previous experiences have clearly shown, therefore, that NTBs create major obstacles to trade. A lesson, in reality, the UK will have to relearn the hard way if it chooses to fall back on WTO rules after Brexit, as these rules do not deal with NTBs.[29]

In the EU, non-tariff barriers are prohibited under articles 34 and 35 TFEU, unless they can be justified under Article 36 TFEU or a rule of reason exception. The next paragraphs will first set out how the CJEU developed these two

27 Case C-221/06 *Stadtgemeinde Frohnleiten* [2007] ECR I-9643, Case 29/87 *Denkavit* [1988] ECR 2965 or Joined Cases 441–442/98 *Mikhailidis* [2000] ECR I-7145. Of course difficulties may arise in practise to dinstinguish, but a choice must then be made. See for example Case 105/75 *Interzuccheri* [1977] ECR 1029 or Case C-28/96 *Fricarnes* [1997] ECR I-4939.

28 See also chapter 10 par. 4.on NTBs in the EAC.

29 Cf also S. Dhingra en T. Sampson, 'Life after Brexit: What are the UK's options outside the European Union?' Centre for Economic Performance, *London School of Economics Working PaperBrexit 01*, HM Government, 'Alternatives to membership: possible models for the United Kingdom outside the European Union' March 2016, available at <https://www.gov.uk/government/uploads/system/uploads/attachment_data/file/504604/Alternatives_to_membership_-_possible_models_for_the_UK_outside_the_EU.pdf>.

provisions into very broad prohibitions that are capable of capturing almost any national rule. Subsequently, they describe the exceptions EU law provides to Member States to defend NTBs that serve a public interest, and the way the CJEU balances restrictions to free movement and such public interests.

10.4.1 *The Prohibition on Quantitative Restrictions and Measures Having Equivalent Effect*

Article 34 TFEU forms the key prohibition behind the free movement of goods in the EU. It provides that:

> Quantitative restrictions on imports and all measures having equivalent effect shall be prohibited between Member States.[30]

The concept of a 'quantitative restriction' thereby refers to measures that directly concern the quantity or the number of products that may be imported or exported.[31] This, of course, includes a total ban, that allows zero products to be imported or exported,[32] but also partial restrictions that allow only a certain number of products to be imported.[33] Like customs duties, however, quantitative restrictions are relatively rare in the EU. The main prohibition in Article 34 TFEU, therefore, concerns 'measures having an equivalent effect to quantitative restrictions' or MEQRs.

As MEQR is a rather vague concept, it was once again up to the CJEU to provide a definition. One route the CJEU could take, in line with Article 18 TFEU, was to interpret this concept narrowly as a prohibition on national measures that discriminated against imported goods. In *Dassonville*, its seminal judgment on the free movement of goods, however, the CJEU took a very different approach and provided a very wide definition of MEQRs as:

> All trading rules enacted by Member States which are *capable* of hindering, directly or *indirectly*, actually or *potentially*, intra-Community trade (...)[34]

---

30 Article 35 TFEU contains an almost identical prohibition for the, less common, restrictions on export, and wil not be discussed separately here.

31 Case 2/73, *Geddo* [1973] ECR 865.

32 Case 34/79, *R Henn and Darby*, [1979] ECR 3795.

33 See for example Case 13/68, *Salgoil* [1968] ECR 453 or Case 170/04, *Rosengren* [2007] ECR I-4701.

34 Case 8/74, *Dassonville*, [1974], ECR 837.

Under this definition, even measures that are *capable* of *potentially* hindering trade in an *indirect* fashion qualify as measures of equivalent effect, and hence are in principle prohibited under Article 34 TFEU. Crucially, the CJEU also did not require any form of (indirect) discrimination to be present, but only looked at the actual or possible effect of a measure on trade.

The broad *Dassonville* definition of MEQR was further developed in *Cassis de Dijon*, another seminal judgment on the free movement of goods. In this case, the applicant wanted to import the liqueur 'Cassis de Dijon' into Germany from France. Under an interesting German approach to consumer protection, however, the liqueur did not contain *enough* alcohol. German law required that liqueurs such as Cassis de Dijon had an alcohol content of at least 25%, whereas the French liqueur only contained 15–20% alcohol. The German authority, therefore, refused to allow the importation. The applicant claimed this constituted a prohibited MEQR. Germany contended, however, that the measure did not discriminate in any way as it applied equally to German and French drinks, and therefore also did not violate Article 34 TFEU. The CJEU was not convinced:

> In practice, the principal effect of requirements of this nature is to promote alcoholic beverages having a high alcohol content by excluding from the national market products of other Member States which do not answer that description
>
> It therefore appears that the unilateral requirement imposed by the rule of Member State of a minimum alcohol content for the purposes of the sale of alcoholic beverages constitutes an obstacle to trade which is incompatible with the provisions of Article [34] of the treaty.[35]

Even measures that in no way distinguish between national and foreign products, therefore, qualify as MEQRs if they in any way hinder foreign goods that want to enter the national market.

Cassis de Dijon also introduced another far reaching doctrine that continued to play an important role in EU free movement law: the principle of mutual recognition.[36] In principle, Member States should trust each other's regulations to be sufficient and adequate, and therefore recognize and allow products that have been legally produced according to the standards of another

35 Case 120/78, *Rewe-Zentrale AG v. Bundesmonopolverwalting für Branntwein* (*Cassis de Dijon*) [1979], ECR 649.

36 See for the importance of this principle for free movement and its role in newer forms of harmonization EU Chapter 9.

Member State. In the case of *Cassis de Dijon*, the fact that the liqueur complied with French legislation should in principle suffice for the German authorities, unless they could prove why in this particular case French products should not be trusted.

It is difficult to exaggerate just how broad the definition of an MEQR under *Dassonville* and *Cassis de Dijon* is. The definition only requires that a national rule in some way makes it more difficult for a product to enter the market, not that the rule is harder on foreign products or imposes a dual burden.[37] In practice, however, almost any rule that is worth having will require something, and therefore make it more difficult to enter the market than if the rule did not exist. For example, any product standard such as requiring real cocoa in chocolate or prohibiting certain additives in baby milk will make it more difficult for foreign producers to enter the market than if these standards did not apply. All such national standards, therefore, qualify as MEQRs under Article 34 TFEU. In addition, the CJEU has also held that Member States have a *positive obligation* to prevent or stop any behaviour by private individuals that might interfere with the free movement of goods. In *Spanish Strawberries*, for example, the French government was found to have violated Article 34 TFEU by not stopping French farmers from attacking and destroying trucks with Spanish fruit that was outcompeting French fruit.[38] Such a general positive obligation to actively remove any restrictions to free movement caused by private individuals could also be a far reaching instrument in the EAC context.

Now as we will see, EU law does not just set aside such eminently desirable rules as health standards for baby milk, as these may often be justified.[39] The only point here is that the very broad definition developed by the Court does qualify all such rules as MEQRs (or NTBs) and therefore brings them under the scope of the prohibition in Article 34 TFEU, and under the scrutiny of EU and national courts.

The benefit of this very broad definition was that it covered all potential NTBs, and removed any space that Member States might have to develop creative NTBs that do protect national products fall outside a narrower definition. The main downside of this definition, however, was that almost all national

37 The MEQR, moreover, may even consist if some practises or factual behaviour of public officials. In one extreme case, even a negative statement by a government official on Italian car lifts was found to constitute an MEQR under Article 34 TFEU. See Case C-470/03 *AGM-COS.MET* [2007] ECR I-2749.

38 Case C-265/95 *Commission / France (Spanish Strawberries)* [1997] ECR I-6959. See also Case C-112/00 *Schmidberger* [2003] ECR I-5659.

39 See paragraph 10.5 below.

rules now qualified as MEQRs and could therefore be challenged on the basis of EU law. After *Dassonville* and *Cassis de Dijon*, therefore, national courts and the CJEU were increasingly flooded with cases. Many of these challenged national rules that did technically qualify as MEQRs, but in reality were not concerned with restricting the free movements of goods. Symbolic in this regard became the Sunday Trading cases in which traders challenged national rules requiring shops to close on Sunday. As this meant traders could not sell their products on a Sunday, this indeed restricted their access to the market, but it was not the kind of restriction Article 34 TFEU was intended to capture.[40]

Consequently, the search was on for a way to limit the definition of an MEQR in a way that would prevent abuse of Article 34 TFEU but would not undermine the effectiveness of Article 34 TFEU in targeting real MEQRs. In the end, the CJEU opted for a less than convincing approach. In *Keck*, another landmark judgment, it introduced a problematic distinction between product norms and selling arrangements, holding that under certain conditions selling arrangements do not fall under the scope of Article 34 TFEU.[41]

Keck concerned two traders, Keck and Mithouard, which were being prosecuted in France for reselling goods at a loss, something that was prohibited under French law. The law, however, only prohibited resellers from doing so, as manufacturers were allowed to sell at a loss. Keck and Mithouard claimed this French rule violated, amongst other things, Article 34 TFEU. Considering its importance, and because it gives a good insight into the reasoning of the Court at this stage of the internal market development, the relevant paragraphs of the judgement are reproduced below:

> By virtue of Article [34], quantitative restrictions on imports and all measures having equivalent effect are prohibited between Member States. The Court has consistently held that any measure which is capable of directly or indirectly, actually or potentially, hindering intra-Community trade constitutes a measure having equivalent effect to a quantitative restriction.

---

40 Case C-145/88 *Torfaen Borough* [1989] ECR I-3851 and Case C-169/91 *B & Q* [2002] ECR I-6635. See for a critical discussion for example A. Arnull, 'What Shall We Do on Sunday?', 26 *European Law Review* (1991), 112 or J. Steiner, 'Drawing the Line: Uses and Abuses of Article 30 EEC', 29 *Common Market Law Review* (1992), 749.

41 Case C-276/91, *Keck and Mithouard*, [1993], ECR 6097.

National legislation imposing a general prohibition on resale at a loss is not designed to regulate trade in goods between Member States.

Such legislation may, admittedly, restrict the volume of sales, and hence the volume of sales of products from other Member States, in so far as it deprives traders of a method of sales promotion. But the question remains whether such a possibility is sufficient to characterize the legislation in question as a measure having equivalent effect to a quantitative restriction on imports.

In view of the increasing tendency of traders to invoke Article [34] of the Treaty as a means of challenging any rules whose effect is to limit their commercial freedom even where such rules are not aimed at products from other Member States, the Court considers it necessary to re-examine and clarify its case-law on this matter.

It is established by the case-law beginning with "Cassis de Dijon" that, in the absence of harmonization of legislation, obstacles to free movement of goods which are the consequence of applying, to goods coming from other Member States where they are lawfully manufactured and marketed, rules that lay down requirements to be met by such goods (such as those relating to designation, form, size, weight, composition, presentation, labelling, packaging) constitute measures of equivalent effect prohibited by Article [34]. This is so even if those rules apply without distinction to all products unless their application can be justified by a public-interest objective taking precedence over the free movement of goods.

By contrast, contrary to what has previously been decided, the application to products from other Member States of national provisions restricting or prohibiting certain selling arrangements is not such as to hinder directly or indirectly, actually or potentially, trade between Member States within the meaning of the Dassonville judgment, so long as those provisions apply to all relevant traders operating within the national territory and so long as they affect in the same manner, in law and in fact, the marketing of domestic products and of those from other Member States.

Provided that those conditions are fulfilled, the application of such rules to the sale of products from another Member State meeting the requirements laid down by that State is not by nature such as to prevent their access to the market or to impede access any more than it impedes the access of domestic products. Such rules therefore fall outside the scope of Article [34] of the Treaty.

> Accordingly, the reply to be given to the national court is that Article 30 of the EEC Treaty is to be interpreted as not applying to legislation of a Member State imposing a general prohibition on resale at a loss.[42]

The CJEU therefore proceeded to create a new category of regulations concerning 'selling arrangements'. Provided such selling arrangements 1) apply to all relevant traders operating within the national territory, and 2) affect the marketing of domestic products and of those from other Member States in the same manner, both in law and in fact, they do not constitute MEQRs under Article 34 TFEU and hence are not prohibited.[43] The concept of selling arrangements, however, was not really defined, but it includes those rules dealing with *how* a product is sold, rather than rules on how the product itself is made.[44]

Keck indeed reduced the scope of Article 34 TFEU, even if it did so in a rather construed and complicated way that has kept lawyers engaged for the past 25 years. One of the opportunities for EAC law, therefore might be to find a better way to delineate the scope of the EAC free movement clauses, even though the more urgent challenge might be to make the prohibitions themselves more coherent and effective first.[45]

One of the questions *Keck* left open concerned the qualification of rules that do not regulate the product itself or the way it is sold, but rather the way a product may be *used* in a Member State. A rule that caps the maximum speed on the highway to a 100 kilometres per hour, for example, does not regulate how a car must be made or how it must be sold. It may affect, however, the

---

42 *Keck*, paras. 11–18.

43 One important application of this requirement concerns the internet. The CJEU has held that restricting sales via the internet will always affect the marketing of foreign prodcuts more negatively since the on-line sales are usually the only channel available to sell foreign products, whereas domestic products usually also have other outlets such as physicial shops. This application of the earlier *De Agostini* case law seriously curtails the application of *Keck* to the on-line market. See Case C-108/09 *Ker-Optika* ECLI:EU:C:2010:725 and Joined Cases C-34/95, C-35/95 and C-36/95, *De Agostini* ECLI:EU:C:1997:344.

44 The CJEU only provided a negative definition by indicating that measures that do *not* form selling arrangement would, inter alia, be those relating to designation, form, size, weight, composition, presentation, labelling and packaging.

45 In this context also see the complex case law of the CJEU on when the effect of a national measure on trade is too uncertain and indirect for the measure to qualifiy as a MEQR. Although not amounting to a real *de minimis* rule, this case law further limits the scope of Article 34 TFEU, although it is difficult to apply and predict in practise. See *inter alia* Case C-379/92, *Peralta* ECLI:EU:C:1994:296, Case 155/80 *Oebel*, [1981] ECR I-1993 as well as the Opinion of AG Kokott in Case C-142/05, *Mickelsson and Roos* ECLI:EU:C:2009:336.

market access of cars. An expensive hyper-car, for example, may become less attractive if you can never really put it to use.

In more recent case law, the CJEU has now confirmed that such rules on use do form MEQRS, and therefore fall under the scope of Article 34 TFEU. One such case concerned the Italian prohibition to use a trailer behind a motorcycle.[46] This rule affected the sale of trailers for motorcycles, as it prohibited their use, even though it did not regulate the product as such. The CJEU held that in addition to product rules, Article 34 TFEU also covers '*any other measure which hinders access of products originating in other Member States to the market of a Member State.*'[47] This more recent case law, therefore, again widens the scope of Article 34 TFEU, and restricts the Keck exception to selling arrangements in the stricter sense.

10.5 Justifying MEQRS

Precisely because Article 34 TFEU captures so many national rules, the question of justification becomes essential. For without a proper doctrine of justification, the EU would run the risk of setting aside a great deal of very welcome national rules that for example protect public health, public security or the environment. The last part of this Chapter, therefore, briefly discusses the question of justification: how can a Member State justify a restriction on the free movement of goods? As the question of justification is often highly context dependent, and as a tremendous wealth of case law exists, this part focuses on the structure and main characteristics of the test used to see if national measures are justified, as understanding this test allows one to independently analyse specific cases on justification.

Restrictions on free movement may be justified if they 1) serve a *legitimate aim*, 2) in a *proportionate* manner.[48] There are two types of legitimate aims,

---

46 Case C-110/05, *Commission v Italy* ECLI:EU:C:2009:66. For another example see Case C-142/05, *Mickelsson and Roos* ECLI:EU:C:2009:336 on the use of jet skis.

47 Case C-110/05, *Commission v Italy*, ECLI:EU:C:2009:66 par. 37. See for further analysis P. Oliver, 'Of Trailers and Jetskis: Is the Case Law on Article 34 TFEU Hurtling in a new Direction?', 33 *Fordham International Law Journal* (2009–2010), 1423, or L. Gormley, 'Free Movement of Goods and their Use—What Is the Use of It?', 33 *Fordham International Law Journal* (2011), 1589–1628.

48 Also note that under the *Tedeschi* principle discussed in EU Chatper 9, Member States may only rely on justifications if the relevant area of law has not yet been harmonized. The moment that secondary EU law has been adopted, for instance on the safety of baby milk, that field is governed by the secondary legislation and no longer by the Treaty

namely Treaty based aims and the judge made aims under the rule of reason. Measures are proportionate, moreover, if they are *suitable* and *necessary* in relation to the legitimate aim they pursue. When applying any of these concepts, furthermore, it should be realized that in general all exceptions to free movement are construed narrowly by the CJEU, and that the Court usually is very strict in applying them.[49] Justifying a restriction, therefore, usually requires a convincing argument from the Member States, particularly demonstrating that the same objective could not have been reached by less restrictive means.

10.5.1 *Treaty Aims and the Rule of Reaon*

Article 36 TFEU provides that:

> The provisions of Articles 34 and 35 shall not preclude prohibitions or restrictions on imports, exports or goods in transit justified on grounds of public morality, public policy or public security; the protection of health and life of humans, animals or plants; the protection of national treasures possessing artistic, historic or archaeological value; or the protection of industrial and commercial property. Such prohibitions or restrictions shall not, however, constitute a means of arbitrary discrimination or a disguised restriction on trade between Member States.

The grounds enumerated in Article 36 TFEU, however, are limitative and interpreted very strictly by the CJEU.[50] Article 36 TFEU, therefore only provides very limited grounds to Member States to justify national measures, which became increasingly problematic after the very broad interpretation given to MEQRS by the CJEU. For where traders could now attack almost any national rule, Member States were severely restricted in their defences. For example, Article 36 TFEU does not even mention consumer protection or the environment, meaning Member States cannot justify any measures based on these clearly desirable and reasonable objectives under the Treaty.

---

provisions on free movement. See for example Case C-309/02, *Radlberger v Land Baden-Württemberg*, [2004] ECR I-11763, Case C-265/06, *Commission v Portugal*, [2008] ECR I-2245 or Case 193/80, *Commission v Italy*, [1981] ECR 3019. For the basis principle see Case 5/77, *Tedeschi* [1977] ECR 1555.

49 See already Case 7/61, *Commission v Italy*, [1961] ECR 317 as well as Case 72/83, *Campus Oil* ECLI:EU:C:1984:256.

50 See amongst many others Case 288/83, *Commission v Ireland*, [1985] ECR 1761, Case C-265/95, *Commission v France*, [1997] ECR I-695 or Case 121/85, *Conegate* [1986] ECR 1007.

In the same *Cassis de Dijon* judgment that confirmed *Dassonville* and introduced mutual recognition, The CJEU recognized this problem and recognized a second, non-Treaty based category of justificatory grounds that Member States could rely on. This category of mandatory requirements has become known as the rule of reason exceptions:

> In the absence of common rules relating to the production and marketing of alcohol (…) it is for the Member States to regulate all matters relating to the production and marketing of alcohol and alcoholic beverages on their own territory.
>
> Obstacles to movement within the community resulting from disparities between the national laws relating to the marketing of the products in question must be accepted in so far as those provisions may be recognized as being necessary in order to satisfy mandatory requirements relating in particular to the effectiveness of fiscal supervision, the protection of public health, the fairness of commercial transactions and the defence of the consumer.[51]

The Court gives the effectiveness of fiscal supervision, the protection of public health, the fairness of commercial transactions and the defence of the consumer as examples of mandatory requirements that may justify restrictions on free movement. Crucially, however, the category of mandatory requirements is an open one. The CJEU is open to accept any reasonable public interest that a Member State may want to serve as a possible ground for justification. Later case law, for example, accepted grounds such as the protection of the environment and of biological resources,[52] consumer protection[53] or freedom of expression[54] as acceptable mandatory grounds.

The rule of reason, therefore, greatly expands the grounds a Member State may rely on to justify restrictions, thereby allowing for a better balancing of free movement and public interests. Some limits, however, do apply. Firstly, the CJEU does accept any purely economic grounds.[55] Secondly, under the

51 *Cassis de Dijon*, par, 8–9.

52 Joined Cases 3/76, 4/76 and 6/76, *Kramer* [1976] ECR 1279, Case 240/83, *ADBHU*, [1985] ECR 531, or Case C-443/10 *Bonnarde* ECLI:EU:C:2011:641.

53 Case C-353/89, *Mediawet Nederland* [1999], ECR I-4069, Case C-161/09, *Kakavetsos-Fragkopoulos* ECLI:EU:C:2011:110, or Case C-481/12 *UAB* ECLI:EU:C:2014:11.

54 Case C-112/00, *Schmidberger*; Case C-71/02, *Karner v Troostwijk* ECLI:EU:C:2004:181.

55 See Case C-109/04 *Kranemann* [2005] ECR I-2421 or Case C-456/10, *ANETT* ECLI:EU:C:2012:241.

orthodox approach, rule of reason grounds may only be used to justify restrictions that are indirectly discriminatory or non-discriminatory. Restrictions that are directly discriminatory may only be justified under a ground listed in Article 36 TFEU, although the CJEU does not always seem to follow this rule religiously.[56]

The main challenge for Member States in justifying an MEQR, however, usually is not to find an acceptable ground under Article 36 TFEU or the rule of reason, but to satisfy the proportionality test that comes next.

10.5.2 *Proportionality of MEQRs*

An MEQR is only justified if it is proportionate in relation to its aim. For internal market cases, the proportionality test asks two questions, relating to the suitability and the necessity of the MEQR. Crucially, both have to be assessed not in abstract but in relation to the specific aim or aims provided as the legitimate aim.

The question of suitability essentially asks if a measure can actually achieve the objective it is supposed to serve. For instance, if the aim is to protect children against too much sugar in soft-drinks, a measure imposing a maximum sugar content is suitable to achieve this aim, a measure just prohibiting French soft-drinks is not. The CJEU has further developed the suitability test by introducing the criterion of consistency, even if the CJEU does not always apply this criterion or does not apply it as stringently as it could. The central idea is that a measure can only be suitable if it achieves its objective in a consistent and systematic manner.[57] This *inter alia* means that a measure should not undermine the very aim it is trying to achieve. An early application of this logic can be seen in *Conegate*, where the UK had seized a consignment consisting 'essentially of inflatable dolls which were clearly of a sexual nature' as these violated public morality.[58] At the same time, however, the UK did allow national production and sale of similar inflatable devices, which led the CJEU to find that:

56 Case 113/80, *Commission v Ireland* ECLI:EU:C:1981:139 or Case 274/87, *Commission v Germany* [1989] ECR 229 for the orthodoxy. For apparent deviations see *inter alia* Case C-573/12, *Ålands Vindkraft* ECLI:EU:C:2014:2037 or Case C-389/96 *Aher-Waggon* ECLI:EU:C:1998:357.

57 See for the introduction of this test in the context of services Case C-243/01 *Gambelli* [2003] ECR I-13031.

58 Case 121/85, *Conegate* ECLI:EU:C:1986:114.

> a Member State may not rely on grounds of public morality within the meaning of Article 36 of the Treaty in order to prohibit the importation of certain goods on the grounds that they are indecent or obscene, where the same goods may be manufactured freely on its territory and marketed on its territory subject only to an absolute prohibition on their transmission by post, a restriction on their public display and, in certain regions, a system of licensing of premises for the sale of those goods to customers aged 18 and over.[59]

If it wants to, a court could impose far reaching scrutiny via a consistency test, as many political measures will not be wholly consistent, either internally or compared to other measures.[60] In practice, however, the real scrutiny takes place in the context of necessity.

The necessity test asks if the same objective could not have been achieved with a less far reaching measure. In other words, is the MEQR the *least restrictive measure* that can be adopted to achive the public aim being pursued?[61] In our example on the requirement to have less sugar in soft-drinks, for example, the question could be asked if the same objective could not be reached by better labeling. Could a clear labeling requirement forcing producers to clearly indicate sugar content and calories perhaps achieve the same objective without needing to impose a maximum sugar content?

It is at this stage that the CJEU can be extremely strict, truly requiring the Member States to show that there was no real alternative.[62] At the same time, the application of the necessity test also gives the CJEU a certain flexibility. For example, in more morally or politically sensitive cases, it may apply a lighter touch and give some more leeway to the Member States, where in other cases it

59 Idem, par. 20.

60 See further on this point A. Cuyvers, Case note to: Joined Cases C-338/04, C-359/04 and C-360/04, Massimiliano Placanica, Christian Palazzese and Angelo Sorricchio (Placanica) 45 (2008) *Common Market Law Review*, 515.

61 See for example Case C-385/99, *Müller-Fauré* [2003] ECR I-4509, or Case C-161/09, *Kakavetsos-Fragkopoulos* ECLI:EU:C:2011:110.

62 Also note that the burden of proof at this stage is on the Member State, so it has to proof that the measure is suitable and necessary. Of course the CJEU can differenitate in how much evidence it requires, sometimes requiring actual statistical evidence, sometimes allowing more general claims about certain effects. See for example Case C-14/02, *ATRAL SA* [2003] ECR I-4431, or Case C-254/05, *Commission v Belgium*, [2007] ECR I-4269.

may be very strict indeed.[63] Predicting the precise application of the necessity test in a particular case therefore requires an analysis of the courts case law in the particular field involved, as well as looking at the general principles and rules for the free movement of goods.

As we will see in Chapters 11, 12 and 13, the other freedoms have all followed the general development of goods, meaning the creation of a wide prohibition, followed by the creation of additional ground for justification and a large body of case law on whether specific national measures may be justified or not.

---

63 Compare for example Case C-434/04, *Anders Ahokainen* [2006] ECR I-9171 and Case C-141/07, *Commission v Germany*, [2008] ECR I-6935 with Case C-297/05, *Commission v the Netherlands*, [2007] ECR I-7467, or Case C-110/05, *Commission v Italy*, ECLI:EU:C:2009:66.

CHAPTER 11

Free Movement of Workers in the EAC

Caroline Kago and Wanyama Masinde

11.1 Introduction

The common market is the third level of economic integration where all barriers to the mobility of people, capital and other resources within the member states are removed, hence creating a single market where all factors of production move freely within the region in question.

The Protocol on the Establishment of the East African Community Common Market (the Common Market Protocol) was signed in Arusha, Tanzania by the Republic of Kenya, Uganda, Rwanda, Burundi and the United Republic of Tanzania, on the 20 November 2009 pursuant to Articles 2(2), 5(2), 151 (1), 76 and 104 of the Treaty for the Establishment of the East African Community (the EAC Treaty) and entered into force in 2010.

The objective of establishing the EAC Common Market through the Common Market Protocols to realise accelerated economic growth and development through the attainment of free movement of goods; free movement of persons; free movement of labour; the right of establishment; the right of residence; the free movement of services; and the free movement of capital.[1] The common market is guided by the principles of National Treatment, Most Favoured Nations Treatment and predictability through transparency and information sharing.[2]

The Common Market Protocol differentiates a "worker" from a person supplying a service. It first commences by defining "labour" to include a worker and a self-employed person. It thereafter defines a "self-employed person" as a person engaged in an economic activity not under any contract of employment or supervision and who earns a living through this activity and a "worker" as a person who performs services for and under the direction of another person in return for remuneration.[3] Hence, a worker is an employee.

In light of the above, when discussing free movement of workers in the context of the East African Community (EAC) one must restrict the discussion to

1 Article 2(4) of Common Market Protocol.

2 Article 3 of the Common Market Protocol.

3 Article 1 of Common Market Protocol.

© CAROLINE KAGO AND WANYAMA MASINDE, 2017 | DOI 10.1163/9789004322073_022
This is an open access chapter distributed under the terms of the CC-BY-NC License.

free movement of an employee. In the context of the EAC, this chapter will therefore commence by discussing free movement of workers and thereafter examine the link between the free movement of service providers and the free movement of workers.

11.2 Free Movement of Workers

The Partner States under the Common Market Protocol guarantee the free movement of workers, who are citizens of the Partner States, within their territories. In addition, they warrant that the said workers shall not be discriminated in their territories based on their nationalities in relation to employment, remuneration and other conditions of work and employment.[4] In this regard, the workers shall be entitled to:

i. *Apply for employment;*
ii. *Accept offers of employment;*
iii. *Conclude contracts and take up employment in accordance with the said contracts, national laws and administrative actions without any discrimination;*
iv. *Move freely within the territories of the Partners States for the purpose of employment;*
v. *Stay in the territory of the Partner State for the purpose of employment (right of residence);*
vi. *Enjoy freedom of association and collective bargaining for better working conditions in accordance with national laws of the Partner State;*
vii. *Enjoy the rights and benefits of social security accorded to workers in that territory;*
viii. *Be accompanied by the spouse and child who are entitled to be employed or engage in any economic activity.*[5]

It should be noted that workers may only take up employment in the private sector, hence they cannot be employed in the public sector.[6] This, therefore

4 Article 10 of the Common Market Protocol.
5 Article 10(3) of the Common Market Protocol.
6 Article 10(10) of the Common Market Protocol.

denies the public sector the benefits that accrue from free movement of workers such as the transfer of skills and experiences from other Partner States.[7]

In addition, Partner States are permitted to limit the free movement of workers on grounds of public policy, public security or public health.[8] However, the state imposing the limitation is required to notify the other Partner States. Although this provision is necessary to provide Partner States with policy space it may be used as a form of disguised discrimination to hinder the free movement of workers from other Partner States.

The provisions of Article 10 of the Common Market Protocol (Free Movement of Workers) are implemented by the EAC Common Market (Free Movement of Workers) Regulations in Annex II. The Regulations cover issues such as work permits; employment of spouses and children of workers; expulsion and deportation of the worker; equal treatment in employment; and categories of workers.

The category of workers covered by the Regulations are administrators and managers; professionals such as engineers, lawyers, statisticians, teachers, accountants and architects; technicians and associate professionals; and crafts and related trades workers. For professions that require accreditation, the workers are subject to clearance by the respective regulatory bodies of the Partner States.

Based on the provisions of the Common Market Protocol and the Regulations, five important issues must be considered in relation to free movement of workers in the EAC:

1. Free movement of persons
2. Mutual recognition of academic and professional qualifications
3. Right of residence
4. Portability of social benefits
5. Labour market information systems

11.2.1 *Free Movement of Persons*

Free movement of persons is one of the fundamental rights guaranteed in the Common Market Protocol. It is the most important right for a worker as it enables him/her to take up a job in another Partner State as the worker is able to move freely within the region with his/her dependents, stay in the territory

7 Compare in this regard the much more limited exception to the EU right of free movement of workers for employment in public service under Article 45(4) TFEU as discussed in EU Chapter 11 par. 2.

8 Article 10 (11) of Common Market Protocol.

of the Partner State together with his/her dependents, be protected while in the territory of the Partner State based on national laws and exit the territory of the Partner State without restrictions.[9]

According to the Common Market Protocol, the Partner States agreed to eliminate all obstacles to the freedom movement of persons by establishing a standard identification system of issuing national identification documents to nationals, which shall be the basis of identifying the citizens of the Partner States in the Community.[10] The citizens of the Partner States will therefore be able to use machine-readable national identity cards as a travel document. Rwanda and Uganda are currently issuing standardized machine readable national identification. However, Kenya, Burundi and Tanzania are yet to commence the issuance of the standardised machine-readable identifications. Nevertheless, there is currently an understanding between Kenya, Uganda and Rwanda that their nationals can use the national identity cards as travel documents across their borders.

The Partner States further agreed to have a common standard travel document for the nationals of Partner States. The common standard travel document, which is the EAC Passport, is currently being used by many nationals of the Partner States. In addition, the Sectoral Council of Ministers responsible for EAC Affairs and Planning, during the 22nd Meeting held on 14th August 2015, developed and adopted a schedule of activities that will ensure that the EAC e-Passport is launched by the 17th Ordinary Summit of the EAC Heads of State.[11]

The provision on free movement of persons contained in Article 7 of the Common Market Protocol is implemented through the EAC Common Market (Free Movement of Persons) Regulations (Annex 1). The Regulations require Partner States to effectively manage their borders through ensuring ease of border crossing for citizens of Partner States; reciprocal opening of border posts; operational hours for the border posts; manning of border posts on 24 hour basis; harmonisation of certain measures, including immigration procedures.[12]

Implementation in some Partner States of border management requirements is ongoing. For example, in Kenya, a recent study reported that seven border posts are operational on a 24 hour basis: Jomo Kenyatta Airport, Mombasa International Airport, Namanga, Lunga Linga, Taveta, Malaba and

9 Article 7, 8 and 9 of the Common Market Protocol.

10 Article 8.

11 Council Report of the 32nd Meeting of the Council of Ministers held on the 10th–14th August 2015 in Arusha, Tanzania at ages 9–11. EAC/CM/32/2015.

12 Regulation 8 of the Regulations on Free Movement of Persons.

Busia. All these borders are electronically interconnected and have integrated border management systems.[13]

11.2.2 *Mutual Recognition of Academic and Professional Qualifications*

The Common Market Protocol requires Partner States to harmonise and mutually recognise academic and professional qualifications, experience obtained, requirements met, and licences or certificates granted in other Partner States.[14] Recognition requires a high level of trust in the education system and professional standards of the home country.[15] Therefore, this means that the Partner States must eventually harmonise their curricula, examinations, standards, certification and accreditation of educational and training institutions. This process is currently ongoing through a four phase project of the EAC which entails harmonising the goals and philosophies of education, curriculum content, education structures, policies and legal frameworks; examining the curricula and approaches of content delivery in order to identify gaps, overlaps and areas to be harmonised; developing of a relevant harmonised curriculum; and making necessary reforms to implement the harmonised curricula.[16]

Recognition of academic and professional qualifications is currently being processed through the conclusion of Mutual Recognition Agreements (MRAs) wherein Partner States agree to accept and recognise each other's requirements, certificates and licences because they are harmonised, considered equivalent or are according to international standards.[17]

In 2013, the Sectoral Council of Education directed the EAC Secretariat to develop legally binding framework for MRAs and mechanisms on how signed MRAs can be formally adopted as instruments of the EAC.[18] A draft Annex VI to the Common Market Protocol, the EAC Common Market (Mutual Recognition of Academic and Professional Qualifications) Regulations 2011, places an

---

13 Victor Ogalo "Achievements and Challenges of Implementation of the EAC Common Market Protocol in Kenya: Case of Free Movement of Labour" (2014) Friedrich Ebert Foundation Research Report.

14 Article 5 (3a) and 11 (1a) of the Common Market Protocol.

15 Cronje, J.B., "Mutual Recognition of Professional Qualifications: The East African Community" (2015) Tralac Brief No. SI5TB04/2015. 2015.

16 This actually forms an area where EAC objectives and ambitions go beyond those in the Europe, as the EU lacks the competence to harmonise curricula, and mutual recognition is based more on trust in the existing systems, as well as secondary legislation. See EU Chapter 11 par. 3.

17 Cronje, J.B. (n 13 above).

18 Report of the 28th Meeting of the Council of Ministers held in Kampala, Uganda on 22nd-29th November 2013 at page 40–41.

obligation on the Partner States to designate competent bodies and to authorise them to enter into MRAs to facilitate the movement of professionals in accordance with the market access commitments made under the Common Market Protocol.[19] It provides guidance on the development of MRAs and the key elements it should contain. The key elements are academic and professional qualification requirements; registration procedures; permitted professional competencies; common code of conduct; disciplinary processes; and administration of the MRA.

This therefore requires that all competent bodies responsible for regulating professional services liberalised by Partner States be identified and required to negotiate MRAs. They include bodies responsible for regulating legal services, accounting services, architectural services, engineering services, integrated engineering services, medical and dental services, nurses and midwives, veterinary services, paramedics and physiotherapists.

So far, accountants, engineers and architects (excluding the Architects' Association of Tanzania) have concluded MRAs.[20] Lawyers are still negotiating their MRA.

11.2.3 *Right of Residence for Workers, Relatives and Non-Economically Active Persons*

A worker and their spouse, children and dependents are entitled to the right of residence.[21] In this regard, a worker with a contract of employment of a period of more than 90 days, his/her spouse, children and dependents are issued with a pass upon the submission of valid travel documents or national identity cards and contract of employment to the immigration officer. Upon entry to the territory of the Partner State, the worker is required to apply for a work permit and dependent pass for his/her spouse, children and dependents. If the contract of employment is for less that 90 days, the worker is issued with a special pass.

Partner States are therefore required to make major reforms in their laws and policies regarding movement of persons to ensure that their laws do not inhibit the free movement of workers and their right of residence. Kenya is a good example of a Partner State that has made efforts towards this end. Following the promulgation of the current Constitution of Kenya in 2010, laws that inhibited the free movement of people such as the Kenya Citizenship Act

19 Cronje, J.B. (n13 above).

20 Report of the 28th Meeting of the Council of Ministers held in Kampala, Uganda on 22nd–29th November 2013 at page 40–41.

21 Article 14 of Common Market Protocol.

(Cap 170); the Immigration Act (Cap 172); Alien Restriction Act (Cap 173) and Visa Regulations were repealed and subsequently replaced with the Kenya Citizenship and Immigration Act No. 12 of 2011 and the Kenya Citizens and Foreign Nationals Management Act No. 31 of 2011.

Currently, the competent authorities in Partner States issue work permits to East Africans wishing to work within the Partner States within 30 days from the date of application.[22] The work permits may be issued for an initial period of up to two years and may be renewed upon application.[23] In addition, Partner States are given the first opportunity, based on merit, in the event they are competing for the same job opportunity with nationals from outside the EAC region.[24] With regard to work permit fees, Rwanda, Kenya and Uganda have waived payment of the fees for East Africans who are workers.[25]

Pursuant to the 20th Meeting of the Sectoral Council of Ministers responsible for EAC and Planning held on 13th July 2014, the EAC Secretariat is coordinating the process of the harmonisation of classification and procedures for issuance of entry/work/residence permits as this is currently still being done in accordance with national laws.[26]

11.2.4 *Labour Laws and Portability of Social Benefits*

The objectives of the Common Market Protocol can only be realised if the Partner States (among other things) harmonise their policies in areas provided for by the Common Market Protocol or determined by the Council.[27] Hence, the Partners States need to harmonise labour policies, programs, legislation, social services, provide for social security benefits, establish common standards and measures for association of workers and employers, establish employment promotion centers and eventually adopt a common employment policy.[28]

The Partners States are therefore required to make major reforms in their labour policies and legislations to address discrimination of citizens and

22 http://www.eac.int/sectors/immigration-and-labour/migration-and-development. Accessed on 1.3.16.

23 http://www.eac.int/sectors/immigration-and-labour/migration-and-development. Accessed on 1.3.16.

24 http://www.eac.int/sectors/immigration-and-labour/migration-and-development. Accessed on 1.3.16 .

25 http://www.eac.int/sectors/immigration-and-labour/migration-and-development. Accessed on 1.3.16.

26 http://www.eac.int/sectors/immigration-and-labour/migration-and-development. Accessed on 1.3.16.

27 Article 4(3) of the Common Market Protocol.

28 Article 5 (2 c) and 12(1) of the Common Market Protocol.

workers from Partner States. Uganda has so far made major labour law reforms for purposes of compliance with the Common Market Protocol. It enacted several statutes and adopted a set of regulations in the area of labour and employment in 2011.[29] Kenya similarly made major labour law reform to facilitate free entry into Kenya of citizens of Partner States to take up jobs, in accordance with the Common Market Protocol.

In addition to the harmonisation of labour laws and policies, the Common Market Protocol envisages a single market in the retirement benefit sector in order to encourage greater movement of workers. The EAC Partner States have different social security schemes operating simultaneously in each Partner State and this therefore creates a major challenge with regard to harmonisation. For example, Burundi has a mandatory public pension scheme, civil service pension scheme, supplementary pension schemes and individual private pensions.[30] Kenya has a mandatory public pension scheme, LAPFUND and LAPTRUST for employees of county governments, public service pension scheme for the civil service, private pension schemes and individual private pensions.[31]

In light of the above, transferability of the benefits of a worker to another Partner State is not possible at the moment until the retirement benefit sector is harmonised and therefore this is a major impediment to the realisation of free movement of workers.

11.2.5 *Labour Market Information Systems*

In order to facilitate access to employment opportunities, the Partner States are required to collect and disseminate information on job vacancies and put in place labour market information systems to facilitate access to employment opportunities by the citizens of the Community.[32]

29 ILO Labour Administration and Inspection Programme, International *Labour Organisation (ILO) Technical Memorandum of the Uganda labour and administration and inspection needs assessment.*

30 Callund Consulting Limited (UK), *Review of the Structure of the Pension Sector in the East African Community* (2013).

31 Callund Consulting Limited (UK), *Review of the Structure of the Pension Sector in the East African Community* (2013).

32 Regulation 12(1) of Annex II of the CMP.

11.3 Service Providers and the Free Movement of Workers

Under the Common Market Protocol Schedule of Commitment on the Progressive Liberalisation of Services (Annex V), services can be traded in the region in four different ways—known as four modes.[33] Service providers or self-employed, as defined in this Chapter, fall under Mode IV—supply of services by a supplier of a Partner State through the presence of a natural person of a Partner State in the territory of another Partner State.

Service providers should be able to move freely within the territory of Partner States; stay in the territory together with his/her dependents; take up and pursue economic activities as self-employed persons; and set up and manage economic undertakings in the territory of another state without being discriminated upon on the basis of nationality.[34]

Common Market Protocol through Annex II and Annex V link the free movement of workers (Annex II) and the service suppliers (Annex V) despite the distinction made under Article 1 of the Common Market Protocol that service providers are not workers. Annex V provides that market access and national treatment commitments in Mode IV are in accordance with Annex II therefore greatly limiting Mode IV to those requirements set in Annex II with regards to entry, stay and exit of workers; acquiring, denial and cancellation of work permits; employment of spouse and children; and equal treatment in employment. Annex II and Annex V need to be delinked in order to enable further separate liberalization negotiations for service suppliers so as to have specific market access and national treatment commitments.

In September 2014, the Council of Ministers directed that specific amendments must be made to the Common Market Protocol hence giving the Partner States an opportunity to review their commitments across all modes of supply but with specific focus on the temporary movement of persons supplying a service (Mode IV) under Annex V of the Common Market Protocol.

---

33 See page 80 of the Schedule on Trade in Services.

34 Article 13 (2) and (3).

CHAPTER 11A

Free Movement of Persons in the EU

Armin Cuyvers

11.1 Introduction

Labour is one of the factors of production that needs to move freely for an internal market to function, and free movement of labour means free movement of persons. Free movement of persons, however, is one of the most complex and challenging of the EU freedoms, both legally and politically. People, after all, are rather more complex than cars, cheese or cassis liqueur. Unlike goods, for example, people get sick, need housing and schooling, have accidents, lose their job, marry and start families, perhaps divorce again, or, in some cases, commit criminal offences. All of these actions affect some of the most sensitive political areas, including social security, healthcare, immigration and public order. Even more than the other freedoms, therefore, free movement of persons has political implications, as the recent debate on Brexit demonstrated in a somewhat tragic manner.[1]

The free movement of persons has developed significantly since its inception in the 1957 Treaty of Rome. Initially, the free movement of persons only concerned workers and other economically active persons. It then became clear that to make the free movement of workers effective, EU law also needed to grant rights to workers' families. Subsequently, the free movement of persons further expanded to include more and more individuals, even if they were not directly economically active. A major development then took place with the introduction of Union citizenship in the Treaty of Maastricht, as several free movement rights were attached directly to the status of EU Citizen.

This Chapter gives a brief overview of the free movement of persons in the EU and its development over time. In line with the other free movement chapters, the overview primarily focuses on the negative integration developed through the seminal case law of the CJEU, but also looks at some of the key

1 See in this context also the deal struck with Cameron before the referendum, in which limiting the right of new workers to social benefits was the key element. The deal can be found in the Conclusions of the European Council of 18–19 February 2016, Annex I, EUCO 1/16. For analysis, see 'Editorial comments: Presiding the Union in times of crisis: The unenviable task of the Netherlands' (2016) 53(2) *Common Market Law Review*, 327–328.

© ARMIN CUYVERS, 2017 | DOI 10.1163/9789004322073_023
This is an open access chapter distributed under the terms of the CC-BY-NC License.

pieces of EU legislation, as harmonization played a relatively big role in this area of EU law.[2]

11.2 Free Movement of Workers

The free movement of workers is laid down in Article 45 TFEU, which has both vertical and horizontal direct effect.[3]

> 1. *Freedom of movement for workers shall be secured within the Union.*
> 2. *Such freedom of movement shall entail the abolition of any discrimination based on nationality between workers of the Member States as regards employment, remuneration and other conditions of work and employment.*
> 3. *It shall entail the right, subject to limitations justified on grounds of public policy, public security or public health:*
>   (*a*) *to accept offers of employment actually made;*
>   (*b*) *to move freely within the territory of Member States for this purpose;*
>   (*c*) *to stay in a Member State for the purpose of employment in accordance with the provisions governing the employment of nationals of that State laid down by law, regulation or administrative action;*
>   (*d*) *to remain in the territory of a Member State after having been employed in that State, subject to conditions which shall be embodied in regulations to be drawn up by the Commission.*
> 4. *The provisions of this Article shall not apply to employment in the public service.'*

---

2 For further information and analysis on this extensive area of EU law see amongst many others S. O'Leary, 'Free movement and persons and services' in P. Craig and G. de Búrca (eds.) *The Evolution of EU law* (2nd edn, OUP 2011), E. Spaventa, *Free Movement of Persons in the EU: Barriers to movement and their constitutional context.* (Kluwer, 2007), A Tryfonidou, 'In search of the aim of the EC free movement of persons provisions: Has the Court of Justice missed the point?' (2009) 46 *Common Market Law Review*, 1591, or J. Shaw, 'Citizenship: Contrasting dynamics at the interface of integration and constitutionalism' in in P. Craig and G. de Búrca (eds.) *The Evolution of EU law* (2nd edn, OUP 2011).

3 Case 41/74 *Van Duyn* [1974] ECR 1337, Case C-281/98, *Angonese* ECR 2000, p. I-4139 and case C-415/93 *Bosman*, [1995] ECR I-4921. Note though that the right only applies to EU citizens moving to another Member State. Third country nationals cannot rely on Article 45 TFEU, nor can EU citizens in their own state.

As with the other free movement provisions, Article 45 TFEU only provides a limited framework that had to be further developed by the CJEU. One of the main open questions was the definition of 'worker' itself. As EU law is autonomous, after all, one may not use national definitions of worker or employee to interpret the concept of worker under EU law.[4] Again in line with the other freedoms, the CJEU developed a very broad and inclusive definition of worker, thereby expanding the group of persons that could rely on it.[5] In *Lawrie Blum*, which concerned the question if a trainee-teacher qualified as a worker, the CJEU for instance held that:

> Since freedom of movement for workers constitutes one of the fundamental principles of the Community, the term 'worker' in article [45] may not be interpreted differently according to the law of each member state but has a community meaning. Since it defines the scope of that fundamental freedom, the community concept of a 'worker' must be interpreted broadly.[6]

The CJEU then continued to provide the following definition of worker:

> The essential feature of an employment relationship, however, is that for a certain period of time a person performs services for and under the direction of another person in return for which he receives remuneration.
>
> In the present case, it is clear that during the entire period of preparatory service the trainee teacher is under the direction and supervision of the school to which he is assigned. (…) The amounts which he receives may be regarded as remuneration for the services provided and for the duties involved in completing the period of preparatory service. Consequently, the three criteria for the existence of an employment relationship are fulfilled in this case.
>
> The fact that teachers' preparatory service, like apprenticeships in other occupations, may be regarded as practical preparation directly related to the actual pursuit of the occupation in point is not a bar to the application of article [45](1) if the service is performed under the conditions of an activity as an employed person.
>
> (…)

4 See also EU Chapter 4.

5 Case C-337/97, *Meeusen* [1999] ECR I-3289.

6 Case 66/85 *Lawrie-Blum* ECR 02121, par. 16.

> The fact that trainee teachers give lessons for only a few hours a week and are paid remuneration below the starting salary of a qualified teacher does not prevent them from being regarded as workers. In its judgment in Levin, the Court held that the expressions 'worker' and 'activity as an employed person' must be understood as including persons who, because they are not employed full time, receive pay lower than that for full-time employment, provided that the activities performed are effective and genuine. The latter requirement is not called into question in this case.[7]

Individuals, therefore, already qualify as workers if they perform relatively small jobs against relatively low wages, as long as the work is 'effective and genuine'. Students that go and study in another Member State and work there for one day a week against minimum wages, for instance as a waiter, therefore qualify as a worker. The broad scope of the concept of worker was further confirmed in *Trojani*, which involved an individual doing some chores for the salvation army in return for housing and some pocket change. The CJEU held that:

> Any person who pursues activities which are real and genuine, to the exclusion of activities on such a small scale as to be regarded as purely marginal and ancillary, must be regarded as a 'worker'. The essential feature of an employment relationship is, according to that case-law, that for a certain period of time a person performs services for and under the direction of another person in return for which he receives remuneration
>
> Moreover, neither the sui generis nature of the employment relationship under national law, nor the level of productivity of the person concerned, the origin of the funds from which the remuneration is paid or the limited amount of the remuneration can have any consequence in regard to whether or not the person is a worker for the purposes of Community law.
>
> With respect more particularly to establishing whether the condition of the pursuit of real and genuine activity for remuneration is satisfied, the national court must base its examination on objective criteria and make an overall assessment of all the circumstances of the case relating to the nature both of the activities concerned and of the employment relationship at issue.

7 Idem, paras. 17–21.

> In this respect, the Court has held that activities cannot be regarded as a real and genuine economic activity if they constitute merely a means of rehabilitation or reintegration for the persons concerned.
>
> However, that conclusion can be explained only by the particular characteristics of the case in question, which concerned the situation of a person who, by reason of his addiction to drugs, had been recruited on the basis of a national law intended to provide work for persons who, for an indefinite period, are unable, by reason of circumstances related to their situation, to work under normal conditions.
>
> In the present case, as is apparent from the decision making the reference, Mr Trojani performs, for the Salvation Army and under its direction, various jobs for approximately 30 hours a week, as part of a personal reintegration programme, in return for which he receives benefits in kind and some pocket money.
>
> (…)
>
> Having established that the benefits in kind and money provided by the Salvation Army to Mr Trojani constitute the consideration for the services performed by him for and under the direction of the hostel, the national court has thereby established the existence of the constituent elements of any paid employment relationship, namely subordination and the payment of remuneration.
>
> For the claimant in the main proceedings to have the status of worker, however, the national court, in the assessment of the facts which is within its exclusive jurisdiction, would have to establish that the paid activity in question is real and genuine.
>
> The national court must in particular ascertain whether the services actually performed by Mr Trojani are capable of being regarded as forming part of the normal labour market. For that purpose, account may be taken of the status and practices of the hostel, the content of the social reintegration programme, and the nature and details of performance of the services.[8]

The ultimate decision whether Trojani qualified as a worker was left to the Belgian referring court, yet the CJEU did provide some criteria to establish the minimum requirements. One key criterion is if the relevant activities are normally provided on the labour market, or if they are more designed to keep

8 Case C-456/02, *Trojani*, ECLI:EU:C:2004:488, paras. 15–24.

certain persons occupied without really forming genuine work.[9] The fact that *Trojani* was even concerned a border case in itself, however, already indicates how broad the concept of worker is interpreted under EU law.

In addition, the CJEU also held that, to ensure Article 45 TFEU can achieve its objective effectively, those seeking work also had to receive some protection. The right to work, after all, is seriously limited where one does not have the right to first seek work. At the same time, one cannot give too many rights solely on the basis that someone is looking for a job. The CJEU balanced both arguments by holding that those objectively qualifying as job seekers have a right of residence for a limited time of six months, after which, if they do not find a job, they have to leave.[10]

As to exceptions, and again in line with the case law on the other freedoms, the CJEU does allow rule of reason exceptions in addition to the exceptions in the TFEU, but interprets both restrictively.[11] The CJEU also gave a very restrictive interpretation to the 'public-service exception' contained in Article 45 paragraph 4 TFEU. This exception only applies where the post in question involves *both* the exercise of a power conferred by public law *and* the safeguarding of the general interests of the State. States can, therefore, not simply bypass Article 45 TFEU by qualifying a position as a public service one: a position in a State school, for instance, will not meet these standards.[12] Instead, the function at stake must entail a real exercise of public authority, such as a judge, a minister or a police officer.

11.3 The Rights of Workers and their Family Members

Once a person qualifies as a worker, both primary and secondary EU law provide several rights to the worker and her family members.[13] Firstly, the worker

---

9 Cf. also Case 344/87 *Bettray* [1989] ECR 1621, par. 17 for an example of a person not qualifying as a worker.

10 Case C-292/89 *Antonissen* ECLI:EU:C:1991:80.

11 As many of the rights on free movement have now been laid down in secondary legislation, however, any exceptions to them must be assessed under the secondary legislation, not the Treaty Articles. See on this relation between primary and secondary law EU Chapter 9 as well as Case C-5/77 *Tedeschi* ECLI:EU:C:1977:144. Where restrictions do fall under primary law, the familiar test for restrictions applies, meaning the restriction must serve a legitimate aim in a proportionate manner.

12 Case 66/85, *Lawrie-Blum v. Land Baden-Würtemberg* [1986], ECR 2121.

13 For the definition of family member now see Article 2 of Directive 2004/38.

and the family members have a right to reside in the Member State.[14] Secondly, the worker is entitled to complete equal treatment with national workers. This includes equal treatment in the areas of remuneration, dismissal, social and tax advantages, trade unions and education rights. These rights already derived from Article 45 TFEU, but are now also laid down in Regulation 492/2011.[15] Based on the right to complete equal treatment of the worker, the family members also enjoy many (derived) social rights and benefits such as student grants and loans and access to child care.[16] The idea is that people would be hindered in accepting a job in another Member State if they would not have the same rights, or if their family members would not receive benefits that nationals do, and the worker would have to cover all kinds of costs for the family members herself.

The rights of workers and their family members, moreover, apply from the very moment an individual becomes a worker. If an Estonian lawyer accepts a job in Hungary, for example, he will have an immediate right to complete equal treatment including all social benefits Hungarian workers are entitled to, and his children will be immediately entitled to student grants or other benefits awarded to children of Hungarian workers.

EU law also tries to support free movement of workers by requiring or simplifying the mutual recognition of diplomas. To begin with, the non-recognition of a diploma can constitute a restriction of Article 45 TFEU, which must be justified and sufficiently motivated.[17] This negative integration has also been complemented by positive integration in the form of elaborate legislation on the mutual recognition of diplomas.[18]

---

14 These rights of residence derive from Article 45 TFEU but are now also laid down in the general Citizens Directive 2004/38 OJ L [2004] 158/77. The right of residence may also extend for a period after the worker becomes unemployed. See Article 7 of Directive 2004/38.

15 Regulation 492/2011 on freedom of movement for workers within the Union OJ [2011] L1/1. This regulation replaced Regulation 1612/68 [1968] OJ L257/2.

16 See also Case C-370/90 *Singh* ECLI:EU:C:1992:296.

17 See for example Case 2/74, *Reyners* [1972], ECR 631 or Case C-340/89, *Vlassopoulou*, ECR 1991, p. 2357.

18 See especially Directive 2005/36 on the recognition of professional qualifications OJ [2005] L255/22.

11.4 Union Citizenship and Directive 2004/38

In line with the economic rationale behind free movement, the rights described above only applied to economically active people, with family members deriving certain rights from the economically active person as well.[19] Gradually, however, free movement rights were extended to persons who were not or no longer economically active.[20] The major expansion of the free movement of persons, and the most far reaching separation of this right from economic activity, took place with the introduction of Union citizenship in the Treaty of Maastricht. Union citizenship is intended to capture and strengthen the bond between the EU and the individual citizen, and is established and bestowed by Article 20 TFEU:

> 1. *Citizenship of the Union is hereby established. Every person holding the nationality of a Member State shall be a citizen of the Union. Citizenship of the Union shall be additional to and not replace national citizenship.*
> 2. *Citizens of the Union shall enjoy the rights and be subject to the duties provided for in the Treaties. They shall have, inter alia:*
>   (*a*) *the right to move and reside freely within the territory of the Member States;*
>   (*b*) *the right to vote and to stand as candidates in elections to the European Parliament and in municipal elections in their Member State of residence, under the same conditions as nationals of that State;*
>   (…)
>
> *These rights shall be exercised in accordance with the conditions and limits defined by the Treaties and by the measures adopted thereunder.*

---

19 Note that service providers and entrepreneurs establishing a business in another Member State also have right to move and reside, and hence fall under the category of economically active people that enjoy free movement rights. Their situation, however, will be discussed in more detail in EU Chapter 12 on services and establishment, even though one could also consider them as part of the free movement of persons.

20 See for example the adoption of three directives in the early nineties extending the free movement rights of non-economically active or no longer economically active persons: Directive 90/364, granting rights of residence for non economically active persons (primarily pensioners); Directive 90/365, granting rights of residence to employees and entrepreneurs having ended their professional activities; Directive 93/96, granting rights of residence to students. All of these have now been replaced by Directive 2004/38.

Article 20 TFEU captures the secondary nature and normative claim of EU citizenship. Even though Union citizenship is 'destined to be the fundamental status' of individuals, it remains subordinated to the national citizenship of a Member State, and does not replace it.[21] This secondary citizenship also symbolizes the constitutional middle-ground occupied by the EU and represents the challenges and opportunities in developing a democracy based on multiple *demoi* instead of one *demos*.[22]

Even though it remains a secondary status,[23] EU citizenship forms an important step in EU integration. Since its creation, moreover, Union citizenship has developed rather spectacularly, and an increasing number of rights have been connected to it, including free movement rights. As Article 21 TFEU provides: 'Every citizen of the Union shall have the right to move and reside freely within the territory of the Member States, subject to the limitations and conditions laid down in the Treaties and by the measures adopted to give them effect.'[24] These limitations and conditions can now mostly be found in Directive 2004/38, known as the Citizens Directive.

Directive 2004/38 gives three 'layers' of movement and residence rights, subject to increasingly stringent criteria. Firstly, Articles 5 and 6 of Directive 2004/38 give a right of entry and the right to reside for up to three months to all Union citizens who move to or reside in a Member State other than that of which they are a national, as well as to their family members. The right of entry under Article 5 entails that Member States may only require a valid identity card or passport, but no other documentation or formalities upon entry.[25] The right to reside for up to three months may also not be subject to any other conditions than to hold a valid identity card or passport. Any EU citizen with

21 See case C-184/99 *Grzelczyk* [2001] ECR I-6193, par. 31.

22 J.H.H. Weiler, 'European democracy and its critics: polity and system', and 'To be a European citizen: Eros and civilization', in: J.H.H. Weiler *The Constitution of Europe: Do the New Clothes have an Emperor?* (CUP 1999), 264, 324, and especially 344 et seq. On the confederal middle-ground occupied by the EU see A. Cuyvers, *The EU as a Confederal Union of Sovereign Member Peoples, Exploring the potential of American (con)federalism and popular sovereignty for a constitutional theory of the EU*, (Diss. Leiden), Zutphen: Wöhrmann 2013.

23 See however cases C-369/90 *Micheletti* [1992] ECR I-4239 and C-135/08) *Rottmann* [2010] ECR I-1449 on the limits imposed by EU citizenship on the rights of Member States to grant or especially to remove national citizenship, and thereby EU citizenship.

24 These rights have direct effect. See for example Case C-413/99, *Baumbast*, ECR I-7091.

25 For third country family members see Article 5(2) a.o.

a passport, therefore, may reside in any other Member State for up to three months.[26]

Secondly, Article 7 of Directive 2004/38 grants a right of residence for *more* than three months to three categories of Union citizens, being those that:

(a) are workers or self-employed persons in the host Member State, or,
(b) have sufficient resources for themselves and their family members not to become a burden on the social assistance system of the host Member State and have comprehensive sickness insurance; or,
(c) Students that have comprehensive sickness insurance and sufficient resources for themselves and their family members not to become a burden on the social assistance system of the host Member State during their period of residence.

As long as a Union citizen falls in one of these categories, he has the right to reside. This right extends, furthermore, to the family members of the Union citizen, even if these family members are not EU citizens themselves.[27]

The main reasoning behind these three categories of citizens with open-ended residence rights is that EU citizens and their family members should have a right to freely reside in the EU as long as they do not become a burden on the host state. This also means that the resources Union citizens need to have under 7(b) and (c) do not have to be very high, they just have to be sufficient for them not to have to rely on the host state for assistance and thereby become a burden.

The third, and most far reaching, right of residence is granted when a citizen has resided legally for a continuous period of at least five years in the host Member State and acquires *permanent residence*.[28] As of that moment, these Union citizens no longer have to meet the requirements under Article 7 of Directive 2004/38 to have residence rights, and they acquire even more rights to equal treatment. Permanent residency can therefore be seen as a very

26 On the possible grounds for expelling citizens, also during this three month period, if they violate certain rules, see the discussion on expulsion below.

27 Directive 2004/38 Art. 7(2).

28 Article 16 2004/38 and Council Directive 2003/109 concerning the status of third-country nationals who are long-term residents OJ [2004] L16/44. For the five year requirement, continuity of residence is not undermined by temporary absences not exceeding a total of six months a year, or by absences of a longer duration for compulsory military service, or by one absence of a maximum of 12 consecutive months for important reasons such as pregnancy and childbirth, serious illness, study or vocational training, or a posting in another Member State or a third country.

substantial status that is one step below acquiring citizenship of another Member State. Once acquired, the right of permanent residency is only lost where the Union citizen leaves is absent from the host state for a period exceeding two consecutive years.

As soon as EU citizens rely on their rights and move to another Member State, they fall under the scope of EU law and under Article 24 of directive 2004/38 also have a right to equal treatment:

1. *Subject to such specific provisions as are expressly provided for in the Treaty and secondary law, all Union citizens residing on the basis of this Directive in the territory of the host Member State shall enjoy equal treatment with the nationals of that Member State within the scope of the Treaty. The benefit of this right shall be extended to family members who are not nationals of a Member State and who have the right of residence or permanent residence.*
2. *By way of derogation from paragraph 1, the host Member State shall not be obliged to confer entitlement to social assistance during the first three months of residence or, where appropriate, the longer period provided for in Article 14(4)(b), nor shall it be obliged, prior to acquisition of the right of permanent residence, to grant maintenance aid for studies, including vocational training, consisting in student grants or student loans to persons other than workers, self-employed persons, persons who retain such status and members of their families.'*

Crucially, Article 24(2) of Directive 2004/38 restricts the rights of EU citizens to entitlements or social assistance in the first three months, for the six month-period granted to job-seekers and to student aid or grants. This restriction ensures that Union citizens cannot simply move to another Member State and then request social benefits, as this would undermine national social security.

Article 27 of Directive 2004/38 allows for certain restrictions on the right of residence on grounds of public policy, public security or public health. In line with the Treaty exceptions, these are interpreted very narrowly, and a proportionality check has to be satisfied. In addition, Articles 28 to 32 of Directive 2004/38 regulate the possible expulsion of Union citizens on the grounds of public policy, public security or public health. Expulsion, however, may only be based on individual behavior and the fact that the individual presents a future risk as well. The protection against expulsion, furthermore, increases with the time the citizen spent in the host Member State.[29]

29 See for example Case C-348/09, *Remscheid* ECLI:EU:C:2012:300.

CHAPTER 12

Freedom of Establishment and the Freedom to Provide Services in the EAC

Kennedy Gastorn

12.1 Introduction

Trade in services is important for the economic growth of the East African Region. This is recognized in the Protocol on the Establishment of the East African Community Common Market ("the Common Market Protocol"), which provides that accelerated economic growth and development of the Partner States can be achieved through the free movement of people and labour; right of establishment and residence; and the free movement of services and capital.[1]

12.2 Right of Establishment

The Common Market Protocol guarantees the right of establishment of nationals of one Partner State in another Partner State and the non-discriminatory treatment of such nationals based on their nationalities.[2] In this regard, this right entitles the nationals of a Partner State to take up and pursue economic activities as self-employed persons, as well as to set up and manage economic undertakings, in the territory of another Partner State. Hence, the right of establishment is divided into two segments. Firstly, the right of natural persons to engage in economic activities not under any contract of employment or supervision and earn a living from such activities. Secondly, the right to set up a legal entity and manage economic activities under it. This Chapter shall therefore discuss the right of establishment under these two headings, namely natural persons and legal persons.

Before discussing the right of establishment as proposed above, it is important to note that the provisions of Article 13 of the Common Market Protocol on the right of establishment are implemented by the East African Community

1 Article 4 (2) of the Common Market Protocol.

2 Article 13 (1 and 2) of the Common Market Protocol.

© KENNEDY GASTORN, 2017 | DOI 10.1163/9789004322073_024
This is an open access chapter distributed under the terms of the CC-BY-NC License.

Common Market (Right of Establishment) Regulations (Annex III). Annex III ensures that there is uniformity among the Partner States in the implementation of Article 13 of the Common Market Protocol.

In addition to Annex III, the Common Market Protocol Schedule of Commitment on the Progressive Liberalisation of Services (Annex V) provides that services can be traded in the region in four different ways—known as four modes.[3] The right of establishment falls under both Mode III (the supply of services by a service supplier of a Partner State, through the commercial presence of the service supplier in the territory of another Partner State) and Mode IV (the supply of the services by a supplier of a Partner State, through the presence of a natural person of a Partner State in the territory of another Partner State). Annex V allows Partner States to make progressive market access and national treatment commitments by selecting the sectors to open up, and sometimes with conditions, hence tailoring the commitments to the particular needs and policy objectives of each Partner State. Therefore, the Partner States are able to control the overall market presence of the other Partner States for different sectors and different modes of supply.[4] The Partner States are however required to make additional commitments on the elimination of restrictions in the service sectors and sub sectors that are not specified in Annex V after the Common Market Protocol enters into force.[5]

Annex V provides that market access and national treatment commitments in Mode IV are in accordance with the East African Community Common Market (Free Movement of Workers) Regulations (Annex II). For purposes of the right to establishment, Annex II covers issues such as entry, stay and exit of workers; acquiring, denial and cancellation of work permits; employment of spouses and children; and equal treatment in employment. There are no specific commitments and therefore there is need to delink Annex V and Annex II in respect to Mode IV to allow for further market access commitments.

12.3 Freedom to Provide Services

The freedom to provide services is provided for under Part F of the Common Market Protocol and further detailed in the Schedule of Commitment on the Progressive Liberalisation of Services (Annex V). Article 16 (7) of the Common Market Protocol defines "services" as encompassing those "in any sector except

3 *See* page 80 of the Schedule on Trade in Services.

4 Article 23 of the Common Market Protocol.

5 Article 23 (2) of the Common Market Protocol.

services supplied in the exercise of governmental authority which are not provided on a commercial basis or in competition with one or more service suppliers" and those which are "normally provided for remuneration, in so far as they are not governed by the provisions relating to free movement of goods, capital and persons."[6] Under Article 16 (1) of the Common Market Protocol, the Partner States guarantee the free movement of services supplied by nationals of Partner States and the free movement of service suppliers who are nationals of the Partner States within the Community. Nationals are defined by Article 1 of the Common Market Protocol as natural or legal persons who are nationals in accordance with the laws of the Partner State.

Nationals of a Partner State provide services to other Partner States in two ways:

(a) By the presence of a service supplier, who is a citizen of a Partner State, in the territory of another Partner State hence a natural person providing the service; or
(b) Commercial presence of the service supplier in the territory of another Partner State hence a legal person providing the service.[7]

This Chapter, will discuss the freedom to provide services along with the right of establishment under these two headings: natural and legal persons.

12.4 Natural Persons

Natural persons for purposes of the right of establishment are referred to as "self-employed persons" under the Common Market Protocol which defines a "self-employed person" as a person engaged in an economic activity not under any contract of employment or supervision and who earns a living through this activity.[8]

Based on the provisions of the Common Market Protocol, Annex II and Annex V, seven important issues must be considered in order to realise the right of establishment and the freedom to provide services for natural persons in the EAC:

6 Article 16 (7) of the Common Market Protocol. See in this regard also the very similar definition under EU law, and the way it has been developed by the Court of Justice of the EU in EU Chapter 12.

7 Article 16 (3 c and d) of the Common Market Protocol.

8 Article 1 of the the Common Market Protocol.

i. Free movement of persons
ii. Right of residence
iii. Non-discrimination,
iv. Removal of restrictions
v. Obtaining licenses and certificates
vi. Portability of social benefits
vii. Right to join professional bodies and trade organisations

12.4.1 *Free Movement of Persons*

A self-employed person, his/her spouse and children can enter and exit the territory of another Partner State in accordance with the national laws and established immigration procedures of the Partner State.[9] The Partner State is required to ensure non-discrimination of the citizens of the Partner States based on their nationalities by ensuring that the citizens of the other Partner States enter its territory without a visa; move freely within its territory; are allowed to stay in the territory; and are allowed to exit the territory without restrictions.[10] In addition, the Partner State must guarantee the protection of the citizens of the other Partner States while in their territories, in accordance with the law. However, if the national of a Partner State commits a crime in their territory, the national is not exempt from prosecution or extradition.

While at the designated entry and exit point of the Partner State, the self-employed person and his/her dependents are required to present to the immigration officer valid travel documents or national identity cards, where a Partner State has agreed to use the national identity card as a travel document, and declare all information required for entry or departure.[11] If the self-employed person and his/her dependents have fulfilled all the legal and procedural requirements, they are each issued with a pass which shall entitle them to enter the territory of the host Partner State for a period of up to six months.[12]

A Partner State can however limit the free movement of persons on grounds of public policy, public security or public health. The Partner State imposing any of the aforesaid permissible limitations must notify the other Partner States immediately.[13]

9 Annex II of the Common Market Protocol Regulation 4 and 5(1).
10 Article 7 of the Common Market Protocol.
11 Annex II of the Common Market Protocol. Regulation 5(2) and Article 9 of the Common Market Protocol. …
12 Annex II of the Common Market Protocol. Regulation 5(3 and 4).
13 Article 7 (5 and 6) of the Common Market Protocol …).

12.4.2 *Right of Residence*

The right of residence is provided for in Article 14 of the Common Market Protocol and implemented in accordance with the East African Common Market (Right of Residence) Regulations—Annex IV of the Common Market Protocol. Annex IV ensures that there is uniformity in the implementation of Article 14 and that the process is transparent, accountable, fair, predictable and consistent with the Common Market Protocol.[14]

Upon entry into the territory of the Partner State, a self-employed person and his/her dependents who intend to reside in the territory of the Partner State are required to apply for a residence permit, within thirty days from the date of entry.[15] The residence permit is however issued by the host Partner State on the basis of the work permit hence a valid work permit must accompany an application for the residence permit.

The procedure and requirements for the application of a work permit by a self-employed person are contained in Annex II of the Common Market Protocol. Annex II provides that a self-employed person who intends to pursue economic activities in the territory of the Partner State is required to apply to the competent authority for a work permit within 30 days from the date of entry.[16] Upon such application, the self-employed person is first issued with a special pass which allows him/her to engage in an economic activity in the territory of the Partner State for the period of the pass as the formalities of establishment are completed.[17] The application for the work permit must be supported by evidence that the self-employed person has sufficient capital and other resources to carry out the economic activity and that the self-employed person is duly licensed or authorized by the host Partner State to engage in the economic activity.[18]

If the application for a work permit is successful, the self-employed person is issued with a work permit within 30 days of application, for an initial period of two years.[19] The competent authority may deny the applicant a work permit however an appeal of the decision is allowed provided it is done in accordance with the national laws of the host Partner State. If the appeal is rejected or the self-employed person is not interested in appealing the decision, the

---

14 Regulation 2 of Annex IV of the Common Market Protocol.

15 Regulation 6(1) of Annex IV of the Common Market Protocol.

16 Regulation 6(1) of Annex IV of the Common Market Protocol.

17 Annex II Regulation 6 (1, 2 and 3) of the Common Market Protocol.

18 Annex II Regulation 6 (4) of the Common Market Protocol.

19 Annex II Regulation 6 (5) of the Common Market Protocol.

self-employed person and his/her dependents are required to leave the territory of the host Partner State within a given reasonable time.[20]

Once the self-employed person is in possession of a valid work permit, he/she is required to apply for a residence permit which is issued within 30 days of the application. The duration of the residence permit for the self-employed person cannot exceed the duration of the work permit. If the self-employed person wishes to reside with his/her spouse and children, he/she is required to apply for a dependents pass for each one of them within 30 days from the date of entry of the spouse and/or children. The dependents pass is issued on the basis of the work permit or residence permit of the self-employed person.[21]

Cancellation of a work permit affects the residence status of a self-employed person. A work permit may be cancelled if the self-employed person is expelled or deported from the territory of the host Partner State; ceases to engage in the economic activity for which the work permit was issued; or obtained the work permit fraudulently. Upon cancellation of the work permit, the self-employed person is required to either regularize his/her status or leave the territory of the host state.[22]

It is not automatic that once a person has a work permit, the residence permit will be issued. The competent authority of the host state may deny the self-employed person a residence permit. The denial must however be done in writing and reasons for such denial given. The self-employed person is permitted to appeal the decision in accordance with the national laws of the host Partner State. If the appeal is unsuccessful or if the self-employed person decides not to appeal the decision, then he/she must leave the territory of the Partner State within a reasonable time.[23]

The residency status of the self-employed person may also be affected by cancellation of the residence permit. A residence permit can be cancelled where a condition of the residence permit is not fulfilled or is breached or on grounds of public policy, public security and public health. In such a case, the self-employed persons and his/her dependents are required to leave the territory of the host state within an indicated reasonable time.[24] If they fail to leave within the time given, then the host Partner State may deport them.[25]

---

20 Annex II Regulation 7 of the Common Market Protocol.

21 Annex II Regulation 8 of the Common Market Protocol.

22 Annex II Regulation 8 of the Common Market Protocol.

23 Annex II Regulation 9 of the Common Market Protocol.

24 Annex II Regulation 11 of the Common Market Protocol.

25 Annex II Regulation 12 of the Common Market Protocol.

As stated earlier, if the work permit or residence permit of the self-employed person is cancelled, it automatically affects the residence status of the dependents. However, there are certain circumstances where the dependents pass may be cancelled independent of the residence status of the self-employed person. These situations include divorce or nullification of the marriage; or if the dependent engages in employment or business.[26] The dependent is however given an opportunity to regularise his/her status (usually 30 days) failure to which he/she must leave the territory of the host Partner State.[27]

12.4.3 *Non-discrimination*

The Partner States are required to ensure that nationals of other Partner States are not discriminated upon on the basis of their nationalities.[28] In addition, services and service suppliers of other Partner States must get similar treatment as that accorded to similar services and service suppliers of the host Partner State unless the difference in treatment is aimed at ensuring the equitable or effective imposition or collection of direct taxes in respect of services or service suppliers of other Partner States.[29] Also, each Partner State must accord unconditionally, to services and service suppliers of other Partner States, treatment no less favourable than that it accords to like services and service suppliers of other Partner States, third parties or custom territories unless the difference in treatment is the result of an agreement on avoidance of double taxation or provisions on the avoidance of double taxation in any other international agreement or arrangement by which the Partner State is bound.[30] Nevertheless, the Common Market Protocol allows for “policy space” in that a host Partner State is allowed to implement measures necessary to protect public morals or to maintain public order; protect human, animal and plant life or health; protect its essential security interests; and secure compliance with laws and regulations which are not inconsistent with the Common Market Protocol such as the prevention of defective and fraudulent practices, the protection of the privacy of individuals in relation to the processing and dissemination of personal data, protection of confidentiality of individual records and accounts, and safety.[31]

---

26 Annex II Regulation 10 of the Common Market Protocol.

27 Annex II Regulation 10 (2) of the Common Market Protocol.

28 Article 13(2) of the Common Market Protocol.

29 Article 17 and 21 (1d) of the Common Market Protocol.

30 Article 18 of the Common Market Protocol.

31 Article 21 and 22 of the Common Market Protocol.

12.4.4 *Removal of Restrictions*

Removal of restrictions is essential for purposes of guaranteeing the free movement of services supplied by nationals of Partner States and the free movement of service suppliers of nationals from other Partner States. In this regard, the Partner States are required to identify the restrictions on the right of establishment and progressively remove the restrictions and not introduce new restrictions after entry into force of the Common Market Protocol.[32] Neither the Treaty for the Establishment of the East African Community (EAC Treaty) nor the Common Market Protocol define what amounts to a progressive removal and how the same can be uniformly implemented. However, Article 76(2) of the EAC Treaty requires the establishment of the common market to be progressive and in accordance with schedules approved by the Council. The reference to the schedules and Article 76(2) of the EAC Treaty are critical and decisive in defining the progressive nature of the services. The schedules of commitment on the progressive liberalization of services provide for elimination dates for market access and national treatment provisions for each liberalised sector and per each country.[33] The Council is therefore the only organ that determines the pace of the progressive removal of restrictions as per the schedules.

Removal of restrictions may also gradually and pragmatically be pursued through the principle of variable geometry. This principle is defined as a principle of flexibility which allows for progression in co-operation among a subgroup of members in a larger integration scheme in a variety of areas and at different speeds.[34] It is therefore applicable at the implementation stage once a policy or a protocol has been concluded consensually by all Partner States.[35] Variable geometry as a rule of flexibility would allow Partner States which are ready to remove some restrictions among themselves and allow the remaining Partner States to join them at a later date.

It needs to be emphasised that the EAC Treaty does not prevent bilateral or trilateral arrangements between and among the Partner States. It is submitted that such arrangements may enrich the cooperation and serve as a foundational base for a strong Community. Some activities under the ongoing Northern Corridor initiatives such as the abolition of work permits between

---

32 Annex III Regulation 10 (1) And Annex V of the Common Market Protocol.

33 Annex V.

34 Article 1 of the Treaty. See also Chapter 6 on the General Principles of EAC Law.

35 *In the Matter of a Request by the Council of Ministers of the East African Community for an Advisory Opinion*, Application No. 1 of 2008, EACJ First Instance Division.

Rwanda, Uganda and Kenya serve as a good example of multilateralism as well as the principle of variable geometry.

12.4.5 *Obtaining Licenses and Other Documents*

For a service provider to be able to provide services in the territory of the host state, he/she needs certain licenses and certificates depending on the national laws and regulations of the host Partner State. The host Partner State is required to ensure that the processes as well as procedures involved in obtaining the relevant licenses and other relevant documents are simplified and the requisite fees to be paid are harmonised.[36] With regard to issues such as proof of financial standing and character of the service provider, the host Partner State is mandated to accept the certifications issued by the banks of the national's Partner State and competent authorities.[37]

12.4.6 *Portability of Social Benefits*

Portability of social benefits is a great incentive for any self-employed person as it guarantees continuity in contribution. The EAC Partner States have different social security schemes operating simultaneously in each Partner State and therefore there is a major challenge with regard to harmonisation of national social security policies, laws and systems to provide for social security for self-employed persons who are nationals of other Partner States.[38] In this regard, transferability of the benefits of self-employed persons to another Partner State is not possible at the moment until the retirement benefit sector is harmonized and hence a major impediment to the realisation of freedom of establishment.

12.4.7 *Right to Join Professional Bodies and Trade Organisations*

Self-employed nationals of other Partner States should be able to join relevant trade organisations and professional bodies of the host Partner State under the same conditions and with the same rights and obligations as a national of the host Partner State.[39] In addition, the self-employed person from a Partner State should be able to vie for any position in the organisation or be appointed for any position available. If any high position in the organisation is connected with the exercise of public authority and hence reserved by any

36 Annex III Regulation 11.

37 Annex II Regulation 13.

38 Article 12 (2) and 13 (3b) of the Common Market Protocol.

39 Annex III Regulation 12 of the Common Market Protocol.

national law of the host Partner State for its nationals, then the position may be declared unavailable.

12.5 Legal Persons

With regard to legal persons, the following three issues must be considered in order to realise the right of establishment for legal persons in the EAC:

i. Non-discrimination
ii. Removal of restrictions
iii. Licenses and Certificates

12.5.1 *Non-discrimination*

According to the Common Market Protocol, companies and firms established in accordance with the national laws of a Partner State and undertaking substantial economic activities in the Partner State must be accorded non-discriminatory treatment in other Partner States, for purposes of establishment.[40]

The requirements with regard to National Treatment and Most Favoured Nation treatment which are applicable to natural persons are also applicable to legal persons.

12.5.2 *Removal of Restrictions*

Partner States are required to ensure that all restrictions on the right of establishment based on the nationality of companies and firms are removed and new restrictions are not introduced.[41] In the event that there are any restrictions in administrative procedures and practices resulting from national laws that restrict the right of establishment, the same should be progressively removed. In this regard, common restrictions such as those on setting up agencies, branches or subsidiaries of companies or firms and the entry of personnel of the companies or firms registered in another Partner State into managerial or supervisory positions in agencies, branches or subsidiaries should be eliminated.

40 Article 13(6) of the Common Market Protocol.

41 Article 13(5) of the Common Market Protocol.

12.5.3 *Licenses and Certificates*

Partner States are required to mutually recognise the relevant experience obtained, requirements met, licenses and certificates granted to a company or firm in another Partner State.[42] Nevertheless, the company or firm of a Partner State must register to be licensed in the host Partner State and disclose the shareholders, partners, directors and financial statements.[43]

42 Article 13(7) of the Common Market Protocol.

43 Annex II Regulation 9 (3 and 4) of the Common Market Protocol.

CHAPTER 12A

Freedom of Establishment and the Freedom to Provide Services in the EU

Armin Cuyvers

12.0 Services: The New Economic Epicenter

When the internal market was established, the European economy primarily revolved around goods.[1] The free movement of services, therefore, was considered to be a residual freedom that applied where the other freedoms did not.[2] In the age of Google and Goldman Sachs, this picture has drastically changed. Services now constitute over 70% of the European economy. Consequently, the free movement of services has also significantly increased in importance.

Considering the increasing importance of services for the EAC as well, this Chapter primarily focuses on the free movement of services as gradually developed by the CJEU. For as we will see, the enormous pluriformity of services, ranging from abortion to construction and from banking to healthcare, raises all kinds of challenges, certainly when one tries to apply the same standard internal market test to all of them. The freedom of services has also given rise to one of the most contested and contorted pieces of EU legislation so far, the Services Directive. In addition to services, this Chapter also covers the main elements of the freedom of establishment, which is closely connected to services.[3]

12.1 The Freedom to Provide Services

This section first discusses the freedom to provide services as laid down in the TFEU and developed by the CJEU. It subsequently outlines what are considered

1 See EU Chapters 9 and 10.

2 This original position can still be seen in the formulation of Article 57 TFEU, and interestingly the residual nature of services seems to have carried over to the EAC as well, see Chapter 12.

3 See for further reading amongst many others V. Hatzopoulos, *Regulating Services in the European Union* (OUP, 2012) or I. Liaonos and O. Odudu, *Regulating Trade in Services in the EU and the WTO: Trust, Distrust and Economic Integration* (CUP, 2012).

© ARMIN CUYVERS, 2017 | DOI 10.1163/9789004322073_025
This is an open access chapter distributed under the terms of the CC-BY-NC License.

restrictions to the free movement of services and how these may be justified. Lastly, the Services Directive is briefly introduced, as it forms one example from EU law that the EAC might not necessarily want to fully emulate.

12.2 The Freedom to Provide Services: Treaty Basis

The freedom to provide services is laid down in Article 56 TFEU:

> Within the framework of the provisions set out below, restrictions on freedom to provide services within the Union shall be prohibited in respect of nationals of Member States who are established in a Member State other than that of the person for whom the services are intended.[4]

Article 57 TFEU adds that:

> Services shall be considered to be "services" within the meaning of the Treaties where they are normally provided for remuneration, in so far as they are not governed by the provisions relating to freedom of movement for goods, capital and persons. (...) Without prejudice to the provisions of the Chapter relating to the right of establishment, the person providing a service may, in order to do so, temporarily pursue his activity in the Member State where the service is provided, under the same conditions as are imposed by that State on its own nationals.

As with the other freedoms, Article 56 and 57 TFEU only provide a very general outline. As a result, it was up to the CJEU to further develop several key issues, including the concept of a service itself, the demarcation between services and establishment and the question of who is allowed to rely on the freedom to provide services.

12.3 The Concept of a Service

Services are defined in the Treaty as all economic activities that are normally provided for remuneration and that are not covered by the other freedoms.

4 Article 56 TFEU has vertical direct effect, see already Case 33/74 *Van Binsbergen* [1974] ECR 129, par. 26. The horizontal effect has not yet been explicitly accepted by the CJEU, as will be discussed further below.

The definition of a service therefore turns on two points: 1) what counts as an economic activity for remuneration and 2) what distinguishes a service from the other freedoms, especially from establishment?

12.3.1 *An Economic Activity for Remuneration*

To qualify as a an economic activity it suffices that an activity is normally done in return for some form of consideration.[5] This consideration may be very little and does not even have to be in money, nor is it required that the service provider seek to make a profit.[6] The CJEU has also found that the consideration itself does not have to be paid by the person receiving the service. The only thing that matters is that the provider receives some form of consideration, not who pays it.[7] Consequently, the consideration may also be paid by a third party, including by the state. This is a particularly important extension of the concept of a service. It means that all kinds of semi-public services, such as healthcare or education, that are provided by private parties but paid for by the state or public insurance schemes, may fall under the free movement of services.[8] Even these sensitive political areas, therefore, have to comply with the EU rules on free movement, and may in principle not restrict foreign providers. Only where an activity is *fully provided* by the state itself, such as in the case of public schools run by the government, it does not constitute a service and therefore falls outside the scope of free movement law.[9]

More generally, the moral dubiousness or political sensitivity of an activity does not remove it from the scope of Article 56 TFEU. As long as an activity is legal and normally provided for remuneration, it qualifies as a service.[10] Consequently, the case law on services reaches some of the more contested

5 See inter alia Case 263/86 *Humbel* [1988] ECR 5365, par. 17, Case C-422/01 *Skandia and Ramstedt* [2003] ECR I-6817, par. 23, and Case C-76/05 *Schwarz and Gootjes-Schwarz* [2007] ECR I-0000, par. 38.

6 See Case C-157/99 *Smits and Peerbooms* [2001] ECR I-5473, paras. 50 and 52 as well as Case C-281/06 *Jundt* ECLI:EU:C:2007:816.

7 Case 352/85 *Bond van Adverteerders and Others* [1988] ECR 2085, par. 16, and Joined Cases C-51/96 and C-191/97 *Deliège* [2000] ECR I-2549, par. 56, *Smits en Peerbooms* par. 58.

8 Case C-157/99 *Smits and Peerbooms* [2001] ECR I-5473, par. 55, Case C-385/99 *Müller-Fauré* [2003] ECR I-4509, ECLI:EU:C:2003:270, par. 103, and especially Case C-372/04 *Watts* [2006] ECLI:EU:C:2006:325. Also see on this point G. Davies, 'Welfare as a Service' (2002) 29 LIEI 27.

9 Case C-263/86 *Humbel* [1988] ECR 5365. Case C-109/92 *Wirth*, however, determined that private education can form a service under art. 56 TFEU.

10 On the exclusion of illegal activities from free movement law see *inter alia* Case C-137/09 *Josemans* [2010] ECR I-13019.

and/or colorful outer reaches of human activity, including abortion, gambling and prostitution.[11] *Grogan*, for example, concerned students handing out information on UK abortion clinics in Ireland. At that time, abortions were illegal in Ireland, as was going abroad for an abortion. This prohibition was based on a moral conviction widely shared by the Irish population, and was laid down in the Irish constitution, yet the large majority of other Member States allowed abortion.[12] Sidestepping the fierce debate on the morality of abortion, the CJEU focused on legality and remuneration to determine if abortion qualified as a service:

> Whatever the merits of those argument on the moral plane, they *cannot influence* the answer to the national court's first question. It is not for the Court to substitute its assessment for that of the legislature in those Member States where the activities in question are practised legally.[13]

Abortion was a 'medical activity which is normally provided for remuneration' and was 'lawfully practiced in several Member States', and therefore qualified as a service.[14] As the relation between the students and the economic activity of the abortion clinic was too remote, however, in this particular case the students could not rely on Article 56 TFEU, providing the CJEU an escape from this moral, legal and political dilemma.[15] After this judgment, a Treaty protocol was adopted that provided legal protection to the Irish ban on abortion against free movement law, providing a targeted political solution without reducing the scope of Article 56 TFEU in general.

The CJEU has been equally been unwilling to limit the scope of Article 56 TFEU based on the social or political sensitivity of certain services.[16] Both

---

11 Case C-159/90, *Grogan* ECLI:EU:C:1991:378, Case C-268/99 *Jany* ECLI:EU:C:2001:616, or Case C-42/07 *Liga Portuguesa* ECLI:EU:C:2009:519. For a discussion on the ensuing struggle of the CJEU in the area of gambling see S.C.G. Van den Bogaert and A. Cuyvers: 'Money For Nothing: The Case Law of the EU Court of Justice on the Regulation of Gambling' *Common Market Law Review* (2011) 48 (4), 1175.

12 *Grogan*, par. 19.

13 *Grogan*, par. 20, emphasis added.

14 *Grogan*, par. 18 and 21.

15 Similarly see Case C-275/92 *Schindler* ECLI:EU:C:1994:119, par. 32, where the CJEU held that 'Even if the morality of lotteries is at least questionable, it is not for the Court to substitute its assessment for that of the legislatures of the Member States where that activity is practised legally.'

16 Case 33/74 *Van Binsbergen* [1974] ECR 129, Case 279/80 *Webb* [1981] ECR 3305, par. 10, and *Kohll*, paragraph 20.

healthcare and education, for example, have been brought under the scope of Article 56 TFEU, even where this brought the CJEU into contested terrain.[17] For example, as healthcare forms a service, individuals may in principle not be restricted from seeking medical treatment in other Member States, which also means that this treatment abroad should, under certain conditions, be covered by national health insurance.[18]

In line with the other freedoms, therefore, the CJEU has developed a very broad definition of a service, and in doing so has greatly extended the scope of Article 56 TFEU. A great many activities qualify as services and therefore are in principle entitled to free movement. As we will see below, however, in return for this very broad concept of a service, the CJEU is often more lenient when assessing restrictions on services in more contested areas.

12.3.2. *Distinguishing Services from Other Freedoms: Temporary Nature*

Article 57 TFEU provides that an activity only qualifies as a service where it is not covered by one of the other freedoms. The primary difficulty in this regard is to distinguish services from establishment.[19] Say for example that a Spanish architect moves to Austria for four months to assist in a large building project, renting a turn-key office space for the duration of his stay. Is he 'merely' a provider of services or has he established himself in Austria?

The essential difference between services and establishment is the *temporary nature* of the activity. Services are intended to be temporary and limited in time. Establishment, on the other hand, is intended to be more permanent and open-ended. Yet in practice it can be difficult to differentiate between the two. The leading, if not always conclusive, judgment on the difference between services and establishment is *Gebhard*, which concerned a German lawyer

---

17 See for healthcare *Joined Cases 286/82 & 26/83, Luisi and Carbone* [1984] ECR 377, par. 16, Case C-158/96 *Kohll* [1998] ECR I-1931) ECLI:EU:C:1998:171, par. 21, Case C-368/98 *Vanbraekel* [2001] ECR I-5363, Case C-157/99 *Geraets-Smits and Peerbooms* [2001] ECR I-5473, C-385/99 *Müller-Fauré* [2003] ECR I-4509, Case C-372/04 *Watts* [2006] ECR I-4325 and Case C-444/05 *Stamatelaki* [2007] ECR I-3185) ECLI:EU:C:2007:231. The Court does make a distinction, however, between hospital and non-hospital healthcare. See also J.W. van de Gronden et al. (eds.), *Health Care and EU Law* (The Hague: Asser, 2011). For education see Case C-109/92 *Wirth* [1993] ECR I-6447, paragraphs 15 and 16 and Case C-76/05 *Schwarz* [2007] ECR I-6849.

18 See also the discussion below on the justification of possible restrictions in this regard.

19 See for financial services and capital Case C-452/04 *Fidium Finanz* [2006] ECR I-9521, ECLI:EU:C:2006:631.

working in Italy.[20] On determining whether Gebhard had established himself in Italy or had remained a service provider the CJEU held the following:

> As the Advocate General has pointed out, the temporary nature of the activities in question has to be determined in the light, not only of the duration of the provision of the service, but also of its regularity, periodicity or continuity. The fact that the provision of services is temporary does not mean that the provider of services within the meaning of the Treaty may not equip himself with some form of infrastructure in the host Member State (including an office, chambers or consulting rooms) in so far as such infrastructure is necessary for the purposes of performing the services in question.
>
> However, that situation is to be distinguished from that of Mr Gebhard who, as a national of a Member State, pursues a professional activity on a stable and continuous basis in another Member State where he holds himself out from an established professional base to, amongst others, nationals of that State. Such a national comes under the provisions of the chapter relating to the right of establishment and not those of the chapter relating to services.[21]

In our example of the Spanish architect moving to Austria, therefore, the architect would still qualify as a service provider. At the same time, *Gebhard* does not mean that the provision of a service can never last for a very long time. In *Schnitzer*, for example, a Portuguese company carried out plastering in Germany for almost three years but still qualified as a service provider:

> Thus, 'services' within the meaning of the Treaty may cover services varying widely in nature, including services which are provided over an extended period, even over several years, where, for example, the services in question are supplied in connection with the construction of a large building. Services within the meaning of the Treaty may likewise be constituted by services which a business established in a Member State supplies with a greater or lesser degree of frequency or regularity, even over an extended period, to persons established in one or more other Member States, for example the giving of advice or information for remuneration.
>
> (...)

20 Case C-55/94 *Gebhard* ECLI:EU:C:1995:411.

21 See also Case C-131/01 *Commission* v *Italy* [2003] ECR I-1659, paragraph 22.

> It follows that the mere fact that a business established in one Member State supplies identical or similar services with a greater or lesser degree of frequency or regularity in a second Member State, *without having an infrastructure there enabling it to pursue a professional activity there on a stable and continuous basis* and, *from the infrastructure*, to hold itself out to, amongst others, nationals of the second Member State, is not sufficient for it to be regarded as established in the second Member State.[22]

No simple criterion or clear time limit exists, therefore, yet the establishment of infrastructure seems to be of particular importance for crossing the thin line between services and establishment.[23] Because of the grey area between both freedoms, it may in some cases be difficult to predict which of the two applies. Considering the significant convergence between the freedoms, however, it will usually also not make a real difference, in terms of outcome, which freeform applies.[24] Sometimes, the CJEU does not even deem it necessary to choose between services and establishment, and simply applies both.[25]

12.4 Who may Rely on Article 56 TFEU?

Once something qualifies as a service, the question remains which individuals are entitled to rely on Article 56 TFEU to demand the free movement of this service. When Article 56 TFEU was drafted, the scenario envisioned was that of a service provider traveling to a customer in another Member State. It would then be the service provider that would rely on Article 56 TFEU to contest any restrictions to her free movement.[26] In *Luisi and* Carbone, however, the CJEU held that not just service providers but also *service recipients* may rely on Article 56 TFEU.[27] This case concerned Italian citizens vacationing in

22 Case C-215/01 *Schnitzer* ECLI:EU:C:2003:662, paras 30–32. Also see Case C-458/08 *Commission v. Portugal* [2010] ECR I-11599.

23 See already Case 205/84 *Commission v. Germany* (*Insurance Services*), where the CJEU also clarified that establishment does not require a formal branch or agency, but that an office or permanent representative may suffice.

24 See EU Chapter 9 on the gradual convergence between the freedoms.

25 See for example Case C-136/00, *Danner* ECLI:EU:C:2002:558, or Case C-334/02, *Commission v. France* ECLI:EU:C:2004:129. For a possible combination of services and goods see Case C-403/08 *Football Association Premier League* ECLI:EU:C:2011:631, par. 79 or Case C-390/99 *Canal Satélite Digital* [2002] ECR I-607, paras. 29 to 33.

26 . See also the early case law of the CJEU fort his assumption, for example Case 33/74 *van Binsbergen* ECLI:EU:C:1974:131 or Case 76/81, *SA Transporoute et travaux* ECLI:EU:C:1982:49.

27 .Joined Cases 286/82 & 26/83, *Luisi and Carbone* [1984] ECR 377.

Germany and France, where they inter alia received some medical treatment. Because they had *received* services there, they could rely on the free movement of services to challenge Italian laws restricting the export of foreign currency:

> It follows that the freedom to provide services includes the freedom, for the recipients of services, to go to another Member State in order to receive a s service there, without being obstructed by restrictions, even in relation to payments and that tourists, persons receiving medical treatment and persons travelling for the purpose of education or business are to be regarded as recipients of services.[28]

As a result of this landmark judgment, *all* individuals that travel to another Member State and receive some kind of services may rely on the free movement of services.[29] Moreover, any national entities that provide a service to such visitors from other Member States may also rely on Article 56 TFEU. For example, if a group of Luxemburgish tourists come to Amsterdam and take a tour on a canal boat, both these tourists and the operator of the canal boat fall under the scope of the free movement of services, and can hence rely on Article 56 TFEU to challenge any restriction they may encounter.[30] As most people that travel to another Member State will receive at least some services, such as transport, lodging or restaurant services, this line of case law has greatly expanded the scope of Article 56 TFEU.

At the same time, the scope of the freedom to provide services does have its limits. To begin with, Article 56 TFEU only applies where a cross-border element is present. Purely internal situations, such as a small Hungarian law firm providing legal advice to a local Hungarian company, are not covered by the freedom to provide services.[31] Four possible cross-border scenarios can be envisioned.[32] Firstly, the service provider may travel to another Member

---

28 Joined Cases 286/82 and 26/83 *Luisi and Carbone* [1984] ECR 377, par. 16.

29 See in this regard also Case C-158/96 *Kohll* [1998] ECR I-1931, Case Case C-372/04 *Watts* [2006] ECR I-4325 and especially Case 186/87 *Cowan* [1989] ECR 195 where the specific services received by a British tourist did not even have to be specified.

30 See for example Case C-98/14 *Berlington* ECLI:EU:C:2015:386, paras. 25 and 26 and Joined Cases C-340/14 and Case C-341/14 *Trijber* ECLI:EU:C:2015:641.

31 Cf. Case C-108/98 *RI.SAN.* [1999] ECR I-5219; ECLI:EU:C:1999:400 or Case 52/79 *Debauve* [1980] ECR 83.

32 Compare also the four 'modes' under the Common Market Protocol Schedule of Commitment on the Progressive Liberalisation of Services (Annex V), as discussed in Chapter 12 par. 2.

State to provide a service.[33] Secondly, under *Luisi and Carbone*, service recipients may travel to another Member State to receive a service. Thirdly, the service itself may cross a border, for example via the internet.[34] Fourthly, the service provider and the service recipient may travel together to another Member State, for example with an Irish consultant joining his Irish client on a business trip to Malta.[35]

In addition, Article 56 TFEU only covers service providers that have the nationality of a Member State *and* are established in a Member State.[36] Service recipients, however, do not have to meet the double requirement of nationality and establishment. Even third-country nationals, therefore, can rely on article 56 TFEU when they receive a service from an EU provider.[37] A Rwandese businesswoman in Brussels may, for example, rely on article 56 TFEU when receiving lobbying services from a UK law firm. Lastly, it seems that Article 56 TFEU still only has *vertical* direct, as its *horizontal* direct effect remains uncertain.[38]

12.5 Restrictions on the Free Movement of Services

The concept of a restriction under Article 56 TFEU is functionally similar to the very broad concept developed by the CJEU in *Dassonville* for goods, and also focuses on market access.[39] The standard definition was provided in *Säger*, were the CJEU held that Article 56 TFEU requires:

---

33 Note that here it is not required that the specific service recipient in that other MS has already been identified. Mere offers of services, without any identified customers as yet, therefore also fall under the freedom. See *Alpine investments* par. 19. In addition, Art. 56 TFEU also applies if a customer moves to another Member State, and hence the service relationship acquires a cross-border element. See Case 15/78 *Koestler* [1978] ECR 1971) ECLI:EU:C:1978:184.

34 Refs *Alpine Investments* par. 22.

35 Cf. Case C-154/89, *Commission v. France* ECLI:EU:C:1991:76 or Case C-398/95, *Syndesmos ton en Elladi Touristikon kai Taxidiotikon Grafeion* ECLI:EU:C:1997:282.

36 See however also the other rights Union citizens and their family members may derive from their citizenship, as discussed in EU Chapter 11.

37 . Case C-484/93, *Svensson and Gustavsson* ECLI:EU:C:1995:379.

38 For vertical direct effect see Case 33/74 *Van Binsbergen* [1974] ECR 1299, par. 27. For the complex case law on horizontal or quasi-horizontal effect see inter alia Case C-309/99 *Wouters* [2002] ECR I-1577, par. 120, Case 36/74 *Walrave and Koch* [1974] ECR 1405 and especially Case C-341/05, *Laval* ECLI:EU:C:2007:809.

39 See EU Chapter 10 as well as Case C-390/99 *Canal Satélite* ECLI:EU:C:2002:34 and T. Connor, 'Goods, Persons, Services and Capital in the European Union: Jurisprudential Routes to Free Movement' (2010) 11 *German Law Journal*, 159. For the earlier case law of the CJEU on this point, which differentiated more between indirect discrimination and

> (...) the abolition of *any restriction* even if it applies without distinction to national providers of services and to those of other Member States, when it is *liable to prohibit or otherwise impede* the activities of a provider of services established in another Member State where he lawfully provides similar services.[40]

No discrimination is therefore required, the criterion only being if there is a *chance* that a national measure will make it more difficult to provide or receive cross-border services.[41] Importantly, this concept also covers any national rule that creates a so-called 'double burden' by replicating safeguards already in place in the home state of the service provider. Consequently, Member States may in principle not impose their own regulations on a foreign service provider on points where the provider is already regulated by its home state.[42] Otherwise, the mere duplication of national rules and requirements would in itself already restrict free movements, such as a free lance pilot that would have to make training hours in five different Member States.

Article 56 TFEU not only provides service providers the right to enter and reside in the Member State, but also to bring all staff they use for providing the service, including Third Country National (TCN) staff.[43] Accidentally, this inclusion of free movement rights for service providers and their staff also means that, if the UK wants to retain the free movement of services after Brexit, they would indirectly also accept a significant amount of free movement of persons.

Although the scope of the prohibition under Article 56 TFEU, therefore, is at least as broad as that under Article 34 TFEU concerning goods, the CJEU has not extended the *Keck* exception to services.[44] Consequently, as with the other

---

non-discriminatory measures, see S.C. Barnard, *The Substantive Law of the EU. The Four Freedoms* (4th edn, OUP 2015), 387 a.o.

40 Case C-76/90 *Säger* [1991] ECR I-4221, par. 12.

41 See also Case C-42/07 *Liga Portuguesa* ECLI:EU:C:2009:519and Case C-384/93 *Alpine Investments* ECLI:EU:C:1995:126.

42 See for example Case C-272/94, *Michel Guiot and Climatec* ECLI:EU:C:1996:147.

43 Case C113/89 *Rush Portuguesa* [1990] ECR I-1417, par. 12, as well as Cases 62/81 and 63/81 Seco *and Desquenne & Giral v Etablissement d'Assurance contre la Vieillesse et l'Invalidité* [1982] ECR 223, Case C-355/98 *Commision v. Belgium* [2000] ECR I-1221, and Case C-43/93 *Vander Elst* [1994] ECR I-3803, par. 21. For the question which labour standards and social laws apply, see Directive 96/71/EC concerning the posting of workers in the framework of the provision of services [1996] OJ L18/1 as well as Case C-341/05, *Laval* ECLI:EU:C:2007:809.

44 See for example Joined Cases C-34–36/95 *De Agostini* ECLI:EU:C:1997:344, Case C-275/92 *Schindler* ECLI:EU:C:1994:119 or Case C-384/93 *Alpine Investments* ECLI:EU:C:1995:126. For the *Keck* exception see EU Chapter 10, par. 4.1. See also W.H. Roth, 'The European Court

freedoms, the main legal debate takes place over the issue of justification, not so much over the existence of a restriction itself.

12.6 Justifications of Restrictions on the Free Movement of Services

As with the other freedoms, a restriction on Article 56 TFEU can be justified if it serves a legitimate aim in a proportionate manner.[45] For services as well, the legitimate aims allowed under Article 51 and 52 TFEU have been judicially complemented by an open category of rule of reason exceptions.[46] Under the rule of reason, the CJEU has already accepted a great variety of aims that may justify a restriction, including consumer protection,[47] cultural policy,[48] preventing abuse of free movement of services,[49] professional rules protecting the recipient of services,[50] or the right to take collective action for the protection of the workers of the host State against possible social dumping.[51] The one main limit is that purely economic aims, such as safeguarding revenue or protecting a certain economic sector, cannot form legitimate aims under the rule of reason.[52] In addition, as in the case of goods, the orthodox doctrine holds

---

of Justice's Case Law on Freedom to Provide Services: is *Keck* Relevant?', in M. Andenas, W.-H. Roth, *Services and Free Movement in EU Law* (OUP, 2002), 1.

45 See amongst many others Case C-678/11 *Commission v Spain* ECLI:EU:C:2014:2434, Case C-523/12 *Dirextra Alta Formazione* ECLI:EU:C:2013:831, par. 24 or Joined Cases C-369/96 and C-376/96 *Arblade* [1999] ECR I-8453, par. 35.

46 For the rule of reason exceptions see Case C-76/90 *Säger* [1991] ECR I-4221. On the strict application of the Treaty exceptions see for example Case C-3/88, *Commission v. Italy* ECLI:EU:C:1992:235, Joined Cases C-430 & 431/99 *Sea-Land Service* ECLI:EU:C:2002:364, Case C-158/96 *Kohll* ECLI:EU:C:1998:171, or Case C-465/05 *Commission v. Italy* ECLI:EU:C:2007:781, par. 49.

47 Case 220/83 *Commission v. France* ECLI:EU:C:1986:461, Case C-393/05 *Commission v. Austria* ECLI:EU:C:2007:722, or Case C-404/05 *Commission v. Germany* ECLI:EU:C:2007:723.

48 Case C-154/89 *Commission v. France* ECLI:EU:C:1991:76, Case C-125/06 *Commission v. Infront* [2008] ECR I-1451, or Case C-195/06 *KommAustria v. ORF* [2007] ECR I-8817.

49 Case C-244/04 *Commission v. Germany* [2006] ECR I-885, par. 38.

50 Case 33/74 *Van Binsbergen* ECLI:EU:C:1974:131, Case C-19/92 *Kraus* ECLI:EU:C:1993:125, or Case C-309/99 *Wouters* ECLI:EU:C:2002:98.

51 Case C-341/05, *Laval* ECLI:EU:C:2007:809.

52 See *inter alia* Case C-338/09 *Yellow Cab* ECLI:EU:C:2010:814, or Case C-347/09 *Dickinger and Ömer* ECLI:EU:C:2011:582. The risk of seriously undermining the financial balance of the social security system does, however, constitute a legitimate aim. See for example Case C-157/99 *Smits and Peerbooms* ECLI:EU:C:2001:404 and Case C-372/04 *Watts* ECLI:EU:C:2006:325.

that directly discriminatory measures can only be justified under Treaty-based exceptions, whereas the rule of reason can only justify indistinctly applicable measures.[53]

One of the main perculiarties in the justification of services, however, is the variation in leeway offered to Member States depending on which service is at stake. This leeway is especially granted via a more relaxed application of the proportionality test, which requires that a restriction is both *suitable* and *necessary* to achieve its objective.[54] These open criteria allow the court to increase or reduce its scrutiny, which in turn allows the CJEU to tweak the formally one-size-fits-all free movement test for different services. In more economic or standard commercial areas, and therefore the majority of cases, the application of the proportionality test is usually very strict, for instance requiring Member States to proof that there really was no less restrictive alternative.[55] In more sensitive areas, the CJEU sometimes satisfies itself with a more limited review, merely checking if the national measure is not manifestly inappropriate.[56] The clearest example of the significant leeway the CJEU can create for Member States, whilst formally remaining within the standard internal market test, can be found in the context of gambling, where Member States have received all but a *carte blanche* to regulate games of chance.[57] This variation in scrutiny allows for the necessary flexibility in such a diverse field as services, but of course also comes at a cost of legal certainty.

---

53 See for example Case C-353/89 *Commission v. Netherlands* ECLI:EU:C:1991:325, or Case C-451/99 *Cura Anlagen* ECLI:EU:C:2002:195, as well as S. O'Leary and J.M. Fernández-Martín, 'Judicially-Created Exceptions to the Free Provision of Services', in M. Andenas, W.-H. Roth, *Services and Free Movement in EU Law* (OUP, 2002), 163. For cases that do not fit this pattern, see for example Case C-118/96 *Safir* ECLI:EU:C:1998:170.

54 See for example Case C-49/98 *Finalarte* ECLI:EU:C:2001:564. The suitability test also includes the requirement of consistency, meaning that the measure may be internally inconsistent or in part undermine the very objective it is trying to realize. See Case C-243/01 *Gambelli* ECLI:EU:C:2003:597, par. 68.

55 Case C-678/11 *Commission v Spain* ECLI:EU:C:2014:2434, par. 43.

56 See for example Case C-262/02 *Commission v. France* (*Loi Evin*) ECLI:EU:C:2004:431, especially the reasoning in paras 33–39.

57 See for an overview S.C.G. Van den Bogaert and A. Cuyvers: 'Money For Nothing: The Case Law of the EU Court of Justice on the Regulation of Gambling' (2011) 48 (4) *Common Market Law Review*, 1175, and for recent developments which may herald some increased scrutiny, S.C.G.Van den Bogaert and A. Cuyvers, 'Let it be? The regulation and allocation of gambling licenses at the EU and Member State level', in: C. Adriaanse, F.J. van Ommeren, W. den Ouden and C.J. Wolswinkel (Eds.), *Scarcity and the State The Allocation of Limited Rights by the Administration* (Intersentia, 2016), 299.

12.7 The Services Directive

The negative integration achieved through Article 56 TFEU as set out above has also been complemented by positive integration, i.e. by EU legislation harmonizing national laws.[58] Of significant importance has been the sectoral legislation, which regulated particular fields such as telecommunication, energy or financial services, the discussion of which is beyond the scope of this Chapter.[59]

In 2006, however, a *general* directive on services in the internal market was adopted, the Services Directive.[60] This Directive became the subject of hitherto unprecedented levels of political contestation and protest, including French plumbers cutting of electricity to the holiday home of then internal market Commissioner Frits Bolkestein as they feared unfair competition from the dreaded 'Polish plumber'.[61] The main bone of contention was the 'country of origin principle' proposed by the Commission, which basically required mutual recognition of home state control. Such mutual recognition would remove many obstacles in one fell swoop, but was also perceived as undermining national protection of workers and service providers.

Under intense political pressure, the final Directive was severely watered down, many services excluded from its scope, and the country of origin principle scrapped.[62] The resulting Directive does not add very much in terms of substantive free movement rights, as the key Article 16 on free movement largely repeats Article 56 TFEU. Nevertheless, the Services Directive has affected the application of the free movement of services and also provides several relevant procedural rights to service procedures in terms of administrative simplification and cooperation.[63] Overall, however, the Directive is far from a success, and the EAC could certainly learn both from the botched political process and

---

58 See EU Chapter 9 for a discussion of this process in general.

59 See in this context also Chapter 16 on sectoral regulation in the EAC.

60 Directive 2006/123/EC of the European Parliament and of the Council on services in the internal market OJ [2006] L376/37. On the preceding debates, see Editorial Comments (2006) CML Rev., 307–311. On the evolution of the proposal, see J.-V. Louis and S. Rodrigues (Eds.) *Les services d'intérêt général et l'Union européenne* Brussels, 2006; O. de Schutter and S. Francq, "La proposition de directive relative aux services dans le Marché intérieur: reconnaissance mutuelle, harmonisation et conflicts de lois dans l'Europe élargie", (2005) CDE, 603–660.

61 On the heated discussions surrounding the Directive see Editorial Comments (2006) *CMLRev*, 307–311.

62 C. Barnard, 'Unravelling the Services Directive', (2008) 45(2) *CMLRev*, 323. On the scope and application see for example Case C-341/14 *Trijber* ECLI:EU:C:2015:641.

63 See chapter II of the Services Directive.

the eventual watered-down compromise. For example, one could first aim for the more limited but pragmatic objective of administrative simplification and cooperation alone, before trying any more radical steps such as introducing a country of origin principle.

12.8 The Freedom of Establishment

Article 49 TFEU contains the right to freedom of establishment, allowing natural and legal persons to establish themselves in other Member States:

> Within the framework of the provisions set out below, restrictions on the freedom of establishment of nationals of a Member State in the territory of another Member State shall be prohibited. Such prohibition shall also apply to restrictions on the setting-up of agencies, branches or subsidiaries by nationals of any Member State established in the territory of any Member State.
>
> Freedom of establishment shall include the right to take up and pursue activities as self-employed persons and to set up and manage undertakings, in particular companies or firms within the meaning of the second paragraph of Article 54, under the conditions laid down for its own nationals by the law of the country where such establishment is effected, subject to the provisions of the Chapter relating to capital.[64]

Article 54 TFEU then further clarifies the concept of a company or a firm:

> Companies or firms formed in accordance with the law of a Member State and having their registered office, central administration or principal place of business within the Union shall, for the purposes of this Chapter, be treated in the same way as natural persons who are nationals of Member States.
>
> 'Companies or firms' means companies or firms constituted under civil or commercial law, including cooperative societies, and other legal persons governed by public or private law, save for those which are non-profit-making.

---

64 The vertical direct effect of Article 49 TFEU was established in Case 2/74 *Reyners* [1974] ECR 631.

As a counterpart to the freedom to provide services, which is temporary in nature, establishment concerns a more *permanent* economic activity in another Member State. In the words of the CJEU, it allows an entity to 'participate, on a stable and continuous basis, in the economic life of a Member State other than his State of origin.'[65]

Article 49 TFEU covers both private individuals (the self-employed), and the legal persons as defined in Article 54 TFEU. Moreover, it covers both primary and secondary establishment, which means that it not just enables one to move completely to a new state to start a new company, but also to set up a second office or to create agencies, branches or subsidiaries in another Member State whilst keeping the primary company in the own Member State.[66] As with services, however, activities connected with the exercise of public authority are excluded.[67]

Just as the free movement of services, the freedom of establishment provides a right to market access and residence which also includes family members.[68] Member States, therefore, are in principle prohibited to adopt any measures that restrict natural or legal persons from primary or secondary establishment.[69] The justification of any such restrictions, as indicated above, is very similar to that of the free movement of services, requiring a legitimate aim that is pursued in a proportionate manner.[70]

One major debate unique to the freedom of establishment concerns the seat of undertakings and the freedom of companies under EU law to change their seat. In part this debate is caused by the fact that some Member States follow the real seat doctrine, whereas others follow the incorporation doctrine to determine the seat. So what happens, for example, if a company first establishes its real seat in Member State A, which follows the real seat doctrine, but then wants to move its seat to Member State B, which follows the incorporation

65 Case C-55/94 *Gebhard* ECLI:EU:C:1995:411, par. 25.

66 See for primary establishment for example Case 2/74 *Reyners* [1974] ECR 631 or Case C-411/03 *SEVIC* [2005] ECR I-10805. For secondary establishment see Case 107/83 *Klopp* [1984] ECR 2971 or Case C-212/97 *Centros* [1999] ECR I-1459.

67 As an exception, this concept is interpreted very narrowly as well, cf. Case 42/92 *Thijssen* [1993] ECR I-4047.

68 See Article 7 of Directive 2004/38.

69 See for examples *inter alia* Case C-161/07 *Commission v. Austria* ECLI:EU:C:2008:759, Case 208/00 *Überseering* [2002] ECR I-9919 or Case C-169/07 *Hartlauer* ECLI:EU:C:2009:141.

70 Free movement of services and the freedom of establishment even share the same Treaty justifications, and many of the same rule of reason grounds apply to both as well. Note in this regard that the Services Directive, as set out above, also applies to establishment, further demonstrating the similarities and connections between both.

doctrine, by merely incorporating its new seat in Member State B whilst keeping its real seat in Member State A? Although the case law is not fully clear yet, so far it seems that Member States remain free to determine which connecting factor they take into account for determining the initial seat as well as the connecting factor they require for maintaining a seat.[71] For the EAC this question may become relevant as well, if differences in incorporation doctrines exist between Partner States, and if companies would increasingly start to use the freedom of establishment, for example for tax purposes.

---

71 See especially Case C-212/97) *Centros* [1999] ECR I-1459, Case C-208/00) *Überseering* [2002] ECR I-9919, and Case C-210/06) *Cartesio* [2008] ECR I-9641.

CHAPTER 13

Free Movement of Capital and East African Monetary Union

Elvis Mbembe Binda

13.1 Introduction

The free movement of capital and the monetary union are closely correlated. Indeed, a successful monetary union is dependent on the effectiveness of capital movement liberalization.[1] At the same time, it is argued that fully liberalized movement of capital and integrated financial markets within a regulatory framework featuring economic policies create tensions in exchange rates, which in turn puts undesirable pressure on monetary policy-makers.[2] Therefore, the East African Monetary Union (EAMU) is a necessary step towards a more stable economic community in the East African Community (EAC).

The free movement of capital is provided by Article 76 on the Establishment of the Common Market, and the monetary union by Articles 82 to 88 of the Treaty for the Establishment of the East African Community. The interrelation between the free movement of capital and the monetary union has been acknowledged in the Treaty under Article 86 entitled 'Movement of Capital' under Chapter Fourteen on monetary and financial cooperation between EAC Partner States. This highlights how the free movement of capital—more than other common market freedoms—is crucial for an effective monetary union. This Chapter, however, is not intended to analyze the correlation between free movement of capital and the monetary union, but considering their close connection, it discusses both fields after one another, shedding light on the provisions governing these two areas in the EAC integration arrangement.

1 Catherine Barnard, *The Substantive Law of the EU: The Four Freedoms* (4th edn, OUP, 2013) 614.

2 *Ibid.*, p. 613.

© ELVIS MBEMBE BINDA, 2017 | DOI 10.1163/9789004322073_026
This is an open access chapter distributed under the terms of the CC-BY-NC License.

13.2 Free Movement of Capital

13.2.1 *Principle*

The free movement of capital is provided in Article 76(1) of the Treaty and further detailed in Articles 24 to 28 of the Protocol on the Establishment of the East African Community Common Market. However, neither the Treaty nor the Common Market Protocol provide a definition for "capital". Article 28 of the Common Market Protocol simply enumerates a non-exhaustive list of operations that should be considered as meaning "capital and related payments and transfers". These are direct investment; equity and portfolio investments; bank and credit transactions; payment of interest on loans and amortization; dividends and other income on investments; repatriation of proceeds from the sale of assets; and other transfers and payments relating to investment flows.[3] This list should be read in conjunction with Annex VI to the Common Market Protocol which enumerates specific operations that the Partner States agreed to liberalize in order to free the flow of capital.[4]

These operations may be categorized into four groups. The first group is related to securities operations which includes securities transactions that are controlled by regulations, the prices of which are regularly published, either by official stock exchanges (quoted securities) or by any other facilities (unquoted securities); some collective investments schemes; money market instruments; and derivatives.[5]

The second group is composed of credit operations meaning, "financing of every kind granted by financial institutions, including financing related to commercial transactions or to the provision of services in which non-residents participate".[6] This group also includes, mortgage loans, consumer credit and financial leasing, as well as back-up facilities and other note issuance facilities.

The third group consists of direct investments. Direct investments are investments of all kinds, by natural or legal persons, that serve to establish or maintain lasting and direct links between the person providing the capital and the entrepreneur or undertaking to which the capital is made available in order to carry on an economic activity.[7] Generally, direct investment involves

---

3 Article 28 of the Protocol on the Establishment of the East African Community Common Market, signed on the 20 November 2009.

4 Compare in this regard also the role of secondary law in de definition of capital, as discussed in EU Chapter 13 par. 2.

5 Explanatory notes of Annex VI to the Common Market Protocol.

6 *Ibid.*

7 *Ibid.*

participation in new or existing undertakings, the establishment and extension of branches or new undertakings belonging solely to the person providing the capital as well as the acquisition in full of existing undertakings, and finally the reinvestment of profits.[8] All these three alternatives should feature an intention of the performer to establish or maintain lasting economic links with the undertaking.[9] This is also the case under European Union law, where these types of capital movements are also considered to be direct investments.[10]

The final group concerns personal capital operations, which include, among others, loans, gifts and endowments, inheritances and legacies, death dues, damages, authors' royalties, etc.[11]

According to Article 24 of the Common Market Protocol, Partner States commit to progressively remove all restrictions and discrimination which could impede the above-mentioned operations, including current payment.[12]

It is noteworthy that, unlike other common market freedoms, which are an exclusive entitlement of the Partner States' nationals, Article 24(1)(e) of the Common Market Protocol opens the free movement of capital to any person who *resides* in the territory of a Partner State. This includes of course nationals, and any other legal or natural person legally living in the territory of a Partner State.

Article 24(1)(b) of the Common Market Protocol prohibits any form of discrimination based on nationality, place of residence or place where the capital is invested. Discrimination based on nationality and place of residence mean that any person of any nationality residing in the territory of the EAC is allowed to move capital within the Community. The question of what "the place where

8 *Ibid.*

9 The guidance provided by IMF and OECD should be taken into consideration to understand the scope of "lasting" and "direct" links referred to by this explanatory note. See IMF, *Balance of Payments Manual* (6th ed., IMF, 2008, updated version of 2011) 100; and OECD, *OECD Benchmark Definition of Foreign Direct Investment* (4th edn, OECD, 2008) 48.

10 Annex I to Council Directive 88/361/EEC for the implementation of Article 67 of the Treaty [1988] OJ L178. Furthermore, for the purpose of implementing Article 63 of the Treaty on the Functioning of the European Union [Ex Article 67 EC, repealed by the Treaty of Amsterdam], the list includes long-term loans with a view to establishing or maintaining lasting economic links.

11 The guidance provided by IMF and OECD should be taken into consideration to understand the scope of "lasting" and "direct" links referred to by this explanatory note. See IMF, *Balance of Payments Manual* (6th edn, IMF, 2008, updated version of 2011) 100; and OECD, *OECD Benchmark Definition of Foreign Direct Investment* (4th edn, OECD, 2008) 48.

12 Article 24(1)(d) of the Common Market Protocol.. This paragraph also highlights the interpenetration between capital movement and other common market freedoms.

the capital is invested" entails is not as clear-cut. It seems clear that this provision advocates for the free movement of capital from the territory of a Partner State to the territory of any other Partner State without discrimination. However, it is not clear whether this provision could be construed as compelling Partner States not to hinder the movement of capital when their residents want to invest in a third country. *Prima facie*, the response would appear negative, as there is no immediate apparent benefit for the EAC to facilitate such an activity, which appears contrary to the common market's aim of creating wealth within the community.

However, a reading of paragraphs (f) and (g) of Article 28 of the Common Market Protocol may suggest otherwise. Article 28 (f) and (g) define "capital and related payments and transfers" to include, the "repatriation of proceeds from the sale of assets" and "other transfers and payments relating to investment flows." Therefore, since it allows, among others, foreign residents in the Community to repatriate the proceeds from the sale of assets or to do other transfers and payments related to investment flows, it can be inferred that the free movement of capital—in terms of the Common Market Protocol—entails that capital is also free to leave the Community. The confinement of the free movement of capital only to intra-EAC operations would affect both inward and outward investment flows in the region. Obviously, such a provision would be contrary to the general expectation of EAC Partner States, who all rely on the attraction of foreign direct investment (FDI) to sustain their national economic development agendas. The free movement of capital between EAC Partner States and third countries would be beneficial, as among other things, it strengthens the control of capital towards third countries, as investors would not attempt to enter or exit the Community market via the most liberal jurisdiction to access their target Partner State.[13]

Therefore, it seems logical to interpret that the EAC lawmakers decided to open the EAC capital market to third countries.[14] Furthermore, Article 25(1)(d), in providing that "[t]he free movement of capital may be restricted upon

13 J. Snell, 'Free Movement of Capital: Evolution as a Non-linear Process' in Paul Craig and Grainne de Burca (eds), *The Evolution of the EU* (OUP 2011) cited by C. Barnard, cited *supra*, p. 584.

14 Note that the free movement of capital is also open in the EU to third countries but its implementation is closely regulated with strong available safeguard measures. C. Hjalmroth and S. Westerberg, 'The Contribution of trade to a new EU growth strategy: Ideas for a more open European Economy' (Part 1 A Common investment policy for the EU), Report, National Board of Trade, p. 11(29) online at http://www.kommers.se/upload/Analysarkiv/Arbetsomr.pdf (accessed on 24 April 2016).

justified reasons related to ... (d) financial sanctions agreed to by the Partner States", confirms the view that free movement of capital is applicable also to third countries.[15] It follows that since free movement of capital is allowed between EAC Partner States and third countries, the former would restrict this free movement in case they decide to take financial sanctions against such third countries. Essentially, the free movement of capital between EAC Partner States and third countries would foster the possibility of business expansion for EAC companies or firms to non-EAC countries. In other words, it could be asserted that this freedom encourages FDI outflows from the EAC. When EAC companies and firms invest abroad, it increases the bloc's competitiveness.[16]

In any event, Article 24(2) compels the Partner States to progressively remove all restrictions to the free movement of capital that existed at the entry into force of the Common Market Protocol and not to introduce new ones. According to the Schedule on the Removal of Restrictions on the Free Movement of Capital, Partner States committed to fully liberalize the movement of capital in the EAC by 31 December 2015. However, the reality on the ground suggests otherwise. In fact, a World Bank Report published in 2014, highlighted that, not only had the Partner States not removed barriers to the free movement of capital existing prior to the entry into force of the Common Market Protocol, new restrictions had actually been introduced.

This Report revealed that out of 20 operations pinpointed by the Common Market Protocol to be liberalized according to the free movement of capital, no EAC Partner State has succeeded to fully liberalize them all. Kenya, the best performer in this domain, has liberalized 17 operations out of 20. All the EAC Partner States restrict the movement of the three remaining operations. Those restrictions are related to the free movement of inward investments, consisting of, for example, the requirement of minimum capital for investors from other Partner States; or the shareholding of nationals in some businesses before they start operating in their territories; as well as the lack of legal framework for the sale or issue of derivative products locally by non-residents and abroad by residents. For instance, Tanzania and Burundi are the countries where restrictions are still preponderant on the free movement of capital, as only four operations have been liberalized.[17] This can be attributed to Burundi and Tanzania's strong reluctance toward the liberalization of capital movement, as displayed

15 Article 25(1)(d) the Common Market Protocolreads "The free movement of capital may be restricted upon justified reasons related to ... (d) financial sanctions agreed to by the Partner States".

16 C. Hjalmroth and S. Westerberg, cited *supra*, p. 8(29).

17 World Bank, *The EAC Common Market Scorecard* [2014], pp. 8–15.

by the fact that these two Partner States took the longest period of time to fully comply with the Common Market Protocol provisions. Burundi's compliance period ran till the end of 2014, while Tanzania's went up to 31 December 2015. In principle, the movement of capital should be now fully liberalized in the EAC and any existing restrictions should be treated as a violation of the Treaty to be addressed by the East African Court of Justice (EACJ).

13.2.2 *Safeguard Measures and Exceptions*

As much as EAC Treaty-makers provided for the free movement of capital, they were also aware of the volatility of this sector and the dramatic impact that a very slight disfunctioning could have on the Partner States' national macro-economy. This is why Article 26(1) and (3) of the Common Market Protocol allow any Partner State to take the necessary steps when the free movement of capital disturbs the functioning of its financial markets or when its balance of payments is "is in difficulties or is seriously threatened with difficulties".[18]

In addition, when the intervention made by a Partner State in the foreign exchange market seriously distorts the condition of competition among Partner States, Article 26(2) of the Common Market Protocol entitles other Partner States to take any necessary measures to counter the consequences of such an intervention. However, according to Article 27(1) of the Common Market Protocol, a safeguard measure taken pursuant to Article 26 should be temporary, proportional, reasonable, and should not discriminate among Partner States or be in favour of third parties. This provision does not however provide for a specific timeframe for what might be considered 'temporary'.[19] Moreover, Article 27(3) prohibits Partner States to adopt or maintain safeguard measures for the purpose of protecting a particular sector, in violation of other provisions of the Common Market Protocol. However, the lack of specification of these provisions may cause Partner States to adopt broad interpretations. For example Article 26(2) which specifies a 'strictly limited period' could be understood as meaning as long as the consequences of such intervention might last.[20]

---

18 Article 26(1) and (3) the Common Market Protocol.

19 Here it may be argued that the measure is temporary until the reasons it is taken to rectify are no longer present. This interpretation would be similar to the application of WTO law.

20 Nevertheless, paragraphs 5 and 6 of Article 27 seem to suggest that the temporariness of safeguard measures have been discussed during the drafting phase of the CMP but that in the end, Partner States decided to entrust the Council with the task of monitoring the necessity of their enforcement. By analogy, in the EU, free movement of capital received

There is no clear indication on the nature of the safeguard measures that a Partner State may take pursuant to Article 26 of the Common Market Protocol, except the restrictions provided for in Article 27(2) and (3). However, once a Partner State decides to take a measure to safeguard its economy from any disturbance or distortion in balance of payments that the free movement of capital may cause, Article 27(4) obliges it to send a notification to both the EAC Secretariat and other Partner States.

In addition to safeguard measures that could interfere with the free movement of capital, according to Article 25(1) of the Common Market Protocol, Partner States are also permitted to restrict this freedom for justified reasons: on the ground of prudential supervision, public policy considerations, money laundering, and financial sanctions agreed among them, provided that the Secretariat and other Partner States are informed. However, the Common Market Protocol raised the bar in allowing the use of restrictions based on any such exception as the concerned Partner State has to "furnish proof that the action taken was appropriate, reasonable and justified".[21] As indicated above, a Partner State that takes such a measure pursuant to Article 25(1) of the Common Market Protocol has an obligation to inform.[22]

Then some questions may arise as to the relevance of the requirement of appropriateness and reasonableness of any measures taken. Two questions remain: firstly, who is entitled to assess whether or not a Partner State's measure impeding the free movement of capital was really justified, appropriate and reasonable, and secondly, what would the sanction be should such a measure be found not to fulfill these requirements. There is no clear regulation on this at the current state of affairs under the EAC law. Unless a case is filed before the EACJ, the full implementation of the free movement of capital will depend, like other community freedoms, on the good will of Partner States.

a distinct treatment by the ECJ and the Commission—the latter sometimes opposing to full liberalization—than the other market freedoms (C. Barnard, cited *supra*, p. 581).

21 Article 25(2) the Common Market Protocol.

22 It appears however that except Burundi, all other Partner States have taken in the past measures restricting the free movement of capital either on the ground of prudential supervision, public policy or anti-money laundering without taking care of informing neither the Secretariat nor the other Partner States (EAC Common Market Scorecard 2014, pp. 44–54). It is worth noting that no Partner State has taken a restrictive measure against the free movement of capital on the ground of financial sanctions.

13.3 Problems Facing the Free Movement of Capital in the EAC Common Market

History has shown that, following trade liberalization between EAC Partner States, industrial agglomeration as a consequence of inequitable FDI inflow is more than hypothetical. Kenya's historical position as the favorite destination for European and Indian FDI during the colonial period is uncontested.[23] This preferential treatment permitted Kenya to become industrially more advanced than the other two founding Partner States, Tanzania and Uganda. While Kenya has been able to maintain its industrial development advantage *vis-à-vis* Tanzania and Uganda, the industrial gap between Partner States has been widened by the accession of Burundi and Rwanda in 2007, and later South Sudan on 15 April 2016. Consequently, the differences in Partner States' development levels remain significant.[24]

Nevertheless, it would be shortsighted to attribute the current differences in Partner States' development levels exclusively to historical decisions. Apart from the colonial decisions that favored the industrial development of one Partner State to the detriment of others, deep structural discrepancies in terms of factor endowments exist between them. The combination of historical events and disproportionate factor endowment distribution between Partner States predisposes the EAC to be an unbalanced region, especially with the implementation of a fully-fledged common market where goods, persons (including workers), services and capital enjoy total free movement rights. In other words, the implementation of free movement of goods, persons, services and capital would foster an inequitable FDI inflow between Partner States.[25]

This inequitable attraction of FDI would create polarization within the EAC, whereby one or two countries with the best combination of FDI determinants, i.e. market access,[26] economic growth, human capital stock, infrastructure,

---

23 Mbembe Binda, *Good Governance and Foreign Direct Investment: A Legal Contribution to a Balanced Economic Development in the East African Community* (EAC) (Uitgeverij BOXPress, 2015), 30.

24 *Ibid.*, pp. 213–240.

25 On more about the impact of regional integration on the location of industries, see P. Krugman, *Development, Geography and Economic Theory* (MIT Press, 1995).

26 It is generally agreed that regional integration affects FDI determinants. For instance, in a common market, a factor like market size becomes less significant as FDI determinant for a single country since companies would focus increasingly on regional rather than local market. See A. Mold, 'The Impact of the Single Market Programme on the Locational Determinants of US Manufacturing Affiliates: An Economic Analysis', [2003] 41 *Journal of Common Market Studies* 38.

regulatory framework, and agglomeration effects would logically attract more FDI than the others. In the new economic geography (NEG), the Partner States which present strong potentials to attract more FDI are considered as 'central' economies, while those with weak potential are called 'peripheral'. According to NEG, structural differences between central and peripheral economies affect their respective ability to attract industrial capacity.[27] Accordingly, *ceteris paribus*, the individual efforts of each Partner State to attract more FDI to foster its own industrial development could not change the balance of power between 'central' and 'peripheral' Partner States. On the contrary, such individual efforts would lead to a fierce intra-EAC competition for FDI inflow, which in the end would unfortunately increase the gap between the two groups. Following the agglomeration effect that underpins the NEG theory, 'central' Partner States would attract more and more FDI—which implies becoming more and more industrialized—while 'peripheral' ones would attract less and less FDI. With no doubt, such a situation would arouse old demons of inequitable sharing of the benefits of the Community between Partner States which compromised previous regional integration initiatives in the EAC.

The occurrence of such a 'central-peripheral' division in FDI inflow in EAC would lead to a Rambo situation.[28] According to an unfolding theory of regional integration between developing countries, "increasing of extra-regional FDI and export flows for one member state cause losses for other members" since FDI are "common pool resources".[29] Consequently, the most frustrated Partner State(s) would become a Rambo with the dominant strategy of defection. Depending on the importance or the number of defected Partner States, the frustration over unbalanced FDI inflow might lead to the collapse of the EAC.

---

27 See also A. Mold, cited *supra*, p. 38. For more details about NEG, see J.P. Neary, 'Of Hype and Hyperbolas: Introducing the New Economic Geography', [2001] 39 *Journal of Economic Literature* 536.

28 S. Krapohl and S. Fink, cited *supra*, 475. It should be recalled that the "term 'Rambo' does not refer to the Hollywood movie, but to a game-theoretical constellation of two actors. A Rambo situation is an asymmetrical game, where one player has a dominant strategy to co-operate, whereas the Rambo's dominant strategy is defection". S. Krapohl, K.I. Meissner and J. Muntschick, 'Regional Powers as Leaders or Rambos? The Ambivalent Behaviour of Brazil and South Africa in Regional Economic Integration' [2014] 52 *Journal of Common Market Studies* 880 referring to K. Holzinger, 'Common Goods, Matrix Games and Institutional Response' [2003] 9 *European Journal of International Relations* 173.

29 S. Krapohl and S. Fink, 'Different Paths of Regional Integration: Trade Networks and Regional Institution-Building in Europe, Southeast Asia and Southern Africa' [2013] 51 *Journal of Common Market* 474.

The threat of an EAC collapse over Partner State's frustration based on inequitable FDI inflow could be accused of overstatement. However, whatever its magnitude, the threat is real and should be taken seriously, at least for two reasons. The first reason is history-based. In fact, previous crises in the EAC were closely related to the inequitable FDI inflow between Partner States,[30] though it must be acknowledged that in the colonial era the terminology FDI was not yet commonly used. The second reason lays with the importance that is accorded to FDI inflow by both the Partner States and the EAC Treaty. For Partner States, it is commonly believed that FDI is the most appropriate supplement, if not alternative, to conditionality-tied Official Development Aid (ODA).[31] This belief motivates most countries, EAC Partner States included, to undergo various reforms to maximize the inflow of FDI in their territories. Consequently, it would not be surprising for a Partner State to vehemently oppose anything that could deter or divert the flow of FDI into its territory, even if it is a regional integration requirement.

As for the EAC Treaty, it mentions the attraction of investment as the means for the realization of a fast and balanced regional development.[32] To understand to the fullest extent the expectations put by the EAC on the attraction of investment, one should remember that the treaty-makers deplored unbalanced regional development as a key factor that caused "continued disproportionate sharing of the benefits of the community among Partner States", which is identified as one of the "main reasons contributing to the collapse" of the EAC.[33] In contemplating the attraction of investment as a remedy against EAC's chronic unbalanced regional development, treaty-makers themselves

---

30 Reference is made to the collapse of the East African Common Services Organizations (EACSO) in 1964 following the Kampala Agreement and the collapse of the former EAC in 1977, as also rightly acknowledged by paragraph 4 of the Preamble to the Arusha Treaty.

31 Despite the controversial econometric results of the impact of FDI on the host country's economy, developing countries—including EAC Partner States—have massively embarked in the battle to secure more FDI inflows. This battle is fought on all grounds, including in particular the reform of national policies and regulations and the availability of various forms of incentives to attract FDI. The attraction of FDI is even considered by some authors as the rationale for regional integration in developing regions. See for instance S. Krapohl and S. Fink, cited *supra*, 474.

32 Paragraph 11 of the Arusha Treaty preamble which reads "And whereas the said countries, with a view to realizing a fast and balanced regional development are resolved to creating an enabling environment in all the Partner States in order to attract investment...". See also articles 79–80 of Arusha Treaty that stress the need for cooperation in investment and industrial development for a balanced industrial growth within the community.

33 Paragraph 4 of the Arusha Treaty Preamble.

had already decided to erect FDI attraction as one of the pillars of the regional integration success.

However, when one confronts these Treaty provisions (where a serious case is made for the attraction of investment) to the practice, the paradox becomes intriguing. As early as 2006, Partner States adopted a well-elaborated five-year Joint Export and Investment Promotion Strategies (JIPS) where most of the threatening issues related to FDI attraction were thoroughly identified and adequate solutions were recommended. At the end of the JIPS implementation period, most of its provisions never came into fruition. The same sad observation could be made regarding the fourth EAC Development Strategy (EAC-DS) which advocated for the enactment of an EAC common investment strategy in tandem with the development of a mechanism for equitable sharing of benefits and costs of EAC integration by 2016.[34] The drafting of the EAC Industrialization Policy (EAC-IP) is another interesting example. While the EAC Treaty mentions the "lack of adequate policies" to address the issue of unbalanced development in the EAC, EAC-IP astonishingly overlooks to mention the differences in Partner States' economic levels as one of the key challenges for the industrialization of the region.[35] Furthermore, no reference is made to the key role that FDI location could play in the industrialization of the Community. Therefore, no single measure is suggested by the EAC-IP to tackle the issue of the uneven distribution of FDI, hence of industries, within the EAC common market.

The fact remains that, despite rhetoric recognition of the need to develop a mechanism related to investment attraction in the EAC in order to foster a balanced regional economic development, Partner States have paradoxically displayed an exasperating nonchalance for the adoption of an adequate framework and for its subsequent implementation.

This lack of regional regulation makes the common market a conducive area for a competition between EAC Partner States for FDI attraction. Unfortunately, as the EAC is characterized by striking economic discrepancies between Partner States, this intra-regional competition would be won

---

34 See EAC, EAC *Development Strategy (2011/2012–2015–2016): Deepening and Accelerating Integration* [August 2011], pp. 65 and 154. (Hereinafter 4th EAC-DS).

35 The challenges facing the industrialization in EAC are exhaustively listed in the EAC-IP. "Development disparities among Partner States is simply marginally listed in the table summarizing the threats to the industrial sector. For more details, see EAC, *East African Community Industrialization Policy 2012–2013* (2011) 9, available online at http://industrialization.eac.int/index.php?option=com_docman&task=cat_view&gid=38&Itemid=70 accessed on 10 February 2015 (hereinafter EAC-IP).

by one or two Partner States offering the best combination of FDI location determinants, including *inter alia* the economic productivity, the availability of qualified human capital, the existence of adequate infrastructure, and the overall observance of good governance principles. To these determinants, it is necessary to add the agglomeration effect professed by NEG. In confronting one Partner State against the other, a twofold observation is made. On the one hand, Kenya leads by far on five out of the six compared determinants, i.e. economic productivity, human capital, infrastructure, good governance and—of course—the agglomeration potential. On the other hand, Burundi seems to be worse off in this FDI attraction intra-EAC competition. As suggested by Krapohl and Fink, the likelihood of a "Rambo situation" (defection) is very high for an unbalanced regional integration like the EAC. Burundi and Tanzania have demonstrated in the past the applicability of this theory in the EAC by their reluctance to join some fast-tracked projects such as single-customs territory, single tourist visa, and the approval of national ID cards to be used as travel documents to cross their mutual borders. As no consensus could be found within the Community settings to fast-track these aspects of integration, Kenya, Rwanda and Uganda—now known as the Coalition of the Willing—decided to make a tripartite intergovernmental deal under the Northern Corridor integration projects. The defectors, Burundi and Tanzania, are allowed to join at their most convenient time. Although, at the beginning, it was perceived as sidelining Burundi and Tanzania, this kind of arrangement is nonetheless allowed by the Treaty under the principle of variable geometry enshrined in the Article 7(e), as one of the operational principles of the Community. Undisputedly, the three projects named above are not directly linked to the flow of inward FDI in the EAC. However, the behavior of some Partner States exemplifies the propensity of defection when regional integration does not, for one reason or another, match the national expectation.

The regional cohesion is even more vulnerable when the object of the competition is external, such as FDI attraction. In this case, if there is no common regional policy to streamline the behavior of member states *vis-à-vis* external actors, the likelihood of fragmentation is high. It is in line with this view that, in order to minimize the risks of defection based on Partner States frustration over the claim of inequitable FDI inflow, it is suggested that there is an urgent need for a regional common investment policy,[36] especially on inward FDI in the area of goods production and services distribution.

36 It should be noted, however, such a regional policy must be within a large framework of common commercial policy which, to some extent, may require the adoption of a common foreign policy that Partner States have failed to make so far.

The adoption of such regional policy is *sine qua non* for the harmonization of Partner States' laws and policies. It is therefore a necessary prerequisite for the establishment of any sustainable mechanism for equitable sharing of benefits and costs of the EAC integration. The regional investment policy would set common rules and principles for the admission and treatment of foreign investment in the EAC.

Since playing by the same rules does not necessarily guarantee the *bona fide* application of those rules by all the players—especially when they are diametrically unequal—it is imperative to have a central referee to monitor the game. For the EAC common regional investment policy to be effectively implemented, it is suggested that the competence on FDI in the production of goods and services distribution should be entrusted to a central regional authority, the Secretariat. This can be easily be based on the—so far unused—principle of subsidiarity contained in Article 7(d) of the EAC Treaty. Indeed, the EAC Treaty defines subsidiarity as a "principle which emphasizes multi-level participation of a wide range of participants in the process of economic integration". Of course, this short definition does not do justice to the rich content encompassed by this principle. To grasp this principle to its fullest extent, a leaf needs to be borrowed from EU law where the principle has been debated, clarified and tested in various areas.[37]

Indeed, in the EU, when it becomes obvious that an action can efficiently achieve its objectives only when it is taken at the supra-national level rather than when it is taken by EU Member States individually or collectively, this forms a compelling argument to transfer an authority to the EU, or for the EU to actually use any competences conferred on it. To assess this efficiency, consideration is given to the scale or the effects of the proposed action.[38]

The principle of subsidiarity has not yet received any substantial attention in the EAC. However, as experienced by the EU, it can be anticipated that the effective development of the EAC's operational framework will much depend on the applicability of this principle in the future.

As the Partner States' individual promotional campaigns for the attraction of FDI would lead to toxic intra-EAC competition, the most efficient alternative way would be to apply the principle of subsidiarity in order to transfer the competence to promote and, to some extent, to protect FDI, to the EAC

---

37 See also EU Chapters 2 and 4. Although in the EU the principle is often used to limit the use of a competence, one can also argue that it may be used to justify why the EAC should be presumed to have a competence and is allowed to use is, namely in those cases where the objectives stated by the EAC Treaty can clearly not be achieved at the national level alone.

38 See Article 5 of the Treaty on the European Union.

Secretariat. Obviously, it is foreseeable that some Partner States would resist that competence transfer as, for many, competence of an area as vital as the attraction of FDI could mean loss of national sovereignty. For this, despite the fact that Partner States decided themselves to give up some national sovereignty by the mere fact of joining the EAC, it is important to indicate that there are channels available in the EAC system for such decision-making. As, due to its predominant political character, the Council might be tempted to block such a competence transfer, the EACJ on the other hand has a very strong potential to play a role in furthering the pro-integration agenda. However, instead of putting the EACJ's legitimacy at stake in trying to impose a position that the primary players of the regional integration would oppose, good governance as a principle may help in reconciling Partner States' diverging points of view about the decision to transfer the competence on FDI in goods and services production from the Partner States to the EAC. On this specific issue, it would be sufficient for all Partner States to think about this transfer not from their individualistic national interests standpoint, but rather as a step towards better governance in the EAC. Better governance would be materialized only through the adoption of better regulations and better institutional framework in order to pursue the objectives of the community.

13.4 East African Monetary Union (EAMU)

13.4.1 *Journey to the Adoption of the EAC Monetary Union Protocol*

According to Article 5(2) of the Treaty, the EAC regional integration can be achieved through four milestones: the customs union, the common market, the monetary union and the political federation.[39] The first step has been achieved through the EAC Customs Union Protocol in 2005. The others remained in a state of dormancy until August 2007 when the EAC Heads of States decided during the 6th Extraordinary Summit that some extra steps should be taken to further the regional integration process. This Summit took a resolution that a common market and a monetary union were to be established by 2012.

Accordingly, the EAC Secretariat was directed to explore measures for the fast implementation of the Summit's resolutions. This led to the adoption and signature of the EAC Common Market Protocol by the Heads of State on 20 November 2009 before it entered into force exactly six months later on 20 May 2010 upon ratification by all the Partner States. Pursuant to this successful progress, in January 2011, the Council put in place the High Level Task Force (HLTF) with the special mandate to initiate negotiations on a protocol

39 See on these steps also Chapter 9 and EU Chapter 9.

establishing a monetary union. As time evolved, it became clear that having this protocol signed within the timeframe directed by the Summit would be very challenging. The negotiation progress was communicated to the Heads of States during their 11th Extraordinary Summit held on 20 April 2013.[40]

This Summit urged the Council to accelerate the drafting process of the East African Monetary Union (EAMU) Protocol in order to have it ready for signature during its scheduled 15th meeting in November 2013. Following this instruction, the HLTF worked so hard that in July 2013 a consensus was reached on all the articles of the draft EAMU Protocol which was then submitted to the Sectoral Council for approval.

On 25 October 2013, a final legal touch was given by the Sectoral Council on Legal and Judicial Affairs in order to prepare the draft of an EAMU Protocol for the signature of EAC Heads of States, which was done as planned on 30 November 2013.

13.4.2 *Highlights of the EAMU Protocol*

The EAMU Protocol entered into force in February 2015, after ratification by all the Partner States in accordance with its Article 30.[41] EAMU is assigned, pursuant to Article 3 of its Protocol, with the objective of promoting and maintaining monetary and financial stability with the aim of facilitating economic integration in order to attain sustainable growth and development of the EAC.

With the adoption of the EAMU Protocol, the Partner States commit to cooperate in monetary and financial matters, including: harmonization and coordination of their fiscal policies; formulation and implementation of a single monetary policy and a single exchange rate policy; development and integration of their financial, payment and settlement systems; adoption of common principles and rules for the regulation and prudential supervision of the financial system; integration of their financial management systems; harmonization of their financial accounting and reporting practices; adoption of common policies and standards on statistics; and adoption of a single currency.[42]

---

40 See in this context also the much longer road to monetary union in the EU, as described in EU Chapter 13.

41 Uganda was the last Partner State to deposit its instruments of ratification with the EAC Secretariat in early February 2015. See C. Ligami, 'Uganda ratifies the monetary union', *The East African*, 7 February 2015, online at http://www.theeastafrican.co.ke/news/Uganda-ratifies-the-monetary-union/-/2558/2616360/-/g05itfz/-/index.html (accessed on 23 April 2016).

42 Art. 4 EAMU Protocol.

Article 5 indicates the necessary steps to be taken by the Partner States prior to the monetary union. These include the full implementation of the Customs Union and the Common Market Protocols in order to ensure close integration of their economies through trade, investments, and factor mobility; the harmonization and coordination of their fiscal policies, and monetary and exchange rate policies; adoption of common principles and rules for payments and settlements; harmonization of their payments and settlement systems, and that of their policies and laws relating to the production, analysis and dissemination of statistical information; introduction of bands and gradual fixation of their bilateral exchange rates to facilitate the conversion of the currencies of the Partner states to the East African Currency Unit (EACU); and the integration of their fiscal systems and adoption of common principles and rules for regulation and supervision of the financial system.[43]

In order to realize an effective monetary union, the Partner States committed—in addition to the prior necessary steps mentioned above—to phase out any outstanding national central bank lending to its government and public entities and to attain and maintain at least for three consecutive years the following macroeconomic convergence criteria:[44]

- A ceiling on headline inflation of 8%;
- A ceiling on fiscal deficit, including grants of 3% of Gross Domestic Product (GDP);
- A ceiling on gross public debt of 50% of GDP in Net Present Value Terms; and
- A reserve cover of 4.5 months of imports.

The Council has full authority to develop measures to ensure regular monitoring, assessment, and enforcement of adherence to the macroeconomic convergence criteria and fostering discipline in the Partner states.[45] In turn, each Partner State has the responsibility of developing a medium term

43 Art. 5(1) EAMU Protocol.

44 Art. 6(1) EAMU Protocol. For the purpose of meeting the Macroeconomic convergence criteria, Partner States agree to monitor the indicative convergence criteria provided by article 5(3) which are (a) a ceiling on core inflation of 5%; (b) a ceiling on fiscal deficit, excluding grants, of 6% of GDP; and (c) a tax to GDP ration of 25%

45 Art. 6(2) EAMU Protocol. See however the difficulties caused in the EU by a reliance on political enforcement of budget norms by the Council of Ministers, as discussed in EU Chapter 13.

convergence programme to facilitate the attainment of the agreed macroeconomic convergence criteria.[46]

The EAMU is a progressive process that is set to run for 10 years starting from the entry into force of the EAMU Protocol in 2014. This process will be completed by the adoption of the EAC single currency in 2024, provided everything goes according plan. The name of the EAC single currency will be determined by the Summit at a later stage.[47] The single currency would be adopted by at least three of the Partner States that meet the prerequisites and the macroeconomic convergence criteria discussed above. Consequently, the Partner States which adopt the EAC single currency will form a single currency area in which that single currency will be the legal tender from a date determined by the Summit upon recommendation of the Council. However, before the single currency becomes the legal tender of the single currency area, the Council will have to fix irrevocable conversion rates at which the single currency will replace the current currencies of the Partner States.[48]

An institutional framework is provided by the EAMU Protocol to mainstream the establishment of the monetary union within the agreed timeframe. The first institution to be established for the purpose of EAMU is the East African Monetary Institute (EAMI) as a provisional institution in charge of the preparatory work for the monetary union.[49] The EAMI was supposed to be operational in 2015. The EAMI will be shortly followed by the setting-up of the institutions provided for in Article 21 of EAMU Protocol, such as the East African Surveillance, Compliance and Enforcement Commission (EASCEM), the East African Statistical Bureau (EASB), and the East African Financial Services Authority (EAFSA) in 2018. These institutions will carry out various activities and initiate relevant reforms leading to the harmonization of Partner States' monetary and financial policies, laws, and systems until the establishment of the East African Central Bank (EACB) in 2024.

The EACB will be established by the Summit upon the recommendation of the Council in order to perform the functions of a central bank in the single currency area.[50] It will form, together with the national central banks of the Partner States in the single currency area, a functionally integrated system of central banks, endowed with full independence *vis-à-vis* the Partner States.[51]

46 Art. 6(4) EAMU Protocol.
47 Art. 18(5) EAMU Protocol.
48 Art. 19 EAMU Protocol.
49 Art. 23 EAMU Protocol.
50 Art. 20(1) and (3) EAMU Protocol.
51 Art. 20(4) EAMU Protocol.

In this sense, the EACB will be mainly in charge of two things. Firstly, the EACB will deal with the formulation of the single monetary policy, binding on the Partner States in the single currency area, with the purpose to achieve and maintain price stability while contributing to the financial stability and economic growth and development of the community.[52] Secondly, the EACB will formulate a single exchange rate policy in compliance with the free-floating exchange rate regime chosen for the single currency area.[53]

It is worth noting that, as far as the financial rights and obligations of the Partner States in the single currency is concerned, Article 20(6) provides that they will be distributed among the Partner States in the single currency area in accordance with the financial key to be determined by the Council and which will be adjusted every three years.

Reiterating, the EAMU entails the formulation of a single monetary policy aimed at achieving and maintaining price stability. The Protocol paves the way for the introduction of a new single currency, which will be the culmination of the EAMU process. *Economic* policy-making competences as such will remain with the Partner States. In the EU, this model of the European Monetary Union featuring centralization of monetary competence while leaving economic policy with the national governments, and relying on mere coordination on their parts, has been criticized.[54] A single monetary policy for the EAC implies the loss of an important tool for individual Partner States to address country specific shocks: nonetheless, strict adherence to the above-mentioned macroeconomic convergence criteria has the potential to avoid these shocks altogether. Consequently, the introduction of a single currency in the EAC is one of the areas where the EAC should pay careful attention to the experiences in the EU, as it is imperative that it learns from the very costly mistakes that have been made there.

---

52 Art. 11 EAMU Protocol.

53 Art. 12(1) and (2) EAMU Protocol.

54 See for example Stefaan Van den Bogaert and Armin Cuyvers, "Of carrots and sticks: From sanctions to rewards in Economic and Monetary Union" *in* Bernard Steunenberg, Wim Voermans & Stefaan Van den Bogaert, *Fit for the Future: Insights on the EU from Leiden University* (Leiden University Press, 2016) (eds) 133.

CHAPTER 13A

Free Movement of Capital and Economic and Monetary Union in the EU

Armin Cuyvers

13.1 Introduction

Full economic integration requires both free movement of capital and Economic and Monetary Union (EMU).[1] Free movement of capital, moreover, is a prerequisite for EMU. Considering their close connection, this Chapter covers both free movement of capital and EMU in the EU. In line with the overall objective of this book, the emphasis of the analysis will be on the early days and the gradual development of the free movement of capital and EMU. In addition, this Chapter briefly analyses the devastating euro crisis that has been plaguing the EU since 2008. Considering its ambition to create a single currency, understanding this crisis and its causes is important to the EAC for two reasons. Firstly, the crisis uncovered several *structural flaws* in the way EMU has been set up in the EU. Secondly, the EAC may learn from the different measures adopted so far to address these structural flaws, even if real structural solutions have not been found yet. Even if the economic and political contexts differ in significant ways, the insights provided by the EU experience may hopefully help the EAC to avoid the staggering financial and political costs the EU has paid so far. In terms of money, the bill already exceeds two trillion euro (€2.000.000.000.000), not even counting lost growth and secondary effects, whereas the full political costs, perhaps including Brexit, are not even fully clear yet. Introducing an EMU, therefore, is a high stakes game, with real benefits, but also very real risks.

13.2 Free Movement of Capital

For a long time, the free movement of capital was the ugly duckling of the four freedoms. Whereas its siblings emerged from the 1957 Treaty of Rome as

1 C. Barnard, *The Substantive Law of the EU: The Four Freedoms* (OUP 2013), 579.

© ARMIN CUYVERS, 2017 | DOI 10.1163/9789004322073_027
This is an open access chapter distributed under the terms of the CC-BY-NC License.

full-fledged prohibitions, the then Articles 67 to 73 on the free movement of capital were markedly less ambitious.[2] Article 67(1), for instance, provided that:

> During the transitional period and *to the extent necessary* to ensure the proper functioning of the common market, Member States shall progressively abolish between themselves all restrictions on the movement of capital belonging to persons resident in Member States and any discrimination based on the nationality or the place of residence of the parties or on the place where such capital is invested.

Only those restrictions *necessary* to ensure the proper functioning of the common market, therefore, were to be *progressively* abolished. Article 68 had a similar ring to it, where it held that Member States should be *as liberal as possible* in granting such exchange authorisations as would still be necessary after the entry into force of the Treaty. Article 71 similarly required that Member States should *endeavour* to avoid introducing within the Community any new exchange restrictions on the movement of capital and current payments connected with such movements or to make existing rules more restrictive.

This restrictive approach to the liberalization of capital movements can be understood from the economic situation in Europe at that time. The Court of Justice of the European Union (CJEU) also respected the more reserved language of the Treaty provisions on capital, and at this stage did not apply the same expansive and effect-driven interpretation it applied to the other freedoms.[3] The limited Treaty provisions and the cautious interpretation by the CJEU left a gap in the free movement of capital, which was gradually filled with secondary legislation. It was not until 1990, however, that free movement of capital was really established as a basic principle of EU law by Council Directive 88/361.[4]

---

2 For more general discussion see *inter alia* Cf. J. Usher, *The Law of Money and Financial Services in the European Community* (OUP, 1994), ch. 1 or L. Flynn, 'Free movement of capital' in Catherine Barnard and Steve Peers (eds.), *European Union Law* (OUP 2014), 443.

3 See, for instance, Case 203/80, *Casati* [1981] ECR 2595. See on the general tendency for expansive interpretations of prohibitions and restrictive interpretations of justifications EU Chapter 9, and for specific examples EU Chapters 10, 11 and 12.

4 Council Directive 88/361, OJ [1988] L178/5, effective as from 1 July 1990. See on this process further J. Snell, 'Free movement of capital: Evolution as a non-linear process' in P. Craig and G. De Búrca (eds), *The Evolution of EU Law* (OUP 2011), 547.

13.2.1 *Directive 88/361 and the Concept of Capital*

Directive 88/361 prohibited all restrictions on movements of capital taking place between persons resident in Member States.[5] In line with the other freedoms, it only allowed several limited exceptions to this general prohibition. Article 4 of Directive 88/361, for instance, allowed Member States to adopt all requisite measures to prevent infringements of their laws and regulations, *inter alia* in the field of taxation and prudential supervision of financial institutions, or to lay down procedures for the declaration of capital movements for purposes of administrative or statistical information.

Directive 88/361 was replaced by the new Treaty provisions on capital in the Treaty of Maastricht and is no longer in force. Yet it remains relevant for the free movement of capital because the CJEU still uses the nomenclature contained in Annex I to the Directive to interpret the current Treaty provisions on capital, especially to define the concept of capital. The nomenclature classifies capital movements according to the economic nature of the assets and liabilities they concern, denominated either in national currency or in foreign exchange, and can hence also be a useful tool to interpret the EAC provisions on free movement of capital. The nomenclature covers direct investments, investments in real estate, operations in securities normally dealt in on the capital market or money market, operations in units of collective investment undertakings, operations in current and deposit accounts with financial institutions, credit cards related to commercial transactions, financial loans and credits, sureties and other guarantees or rights or pledge, transfers in performance of insurance contracts, personal capital movements, as well as the physical import and export of financial assets.

13.2.2 *From Ugly Duckling to Global Swan: The Treaty of Maastricht and Beyond*

The next major step in liberalizing the movement of capital was taken with the 1992 Treaty of Maastricht.[6] With Maastricht, the free movement of capital leapfrogged from the least developed freedom to the most far reaching one. Capital became the only freedom that also applies to third countries, meaning that it not only prohibits restrictions to the movement of capital within the EU, but also to the movement of capital to and from third countries, albeit with some extra exceptions. Later Treaties, including the 2009 Treaty of Lisbon, retained this broad scope for the free movement of capital, which now is contained in Article 63 TFEU:

---

5 See Council Directive 88/361 Article 1.

6 See also EU Chapter 1 for the broader importance of this Treaty for European integration, and capital and EMU in particular.

> 1. *Within the framework of the provisions set out in this Chapter, all restrictions on the movement of capital between Member States and between Member States and third countries shall be prohibited.*
> 2. *Within the framework of the provisions set out in this Chapter, all restrictions on payments between Member States and between Member States and third countries shall be prohibited.*

Capital movements include all financial operations essentially concerned with the investment of funds. Payments, on the other hand, concern transfers of foreign exchange which form the consideration for an underlying transaction.[7][8] As indicated above, both concepts are further fleshed out by the non-exhaustive nomenclature in Annex I of Directive 88/361.[9] Sometimes, moreover, it may be difficult to determine whether a certain activity, such as providing credit, falls under services, establishment or capital, as these freedoms often overlap. In such cases, the CJEU generally looks at the 'predominant' freedom, even if the case law is not yet wholly clear and consistent, and sometimes applies multiple freedoms simultaneously.[10]

In contrast to the original provisions, the CJEU has held that Article 63 TFEU has vertical direct effect.[11] So far, however, Article 63 TFEU does not seem to have horizontal direct effect.[12]

---

7 See on this difference Joined cases 286/82 and 26/83 *Luisi and Carbone* [1984] ECR 00377 and Case 308/86 *Lambert* [1988] ECR-04369.

8 Case 308/86 *Criminal proceedings against R. Lambert* [1988] ECR-04369.

9 For examples of categories that have given rise to doubts and litigation see Case C-318/07 *Persche* [2009] ECR I-00359, Case C-256/06 *Jäger* [2008] ECR I-123, Case C-513/03 *Van Hilten-van der Heijden* [2006] ECR I-01957, Case C-364/01 *Barbier* [2003] ECR I-15013, and Case C-35/98 *Verkooijen* [2000] ECR I-4071.

10 See for example Case C-196/04 *Cadbury Schweppes* [2006] ECR I-7995, and Case 452/04 *Fidium Finanz* [2006] ECR I-9521, Case C-244/11 *Commission v Greece*, Case C-212/09 *Commission v Portugal* [2011] ECR I-10889, Case C-326/07 *Commission v Italy* [2009] ECR I-02291, or Case C-251/98 *Baars* [2000] ECR I-02787.

Case C-212/09 *Commission v Portugal* (n. 54) para 43; Case C-112/05 *Commission v Germany* (n. 33) para 18 and the cited case law; Case C-326/07 *Commission v Italy* (n. 54) para 35; Case C-543/08 *Commission v Portugal* (n. 54) para 42.

11 See for the first time accepting this vertical direct effect Joined cases C-163/94, C-165/94 and C-250/94 *Sanz de Lera* [1995] ECR I-04821 par. 41, and later Case C-101/05 *Skatteverket* [2007] ECR I-11531 para 21.

12 See for example Case C-478/98 *Commission v Belgium (Eurobond)* [2000] ECR I-07587, Joined cases C-282/04 and C-283/04 *Commission v The Netherlands* [2006] ECR I-09141, Case C-112/05 *Commission v Germany* [2007] ECR I-08995, and C. Barnard, *The Substantive Law of the EU: The Four Freedoms* (OUP 2013), 586. For a different, if not as authoritative,

13.2.3 *Restrictions and Justifications for the Free Movement of Capital*

After the broadening of the Treaty provisions in Maastricht, the CJEU also started to apply the familiar expansive interpretation to the concept of a restriction in the context of capital. Any national measure that may affect the market access of foreign investors qualifies as a restriction under Article 63 TFEU, and is therefore in principle prohibited. This includes any measures that may deter or discourage foreign investors from investing in undertakings in a Member State.[13]

As with the other freedoms, however, restrictions on the free movement of capital may be justified if they serve a legitimate aim in a proportionate manner. The legitimate aims are partially laid down in the Treaty, but the CJEU also applies the rule of reason to capital, which means that Member States may suggest any reasonable public objective to try and justify restrictions that are not directly discriminatory.[14]

Partially because it also applies to non-EU Member States, the express Treaty derogations for capital are more extensive than those for the other freedoms. To begin with, Article 65(1)(a) TFEU allows Member States to distinguish between resident and non-resident taxpayers in relation to matters of taxation, reflecting the Member States' competence over taxation.[15] Article 65(1)(a) TFEU, however, is strictly interpreted by the Court, especially as far as comparability is concerned.[16] Article 65(1)(b) TFEU contains the general aims of public policy and public security that may justify restrictions, and is similar to the aims mentioned in Articles 36, 45 (3) and 52 TFEU. In addition, it provides that restrictions may be justified in order to prevent infringements of national law and regulations, in particular in the field of taxation and prudential supervision of financial institutions, and to require declarations of capital movements for purposes of administrative or statistical information.[17]

---

view see J. Rickford, 'Protectionism, Capital Freedom, and the Internal Market', in Bernitz & Ringe (eds), *Company Law and Economic Protectionism* (OUP 2010) p. 77.

13 See for example Case C-543/08 *Commission v Portugal* ECLI:EU:C:2010:669, par. 69, Case C-464/98, *Westdeutsche Landesbank Girozentrale v Stefan and Republik Österreich* [2001] ECR I-173, or Case C-439/97, *Sandoz* [1999] ECR I-7041.

14 See on the development of the rule of reason in general also EU Chapter 9 and 10, as it was first established in the context of the free movement of goods.

15 See also Case C-35/98 *Verkooijen* [2000] ECR I-4071.

16 See for example Case C-315/02 *Lenz* [2004] ECR I-7063 or Case C-559/13 *Grünewald* ECLI:EU:C:2015:109.

17 See for example Case C-439/97 *Sandoz* [1999] ECR I-7041, Joined cases C-358/93 and C-416/93 *Bordessa* ECLI:EU:C:1995:54, Case C-54/99 *Association Eglise de scientologie de Paris* [2000] ECR I-1335. In the recent restrictions imposed in Greece to protect its

When it comes to capital movements to and from third countries, moreover, the Treaty allows four additional types of restrictions, some to be imposed at the EU level. Firstly, Article 64 (1) TFEU allows Member States to maintain restrictions that already existed on 31 December 1993, and is known as the grandfather clause. Secondly, Article 64 (2) and (3) and Article 65 (4) TFEU allow the EU, and especially the Council, to adopt measures regarding capital movements with third countries. Thirdly, Article 65 (4) TFEU concerns Council approval of restrictive tax measures concerning third countries. Lastly, Article 66 TFEU allows the Council, on a proposal from the Commission and after consulting the European Central Bank, to take safeguard measures in exceptional circumstances where movements of capital to or from third countries cause, or threaten to cause, serious difficulties for the operation of Economic and Monetary Union.

As to the rule of reason grounds for restricting the free movement of capital, the CJEU again follows the open-ended approach developed in the context of goods, allowing Member States to put forward any public interest that may potentially justify a restriction. So far, for example, the CJEU has accepted *inter alia* the protection of the environment, the promotion of research and development, or the safeguarding public housing as legitimate aims.[18]

Again in line with the other freedoms, the real bottleneck for justifying restrictions remains the proportionality test, which requires that a national measure is both *suitable* and *necessary* to achieve its legitimate aim. Especially the necessity test, which requires that there is no less restrictive way to achieve the same legitimate aim, can be difficult to satisfy.[19] For example, systems of prior authorisation will generally be disproportionate as a system of *post-facto* declaration will often be able to safeguard the same public interests.[20] When defending a restriction, therefore, the Member State has to convince the CJEU that there really is no less restrictive measure possible that may achieve the same result, whereby the CJEU tends to be more lenient if it is obvious that

banks and financial system, see European Commission, Statement /15/5271, Brussels, 29 June 2015.

18 Joined cases C-515/99 *Reisch* [2002] ECR I-2157, Case C-10/10 *Commission v Austria* [2011] ECR I-5389, or Case C-567/07 *Sint Servatius* [2009] ECR I-9021.

19 In the context of capital, moreover, the CJEU sometimes separately applies legal certainty as a third criterion. See for example Case C-54/99 *Association Eglise de scientologie de Paris* [2000] ECR I-1335. For an example of a measure that was found proportionate see Case C-503/99 *Commission v Belgium* [2002] ECR I-4809.

20 Joined cases C-358/93 and C-416/93 *Bordessa* ECLI:EU:C:1995:54. See also Case C-483/99 *Commission v France* [2002] ECR I-4781, for a somewhat more flexible approach.

a national measure is *bona fides* and does not (also) serve protectionist aims such as protecting national champions or particular sectors of the economy.

13.3 Economic and Monetary Union: The Legal Framework Behind the Euro

As indicated in EU Chapter 9, an Economic and Monetary Union forms the most far reaching form of economic integration. Member States create a single currency (the euro) and transfer all monetary policy and significant parts of economic policy to the central authority. EMU can provide significant benefits, and becomes increasingly necessary as national markets become integrated. For example, EMU removes the problem of fluctuating exchange rates that may hinder free movement, and further enables and supports free movement of capital. At the same time, EMU can cause serious damage if not done correctly. Indeed, the euro simultaneously constitutes one of the crowning achievements and one of the most existential challenges facing European integration today.

The following section first discusses the long road towards EMU, followed by an overview of the legal structure eventually adopted to support the euro. Subsequently this section looks at the structural flaws in the way EMU has been structured in the EU, which have come into sharper focus since the euro crisis, as well as the attempts so far to remedy these flaws.[21] As the euro crisis is still far from resolved at the time of writing, no final conclusions can yet be drawn, but the EAC can surely benefit from the many insights generated in the EU so far, and the cautionary tales some of these insights tell.[22]

---

21 Parts of this discussion builds on the description given in S. Van den Bogaert and A. Cuyvers, 'Of Carrots and Sticks: What Direction to take for Economic and Monetary Union?', in: B. Steunenberg, W. Voermans and S. Van den Bogaert, *Fit for the Future: Insights on the EU from Leiden University* (Leiden University Press, 2016), as well as A. Cuyvers, *The EU as a Confederal Union of Sovereign Member Peoples, Exploring the potential of American (con)federalism and popular sovereignty for a constitutional theory of the EU*, (2013, Diss. Leiden), Ch 13. In addition I gratefully acknowledge the great research assistance provided by my (former) students Carlota Marianne Wolters Corte Real de Paula Coelho and Victoria Trifonchovska.

22 Clearly this Chapter can only provide a brief introduction to this vast, complex and contested topic. For further reading see *supra* 21 as well as the excellent discussions in K. Tuori & K. Tuori, *The Eurozone Crisis, A Constitutional Analysis*, (CUP, 2014), A. Hinarejos, *The Euro Area Crisis in Constitutional Perspective* (OUP, 2015) and F. Snyder, 'EMU-Integration and differentiation: Metaphor for European Union", in P. Craig and G. De Búrca (eds.), *The Evolution of EU Law* (2nd. Ed, OUP 2011).

13.3.1 *The Long Road to EMU*

Long before the Treaty of Maastricht in 1992, a single European currency was being considered. Already in 1969 very concrete plans were developed by the Werner Commission, which produced a detailed and well-considered road-map towards establishing an Economic and Monetary Union by 1 January 1981.[23] This plan suggested that EMU would be achieved in three successive stages, and found *inter alia* that EMU could only work if it was accompanied by a transfer of all monetary and significant economic competences to the EU. With the benefit of hindsight, the Werner Report already pointed to many of the risks and weaknesses that would later plague the euro, and therefore might also be of great interest to the EAC.

Although the Werner plan was actually taken over in a 1971 Council Resolution on the attainment of the EMU, this resolution was never implemented.[24] This failure was partially due to the economic circumstances at the time. Economic problems in the US caused the European currencies to float, taking away one of the central assumptions underlying the proposed EMU, namely the fixed exchange rates of European currencies. Instead of a Monetary Union, another mechanism was therefore adopted, which is generally referred to as the 'Snake'. The crux of this Snake was that the difference between the exchange rates of two Member States should never exceed 2.25%. Already by 1977, however, it was apparent that the snake had failed and was unable to stop the fluctuations between Member State currencies.

Besides these economic problems, the development of a real EMU was also hindered by political resistance to the transfer of economic policy to the EU level. Economic policy involves decisions on national spending, budgets and revenue. In other words, it concerns intensely political questions on how much money to spend and how to spend it, and consequently touches directly on national parliaments' power of the purse, the bedrock of parliamentary power. One can understand, therefore, that Member States proved rather unwilling to transfer control over economic policy to the EU, even if pooling part of their economic competences at the EU level might be necessary for EMU or beneficial in the longer run.

Even after the failure of the Snake, therefore, establishing a real EMU did not prove politically feasible. Two parallel tracks now emerged. Firstly, the European Monetary System (EMS) was introduced to combat the problem

---

23 For a more detailed overview of the entire process leading up to the euro *see* O. Issing, *The Birth of the Euro*, (CUP, 2008).

24 [1971] OJ C28/1.

of floating exchange rates.[25] The EMS created the Exchange Rate Mechanism (ERM) and the European Currency Unit (ECU). The value of the ECU was dependant on a combination of several Member State currencies. The ERM then contained some complex provisions to try and keep Member State currencies within 2.25% of their value as against the ECU. The ESM, however, did not prove robust enough to survive the currency crises of 1992 and 1993.

Secondly, a new process was started to establish full EMU in the medium term. This plan to create a currency union regained momentum in the wake of the Single European Act of 1986.[26] In 1989, a committee headed by Delors, then the very influential president of the European Commission, submitted its report on how to establish an EMU.[27] It proposed that EMU should be established in three phases. The first phase comprised the completion of the internal market and membership of states in the ERM, which did not require Treaty amendments. The second phase entailed the creation of a European System of Central Banks (ESCB) which was to be entrusted with the task of coordinating national monetary policy and conducting monetary policy. The third and final phase would permanently fix the exchange rates and introduce a new single currency under the auspices of the European Central Bank (ECB), which would also be established under the third phase. With its three phases, the Delors Report bears great resemblance to the earlier Werner Report. Crucially, however, Delors concluded that an effective EMU required far less transfers of economic policy competences to the EU and far less economic convergence than previously indicated by the Werner Report.

By requiring less transfers of economic policy competences, the Delors Report reduced the political costs of EMU. The Delors Report also came at an economically and politically opportune moment. Economically, the internal market project was close to completion and the Member States were experiencing high economic growth. Politically, the Berlin Wall had just come down, which fundamentally changed the nature and dynamic of European integration. Afraid of the political and economic might of a united Germany, France wanted a single European currency to bind Germany to Europe. Germany accepted to give up its very strong *Deutschmark* as a price for its unification, but in return did insist that the legal framework behind the new currency would follow the German model, which included a strong and independent

25 Bulletin EC 12–1978.

26 See on the broader importance of the SEA for revitalizing European integration and especially the internal market also EU Chapters 1 and 9.

27 Report on Economic and Monetary Union in the European Community (EC Commission 1988).

central bank and a primary focus of monetary policy on price stability. At this stage already, therefore, the euro was based more on political considerations than on economic ones, as well as on the rather optimistic assumptions in the Delors Report as to the economic coordination and economic convergence required to make a supranational currency work.[28]

With the political support of Germany and France, and on the basis of the Delors Report, the first stage of the EMU started in July 1990. In the mean time, an intergovernmental conference was set up to determine the necessary Treaty revisions to proceed to the second and third stages of EMU as set out in the Delors Report. This conference ultimately led to the commitment to a single European currency in the 1992 Treaty of Maastricht.

13.3.2 *Maastricht and the Birth of the Euro*

The Maastricht Treaty contained a clear commitment to EMU, and provided the Treaty amendments necessary for the second and third phase of the Delors Report. 1 January 1994 was set as the starting date for the second phase. Stage three, which included the creation of the European Central Bank and the introduction of the single currency, was to start no later than 1 January 1999.

Directly after the start of the third stage on 1 January 1999, the Council adopted the conversion rates at which the European currencies were irrevocably fixed and would later be exchanged for the single currency, which was still called ECU at this point. From this moment onwards, the ECU became a real currency, and exchange rate fluctuations became a thing of the past, even though Member States formally retained their own national currency. Even though the Dutch were still paying with their guilders and the Italians with their liras, in other words, these were in reality no longer different currencies, but rather different variants of the ECU, even if most people did not realize this yet.

---

28 On the economics of EMU, including the problem of an optimum currency union and the debates between monetarists and economists and between German ordoliberalism and French *dirigisme*, see *inter alia* K. Tuori and K. Tuori, *The Eurozone Crisis, a Constitutional Analysis* (CUP, 2014), D. Daianu, C. D'Adda, G. Basevi, and R. Kumar, *The Eurozone crisis and the future of Europe: the political economy of further integration and governance.* (Palgrave Macmillan, 2014), H. Snaith, 'Narratives of Optimum Currency Area Theory and Eurozone Governance' 19(2) 2014 *New Political Economy*, 183, B. Eichengreen, 'European Monetary Integration with Benefit of Hindsight', 50 (2012) *Journal of Common Market Studies*, 123, J. Rodden, *Hamilton's Paradox: The Promise and Peril of Fiscal Federalism* (CUP, 2006), W.E. Oates, 'Toward A Second-Generation Theory of Fiscal Federalism', 12 (2005) *International Tax and Public Finance*, 349, and R. Mundell, 'A Theory of Optimum Currency Areas' 51 (1961) *American Economic Review* 657.

The start of stage three also entailed the establishment of the European Central Bank (ECB) to replace the European Monetary Institute (EMI). This institute had done preparatory work during stage 2, but in phase three it was time for the independent ECB to step in and take control of the single currency. The ECB heads the European System of Central Banks (ESCB) and has the exclusive competence to determine EU monetary policy.[29] Member States, therefore, have lost all competences regarding monetary policy.[30] The primary objective of the ESCB is to maintain price stability. The ECB's primary instrument thereby is its control over the interest rate in the Euro zone. Without prejudice to this objective of price stability, the ESCB also aims to support the general economic policies in the Community, acting in accordance with the principle of an open market economy with free competition. Further ESCB tasks include conducting foreign-exchange operations, holding and managing the official foreign reserves of the Member States and promoting the smooth operation of payment systems. The exclusive right to authorise the issue of banknotes within the Community also lies with the ECB. Coins may be issued by the Member States, subject to approval by the ECB on the volume of the issue.

As of 1 January 2002, the euro was introduced in all Member States participating in the EMU and, after a short transitional period, became the only legal tender in these countries, fully replacing the former Member State currencies.

To join the euro, Member States had to fulfil several legal and economic requirements. Amongst other things, they had to establish completely independent national central banks and meet the 'convergence criteria' laid down in Article 140(1) TFEU and Protocol No. 13. These *inter alia* required a high degree of price stability, normal fluctuation margins (ERM II), and durable convergence of interest rates. Most famously, these criteria imposed the famous deficit limit of 3% and debt limit of 60% of GDP to ensure the sustainability of the government's financial position.

On 1 January 1999, so at the start of phase three, the Council, meeting at the level of heads of state and government, found that 11 of the then 15 EU Member States met these criteria and were allowed to join the euro. At this stage, Greece was not yet allowed to join, whereas the UK, Denmark and Sweden did not want to join. One and a half years later, however, in July 2000, Greece was already allowed in, joining therefore even before the euro would be physically

29 See Article 127 TFEU.

30 See EU Chapter 3 on the nature of EU exclusive competences. Please note though that the national central banks are represented in the ESCB, and therefore it is the independent national central banks that set EU Monetary policy, together with the ECB board.

introduced on 1 January 2002. Currently, 19 out of the 28 Member States have the euro as their currency.[31]

For Member States, joining the euro meant going beyond coordination of national economic policies. Most importantly, Member States that participate in the euro are under a binding legal obligation to keep their deficits under 3% and their debt under 60% of GDP. This stricter coordination, however, is a far cry from the real Economic Union envisioned by Werner. Member States still set their own economic policies, albeit that they have to do so within an increasingly tight framework of EU coordination and supervision. As we will see, it is precisely this gap between an exclusive EU monetary policy and an essentially intergovernmental coordination of economic policy that turned out to be one of the key flaws in the euro.

13.3.3 *The Asymmetry Between Monetary and Economic Union: The Fault Lines of the Euro*

As indicated above, the legal framework behind the euro is fundamentally asymmetric.[32] Monetary policy became an exclusive EU competence, but economic policy largely remained a Member State competence. Economic and monetary policies are therefore regulated at different levels, even though both are essential for a stable euro. The primary reason for this asymmetry is that Member States did not want to transfer control over economic policy to the EU, as it is so central to national politics. In addition, because economic policy is so connected to national politics, it also remains the question if the EU could be legitimate enough to wield far reaching competences over national economic policy.[33]

Member States, therefore, were fully aware of this asymmetry at Maastricht, but thought it could be compensated by two control mechanisms: market discipline and public discipline.

Market discipline was to be ensured by Articles 123 to 125 TFEU. Article 123 TFEU prohibits monetary financing, meaning that the ECB and national central banks are not allowed to provide financial assistance, directly or indirectly, to Member States. Member States, therefore, cannot turn on the printing presses

---

31 See for an overview <http://europa.eu/european-union/about-eu/money/euro_en>.

32 See also J.-V. Louis, 'The Economic and Monetary Union: Law and Institutions', 41 (2004) *Common Market Law Review*, 1075.

33 See on the limited capacity of the EU, due to its confederal basis, A. Cuyvers, *The EU as a Confederal Union of Sovereign Member Peoples, Exploring the potential of American (con)federalism and popular sovereignty for a constitutional theory of the EU*, (2013, Diss. Leiden), Ch 13.

when they need more money. Article 124 TFEU prohibits privileged access to financial institutions for the EU or Member States, again preventing them from getting easy money in this manner. Article 125 TFEU, the famous no-bail-out clause, prohibits the Union and Member States from assuming liability for financial commitments of other Member States. This clause was essentially designed to signal to the markets that each Member State would remain responsible for its own debts, and would not be helped by other Member States in case of default. If a bank lends money to Greece, therefore, it should only look at the financial situation of Greece, and should not expect Germany to pay back the loan if it turns out Greece cannot do so itself. Jointly, these provisions should ensure that Member States can only get additional money from the markets, and can therefore also be disciplined by those same markets. For if a Member States spends too much, and the markets know that this Member States remains solely responsible for its own debts, the expectation was that markets would ask higher and higher interest when buying the bonds of this Member State (i.e. lending it money). The higher interest would then make money more expensive, and force the Member State to borrow and spend less, so the theory went.

Public discipline was to be ensured via Articles 121 and 126 TFEU. Article 121 TFEU contains the multilateral surveillance procedure, which essentially tries to ensure closer coordination of economic policies via soft law instruments. Article 126 TFEU provides for the now infamous excessive deficit procedure.[34] Under this procedure, the Commission examines if a Member State has or will have an excessive deficit. If this is the case, the Council may issue recommendations to the Member State concerned. If the excessive deficits persist, the Council may eventually impose serious sanctions, including fines of up to 0.5% of GDP. The fines, therefore, are to be imposed by the Council, i.e. by the Ministers of Finance of the Member States themselves. Consequently, this system of public enforcement ultimately depended on a form of *political self-policing*. It required politicians to fine their colleagues for having excessive deficits, even as they knew full well that they might have excessive deficits themselves at some point in the future.[35]

---

34 See Article 126(1) TFEU and the now infamous Stability and Growth Pact, originally comprised of three elements, being a resolution by the European Council on the Stability and Growth Pact OJ [1997] C236/1, Regulation 1466/97 [1997] OJ L209/1, and Regulation 1467/97 [1997] OJ L209/6.

35 Compare for the inherent weakness of such systems also the extremely limited use of Article 259 TFEU, which allows Member States to start infringement proceedings against each other, as discussed in EU Chapter 8.

Despite the fundamental asymmetry at its core, the euro initially performed well. Problems arose, however, when the global financial crisis erupted after the fall of Lehman Brothers in 2008, and the euro came under increasing pressure. The main trigger for the subsequent euro crisis was the near bankruptcy of Greece. After previous fraudulent figures were re-examined, it turned out that in 2009 Greece's budget deficit reached 15.4% of GDP, more than five times the maximum allowed. Because of its financial difficulties, interest rates on Greek bonds rose sharply, threatening to cut off Greece from the capital markets completely. The critical situation in Greece, moreover, led to general insecurity and instability in the markets, also causing financial difficulties for other euro area Members, in particular Ireland, Portugal, Cyprus, and Spain. It was, therefore, feared that a Greek default would cause a domino affect, leading to further defaults in much bigger euro economies that could no longer be contained or absorbed. At the height of the crisis, a complete melt-down of the European economy and the euro itself was considered a very real possibility.[36]

The depth, intensity and abruptness of the euro crisis pinpointed several structural flaws in the fabric of the euro, and demonstrated that several political, economic and legal assumptions underlying EMU were incorrect.[37] To begin with, the financial markets had not disciplined national budgets. Quite the contrary, for a long time, most euro zone members had paid almost the same interest on their government debt as Germany, even though they were not as stable. Between 2001 and 2009, for example, even Greece could borrow against close to the same rates as Germany, even though Greece clearly had not become as economically developed as Germany overnight. Instead of disciplining Greek spending, the markets had rather facilitated a significant increase in borrowing and spending.[38]

Secondly, the mechanisms for public discipline had also failed to contain the economic policy of Member States within the agreed boundaries. The first signs of this failure had already been visible when in 2003 the Council, for political reasons, decided not to sanction France and Germany for their excessive deficits.[39] The overall failure of this political enforcement mechanism, however, becomes even clearer when one realizes that by now all but

36 Cf. M. Ruffert, 'The European Debt Crisis and European Law' 48 (2011) *CMLRev*, 1777.

37 See for an excellent overview of these assumptions K. Tuori & K. Tuori, *The Eurozone Crisis, A Constitutional Analysis* (CUP, 2014), as well as the literature cited *supra* note 28.

38 Note that if this windfall had just been used by Greece to refinance its debt and invest in structural reforms, the euro would have had a very positive impact. Instead, this golden economic opportunity was wasted largely on consumption, leading to bubbles.

39 See on this issue also Case C-27/04, *Commission v Council*, [2004] ECR I-6649.

two euro zone members have had excessive deficits at least once, but no fine has ever been imposed.

Thirdly, it became clear that the EMU framework did not contain any mechanisms to deal with crises, such as Member States in financial distress. The system was premised on the idea that private and public discipline would always work, and that Member States would not fail. As soon as they did, however, it turned out that certain strict rules such as the 'no-bailout clause' of Article 125 TFEU became untenable. By introducing the euro, the members of the Eurozone had become so interconnected that they could not allow any euro state to default. Even discounting any arguments based on solidarity, due to contagion and spill-over effects the costs of letting one state default would simply be too great. The euro, therefore, had created the need to help euro states in crisis, but not the means to do so.

Fourthly, the original EMU framework was preoccupied with preventing *public* deficits and debts. Consequently, it was not sufficiently capable of detecting and dealing with macro-economic imbalances, including imbalances in competitiveness and private debt. In addition, the assumption that the euro would automatically lead to sufficient economic convergence also proved wrong. As it turned out, macro-economic imbalances had only increased and significantly contributed to the crisis, for example in Ireland and Spain, where cheap money from several Western Member States had caused enormous bubbles. Many of the economic assumptions underlying the euro, which were *inter alia* relied upon to assuage worries about the fact that the EU does not form an optimum currency area, therefore also proved incorrect.

13.3.4 *Fixing the Euro?*

Even though it had started with a financial melt-down in the US, the euro crisis therefore demonstrated several structural flaws in EMU and the carnage these flaws could cause.[40] As abandoning Greece or the euro itself were politically and economically impossible, work was started to repair the EMU and to address, to the extent possible, the structural flaws that had been identified. This section briefly discusses the different measures adopted or proposed to address these flaws. As it can obviously not go into great detail, it focusses on the key objectives and assumptions underlying the different measures, as these will be of primary interest to the EAC. We start with a discussion of the crisis measures that were taken in the heat of the crisis, and then move on to the more structural measures adopted later on. These structural measures will

40 For a powerful and concise economic analysis, *see* B. Eichengreen, 'European Monetary Integration with Benefit of Hindsight', 50 (2012) *Journal of Common Market Studies*, 123.

be further subdivided into measures that focus on the EU level and measures that focus on the national level.

13.3.4.1 Crisis Measures to Save the Euro

The first crisis measures concerned direct aid to Greece, so as to avoid Greece from defaulting and potentially dragging the entire euro down with it. On 2 May 2010, the euro area Member States, together with the United Kingdom, Sweden and Denmark, established the first Greek Loan Facility (GLF) of €80 billion.[41] In addition, within one week of the GLF, the euro area Member States and the IMF set up a general €750 billion emergency fund to assist any other euro state that would run into difficulties. This emergency fund consisted of the European Financial Stabilization Mechanism (EFSM) and the European Financial Stability Facility (EFSF).[42] The smaller EFSM was an EU instrument, established by Regulation 407/2010 and based on the emergency clause of Article 122(2) TFEU. The EFSF, on the other hand, formally was not an EU instrument at all, but a 'special purpose vehicle' under Luxembourg private law, based on an international agreement between participating Member States: the crisis required a certain amount of legal ingenuity and flexibility at this stage. The EFSF had an effective lending capacity of €440 billion.[43] Financial assistance could only be given on the basis of strict conditionality, entailing *inter alia* the adoption of austerity measures and structural economic reforms. Recourse to the EFSF, therefore, meant accepting far reaching influence by the creditors on national economic policy, and probably painful spending cuts and other austerity measures. In addition to Greece, who was the first to receive assistance from the EFSF, Ireland, Portugal, Cyprus, and Spain also received financial assistance from these emergency funds at some point, often to bail out their own banks.

---

41 The GLF is founded on two agreements concluded on 8 May 2010, available at: <www.eurocrisismonitor.com/Downloads/GLF.pdf>. The first concerns an inter-creditor agreement among the euro area lender Member States, containing the modalities of their involvement in the loan facility. The second forms a loan facility agreement which sets out the provisions governing the pooled bilateral loans.

42 The basic arrangements concerning the European System of Financial Supervision (EFSF) are laid down in a framework agreement between the EFSF as a legal entity and the euro area Member States as its shareholders. Statement by the Eurogroup, Brussels, 2 May 2010. See also A. de Gregorio Merino, 'Legal Developments in the Economic and Monetary Union During the Debt Crisis: The Mechanisms of Financial Assistance', 49 (2012) *CMLRev*, 1613.

43 European Financial Stability Facility, EFSF Framework Agreement, available at: <www.efsf.europa.eu/about/legal-documents/index.htm> (last visited on 1 February 2016).

In addition to these emergency funds, the ECB also played a vital role in crisis management, often throwing its full weight behind the euro. It was ECB president Mario Draghi who famously pledged that the ECB would 'do whatever it takes to preserve the euro' and that 'it will be enough'. Even though the ECB could never directly support euro states in need, it did commit trillions of euros in buying up bonds on the secondary market and other unconventional monetary instruments, relieving pressure on euro states in distress and calming markets.[44]

These ad hoc bilateral loans, emergency funds and interventions by the ECB managed to prevent a complete melt-down, but it quickly became obvious that overcoming the crisis required more structural solutions as well, both at the EU and at the national level.[45]

13.3.4.2 Structural Measures at the EU Level

One of the first structural steps taken at the EU level was to set up a permanent fund to support euro states in crisis, also to signal to the markets that the EU was committed to the euro and to stop speculation against the single currency. The creation of a permanent stability mechanism first required a simplified Treaty revision to insert a new third paragraph in Article 136 TFEU, actually allowing the creation of such a permanent fund by the Member States. On 2 February 2012, even before this new Treaty provision formally entered into effect, the European Stability Mechanism (ESM) was established in an international treaty concluded by the euro Member States, and eventually given an effective lending capacity of €750 billion. Like the EFSF, however, it only provides financial assistance on the basis of strict conditionality. In light of the, often far reaching, conditions that must be met, Member States will only ask for assistance from the ESM where they have no other options left. This is also intended to counter the moral hazard of States simply spending too much as they expect to be bailed out by the ESM anyway.[46]

---

44 For the legal tension this created between the ECB, the CJEU and the German Constitutional Court see the OMT Saga, played out in BVerfGE 2 BvR 2728/13 (2014) OMT (referral CJEU), Case C-62/14, *Gauweiler* (OMT), ECLI:EU:C:2015:400, and BVerfGE, 2 BvR 2728/13, 2 BvR 2729/13, 2 BvR 2730/13, 2 BvR 2731/13, 2 BvE 13/13 (2016) *OMT* (final decision).

45 See also K. Armstrong, 'The New Governance of EU Fiscal Discipline', 38 (2013) *European Law Review*. 601, or S.C.G. Van den Bogaert and V. Borger, 'Twenty Years After Maastricht: The Coming of Age of the EMU?', in M. de Visser & A.P. van der Mei (eds.), *The Treaty on European Union 1993–2013: Reflections from Maastricht* (Intersentia, 2014), 451.

46 Cf on this risk T.J. Goodspeed, 'Bailouts in a Federation,' 9 (2012) *International Tax and Public Finance*, 409.

In addition, measures were adopted to strengthen the control over Member States' budgets and to improve overall economic policy coordination. For, if the fundamental asymmetry between economic and monetary union could not be removed on the short or medium term, the idea was to make EU control over national economic policy more effective, in a sense trying to fix the system of public control introduced at Maastricht. One important initiative in this regard is the so-called 'six-pack', which consists of six legislative measures that jointly increase budgetary discipline and create a system to prevent and detect macro-economic imbalances.[47] The six-pack inter alia introduced the possibility to impose sanctions for excessive deficits by reversed qualified majority voting in the Council.[48] Under this new system, any sanctions that the Commission recommends for excessive deficits will be adopted unless a qualified majority in the Council votes *against* the imposition of fines within 10 days.[49] This mechanism increases the power of the Commission, as in theory it should be hard to find a qualified majority to block sanctions. In practice, however, even under this new mechanism no sanctions have yet been imposed, despite several Member States showing excessive deficits.

The six-pack also created the possibility of imposing sanctions in the *preventive* arm of the Stability and Growth Pact (SGP) and in the newly created macro-economic imbalance procedure. It also strengthened the corrective arm of the SGP, allowing sanctions that range from an interest-bearing deposit of 0.2% of GDP to an irreversible fine of 0.2% of GDP.[50] In light of the important role played by fraud in the Greek tragedy, Article 8 of Regulation

47 Regulation (EU) 1173/2011 of the European Parliament and of the Council of 16 November 2011 on the effective enforcement of budgetary surveillance in the euro area OJ 2011 L306/1; Regulation (EU) 1174/2011 of the European Parliament and of the Council of 16 November 2011 on enforcement measures to correct excessive macro-economic imbalances in the euro area OJ 2011 L306/8; Reg. 1175/2011; Regulation (EU) 1176/2011 of the European Parliament and of the Council of 16 November 2011 on the prevention and correction of macro-economic imbalances OJ 2011 L306/25; Reg. 1177/2011; Council Directive 2011/85/EU of 8 November 2011 on requirements for budgetary frameworks of the Member States OJ 2011 L306/41.

48 See Articles 4(2), 5(2) and 6(2) of Regulation 1173/2011. The system of reverse qualified majority voting has also been introduced in the macro-economic imbalances procedure in relation to euro area Member States. See Article 3(3) of Regulation 1174/2011.

49 R. Palmstorfer, 'The Reverse Majority Voting under the 'Six Pack': A Bad Turn for the Union?' 20 (2013) *European Law Journal*, 186.

50 See especially Regulation 1173/2011. For macro-economic imbalances see Regulation 1176/2011.

1173/2011 also introduced a possible fine of up to 0.2% of GDP for the manipulation of statistics.

In addition to the six-pack, a so called two-pack was also adopted in May 2013.[51] These two regulations primarily aim to improve the coordination of national budgets, and *inter alia* help establish the 'European Semester'. Under the European Semester, euro zone members must submit their draft budgets to the Commission and the Eurogroup following a standard time-line, and take Commission and Council opinions and recommendations into account when adopting their final budgets. This mechanism ensures that the Commission and the Council already become involved in the national budget procedure at a relatively early stage. The opinions and recommendations of the Commission and Council are not formally binding, but the main idea is that increased transparency, supervision and dialogue will guide Member States towards an economic policy that is more in line with their EU obligations.

13.3.4.3 Structural Measures at the National Level

One interesting measure that has also been adopted so far does not focus on the EU level, but rather tries to improve economic policy and budgetary controls at the national level. In 2012, all EU Member States except the UK and the Czech Republic signed the Treaty on Stability, Coordination and Governance (TSCG), also known as the Fiscal Compact. Although the TSCG was rushed through to appease financial markets, and therefore has many limitations, the intuition behind the Treaty is valuable.

The TSCG firstly formulates the so-called 'Golden Rule', which requires all parties to create a rule of *national* law which demands that the budget is either balanced or in surplus. This rule, moreover, must either be incorporated in the constitution, or else in a law guaranteeing equivalent effectiveness to a constitutional rule.[52] The central idea is that the only legal instrument legitimate and powerful enough to limit national spending is the national constitution, as all lower legislation can be set aside by the same government and parliament

---

51 Regulation 472/2013 on the strengthening of economic and budgetary surveillance of Member States in the euro area experiencing or threatened with serious difficulties with respect to their financial stability, OJ 2013 L140/1 and Regulation 473/2013 on common provisions for monitoring and assessing draft budgetary plans and ensuring the correction of excessive deficit of the Member States in the euro area, OJ 2013 L 140/11.

52 SCG Treaty Art. 3(1)(a) and (b). For discussion see M. Adams, F. Fabbrini, and P. Larouche (eds), *The Constitutionalization of European Budgetary Constraints* (Oxford, Hart 2014). SCG Treaty Art. 3(1)(e). Note that this obligation, and hence the Golden Rule, only concerns the deficit, and not the debt ratio.

adopting the budget. In addition to the golden budget rule, the signatories of the TSCG are also obligated to create a national correction mechanism that kicks in whenever an excessive deficit nevertheless occurs.[53] Lastly, and together with the two-pack, the TSCG also requires that states create independent Fiscal Councils at the national level, which must monitor national economic policy.

The TSCG is often dismissed as a mere political gesture, largely intended to calm markets and acquire the support of Germany and the ECB for the creation of the ESM.[54] Indeed the TSCG has multiple flaws and has not been implemented properly in most contracting states.[55] However, at the same time, it also represents a valuable political intuition that as long as the EU lacks the democratic legitimacy to directly control budgets, effective budget controls must be primarily established at the national level, and then perhaps supported by secondary EU controls.[56] Considering the political realities in the EAC, including the sensitivities surrounding sovereignty, such a more confederal approach to budget discipline might also fit better in the EAC, or at least provide an interesting addition to more centralizing measures.

13.3.5 *EMU and the Road Ahead*

As indicated above, all the measures adopted so far have strengthened EMU in the EU, but have not yet addressed the fundamental asymmetry at the heart of EMU. Economic policy still remains a national competence, even if supervision and coordination has improved. Consequently, the debate continues as to the future of the euro and EMU in Europe. Three general schools of thought can be distinguished in this debate. On the one extreme is the school that reasons that a monetary union can only survive as part of a full political and economic

53 SCG Treaty Art. 3(1)(e).

54 Cf for example S. Peers, 'The Stability Treaty: Permanent Austerity or Gesture Politics?', 2012 *EuConst*, 404.

55 See for instance P. Craig, 'The Stability, Coordination and Governance Treaty: Principle, Politics and Pragmatism', (2012) *European Law Review*, 231, J-H. Reestman, 'The Fiscal Compact: Europe's Not Always Able to Speak German. On the Dutch Implementing Act and the Hazardous Interpretation of the Implementation Duty in Article 3(2) Fiscal Compact', (2013) 9 *European Constitutional Law Review*, 480, or H.T. Burret and J. Schnellenbach, 'Implementation of the fiscal compact in the Euro area Member States: Expertise on behalf of the German Council of Economic Experts', 2014 No. 08/2013e.

56 See for a further development of this confederal take on budget controls A. Cuyvers, *The EU as a Confederal Union of Sovereign Member Peoples, Exploring the potential of American (con)federalism and popular sovereignty for a constitutional theory of the EU*, (2013, Diss. Leiden), Ch 13.

union, but that full economic and political union is neither feasible nor desirable. Consequently, this school comes to the conclusion that the euro should be abolished, or a new currency set up between the strongest EU economies.[57]

The other extreme position agrees that a monetary union can only survive as part of a full political and economic union, but draws the opposite conclusion, namely that the EU should therefore take the leap of faith towards full political and economic union.[58] This perspective is epitomized by the 'five presidents report' (FPR), the most recent high level proposal on the future of EMU.[59] Although it does not seem to have the full political support of all five presidents, the FPR essentially suggests the 'leap of faith' solution of creating the economic and political union needed for a stable euro. To this end, the FRP proposes four interrelated unions, being 1) a 'genuine Economic Union', 2) a Financial Union, 3) a Fiscal Union, and 4) a Political Union. Although the political union proposed is not really defined in the FPR, the measures suggested go a long way towards creating a European federation, raising serious questions about feasibility and national democracy.[60]

The third school basically rejects the assumption that one needs full economic and political union to create a sufficiently stable euro. Consequently, this school focusses on intermediate solutions and trying to find a middle ground that can both respect the primary sovereignty and democratic process at the national level, whilst also providing sufficient coordination and safeguards at the European level. Such solutions may look to combine insights

---

57 See for example P. Krugman, 'Revenge of the Optimum Currency Area' 27 (2013) *NBER*, 441.

58 See S. Van den Bogaert and A. Cuyvers, 'Of Carrots and Sticks: What Direction to take for Economic and Monetary Union?', in: B. Steunenberg, W. Voermans and S. Van den Bogaert, *Fit for the Future: Insights on the EU from Leiden University* (Leiden University Press, 2016).

59 Jean-Claude Juncker, in close cooperation with Donald Tusk, Jeroen Dijsselbloem, Mario Draghi and Martin Schulz 'Completing Europe's Economic and Monetary Union' (Five Presidents Report), 22 June 2015, available via: <http://ec.europa.eu/priorities/economic-monetary-union/docs/5-presidents-report_en.pdf.>. Also seem the accompanying analytical note: Juncker, 'Preparing for Next Steps on Better Economic Governance in the Euro Area', Informal European Council 12 February 2015. The FPR forms an important evolution compared to the previous Commission 'blueprint for a deep and genuine economic and monetary union.' COM(2012) 777 final, and the 2012 'Van Rompuy plan', also known as the Four Presidents Report. The Van Rompuy plan was later adopted, in an even softer version, as the 'Roadmap for the *completion* of EMU' in the European Council conclusions on completing EMU of 14 December 2012, EUCO 205/12.

60 Cf B. Crum, 'Saving the Euro at the Cost of Democracy' 51 (2013) *Journal of Common Market Studies* 614 or G. Majone, *Rethinking the Union of the Europe Post-Crisis* (CUP, 2014).

from the European Semester and the TSCG in an attempt to develop a hybrid, or confederal, system that can square the circle of a single European currency based on multiple national democracies and economic policies.[61] If successful, such systems could preserve the unique nature and potential of regional integration without slipping back into intergovernmentalism or leaping ahead towards uncertain federation. Yet to be successful this third school must also challenge the weight of history, and those economic schools that suggest a currency can only exist in a political union.

With Brexit, the euro crisis therefore remains one of the main challenges facing European integration today. The euro forces the EU to keep evolving and improving in its search for a new form of supranational governance that can respect national identities and democracy as the cradle of political legitimacy but that can also provide an effective answer to our globalizing reality in which public authority must be exercised above the state in order to retain its relevance and influence. As the EAC joins the rest of the world in this quest, also in the context of EMU, it may already take advantage of several practical improvements developed in the EU. For example, it may, as currently envisioned, include an emergency fund like the ESM directly from the start, instead of only creating it when a crisis hits. In addition, it can create more effective tools for coordination and supervision of national economic policy at the EAC level by taking the lessons from the Stability and Growth Pact, the six-pack and the two-pack into account. These lessons can be combined with the sound intuition of the TSCG to also try and embed primary checks on economic policy at the national level, preferably via independent institutions. Equally, it would be wise to broaden review and coordination to macro-economic imbalances right from the start, as the EAC also does not form an optimal currency union.

None of these mechanisms, however, will sufficiently solve the fundamental asymmetry between national economic policies and an EAC monetary union,

---

61 See for a discussion of this approach A. Cuyvers, *The EU as a Confederal Union of Sovereign Member Peoples, Exploring the potential of American (con)federalism and popular sovereignty for a constitutional theory of the EU*, (2013, Diss. Leiden), Ch 13, and for a more general overview of these debates. K. Tuori and K. Tuori, *The Eurozone Crisis, a Constitutional Analysis* (OUP, 2014), G. Majone, *Rethinking the Union of the Europe Post-Crisis* (CUP, 2014), B. Eichengreen 'European Monetary Integration with Benefit of Hindsight', 50 *Journal of Common Market Studies*, 123, M. Hallerberg, 'Fiscal federalism reforms in the European Union and the Greek crisis', 12 (2011) *European Union Politics*, 127, W.E. Oates, 'Toward A Second-Generation Theory of Fiscal Federalism', 12 (2005) *International Tax and Public Finance*, 349, M. Adams, F. Fabbrini and P. Larouche (eds), *The Constitutionalization of European Budgetary Constraints* (Hart, 2014), A J. Menendez, 'The existential crisis of the European Union', 14 (2013) *German Law Journal*, 453.

which, as in the EU, will persist as long as the EAC does not evolve into a full political union. Consequently, on this point, as on many of the other challenges facing European integration, the EAC will join the EU in the fray of regional integration, where its unique contributions and perspectives will be warmly welcomed. For, as far as regional integration is concerned, both the challenges and opportunities are more than big enough for all of us, and certainly too big for each of us individually.

CHAPTER 14

EAC Competition Law

Joyce Karanja-Ng'ang'a

14.1 Introduction and Background

Competition law is concerned with the structure and behaviour of enterprises in the market.[1] It aims to create a market in which producers and traders would compete freely on the quality of products and services they offer and the prices they charge rather than through the improper exercise of market power, whether acquired unilaterally or in concert with others.[2] Further, competition law is important to provide a framework for competitive activity as it seeks to encourage and improve the competitive environment, create a conducive environment for investment and promote the transfer of the benefits to consumers. More broadly, competition policy is designed to address "industry structures and practices that give excessive market power to sellers to raise prices above, or reduce quantities below the levels that would prevail in competitive markets."[3]

The increasing number of regional trade agreements for closer economic integration through removal of barriers against free movement of goods and services and labour, has raised the need for competition law and policy at the regional level.[4] The Secretary General of the Common Markets for Eastern and Southern Africa ("COMESA") in 2004 stated the issue as follows:

> as the regional economy integrates more deeply, the necessity for appropriate policy instruments and tools is becoming increasingly urgent and, in this regard, a competition policy is important to ensure observance

1 Melaku Geboye Desta, 'Exemptions from Competition Law in Regional Trade Agreements: A study based on experiences in agriculture and energy sectors' in Philippe Bruisk, Ana Maria Alvarez, Lucian Cernat (eds), in *United Nations Conference on Trade and Development, Competition Provisions in Regional Trade Agreements: How to Assure Development Gains* (United Nations 2005).

2 *Ibid.* 2.

3 Tarullo, D.K. (2000), Norms and Institutions in global competition policy, American Journal of International Law, 94, 478–504.

4 *Supra.* 1.

© JOYCE KARANJA-NG'ANG'A, 2017 | DOI 10.1163/9789004322073_028
This is an open access chapter distributed under the terms of the CC-BY-NC License.

of good corporate governance and promoting equitable and harmonious economic development.[5]

This Chapter examines competition law in the East African Community ("EAC") which is the regional intergovernmental organization of the Republics of Burundi, Kenya, Rwanda, Tanzania, Uganda and South Sudan[6] (the "Partner States"),[7] headquartered in Arusha, Tanzania. In order to ensure, protect and promote fair trade and consumer welfare in the EAC region, the Council of Ministers of the EAC adopted a competition policy in 2004.[8] Subsequently the East African Legislative Assembly (the "Assembly") enacted the East African Community Competition Act in 2006[9] (the "EAC Competition Act"). Additionally, the East African Community Regulations (the "EAC Competition Regulations") were adopted in 2010 by the Council of Ministers. The EAC Competition Regulations mainly contain procedural requirements on the various applications of the East African Community Competition Authority (the "EAC Competition Authority") as provided in the EAC Competition Act. The EAC Competition Regulations are to come into force on such date as the EAC Council of Ministers may appoint by notice in the EAC Gazette.

The EAC Competition Act came into effect on 1 December 2014 by an EAC Gazette notice dated 23 January 2015. It has been ratified by all Partner States but the enforcement and operationalization of the EAC Competition Act has not yet commenced. This is primarily linked to the delay in constituting the EAC Competition Authority which is established under the EAC Competition Act[10] and charged with enforcing the EAC Competition Act.[11] Notably, the Council of Ministers has now approved commissioners to the EAC Competition Authority and appointed a secretariat which is currently in the process of recruiting technical staff.[12] The EAC Competition Authority is expected to begin operations in the third or fourth quarter of 2016.

5 Erastus Mwencha, Secretary General, COMESA: Ministerial Roundtable, (Cairo 2004).

6 South Sudan was admitted into the EAC by a resolution of the 17th Ordinary session of the EAC Heads of State Summit held in Arusha, Tanzania on 3 February 2016.

7 Somalia has also applied in 2011 for entry into the EAC but they have not yet been admitted.

8 East African Community Competition Policy, 2004.

9 Gazette of the East African Community No. 002 Vol AT 1-003 dated September 2007.

10 EAC Competition Act, s 37.

11 An interim organisational structure and budget for the EAC Competition Authority for the 2016/2017 financial year has also been approved by the Partner States.

12 Adam Ihucha, 'EAC Competition Authority to Start Operations in July' (The East African Standard 18 June 2016) <http://www.theeastafrican.co.ke/business/EAC-competition-

According to TradeMark East Africa,[13] there have been other major challenges that have contributed to delays in operationalizing the EAC Competition Act. To begin with, there has been inadequate funding from Partner States to enable the EAC Competition Authority to start its operations and function effectively across the region.[14] Furthermore, there are jurisdictional conflicts between the EAC competition regime and the national competition regimes leading to disharmony and enforcement hurdles. Similarly, amendments to the EAC competition legislation that would bring regional harmony have been delayed by national governments.[15] In addition, the economies of the Partner States are at different levels of development, and there is still a quest for protectionism by the governments of some of the Partner States.[16]

More importantly, there has been a lack of political will and vested interests by the governments of some Partner States, who have shown reluctance to be supervised at the regional level on national economic matters such as national procurement law and industrial policy.[17] Another major challenge is that the interface between sector regulators and national competition authorities has not been properly established in the Partner States.

The EAC Competition Act gives the EAC Competition Authority exclusive original jurisdiction in the determination of violations of the EAC Competition Act. This means that national competition authorities in the Partner States will not have the jurisdiction to make determinations or findings based on the East African Competition Act. Therefore, the jurisdiction of national competition authorities is limited to enforcement of their own national laws. The enforcement authorities of Partner States are also obliged to enforce the decisions made by the EAC Competition Authority.[18] Consequently, each Partner State

authority-to-start-operations-in-July-/-/2560/3255818/-/b6nmku/-/index.html> accessed 12 July 2016.

13 Elizabeth Sisenda, 'Why EAC Competition Law is Key in Efforts to Spur Growth' (The Business Daily, 2 November 2015)<h http://www.businessdailyafrica.com/Opinion-and-Analysis/EAC-competition-law-to-spur-growth/-/539548/2939986/-/12kt4ny/-/index.html> accessed 27 January 2016.

14 *Ibid.* The EAC Legislative Assembly approved a budget of USD 587,565 for the operationalization of the EAC Competition Authority in the 2016/2017 financial year which begins on 1 July 2016 and ends on 30 June 2017. Please also see <http://www.theeastafrican.co.ke/news/EAC-unveils-austere-budget-for-2016-17-/-/2558/3222616/-/14lj4l9z/-/index.html>.

15 *Ibid. 15.*

16 *Ibid. 15.*

17 *Ibid. 15.*

18 EAC Competition Act, s 44(6).

is required to establish its own competition legislation, policy and regulatory authority.

At present, all Partner States have enacted national competition laws except Uganda. However, the Partner States are at different stages of implementing their competition laws. Kenya and Tanzania have functioning competition enforcement organs charged with enforcing their respective national competition laws. These are the Competition Authority of Kenya[19] (the "CAK") and the Fair Competition Commission[20] (the "FCC"), respectively.

Rwanda is in the process of setting up an enforcement authority, the Rwanda Competition and Inspectorate Authority, to deal specifically with competition matters. In the meantime, Rwanda's competition law, Law N°36/2012 Relating to Competition and Consumer Protection of 21 September 2012, is being enforced by the Ministry of Trade and Industry. In Burundi, the relevant competition legislation is the Competition Act, Law N° 1/06 of 25 March 2010, which establishes the Competition Commission. However, to date, the Burundi Act has not yet been implemented nor has the Competition Commission been operationalised.

As for Uganda, no specific competition regime has been put in place to date, even though over the years Bills have been submitted to Uganda's Cabinet and Parliament, in particular a Competition Bill issued by the Uganda Law Reform Commission, so far unsuccessfully.[21] Uganda, however has in place sector specific laws which address competition regulation in particular industries. These include, the Uganda Communications Act (Cap 106 of the laws of Uganda), the Electricity Act, 1999 (Cap. 145); the Financial Institutions Act (Cap. 54); the Petroleum Supply Act, 2003 and the Insurance Act (Cap. 213) as amended by the Insurance (Amendment) Act, 2011.

In light of the above, any comparative analysis to the practice of a Partner State in this Chapter will focus on the practice in Kenya and Tanzania, which already have competition regulation that is actively being enforced.

Kenya, Rwanda and Uganda are also members of COMESA and are subject to the COMESA competition regime comprised of the COMESA Competition Regulations, 2004 and the COMESA Competition Rules, 2004.[22] Further,

19 Established under section 7 of the Kenyan Competition Act, Act No.12 of 2010.

20 Established by the Fair Competition Act, No.8 of 2003.

21 Anne Brigot-Laperrousaz, 'East-Africa and Antitrust: Enforcement of EAC Competition Act', (*African Antitrust & Competition Law*, 14 January 2016), <http://africanantitrust.com/category/burundi/> accessed 8 January 2016.

22 The COMESA competition regime is enforced by the COMESA Competition Commission established under Article 6 of the COMESA Competition Regulations, 2004.

Tanzania is a member of the Southern African Development Community ("SADC"). Although SADC does not have a binding competition law in force, it signed a Declaration on Regional Cooperation in Competition and Consumer Policies in September 2009, which sets out a cooperation framework on competition policy for the SADC Free Trade Area that helps streamline international trade and support economic growth.[23] Similarly, Tanzania is required to act within the spirit of this Declaration.

Therefore, an additional challenge with implementation of the EAC competition regime, in particular for Kenya and Tanzania is that no mechanism has yet been established to facilitate the interaction between the EAC Competition law, their national competition laws and COMESA (in the case of Kenya). As such, a merger transaction in Kenya, for example, may fall within the ambit of three separate regimes, and in theory would need to be notified to the EAC Competition Authority, the Competition Authority of Kenya and COMESA Competition Commission. This multiplicity of notifications would result in increased transaction costs and possible delays in obtaining merger clearances, making these regions potentially less attractive to investments. This is contrary to the objectives of the EAC competition regime which we examine in detail below. Further, there is the risk of contradicting decisions being issued by the different regulators and forum shopping where merger parties choose to notify only to the regulator they think is most likely to approve their transaction.

14.2 Objectives and Application of the EAC Competition Act

The EAC Competition Act states that the objectives of the competition policy and practice in the EAC shall be, among other things:

(*a*) *to enhance the welfare of the people in the EAC by protecting all market participants' freedom to compete by prohibiting anti-competitive practices; protecting the opening of Partner States' markets against the creation of barriers to interstate trade and economic transactions by market participants; guaranteeing equal opportunities in the EAC to all market participants in the EAC and especially to small and medium-sized enterprises; guaranteeing a level playing field for all market participants in the EAC by eliminating any discrimination by Partner States on the basis of nationality or residence;*

23 Southern African Development Community, 'Competition Policy', <http://www.sadc.int/themes/economic-development/trade/competition-policy/> accessed 8 January 2016.

(*b*) *to enhance the competitiveness of* EAC *enterprises in world markets by exposing them to competition within the* EAC*;*
(*c*) *to create an environment which is conducive to investment in the* EAC*;*
(*d*) *to bring the* EAC*'s competition policy and practice in line with international best practice; and*
(*e*) *to strengthen the Partner States' role in relevant international organizations.*[24]

The EAC Competition Act applies to all economic activities and sectors having cross-border effect.[25] The extent of the cross-border effect is not expressly defined but it is implied from the provisions of the EAC Competition Act to be within the East African Community.

The EAC Competition Act does not apply to: any conduct of persons acting in their capacity as consumers; collective industrial bargaining; and sovereign acts of the Partner States.[26] It also excludes its application to restraints on competition imposed by and resulting from a Partner State's regulation of specific sectors or industries to the extent that the anti-competitive conduct is required by such regulation within that Partner State's own jurisdiction,[27]—presumably a carve-out for parastatal monopolies or state aided firms.

The EAC Competition Act deals with specific aspects which would affect competition in the EAC including: mergers and acquisitions, prohibited trade practices, abuse of dominance, Partner State subsidies and public procurement. Most of the provisions contained in the EAC Competition Act are broadly drafted and do not provide the means of interpretation or procedures for implementation. Once operationalized, it is expected that the EAC Competition Authority, will publish guidelines, rules or regulations setting out its application of the provisions of the EAC Competition Act and providing more specific details of the way in which the EAC Competition Act is to be applied; this was the approach taken by the COMESA Competition Commission to which Kenya, Rwanda and Uganda are members. It will be critical that any such guidelines, rules and regulations are developed whilst taking into account the competition legislation in Partner States.

We consider the specific provisions of the EAC Competition Act governing cartels, abuse of dominance and concentrations below.

---

24 EAC Competition Act, s 3.
25 EAC Competition Act, s 4(1).
26 EAC Competition Act, s 4(2).
27 EAC Competition Act, s 4(3).

Central to each of these provisions is the definition of the relevant market. The concept of relevant market is defined in Section 5(5) of the EAC Competition Act. For the purposes of the Act, the area of the relevant market is to be determined by *"the substitutability of goods or services for consumers in light of their intended use, characteristics and prices as well as by the substitutability of different sources of supply located in different regions."*[28]

14.3 Cartels

Black's Law Dictionary defines a cartel as, '*a combination of producers or sellers that join together to control a product's production or price*'.[29] It is also defined as an association of firms with common interest seeking to prevent extreme competition, allocate markets or share knowledge.[30]

OECD explains a cartel as a formal agreement among firms in an oligopolistic industry.[31] Cartel members may agree on such matters as prices, total industry output, market shares, allocation of customers, allocation of territories, bid-rigging, establishment of common sales agencies, and the division of profits or combination of these.[32] Cartels or cartel behaviour attempts to emulate that of a monopoly by restricting industry output, raising or fixing prices in order to earn higher profits.[33] This then hinders competition by limiting the supply of specific trade goods or increasing the prices of such goods and services, making them unnecessarily expensive and hence injuring the consumer.[34]

Cartel conduct is prohibited in most competition laws around the world including those in the Partner States that presently have competition legislation; and the EAC Competition Act is no different. The EAC Competition Act provides that a person shall not engage in a concerted practice if that practice has, or is intended to have, an anti-competitive effect in the relevant market,[35] unless permitted by the EAC Competition Authority.[36] A "concerted practice"

28 EAC Competition Act, s 5(5).

29 Bryan A. Garner, *Black's Law Dictionary*, (8th edn, West Publishing Co., 2004).

30 *Ibid.*

31 R.S. Khemani and D.M. Shapiro, 'Glossary of Industrial Organisation Economics and Competition Law' (Directorate for Financial, Fiscal and Enterprise Affairs, OECD, 1993), <https://stats.oecd.org/glossary/detail.asp?ID=3157> accessed on 8 February 2016.

32 *Ibid.*

33 *Ibid.*

34 'Cartels and anti-competitive agreements' www.oecd.org.

35 EAC Competition Act, s 5(1).

36 EAC Competition Act, s 7.

is defined to mean, "*any agreement, arrangement or understanding, formal or informal, written or oral, open or clandestine, between competitors.*"[37] From the definition, the cartel provisions of the EAC Competition Act appear to cover only cooperation among competitors, that is, horizontal agreements. However, this may arguably include vertical arrangements with underlying horizontal purposes.[38]

More specifically, the EAC Competition Act prohibits the following practices:[39]

(a) collusion by competitors to fix prices;
(b) collusive tendering and bid rigging;
(c) collusive market or customer allocation;
(d) quantitative restraints on investment, input, output or sales;
(e) barring competitors from access to the market or from access to an association or arrangement which is essential for competition; and
(f) concerted practice restricting movement of goods within the EAC.

Additionally, any concerted practice by undertakings restricting exports to or imports from foreign countries is prohibited, if it is intended to have anti-competitive effects on the relevant market within the EAC or on access of EAC undertakings to exports or imports.

Any person who contravenes the above provisions is liable to a fine of not more than USD 100,000. In this respect, the EAC Competition Act does not expressly provide an appeal mechanism for a person dissatisfied with the decision of the EAC Competition Authority. However, the EAC Competition Act generally empowers the East African Court of Justice (the "EACJ")[40] to determine any question with respect to any action of the EAC Competition

37 EAC Competition Act, s 2.

38 Please note however, the provisions of the EAC Competition Act relating to abuse of dominance also consider the vertical effects of the actions of an undertaking holding a dominant position by prohibiting a dominant firm from engaging in practices whereby: (a) the resale prices or conditions are directly or indirectly fixed; (b) customers or competitors are foreclosed from access to sources of supply or from access to outlets; (c) movement of goods or services between different geographical areas are restricted; and (d) an intellectual property right is used in any way that goes beyond the limits of its legal protection.

39 EAC Competition Act, s 5(2).

40 The East African Court of Justice is one of the organs of the EAC established under Article 9 of the Treaty for the Establishment of the East African Community. EACJ's major responsibility is to ensure the adherence to law in the interpretation and application of and compliance with the EAC Treaty.

Authority. Consequently, an aggrieved person may appeal a decision of the EAC Competition Authority pursuant to this provision, to the EACJ.

However, the EAC Competition Act exempts certain practices from the application of the provisions stated above. Thus, in situations where the combined market share of the competitors does not exceed 10% of the relevant market, the undertakings will not be prohibited from engaging in quantitative restraints on investment, input, output or sales or from engaging in concerted practices restricting movement of goods within the EAC.[41]

Additionally, where the combined market share of the parties involved in the concerted practice does not exceed 20% of the relevant market and the agreement relating to the concerted practice does not contain any of the specifically prohibited practices outlined in (a)–(f) above, the prohibition will not apply to the following practices: joint research and development; specialization or distribution; and standardization of products or services.[42]

The EAC Competition Authority may also exempt any other category of concerted practice, provided it has objectives which lead to the improvement of production or distribution and whose beneficial effects, in the opinion of the EAC Competition Authority, outweighs its negative effects on competition provided that the combined market share of the parties involved in the concerted practice does not exceed 20% of the relevant market.[43]

Any person[44] who intends to engage in a concerted practice which does not fall into the exemptions discussed above, must apply to the EAC Competition Authority for permission. The procedure for the exemption application is provided in the EAC Competition Regulations. The application must be made in the prescribed form[45] provided in the EAC Competition Regulations, filed together with a detailed statement setting out the reasons why the concerted practice should be permitted and accompanied by the prescribed fee[46] (which has not yet been prescribed).

Under the EAC Competition Act, the EAC Competition Authority is required to determine the exemption application within 45 days from the receipt of

41 EAC Competition Act, s 6(1).

42 EAC Competition Act, s 6(2).

43 EAC Competition Act, s 6(4).

44 The Laws of The Community (Interpretation) Act, 2004, section 2, a person is defined to include a company, corporation and association or body of persons, corporate or unincorporated.

45 EAC Competition Regulations, Regulation 16(1).

46 EAC Competition Regulations, Regulation 16(2).

the application and communicate the decision to the applicant.[47] If the EAC Competition Authority does not communicate a decision on the application within the stipulated time, the exemption application shall be deemed to have been approved.[48] Notably, unlike most of the Partner States' existing competition laws, for example Kenya, neither the EAC Competition Act nor the EAC Competition Regulations provide for an extension of the prescribed timelines. This means that the EAC Competition Authority would need to make any requests for additional information, raise any queries or hold any conference hearings within the 45 day period in which it is required to make and communicate its decision.

A person who engages in a concerted practice without the permission of the EAC Competition Authority commits an offence and is liable to a fine of not more than USD 10,000. It is not clear from the EAC Competition Act whether this penalty is in addition to, or instead of the USD. 100,000 penalty prescribed for breach of the provisions on concerted practices stated above. This is an issue that will perhaps be clarified by the EAC Competition Authority once it is operationalized.

In addition, any agreement that constitutes a concerted practice is void.[49]

14.4 Abuse of a Dominant Position

The EAC Competition Act defines a dominant position as:

> a position of economic strength enjoyed by one undertaking individually or by more undertakings collectively which enables them to prevent effective competition being maintained in the relevant market by giving the undertaking the power to behave to a material extent independently of its competitors, customers and consumers and in particular to foreclose other undertakings from competing in the relevant market.[50]

The definition of dominant position above is broad and gives the EAC Competition Authority a lot of discretion in determining whether a firm holds a dominant position. Notably, this can be compared to the EU where the relevant provisions do not provide a definition of "dominant position" and the

47 EAC Competition Act, s 7(3); EAC Competition Regulations, Regulations 16(3).

48 EAC Competition Act, s 7(5); EAC Competition Regulations, Regulations 16(4).

49 EAC Competition Act, s 26(1).

50 EAC Competition Act, s 2.

concept of dominance has been elaborated on in case-law and European Commission Guidance Papers.[51]

The definition provided by the EAC Competition Act is different from that in Kenya and Tanzania where the market share held by the relevant firm is one of the main elements taken into account in determining if an entity is a dominant undertaking.

In Kenya, the Competition Act of Kenya defines a dominant undertaking as an undertaking which:[52]

(*a*) *produces, supplies, distributes or otherwise controls not less than one-half of the total goods of any description which are produced, supplied or distributed in Kenya or any substantial part thereof; or*
(*b*) *provides or otherwise controls not less than one-half of the services which are rendered in Kenya or any substantial part thereof.*[53]

Additionally, and notwithstanding the above definition, an undertaking in Kenya will be deemed to be dominant if:[54]

(*i*) *though not dominant it controls at least 40% but not more than 50% of the market share (unless it can show that it does not have market power); or*
(*ii*) *it controls less than 40% of the market share but has market power.*

Similarly, in Tanzania an undertaking is deemed to have a dominant position if: acting alone, it can profitably and materially restrain or reduce competition in that market for a significant period of time; and the person's share of the relevant market exceeds 35%. It remains to be seen whether the EAC Competition Authority will apply a market share test when interpreting the dominance of an undertaking.

From the definition of dominant position above, it is clear that the EAC Competition Act covers both the conduct of a single dominant firm as well as collective dominance. This is distinct from Tanzania's Fair Competition Act

51 Case 102/77, *Hoffmann-La Roche & Co AG v Commission* [1979] ECR 461; Guidance on the Commission's Enforcement Priorities in Applying Article 82 of the EC Treaty to Abusive Exclusionary Conduct by Dominant Undertakings [2009] OJ C 45/2. See also EU Chapter 14.

52 Competition Act of Kenya, s 4(3).

53 Pursuant to sec.4 of the Competition Act of Kenya, No. 12 of 2010.

54 Competition Act of Kenya, s 34(2).

whose provisions on dominance are restricted to the conduct of a single firm.[55] Due to the delicacy of making a finding of collective dominance, which would place a considerable burden of proof on the EAC Competition Authority, especially in establishing a concerted practice affording the parties the power to behave to an appreciable extent independently of their competitors and the consumers, the EAC Competition Authority will need to adopt rules or guidelines setting out the criteria for economic assessment particularly an assessment of the structure of the market.[56]

In addition, an undertaking on which small or medium sized undertakings (SMES) are dependent on is deemed to be a dominant undertaking and is also bound by the prohibitions set out in (a) and (b) below.[57]

The provisions of the EAC Competition Act on abuse of dominance can be classified into three categories:

(a) prohibitions against exploitation of consumers—under the EAC Competition Act, a dominant undertaking should not: directly or indirectly impose unfairly high selling or unfairly low purchasing prices or other unfair trading conditions; limit production or technical development and innovation to the prejudice of consumers; and discriminate between consumers or suppliers according to non-commercial criteria such as nationality or residence.[58]
(b) prohibition against exclusion of competitors—a dominant undertaking should not engage in any practice that excludes, or is intended to exclude, its competitors from the market by means of: predatory pricing; price squeezing or cross subsidization.[59] Further, a dominant undertaking in the relevant market should not engage in a practice that harms the competitive position of competitors on downstream or upstream markets by: a refusal to deal; a refusal of access to an essential facility; tying arrangements; or unjustifiably discriminating among customers or suppliers.
(c) prohibitions relating to vertical agreements that is, agreements within the supply chain—a dominant undertaking in the relevant market should not engage in a practice whereby: the resale prices or conditions

55 United Nations Conference for Trade and Development, (2012) Voluntary Peer Review Of Competition Law And Policy: United Republic Of Tanzania, UNCTAD/DITC/CLP/2012/1.

56 Carina Olsson, 'Collective Dominance—Merger Control on Oligopolistic Markets' (2000) Göteborgs Universitet.

57 EAC Competition Act, s 8(2), 9(3).

58 EAC Competition Act, s 8(1).

59 EAC Competition Act, 9(1).

are directly or indirectly fixed; customers or competitors are foreclosed from access to sources of supply or from access to outlets; movement of goods or services between different geographical areas are restricted; or an intellectual property right is used in any way that goes beyond the limits of its legal protection.

Any contravention of the above provisions on abuse of dominance is an offence punishable by either a fine of not more than USD 10,000 or imprisonment for a term of not more than 2 years or both. It is noteworthy that, as in mergers, the national courts in Partner States have jurisdiction in relation to criminal offences under the EAC Competition Act.[60]

14.5 Concentrations

Concentrations in the EAC are subject to merger control and the EAC Competition Authority must be notified of them promptly upon the conclusion of the agreement in respect of a merger or an acquisition.[61] It is notable that an agreement will be considered to be as such, irrespective of whether it is in writing or not. This notification is required to be made by the undertaking acquiring control through the merger or acquisition.[62]

The EAC competition regime is suspensory and therefore parties cannot implement a proposed merger or acquisition before obtaining the approval of the EAC Competition Authority. However, the EAC Competition Act contains deemed approval provisions discussed under this heading below.

The EAC Competition Act defines a merger as "*… an amalgamation or joining of two or more firms into an existing firm or to form a new firm.*"[63] Furthermore, it defines an acquisition as "*any acquisition by an undertaking of direct or indirect control of the whole or part of one or more other undertakings, irrespective of whether the acquisition is effected by merger, consolidation, take-over, purchase of securities or assets, contract or by any other means.*"[64]

The EAC Competition Act does not contain a definition of "control". However, it grants the Council of Ministers the power to make regulations generally for

60 EAC Competition Act, s 48(2).

61 EAC Competition Act, s 11(1) (2).

62 EAC Competition Act, s 11(3).

63 EAC Competition Act, s 2.

64 EAC Competition Act, s 2.

the carrying into effect of the provisions of the EAC Competition Act.[65] The Council of Ministers, exercising this power, may also pass regulations providing a definition of control for purposes of the EAC Competition Act.

Hopefully, such rules or regulations will be developed through a process of consultation with stakeholders in Partner States. As stated above, it is likely that the EAC Competition Authority will be influenced by the interpretation of control in the competition laws and decisions of the competition authorities of the EAC Partner States,[66] as well as the general practices of other regional regulators such as the COMESA Competition Commission.[67]

The other likelihood is that rules or guidelines will be issued by the EAC Competition Authority to provide further guidance in this respect. It is useful to note that this is the approach that was taken by the COMESA Competition

---

65 EAC Competition Act, s 49.

66 Section 41(3) of the Kenyan Competition Act defines control in terms of the specific circumstances in which a person would be deemed to have control of an undertaking. Thus, a person 'controls' an undertaking if that person: (i) beneficially owns more than one half of the issued share capital of the undertaking; (ii) is entitled to vote a majority of the votes that may be cast at a general meeting of the undertaking, or has the ability to control the voting of a majority of those votes, either directly or through a controlled entity of that undertaking; (iii) is able to appoint, or to veto the appointment of, a majority of the directors of the undertaking; (iii) is a holding company, and the undertaking is a subsidiary of that company as contemplated in the Companies Act; or (iv) in the case of the undertaking being a trust, has the ability to control the majority of the votes of the trustees or to appoint the majority of the trustees or to appoint or change the majority of the beneficiaries of the trust; (v) in the case of the undertaking being a nominee undertaking, owns the majority of the members' interest or controls directly or has the right to control the majority of members' votes in the nominee undertaking; or (vi) has the ability to materially influence the policy of the undertaking in a manner comparable to a person who, in ordinary commercial practice, can exercise an element of control referred to above.

Section 4(2) of Tanzania's Fair Competition Act provides that, 'a *body corporate shall control another body corporate within the meaning of sub-section (1) if the first-mentioned body corporate: (i) owns or controls a majority of the shares carrying the right to vote at a general meeting of the other body corporate; or (ii) has the power to control the composition of a majority of the board of directors or other governing organ of the other of body corporate; or (iii) has the power to make decisions in respect of the conduct of the affairs of the other body corporate.*'

67 In COMESA (which affects Kenya, Rwanda and Uganda), the COMESA Competition Commission published guidelines, the COMESA Merger Assessment Guidelines, 2014 which confirmed the COMESA Competition Commission's previous practice as at the time of their adoption that, whether a transaction is a 'merger' depends on whether control is acquired—and 'control' is based on whether a party has the possibility of exercising decisive influence over an undertaking or asset.

Commission. At the moment, there are no merger thresholds specified by either the EAC Competition Act or the EAC Competition Regulations and consequently, all mergers having a cross-border effect within the EAC are notifiable to the EAC Competition Authority. The EAC Competition Act also does not provide the meaning of "cross-border effect". It is not clear whether cross-border effect means that the proposed merger or acquisition affects at least two Partner States or whether it must affect more than two Partner States. Again, this will hopefully be clarified by the EAC Competition Authority once it is operationalized. However, this means that mergers and acquisitions that are confined within the national boundaries of a Partner State would not be subject to the application of the EAC Competition Act; instead, national competition laws (if any) would apply. However, the lack of merger thresholds means that every transaction that qualifies as a merger or an acquisition with cross-border effect under the EAC Competition Act would be notifiable and would result in the EAC Competition Authority utilizing its limited resources on transactions that are too small to affect trade between the Partner States. By way of observation, this is how the COMESA Competition Regulations were initially operationalized and the period following their commencement caused chaos and uncertainty for transactions affecting businesses in the Common Market. It is hoped that the EAC Competition Authority would learn from the shortcomings of the COMESA Competition Commission. Furthermore, this can be contrasted to the EU system in which the EU Merger Regulation establishes certain turnover thresholds which need to be satisfied in order to trigger notification to the EU Competition Authority.[68]

A merger or acquisition carried out in the absence of an authorizing order by the EAC Competition Authority is of no legal effect.[69] The EAC Competition Authority is mandated to order the divestiture of any merger or acquisition undertaken in contravention of the EAC Competition Act.[70]

Any person found guilty of failing to obtain an authorising order from the EAC Competition Authority prior to a merger will be liable upon conviction to imprisonment for a term not exceeding 2 years or to a fine not exceeding USD 10,000, or both.[71] The national courts in Partner States have jurisdiction in relation to criminal offences under the EAC Competition Act.[72]

68 Articles 1(2) and (3) of Council Regulation (EC) No. 139/2004.See also EU Chapter 14.

69 EAC Competition Act, s 12(1)(4).

70 EAC Competition Act, s 26(2).

71 EAC Competition Act, s 48.

72 EAC Competition Act, s 48(2).

The test that the EAC Competition Authority will use when assessing a merger is whether it will lead to the creation, or strengthening of an already dominant position, thereby lessening competition in the relevant market. More particularly, Section 13(2) of the EAC Competition Act provides that the EAC Competition Authority will consider the following factors:

(*a*) *the competitive structure of all markets affected by the merger or acquisition, including the potential competition from both inside and outside the EAC in light of legal or other barriers to entry;*
(*b*) *the undertakings in the markets affected, their control of essential facilities, their integration in upstream and downstream markets, and their financial resources;*
(*c*) *the competitors and the alternatives available to suppliers and consumers; and*
(*d*) *any pro-competitive effects of the merger or acquisition which may outweigh the harmful effects on competition.*

The merger notification must be made in the form prescribed in the EAC Competition Regulations,[73] and submitted to the EAC Competition Authority together with any relevant documents supporting the intended merger or acquisition.[74] Upon the issuance of an acknowledgment of receipt of notification of an intended merger or acquisition, the EAC Competition Authority is mandated to publish a notice of the intended merger in at least two newspapers of national circulation in each Partner State and on the EAC website.[75] The purpose of this notice is to invite interested persons to express their views on the proposed merger or acquisition within 14 days of publication of the notice.

The EAC Competition Regulations also allow any interested person to submit any relevant document to the EAC Competition Authority expressing their views on the merger or acquisition at hand.[76] The EAC Competition Authority may then utilize this information in considering the merger or acquisition as it deems fit.

---

73 Form EACCA 1 provided in the Schedule to the EAC Competition Regulations.

74 The prescribed form (Form EACCA 1) prescribes the following supporting documents: memorandum and articles of association, copies of audited annual financial statements for the last three years, strategic business plans, certificates of incorporation/registration, merger agreement, and other relevant documents.

75 EAC Competition Regulations, Regulation 7.

76 EAC Competition Regulations, Regulation 8(1).

Upon assessing the intended merger or acquisition, the Authority may either: approve the merger or acquisition with or without conditions; decide that the intended merger or acquisition falls outside the jurisdiction of the EAC Competition Act; or reject the intended merger or acquisition.[77] In the event that the EAC Competition Authority decides that the merger is outside the jurisdiction of the EAC Competition Act, then it is required to refund 75% of the filing fee paid in respect of the merger notification. No fees have yet been prescribed for filing a merger notification to the EAC Competition Authority.

The EAC Competition Authority is required to make a decision within 45 calendar days of the notification requirements being satisfied.[78] If the EAC Competition Authority has not communicated its decision within the stipulated time period,[79] the merger or acquisition may be implemented. This provision will help to deal with any potential delays in determining applications. Due to the lack of merger thresholds it is expected that the EAC Competition Authority may initially be inundated with applications since, in the absence of any thresholds or contrary legislative instruments, all mergers and acquisitions having cross-border effects would be notifiable to it.

Where the EAC Competition Authority rejects a merger or acquisition application, the merging parties may appeal the decision of the EAC Competition Authority to the Council of Ministers.[80] The Council of Ministers may only approve a merger or acquisition if it is satisfied that the merger or acquisition is to fulfil an overriding public interest.[81]

The EAC Competition Act does not expressly stipulate the factors to be considered by the Council of Ministers in determining whether a merger or acquisition fulfils an overriding public interest. However, it is expected that the Council of Ministers will be guided by the objectives of the EAC as set out in the Treaty for the Establishment of the East African Community. These objectives are to develop policies and programmes aimed at widening and deepening co-operation among the Partner States in political, economic, social and cultural fields, research and technology, defence, security and legal and judicial affairs, for their mutual benefit.[82] In this respect, the EAC seeks to, among

77 EAC Competition Regulations, Regulation 8(2).

78 Articles 1(2) and (3) of Council Regulation (EC) No. 139/2004. See also EU Chapter 14.

79 EAC Competition Act, s 12(1)(4).

80 EAC Competition Act, s 26(2).

81 EAC Competition Act, s 48.

82 EAC Competition Act, s 48(2).

other things, ensure: the attainment of sustainable growth and development of the Partner States by the promotion of a more balanced and harmonious development of the Partner States; and the strengthening and consolidation of co-operation in agreed fields that would lead to equitable economic development within the Partner States and which would in turn, raise the standard of living and improve the quality of life of their populations.[83]

14.6 State Aids as a Prohibited Business Practice

The EAC Competition Act does not define "state aid". State aid is also not provided in the national competition laws of the Partner States. The EAC Competition Authority would perhaps need to look to other jurisdictions with more developed competition law in implementing the State aid provisions of the EAC Competition Act, including the European Union. The European Commission defines state aid as an advantage in any form whatsoever conferred on a selective basis to undertakings by national public authorities.[84] According to the European Commission, to constitute State aid, a measure needs satisfy the following:

> there has been an intervention by the State or through State resources which take the forms of either a tax relief, grant, government holding of all or part of a company, or providing goods and services on preferential terms; the intervention gives the recipient an advantage on a selective basis, for example to specific companies or industry sectors, or to companies located in specific regions; competition has been or may be distorted; and the intervention is likely to affect trade between Member States.[85]

83 Form EACCA 1 provided in the Schedule to the EAC Competition Regulations.

84 The prescribed form (Form EACCA 1) prescribes the following supporting documents: memorandum and articles of association, copies of audited annual financial statements for the last three years, strategic business plans, certificates of incorporation/registration, merger agreement, and other relevant documents.

85 EAC Competition Regulations, Regulation 7.

However, in some circumstances, state aid can promote a well-functioning and equitable economy.[86]

Articles 107 to 109 of the Treaty on the Functioning of the European Union (the "TFEU") contain the substantive and procedural rules on distortions of competition as a result of State measures involving any form of aid to undertakings.

Article 107(1) of the TFEU provides that aid granted by a member state or through State resources, in any form whatsoever, which distorts, or threatens to distort, competition by favouring certain undertakings or the production of certain goods, is incompatible with the internal market insofar as such aid affects trade between member states. There are several types of aid which are *de jure* exempt from the prohibition and which are enumerated in Article 107(2) of the TFEU.[87] In addition, Article 107(3) of the TFEU provides for the possibility of exemption from the prohibition with the approval of the European Commission. It sets out a number of policy objectives for which state aid may be considered compatible with the internal market, including state aid aimed at: (a) promoting the economic development of areas where the standard of living is abnormally low or where there is serious underemployment; (b) remedying a serious disturbance in the economy of a member state; or (c) promoting the execution of an important project of common European interest.

The European Commission enjoys a wide discretion in assessing the compatibility of aid under Article 107(3) of the TFEU. To this end, the European Commission must conduct a balancing test between economic and social interests on the one hand, against the effects on competition and trade between member states on the other hand. The European Commission also ensures that there is frequent review of the law in ensuring that state aid is boosting the European economy. In this respect, it has adopted policies for assessing specific types of aids such as rescue and restructuring aid, government guarantees, and aid for the sale of land by public bodies.

Similarly, the EAC Competition Act allows each Partner State to grant subsidies to any undertaking if it is of the opinion that it is in the public interest to do so.[88]

86 EAC Competition Regulations, Regulation 8(1).

87 EAC Competition Regulations, Regulation 8(2).

88 EAC Competition Act, s 14.

A Partner State may grant subsidies to/for:[89]

(*a*) *consumers of certain categories of products or services in order to promote social services;*
(*b*) *the development of small and medium-sized enterprises;*
(*c*) *the restructuring, rationalizing and modernizing of specific sectors of the Partner State's economy;*
(*d*) *less developed regions;*
(*e*) *research and development;*
(*f*) *the financing of a public sector;*
(*g*) *the promotion and protection of food security;*
(*h*) *the protection of the environment;*
(*i*) *the education and training of personnel;*
(*j*) *the conservation of the cultural heritage; and*
(*k*) *the compensation of damages caused by natural disasters or by macroeconomic disturbances.*

The instances listed above essentially comprise the public interest concerns that a Partner State would consider in determining whether to grant a subsidy or not. This list is not exhaustive. Under Section 17(2) of the EAC Competition Act, the Council of Ministers may exempt other categories of subsidies on the recommendation of the EAC Competition Authority. In granting the exemption, the Council of Ministers shall take into account: the materiality of the subsidy for the achievement of its objective; the compatibility of the subsidy with the objectives of the EAC, including the opening of Partner States' markets; and the establishment of a competitive environment in the EAC. For these cases, the Council of Ministers shall determine the duration of every exemption of subsidy so granted.[90]

However, Partner States are prohibited from applying any subsidies which distort or threaten to distort competition within the EAC.[91] More specifically, the following subsidies are expressly not allowed:[92]

89 EAC Competition Act, s 17.
90 EAC Competition Act, s17(4).
91 EAC Competition Act, s 16(1).
92 EAC Competition Act, s 16(2).

(a) any subsidy for the promotion of exports or imports between the EAC Partner States; and

(b) any subsidy which is granted on the basis of the nationality or residence of persons or country of origin of goods or service.

Before granting any subsidy, a Partner State must notify the EAC Competition Authority.[93] Where the EAC Competition Authority considers that the subsidy falls under the exemption stated above, it will communicate its decision to the Partner State. If the Partner State is dissatisfied with the EAC Competition Authority's decision, it may refer the matter to the EACJ.[94] In the case that the EACJ determines that the subsidy is illegal, a Partner State will be required to recover the subsidy from its recipient.[95]

93 EAC Competition Act, s 15(1).

94 EAC Competition Act, s 15(3).

95 EAC Competition Act, s 15(4).

CHAPTER 14A

EU Competition Law

Pieter Van Cleynenbreugel

14.1 Introduction

The European Union's ambition to establish a single market always extended beyond the abolition of State rules restricting the free movement of persons and commodities. Convinced that restrictive agreements between or unilateral practices of private businesses as well as State measures subsidising particular enterprises could be equally harmful to the smooth functioning of an internal market, the Treaties have always incorporated competition law provisions.[1] Current Articles 101–109 TFEU[2] prohibit cartel agreements (2.), unilateral abusive behaviour (3.) as well as certain forms of State aid (4.)[3] and contain legal bases for the setup of a supranational enforcement mechanism (5.).

14.2 Article 101 TFEU: prohibited collusion

Article 101 TFEU states that "shall be prohibited as incompatible with the internal market: all agreements between undertakings, decisions by associations of undertakings and concerted practices which may affect trade between Member States and which have as their object or effect the prevention, restriction or distortion of competition within the internal market. More particularly,

* Professor (chargé de cours) of European Union law, Université de Liège, Belgium; Ph.D (KU Leuven); LL.M. (Harvard); LL.M., LL.B. (KU Leuven); pieter.vancleynenbreugel@ulg.ac.be.

1 Contrary to s3 of the East African Community Competition Act (see previous chapter), which outlines the objectives of EAC Competition law, the EU Treaties remain silent about the exact objectives of EU competition law; the only thing they seem to hint at—in Protocol No. 26—is that competition law constitutes an inherent part of the EU internal market.

2 Those provisions can be found in Chapter I, Title VII, Part III (Union policies and internal actions) of the Treaty on the Functioning of the European Union.

3 In addition, Article 106 also states that competition law applies, in principle, without exception to undertakings entrusted with services of general economic interest. In some situations, however, exceptions to the full-fledged application of those rules could obstruct the performance, in law or in fact, of the particular tasks assigned to them; in that situation, exceptions to the full application of competition law rules can be proposed.

© PIETER VAN CLEYNENBREUGEL, 2017 | DOI 10.1163/9789004322073_029
This is an open access chapter distributed under the terms of the CC-BY-NC License.

the provision adds a few examples of such agreements, decisions or practices. Those include, yet are not limited to:[4]

(a) directly or indirectly fixing purchase or selling prices or any other trading conditions;
(b) limiting or controlling production, markets, technical development, or investment;
(c) sharing markets or sources of supply;
(d) applying dissimilar conditions to equivalent transactions with other trading parties, thereby placing them at a competitive disadvantage;
(e) making the conclusion of contracts subject to acceptance by the other parties of supplementary obligations which, by their nature or according to commercial usage, have no connection with the subject of such contracts.

In order for Article 101(1) to apply, the behaviour concerned has to produce effects within the internal market[5] and, similar to s4(1) EAC Competition Act, affect trade between Member States. Within that territorial context, the provision prohibits all agreements fixing prices, quantities or territorial areas between different businesses, or which would otherwise restrict the normal processes of competition on a market. The Treaty did not define the notions of agreement between undertakings, decision of an association of undertakings, concerted practice, and restriction of competition. It has fallen upon the European Commission and the Court of Justice of the European Union to explain the scope of those notions following the entry into force of the Treaties. In doing so, both institutions continuously opted for a functional approach, seeking to capture as many varieties of cartel-like behaviour within the scope of the prohibition.

In order for Article 101 TFEU to apply, the behaviour of at least two undertakings has to be at stake. According to consistent case law, an undertaking comprises any entity engaged in economic activity, regardless of its legal status and the way in which it is financed.[6] The entity definition looks beyond the

4 As confirmed in Case C-49/92 P, *Commission of the European Communities v Anic Partecipazioni SpA*, ECLI:EU:C:1999:356, para 108.

5 On that notion, see Joined Cases 89, 104, 114, 116, 117 & 125–129/85, *A. Ahlström Osakeyhtio and Others v Commission (Woodpulp-I)*, ECLI:EU:C:1988:447, para 11–18 and Case T-102/96, *Gencor Ltd v Commission*, ECLI:EU:T:1999:65, para 90–100.

6 Case C-41/90, *Klaus Höfner and Fritz Elser* v. *Macrotron GmbH.*, ECLI:EU:C:1991:161, para 21.

legal corporate or association law categories determined across the different national legal orders, identifying economic realities over legal form. As a result, a parent company and its fully-owned subsidiary will be considered a single undertaking; intra-enterprise contracts are thus excluded from the scope of Article 101 TFEU.[7] Economic activity is defined as any offering of goods or services that can take place in a market environment.[8] As such, marketable activities engaged in by public entities also qualify as economic, bringing those entities within the undertaking definition.[9] The Court of Justice consistently maintains a similar non-formal approach when identifying an agreement. From its early case law onwards, it confirmed that any concurrence of wills, regardless its form or scope, could be considered an agreement.[10] In the seminal *Consten and Grundig* judgment, the Court added that both horizontal (concluded at the same level of production/distribution chain) and vertical agreements (concluded between operators on different levels of that chain) are covered by the prohibition.[11]

An association of undertakings comprises any grouping of economic operators which could potentially be used as an intermediary, a shield or an alternative means to maintain, monitor and develop prohibited collusive practices.[12] Trade associations or other professional associations acknowledged as such by national law and created to protect and promote the interests of particular economic operators are the most obvious examples of such groupings.[13] EU competition law nevertheless goes beyond those formal distinctions. Recently, the Court of Justice even argued that, in assembling banks in one of its committees deciding on fees applied across the payment card network, a credit card company—itself an undertaking—acted as an association of banks, thus qualifying as an association of undertakings. Any calculated decision,

7 Case C-73/95 P, *Viho Europe BV* v. *Commission*, ECLI:EU:C:1996:405, paras. 6 and 16.

8 See M. Szydlo, 'Leeway of Member States in Shaping the Notion of an 'Undertaking' in Competition Law', 33 *World Competition* (2010), 549–568.

9 See e.g. Case C-475/99 *Firma Ambulanz Glöckner v Landkreis Südwestpfalz*, ECLI:EU:C:2001:577, para 20.

10 Joined Cases C-2 & 3/01 P, *Bundesverband der Arzneimittel-Importeure eV & Commission* v. *Bayer*, ECLI:EU:C:2004:2, para 69.

11 Joined Cases 56 & 58/64, *Consten and Grundig* v. *Commission*, ECLI:EU:C:1966:41, p. 339.

12 Case T-39/92, *Groupement des Cartes Bancaires CB v Commission of the European Communities*, ECLI:EU:T:1994:20, para 77.

13 Case 246/86, *Societé Cooperative des Asphalteurs Belges (Belasco SC) v Commission of the European Communities*, ECLI:EU:C:1989:301 or Case C-309/99, *Wouters v Algemene Raad van de Nederlandse Orde van Advocaten*, ECLI:EU:C:2002:98.

recommendation or advisory practice in the interest of its members, it will be considered to represent the "private interests" of participating undertakings.[14]

In order to avoid situations where parties refrain from concluding an agreement or reverting to their trade association in order to adopt potentially anticompetitive behaviour, the Treaty also prohibits concerted practices. According to the Court, a concerted practice refers to any form of coordination between undertakings, by which, without it having been taken to the stage where an agreement properly so-called has been concluded, practical cooperation between them is knowingly substituted for the risks of competition.[15] The mere proof of contact followed by prima facie coordinated behaviour suffices for the European Commission to prove the existence of such practice.[16] A case in point is *T-Mobile*, in which the Court held that the coordinated price increase of Dutch telecom operators following known contacts between representatives of the different undertakings gave rise to the existence of such practice.[17]

The notion of restriction of competition has never been defined in an exhaustive manner. The European Commission and the EU Courts have rather analysed, in each individual case, to what extent a restriction can be deemed in place, inter alia relying on the examples listed in the Treaty.[18] An important distinction is made between restrictions by object and by effect in that regard. Object restrictions are practices deemed quasi-always to restrict competition, without the need for an in-depth analysis of the actual effects the behaviour concerned produces on the relevant market.[19] Price-fixing, market segmentation and output restrictions, also listed in Article 101(1) TFEU, are the most obvious examples in this regard. Effect restrictions require a more in-depth economic "counterfactual" analysis. The European Commission in those cases has to prove that competition has been harmed in a way that would not have

14 Case C-382/12 P, *MasterCard v Commission*, ECLI:EU:C:2014:2201, para 71–73.

15 Joined Cases 40–48, 50, 54–56, 111, 113 & 114/73, *Suiker Unie and Others* v. *Commission*, ECLI:EU:C:1975:174, para 26.

16 Joined Cases C-89, 104, 114, 116, 117, 125–129/85, *Ahlström Osakeyhtiö and Others* v. *Commission* (*Woodpulp* II), ECLI:EU:C:1993:120, para 126–127.

17 Case C-8/08, *T-Mobile*, ECLI:EU:C:2009:343.

18 See for a more elaborate analysis, P. Van CleynenbrEUgel, 'Article 101 TFEU and the EU Courts: adapting legal form to the realities of modernization?', 51 *Common Market Law Review* (2014), 1409.

19 Case C-209/07, *Competition Authority* v. *Beef Industry Development Society Ltd and Barry Brothers (Carrigmore) Meats Ltd.*, ECLI:EU:C:2008:643, para 17.

been the case had the restrictive behaviour not been engaged in.[20] In addition, such restrictions have to be appreciably affecting interstate trade within the internal market. To the extent that undertakings have a market share below 10% (horizontal agreements) or 15% (vertical and mixed agreements), the Commission will not take enforcement action.[21] Object restrictions nevertheless never benefit from *de minimis*.[22]

In addition to the prohibition, Article 101(2) TFEU contains a specific civil law sanction, stating that any agreements or decisions prohibited pursuant to this Article shall be automatically void. The sanction outlined in this provision complements the administrative enforcement framework set up by the Commission from the early 1960s onwards. By virtue of the direct effect of that provision, the voidness of anticompetitive agreements can be invoked directly before and by national jurisdictions.[23]

The prohibition outlined in Article 101(1) is not absolute. Article 101(3) TFEU confirms that agreements, decisions or practices which contribute to improving the production or distribution of goods or to promoting technical or economic progress, while allowing consumers a fair share of the resulting benefit, and which do neither impose on the undertakings concerned restrictions which are not indispensable to the attainment of these objectives nor afford such undertakings the possibility of eliminating competition in respect of a substantial part of the products in question, can be justified. It results from this provision that any restrictive agreement, decision or practice can—at least in theory—be justified. Prior to 2004, only the European Commission could decide on the existence of such justification, called an exemption decision. Since 2004, undertakings will have to self-assess whether their agreement can be deemed justified.[24]

In order to render this assessment more predictable, the European Commission adopted, after having been granted those powers by the Council in accordance with Article 103 TFEU, so-called block-exemption regulations, excluding categories of agreements from the Article 101(1) TFEU prohibition.

---

20 2004 *Commission Guidelines on the application of Article 81(3) of the Treaty*, [2004] O.J. C101/97, para 24.

21 See 2014 Notice on agreements of minor importance which do not appreciably restrict competition under Article 101(1) of the Treaty on the Functioning of the European Union (de minimis Notice), [2014] O.J. C291/1 .

22 Case C-226/11, *Expedia Inc.* v. *Autorité de la concurrence and Others*, ECLI:EU:C:2012:795, para 38.

23 Case C-127/73, *BRT v Sabam*, ECLI:EU:C:1974:25.

24 Case C-68/12, *Protimonopolný úrad Slovenskej republiky* v. *Slovenská sporiteľňa a.s.*, ECLI:EU:C:2013:71, para 36.

By way of example, all vertical agreements between undertakings having a market share of less than 30% are thus excluded, except for agreements containing so-called "hardcore restrictions".[25] Hardcore restrictions can only very rarely be justified on the basis of Article 101(3) TFEU.

14.3 Article 102 TFEU: Prohibited Unilateral Market Behaviour

Article 102 TFEU states that any abuse by one or more undertakings of a dominant position within the internal market or in a substantial part of it shall be prohibited as incompatible with the internal market in so far as it may affect trade between Member States. The Treaty again provides a non-exhaustive list of examples,[26] referring to:

(a) directly or indirectly imposing unfair purchase or selling prices or other unfair trading conditions;
(b) limiting production, markets or technical development to the prejudice of consumers;
(c) applying dissimilar conditions to equivalent transactions with other trading parties, thereby placing them at a competitive disadvantage;
(d) making the conclusion of contracts subject to acceptance by the other parties of supplementary obligations which, by their nature or according to commercial usage, have no connection with the subject of such contracts.

Prohibiting above all the unilateral behaviour of one undertaking or of a group of undertakings presenting itself on the market as a single economic operator,[27] Article 102 TFEU contains additional non-defined concepts, which have been clarified early on in the Commission's decision-making practice and the Court of Justice's case law. More specifically, the notions of dominance and abuse are particularly relevant in that respect.

---

25 Commission Regulation 330/2010 of 20 April 2010 on the application of Article 101(3) of the Treaty on the Functioning of the European Union to categories of vertical agreements and concerted practices, [2010] O.J. L102/1.

26 Compare with s8 EAC Competition Act, which defines and classifies, in a more direct way, different types of abuses.

27 See Joined Cases C-395/96 P and C-396/96 P, *Compagnie maritime belge transports and Others* v *Commission*, ECLI:EU:C:2000:132, para 36.

Dominance is a precondition in order for the Article 102 TFEU prohibition to be applicable. Indeed, a non-dominant undertaking engaging in behaviour deemed as abusive under that provision will not be subject to competition law scrutiny. An undertaking is said to have a dominant position if it can prevent effective competition from being maintained on the relevant market by virtue of it having the power to behave to an appreciable extent independently of its competitors, its customers and ultimately of the consumers.[28] In order to determine the existence of such position, the EU Courts accepted that the Commission established, on a case-by-case way, the existence of dominance on a relevant product and geographical market.[29]

Once the market determined, the finding of dominance is above all premised on market shares. The Court established that an undertaking maintaining a market share of 50% or more is presumed to be dominant while a share between 40% and 50% may indicate dominance depending on other factors. An undertaking with a market share below 40% can still be dominant but only in exceptional circumstances in light of other market features.[30] In addition, the market structure may have to be looked at, even when market shares do not permit to derive that the undertaking concerned is dominant.[31]

In its early *Hoffmann LaRoche* judgment, the Court has defined abuse as an objective concept relating to the behaviour of an undertaking in a dominant position which is such as to influence the structure of a market where, as a result of the very presence of the undertaking in question, the degree of competition is weakened and which, through recourse to methods different from those which condition normal competition in products or services on the basis of the transactions of commercial operators, has the effect of hindering the maintenance of the degree of competition still existing in the market or the growth of that competition.[32]

From that definition, two types of abuses have been identified. On the one hand, it captures exploitative abuses, e.g. the charging of monopolist prices to

28 Case 85/76, *Hoffmann-La Roche & Co. AG v Commission of the European Communities*, ECLI:EU:C:1979:36, para 38.

29 Commission Notice on the definition of relevant market for the purposes of Community competition law, [1997] O.J. C372/5.

30 Communication from the Commission—Guidance on the Commission's enforcement priorities in applying Article 82 of the EC Treaty to abusive exclusionary conduct by dominant undertakings, [2009] O.J. C45/7, recital µ&'.(hereinafter 2009 enforcement priorities notice).

31 2009 enforcement priorities notice, recital 15.

32 Case 85/76, *Hoffmann-La Roche & Co. AG v Commission of the European Communities*, ECLI:EU:C:1979:36, para 91.

consumers or clients,[33] On the other hand, it also encompasses exclusionary abuses targeting (potential) competitors.[34] Examples that have been identified throughout the case law include predatory pricing,[35] loyalty discounts,[36] exclusivity agreements, and refusal of access to essential facilities necessary to the creation of a new product or service.[37]

Contrary to Article 101 TFEU, Article 102 does not contain a specific civil law sanction or possibilities for exception. In practice, the administrative enforcement regime will nevertheless apply and the EU Courts have accepted—at least in theory—that abusive behaviour can be justified objectively, for example if it contributes to a more efficient functioning of the market in which the undertaking concerned is active.[38]

14.4 State Aid

Article 107(1) TFEU considers any aid granted by a Member State or through State resources in any form whatsoever which distorts or threatens to distort competition by favouring certain undertakings or the production of certain goods, in so far as it affects trade between Member States, to be incompatible with the internal market.[39] Again, the Treaty did not define the notions of aid and of 'certain' undertakings. The other notions—undertaking, internal market and affectation of trade—are interpreted in coherence with the interpretations of those concepts in Articles 101 and 102 TFEU.

According to consistent case law, any advantage granted by or attributed to a public authority to one or more selected undertakings will be considered as incompatible aid. As such, direct subsidies, but also interest-free loans, interest reductions or tax breaks are considered advantages.[40] Applied in this regard,

33 2009 enforcement priorities notice, recital 7.

34 2009 enforcement priorities notice, recital 6.

35 See Case C-62/86, *AKZO Chemie BV v Commission of the European Communities*, ECLI:EU:C:1991:286.

36 Case C-95/04, *British Airways plc v Commission of the European Communities*, ECLI:EU:C:2007:166.

37 Case C-418/01, *IMS Health GmbH & Co. OHG v NDC Health GmbH & Co. KG*, ECLI:EU:C:2004:257.

38 Case C-52/09, *Konkurrensverket v TeliaSonera Sverige AB*, ECLI:EU:C:2011:83.

39 S14 et seq. of the EAC Competition Act rather refer to subsidies, which potentially are more limited in scope than advantages envisaged by EU law.

40 For more detailed examples of what constitutes aid, see Commission Notice on the notion of State aid as referred to in Article 107(1) of the Treaty on the Functioning of the European Union, [2016] O.J. C262/1.

the existence or not of aid is dependent on the so-called "private investor" test. To the extent that a private undertaking would have made the same investment or transcation as a public authority, the measure at hand is not considered aid.[41]

In order to be prohibited, an aid measure also necessarily has to be selective. Selectivity means that the advantage will only be granted to an individual undertaking or to a particular group of undertakings active within a Member State's territory. A measure targeting a specific sector of the economy or a certain region within a Member State is also deemed selective.[42]

The general prohibition outlined in Article 107(1) TFEU is again not absolute. Articles 107(2) and (3) TFEU contain a list of exceptions excluding measures from the prohibition. The second paragraph contains per se exceptions, i.e. exceptions that do not leave any discretion for the Commission to judge their compatibility (e.g. aid relating to natural disasters), whereas the third allows the Commission some discretion whether or not to accept them. This has given rise to the emergence of soft law instruments outlining how the Commission will use its discretion.[43] In addition, block exemption regulations excluding certain categories of aid up to a certain quantified amount have excluded specific categories of aid from the prohibition.[44]

14.5 Enforcement

The mere inscription of rules in the Treaty framework has not as such given rise in itself to the creation of a competition law culture across the EU internal market. A dedicated enforcement system was necessary in that respect, coupled with a supranational court—the Court of Justice—willing to review and interpret vague notions included in the Treaty. It deserves to be mentioned that the enforcement system gradually grew from being a strong *ex ante* authorisation-focused to a more *ex post* enforcement regime.

---

41 The Court often refers to the 'market economy investor principle', see e.g. Case C482/99, *France v Commission*, ECLI:EU:C:2002:294.

42 Among others Case C-88/03, *Portugal* v *Commission*, ECLI:EU:C:2006:511, para 54.

43 For an overview, see http://ec.europa.eu/competition/state_aid/legislation/legislation.html.

44 Most notably, Commission Regulation (EU) No. 651/2014 of 17 June 2014 declaring certain categories of aid compatible with the internal market in application of Articles 107 and 108 of the Treaty, [2014] O.J. L187/1.

14.5.1 Ex ante *Authorisation as Enforcement Starting Point*

Upon its entry into force in 1958, the EEC Treaty did not envisage one singularly structured enforcement regime for EU competition law.

On the one hand, in relation to State aid, Article 108 TFEU determines that the Commission is to keep under review existing aid schemes, yet, above all, mustbe informed of any plans by Member States to grant or alter aid. Informed in this context actually implies that the advantage to be granted has to be notified to it, following which an approval or rejection decision will be adopted. As such, absent a Commission approval decision, Member States can not proceed in granting aid to the undertakings concerned.[45]

On the other hand, in relation to restrictive agreements and abusive behaviour, Article 103 provides a legal basis for the Council to adopt measures aimed at ensuring compliance with the prohibitions laid down in Article 101(1) and in Article 102 by making provision for fines and periodic penalty payments and delineating the role of Commission and Court of Justice in this regard. In 1962, the Commission was entrusted with the task, by virtue of Regulation 17/62, directly to grant exemptions in accordance with Article 101(3) TFEU. As a result, every agreement which was potentially anticompetitive had to be notified to the Commission, which by virtue of a decision could exempt it from the Article 101(1) TFEU prohibition.[46] Only the Commission was competent to apply Article 101(3) TFEU, which did not have direct effect.[47] The notification obligation allowed the Commission to establish a more or less consistent line of decisions, in which it interpreted Article 101 TFEU. The Court of Justice, in reviewing those decisions, further confirmed or modified the Commission's interpretation of those provisions. The lack of clear time limits for taking a decision and, the continuous increase of notifications nevertheless triggered a reform towards a more ex post enforcement system in 2004.

Article 102 TFEU practices were not subject to a similar notification obligation. In practice, however, the European Commission, from the early days onwards, actively used its freshly conferred enforcement powers also to target dominant undertakings and to penalise their abusive practices. Being allowed to impose fines of up to 10% of the annual turnover of each undertaking, the

---

45 Confirmed in Council Regulation (EU) 2015/1589 of 13 July 2015 laying down detailed rules for the application of Article 108 of the Treaty on the Functioning of the European Union, [2015] O.J. L248/9.

46 Article 9 Council Regulation 17 implementing Articles 85 and 86 of the Treaty, [1962] O.J. L 13/204 (English Special Edition, Chapter 1959–1962, 87) (Hereafter referred to as Regulation 17/62).

47 Article 4 Regulation 17/62.

Commission succeeded in interpreting and enforcing this provision at the same time.[48] Along the way, it shaped the notions of dominance and abuse that are still being applied today.

In addition, Regulation 17/62 set up an elaborate administrative enforcement regime, allowing the Commission to inspect undertakings' premises, to seize documents and to impose fines and periodic penalty payments on those undertakings for having infringed Articles 101 and 102 TFEU. Those fines could be as high as 10% of the undertaking's global annual turnover, a rule that remains in force until today.[49]

14.5.2 *Moving Towards More* ex post *Enforcement*

The focus on ex ante enforcement and the accompanying notification/authorisation obligations imposed on the Commission services became increasingly burdensome, as more and more notifications were made and the Commission's resources were not extended at a comparable pace. Anticipating the accession of ten new Member States in 2004 and the most likely unmanageable increase in Article 101(3) TFEU authorisation requests, the European Commission decided that a reform of the Article 101 TFEU enforcement system was necessary.[50] Emphasising how the basic competition law provisions had become well-established throughout the Union, it proposed to decentralise the application and enforcement of Articles 101 and 102 TFEU, by giving national competition authorities and courts direct powers under Article 101(3) TFEU.

Regulation 1/2003 effectively made this happen from 1 May 2004 onwards. It since obliges national competition authorities and courts to apply Articles 101 and 102 TFEU in full and to ensure that those provisions are interpreted in accordance with the established case law of the Court of Justice and decision-making practice of the Commission.[51] In addition, national competition authorities have been conferred specifically circumscribed powers as regards the types of EU competition law decisions they can/have to adopt.[52]

48 Article 3 Regulation 17/62; see on that development, P. Ibanez Colomo, The Law on Abuses of Dominance and the System of Judicial Remedies, available at http://papers.ssrn.com/sol3/papers.cfm?abstract_id=2270099.

49 Article 15(2)b Regulation 17/62.

50 For the proposal and its background, again see Commission White Paper on the Modernisation of the Rules implementing Articles 85 and 86 of the EC Treaty.

51 Article 3 Council Regulation 1/2003 of 16 December 2002 on the implementation of the rules on competition laid down in Articles 81 and 82 of the Treaty, [2003] O.J. L 1/1.

52 Article 5 Regulation 1/2003.

Although Member States' authorities apply those rules autonomously, the Commission provides for tools to take away a case from national authorities and take over the investigation or to intervene in pending litigation before Member States' courts.[53] Although the Commission now no longer authorises agreements in the realm of Article 101(3) TFEU, the increased adoption of soft law instruments and Commission "help lines" allow it to keep an eye on whether or not the application of EU competition law develops in a coherent way across different Member States' jurisdictions.[54] To that extent, the Commission also assembles all national authorities in a European Competition Network (ECN), within which decisions on case allocation are made in an informal way. Following the allocation decision, the designated authority will initiate or proceed its infringement proceedings, whereas other authorities will refrain from continuing their actions. As such, the Commission seeks to control who deals with a specific case at what time.[55]

Regulation 1/2003 also confirms and extends the Commission's investigative and sanctioning powers, inviting Member States' to streamline theirs in line with the Commission's.[56]

14.6 Concentrations

The Treaty did not mention anything on those concentrations, including acquisitions and certain joint ventures. Their assessment under the Article 101(3) TFEU exemption mechanism or, *ex post* under Article 102 TFEU, was not conducive to legal certainty. For that reason, and responding directly to the limits enounced in the Court's case law,[57] the EU adopted Concentration Control Regulation 4064/89, which has been modified into Regulation 139/2004.[58] The

53 Article 11(6) Regulation 1/2003.

54 For an introductory overview of those help lines, P. Van Cleynenbreugel, 'National courts and EU competition law: lost in multilevel confusion?' in N. Bodiroga-Vukobrat, S. Rodin and G. Sander, *New Europe, Old Values? Reform and Perseverance* (Heidelberg, Springer, 2016), 181–198.

55 On the operations of the European Competition Network, see Joint Statement of the Council and the Commission on the Functioning of the Network of Competition Authorities, http://ec.europa.eu/competition/ecn/joint_statement_en.pdf.

56 See Articles 17–24 Regulation 1/2003.

57 E.g. Case 6/72, *Europemballage Corporation and Continental Can Company Inc. v Commission of the European Communities*, ECLI:EU:C:1973:22.

58 Council Regulation (EEC) No. 4064/89 of 21 December 1989 on the control of concentrations between undertakings, [1989] O.J. L395/1, replaced by Council Regulation (EC) No. 139/

notion of concentration captures any change in control or ownership over an undertaking, through mergers and other forms of control through acquisitions and certain joint ventures.[59]

Turnover thresholds are used to determine whether or not the concentration has a so-called "Union dimension".[60] All intended concentrations with a Union dimension now have to be notified to the European Commission, which is called upon to authorise or prohibit them by means of a decision, to be adopted within strict time limits.[61] Concentrations which do not have a Union dimension, have to be notified to Member State competition authorities, which almost all adopted a similar notification procedure at national level. The test applied in this regard originally focused on whether or not the envisaged concentration would result in a dominant position on the relevant market.[62] The 2004 Regulation explicitly broadened that test, asking the Commission to assess whether the envisaged concentration does not result in a significant impediment of effective competition on a relevant market.[63]

2004 of 20 January 2004 on the control of concentrations between undertakings (the EC Merger Regulation), [2004] O.J. L24/1.

59 Article 3 Regulation 139/2004.

60 Articles 1(2) and (3) Regulation 139/2004.

61 Articles 4 and 10 Regulation 139/2004.

62 Article 2 Regulation 4064/89.

63 Article 2 Regulation 139/2004.

CHAPTER 15

Judicial Enforcement and Implementation of EAC Law

James Otieno-Odek

15.1 Introduction

The East African Community law is found in the Treaty for the Establishment of the East African Community (the EAC Treaty), its Protocols, Directives of the Council of Ministers and Acts of the East African Legislative Assembly (the Assembly) and decisions of the East African Court of Justice (EACJ). The Protocol on the Establishment of the East African Customs Union sets out the customs law of the Community to include the relevant provisions of the Treaty; the Customs Union Protocol; regulations and directives made by the Council; applicable decisions of the EACJ; Acts of the Community enacted by the Assembly and relevant principles of international law.[1] On matters pertaining to implementation of the Treaty, Community organs, institutions and laws take precedence over similar national ones.[2]

The EAC Treaty establishes the EACJ as the judicial organ of the Community.[3] The Court is made up of two divisions: First Instance Division and the Appellate Division. Cases are lodged before the First Instance Division and an aggrieved party may institute appeal before the Appellate Division. The First Instance Division is at any given time composed of not more than ten Judges whereas the Appellate Division is comprised of five Judges.[4] The EAC Treaty allows national courts of the Partner States to adjudicate on issues involving the Community. However, decisions of the EACJ on the interpretation and application of the Treaty take precedence over decisions of national courts on similar matters.[5]

1 Article 39 of the Customs Union Protocol.

2 Article 8 (4) of the EAC Treaty.

3 Article 23 of the EAC Treaty stipulates that the Court shall be a judicial body which shall ensure the adherence to law in the interpretation and application of and compliance with the Treaty.

4 Article 24 (2) of the EAC Treaty.

5 Article 33 (2) of the EAC Treaty.

© JAMES OTIENO-ODEK, 2017 | DOI 10.1163/9789004322073_030
This is an open access chapter distributed under the terms of the CC-BY-NC License.

Primarily, the EACJ has jurisdiction over interpretation and application of the EAC Treaty.[6] The Court's jurisdiction includes advisory and arbitral jurisdiction and any such jurisdiction that may be conferred upon it any time by the Council of Ministers. The jurisdiction of the Court has since been extended to cover trade and investment disputes.[7]

The execution of a judgment of the EACJ which imposes pecuniary obligation on a person is governed by the rules of civil procedure in force in the Partner State in which execution is to take place.[8] Judgments of the Court are enforced and executed at national level by the Partner States.

This Chapter is a snapshot of the emerging jurisprudence from the EACJ and a preview of how EAC Partner States are enforcing and implementing the Community law in their national jurisdictions. In appraising how the Partner States are enforcing and implementing the community law, it is vital to note that in the case of *Timothy Alvin Kahoho—v- The Secretary General of the* EAC,[9] the EACJ observed that the Summit[10] is the driver of of East African integration and political federation. In *Peter Anyang Nyongo—v- The Attorney General of the Republic of Kenya,*[11] the EACJ held that a Partner State may not invoke the provisions of its internal law as a justification for its failure to perform obligations under the EAC Treaty. The Court expressed that it cannot be lawful for a State which has voluntarily entered into a Treaty with other States by which rights and obligations are vested not only on the State parties but also on their people, to plead that it is unable to perform its obligations because its laws do not permit it to do so. In *Henry Kyarimpa—v- Attorney General of Uganda,*[12] the Appellate Division of the EACJ expressed that in adjudging an impugned State action as being internationally wrongful, the Court asks itself the question not whether such action is in conformity with internal law, but rather whether it is in conformity with the EAC Treaty. The Court found that where the complaint

6 Article 21 (1) of the EAC Treaty.

7 On 30th November, 2013, the Summit of the EAC Head of States approved the Council of Ministers' decision to extend the Courts jurisdiction to include matters of trade, investment and EAC Monetary Union. To this end, the Partner States of the Community will need to agree a Protocol tooperationalize the extended jurisdiction as per Article 27(2).

8 Article 44 of the EAC Treaty.

9 Appeal No. 2 of 2013.

10 Article 9 (1) (a) of the EAC Treaty establishes the Summit as an organ of the Community. In Article 10 (1), the Summit consists of the Heads of State or Government of the Partner States. In Article 11 (1), the Summit gives the general directions and impetus as to the development and achievement of the objectives of the Community.

11 EACJ Reference No. 1 of 2006.

12 EACJ Appeal No. 6 of 2014.

is that the action was inconsistent with internal law and, on that basis, a breach of a Partner State's obligation under the EAC Treaty to observe the principle of the rule of law, it is the Court's inescapable duty to consider the internal law of such Partner State in determining whether the conduct complained of amounts to a violation or contravention of the Treaty.[13]

15.2 Emerging Jurisprudence from the EACJ on Interpretation of the Treaty

The EACJ is very active in the interpretation of the EAC Treaty. The Court has expressed that the Community is a people centered and market-driven cooperation,[14] and in this regard, consultation and participation of the people outside the Summit and other organs of the Community is imperative. In the case of *East Africa Law Society and 4 others v. Attorney General of Kenya and 3 others*,[15] the Court expressed:

> It is common knowledge that the private sector and civil society participated in the negotiations that led to the conclusion of the Treaty among the Partner States and, as we have just observed, that they continue to participate in the making of Protocols thereto. Furthermore, as we noted earlier in this judgment, Article 30 entrenches the people's right to participate in protecting the integrity of the Treaty. We think that construing the Treaty as if it permits sporadic amendments at the whims of officials without any form of consultation with stakeholders would be a recipe for regression to the situation lamented in the preamble of "lack of strong participation of the private sector and civil society" that led to the collapse of the previous Community….Failure to carry out consultation outside the Summit, Council and the Secretariat was inconsistent with a principle of the Treaty and therefore constituted an infringement of the Treaty (…)

13 The Court took a similar view in the case of Plaxeda Lugumba v. The Secretary General of the East African Community, Reference No. 8 of 2010 (First Instance Division); and The Attorney General of Rwanda v. Plaxeda Lugumba, Appeal No. 1 of 2012 (Appellate Division).

14 Article 7 (1) of the EAC Treaty.

15 EACJ Reference No. 3 of 2007.

Another notable statement from the EACJ relates to the interpretation of the principle of variable geometry. Article 7(1) of the EAC Treaty identifies the principle of variable geometry as one of the operational principles in the integration of the Community. Variable geometry is defined in Article 1 of the EAC Treaty to mean the principle of flexibility which allows for progression in co-operation among a sub-group of members in a larger integration scheme in a variety of areas and at different speeds. Article 7(1) (e) of the EAC Treaty describes the principle of variable geometry as one which allows for progression in co-operation among groups within the Community for wider integration schemes in various fields and at different speeds.

In the *Advisory Opinion in Reference by Council of Minister,*[16] the Court opined that variable geometry is intended to allow those Partner States who cannot implement a particular decision simultaneously or immediately to implement it at a suitable certain future time or simply at a different speed while at the same time allowing those who are able to implement immediately to do so. The Court held that the principle of variable geometry is a strategy of implementation of Community decisions and a guide to the integration process.

On *locus standi* of individuals to bring action alleging violation of the EAC Treaty, the Court in *Peter Anyang Nyongo—v- The Attorney General of the Republic of Kenya*[17] expressed that under Article 30 (1) of the EAC Treaty, a claimant is not required to show a right or interest that was infringed or damage that was suffered as a consequence of the matter complained about but that it is enough if it is alleged that the matter complained of infringes a provision of the Treaty in a relevant manner. This principle was equally applied in *Samuel Mukira Muhochi—v- Attorney General of the Uganda*[18] where the Court held that once there is an allegation of infringement of the provision of the EAC Treaty, the Court has jurisdiction to interpret and apply the provisions alleged to be infringed under the powers conferred on it by Articles 23 (1) and 27 (1) of the EAC Treaty. It must be noted that in *Peter Anyang' Nyong'o—v- The Attorney General of the Republic of Kenya,*[19] the EACJ held that exhaustion of local remedies is not a pre-condition for accessing the Court.

In relation to Bills presented before the Assembly, the EACJ in the case of *Callist Andrew Mwatella & 2 others vs. East African Community,*[20] held that all

16 EACJ Application No. 1 of 2008.

17 EACJ Reference No. 1 of 2006.

18 EACJ Reference No. 5 of 2011.

19 EACJ Reference No. 1 of 2006.

20 EACJ Reference No. 1 of 2005.

Bills introduced into the Assembly belong to the Assembly, whether tabled initially by way of Private Members' Bills, Community Bills or by the Council of Ministers. As such, permission of the Assembly is required to withdraw any Bill from the House.

15.3 Emerging EACJ Jurisprudence on the Rule of Law and Human Rights

The rule of law is the *sine qua non* of any democratic society. In *Baranzira Raphael & another—v- Attorney General of the Republic of Burundi*,[21] the First Instance Division of the Court examined the concept of rule of law. Quoting from a UN Report, the court stated:

> The concept of the rule of law refers to the principle of governance to which all persons, institutions and entities, public or private, including the State itself, are accountable to laws that are publicly promulgated, equally enforced and independently adjudicated and which are consistent with international human rights norms and standards. It requires, as well, measures to ensure adherence to the principle of supremacy of the law, equality before the law, accountability to the law, fairness in the application of the law, separation of power, participation in decision making, legal certainty, avoidance of arbitrariness and procedural and legal transparency. (See Report of the (UN) Secretary General on the Rule of Law and Transitional Justice in Conflict and Post-Conflict Societies, UN Doc.5/2004/616 (2004) para.6)

The Appellate Division of the EACJ has had occasion to pronounce itself on the need for an applicant to prove the allegations made in a complaint or reference. In *Union Trade Centre Limited—v- The Attorney General of Uganda*,[22] the Appellate Division observed that in law, pleadings in court (whether in the form of Reference, Response to Reference, Notice of Motion, Statement of Claim or by whatever name called) are not evidence. They are averments of the proof of which is submitted to the trier of fact. Evidence is the means by which those averments are proved or disproved. The Court opined on the need to dispense justice effectively before the national courts. In discharging

21 EACJ, First Instance Division Reference No. 15 of 2014.

22 EACJ Appeal No. 1 of 2015.

judicial duties, the Court expressed, although speed is good justice is even better and often, justice hurried is justice buried.

Notable features from the jurisprudence of the EACJ appertain to its human rights jurisdiction. In *James Katabazi—v- Secretary General of the* EAC,[23] the Court held that while it did not have jurisdiction over human rights violations *per se*, it may still consider human rights violation if it falls under the provisions of Article 27(1) of the EAC Treaty. It was noted that one role of the Court is to interpret the Treaty (Article 27(1)), which includes "respect for the rule of law" as per Article 6(d).[24] The Court stated that the overriding consideration of the rule of law is that both the rulers and the governed are equally subject to the same law of the land. In *Attorney General of Rwanda—v- Plaxeda Rugumba*,[25] the Appellate Division found that although the EACJ does not yet have jurisdiction to adjudicate disputes concerning human rights *per se*, Article 6(d) of the EAC Treaty and Article 6 of the African Charter allow the Court to assert jurisdiction over human rights claims. In *Samuel Mukira Mohochi v. Attorney-General of Uganda*,[26] the Court re-iterated that whereas there are no human rights provisions in the EAC Treaty, the Court does have jurisdiction over breaches of the State's obligations under Articles 6(d), 7(2) and 104 of the Treaty and Article 7 of the East African Common Market Protocol. The Court in expressing that human rights infringements establish a legal foundation for jurisdiction under Article 27(1) of the Treaty stressed that the obligations in Article 6(d) are serious government obligations of immediate and consistent conduct.

In *Mary Ariviza and Okotch Mondoh v. Attorney General of Kenya and Secretary General of the East African Community*,[27] the EACJ affirmed that "due process" is a component of the "rule of law" and defined it as the "following of laid down laws and procedures." In *Henry Kyarimpa—v- Attorney*

23 EACJ, First Instance Division, Reference No. 1 of 2007.

24 Article 6 (d) of the EAC Treaty provides that one of the fundamental principles of cooperation in the Community is good governance including adherence to the principles of democracy, the rule of law, accountability, transparency, social justice, equal opportunities, gender equality, as well as the recognition, promotion and protection of human and peoples rights in accordance with the provisions of the African Charter on Human and Peoples' Rights.

25 EACJ Appellate Division, Appeal No. 1 of 2012.

26 EACJ First Instance Division, Reference No. 5 of 2011.

27 EACJ First Instance Division, Ref. No. 7 of 2010.

General of Uganda,[28] the EACJ Appellate Division expressed that the Court cannot act in vain. The Court affirmed:

> We must say that when we don our gowns, step out of our chambers, and enter the temple of justice to do our sacred duty of dispensing justice, we never ever leave our common sense outside. As a Court of Law, we cannot act in vain… Decisions of this Court under Article 30 of the Treaty are decisions in rem (binding as against both the parties and non parties alike) and not in personam (binding only on the parties before the court). The Court cannot shirk its duty to make such decisions because third parties who have not been afforded an opportunity to be heard are thereby affected.[29]

In *Henry Kyarimpa—v- Attorney General of Uganda*,[30] the Appellate Division further expressed that:

> …When the Court has to consider whether particular actions of a Partner State are unlawful and contravene the Principle of the Rule of Law under the Treaty, the Court has jurisdiction, and, indeed, a duty to consider the internal laws of the Partner State and apply its own appreciation thereof to the provisions of the Treaty. The Court does not and should not abide the determination of the import of such internal law by the National Courts. By parity of reasoning, it should be equally obvious that when what is alleged to be a violation of the Treaty Principle of the Rule of Law is the disobedience of an order of the Court of a Partner State, the Court should not abide the determination, if any, by such National Court on whether such Court's order has been disobeyed. It is for this Court to satisfy itself, without the input of the National Court, whether there has been disobedience or disregard of a Court order and to apply that finding in the interpretation of the Treaty.

---

28 EACJ Appeal No. 6 of 2014.

29 Article 30 of the EAC Treaty stipulates that any person who is a resident in a Partner State may refer for determination by the Court, the legality of any Act, regulations, directive, decision or action of Partner State or an institution of the Community on the grounds that such Act, regulation, directive, decision or action is unlawful or is an infringement of the provisions of the Treaty.

30 EACJ Appeal No. 6 of 2014.

15.4 Emerging Jurisprudence from National Courts on Enforcement and Implementation of Community Law

The national courts of the EAC Partner States have jurisdictional competence to consider and determine matters relevant to the Community.[31] Most of the cases that have been urged before national courts pertain to the implementation and enforcement of the EAC Customs Management Act. The Act provides the legal framework for the trade regime of the Community. The Act is the foundation for private sector engagement and involvement in the Community; it embodies the market driven component of the EAC cooperation.

In criminal matters, unless otherwise expressly specified, offences under the Act are dealt with in accordance with the laws on criminal procedure of a Partner State.[32] In civil cases, the applicable law is the law of the Partner State with the relevant court being the national court with national pecuniary jurisdiction.

The EAC Customs Management Act lays out procedures to be followed in the resolution of customs disputes. Any suit or action under the Act may be brought in the name of the Commissioner and the Commissioner may sue and be sued in the name of the Commissioner.[33] The Commissioner may, where satisfied that a person has committed an offence under the Act in respect of which a fine is provided or in which anything is liable to forfeiture, compound the offence and may order such person to pay an amount of money not exceeding the fine which the person would have paid if prosecuted or convicted of the offence.[34] However the Commissioner may not exercise the power to compound unless the person admits he has committed the offence and requests the Commissioner to compound the offence.

In the Tanzanian case of *Tanzania Revenue Authority—v- Murtazar Hussein Budha*,[35] the Revenue Authority in the exercise of its powers under section 219 (1) of the EAC Customs Management Act charged the respondent with the offence of being found in possession of uncustomed goods contrary to Section 200 of the Act and Section 47 of the Value Added Tax (VAT) Act. The trial court held that "orders emanating from compounded offences under Section 219 of the Customs Management Act lack forum of enforcement." This finding by the Tanzania national court portends a challenge to enforcement of the EAC

31 Article 33 of the EAC Treaty.

32 Section 220 (2) of the EAC Customs Management Act.

33 Section 221 of the EAC Customs Management Act.

34 Section 221 of the EAC Customs Management Act.

35 Tanzania Criminal Appeal No. 285 of 2008.

Customs Management Act. From the perspective of the Revenue Authority, the ruling diminishes the advantages of compounding offences.

Where a person is dissatisfied with the decision of the Commissioner, he or she may lodge an application for review to the Commissioner within 30 days of the decision. Section 230 (1) of the EAC Customs Management Act provides that appeals from the decision of the Commissioner under Section 229 of the Act lie to the Tax Appeals Tribunal established under Section 231. The appeal ought to be lodged within 45 days of the Commissioner's decision.

In the Ugandan case of *Kawuki Mathias—v- Commissioner General of Uganda Revenue Authority*,[36] the Ugandan High Court held that the statutory procedure under the EAC Customs Management Act must be followed; that when statute prescribes a certain procedure, it is unlawful to follow a different procedure. In the Uganda case, the applicant Mr. Kawuki Mathias filed an originating Notice of Motion before the Commercial Division of the High Court under Section 98 of the Civil Procedure Act seeking release of his container of imported cargo comprising of sandals. The Ugandan Revenue Authority objected to the suit on the ground that the suit was prematurely instituted, bad in law and ought to be dismissed. It was contended that the Applicant should have exhausted the procedures provided for under the EAC Customs Management Act before filing the application. Section 230 (1) of the EAC Customs Management Act provides that appeals from a decision of a Commissioner under Section 229 of the Act lie to the Tax Appeals Tribunal established under Section 231. Taking into consideration the above provisions, the Ugandan High Court held that the application was prematurely filed for not having exhausted the appeal procedures under Section 231 of the EAC Customs Management Act.

Principles and concepts from administrative law have been adopted and applied by the national courts in the enforcement and implementation of Community law. It has been expressed that in the implementation of the EAC Customs Management Act, the trading parties have a legitimate expectation that they would not be compelled to meet tax obligations which are not imposed by the law; that the revenue authorities shall not demand taxes or import duty when the law does not provide for the same; and that nationals would not be made to bear unlawful tax obligations.

In *Greenberg Trading Limited—v- Kenya Revenue Authority*,[37] it was held that the doctrine of legitimate expectations applies in the implementation of the

36 HC Miscellaneous Cause No. 14 of 2014.

37 Mombasa HC Misc. App. No. 52 of 2010.

EAC Customs Management Act.[38] The Court expressed that it is a legitimate expectation of an import duty payer that, once a tax liability arises, the Revenue Authority would notify the tax payer and demand payment of the same and in doing so, the Authority would specify how the liability arose, the transactions in question and how the same is payable. The Court expressed that it is a legitimate expectation that the regular practice of the Revenue Authority is that once goods have been verified and duty thereon paid, the Authority would release the goods to the importer. It must be noted that in *Coastal Bottlers Limited—v- Commissioner of Domestic Taxes*,[39] it was held that when an act is against the law, the doctrine of legitimate expectations is inapplicable.

Apart from the doctrine of legitimate expectations, national courts have held that in implementation of the EAC Customs Management Act, the Revenue Authority is under obligation to observe the rules of natural justice. Under the Act, the Commissioners of Revenue Authorities in all the EAC Partner States have wide powers to assess and levy import duty, VAT, to seize goods and to compound offences. It has been expressed that these powers must be exercised in accordance with the rules of natural justice and fair administrative action. In *Major General David Tinyefuza—v- Attorney General*,[40] the Uganda Constitutional Court expressed that

> the notion of a subjective or unfettered discretion is contrary to the rule of law. All power has legal limits and the rule of law demands that the Courts should be able to examine the exercise of discretionary power. If therefore the executive in exercising its discretion under an Act of Parliament has exceeded the four corners within which the Parliament has decided it can exercise its discretion, such an exercise of discretion would be ultra vires the Act and a court of law must be able to hold it to be so.

In *Kenya Revenue Authority v. Spectre International Limited*,[41] the Kenya Court of Appeal re-affirmed that:

---

38 The concept of legitimate expectation arises where in a particular situation a person has an expectation that a public body or private parties will retain a long-standing practice or keep a promise. Legitimate or reasonable expectation may arise either from an express promise given on behalf of a public authority or the existence of a regular practice which the claimant can reasonably expect to continue.

39 Nairobi High Court Miscellaneous Application No. 1756 of 2005.

40 Uganda Constitutional Petition No. 1 of 1996.

41 Civil Appeal No. 235 of 2010.

> it is trite law that persons charged with statutory powers and duty ought to exercise the same reasonably and fairly and the discretion ought not to be exercised whimsically, unreasonably, arbitrarily or against the tenets of natural justice. If the discretion is used arbitrarily or unreasonably, the court may step in to remedy the situation.

An aspect of the EAC trade regime that has been adjudicated by a Partner State court relates to product classification and product valuation under the EAC Customs Management Act. Article 8 (2) of the Customs Union Protocol stipulates that the Partners States shall adopt the "Harmonized Commodity Description and Coding System" for product classification and follow the opinion of the World Customs Organization.

In *BETA Healthcare International Limited—vs- Kenya Revenue Authority*,[42] the dispute related to classification of a product either as a medicament or a food supplement. The applicant had imported Sandoz Calcium Forte—500 and declared the goods as medicaments and paid zero import duty. On the other hand, the Revenue Authority upon conducting a post clearance audit classified the imported goods as food supplement liable to import duty Ksh. 127, 795,427. The applicant requested for an opinion of the classification of the goods from the World Customs Organization. The High Court held that the opinion of the World Customs Organization classifying the product as food supplement was binding. The Court observed that under Section 126 of the EAC Customs Management Act the customs authority is required to apply or interpret the section and the 4th Schedule on product classification after taking into account the decisions, rulings, opinions and interpretations given by the directorate, WTO or the Customs Cooperation Council.

The Uganda High Court has had an opportunity to consider and determine the implementation of EAC Customs Management Act in relation to product valuation. In *Testimony Motors—v- Commissioner of Customs Uganda Revenue Authority*,[43] the Ugandan Revenue Authority unilaterally suspended the use of the transaction value and adopted the alternative method for customs valuation. The action against the Revenue Authority was for a declaration that the directive to unilaterally suspend the operation of the transaction value method provided in Section 122 and the 4th Schedule of the EAC Customs Management Act was arbitrary and unlawful. The interpretative notes of the Act provides that the methods of valuation are set out in sequential order of application and the primary method of customs valuation is defined in paragraph 2 to be

42 Miscellaneous. Application No. 4 of 2009.

43 High Court Case No. 212 of 2012.

the transaction value method. The Ugandan Court issued a declaration that the directive of the Commissioner of Customs of the Uganda Revenue Authority to suspend the operation of the transaction value method was unlawful to the extent that it excluded the application of the transaction value method for assessment of customs duty.

The relationship between the EAC Customs Management Act and the fundamental right to property and detention of goods for non-payment of duty has been considered by the national court in Kenya. In *Cyrwan Enterprises—v- Kenya Revenue Authority*,[44] the petitioner challenged the constitutionality of the provisions of the EAC Customs Management Act that permitted the Kenya Revenue Authority officials to intercept and detain goods they considered suspicious until duty was paid. It was argued that the Act was contrary to Article 40 of the Kenya Constitution that protects the right to property.[45] It was argued that the powers of the Revenue Authority to intercept and detain goods were an arbitrary detention of one's property. The Court held that collection of taxes was an important component of the modern state and statutes governing collection of taxes are consistent with the letter and spirit of the Constitution. It was observed that the provisions of EAC Customs Management Act were part of a statutory scheme aimed at efficient and effective collection of customs duty; that Section 210 of the Act only set out the kind of goods liable to forfeiture and did not empower the revenue authority to arbitrarily take a person's property. It was noted that taking the provisions of impugned sections within the context of the entire Act, the EAC Customs Management Act demonstrates that forfeiture is not arbitrary but is subject to reasonable grounds. Moreover, the Court observed that there was a procedure for determining the rights of a party whose property had been seized on account of suspicion of breach of the EAC Customs Mangement Act and for the Commissioner to secure the collection of taxes. The Court concluded that Sections 210 and 211 of EAC Customs Management Act were not unconstitutional or in violation of Article 40 of the Constitution of Kenya. In *Kasibo Joshua—v- Commissioner of Customs, Uganda Revenue Authority*,[46] it was held that it was wrong to forfeit and condemn the goods if the fines and penalties imposed were wrong in the first place.

---

44 High Court Constitutional Petition No. 322 of 2011.

45 Article 40 (1) of the Kenya Constitution provides inter alia that every person has the right either individually or in association with others to own and acquire property. Article 40 (1) stipulates that the State shall not deprive a person of property of any description or of any interest in or right over property of any description unless the deprivation is for a public purpose and provision is made for compensation.

46 Uganda HC Misc. App. No. 44 of 2007.

Apart from the adopting principles of administrative law, the practical aspects of regional trade integration has been a subject of adjudicate by national courts. One of the factors determining successful regional integration is trade facilitation. Trade facilitation provides an important opportunity for integrating countries to increase the benefits from open trade, and contributing to economic growth and poverty reduction.[47] The infrastructural and logistical aspects of trade facilitation have impact on efficient and effective movement of goods within and among the integrating States.

Trade facilitation focuses inter alia on transactions at the border, such as documentary requirements, transparency of customs clearance and transit procedures, and disciplines on fees and taxes. Comprehensive trade facilitation examines the costs that traders and producers face from production until the delivery of their goods and services to the overseas buyer and thereby includes all the transaction costs both directly and indirectly associated with the trading process. In regional integration, the legal framework for trade facilitation is significant. A vital logistical aspect for regional trade is clearance of goods at the port of entry either for domestic consumption, transit to frontier states or goods destined for Export Processing Zones in a Partner State.

Port clearance of goods is largely handled by clearing agents and the issue liability of owner of goods for acts of a duly authorized agent is a pertinent question in customs law. Once goods have entered a Partner State, Regulation 174 of the EAC Customs Management Act provides that a security bond shall be furnished to cover movement of goods between points of importation and re-exportation or transit.

In *Alltex EPZ Ltd.—v- Kenya Revenue Authority*,[48] the applicant was licensed to manufacture goods under bond as an Export Processing Zone (EPZ) within the meaning of Section 160 of the EAC Customs Management Act. An employee of Alltex fraudulently cleared some goods destined for the EPZ and diverted them into the Kenya domestic market. The Revenue Authority demanded import duty for the fraudulently cleared goods. The legal issue was whether a licensee must pay taxes secured by the security bond when the imported goods destined to the EPZ are diverted by criminal or delinquent acts of an employee. It was argued that the licensee was not liable to pay taxes as the criminal acts of the employee were not done in the course of employment; that once an employee is engaged in fraud he was outside the scope of his employment. The Revenue Authority submitted that there are judicial decisions to support the position that a tax payer is liable to pay tax notwithstanding the criminal or

47 World Bank, Policy Note No: 27 by Barbara Rippel November, 2011.

48 Miscellaneous Application No. 709 of 2008.

delinquent conduct of the employee (See *R v. Kenya Revenue Authority ex parte Africa Boot Limited, HC Misc. App No. 24 of 2010; R- v- Commissioner of Customs ex parte Transami (K) Limited.*[49] The Kenya High Court citing *R- v- Commissioner of Customs ex parte Transami (K) Limited,*[50] held that an owner of any goods who authorizes an agent to act for him is liable for the acts and declarations by the agent. Citing with approval the decision in *R v. Kenya Revenue Authority ex parte Africa Boot Limited,*[51] the Court emphasized that when a customs agent engages in fraudulent activities, the importer has to bear the loss with fortitude and find a way of recovering the money misappropriated from the customs agent; that a prudent tax payer will always monitor the activities of its agent so as to ensure compliance with the law.

In the realm of intellectual property, the case of *R- v-Kenya Revenue Authority ex parte Bata Shoe Company (K) Ltd,*[52] provides a case study on the interface between intellectual property rights, customs and value added tax in the context of the EAC Customs Management Act. One of the grounds raised by Bata Shoe Co. (K) Limited as the applicant was that the Revenue Authority's decision to demand payment of taxes on royalties the applicant paid to an entity known as Bata Brands was ultra vires the EAC Customs Management Act and the Revenue Authority's powers. According to the applicant, the distribution royalties is not subject to customs duty as they are not royalties related to the goods being valued that the buyer must pay within the meaning of Rule 9(i) (c) of the 4th Schedule to the EAC Customs Management Act. It was contended that subparagraph 1(c) to the Note on Interpretation of Rule 9(i) (c) of the 4th Schedule provides that—

> Payments made by the buyer, for the right to distribute or resell the imported goods shall not be added to the price actually paid or payable for the imported goods if such payments are not a condition of sale for export to Partner state of the imported goods.

The applicant maintained it was not obliged to pay the customs and VAT on the buying commission by virtue of the provisions of Paragraph 1 of the Note of Interpretation of Paragraph 2(1) of the 4th Schedule which provides that:

49 Nairobi High Court Miscellaneous Application No. 81 of 2011.

50 Nairobi High Court Miscellaneous Application No. 81 of 2011.

51 High Court Miscellaneous Application No. 24 of 2010.

52 Judicial Review Case No. 36 of 2011.

> the price actually paid or payable is the total payment made by the buyer to or for the benefit of the seller for the imported goods.

The Revenue Authority in demanding customs duty contended that payment of duty was permitted under Section 122 and paragraph 9(1) (c) of the 4th Schedule. It was submitted that the Interpretive Notes to paragraph 9(1) (c) clarify that royalties and licence fees may include among other things payment in respect of patents, trademarks and copyrights. The Revenue Authority asserted that two conditions must be established for chargeability of royalties namely, the royalty payment relates to the goods being valued and the royalty is paid pursuant to a condition of sale. It was the Revenue Authority's case that both conditions were satisfied in relation to the goods sold by the applicant. The Revenue Authority cited the case of *Republic v Kenya Revenue Authority ex-parte Beirsdorf East Africa Ltd*,[53] where it was expressed:

> .... payment of royalties by the applicant to Biersdorf is a condition of sale of their imported patented goods. I agree with the respondent that if royalties were not a condition of sale anyone would be at liberty to import, manufacture or even distribute Biersdorf's products without permission of the patent holder. That would be an unacceptable trade practice. The relevant law must be interpreted in a manner that makes economic sense. The only instance in which payments made by a buyer for the right to distribute or resale imported goods may not be added to the price actually paid or payable for purposes of determining custom value is where the payments (including royalties) are not a condition of sale.

The trial court in *R—v- Kenya Revenue Authority ex parte Bata Shoe Company (K) Ltd*,[54] observed that the royalty fees paid to Bata Brands by Bata Shoe (K) Limited were payable in respect of imported goods as well as goods manufactured locally. The Court held that the royalty fees were paid for the use of the trademarks in Kenya and they had nothing to do with the prices of imported products. The Court expressed that it would be a herculean exercise to try and separate royalties for locally manufactured goods and imported goods so as to find out what the price payable for the imported goods is. The Court concluded that the Court was not the forum for assessment of taxes, that it is the duty of

53 Nairobi High Court Miscellaneous Application No. 413 of 2009.

54 Judicial Review Case No. 36 of 2011.

the Revenue Authority to assess the tax due and payable and the court will not interfere with the statutory functions of the Revenue Authority.

Aside from trade in goods, the trade regime of the EAC incorporates trade in services. Partner States have undertaken to adopt measures to achieve free movement of services.[55] The case of *Barclays Bank of Kenya Limited—v- Kenya Revenue Authority*,[56] is a pointer on how Kenyan courts deal with taxation of service charge on credit card transactions in cross border trade in services. The relevant facts of the case are that Barclays Bank (K) Limited enables its customers to make payment for goods and services in Kenya and elsewhere using credit card instead of cash. To provide credit card services, the Bank is a member of a wide network operated by international credit card companies such as VISA CARD, American Express (AMEX) and Master Card. These companies administer a world-wide consumer payment system which enables their members to provide their customers with the means of making payment. Barclays Bank (K) Limited pays various fees to the Card companies to access the networks. The fees paid to the card companies include Association Fees, Quarterly Service Fees, International Service Fee, and VISANET (internet software licence) Service fee, Interchange fees (for clearing and settlement fees, risk monitoring) and compliance fee between issuers of the card and the networks. The issue in the *Barclays* case was whether such fees are royalty or professional management fee subject to withholding tax under the provisions of the EAC Customs Management Act and the relevant Kenya revenue laws. The Kenyan High Court held that such fees are not royalty and are not professional management fees subject to withholding tax.

15.5 Emerging Jurisprudence on Recognition and Enforcement of Foreign Judgments in EAC

The EAC Treaty calls for "standardization of judgments of courts within the Community" and cooperation in "judicial and legal matters with a view to harmonizing their judicial and legal systems".[57] Each of the Partner States has national courts which delivers judgments that may need to be enforced and executed in another Partner State's national jurisdiction. The EAC Treaty in Article 44 provides the legal framework for execution of EACJ judgments in the Partner States. However, the legal framework for execution of a Partner State

55 Article 104 (1) of the EAC Treaty.

56 Misc. Appl. No. 1223 of 2007.

57 Article 126 (1) of the EAC Treaty.

national judgment in the territory of another Partner State is a subject that is not dealt with by the Treaty. This issue depends on the national legal framework for execution of foreign judgments.

Kenya, Uganda and Tanzania have Foreign Judgment Reciprocal Enforcement Acts which permit judgments of each Partner State's national court to be enforced and executed in another Partner State.[58] The respective Acts of each country has designated the other countries as designated countries for purposes of foreign judgment reciprocal enforcement.

In Kenya, enforcement of foreign judgments is the subject of *The Foreign Judgments (Reciprocal Enforcement) Act (Cap 43 of the Laws of Kenya)*. The objective of the Act is to make provision for enforcement of judgments given in countries outside Kenya which accord reciprocal treatment to judgments given in Kenya. Litigation on enforcement of foreign judgment has been considered in various cases in Kenya. In *Intalframe Ltd—v- Mediterranean Shipping Company,*[59] it was held that the basic principle upon which neighbouring or other states provide enforcement of foreign judgments is one of reciprocity. (See *also Ssebaggala & Sons Electric Centre Limited—v- Kenya National Shipping Lime Limited;*[60] *Pioneer General Assurance Society Limited—v- Zilfikarali Nimji Javer;*[61] *Societe de Transports International Rwanda—v- H. Abdi.*[62]

In *Jayesh Hasmukh Shah—v- Navin Haria & another,*[63] enforceability of a foreign judgment from non-designated country was considered. The appellant sought to enforce and execute in Kenya a judgment from Ethiopia which is not a designated country under the provisions of Foreign Judgments (Reciprocal Enforcement) Act (Cap 43 of the Laws of Kenya). The Kenya Court of Appeal held that in the absence of a reciprocal enforcement arrangement, a foreign judgment is enforceable in Kenya as a claim in common law. The common law principles on enforcement of foreign judgments were extensively elaborated in the case of *Adams & Others—v- Cape Industrials PLC.*[64] Another relevant case law on enforceability of foreign judgment from a non-designated country is the Uganda case of *Christopher Sales & Another—v- The Attorney Genera.*[65]

58 See Tanzania, The Reciprocal Enforcement of Foreign Judgments Act, Chapter 8 of the Laws of Tanzania; see Uganda Foreign Judgments (Reciprocal Enforcement) Act Chapter 9 of the Laws of Uganda.

59 (1986) KLR.

60 (2000) LawAfrica LR 931.

61 (2006) eKLR.

62 Civil Application No. NAI 298 of 1997.

63 [2016] eKLR, Nairobi Civil Appeal No. 147 of 2009.

64 (1990) Ch. 433.

65 Uganda HCCC No. 91 of 2011.

In this case, the Uganda High Court held that a foreign judgment from the United States of America (USA) was enforceable in Uganda despite the fact that the USA was not a designated country under the provisions of Uganda Foreign J*udgments* (*Reciprocal Enforcement*) *Act* (*Cap 9, Laws of Uganda*).

15.6 Conclusions and Recommendations

The emerging jurisprudence from the EACJ and the national courts of the Partner States depict a positive trend towards development of local jurisprudence in the interpretation and application of Community law. Most of the cases before the EACJ are premised on violation of EAC Treaty provisions particularly the Articles on good governance and rule of law. Through the craft of judicial interpretation, human rights litigation has found its way into the EACJ jurisdictional competence. It is observable that the EACJ is making positive contribution to Community jurisprudence on the rule of law, good governance and respect for human rights. The Court's decisions play a role in putting the national governments of the Partner States under check and control. Likewise, the residents of the EAC Partner States have found a supranational forum at which they can ventilate grievances on violation of their fundamental rights and freedoms. The Bar Associations have also found an additional forum in which to practice and sharpen their advocacy skills. To this end, the EACJ plays a significant role in human resource capacity building on regional integration issues within the Community. The Court is incrementally institutionalizing the rule of law within the Community.

On trade liberalization, disputes on interpretation and application of the EAC Customs Management Act have rarely found their way before the EACJ. There is limited litigation before the Court on the EAC Trade Regime. The EACJ has received no single case on the EAC Customs Union. In 2008, *Mordern Holdings—v- Kenya Ports Authority*,[66] filed a customs union reference case but the Court dismissed it for want of jurisdiction. The dismissal of this case by the Court for lack of jurisdiction was a big blow to the business community that has since shunned the Court.

In a majority of the cases before the EACJ, the applicants are natural persons or Bar Associations of the Partner States. Litigation by the business community or commercial corporate entities is very limited before the Court. There is need to encourage the private sector to be active before the Court. The limited participation of the business community may be explained by the establishment

66 Reference No. 1 of 2008.

of parallel EAC Dispute Resolution Mechanisms (Quasi Judicial Bodies). Much as the EACJ is the main judicial organ of the Community, the EAC Partner States continue to establish other quasi-judicial bodies or mechanisms with the same mandate as the EACJ. The Customs Union and Common Market Protocols are an example where parallel mechanisms have been established with potentialities of making EACJ redundant or be a cause for conflicting decisions in the region.[67] Under Article 54 (2) of the EAC Common Market Protocol, jurisdiction to entertain Common Market related disputes has mainly been given to national courts and this undermines the EACJ.

From an administrative point of view, one of the challenges facing the EACJ is its intermittent and an ad-hoc nature. The EACJ does not have any continuous sittings; the court sits in sessions and this delays disposal of cases and hinders efficiency. The current work load of the EACJ does not require all the Judges to reside permanently in Arusha where the seat of the Court is located. However, it is recommended that when the work load of the Court increases, the possibility of continuous sitting should be explored. Another challenge is the reluctance of the Partner States to explicitly extend the jurisdiction of the EACJ to include human rights issues.

At the national level, disputes before the Partner States court are customs related and are founded on the EAC Customs Management Act. Rarely has an issue relating to interpretation and application of the EAC Treaty been considered for determination by the national courts. In most cases, the private sector is active as the applicants before the national courts. The active participation is due to enforcement of the EAC Customs Management Act by national Revenue Authorities as they collect revenue for their national governments. Time lag between the filing of complaint before the national court and the determination of the dispute is a factor that should be considered if dispute resolution before national courts can effectively contribute to regional integration.

67 The dispute resolution mechanism put in place by the EAC Customs Union Protocol is in Annex IX of the Protocol. See also the East African Committee on Trade Remedies established under Article 24 of the EAC Customs Union Protocol.

CHAPTER 16

Harmonization in the EAC

Aleem Tharani

16.1 Introduction

Regional integration is a major development strategy for African countries who share the aim of continent-wide economic, social and cultural integration by 2028. An important aspect of this is trade liberalization. This is to be achieved through regional free trade areas, progressing towards a customs union, a common market and ultimately monetary union. The East African Community (EAC) is a regional intergovernmental organisation of five Partner States, comprising Burundi, Kenya, Rwanda, Tanzania and Uganda (the Partner States), headquartered in Arusha, Tanzania. The broad goal of the EAC is to widen and deepen cooperation among the Partner States. The EAC is one of eight regional economic communities recognised by the African Union (AU), and the only one that has a vision of the creation of a political federation within the EAC. This Chapter will look at how the EAC can use harmonisation to further integration by focusing on the energy sector.

It is well established that Africa is rich in resources, however, has poor infrastructure. In the energy sector, while the EAC is focused on laying the groundwork to ensure that energy and power are harnessed by all Partner States, what additionally will need to be harnessed is regional integration and the harmonisation not only of policy but of laws. Harmonization is necessary in order to ensure that within the EAC, no deterrent Partner States that have not been on the strongest footing in terms of legislation and those Partner States traditionally regarded as "legally safe" are both regarded equally.

16.2 The Rationale for Harmonization

There can be little doubt that the increase in inter-state trade promotes economic development and growth. In order to further economic growth, developed and developing countries alike have entered into relationships characterised by interdependence. This interdependence has prompted a move towards economic convergence and this is where the idea of regionalism originates; it is rooted in the observation that small and fragmented markets

© ALEEM THARANI, 2017 | DOI 10.1163/9789004322073_031
This is an open access chapter distributed under the terms of the CC-BY-NC License.

hamper economic development and trade, and that economic development is measured, *inter alia*, by the ability of a country to create a good environment for the private sector. Regional integration arrangements are intended to pave the way towards the creation of larger regional markets. A larger market benefits the participating countries in that it enhances domestic competition, encourages economic diversification, increases return on investment, thereby attracting more investment.

Evidence from the harmonization of energy laws in other trade communities globally suggests that harmonization results in increased efficiency and approvals for the energy sector thereby cutting one or two years off the overall approval process (thereby allowing project development to occur quicker) and enhancing domestic GDP by upwards of 8%-10%.

There is a tremendous variation across East Africa in the legal framework and policy when the fundamentals of the energy industry and how a developer goes about exploration, project development, operations and decommissioning are considered. These variations, combined with the economic consequences of mismanagement of the sector create investment uncertainty. This investment uncertainty is increased by "inefficient and cumbersome" legislation found in some East African States. Even if a potential investor (and a potential trader for that matter) is not deterred by the unfamiliarity or possible complexity of a foreign legal system, he may be loathed to invest in a state whose laws have not been brought up to date with the developments in economic and international relations. Of course, once attracted, investor interests must be protected and each African state must have laws that provide such security to all investors.

Harmonization is also important to deal with global transboundary issues such as climate change. Climate change resulting from energy-related greenhouse gas emissions is a global challenge without physical or geographical borders which pose various threats to vulnerable regions such as the EAC. The transboundary nature of climate change and its effects necessitates regulatory action in the form of harmonized law and policy responses among the EAC Partner States. The role of the energy sector in climate change mitigation in developing regions such as the EAC pertains to a shift from overtly fossil fuel-based energy sectors to more renewable energy sources. The energy sector reforms needed to achieve this transition to a low carbon economy based on less carbon-intensive energy sources should be regulated in terms of harmonized sub-regional law and policy.

Many African countries already have institutions, legislations and regulations which allowed interconnection and electricity market. Benchmark national legislation and best practices identified represent good examples for less advanced countries, regarding the different framework conditions, for cooperation and harmonization. The power sector of the Sub-Saharan countries, with the exception of South Africa, is comprised of relatively small systems which are characterized by technical, operational and financial problems. The creation of regional markets is essential for creating the environment to attract the needed (funds) capital, technology and expertise to help fix the challenges of the electricity deficit. Many countries under perform in rate and level of electricity access, because of weak means and also due to a lack of policies, poor enabling environment for private sector investments, and institutions for development and roll-out of related programmes, in particular through innovative ways, including renewable energy and mini-grid solutions. Despite a large number of best practices, there are a range of remaining barriers hindering the development and access to modern and sustainable energy services on the continent, including: low levels and lack of effective policy, regulatory and institutional frameworks; unattractive energy market to potential investors due to high investment costs and low technical skills and implementation capacity, amongst others.

Harmonization is not only a public sector led initiative. The role of the private sector in African regional integration (which has to date been largely in the hands of governments and non-governmental organisations) is gradually increasing. Apart from its contribution to policymaking and advice to governments, the private sector can participate in the implementation of regional projects and provide financial and human resources, spread of expertise, and technological and management knowledge. It can also contribute to production of goods, job creation and increased market size and cross-border investment. The harmonization of legal regimes improves the capacity of states to coordinate their economic policies. If harmonization of laws is extended beyond the coordination of economic policies to include substantive business laws among Partner States, individual traders will be encouraged, but so will potential investors who will have the needed assurance that they will be familiar with the legal procedure and consequences. Every investor, creditor or trader wants to be aware of the risks inherent in the undertaken commercial transaction. Where the content and effect of legal rights and obligations are more predictable, the legal risks and thus the transaction costs are reduced.

Regional harmonization is a necessary corollary to the overall aim to promote trade and investment and increase economic growth. In order to make the process of regional integration meaningful, traders and investors must be given the opportunity to avoid the doldrums of legal diversity, they must be allowed to rely on laws which are in line with the realities of business practice and which are up to date with international standards. This should involve the harmonization of domestic substantive legal provisions. What remains for East African states is to find the most appropriate method by which such harmonization would take place.

16.3 EAC Approach to Integration and Harmonization in the Energy Sector

Co-operation in the energy sector among the Partner States is governed by Article 101 of the Treaty for the Establishment of the East African Community (the Treaty).

Article 101 of the Treaty provides that the Partner States shall adopt policies and mechanisms to promote the efficient exploitation, development, joint research and utilisation of various energy resources available within the region and shall in particular promote within the Community:

1. the least cost development and transmission of electric power, efficient exploration and exploitation of fossil fuels and utilisation of new and renewable energy sources;
2. the joint planning, training and research in, and the exchange of information on the exploration, exploitation, development and utilisation of available energy resources,
3. the development of integrated policy on rural electrification,
4. the development of inter-Partner State electrical grid interconnections,
5. the construction of oil and gas pipelines, and
6. all such other measures to supply affordable energy to their people taking cognisance of the protection of the environment as provided for by this Treaty.

In order to achieve the Article 101 objectives, the sector has been organised into three sub-sectors, namely:

1. Power (including transmission and interconnectivity);
2. New and Renewable Energy Sources, Energy Conservation and Energy Efficiency; and
3. Fossil fuels.

16.3.1 *The Power Sector*

The following have been identified as the key harmonization objectives for the Power sub-sector:

1. Cooperation on power sector issues of regional interest;
2. Development of regional interconnections;
3. Joint development of power projects for regional benefit;
4. Development of regional power markets; and
5. Exchange of technical and strategic information.

In order to foster power system interconnectivity by the Heads of States of the Common Market for Eastern and Southern Africa (COMESA) region, a specialised institution named the Eastern Africa Power Pool (the EAPP) was established in 2005 with the signing of an Inter-Governmental Memorandum of Understanding (IGMOU) by seven Eastern Africa countries, namely: Burundi, Democratic Republic of Congo (DRC), Egypt, Ethiopia, Kenya, Rwanda and Sudan. Since the IGMOU, Tanzania, Libya and Uganda have also joined the EAPP.

The main objective of the EAPP is the optimum development of energy resources in the region and to ease the access to electricity power supply to all people of the countries in the Eastern Africa region through regional power interconnections. The EAPP has also been formed to achieve the following goals:

1. To be a framework for pooling energy resources, promoting power exchanges between utilities in Eastern Africa and reduce power supply costs based on an integrated master plan and pre-established rules (Grid code);
2. Optimize the usage of energy resources available in the region by working out regional investment schemes in Power Generation, Transmission and Distribution;
3. Reduce electricity cost in the region by using power systems interconnection and increasing power exchanges between countries; and
4. Provide efficient co-ordination between various initiatives taken in the fields of power production, transmission as well as exchanges in the region.

Well on its ways to achieving its objectives, the EAPP has so far:

1. Together with the EAC, developed a Regional Power Master Plan and Interconnection Code that will allow the EAC and EAPP to identify sources of cheap electricity from ten Eastern Africa countries that the EAC could use to interconnect to and complement the development of locally available resources; and
2. Developed a gap analysis tool to assist member country power utility companies to assess their compliance to the Interconnection Code. This is useful to member countries because the complete interconnectivity of the East African region is scheduled for the end of 2017 and in readiness for this, all power utility companies in the EAC and are working closely to be fully compliant to the Interconnection Code.

In addition to the work of the EAPP, the EAC works closely with other regional organisations in promoting regional projects and programmes. The aim of these projects, as with the EAPP is regional interconnection through the establishment of transmission lines in order to facilitate a vibrant regional power trade. In this regard, the EAC energy department works closely with the Nile Equatorial Lakes Subsidiary Action Programme, the Eastern Africa Power Pool, the Energy for Great Lakes and neighbouring Regional Economic Communities in collaboration with development partners.

One additional initiative of the EAC worth mentioning is the development of a cross-border electrification programme. This programme enables border towns to connect from the neighbouring Partner State at the distribution voltage when it is more economical than connecting with the grid within its own country. This initiative hopes to increase access in a cost effective manner. The EAC Cross-Border Electrification Policy governs the implementation of this programme as well as development of shared renewable energy resources such as small hydro power projects.

16.3.2 *Renewable Energy*

The objective of the EAC for the New and Renewable Energy Sources, Energy Conservation and Energy Efficiency sub-sector is to increase the deployment of renewable energy and the adoption of energy conservation and energy efficiency practices. Specific objectives include:

1. To promote development of New and Renewable Energy Sources;
2. To initiate programmes on Energy Conservation and Energy Efficiency;

3. To develop a comprehensive energy conservation and efficiency strategy and plan; and
4. To develop a Renewable Energy Master Plan.

The following initiatives have been adopted to meet the above objectives:

1. Regional Strategy on Scaling-Up Access to Modern Energy Services
2. Technical Capacity Building for Small Hydropower projects
3. Establishment of the East Africa Centre for Renewable Energy and Energy Efficiency

To achieve its objectives and contribute towards increased access to modern, affordable and reliable energy services, in March 2014, the Sectoral Council on Energy approved the Project Document for the Establishment of the EAC Centre for Renewable Energy and Energy Efficiency (EACREEE). EACREEE is expected to be operational by end of 2016.

16.3.3 *Fossil Fuels*

In order to facilitate the provision of efficient and reliable delivery of oil products throughout the region, a Regional Strategy on development of regional refineries was developed. It addresses all aspects of petroleum distribution systems in the region, including refineries and storage facilities in a holistic way in order to improve its effectiveness and efficiency. The Strategy reveals the clear interdependence between various forms of infrastructure in the delivery of petroleum products. Key recommendations for the strategy include:

1. The development a new refinery in Uganda in order for the oil already discovered in Uganda to benefit the region financially;
2. The acceleration of planned upgrading of the Mombasa refinery; and
3. The improvement in the handling, transportation, storage and distribution facilities in the region for efficient and economic distribution of petroleum products.

Important discoveries made in Kenya, Tanzania and Uganda are expected to enhance the resource potential for the region towards energy self-sufficiency. This has resulted in the scaling up of regional exploration efforts in the oil and gas sector.

The EAC has identified priority oil and gas pipeline projects as follows:

1. Crude oil pipeline: Feasibility studies for a crude oil pipeline to transport crude oil from the Albertine Graben to the Indian Ocean for export have been completed. In addition, networks of crude oil pipelines which will transport crude oil from oil fields in the EAC to the refinery are currently under development. Also in development is an oil products pipeline from the refinery to Kampala, Uganda which will facilitate delivery to the market.
2. Upgrading existing oil products pipeline: The existing pipeline system runs from the Mombasa port to Eldoret and Kisumu in Western Kenya. The upgrade project covers construction of a new pipeline from Mombasa to Nairobi and between Sinendat and Kisumu as capacity enhancement for the Eldoret depot. These projects will contribute to planned expansion to other EAC Partner States and other countries that rely on the region for their petroleum imports. Further information on the development of the pipeline can be found on the Kenya Power (KPLC) website.
3. Kenya—Uganda—Rwanda—Burundi oil products pipeline: Feasibility studies and tender documents for the extension of the existing oil products pipeline from Kenya to Uganda and Rwanda have been completed and resources for EPC contracting are being mobilised. Procurement for consultancy services to carry out feasibility study for extension from Rwanda to Burundi is ongoing. The project sections include Eldoret (Kenya)—Kampala (Uganda), Kampala—Kigali (Rwanda) and Kigali—Bujumbura (Burundi). In addition, an oil products pipeline will link a new refinery in Hoima (Uganda) to Kampala making it a hub for refined oil products from the discoveries in the Albertine Graben for distribution in the region through the planned pipeline network. These projects will facilitate efficient, safe, cost-effective and environmentally-friendly distribution of the oil products.
4. Proposed Uganda—Tanzania oil products pipeline: EAC plans to link all its Partner States to the planned refinery development in Hoima, Uganda. It is in this context that an oil products pipeline is planned from Mbarara (Uganda) to Mwanza, Isaka and Dar es Salaam (Tanzania). The planned pipeline system from Kampala (Uganda) to Kigali (Rwanda) and Bujumbura (Burundi) will create a major depot in Mbarara (Uganda). The planned pipeline to Tanzania is proposed to start from this depot. Resources are being mobilised to carry out a feasibility study on the project.

16.4 Harmonisation in the Energy Sector from an EAC Perspective: Progress and Challenges

The EAC faces several challenges in achieving its development vision. Energy has been recognised as one of the key elements in achieving this vision. Lack of electrical and motive power means that a majority of the population cannot participate in economic and social activities to improve their standards of living. Access to clean, affordable, and reliable energy has a profound bearing on living standards and human wellbeing. It is therefore necessary to move away from the 'business-as-usual' scenario to a more determined energy services driven approach that addresses some of the key barriers that hinder increased access to modern energy services.

An argument has also been made in favour of EAC Partner States entering into a multi-lateral investment treaty with a focus on trade and investment in energy. A number of factors combine in varying degrees to make a cooperative approach toward the harnessing of resources (and, therefore, policies) for sustainable energy development in the EAC. These include the underdevelopment and uneven distribution of energy resources across the region; the landlocked position of Uganda, Rwanda and Burundi and the consequent difficulties of importing commercial energy; the poverty of the consumers and a small sized market; the poor development of commercial energy infrastructure; and the lack of skilled technical expertise in the region. The guiding principles for investment regulation/liberalization towards a regional investment agreement for the EAC can be similar to those of the OECD's multilateral agreement, which have been described as follows: (1) Promoting a more secure, predictable, and transparent environment in which to plan and operate cross-border investments; (2) Ensuring greater protection for investors and their investments; (3) Promoting the progressive liberalization of barriers restricting the entry and conduct of foreign firms in domestic markets; (4) Reducing or eliminating measures that distort trade and investment decisions and reduce allocative efficiency; (5) Developing credible institutions and rules for solving potential disputes; (6) Ensuring adequate consideration for environmental issues, core labour standards and other related issues; and (7) Ensuring that the relationship between the agreement and other related international instruments is clarified. By providing greater predictability, transparency and legal security for investors, a regional investment agreement would have the added benefit of attracting more foreign direct investment in the region.

Although some progress has been made in achieving harmonisation, substantial challenges remain which are not specific to the energy sector. These include:

1. The original EAC is a regional intergovernmental organisation that dates back to 1917 and collapsed in 1977 due to various political and economic reasons. The present EAC was established in 2000 with the aim of become an economic area (including customs and monetary unions, with harmonized macroeconomic policies, and ultimately a political federation). However, no overall timetable has been established for this process. EAC Partner States are yet to fully implement some of the provisions within the legal framework of the EAC, such as the harmonization of customs procedures, other duties and charges on imports, internal indirect taxes and fees on production.
2. Differences in implementation capacity among the various EAC Partner States has also affected the ability to fully implement the EAC Treaty into national law.
3. Membership in multiple trade agreements has also proved problematic from a harmonization and integration perspective. Kenya, Tanzania and Uganda participate in different regional trade agreements. For instance, Kenya and Uganda are members of the COMESA while Tanzania is a member of the Southern African Development Community (SADC) and a signatory to the Agreement on the Global System of Trade Preferences among Developing Countries (GSTP). Tanzania is also considering re-entering COMESA after its withdrawal in 2000. While each country is free under the provisions of the EAC to negotiate bilateral agreements provided they notify the other two members, in practice, overlapping membership has created problems. For instance, the agreements use different types of rules of origin, i.e. the criteria used to define where a product was made to determine whether it is eligible to benefit from liberalised trade within a regional trade agreement. The terms of entry of goods into the EAC can also vary for different importing countries since SADC and COMESA are governed by different protocols of trade.

From an energy sector perspective, the following observations can be made around harmonisation and integration:

1. EAC Partner States have more or less the same development and energy needs, with few disparities in the levels of each. What is required to achieve sustainable development in one country is not very different from what is required in another. For energy supply to be dependable enough to foster sustainable economic development

in the EAC, there should be an effective and unified energy policy in place. This is lacking in the EAC. Each country has its own approaches to energy trade and investment. These, however, are neither effective nor uniform. Each country operates alone and the results do not promote economic development. It is of paramount importance, therefore, that the EAC puts in place a viable and harmonized energy policy, which will address the problems of trade and investment in sustainable energy. Harmonized and well thought out strategies will go a long way to promote sustainable development in the EAC

2. There is a further need amongst the EAC Partner States to harmonize the investment climate in the energy sector and thereby promote foreign investment in the energy sector. Measures are required to be taken in respect of expanding and upgrading the energy infrastructure; promoting energy efficiency and conservation; mobilising requisite financial resources for the operation and expansion of energy services consistent with rising demands; ensuring security of supply through diversification of sources and mixes in a cost effective manner; increasing accessibility to all sectors of the population; and improving corporate governance and accountability.

3. The divergence in energy related policies across the EAC has resulted in different standards of bankability being applied across the EAC Partner States thereby requiring investors to undertake detailed due diligence in respect of various issues across the EAC Partner States. The impact of this is that invariably, investors end up favouring one jurisdiction over another for purposes of investing in different segments of the energy sector. An example of such varying bankability thresholds is nowhere more evident than in the power sector. The potential of the power sector to be the driving force behind economic growth for each EAC Partner State cannot be disputed. The Eastern Africa region has more than 15,000MW of geothermal power potential, located primarily in the Rift Valley areas. The untapped energy potential for the latter is estimated at more than 7,000MW of electric power. Notwithstanding this, geothermal energy is currently under-exploited due to a number of challenges, including: (i) lack of an enabling policy, legal and regulatory framework that would attract investment into the region; (ii) colossal start-up investment outlays for geothermal exploration and development; and (iii) risks inherent with resource

exploration and power development projects. In terms of the disparity between EAC Partner States in harnessing and exploiting this potential one need only look at the varying fortunes of the national offtakers in Kenya and Tanzania. The electricity sector in Tanzania is dominated by the Tanzania Electric Supply Company Limited (TANESCO) in a vertically integrated market structure carrying out generation, transmission, distribution and supply. In 1992, the Tanzania National Energy Policy ended the monopoly held by the public utility and allowed private sector involvement in the electricity industry. Although opportunities for economic growth are created by Tanzania's approximately US$75 billion gas reserves, it is widely accepted that any TANESCO power purchase agreement (PPA) may be difficult to bank and any greenfield independent power producer (IPP) project will need government support in the form of a sovereign guarantee for all TANESCO payments under the PPA. By contrast, the Kenyan IPP market, which was unbundled in the mid-2000s, has largely moved away from any requirement for a government guarantee to backstop offtaker payments under the PPA. KPLC's ability to build this internal capacity and balance sheet strength is largely seen to have resulted from the 2007 unbundling. Besides being responsible for system operations, KPLC was mandated to prepare long-term generation plans (under the supervision of the regulator) and to procure new generation capacity from either Kenya Electricity (KenGen) or IPPs. Initially, KPLC relied on transaction advisers but has over time become an effective independent entity capable of running competitive international tenders and negotiating contracts with winning bidders.

4. Notwithstanding point 3 above, there are areas of common difficulties experienced amongst the EAC Partner States. Several studies have concluded that the biggest impediment to regional and intra-Africa trade is poor infrastructure, both in terms of missing links in existing regional networks and inadequate maintenance of existing infrastructure. The supply-side constraints include poor transport infrastructure, logistical problems, energy deficit, poor access to ICT, and water scarcity. Sustainable infrastructure will help remove those constraints and enhance trade. The focus on infrastructure is also consistent with continental initiatives. The financing needs of infrastructure development in Africa are huge. For example, weak power transmission and distribution infrastructure is due to limited

> investments in power system upgrading. The economies, therefore, experience high electrical power system losses, extreme voltage fluctuations and intermittent power outages that cause equipment and material damage and losses in production. The low level of electricity access explains the need for sustainable energy investment projects. The energy policies and legislation for EAC countries are supposed to respond to these challenges. Yet, much as these policies and legislation have been in place for some time, the challenges continue. To achieve sustainable development, the strong points of each policy, strategy and law should be put together and weak points dropped, to form a single unified energy policy, as well as strategies and legislation for the EAC.

The disparity in investment terms is also evident in the oil and gas sector where no EAC model form exploration law or production sharing agreement has been put into place. The existing upstream exploration regime between EAC Partner States differs significantly. For example:

> each jurisdiction applies differing models in respect of matters such as signature bonuses, royalties as well as the applicable formula for production sharing;

differing rates of income tax apply to contractors across the different jurisdictions (Kenya: The income tax rate for branches is 37.5% (rather than 30% for resident companies); Tanzania: 10% of profits deemed to be repatriated; and Uganda: 15% of profits deemed to be repatriated); and

> each country also applies different requirements in respect of local content requirements in the extractives industry.

16.5 Conclusion

The benefits of a regional approach to energy access have been well articulated. The potential economic benefits of a harmonized approach to legislation in this sector can have a domino effect that results in greater and large investments, which then results in positive economic benefits, which in turn has the potential to lead to better regulation, increased monitoring especially of environmental impacts and greater ownership by Partner States in the future of resources that they have been privileged to be entrusted with.

References

African Development Bank—Eastern Africa Regional Integration Strategy Paper 2011–2015.

EAC Annual Report 2013–2014.

http://www.eac.int/energy/index.php?option=com_content&view=article&id=107&Itemid=68.

http://www.tralac.org/.

http://eappool.org/.

Regional Strategy on Scaling-up Access to Modern Energy Services-EAC.

Similar Solutions for Similar Problems: Harmonising Energy Trade and Investment Policies and Strategies in the East African Community—Kikonyogo (2009).

The need to harmonise trade-related laws within countries of the African Union: an introduction to the problems posed by legal divergence—Polina Dlagnekova (2012).

World Trade Organization—East African Community—trade policy review report by the secretariat.

Bibliography

Adams M., Fabbrini F. and Larouche P. (eds), *The Constitutionalization of European Budgetary Constraints* (Hart 2014).

African Development Bank, 'Eastern Africa Regional Integration Strategy Paper (2011–2015) Regional Departments—East I & East II (OREA/OREB)' (September 2011).

African Development Bank, 'Eastern Africa Regional Integration Strategy Paper (2011–2015) Regional Departments—East (OREA/OREB)' (2016).

African Development Bank Group, 'Is Variable Geometry Leading to the Fragmentation of Regional Integration in East Africa?' <http://www.afdb.org/en/blogs/integrating-africa/post/is-variable-geometry-leading-to-the-fragmentation-of-regional-integration-in-east-africa-12524/> accessed 20 November 2016.

AFRODAD, *Regional Integration and Debt in East Africa* (High Gloss Prints Harare 2003).

Alter A.J., 'Who are the "Masters of the Treaty"? European Governments and the European Court of Justice' (1998) 52 International Organization 121.

Alter K., *The European Court's Political Power: Selected Essays* (OUP 2009).

Amerasinghe C.F., *Principles of the Institutional Law of International Organizations* (2nd edn, Cambridge University Press 1996).

Amtenbrink F., Blokker N., Van den Bogaert S., Cuyvers A., Heine K., Hillion C., Kantorowicz K., Lenk H. and Repasi R., *The European Union's Role in the G20* (Working paper for the scientific bureau of the European Parliament 2015).

Anadi S.K., 'Regional Integration in Africa: the case of ECOWAS' (DPhil thesis, University of Zürich 2005).

Apuuli D.P., 'Fast Tracking East African Federation: Asking the Difficult Questions' (Development Network of Indigenous Voluntary Associations (DENIVA), Public Dialogue on Fast Tracking East African Federation Dialogue, Kampala, November 2006).

Armstrong K., 'The New Governance of EU Fiscal Discipline' (2013) 38 European Law Review 601.

Arnull A., 'What Shall We Do on Sunday?'(1991) 26 European Law Review 112.

Arnull A., *The European Union and its Court of Justice* (2nd edn, OUP 2006).

August R. et al., *International Business Law: Text, Cases and Readings* (5th edn, Pearson Education International 2009).

Avbelj M., Fontanelli F. and Martinico G. (eds), *Kadi on Trial* (Routledge 2014).

Ayeko F., 'East African States Still Negotiate Trade Pacts as One Despite 2008 Law' (*The East African*, 4 October 2010) <http://www.theeastafrican.co.ke/news/EAC-states-still-to-negotiate-trade-pacts/2558-1024814-fxbemj/index.html> accessed 20 November 2016.

Babarinde O.A., *The Lomé Convention and Development: An Empirical Assessment* (Avebury Press 1994).

Balassa B., *The Theory of Economic Integration* (Routledge 2011).

Balthasar S., '*Locus Standi* Rules for Challenges to Regulatory Acts by Private Applicants: The New Article 263(4) TFEU' (2010) 35 European Law Review 542.

Bangaba J., 'Leaders Urge Review of EU-EAC Trade Deal' (*The East African* 23 July 2016) <http://www.theeastafrican.co.ke/news/Leaders-urge-review-of-EAC-EU-trade-deal/2558-3307650-uaooovz/index.html> accessed 20 November 2016.

Barnard C., 'Unravelling the Services Directive' (2008) 45(2) Common Market Law Review 323.

Barnard C., 'Derogations, justifications and the Four Freedoms' in Barnard and Odudu (eds.) *The Outer Limits of European Union Law* (OUP 2009).

Barnard C., *The Substantive Law of the EU: The Four Freedoms* (4th edn, OUP 2013).

Barton O., 'An analysis of the principle of subsidiarity in European Union law' (2014) 2 North East Law Review 83.

Baumol W.J. and Blinder S.A., *Economics: Principles & Policy* (11th edn, South-Western Cengage Learning 2008).

Berglund S., 'Prison or Voluntary Cooperation? The Possibility of Withdrawal from the European Union' (2006) 29 Scandinavian Political Studies 147.

Bermann G.A., 'Subsidiarity and the European Community' (1994) 17 Hastings International & Comparative Law Review 97.

Berry, Homewood and Bogusz, *EU Law—Text, Cases and Materials* (2nd edn OUP 2015).

Besselink L.F.M., 'Beyond Notification: How to Leave the Union without Using Article 50 TEU', (U.K. Const. L. Blog, 30th Jun 2016) < http://ukconstitutionallaw.org> accessed 20 November 2016.

Binda M., 'Good Governance and Foreign Direct Investment: A Legal Contribution to a Balanced Economic Development in the East African Community' (DPhil thesis, Utrecht University 2015).

Binda M., *Good Governance and Foreign Direct Investment: A Legal Contribution to a Balanced Economic Development in the East African Community (EAC)* (Uitgeverij BOXPress 2015).

Bobek M., 'Learning to talk: Preliminary Rulings, the Courts of the New Member States and the Court of Justice' (2008) 45 Common Market Law Review 1611.

Bomberg E. et al., *The European Union: How does it work?* (OUP 2012).

Brigot-Laperrousaz A., 'East-Africa and Antitrust: Enforcement of EAC Competition Act' (*African Antitrust & Competition Law*, 14 January 2016), <https://africanantitrust.com/2016/01/14/the-big-picture-aat-east-africa-antitrust-enforcement/> accessed 20 November 2016.

Broberg M. and Fenger N., *Preliminary References to the European Court of Justice* (2nd end, OUP 2014).

Brownlie I., *Basic Documents in International Law* (4th edn, OUP 1995).

Brownlie I., *Principles of Public International Law* (7th edn, OUP 2008).

Burret H.T. and Schnellenbach J., 'Implementation of the fiscal compact in the Euro area Member States' (German Council of Economic Experts Working Paper 2014 No. 08/2013e).

Busuioc M., *European Agencies: Law and Practises of Accountability* (OUP 2013).

Byamukama D., 'The EAC Treaty has the force of law in Uganda' (*New Vision*, 25 November 2015) <http://www.newvision.co.ug/new_vision/guest-blog-blog/1408032/eac-treaty-force-law-uganda> accessed 20 November 2016.

Callund Consulting Limited (UK), *Review of the Structure of the Pension Sector in the East African Community* (2013).

Cappelletti M., Seccombe M., Weiler J.H.H., *Integration Through Law—European and the American Federal Experience, Vol. I* (De Gruyter 1986).

Cardozo R., 'The Project for a Political Community' (1952–2) in Pryce R (ed), *The Dynamics of European Union* (Croom Helm 1987).

Cass D., 'The Word that Saves Maastricht? The Principle of Subsidiarity and the Division of Powers within the European Community' (1992) 29 Common Market Law Review 1107.

Cecchini P., *The European Challenge 1992: The Benefits of a Single Market* (Gower 1988).

Chalmers D., Davies G. and Monti G., *European Union Law* (CUP 2010).

Connor T., 'Goods, Persons, Services and Capital in the European Union: Jurisprudential Routes to Free Movement' (2010) 11 German Law Journal 159.

Corbett R., Jacobs F and Shackleton M. (eds), *The European Parliament* (7th edn, John Harper Publishing 2007).

Cosgrove-Twitchett C., *Europe and Africa: From Association to Partnership* (Saxon House 1978).

Craig P., 'Integration, Democracy and Legitimacy' in Craig and de Búrca (eds), *The Evolution of EU Law* (2nd edn, OUP 2010).

Craig P., 'The European Union Act 2011: Locks, limits and legality' (2011) 48 Common Market Law Review 1881.

Craig P., 'The Stability, Coordination and Governance Treaty: Principle, Politics and Pragmatism' (2012) 37 European Law Review 231.

Craig P., 'Brexit: a drama in six acts' 2016 (4) European Law Review 447.

Craig P. and De Búrca G. (eds), *The Evolution of EU Law* (2nd edn, OUP 2011).

Craig P. and De Búrca G., *EU Law* (6th edn, OUP 2015).

Cronje J.B., 'Mutual Recognition of Professional Qualifications: The East African Community' (2015) Trade Law Centre Brief No. SI5TB04/2015.

Crum B., 'Saving the Euro at the Cost of Democracy' (2013) 51 Journal of Common Market Studies 614.

Curtin D., *Executive Power in the European Union: Law, Practises and the Living Constitution* (OUP 2009).

Curtin D. and Egeberg M., 'Tradition and Innovation: Europe's Accumulated Executive Order' (2008) 31 *West European Politics* 639.

Cuyvers A., 'Case note to: Joined Cases C-338/04, C-359/04 and C-360/04, Massimiliano Placanica, Christian Palazzese and Angelo Sorricchio (Placanica)' (2008) 45 Common Market Law Review 515.

Cuyvers A., 'The Kadi II judgment of the General Court: the ECJ's predicament and the consequences for Member States' (2011) 7 European Constitutional Law Review 481.

Cuyvers A., 'The EU as a Confederal Union of Sovereign Member Peoples, Exploring the potential of American (con)federalism and popular sovereignty for a constitutional theory of the EU' (DPhil thesis, Leiden University 2013).

Cuyvers A., '"Give me one good reason": The unified standard of review for sanctions after Kadi II' (2014) 51(6) Common Market Law Review 1759.

Daianu D., D'Adda C., Basevi G. and Kumar R., *The Eurozone crisis and the future of Europe: the political economy of further integration and governance* (Palgrave Macmillan 2014).

Damrosch L.F. et als., *International Law: Cases and Materials* (4th edn, American Casebook Series 2001).

Dann P., 'The Political Institutions' in Von Bogdandy A and Bast J (eds), *Principles of European Constitutional Law* (2nd edn Hart Publishing 2010).

Davies G., 'Welfare as a Service' (2002) 29 Legal Issues of Economic Integration 27.

Davies G., 'What Does It All Mean?' (2016) German Law Journal Brexit Supplement 7.

De Baere G., *Constitutional Principles of EU External Relations* (OUP 2008).

De Búrca G., 'The Institutional Development of the EU: A Constitutional Analysis' in Craig and de Búrca (eds), *The Evolution of EU law* (OUP 1999).

De Búrca G., 'Sovereignty and the Supremacy Doctrine of the European Court of Justice', in Walker (ed), *Sovereignty in Transition* (Hart Publishing 2006).

De Búrca G. and Scott J., *Constitutional Change in the EU. From Uniformity to Flexibility?* (Hart Publishing 2000).

De Búrca G. and Weiler J.H.H., *The European Court of Justice* (OUP 2001).

De Gregorio Merino A., 'Legal Developments in the Economic and Monetary Union During the Debt Crisis: The Mechanisms of Financial Assistance' (2012) 49 Common Market Law Review 1613.

De Rougemont D., *The Idea of Europe* (MacMillian 1965).

De Schutter O. and Francq S., 'La proposition de directive relative aux services dans le Marché intérieur: reconnaissance mutuelle, harmonisation et conflicts de lois dans l'Europe élargie' (2005) Cahiers de droit européen 603.

De Witte B., 'Direct Effect, Supremacy, and the Nature of the Legal Order' in Craig and De Búrca (eds), *The Evolution of EU Law* (OUP 1999).

De Witte B., 'Non-Market Values in Internal Market Legislation', in Nic Shuibhne (ed), *Regulating the Internal Market* (Edward Elgar 2006).

De Witte B., 'The Continuous Significance of *Van Gend en Loos*' in Maduro M.P. and Azoulai L. (eds) *The Past and Future of EU Law: The Classics of EU law Revisited on the* 50th *Anniversary of the Rome Treaty* (Hart Publishing 2010).

De Witte B., 'Direct Effect, Supremacy, and the Nature of the Legal Order', in Craig and De Búrca (eds), *The Evolution of EU Law* (2nd edn, OUP 2011).

De Witte B., 'The European Union as an international legal experiment', in de Búrca G. and Weiler J.H.H., *The Worlds of European Constitutionalism* (CUP 2012).

De Witte B., 'Near-membership, partial membership end the EU constitution' (2016) 4 European Law Review 471.

Delanty G., *Inventing Europe: Idea, Identity, Reality* (Macmillan 1995).

Desta M.G., 'Exemptions from Competition Law in Regional Trade Agreements: A study based on experiences in agriculture and energy sectors' in Bruisk, Alvarez and Cernat (eds), *United Nations Conference on Trade and Development, Competition Provisions in Regional Trade Agreements: How to Assure Development Gains* (United Nations 2005).

Dhingra S. and Sampson T., 'Life after Brexit: What are the UK's options outside the European Union?' (Centre for Economic Performance London School of Economics Working Paper Brexit 01 February 2016).

Dougan M., 'Minimum Harmonization and the Internal Market' (2000) 37 Common Market Law Review 853.

Dougan M., 'The Treaty of Lisbon 2007: Winning Minds, not Hearts' (2008) 45 Common Market Law Review 617.

Douglas-Scott S., *Constitutional Law of the European Union* (Pearson 2002).

Dworkin R., *Taking Rights Seriously* (Duckworth 1977).

Earnshaw D. and Judge D., *The European Parliament* (2nd edn, Palgrave 2008).

East African Community, *The East African Community: A Handbook 1972* (Information Division, EA Community 1972).

East African Community, *Communiqué of the* 6th *Extraordinary Summit of East African Community Heads of State* <http://www.eac.int/news/index.php?option=com_docman&task=doc_view&gid=142&Itemid=77> accessed 20 November 2016.

East African Community, *Joint Communiqué 17th Ordinary Summit of the East African Community Heads of State* <http://www.eac.int/news-and-media/statements/20160302/joint-communique-17th-ordinary-summit-east-african-community-heads-state> accessed 20 November 2016.

East African Community, *Report of the* 28th *Meeting of the Council of Ministers* EAC/CM/28/2013 (2013).

East African Community, *Report of the 32nd Meeting of the Council of Ministers* EAC/CM/32/2015 (2015).

East African Community, *East African Community Facts and Figures—2012* <www.eac.int/statistics/index.php?option=com_docman&task=doc_view&gid=142&tmpl=component&format=raw&Itemid=153> accessed 20 November 2016.

East African Community, *Report of the Capacity Building Workshop for the Committee on General Purpose: "The Legislative process of Bills: From Initiation, enactment to oversight on enacted law* <http://www.eala.org/new/index.php/key-documents/reports/500-capacity-building-workshop-for-the-eala-committee-on-general-purpose?path> accessed 20 November 2016.

East African Community, EAC *Development Strategy (2011/2012–2015–2016): Deepening and Accelerating Integration* (August 2011).

Editorial Comments, 'The services directive proposal: Striking a balance between the promotion of the internal market and preserving the European social model' (2006) 43(2) Common Market Law Review 307.

Editorial Comments 'An ever Mighty European Council' 46 Common Market Law Review (2009).

Editorial Comments, 'Presiding the Union in times of crisis: The unenviable task of the Netherlands' (2016) 53(2) Common Market Law Review 327.

Editorial Comments, 'True is it that we have seen better days' (2016) 53(4) Common Market Law Review 875.

Edward D., '*CILFIT* and *Foto-Frost* in their Historical and Procedural Context', in Maduro M.P. and Azoulai L. (eds), *The Past and Future of EU Law: The Classics of EU law Revisited on the 50th Anniversary of the Rome Treaty* (Hart Publishing 2010).

Eeckhout P., *EU External Relations Law* (OUP 2011).

Eiassen K.A. and Monsen B., 'Comparison of European and Southeast Asian Integration' in M. Telò (ed), *European Union and New Regionalism: Regional Actors and Global Governance in a Post-Hegemonic Era* (Ashgate 2001).

Eichengreen B., 'European Monetary Integration with Benefit of Hindsight' (2012) 50 Journal of Common Market Studies 123.

El-Affendi A., 'The Perils of Regionalism: Regional Integration as a Source of Instability in the Horn of Africa?' (2009) 3 Journal of Intervention and Statebuilding 1.

Emerson M., Aujean M., Catinat M., Goybet P., and Jacquemin A., *The Economics of 1992: The EC Commission's Assessment of the Economic Effects of Completing the Internal Market* (OUP 1988).

European Commission, 'Completing the Internal Market' (Commission White Paper 1985, COM(85)310).

European Commission, 'Commission Notice on the definition of relevant market for the purposes of Community competition law' (1997) O.J. C372/5.

European Commission, 'The Period of Reflection and Plan D' (2006) Com(2006) 212.

European Commission, 'Guidance on the Commission's Enforcement Priorities in Applying Article 82 of the EC Treaty to Abusive Exclusionary Conduct by Dominant Undertakings' (2009) OJ C 45/2.

European Commission, 'Commission Notice on agreements of minor importance which do not appreciably restrict competition under Article 101(1) of the Treaty on the Functioning of the European Union (de minimis Notice)' (2014) O.J. C291/1.

European Commission, 'Commission Notice on the notion of State aid as referred to in Article 107(1) of the Treaty on the Functioning of the European Union' (2016) O.J. C262/1.

European Commission, *What is the Common Customs Tariff* < http://ec.europa.eu/taxation_customs/customs/customs_duties/tariff_aspects/index_en.htm> accessed 20 November 2016.

European Commission, *Economic Partnership Agreement between the EU and the Eastern Africa Community* (EAC) <http://trade.ec.europa.eu/doclib/html/142194.htm> accessed 20 November 2016.

Fennely N., 'The European Court of Justice and the Doctrine of Supremacy: *Van Gend en Loos; Costa v. ENEL; Simmenthal*' in Maduro M.P. and Azoulai L. (eds) *The Past and Future of EU Law: The Classics of EU law Revisited on the 50th Anniversary of the Rome Treaty* (Hart Publishing 2010).

Flynn L., 'Free movement of capital' in Barnard C and Peers S (eds), *European Union Law* (OUP 2014).

Franck T.M., *East African Unity Through Law* (Yale University Press 1964).

Frankenberg G., 'Comparing constitutions: Ideas, ideals, and ideology—toward a layered narrative', International Journal of Constitutional Law (2006) International Journal of Constitutional Law 439.

Friel R.J., 'Providing a Constitutional framework for withdrawal from the EU: Article 59 of the Draft European Constitution' (2004) 53 International Comparative Law Quarterly 407.

Fursdon E., *The European Defence Community: A History* (Macmillan, 1980).

Gamble A., 'Regional Blocs, World Order and the New Medievalism' in M. Telò (ed), *European Union and New Regionalism: Regional Actors and Global Governance in a Post-Hegemonic Era* (Ashgate 2001).

Gastorn K., 'The Legal Analysis of the Common Market of the East African Community as Market Freedoms in the Open Market Economy' (2011) Law in Africa 143.

Gathi J.T., 'African regional trade agreements as flexible legal regimes' (2010) 35 North Carolina Journal of International Law and Commercial Regulation 571.

Ghai Y.P. and McAuslan J.P.W.B., *Public Law and Political Change in Kenya: A Study of the Legal Framework of Government from Colonial Times to the Present* (OUP 1970).

Gingsberg, *Demystifying the European Union: the Enduring Logic of Regional Integration* (2nd edn, Rowman & Littlefield Publishers 2010).

Goodspeed T.J., 'Bailouts in a Federation' (2012) 9 International Tax and Public Finance 409.

Gormley L., 'Free Movement of Goods and their Use—What Is the Use of It?' (2011) 33 Fordham International Law Journal 1589.

Grimm D., 'Comments on the German Constitutional Court's Decision on the Lisbon Treaty. Defending Sovereign Statehood against Transforming the European Union into a State' (2009) 5 European Constitutional Law Review 353.

Grimm D., 'Types of Constitutions', in Rosenfeld M. and Sajó A. (eds), *The Oxford Handbook of Comparative Constitutional Law* (OUP 2012).

Groussot X., *General Principles of Community Law* (Europa Law Publishing 2006).

Grynberg, R., 'The WTO incompatibility of the Lomé Convention Trade Provisions' (1998) Asia Pacific School of Economics and Management Working Paper 98/3 <https://crawford.anu.edu.au/pdf/wp98/sp98-3.pdf> accessed 20 November 2016.

Gyekye K., *Tradition and Modernity: Philosophical Reflections on the African Experience* (OUP 1997).

Halberstam D., 'Pluralism in *Marbury* and *Van Gend*' in Maduro M.P. and Azoulai L. (eds) *The Past and Future of EU Law: The Classics of EU law Revisited on the 50th Anniversary of the Rome Treaty* (Hart Publishing 2010).

Hallerberg M., 'Fiscal federalism reforms in the European Union and the Greek crisis' (2011) 12 European Union Politics 127.

Harbo F., 'Secession Right—An Anti-Federal Principle? Comparative Study of Federal States and the EU' (2008) 1 Journal of Politics and Law 132.

Hargreaves S., *EU Law* (OUP 2009).

Hatzopoulos V., *Regulating Services in the European Union* (OUP 2012).

Hayes-Renshaw F., van Aken W. and Wallace H., 'When and Why the Council of Ministers of the EU Votes Explicitly' (2006) 44 Journal of Common Market Studies 161.

Hayes-Renshaw F. and Wallace H., *The Council of Ministers* (2nd edn, Macmillan 2006).

Heitne B., 'Development Regionalism in New Directions' in M. Lundahl and B.J. Ndulu (eds), *Development Economics (Growth, Environmental Concerns and Government in the 1990s)* (London Routledge 1996).

Herbst J., 'Observations on the Right to Withdraw from the European Union: Who are the "Masters of the Treaties"?' (2005) 6 German Law Journal 1755.

Hillion C., 'Tous pour un, un pour tous! Coherence in the External Relations of the European Union' in Cremona M. (ed), *Developments in EU External Relations Law* (OUP 2008).

Hillion C., 'EU Enlargement' in Craig P. and De Búrca G. (eds), *The Evolution of EU Law* (2nd edn, OUP 2011).

Hillion C., 'Accession and Withdrawal in the Law of the European Union' in Arnull A. and Chalmers D. (eds), *The Oxford handbook of European Law* (OUP 2015).

Hillion C., and Koutrakos P. (eds), *Mixed Agreements Revisited* (Hart 2010).

Hinarejos A., *The Euro Area Crisis in Constitutional Perspective* (OUP 2015).

HM Government, 'Alternatives to membership: possible models for the United Kingdom outside the European Union' (March 2016).

Hoffmann H. and Türk A. (eds), *EU Administrative Governance* (Edward Elgar 2006).

Hofmeister H., '"Should I Stay or Should I Go?"—A Critical Analysis of the Right to Withdraw From the EU' (2010) 16 European Law Journal 589.

Holzinger K., 'Common Goods, Matrix Games and Institutional Response' (2003) 9 European Journal of International Relations 173.

Hooghe L., *The European Commission and the Integration of Europe* (CUP 2002).

Ibanez Colomo P., 'The Law on Abuses of Dominance and the System of Judicial Remedies' (2013) LSE Legal Studies Working Paper No. 13/2013 <http://papers.ssrn.com/sol3/papers.cfm?abstract_id=2270099> accessed 20 November 2016.

Idriz-Tescan, 'Legal constraints on EU Member States as primary law makers: a case study of the proposed permanent safeguard clause on free movement of persons in the EU negotiating framework for Turkey's accession' (DPhil thesis, University of Leiden 2015, Meijersreeks:MI-247) Ihucha A., 'Comesa, Sadc imports get tariff relief again' (*The East African,* January 2013) < http://www.theeastafrican.co.ke/news/Comesa-Sadc-imports-get-tariff-relief-again-/-/2558/1658344/-/ugt2mi/-/index.html> accessed 20 November 2016.

Ihucha A., 'EAC unveils austere budget for 2016/17' (*The East African*, 28 May 2016) <http://www.theeastafrican.co.ke/news/EAC-unveils-austere-budget-for-2016-17-/-/2558/3222616/-/14lj4l9z/-/index.html> accessed 20 November 2016.

Ihucha A., 'EAC Competition Authority to Start Operations in July' (*The East African* Standard, 18 June 2016) <http://www.theeastafrican.co.ke/business/EAC-competition-authority-to-start-operations-in-July-/-/2560/3255818/-/b6nmku/-/index.html> accessed 20 November 2016.

IMF, *Balance of Payments Manual* (6th edn, IMF, 2008, updated version of 2011).

International Labour Organisation, *Technical Memorandum of the Uganda labour and administration and inspection needs assessment* (Labour Administration and Inspection Programme).

Issing O., *The Birth of the Euro* (CUP 2008).

Jackson V.C., 'Methodological Challenges in Comparative Constitutional Law' (201) 28 Penn State International Law Review 319.

Jackson V.C., 'Comparative Constitutional Law: Methodologies', in Rosenfeld M. and Sajó A. (eds) *The Oxford Handbook of Comparative Constitutional Law* (OUP 2012).

Janning J., European Democracy and Variable Geometry. How a multi-speed Europe complicates the Union's democratic legitimacy' (2013) <https://ip-journal.dgap.org/en/ip-journal/topics/European-democracy-and-variable-geometry> accessed 25 December 2013.

Janssens C., *The Principle of Mutual Recognition in EU Law* (OUP 2013).

Jarass H.D., 'A Unified Approach to the Fundamental Freedoms' in Andenas and Roth (eds), *Services and Free Movement in EU Law* (OUP 2002).

Jenkins C and Thomas L, 'African Regionalism and the SADC' in M. Telò (ed), *European Union and New Regionalism: Regional Actors and Global Governance in a Post-Hegemonic Era* (Ashgate 2001).

Kahn-Freund O, 'On Uses and Misuses of Comparative Law' (1974) 37 Modern Law Review 1.

Kapteyn P.J.G., McDonnell A.M., Mortelmans K.J.M., and Timmermans C.W.A. (eds), *The Law of the European Union and the European Communities* (4th edn, Kluwer Law International 2008).

Karakamisheva-Jovanovska T., 'Legal Principles versus Fundamental Rights Post Lisbon' (2013) 15 Rev. Eur. L. 41.

Kasaija P., 'The State of Constitutionalism in East Africa: The Role of the East African Community—2007' in W Kioko (ed) *Constitutionalism in East Africa* (Kampala Foundation Publishers 2009) Kenya Human Rights Commission, *The ABC of the EAC_EU Economic Partnership Agreement (EPA)* <http://www.khrc.or.ke/mobile-publications/economic-rights-and-social-protection-er-sp/59-the-abc-of-eac-eu-economic-partnership-agreements-epa/file.html> accessed 20 November 2016 Khemani R.S. and Shapiro D.M., '*Glossary of Industrial Organisation Economics and Competition Law*' (*Directorate for Financial, Fiscal and Enterprise Affairs*, (OECD, 1993).

Kidanka C., 'Tanzania dodges EPA to Protect Industrialisation, budget' (*The East African*, 16 July 2006) <http://www.theeastafrican.co.ke/news/Dar-dodges-EPA-to-protect-industrialisation--budget/2558-3297388-9egi70/index.html> accessed 20 November 2016.

Kiraso B.B., 'EAC Integration—Enabling Peace and Security Architecture' (EAC Peace and Security Conference, Kampala, October 2009).

Kivuva J.M., 'East Africa's dangerous dance with the past: Important lessons the new East African Community has not learned from the defunct' (2014) 10 European Scientific Journal 359.

Komárek J., 'Judicial Lawmaking and Precedent in Supreme Courts' (2011) LSE Legal Studies Working Paper No. 4/2011, <http://ssrn.com/abstract=1793219> accessed 20 November 2016.

Komárek J., 'Czech Constitutional Court Playing with Matches: the Czech Constitutional Court Declares a Judgment of the Court of Justice of the EU Ultra Vires' (2012) 8 European Constitutional Law Review (2012).

Komárek J., 'Federal Elements in the Community Judicial System: Building Coherence in the Community Legal System' (2005) 42 Common Market Law Review 9.

Kostoris Padoa Schioppa F. (ed), *The Principle of Mutual Recognition in the European Integration Process* (Palgrave MacMillan 2005).

Krapohl S. and Fink S., 'Different Paths of Regional Integration: Trade Networks and Regional Institution-Building in Europe, Southeast Asia and Southern Africa' (2013) 51 Journal of Common Market 474.

Krapohl S., Meissner K.I. and Muntschick J., 'Regional Powers as Leaders or Rambos? The Ambivalent Behaviour of Brazil and South Africa in Regional Economic Integration' (2014) 52 Journal of Common Market Studies 880.

Krugman P., *Development, Geography and Economic Theory* (MIT Press 1995).

Krugman P., 'Revenge of the Optimum Currency Area' (2013) 27 NBER 441.

Lawson F.H., *Comparative Regionalism* (Ashgate 2009).

Lazowski A., 'Withdrawal from the European Union and Alternatives to Membership' (2012) 37 European Law Review 523.

Le Goff J., *The Birth of Europe* (Blackwell 2005).

Lechner S. and Ohr R., 'The Right of Withdrawal in the Treaty of Lisbon: A Game Theoretic Reflection on Different Decision Processes in the EU' (2011), 32 Eur J Law Econ 357. doi: 10.1007/s10657-009-9139-1.

Legrand P., 'The Impossibility of "Legal Transplants"' (1997) 4 Maastricht Journal of European and Comparative Law 111.

Lenaerts K., 'Constitutionalism and the Many Faces of Federalism' (1990) 4 American Journal of Comparative Law 208.

Lenaerts K., 'Exploring the Limits of the EU Charter of Fundamental Rights' (2012) 8 European Constitutional Law Review 375.

Lenaerts K., 'The Court's Outer and Inner Selves: Exploring the External and Internal Legitimacy of the European Court of Justice' in Adams, De Waele, Meeusen and Straetmans (eds), *Judging Europe's Judges, The Legitimacy of the Case Law of the European Court of Justice* (Hart 2013).

Lenaerts K., 'The Court of Justice as the Guarantor of the Rule of Law Within the European Union' in De Baere and Wouters, *The Contribution of International and Supranational Courts to the Rule of Law* (Edward Elgar Publishing Limited 2015).

Lenaerts K. and Gutierrez-Fons, 'The Constitutional Allocation of Powers and General Principles of EU law' (2010) Common Market Law Review 1631.

Lenaerts K. and van Nuffel P., *Constitutional Law of the European Union* (Thomson 2005).

Liaonos I. and Odudu O., *Regulating Trade in Services in the EU and the WTO: Trust, Distrust and Economic Integration* (CUP 2012).

Ligami C., 'Uganda ratifies the monetary union' (*The East African*, 7 February 2015) <http://www.theeastafrican.co.ke/news/Uganda-ratifies-the-monetary-union/-/2558/2616360/-/g05itfz/-/index.html> accessed 20 November 2016.

Lloyd P., 'The Variable Geometry Approach to International Economic Integration' (2009) 1 International Journal of Business and Development Studies 51.

Louis J.V., 'The Economic and Monetary Union: Law and Institutions' (2004) 41 Common Market Law Review 1075.

Louis J.V. and Rodrigues S (eds), *Les services d'intérêt général et l'Union européenne* (Bruylant 2006).

Lumumba P.L.O. 'The East African Community Two: Destined to Succeed or Doomed to Fail?' (2009) 5(1) Law Society of Kenya Journal 105.

Maalim M.J., "The United Republic of Tanzania in the East African Community: Legal Challenges in Integrating Zanzibar ('DPhil thesis, University of Dar es Salaam 2013).

MacCormick N., *Questioning Sovereignty: Law, State and Nation in the European Commonwealth*' (OUP 1999).

Maduro M.P., 'Contrapunctual Law: Europe's Constitutional Pluralism in Action' in Walker (ed), *Sovereignty in Transition* (Hart 2006).

Maduro M.P. and Azoulai L. (eds), *The Past and Future of EU Law: The Classics of EU law Revisited on the 50th Anniversary of the Rome Treaty* (Hart Publishing 2010).

Majone G., *Dilemmas of European Integration: The Ambiguities and Pitfalls of Integration by Stealth* (OUP 2005).

Majone G., *Rethinking the Union of the Europe Post-Crisis* (CUP 2014).

Mancini F. and Keeling D., 'From *CILFIT* to *ERT*: The Constitutional Challenge Facing the European Court' (1991) 11 Yearbook of European Law 1.

Mathinjsen, P.S.R.F., *A Guide to European Union Law* (Thomson Sweet & Maxwell 2007).

Matilla M., 'Contested Decisions: Empirical Analysis of Voting in the Council of Ministers' (2004) 43 European Journal of Political Research 29.

Mattli, *The Logic of Regional Integration: Europe and Beyond* (Cambridge University Press 1999).

Mayer F.C., 'Van Gend en Loos: The Foundation of a Community of Law' in Maduro M.P. and Azoulai L. (eds) *The Past and Future of EU Law: The Classics of EU law Revisited on the 50th Anniversary of the Rome Treaty* (Hart Publishing 2010).

McAllister R., *European Union: An Historical and Political Survey* (Routledge 2010).

McCormick J., *The European Union, Politics and Policies* (4th edn, Westview Press 2008).

Mchome S.E., 'The Treaty of the East African Community: Is it the Equivalent of a National Constitution?' in Gastorn, Sippel and Wanizek (eds), *Processes of Legal Integration in the East African Community* (Dar es Salaam University Press 2011).

McKitterick R., *Charlemagne: the Formation of a European Identity* (CUP 2008).

Mendez-Pinedo M.E., *EC and EEA Law: A Comparative Study of the Effectiveness of European Law* (Europa Law Publishing 2009).

Menendez A.J., 'The existential crisis of the European Union' 14 (2013) German Law Journal 453.

Mold A., 'The Impact of the Single Market Programme on the Locational Determinants of US Manufacturing Affiliates: An Economic Analysis' (2003) 41 Journal of Common Market Studies 38.

Molle W., *The Economics of European Integration* (Aldershot 2006).

Monti M., 'A New Strategy for the Single Market, At the Service of Europe's Economy and Society' (Report to the President of the European Commission José Manuel Barroso, 2010).

Moravcsik, *The Choice for Europes: Social Purpose and State Power from Messina to Maastricht* (Cornell University Press 1998).

Moregenathu H., *Politics Among Nations* (Alfred Knoff 1950).

Mortelmans K.J.M., 'The Relationship between the Treaty Rules and Community Measures for the Establishment and Functioning of the Internal Market: Towards a Concordance Rule' (2002) Common Market Law Review 1303.

Mugomba A.T., 'Regional Organizations and African Underdevelopment: the Collapse of the East African Community' (1978) 16(2) The Journal of Modern African Studies 261.

Mukandala R., 'Political Co-operation' in EAC*: Perspectives on Regional Integration and Co-operation in East Africa* (EAC Secretariat 2000).

Mukwaya A.K.K., 'A Survey of Relationships between the European Union and the East African States, 1961–1980' (1997) 19(2) East African Geographical Review 73.

Mundell R., 'A Theory of Optimum Currency Areas' (1961) 51 American Economic Review 657.

Mutai H.K., *Compliance With International Trade Obligations: The Common Market For Eastern and Southern Africa* (Kluwer Law International 2007).

Mutai H.K., 'Regional trade integration strategies under SADC and the EAC: A comparative analysis' (2011) 1 SADC Law Journal 81.

Mwapachu J.V., 'Ten Years of the EAC—Achievements, Challenges and Prospects' in Gastorn, Sippel and Wanizek (eds), *Processes of Legal Integration in the East African Community* (Dar es Salaam University Press 2011).

Mwapachu J.V., *Challenging The Frontiers of African Integration: The Dynamics of Policies, Politics and Transformation in the East African Community* (E&D Vision Publishing Limited 2012).

Mwase N., 'Regional Economic Integration and the Unequal Sharing of Benefits: Background to the Disintegration and Collapse of the East African Community' (1979) 4 Africa Development 2.

Nahamya S.G., *Regional Economic Disintegration: Tensions, Conflicts and Causes—the Case of the East African Community* (DPhil thesis, Colorado State University 1980).

Ndegwa P., *The Common Market and Development in East Africa* (Eastern Africa Publishing House, 1965).

Neary J.P., 'Of Hype and Hyperbolas: Introducing the New Economic Geography'(2001) 39 Journal of Economic Literature 536.

Newman P., 'The Economics of Integration in East Africa' in Leys and Robson (eds), *Federation in East Africa: Opportunities and Problems* (OUP 1965).

Nic Shuibhne N., *The Coherence of EU Free Movement Law. Constitutional Responsibility and the Court of Justice* (OUP 2013).

Nicolaides P., 'Withdrawal from the European Union: A Typology of Effects' (2013) 20 MJ 209.

Nielsen H.K., 'The Protection of Fundamental Rights in the Law of the European Union' (1994) 63 Nordic Journal of International Law 213.

Nsekela H.R., 'Overview of the East African Court of Justice' (Sensitisation Workshop on the Role of the EACJ in the EAC Integration, Kampala, November 2011).

Nsekela H.R., 'Cooperation between the East African Court of Justice and the national courts of Partner States' (*United Republic of Tanzania Judges Conference*, Arusha, August 2009).

Nyman-Metcalf and Papageorgiou, *Regional Integration and Courts of Justice* (Insertia 2005).

Oates W.E., 'Toward A Second-Generation Theory of Fiscal Federalism' 12 (2005) International Tax and Public Finance 349.

OECD, *OECD Benchmark Definition of Foreign Direct Investment* (4th edn, OECD, 2008).

Ogalo V., 'Achievements and Challenges of Implementation of the EAC Common Market Protocol in Kenya: Case of Free Movement of Labour' (2014) Friedrich Ebert Foundation Research Report.

O'Leary S. and Fernández-Martín J.M., 'Judicially-Created Exceptions to the Free Provision of Services' in Andenas M., Roth W.H., *Services and Free Movement in EU Law* (OUP 2002).

O'Leary S., 'Free movement and persons and services' in Craig and de Búrca (eds), *The Evolution of EU law* (2nd edn, OUP 2011).

Oliver P., 'Of Trailers and Jetskis: Is the Case Law on Article 34 TFEU Hurtling in a new Direction?' (2009–2010) 33 Fordham International Law Journal 1423.

Oliver P. (ed), *Oliver on Free Movement of Goods in the European Union* (5th edn, Hart 2010).

Olivier G., 'Regional Integration in Africa: A Political Perspective' (unpublished manuscript).

Olsson C., 'Collective Dominance—Merger Control on Oligopolistic Markets' (DPhil thesis, Göteborgs Universitet 2000).

Ongónge L., 'The EAC-EU Economic partnership Agreement: Context, Content and Consequences' (2015) Institute of Economic Affairs Trade Notes <http://www.ieakenya.or.ke/publications/notes/1/2015/09> accessed 20 November 2016.

Onoria H., 'Botched-up Elections, Treaty Amendments and Judicial Independence in the East African Community' (2010) 54 Journal of African Law 74.

Oppenheimer A. (ed), *The Relationship Between European Community Law and National Law: The Cases Vol I and II* (CUP 1994 and 2003).

Oppong R.F., 'Re-imagining International Law: An Examination of Recent Trends in the Reception of International Law Into National Legal Systems in Africa' (2006) 30 Fordham International Law Journal 296.

Organisation of African Unity, *Lagos Plan of Action for Economic Development of Africa 1980–2000* (Lagos 1980).

Osoro P., 'The East African Community and Non-Tariff Barriers A Hindrance to the Trade Liberalisation Policy and Legal Proposals for Eliminating Non-Tariff Barriers' (LLM thesis, University of Nairobi 2015).

Ottervanger T. and Cuyvers A., *The functioning of the East African Community: Common market, Court of Justice and fundamental rights, a comparative perspective with the European Union* (Europa Instituut Leiden 2013).

Ottervanger T., Cuyvers A., Ammeloot C., Croft M., Etienne V., Gallerizzo A., Harrer M., Wernitzki N-J., *'The functioning of the East African Community: Common Market, Court of Justice and fundamental rights, a comparative perspective with the European Union'* (Leiden Centre for the Legal and Comparative Study of the East African Community, November 2012).

Oumar Sy S., 'The Birth of the ACP Group' (The Courier No. 93 September-October 1985).

Oyugi E., 'East African Community—the Third Round: A People, Market or State-driven Regionalisation project?' in *EAC 10th Anniversary Symposium: Role of Non-State Actors in Deepening EAC Integration* (Arusha:East African Community 2009).

Padoan P.C., 'Political Economy of New Regionalism and World Governance' in M. Telò (ed), *European Union and New Regionalism: Regional Actors and Global Governance in a Post-Hegemonic Era* (Ashgate 2001).

Palavret J-M et al. (eds), *Visions, Votes and Vetoes: Reassessing the Luxembourg Compromise 40 Years On* (Peter Lang 2006).

Palmstorfer R., 'The Reverse Majority Voting under the 'Six Pack': A Bad Turn for the Union?'(2013) 20 European Law Journal 186.

Peers S., 'The Stability Treaty: Permanent Austerity or Gesture Politics?' (2012) 8 European Constitutional Law Review 404.

Pelkmans J., 'The New Approach to Technical Harmonization and Standardization' (1987) 25 CCMS, 249.

Pelkmans J., *European Integration: Methods and Economic Analysis* (Longman 1997).

Pelkmans J., 'Mutual Recognition in Goods: On Promises and Disillusions' (2007) 14 JEPP, 699.

Pernice I., '*Costa v. ENEL* and *Simmenthal*: Primacy of European Law' in Maduro M.P. and Azoulai L (eds) *The Past and Future of EU Law: The Classics of EU law Revisited on the 50th Anniversary of the Rome Treaty* (Hart Publishing 2010).

Pescatore P., 'Van Gend en Loos, 3 February 1963—A View from Within' in Maduro M.P. and Azoulai L (eds) *The Past and Future of EU Law: The Classics of EU law Revisited on the 50th Anniversary of the Rome Treaty* (Hart Publishing 2010).

Philippe X., 'The Principles of Universal Jurisdiction and Complementarity: How Do The Two Principles Intermesh?' (2006) 88 International Review of the Red-cross 375.

Pierson P., 'The Path to European Integration: A Historical Institutionalist Analysis' (1996) 29 Comparative Political Studies 123.

Piris J.C., 'Should the UK withdraw from the EU: legal aspects and effects of possible options' (Fondation Robert Schuman / European Issues n°355, May 2015).

Possi A., 'Striking a Balance between Community norms and Human Rights: The Continuing struggle of the East African Court of Justice' (2015) 15 African Human Rights Law Journal 192.

Prechal S., 'Does Direct Effect Still Matter?' (2000) Common Market Law Review 1047.

Prechal S., *Directives in EC law* (2nd edn, OUP 2005).

Puetter U., *The European Council and the Council: New Intergovernmentalism and Institutional Change* (OUP 2014).

Ravo L.M., 'The Role of the Principle of Effective Judicial Protection in the EU and its Impact on National Jurisdictions' (DPhil thesis, University of Trieste 2012).

Raz J., 'Legal Principles and the Limits of Law' (1972) 81 Yale Law Journal 82.

Reestman J.H., 'The Fiscal Compact: Europe's Not Always Able to Speak German. On the Dutch Implementing Act and the Hazardous Interpretation of the Implementation Duty in Article 3(2) Fiscal Compact' (2013) 9 European Constitutional Law Review 480.

Reith S. and Boltz M., 'The East African Community Integration: Between Aspiration and Reality. Ambition for and Reality of the East African Community in a Globalized World' (Knorad Adenauer Stiftung International Reports 2011).

Rickford J., 'Protectionism, Capital Freedom, and the Internal Market' in Bernitz and Ringe (eds), *Company Law and Economic Protectionism* (OUP 2010).

Rodden J., *Hamilton's Paradox: The Promise and Peril of Fiscal Federalism* (CUP 2006).

Rosas A. and Armati L., *EU Constitutional Law* (Hart 2010).

Roth W.H., 'The European Court of Justice's Case Law on Freedom to Provide Services: is *Keck* Relevant?' in Andenas M, Roth W.H., *Services and Free Movement in EU Law* (OUP 2002).

Ruffert, 'The European Debt Crisis and European Law' (2011) 48 Common Market Law Review 1777.

Ruhangisa, J.E., *The Institutions of the East African Community with Emphasis on the East African Court of Justice—A Course Material for TGCL Students* (University of Dar es Salaam 2010, unpublished).

Ruhangisa J.E., 'Procedures and Functions of the East African Court of Justice' in Gastorn, Sippel and Wanizek (eds), *Processes of Legal Integration in the East African Community* (Dar es Salaam University Press 2011).

Ruhangisa J.E., 'Establishing Independent and Effective Regional Courts: Lessons for the SADC Region from the EAC and ECOWAS' (SADC Regional Colloquium on the SADC Tribunal, Johannesburg, March 2013).

Ruhangisa J.E., 'From Rules to Reality: Creating a Legal Community for the EAC' (A Key Note Address to the Second LEAC Conference on East African Integration Through law, organized by Leiden University in Collaboration with the East African Court of Justice, Arusha, May 2016).

Sandry R., 'Intra-REC trade and overlapping membership: review of COMESA, EAC, SADC' (*Trade Law Centre,* August 2015) <https://www.tralac.org/publications/article/7885-intra-rec-trade-and-overlapping-membership-review-of-comesa-eac-and-sadc.html> accessed 20 November 2016.

Schauer F., 'Do Cases Make Bad Law?' (2006) 73 The University of Chicago Law Review 883.

Schermers H.G. and Blokker N.M., *International Institutional Law* (Martinus Nijhoff Publishers, 1995).

Schönberger C., 'Lisbon in Karlsruhe: Maastricht's Epigone at Sea' (2009) 10 German Law Journal 1201.

Schorkopf F., 'The European Union as An Association of Sovereign States: Karlsruhe's Ruling on the Treaty of Lisbon' (2009) 10 German Law Journal 1220.

SEATINI, *Uganda's Trade Negotiation Framework,* September 2013.

Seyersted F., 'Objective International Personality of Intergovernmental Organizations: Do their Capacities Depend Upon The Conventions Establishing Them?' (1964) 34 Nordisk Tidsskrift for International Ret 1.

Shaw J., 'Citizenship: Contrasting dynamics at the interface of integration and constitutionalism' in in Craig and de Búrca (eds.) *The Evolution of EU law* (2nd edn, OUP 2011).

Shaw M.N., *International Law* (Cambridge University Press 1997).

Shivji I.G., 'Pan-Africanism and the Challenge of East African Integration' in *EAC 10th Anniversary Symposium: Role of Non-State Actors in Deepening EAC Integration* (Arusha:East African Community 2009).

Sisenda E., 'Why EAC Competition Law is Key in Efforts to Spur Growth' (*The Business Daily,* 2 November 2015) <http://www.businessdailyafrica.com/Opinion-and-Analysis/EAC-competition-law-to-spur-growth/-/539548/2939986/-/12kt4ny/-/index.html> accessed 20 November 2016.

Smith K.E., 'The Evolution and Application of EU Membership Conditionality' in Cremona M (ed), *The enlargement of the European Union* (OUP 2003).

Snaith H., 'Narratives of Optimum Currency Area Theory and Eurozone Governance' (2014) 19(2) New Political Economy 183.

Snell J., *Goods and Services in EC Law: A Study of the Relationship between the Freedoms* (OUP 2002).

Snell J., 'Free Movement of Capital: Evolution as a Non-linear Process' in Craig and de Burca (eds), *The Evolution of the EU* (OUP 2011).

Snyder F, 'EMU-Integration and differentiation: Metaphor for European Union' in Craig and de Búrca (eds), *The Evolution of EU Law* (2nd edn, OUP 2011).

Spaventa E., *Free Movement of Persons in the EU: Barriers to movement and their constitutional context* (Kluwer 2007).

Spence D. (ed), *The European Commission* (3rd edn, Harper 2006).

Ssempebwa E.F., East African Community Law' (Lexis Nexis2015).

Ssemuwemba A.M., 'EPA Negotiations: Is EAC at the crossroad?' (*The Daily Monitor,* 2 August 2016 <http://www.monitor.co.ug/Business/Prosper/EPA-negotiations--Is-EAC-at-the-crossroads-/688616-3325520-kg10mdz/index.html> accessed 20 November 2016.

Steiner J., 'Drawing the Line: Uses and Abuses of Article 30 EEC' (1992) 29 Common Market Law Review 749.

Stone Sweet A. and Caporaso J.A., 'From Free Trade to Supranational Policy: The European Court and Integration' in Waynes, Sandholtz and Stone Sweet (eds), *European Integration and Supranational Governance* (OUP 1998).

Strayer R.W., 'The Failure of Closer Union in East Africa 1919–1931' (DPhil thesis, University of Wisconsin-Madison 1966).

Szydlo, 'Leeway of Member States in Shaping the Notion of an 'Undertaking' in Competition Law' (2010) 33 World Competition 549.

Tarullo, D.K., 'Norms and Institutions in Global Competition Policy' (2000) 94 American Journal of International Law 478.

Tatham A., '"Don't Mention Divorce at the Wedding, Darling!" EU Accession and Withdrawal after Lisbon' in Biondi, Eeckhout and Ripley (eds), *EU Law after Lisbon* (OUP 2012).

Tax S.L., 'East African Community Integration: Marching towards a Common Market' (Paper Presented at the University of Dar es Salaam, East African Community Students' Union, June 2010, unpublished).

Telò M. (ed), *European Union and New Regionalism: Regional Actors and Global Governance in a Post-Hegemonic Era* (Ashgate 2001).

Temple Lang J., 'How Much do the Smaller Member States Need the European Commission: The Role of the Commission in a Changing Europe' (2002) 39 Common Market Law Review 315.

Tiersky R., 'Europe: International Crisis and the Future of Integration' in R. Tiersky (ed), *Europe Today* (2nd edn, Rowman & Littlefield Publishers Inc. 2004).

Tomuschat C., 'Calling Europe by Phone' Guest Editorial' (2010) 47 Common Market Law Review 3.

Toth A.G., 'The Principle of Subsidiarity in the Maastricht Treaty' (1992) 29 Common Market Law Review 1079.

Trabelsi I., 'Agricultural trade face to Non-Tariff barriers: A gravity model for the Ero-Med area' (2013) 3 Journal of Studies in Social Sciences 1.

Tridimas T., *The General Principles of EU Law* (2nd edn, OUP 2006).

Tridimas T. and Poli S., '*Locus Standi* of Individuals under Article 230(4): The Return of Eurydice?' in Arnull, Eeckhout, and Tridimas (eds), *Continuity and Change in EU law: Essays in Honour of Sir Francis Jacobs* (OUP 2008).

Tridimas T., 'Constitutional Review of Member State Action: The Virtues and Vices of an Incomplete Jurisdiction' (2011) 9 I-CON 737.

Tryfonidou A., 'In search of the aim of the EC free movement of persons provisions: Has the Court of Justice missed the point?' (2009) 46 Common Market Law Review 1591.

Tuori K., *The Eurozone Crisis, a Constitutional Analysis* (CUP 2014).

Tushnet M., 'Comparative Constitutional Law', in Reimann M. and Zimmermann R. (eds), *The Oxford Handbook of Comparative Law* (OUP 2006).

United Nations Conference for Trade and Development, 'Voluntary Peer Review Of Competition Law And Policy: United Republic Of Tanzania' (2012) UNCTAD/DITC/CLP/2012/1.

United Nations Economic Commission for Africa, *Assessing Regional Integration in Africa V Towards an African Continental Free Trade Area* (Addis Ababa 2012).

Usher J., *The Law of Money and Financial Services in the European Community* (OUP 1994).

Usui Y., Constructing an East Asian Acquis' in Nkamura (ed), *East Asian Regionalism from a Legal Perspective: Current features and a vision for the future* (Routledge 2009).

Valk M., 'The Rule of the European Court of Justice and the East African Court of Justice: Comparing Potential Judicial Strategies for Early Stage Integration' (DPhil thesis, Leiden University 2015).

Van Cleynenbreugel P., 'Article 101 TFEU and the EU Courts: adapting legal form to the realities of modernization?' (2014) 51 Common Market Law Review 1409.

Van Cleynenbreugel P., 'National courts and EU competition law: lost in multilevel confusion?' in Bodiroga-Vukobrat N., Rodin S. and Sander G., *New Europe, Old Values? Reform and Perseverance* (Springer, 2016).

Van de Gronden J.W. et al. (eds), *Health Care and EU Law* (Asser 2011).

Van den Bogaert S. and Borger V., 'Twenty Years After Maastricht: The Coming of Age of the EMU?', in de Visser and van der Mei (eds), *The Treaty on European Union 1993–2013: Reflections from Maastricht* (Intersentia 2014).

Van den Bogaert S. and Cuyvers A., 'Money For Nothing: The Case Law of the EU Court of Justice on the Regulation of Gambling' (2011) 48(4) Common Market Law Review 1175.

Van den Bogaert S. and Cuyvers A., 'Let it be? The regulation and allocation of gambling licenses at the EU and Member State level' in Adriaanse C., van Ommeren F.J., den Ouden W. and Wolswinkel C.J. (eds), *Scarcity and the State The Allocation of Limited Rights by the Administration* (Intersentia, 2016).

Van den Bogaert S. and Cuyvers A., 'Of carrots and sticks: From sanctions to rewards in Economic and Monetary Union' in Steunenberg, Voermans and Van den Bogaert (eds), *Fit for the Future: Insights on the EU from Leiden University* (Eleven International Publishing 2016).

Van Elsuwege L.P., 'EU External Action after the Collapse of the Pillar Structure: In Search of a New Balance Between Delimitation and Consistency' (2010) 47 Common Market Law Review 987.

Van Middelaar L., *The Passage to Europe, How a Continent became a Union* (Yale University Press 2014).

Van Middelaar L., 'The return of politics: The European Union after the crises in the euro zone and Ukraine' (2016) Journal of Common Market Studies 54.

Van Middelaar L., 'Taking decisions or setting norms. EU Presidencies between executive and legislative power in a crisis-driven Union', in Steunenberg, Voermans and Van den Bogaert (eds), *Fit for the Future: Insights on the EU from Leiden University* (Eleven International Publishing 2016).

Van Vooren B. and Wessel R.A., *EU External Relations Law: Text, Cases and Materials* (CUP 2014).

Vasconcelos Á.d, 'European Union and Mercosur' in M. Telò (ed), *European Union and New Regionalism: Regional Actors and Global Governance in a Post-Hegemonic Era* (Ashgate 2001).

Vines A., 'A Decade of African Peace and Security Architecture' (2013) 89 International Affairs 1.

Von Bogdandy A., 'Founding Principles' in Von Bogdandy A. and Bast J. (eds), *Principles of European Constitutional Law* (2nd edn, Hart 2010).

Von Bogdandy A. and Schill S., 'Overcoming Absolute Primacy: Respect for National Identity Under the Lisbon Treaty' (2011) Common Market Law Review 1417.

Von Borries R. and Hauschild M., 'Implementing the Subsidiarity Principle' (1999) 5 Columbia Journal of European Law, 369.

Walker N., 'The Idea of Constitutional Pluralism' (2003) 65 The Modern Law Review 317.

Walker N., 'Big 'C' or small 'c'' (2006) 12 European Law Journal 12.

Walker N., 'The European Fallout' (2016) German Law Journal Brexit Supplement 126.

Ward A., *Judicial Review and the Rights of Private Parties in EU law* (2nd edn, OUP 2007) Warntjen A., 'Steering the Union: The Impact of the EU Presidency on Legislative Activity' (2007) 45 Journal of Common Market Studies 1135.

Weiler J.H.H., 'The Transformation of Europe' (1991) Yale Law Journal 100.

Weiler J.H.H., 'The Tranformation of Europe' (1991) Yale Law Journal 2414.

Weiler J.H.H., 'European democracy and its critics: polity and system' in Weiler J.H.H., *The Constitution of Europe: Do the New Clothes have an Emperor?* (CUP 1999).

Weiler J.H.H., 'To be a European citizen: Eros and civilization' in Weiler J.H.H., *The Constitution of Europe: Do the New Clothes have an Emperor?* (CUP 1999).

Weiss F., 'Greenland's Withdrawal from the European Communities' (1985) 10 European Law Review 173.

Werts J., *The European Council* (Harper 2008).

Wessel R. and Van Vooren B., *EU External Relations Law: Text, Cases and Materials* (CUP 2014).

Westlake M., '"The Style and the Machinery": The Role of the European Parliament in the EU's Legislative Process', in: P. Craig and C. Harlow (eds), *Lawmaking in the European Union* (Kluwer 1998).

Westlake M. and Galloway D., *The Council of the European Union* (3rd edn, Harper Publishing 2004).

Widdows K., 'The Unilateral Denunciation of Treaties Containing no Denunciation Clause' (1983) 53 British Ybk Intl L 102.

World Bank, 'Why Trade Facilitation is Important for Africa, (Policy Note No: 27, November 2011).

World Bank, *East African Common Market Scorecard 2014: Tracking EAC Compliance in the Movement of Capital, Services and Goods* < http://documents.worldbank.org/curated/en/2014/01/23862386/east-african-common-market-scorecard-2014-tracking-eac-compliance-movement-capital-services-goods-vol-2-main-report> accessed 20 November 2016.

Wouters J., Odermatt J. and Ramopoulos T., 'The EU in the World of International Organizations: Diplomatic Aspirations, Legal Hurdles and Political Realities', in Smith, Keukeleire, Vanhooacker (eds), *The diplomatic system of the European Union: evolution, change and challenges* (Routledge 2015).

Zartman W., *The Politics of Trade Negotiations between Africa and the European Economic Community* (Princeton University Press 1971).

EU

Court of Justice

C-1/58 *Stork & Cie v High Authority of the European Coal and Steel Community* ECLI:EU:C:1959:4.

C-2/62 and 3/62 *Commission v Belgium and Luxemburg* ECLI:EU:C:1962:45.

C-25/62 *Plaumann* ECLI:EU:C:1963:17.

C-26/62 *Van Gend en Loos v Netherlands Inland Revenue Administration* EU:C:1963:1.

C-28–32/62 *Da Costa* ECLI:EU:C:1963:6.

C-31/62 and 33/62 *Wöhrmann v Commission of the EEC* ECLI:EU:C:1962:49.

C-6/64 *Costa v E.N.E.L* ECLI:EU:C:1964:66.

C-56 and 58/64 *Consten and Grundig v Commission* ECLI:EU:C:1966:41.
C-27/67 *Fink-Frucht* [1968] ECR 223.
C-7/68 *Commission v. Italy* [1968] ECR 617.
C-13/68 *Salgoil* [1968] ECR 453.
C-24/68 *Commission v Italy* [1969] ECR 193.
C-2/69 *Sociaal fonds voor de Diamantarbeiders* [1969] ECR 211.
C-4/69 *Lütticke v Commission* ECLI:EU:C:1971:40.
C-9/70 *Franz Grad v Finanzamt Traunstein* ECLI:EU:C:1970:78.
C-11/70 *Internationale Handelsgesellschaft,* [1970] ECR 1125.
C-22/70 *AETR* [1971] ECR 263.
C-6/72 *Europemballage Corporation and Continental Can Company Inc. v Commission of the European Communities,* ECLI:EU:C:1973:22.
C-21–24/72 *International Fruit Company* [1972] ECR 1219.
C-2/73 *Geddo* [1973] ECR 865.
C-4/73 *Nold* ECLI:EU:C:1974:51.
C-40–48, 50, 54–56, 111, 113 & 114/73 *Suiker Unie and Others* v. *Commission* ECLI:EU:C:1975:174.
C-127/73 *BRT v Sabam* ECLI:EU:C:1974:25.
C-166/73 *Rheinmühlen-Düsseldorf* ECLI:EU:C:1974:3.
C-167/73 *Commission v France* (Merchant Navy) ECLI:EU:C:1974:35.
C-181/73 *Haegeman* [1974] ECR 449.
C-2/74 *Reyners* [1972], ECR 631.
C-8/74 *Dassonville* [1974], ECR 837.
C-33/74 *Van Binsbergen* [1974] ECR 129.
C-36/74 *Walrave and Koch* [1974] ECR 1405.
C-41/74 *Van Duyn* ECLI:EU:C:1974:133.
C-45/75 *Rewe-Zentral* [1976] ECR 181.
C-87/75 *Bresciani* [1976] ECR 129.
C-105/75 *Interzuccheri* [1977] ECR 1029.
C-3/76, 4/76, and 6/76 *Kramer* [1976] ECR 1279.
C-41/76 *Donckerwolcke* [1976] ECR 1921.
C-52/76 *Benedetti* ECLI:EU:C:1977:16.
C-85/76 *Hoffmann-La Roche & Co. AG v Commission of the European Communities* ECLI:EU:C:1979:36.
C-5/77 *Tedeschi* ECLI:EU:C:1977:144.
C-106/77 *Simmenthal* ECLI:EU:C:1978:139.
C-112/77 *Töpfer* ECLI:EU:C:1978:94.
C-149/77 *Defrenne* EU:C:1978:130.
C-15/78 *Koestler* ECLI:EU:C:1978:184.
C-120/78, *Cassis de Dijon* ECLI:EU:C:1979:42.

C-128/78 *Commission v United Kingdom* (Tachographs), ECLI:EU:C:1979:32.
C-148/78 *Criminal proceedings against Tullio Ratti* ECLI:EU:C:1979:110.
C-168/78 *Commission* v *France* [1980] ECR 347.
C-169/78 *Commission v Italy* [1980] ECR 385.
C-170/78 *Commission v UK* [1983] ECR 2265.
C-171/78 *Commission v Denmark* [1980] ECR 447.
C-34/79 *R Henn and Darby*, [1979] ECR 3795.
C-52/79 *Debauve* [1980] ECR 83.
C-140/79 *Chemial Farmaceutici v DAF* [1981] ECR 1.
C-113/80 *Commission v Ireland* ECLI:EU:C:1981:139.
C-155/80 *Oebel* [1981] ECR I-1993.
C-193/80 *Commission v Italy* [1981] ECR 3019.
C-203/80 *Casati* [1981] ECR 2595.
C-244/80 *Foglia* ECLI:EU:C:1981:302.
C-279/80 *Webb* [1981] ECR 3305.
C-15/81 *Schul* [1982] ECR 1982, 1409.
C-62/81 and 63/81 Seco *and Desquenne & Giral v Etablissement d' Assurance contre la Vieillesse et l' Invalidité* [1982] ECR 223.
C-76/81 *SA Transporoute et travaux* ECLI:EU:C:1982:49.
C-102/81 *Nordsee* ECLI:EU:C:1982:107.
C-283/81 *CILFIT* ECLI:EU:C:1982:335.
C-132/82 *Commisison v Belgium* ECLI:EU:C:1983:135.
C-286/82 & 26/83 *Luisi and Carbone* [1984] ECR 377.
C-13/83 *Parliament v Council* (Transport Policy) ECLI:EU:C:1985:220.
C-14/83 *Von Colson & Kamann* ECLI:EU:C:1984:153.
C-107/83 *Klopp* [1984] ECR 2971.
C-220/83 *Commission v. France* ECLI:EU:C:1986:461.
C-240/83 *ADBHU* [1985] ECR 53.
C-288/83 *Commission v Ireland* [1985] ECR 1761.
C-294/83 *Les Verts* ECLI:EU:C:1986:166.
C-112/84 *Humblot* ECLI:EU:C:1985:185.
C-152/84 *Marshall* EU:C:1986:84.
C-205/84 *Commission v. Germany* ECLI:EU:C:1986:463.
C-243/84 *Johnnie Walker* [1986] ECR 875.
C-66/85 *Lawrie-Blum* ECR 02121.
C-89/85, C-104/85, C-114/85, C-116/85, C-117/85, C-125/85, C-126/85, C-127/85, C-128/85 and C-129/85 *Woodpulp I* ECLI:EU:C:1993:120.
C-121/85 *Conegate* [1986] ECR 1007.
C-184/85 *Commission v Italy* [1987] ECR 2013.
C-293/85 *Commission v Belgium* ECLI:EU:C:1988:40.

C-311/85 *Vereniging voor Vlaamse reisbureaus* [1987] ECR 3801.
C-314/85 *Foto-Frost* [1987] ECR 4199.
C-352/85 *Bond van Adverteerders and Others* [1988] ECR 2085.
C-12/86 *Demirel* ECLI:EU:C:1987:400.
C-14/86 *Pretore di Salò* ECLI:EU:C:1987:275.
C-45/86 *Commission v. Council* [1987] ECR 493.
C-62/86 *AKZO Chemie BV v Commission of the European Communities* ECLI:EU:C:1991:286.
C-246/86, *Societé Cooperative des Asphalteurs Belges (Belasco SC) v Commission of the European Communities*, ECLI:EU:C:1989:301.
C-249/86 *Commission v. Germany* [1989] ECR 1263.
C-252/86 *Bergandi* ECLI:EU:C:1988:112.
C-263/86 *Humbel* [1988] ECR 5365.
C-308/86 *Lambert* [1988] ECR-04369.
C-18/87 Commission v Germany, ECLI:EU:C:1988:453.
C-29/87 *Denkavit* [1988] ECR 2965.
C-186/87 *Cowan* [1989] ECR 195.
C-247/87 *Star Fruit* ECLI:EU:C:1989:58.
C-274/87 *Commission v Germany* [1989] ECR 229.
C-344/87 *Bettray* [1989] ECR 1621.
C-379/87 *Groener* ECLI:EU:C:1989:599.
C-3/88 *Commission v. Italy* ECLI:EU:C:1992:235.
C-5/88 *Wachauf* [1989] ECR 2609.
C-145/88 *Torfaen Borough* [1989] ECR I-3851.
C-170/88 *Ford España v Spain* ECLI:EU:C:1989:306.
C-262/88 *Barber* ECLI:EU:C:1990:209.
C-69/89 *Nakajima* [1991] ECR I-2069.
C-106/89 *Marleasing* ECLI:EU:C:1990:395.
C-113/89 *Rush Portuguesa* [1990] ECR I-1417.
C-154/89 *Commission v France* ECLI:EU:C:1991:76.
C-188/89 *Forster* [1990] ECR I-3313.
C-260/89 *ERT* [1991] ECR I-2925.
C-292/89 *Antonissen* ECLI:EU:C:1991:80.
C-300/89 *Commission v Council* (Titanium Dioxide) ECLI:EU:C:1991:244.
C-309/89 *Codorniu* ECLI:EU:C:1994:197.
C-340/89 *Vlassopoulou* ECLI:EU:C:1991:193.
C-353/89 *Mediawet Nederland* [1999] ECR I-4069.
C-2/90 *Commission v. Kingdom of Belgium* ECLI:EU:C:1992:310.
C-6/90 and 9/90 *Francovich* [1991] ECR I-5357.
C-41/90 *Klaus Höfner and Fritz Elser* v. *Macrotron GmbH* ECLI:EU:C:1991:161.

C-76/90 *Säger* [1991] ECR I-4221.
C-159/90 *Grogan* ECLI:EU:C:1991:378.
C-369/90 *Micheletti* [1992] ECR I-4239.
C-370/90 *Singh* ECLI:EU:C:1992:296.
C-169/91 *B & Q* [2002] ECR I-6635.
C-267 & 268/91 *Keck and Mithouard* ECLI:EU:C:1993:905.
C-19/92 *Dieter Kraus* ECLI:EU:C:1993:125.
C-42/92 *Thijssen* [1993] ECR I-4047.
C-49/92 P *Commission of the European Communities v Anic Partecipazioni SpA* ECLI:EU:C:1999:356.
C-91/92 *Faccini Dori* [1994] ECR I-3325.
C-109/92 *Wirth* ECLR:EU:C:1993:916.
C-137/92 P *Commission v. BASF* [1994] ECR I-2555.
C-275/92 *Schindler* ECLI:EU:C:1994:119.
C-379/92 *Peralta* ECLI:EU:C:1994:296.
C-43/93 *Vander Elst* [1994] ECR I-3803.
C-46/93 and 48/93 *Brasserie du Pêcheur* [1996] ECR I-1029.
C-363/93 *Lancry* [1994] ECR I-3957.
C-280/93 *Germany v. Commission* [1994] ECR I-4873.
C-358/93 and C-416/93 *Bordessa* ECLI:EU:C:1995:54.
C-384/93 *Alpine Investments* ECLI:EU:C:1995:126.
C-479/93 *Francovich* [1995] ECR I-3843.
C-484/93 *Svensson and Gustavsson* ECLI:EU:C:1995:379.
C-55/94 *Gebhard* ECLI:EU:C:1995:411.
C-163/94, C-165/94 and C-250/94 *Sanz de Lera* [1995] ECR I-04821.
C-189/94 and 190/94 *Dillenkofer v Germany*, ECLI:EU:C:1996:375.
C-194/94 *CIA Security* [1996] ECR I-220.
C-272/94 *Michel Guiot and Climatec* ECLI:EU:C:1996:147.
C-321/94 *Pistre*, [1997] ECR I-2343.
C-34/95, C-35/95 and C-36/95, *De Agostini* ECLI:EU:C:1997:344.
C-73/95 P *Viho Europe BV* v. *Commission* ECLI:EU:C:1996:405.
C-185/95 P *Baustahlgewebe* ECLI:EU:C:1998:608.
C-250/95 *Futura* ECLI:EU:C:1997:239.
C-265/95 *Commission v France* (Spanish Strawberries) [1997] ECR I-6959.
C-299/95 *Kremzow* EU:C:1997:25.
C-398/95 *Syndesmos ton en Elladi Touristikon kai Taxidiotikon Grafeion* ECLI:EU:C:1997:282.
C-28/96 *Fricarnes* [1997] ECR I-4939.
C-51/96 and C-191/97 *Deliège* [2000] ECR I-2549.
C-118/96 *Safir* ECLI:EU:C:1998:170.

C-129/96 *Inter-Environment Wallonie* ECLI:EU:C:1997:628.

C-149/96 *Portugal v Council* [1999] ECR I-8395.

C-158/96 *Kohll* ECLI:EU:C:1998:171.

C-369/96 and C-376/96 *Arblade* [1999] ECR I-845.

C-386/96 P *Dreyfus v Commission* [1998] ECR I-2309.

C-389/96 *Aher-Waggon* ECLI:EU:C:1998:357.

C-395/96 P and C396/96 P *Compagnie maritime belge transports and Others v Commission* ECLI:EU:C:2000:13.

C-10/97 to C-22/97 *Ministero delle Finanze v IN.CO.GE.'90 Srl and 12 others* ECLI:EU:C:1998:498.

C-126/97 *Eco Swiss v Benneton* ECLI:EU:C:1999:269.

C-212/97 *Centros* [1999] ECR I-1459.

C-337/97 *Meeusen* [1999] ECR I-3289.

C-387/97 *Commission v Greece*, ECLI:EU:C:2000:356.

C-439/97 *Sandoz* [1999] ECR I-7041.

C-35/98 *Verkooijen* [2000] ECR I-4071.

C-49/98 *Finalarte* ECLI:EU:C:2001:564.

C-97/98 *Jägerskiöld* [1999] ECR I-7319.

C-108/98 *RI.SAN* ECLI:EU:C:1999:400.

C-251/98 *Baars* [2000] ECR I-02787.

C-281/98 *Angonese* [2000] ECR I-4139.

C-352/98P *Bergadem* [2000] ECR I-5291.

C-355/98 *Commision v. Belgium* [2000] ECR I-1221.

C-368/98 *Vanbraekel* [2001] ECR I-5363.

C-376/98 *Tobacco Advertising I* [2000] ECR I-8419.

C-379/98 *PreussenElektra* ECLI:EU:C:2001:160.

C-403/98 *Azienda Agricola Monte Arcosu v Regione Autonoma della Sardegna* ECLI:EU:C:2001:6.

C-408/98 *Abrahamsson* ECLI:EU:C:2000:367.

C-441–442/98 *Mikhailidis* [2000] ECR I-7145.

C-464/98, *Westdeutsche Landesbank Girozentrale v Stefan and Republik Österreich* [2001] ECR I-173.

C-478/98 *Commission v Belgium* (Eurobond) [2000] ECR I-07587.

C-54/99 *Association Eglise de scientologie de Paris* [2000] ECR I-1335.

C-157/99 *Smits and Peerbooms* [2001] ECR I-5473.

C-268/99 *Jany* ECLI:EU:C:2001:616.

C-184/99 *Grzelczyk* [2001] ECR I-6193.

C-309/99 *Wouters* [2002] ECR I-1577.

C-385/99 *Müller-Fauré* [2003] ECR I-4509.

C-390/99 *Canal Satélite Digital* [2002] ECR I-607.
C-413/99 *Baumbast* ECR I-7091.
C-430 & 431/99 *Sea-Land Service* ECLI:EU:C:2002:364.
C-451/99 *Cura Anlagen* ECLI:EU:C:2002:195.
C-475/99 *Firma Ambulanz Glöckner v Landkreis Südwestpfalz* ECLI:EU:C:2001:577.
C482/99 *France v Commission* ECLI:EU:C:2002:294.
C-483/99 *Commission v France* [2002] ECR I-4781.
C-503/99 *Commission v Belgium* [2002] ECR I-4809.
C-515/99 *Reisch* [2002] ECR I-2157.
C-11/00 *Commission v European Central Bank*, ECLI:EU:C:2003:395.
C-50/00 P *Union de Pequeños Agricultores v Council*, ECLI:EU:C:2002:462.
C-99/00 *Kenny Roland Lykkeskog*, ECLI:EU:C:2002:329.
C-112/00 *Schmidberger* [2003] ECR I-5659.
C-136/00 *Danner* ECLI:EU:C:2002:558.
C-208/00 *Überseering* [2002] ECR I-9919.
C-453/00 *Kühne & Heitz* [2004] ECR I-837.
C-472/00 P *Fresh Marine* ECLI:EU:C:2003:399.
C-2 and 3/01 P *Bundesverband der Arzneimittel-Importeure eV & Commission v Bayer* ECLI:EU:C:2004:2.
C-131/01 *Commission* v *Italy* [2003] ECR I-1659.
C-189/01 *Jippes* ECLI:EU:C:2001:420.
C-215/01 *Schnitzer* ECLI:EU:C:2003:662.
C-243/01 *Gambelli* [2003] ECR I-13031.
C-338/01 *Commission v. Council* (AGGF) [2004] ECR I-4829.
C-364/01 *Barbier* [2003] ECR I-15013.
C-397–403/01 *Pfeiffer* [2004] ECR I-8835.
C-418/01 *IMS Health GmbH & Co. OHG v NDC Health GmbH & Co. KG*, ECLI:EU:C:2004:257.
C-422/01 *Skandia and Ramstedt* [2003] ECR I-6817.
C-491/01 *British American Tobacco* [2002] ECR I-11453.
C-14/02 *ATRAL SA* [2003] ECR I-4431.
C-71/02 *Karner v Troostwijk* ECLI:EU:C:2004:181.
C-201/02 *Wells* [2004] ECR I-723.
C-225/02 *Garcia Blanco* ECLI:EU:C:2005:34.
C-262/02 *Commission v. France* (Loi Evin) ECLI:EU:C:2004:431.
C-304/02 *Commission v France*, ECLI:EU:C:2005:444.
C-309/02 *Radlberger v Land Baden-Württemberg*, [2004] ECR I-11763.
C-315/02 *Lenz* [2004] ECR I-7063.
C-334/02 *Commission v. France* ECLI:EU:C:2004:129.
C-350/02 *Commission v Netherlands*, ECLI:EU:C:2004:389.

C-434/02 *Arnold André* [2004] ECR I-11825.

C-456/02 *Trojani* ECLI:EU:C:2004:488.

C-72/03 *Carbonati Apuani* ECLI:EU:C:2004:506.

C-88/03 *Portugal* v *Commission* ECLI:EU:C:2006:511.

C-152/03 *Ritter-Coulais* ECLI:EU:C:2006:123.

C-176/03 *Commission v Council* (Ship Source Pollution I) [2005] ECR I-7879.

C-210/03 *Swedish Match* [2004] ECR I-11893.

C-266/03 *Commission v Luxemburg* [2005] ECR I-4805.

C-293/03 *My* ECLI:EU:C:2004:821.

C-380/03 *Tobacco Advertising* II [2006] ECR I-11573.

C-433/03 *Commission v Germany* [2005] ECR I-6985.

C-459/03 *Commission v Ireland* [2006] ECR I-4635.

C-470/03 *AGM-COS.MET* [2007] ECR I-2749.

C-513/03 *Van Hilten-van der Heijden* [2006] ECR I-01957.

C-27/04 *Commission v Council*, [2004] ECR I-6649.

C-95/04 *British Airways plc v Commission of the European Communities* ECLI:EU:C:2007:166.

C-109/04 *Kranemann* [2005] ECR I2421.

C-144/04 *Mangold* EU:C:2005:709.

C-155/04 *Alliance for Natural Health* [2005] ECR I-6451.

C-170/04 *Rosengren* [2007] ECR I-4701.

C-180/04 *Vasallo* ECLI:EU:C:2006:518.

C-196/04 *Cadbury Schweppes* [2006] ECR I-7995.

C-234/04 *Kapferer* [2006] ECR I-2585.

C-244/04 *Commission v Germany* [2006] ECR I-88.

C-282/04 and C-283/04 *Commission v The Netherlands* [2006] ECR I-09141.

C-351/04 *Ikea Wholesale* [2007] ECR I-7723.

C-372/04 *Watts* [2006] ECLI:EU:C:2006:325.

C-432/04 *Commission v Cresson* [2006] ECR I-6387.

C-434/04 *Anders Ahokainen* [2006] ECR I-9171.

C-452/04 *Fidium Finanz* ECLI:EU:C:2006:631.

C-51/05 P *Cantina Sociale* ECLI:EU:C:2008:409.

C-65/05 *Commission v. Greece* [2006] ECR I-10341.

C-76/05 *Schwarz and Gootjes-Schwarz* [2007] ECR I-0000.

C-101/05 *Skatteverket* [2007] ECR I-11531.

C-110/05 *Commission v Italy* ECLI:EU:C:2009:66.

C-112/05 *Commission v Germany* [2007] ECR I-08995.

C-142/05 *Mickelsson and Roos* ECLI:EU:C:2009:336.

C-220/05 *Auroux* ECLI:EU:C:2007:31.

C-254/05 *Commission v Belgium* [2007] ECR I-4269.

C-297/05 *Commission v the Netherlands* [2007] ECR I-7467.
C-341/05 *Laval un Partneri* ECLI:EU:C:2007:809.
C-393/05 *Commission v. Austria* ECLI:EU:C:2007:722.
C-402/05 P & C-415/05 P *Kadi I* [2008] ECR I-6351.
C-404/05 *Commission v. Germany* ECLI:EU:C:2007:72.
C-440/05 *Ship Source Pollution* II [2007] ECR I-9097.
C-444/05 *Stamatelaki* ECLI:EU:C:2007:231.
C-465/05 *Commission v. Italy* ECLI:EU:C:2007:781.
C-120/06 and 121/06 *FIAMM* [2008] ECR I-6513.
C-125/06 *Commission v Infront* [2008] ECR I-1451.
C-133/06 *Parliament v Council* (Secondary Legal Basis) [2008] ECR I-3189.
C-195/06 *KommAustria v ORF* [2007] ECR I-8817.
C-210/06 *Cartesio* ECLI:EU:C:2008:723.
C-221/06 *Stadtgemeinde Frohnleiten* [2007] ECR I-9643.
C-256/06 *Jäger* [2008] ECR I-123.
C-265/06 *Commission v Portugal,* [2008] ECR I-2245.
C-281/06 *Jundt* ECLI:EU:C:2007:816.
C-301/06 *Ireland v Parliament and Council* (Data Retention), ECLI:EU:C:2009:68.
C-411/06 *Commission v. Parliament and Council* (shipment of waste) ECLI:EU:C:2009:518.
C-42/07 *Liga Portuguesa* ECLI:EU:C:2009:519.
C-141/07 *Commission v Germany* [2008] ECR I-6935.
C-161/07 *Commission v. Austria* ECLI:EU:C:2008:759.
C-166/07 *Parliament v. Council* (Irish Fund) [2009] ECR I-7135.
C-169/07 *Hartlauer* ECLI:EU:C:2009:141.
C-209/07 *Competition Authority* v. *Beef Industry Development Society Ltd and Barry Brothers (Carrigmore) Meats Ltd* ECLI:EU:C:2008:643.
C-246/07 *Commission v Sweden (PFOS)* ECLI:EU:C:2010:203.
C-318/07 *Persche* [2009] ECR I-00359.
C-326/07 *Commission v Italy* [2009] ECR I-02291.
C-385/07 P *Der Grüne Punkt* ECLI:EU:C:2009:456.
C-402/07 *Sturgeon* ECLI:EU:C:2009:716.
C-445/07 P and C-455/07 P *Ente per le Ville vesuviane* [2009] ECR I-7993.
C-555/07 *Seda Kücükdeveci v Swedex GmbH & Co. KG,* [2010] ECR I-365.
C-567/07 *Sint-Servatius* ECLI:EU:C:2009:593.
C-8/08 *T-Mobile* ECLI:EU:C:2009:343.
C-135/08 *Rottmann* [2010] ECR I-1449.
C-403/08 *Football Association Premier League* ECLI:EU:C:2011:631.
C-458/08 *Commission v. Portugal* [2010] ECR I-11599.
C-543/08 *Commission v Portugal* ECLI:EU:C:2010:669.
C-578/08 *Chakroun* [2010] ECR I-1839.

C-34/09 *Zambrano* [2011] ECR I-1177.
C-52/09 *Konkurrensverket v TeliaSonera Sverige AB* ECLI:EU:C:2011:83.
C-108/09 *Ker-Optika* ECLI:EU:C:2010:725.
C-137/09 *Josemans* [2010] ECR I-13019.
C-161/09 *Kakavetsos-Fragkopoulos* ECLI:EU:C:2011:110.
C-212/09 *Commission v Portugal* [2011] ECR I-10889.
C-338/09 *Yellow Cab* ECLI:EU:C:2010:814.
C-347/09 *Dickinger and Ömer* ECLI:EU:C:2011:582.
C-348/09 *Remscheid* ECLI:EU:C:2012:300.
C-391/09 *Runevič-Vardyn and Wardyn* [2011] ECLI:EU:C:2011:291.
C-402/09 *Tatu* ECLI:EU:C:2011:219.
C-10/10 *Commission v Austria* [2011] ECR I-5389.
C-188/10 *Melki en Abdeli* ECLI:EU:C:2010:363.
C-282/10 *Dominguez*, ECLI:EU:C:2012:33.
C-364/10 *Hungary v. Slovak Republic* ECLI:EU:C:2012:3798.
C-443/10 *Bonnarde* ECLI:EU:C:2011:641.
C-456/10 *ANETT* ECLI:EU:C:2012:241.
C-584/10 P *Commission v Kadi* (Kadi II).
C-617/10 *Akerberg Fransson*, ECLI:EU:C:2013:105.
C-40/11 *Lida* ECLI:EU:C:2012:691.
C-171/11 *Frabo* ECLI:EU:C:2012:453.
C-226/11 *Expedia Inc v Autorité de la concurrence and Others* ECLI:EU:C:2012:795.
C-244/11 *Commission v Greece* ECLI:EU:C:2012:694.
C-300/11 *ZZ* ECLI:EUC:2013:363.
C-399/11 *Melloni* ECLI:EU:C:2013:107.
C-583/11 P *Inuit* ECLI:EU:C:2013:625.
C-678/11 *Commission v Spain* ECLI:EU:C:2014:2434.
C-68/12 *Protimonopolný úrad Slovenskej republiky v Slovenská sporitel'n ̌a a.s.* ECLI:EU:C:2013:71.
C-87/12 *Ymeraga* ECLU:EU:C:2013:291.
C-131/12 *Google v Spain* ECLI:EU:C:2014:317.
C-176/12 *AMS* ECLI:EU:C:2014:2.
C-270/12, *UK v Parliament and Council* (*ESMA*), ECLI:EU:C:2014:18.
C-286/12 *Commission v Hungary*, ECLI:EU:C:2012:687.
C-293/12 and 594/12 *Data Retention Directive* ECLI:EU:C:2014:238.
C--382/12 P *MasterCard v Commission* ECLI:EU:C:2014:2201.
C-390/12 *Pfleger* EU:C:2014:281.
C-427/12 *Commission v Parliament and Council* (Biocidal Products), ECLI:EU:C2014:170.
C-481/12 *UAB* ECLI:EU:C:2014:11.

C-523/12 *Dirextra Alta Formazione* ECLI:EU:C:2013:831.
C-573/12, *Alands* ECLI:EU:C:2014:2037.
C-198/13 *Julian Hernandez* ECLI:EU:C:2014:2055.
C-206/13 *Cruciano Siragusa* ECLI:EU:C:2014:126.
C-377/13 *Ascendi Beiras* ECLI:EU:C:2014:1754.
C-559/13 *Grünewald* ECLI:EU:C:2015:109.
C-62/14 *Gauweiler* (OMT) ECLI:EU:C:2015:400.
C-98/14 *Berlington* ECLI:EU:C:2015:386.
C-160/14 *Ferreira da Silva* ECLI:EU:C:2015:565.
C-340/14 *Trijber* ECLI:EU:C:2015:641.
C-358/14, *Poland v Parliament and Council* (Tobacco Advertising III) ECLI:EU:C:2016:323.
C-394/15 P *Dalli v Commission* ECLI:EU:C:2016:262.

General Court

T-39/92 *GrOUPement des Cartes Bancaires CB v Commission of the European Communities*, ECLI:EU:T:1994:20.
T-102/96 *Gencor Ltd v Commission* ECLI:EU:T:1999:65.
T-260/97 *Camar* ECLI:EU:T:2005:283.
T-177/01 *Jégo-Quéré* [2002] ECLI:EU:T:2002:112.
T-315/01 *Kadi I* [2005] ECR II-3649.
T-395/04 *Air One* ECLI:EU:T:2006:123.
T-262/10 *Microban* ECLI:EU:T:2011:623.

Opinions

Opinion 1/76 *Laying-up fund* [1977] ECR 741.
Opinion 1/91 (*EEA Agreement*) [1991] ECR 6079.
Opinion 2/94 *Accession to the ECHR* [1996] ECR I-1759.
Opinion 1/03 ECLI:EU:C:2006:81.
Opinion 1/09 *Patents court* ECLI:EU:C:2011:123.
Opinion 2/13 *on the draft agreement providing for the accession of the European Union to the Convention for the Protection of Human Rights and Fundamental Freedoms* ECLI:EU:C:2014:2454.

Belgium

Cour de Cassation (Belgium), 27 May 1971, S.A. *Fromagerie franco-suisse 'Le Ski'* (1971) RTD sur 495.
Cour Constitutionnelle, 3 February 1994, No. 12/94.
Cour de Cassation, 9 Nov. 2004, Pas., 2004, 1745.
Cour de Cassation, 16 Nov. 2004, Pas., 2004, 1802.

Czech Republic

Czech Constitutional Court, Pl. ÚS 19/08, 26 November 2008 *Lisbon I.*

Czech Constitutional Court, Pl. ÚS 29/09, 3 November 2009 *Lisbon* II.

Czech Constitutional Court, Pl. ÚS 5/12, 31 January 2012 *Landtova.*

Estonia

Constitutional Chamber of the Supreme Court of Estonia, Opinion No. 3-4-1-3-06 of 11 May 2006 Euro.

France

Conseil constitutionnel, Decision 2004–2005 DC of 19 November 2004, *Traité établissant une Constitution pour l'Europe.*

Conseil constitutionnel, Decision 2600–540 DC of 27 July 2006, *Loi transposant la directive sur le droit d'auteur.*

Germany

BVerfGE 37, 271 (1974) *Solange I.*

BVerfGE 89, 155 (1993) *Maastricht Urteil.*

BVerfGE, 2 BvE 123,267, 2 BvE 2/08 (2009) *Lissabon Urteil.*

BVerfGE 2 BvR 2728/13 (2014) *OMT* (referral CJEU).

BVerfGE, 2 BvR 2728/13, 2 BvR 2729/13, 2 BvR 2730/13, 2 BvR 2731/13, 2 BvE 13/13 (2016) *OMT* (final decision).

Hungary

Hungarian Constitutional Court, Decision 143/2010 (VII. 14.) AB, of 12 July 2010 *Lisbon Treaty.*

Italy

Italian Corte Costituzionale, Decision No. 348 and No. 349, 24 of October 2007.

Poland

Polish Constitutional Court, K18/04 of 11 May 2005, *EU Accession.*

Spain

Spanish Constitutional Court Declaration 1/2004 of December 13 2004 on the Constitutional Treaty, (BOE number 3 of 4 January 2005).

The Netherlands

Hoge Raad, 2 November 2011, LJN AR1797.

Hoge Raad, 1 October 2004, LJN AO8913.

Raad van State, 7 July 1995, AB 1997.

United Kingdom

Adams & Others v Cape Industrials PLC [1990] Ch. 433.

R v Secretary of State for Transport ex. p. Factortame (No. 2) [1991] A.C. 603.

R (on the application of HS2 Action Alliance Limited) (Appellant) v The SECRetary of State for Transport and another (Respondents) [2014] UKSC 3.

R (on the application of Miller and Dos Santos) v Secretary of State for Exiting the European Union [2016] EWHC 2768.

EAC

East African Court of Justice

EACJ Ref No. 1 of 2005, *Calist Mwatela and 2 Others v East African Community.*

EACJ Ref No. 1 of 2006, *Prof. Peter Anyang' Nyong'o & 10 others v Attorney General of Kenya & 2 Others.*

EACJ Ref No. 1 of 2007, *Katabazi & 21 Others v the Attorney General of the Republic of Uganda and the Secretary General of the East African Community.*

EACJ Ref No. 2 of 2007, *Christopher Mtikila v The Attorney General of the United Republic of Tanzania and the Secretary General of the East African Community.*

EACJ Ref No. 3 of 2007, *The East Africa Law Society & 5 Others v the Attorney General of the Republic of Kenya & 4 Others.*

EACJ Ref No. 1 of 2008, *Mordern Holdings v Kenya Ports Authority.*

EACJ Ref No. 1 of 2010, *Honorable Sitenda Sibalu v the Secretary of the EAC, Attorney General of Uganda, Honorable Sam Njuba, and the Electoral Commission of Uganda.*

EACJ Ref No. 7 of 2010, *Mary Ariviza and Okotch Mondoh v Attorney General of kenya and Secretary General of the East African Community,* (*First Instance Division*).

EACJ Ref No. 8 of 2010, *Plaxeda Rugumba v the Attorney General of the Republic of Rwanda.*

EACJ Ref No. 30 of 2010, *Independent Medico Legal Unit v. Attorney General of Kenya.*

EACJ Ref No. 1 of 2011, *East Africa Law Society v Secretary General East Africa Law Society.*

EACJ Ref No. 4 of 2011, *Omar Awadh and Six Others v Attorney General of Kenya and Attorney General of Uganda.*

EACJ Ref No. 5 of 2011, *Samuel Mukira Muhochi v Attorney General of the Uganda.*

EACJ Ref No. 6 of 2011, *Democratic Party and Mukasa Mbidde v Secretary General of the East African Community & Attorney General of Uganda.*

EACJ Ref No. 1 of 2012, *Timothy Alvin Kahoho v Secretary General.*

EACJ Ref No. 2 of 2012, *Angela Amudo v. the East African Community.*

EACJ Ref No. 6 of 2012, *Among A. Anita v The Attorney General of Uganda and Secretary General of the East African Community.*

EACJ Ref No. 7 of 2012, *Antony Calist Komu v Attorney General of The United Republic of Tanzania.*

EACJ Ref No. 9 of 2012, *East African Center for Trade Policy and Law v Secretary General.*

EACJ Ref No. 1 of 2014, *Attorney General of Uganda v Tom Kyahurwenda.*

EACJ Ref Nos. 5 and 10 of 2014, *Mbidde Foundation Limited and Rt Hon Margaret Zziwa v Secretary General of the East African Community and The Attorney General of Uganda.*

EACJ Ref No. 15 of 2014, *Baranzira Raphael & another v Attorney General of the Republic of Burundi.*

Appellate Division

Appeal No. 1 of 2011, *Independent Medical Legal Unit v Attorney-General of Kenya.*

Appeal No. 1 of 2012, *Attorney General of Rwanda v Plaxeda Rugumba.*

Appeal No. 3 of 2013, *Alcon International Limited v Standard Chartered Bank of Uganda and 2 Others.*

EACJ Appeal No. 6 of 2014, *Henry Kyarimpa v Attorney General of Uganda.*

EACJ Appeal No. 1 of 2015, *Union Trade Centre Limited v the Attorney General of Uganda.*

Arbiration

Arbitration Cause No. 1 of 2012, *Nayebare Alice v East Africa Law Society.*

Advisory Opinion

Application No. 1 of 2008, *In the Matter of a Request by the Council of Ministers of the East African Community for an Advisory Opinion.*

Kenya

Civil Appeal No. 18 of 1985, *Intalframe Ltd -v- Mediterranean Shipping Company.*

Civil Application No. NAI 298 of 1997, *Societe de Transports International Rwanda v H. Abdi.*

Civil Case No. 916 of 1997, *Pioneer General Assurance Society Limited v Zilfikarali Nimji Javer.*

Civil Case No. 1723 of 2000, *Ssebaggala & Sons Electric Centre Limited v Kenya National Shipping Lime Limited.*

Nairobi High Court Miscellaneous Application No. 1756 of 2005, *Coastal Bottlers Limited v Commissioner of Domestic Taxes.*

Miscellaneous Application No. 1223 of 2007, *Barclays Bank of Kenya Limited v Kenya Revenue Authority.*

Miscellaneous. Application No. 4 of 2009, *BETA Healthcare International Limited v Kenya Revenue Authority.*

Miscellaneous Application No. 709 of 2008, *Alltex EPZ Ltd. v Kenya Revenue Authority* High Court.

Nairobi Civil Appeal No. 147 of 2009, *Jayesh Hasmukh Shah v Navin Haria & another.*

Miscellaneous Application No. 413 Of 2009, *Republic v Kenya Revenue Authority ex-parte Beirsdorf East Africa Ltd* Nairobi High Court.

Miscellaneous Application No. 24 of 2010, *R v Kenya Revenue Authority ex parte Africa Boot Limited.*

Mombasa HC Misc. App. No. 52 of 2010, *Greenberg Trading Limited v Kenya Revenue Authority.*

Civil Appeal No. 235 of 2010, *Kenya Revenue Authority v Spectre International Limited.*

Nairobi High Court Miscellaneous Application No. 81 of 2011, *R v Kenya Revenue Authority ex parte Africa Boot Limited, HC Misc. App No. 24 of 2010.*

Judicial Review Case No. 36 of 2011, *R v Commissioner of Customs ex parte Transami (K) Limited.R- v-Kenya Revenue Authority ex parte Bata Shoe Company (K) Ltd.*

High Court Constitutional Petition No. 322 of 2011, *Cyrwan Enterprises v Kenya Revenue Authority.*

Tanzania

Tanzania Criminal Appeal No. 285 of 2008, *Tanzania Revenue Authority v Murtazar Hussein Budha.*

Uganda

Constitutional Appeal No. 3 of 2004, *The Attorney General v Paul K. Ssemogerere and Hon. Zachary Olum.*

Uganda Constitutional Court Petition No. 28 of 2006, *Jacob Oulanyah v Attorney General of the Republic of Uganda.*

Uganda HC Miscellaneous Application No. 44 of 2007, *Kawuki Mathias v Commissioner General of Uganda Revenue Authority.*

High Court Case No. 212 of 2012, *Testimony Motors v Commissioner of Customs Uganda Revenue Authority.*

HC Miscellaneous Cause No. 14 of 2014, *Kasibo Joshua v Commissioner of Customs, Uganda Revenue Authority.*

Index

Abuse of a dominant position 442
Acte clair doctrine 269, 280
Acte éclairé doctrine 269, 280
Action for annulment 232, 254–258, 260
Advisory opinions 60, 64, 142, 232, 242, 250–252, 273
Assembly *see* East African Legislative Assembly (EALA)
Asymmetry 77, 111, 306, 309, 421, 423, 427, 429, 431

Brexit 21–24, 33–36, 86–87, 90 n. 34, 95, 119, 132 n. 42, 133, 181, 332, 354, 385, 410, 431
Budget 50, 59, 145 n. 18, 233 n. 16

Capital, free movement of 105, 110 n. 27, 289–290, 303, 307, 345, 367, 392–399, 410–412, 414–416
Cassis de Dijon criterion 334–337, 341
Charges having equivalent effect to Customs Duties 328
Charter of Fundamental Rights of the EU 31, 170 n. 30, 218, 220, 224
Citizenship 30, 39, 288, 350–351, 354–355, 361–362, 364, 384 n. 36
Citizenship Directive 361–362, 364
Civil Society 16, 18, 20, 46, 48, 56, 60, 75, 117, 243, 469
Co-ordination Committee 46–47, 48 n. 29, 62, 67, 74, 75 n. 150
Colonialism 7, 12, 14, 16
Collusive behaviour 440, 456
Common Market 13, 17, 58 nn. 80–81, 65, 110 n. 27, 288, 322, 345, 347–349, 365–366, 369
Common Market for Eastern and Southern Africa (COMESA) 9, 43, 312, 490
Community Law 217 n. 2
Competences 19, 26, 29, 33, 80, 89, 92, 104 n. 5, 105, 119–123, 125–132, 162, 183 n. 7, 185 n. 15, 196, 198, 200–201, 206, 218, 404, 409, 417–418, 420–421
Competition law 96, 100, 134, 164 n. 16, 256, 277, 433–434, 436–437, 439, 442, 446–447, 450, 454 nn. 1, 3, 456, 460, 462–465
Confederation ix
Confederalism 8, 25, 181 n. 76, 362 n. 22, 421, 429, 431
Concerted Practices 441–442, 454, 457, 459 n. 25
Council of Ministers 18, 47, 62, 82, 86–89, 114, 116, 126, 142–145, 187, 197, 208, 209 n. 29, 233, 236–237, 245, 250–251, 289, 292, 322, 348, 349 n. 18, 350 n. 20, 351, 353, 407 n. 45, 434, 445–446, 449, 452, 467–468, 471
Court of Appeal for Eastern Africa 15, 44
Customs duty 328–329, 332, 478, 480–481
Customs Union 13, 17, 65, 110, 285 n. 3, 305, 308, 313, 314 n. 64–65, 315 nn. 66–67, 69–72, 316 n. 76

Dassonville formula 333–337, 341, 385
Decisions 19, 27–28, 40, 55, 57–62, 64–65, 67, 74–77, 86, 88, 96, 101, 103, 106, 113, 117–118, 133–134, 140–142, 144–145, 147, 152–155, 157–159, 163, 170, 173–174, 188, 206–208, 215, 232–237, 239–242, 250–252, 265, 267–268, 270, 278, 280–282, 294, 308, 399, 417, 435, 437, 446, 454–455, 458, 463–465, 467, 470, 473, 477, 479, 484–485, 494
Democratic legitimacy 22, 30, 80, 83, 429, 437
Direct effect of EAC law 151–152
Direct effect of EU law 29, 151 n. 39, 161–162, 165, 167, 169–171, 173–174, 217, 219, 298, 328
Direct foreign investment 404, 496
Discrimination 169 n. 30, 175, 218, 290, 318, 330, 334, 340, 346–347, 351, 385, 394–395, 411, 437

East African Central Bank 74, 408
East African Common Services Organizations 401 n. 30
East African Community 1967–1977 45
East African Community Committee on Trade Remedies 319, 485 n. 67
East African Community Competition Act 2006 50

East African Community Competition Authority 434–435, 437, 439–450, 452–453
East African Community Customs Management Act 2004 50, 154, 308 n. 28
East African Community Development Strategy 402, 480
East African Court of Appeal 187–188
East African Court of Justice 47, 54, 141, 156 n. 58, 189, 230, 265, 397, 440, 467
East African Currency board 15
East African Development Bank 15, 44, 46, 68–69
East African Federation 62, 287 n. 5, 288
East African Legislative Assembly (EALA) 43, 46–47, 48, 75, 114, 140–141, 187, 190, 232, 307, 318 n. 86, 319, 434, 467
East African Monetary Institute 74, 408
East African Postal Union 15, 287
Economic and Monetary Union 30, 107, 410, 415–417, 427
Economic Community of Central African States 312
Economic Community of West African States 8, 51
Economic integration, types of 294, 300, 416
Effectiveness 92, 98, 122, 127–128, 130, 169, 172, 177, 200–201, 204 n. 7, 219–220, 275, 300, 305, 328, 336, 341, 392, 428, 492
Enforcement of EAC law 434–435, 474, 485
Enforcement of EU law 96, 167, 463
Enhanced cooperation 106, 132
Equitable division of benefits ix
Establishment, freedom of 109, 373, 376, 389
Equal treatment 120, 347, 353, 360, 363–364, 366
Euro (*see* Economic and Monetary Union)
European Central Bank 88, 101, 107, 255, 415, 418–420
European Commission 63, 81–82, 85–86, 88–89, 92 n. 43, 197, 260, 418, 443, 450–451, 455–458, 463–464, 466
European Community (EC) 30, 33
European Council 31, 37–40, 45, 82–89, 93, 95, 97, 197, 224, 258
European Court of Justice 29, 97 n. 68, 203, 275 n. 1, 298 n. 20
European Economic Community (EEC) 28, 183, 191, 293
European Parliament 30, 31, 41, 52, 79–84, 88–89, 92, 97, 120–122, 129, 135–138, 197, 255, 258–259, 274
European Union (EU) 6, 22, 43, 182, 185, 202
Export, restrictions on 333 n. 30

Free movement 105, 290, 299, 303–304, 306, 315, 327, 347, 354, 355 n. 2, 368, 390 n. 70, 410, 411 nn. 2, 4
Fundamental principles of the EAC 243
Fundamental rights 26, 33, 163, 170 n. 30, 178–180, 211–212, 217–228, 279, 347, 484

General Principles 112, 165, 169 n. 30, 202–205, 214–225, 228, 344
Good governance 54, 57, 110–113, 159, 202, 205, 213, 216, 230, 289, 403, 405, 484

Human rights 64, 66, 70, 112–113, 115, 188, 192, 205, 210–214, 218, 222, 230–231, 244–245, 249, 292, 471–472, 484–485

Keck exception 301, 339, 385

Lake Victoria 46, 50, 52 n. 49, 68, 72–73, 77, 247 n. 53
Legal basis 41, 46, 82, 120, 122–124, 129, 137, 175, 178, 218, 224 n. 20, 255, 463

Member State liability 173, 220, 278 n. 11
Member States 5, 10–11, 13, 16, 18–22, 24, 31–39, 41–42, 81–83, 86–87, 88–103, 107–109, 119, 127–134, 137–139, 163, 166–169, 171–173, 175–179, 194, 196–201, 218–219, 221–222, 226–227, 243, 245, 255, 258–260, 262–264, 280–282, 291, 293–297, 299–300, 307, 318, 328–343, 345, 355, 361–362, 377–381, 383, 385, 387, 389–390, 403–404, 411–428, 450–451, 454–455, 459, 461, 463–465
Mergers and acquisitions 438, 447, 449
Monetary Union 13, 17, 19, 30, 46, 50, 59, 64, 74, 76, 107, 109–110, 186, 214, 285, 287, 289, 306–307, 392, 405–410, 415–417, 427, 429–431, 486, 495
Mutual recognition 200, 300–301, 324, 334, 341, 347, 349, 360, 388

National Courts 64–66, 98, 100, 142, 146–147, 149, 152, 154–159, 162, 165, 168–169, 172 n. 39, 173, 176, 178, 180, 222, 232, 239–243, 246, 254, 265–270, 272–276, 278–284, 298, 328, 335–336, 445, 447, 465, 467, 471, 473–476, 479, 482, 484–485
Necessity 21, 77, 269, 282, 342–344, 397 n. 20, 415, 433
Non-Tariff Barriers (NTB's) 51, 109, 209, 290, 304, 306, 309, 315–319, 332

Objective justification 414
Operational principles of the EAC 111, 210, 212
Opinion of the EACJ 441
Opinions of the CJEU 264

Partner States 16, 18, 24, 47–50, 54, 57–59, 62–74, 76–78, 103–106, 109–115, 139–140, 142–160, 182–195, 200, 204–207, 209–216, 230, 232–243, 248–249, 265–266, 268, 271–274, 289–292, 303–304, 306–308, 311–325, 346–353, 365–368, 371–375, 391–409, 434–439, 442, 445–447, 449–450, 453, 467–470, 474, 476, 482, 484–489, 493–498
Permanent Tripartite Commission 17, 44–45
Persons, free movement of 31, 105, 107, 290, 301, 345, 347–348, 354, 361, 368, 385, 454
Political federation 17, 19, 46, 48, 54–55, 75–76, 110, 117, 182, 186, 189, 193, 195, 214, 252, 285, 287–289, 306, 405, 468, 486, 495
Precedent 35, 83–84, 141, 152, 269–270, 272, 284
Predatory pricing 444, 461
Preliminary ruling 64, 142, 154–156, 239, 242, 243, 265, 267, 269–276, 282, 284
Price fixing 457
Principles of the Community 47, 110–111, 140, 186, 208, 232, 252, 306, 356, 403
Private Sector 16, 18–19, 46, 48, 56, 243, 318, 346, 469, 474, 484–485, 487, 488, 497
Product requirements 300
Proportionality 130–131, 217–218, 284, 301, 342, 364, 387, 415
Public policy 121, 340, 347, 355, 364, 368, 370, 398, 414

Regulations 348, 366, 434
Representation 53, 76–77, 80, 153, 197, 234, 238
Residence 105, 109–110, 133, 290–291, 345–347, 350–351, 359, 361–365, 368–371, 390, 394, 411, 437, 444, 453
Restriction 49, 63, 164, 298, 318, 329, 333, 336–337, 339–340, 343, 351, 359–360, 364, 383–387, 414–415, 454–455, 457
Rule of Reason 340

Secretariat (*see* EAC Secretariat)
Secretary General 49, 53, 55, 57, 59–62, 64–66, 113, 117, 144, 149, 153, 187, 190, 194, 230, 233, 239, 245, 247–248, 250–252, 266, 268, 272, 319, 433–434, 471–472
Sectoral Committees 46–47, 58, 62, 67, 187, 317
Sectoral Councils 58, 142, 233–234, 236
Selling arrangements (*See* Keck)
Service recipients 382, 384
Services, free movement of 289–290, 345–346, 365, 367, 372, 376–378, 383–386, 388, 390, 482
Services Directive 376–377, 388, 390
Single European Act 29, 80, 91, 299, 418
Single Market 29, 48, 285, 294, 345, 352, 454
Southern African Development Community 43, 312, 437, 495
Sovereignty 3–5, 7–8, 10, 12, 25, 37, 43, 78, 81, 143, 146, 160, 182, 186, 189, 195, 206, 237, 405, 416, 429–430
Special legislative procedure 129, 137
State aid 96, 450–451, 454, 461, 463
Subsidiarity 47, 104, 111, 119, 130–131, 206–207, 217–218, 226, 404
Suitability 99, 342, 387 n. 54
Summit 9, 11, 18, 46–48, 50–51, 54–63, 68, 74–76, 78, 83–85, 109, 113, 117–119, 140–141, 144, 145, 185–187, 190, 194–195, 197, 235, 237, 244, 251, 292, 319, 348, 405–406, 408, 434, 468–469
Supremacy of EAC law 211
Supremacy of EU law 29, 128 n. 30, 154 n. 51, 162, 175–176, 178, 222, 278, 328 n. 10

Taxation 88, 313, 328, 330, 371, 412, 414, 482
Transparency 91, 110, 159, 205, 345, 428, 471–472, 479, 494

Treaty establishing a Constitution for Europe (Constitutional treaty) 31
Treaty of Lisbon 32–33, 36–37, 39, 84–85, 89, 197, 200, 224, 257, 412
Treaty of Maastricht 30–31, 33, 85, 218, 223, 354, 361, 412, 417, 419
Treaty of Nice 31
Treaty of Paris 79 n. 2
Treaty of Rome 28 n. 13, 34 n. 34, 103 n. 1, 198, 293, 354, 410

Union Citizenship 354, 361–362

Variable Geometry 105–108, 111–112, 119, 131, 133, 207–209, 251–252, 306, 372–373, 470

Withdrawal from the EU 36
Workers, free movement of 200, 290, 345–347, 349–355, 360, 366

www.ingramcontent.com/pod-product-compliance
Lightning Source LLC
LaVergne TN
LVHW012050011026
849162LV00017B/32
* 9 7 8 9 0 0 4 3 2 2 0 6 6 *